CAMBRIDGE GREEK AND

GENERAL EDITORS

P. E. EASTERLING
Regius Professor Emeritus of Greek, University of Cambridge

PHILIP HARDIE
*Fellow, Trinity College, and Honorary Professor of Latin Emeritus,
University of Cambridge*

†NEIL HOPKINSON

RICHARD HUNTER
Regius Professor of Greek Emeritus, University of Cambridge

S. P. OAKLEY
Kennedy Professor of Latin, University of Cambridge

OLIVER THOMAS
Associate Professor in Classics, University of Nottingham

CHRISTOPHER J. WHITTON
Professor of Latin Literature, University of Cambridge

FOUNDING EDITORS

P. E. EASTERLING

†E. J. KENNEY

THUCYDIDES
THE PELOPONNESIAN WAR

BOOK VI

EDITED BY
CHRISTOPHER PELLING
Emeritus Regius Professor of Greek, University of Oxford

CAMBRIDGE
UNIVERSITY PRESS

University Printing House, Cambridge CB2 8BS, United Kingdom

One Liberty Plaza, 20th Floor, New York, NY 10006, USA

477 Williamstown Road, Port Melbourne, VIC 3207, Australia

314–321, 3rd Floor, Plot 3, Splendor Forum, Jasola District Centre, New Delhi – 110025, India

103 Penang Road, #05–06/07, Visioncrest Commercial, Singapore 238467

Cambridge University Press is part of the University of Cambridge.

It furthers the University's mission by disseminating knowledge in the pursuit of education, learning, and research at the highest international levels of excellence.

www.cambridge.org
Information on this title: www.cambridge.org/9781107176911
DOI: 10.1017/9781316819067

© Cambridge University Press 2022

This publication is in copyright. Subject to statutory exception and to the provisions of relevant collective licensing agreements, no reproduction of any part may take place without the written permission of Cambridge University Press.

First published 2022

Printed in the United Kingdom by TJ Books Limited, Padstow Cornwall

A catalogue record for this publication is available from the British Library.

Library of Congress Cataloging-in-Publication Data
NAMES: Thucydides, author. | Pelling, C. B. R., editor.
TITLE: The Peloponnesian War, Book VI / edited by Christopher Pelling.
Other titles: History of the Peloponnesian War. Book 6
DESCRIPTION: Cambridge, United Kingdom ; New York, NY : Cambridge University Press, 2022. | Series: Cambridge Greek and Latin classics | Includes index.
IDENTIFIERS: LCCN 2021032828 (print) | LCCN 2021032829 (ebook) | ISBN 9781107176911 (hardback) | ISBN 9781316630211 (paperback) | ISBN 9781316819067 (ebook)
SUBJECTS: LCSH: Greece – History – Peloponnesian War, 431–404 B.C.
CLASSIFICATION: LCC DF229.T56 G74 2022 (print) | LCC DF229.T56 (ebook) | DDC 938/.05–dc23
LC record available at https://lccn.loc.gov/2021032828
LC ebook record available at https://lccn.loc.gov/2021032829

ISBN 978-1-107-17691-1 Hardback
ISBN 978-1-316-63021-1 Paperback

Cambridge University Press has no responsibility for the persistence or accuracy of URLs for external or third-party internet websites referred to in this publication and does not guarantee that any content on such websites is, or will remain, accurate or appropriate.

CONTENTS

List of Maps	page vi
List of Figures	vii
Preface	ix
List of Abbreviations	xi
Maps	xiv
Introduction	1
1 Thucydides and the Sicilian Expedition	1
2 Author, Audience, and Performance	8
3 Book 6 in the History	14
(a) Books 6–7	14
(b) Book 5 and Book 6	17
(c) Book 6 in the Whole	20
4 The Speeches	22
5 Athens and Syracuse	29
6 The Text	36
Deviations from Alberti	38
Sigla	40
THUCYDIDES: BOOK VI	41
Commentary	93
Works Cited	321
Indexes	
1 General	342
2 Language, Style, and Narrative Technique	348
3 Greek	350

MAPS

1 Sicily *page* xiv
2 Southern Italy xv
3 Greece xvi
4 Syracuse xviii

FIGURES

1. Vase of satyr attacking Herm. Musée cantonal d'archéologie et d'histoire, Lausanne. Inv. 3250. *page* 173
2. Harmodius and Aristogeiton. Roman copy of fifth-century BCE statues by Critius and Nesiotes. Napoli, Museo Archeologico Nazionale. 222

PREFACE

'Tacitus was a great man', said Macaulay; 'but he was not up to the Sicilian expedition'.[1] To write commentaries on Thucydides' Sicilian books is a daunting privilege. The excellence of the narrative is beyond doubt: as Plutarch says (*Nicias* 1.1), these show Thucydides at his 'most emotional, most vivid, and most varied'. To try to explain how that excellence is achieved risks labouring the obvious and compromising that immediacy. Nor is it exactly untrodden territory. The great nineteenth- and early twentieth-century commentaries – Krüger, Poppo and Stahl, and Classen and Steup, all still immensely useful – had mighty successors: Dover's 1970 contribution to Gomme, Andrewes, and Dover's *Historical Commentary on Thucydides* (hereafter, *HCT*) and Hornblower's 2008 third volume of his *Commentary on Thucydides* (hereafter, *CT*). Dover has many textual and Hornblower many literary comments to complement their thorough treatment of the history. Yet the attempt to add two more commentaries is still worthwhile. Books 6 and 7 are natural choices for those coming to Thucydides for the first time, perhaps in an undergraduate or graduate class; but Thucydides' Greek is notoriously difficult, especially in the speeches, and Book 6 has the most speeches of them all. It is not just the novice reader that often needs, or at least welcomes, help, and even Dover's shorter school commentaries (1965) took too much prior facility for granted. I have therefore included more linguistic explanation than in two earlier 'green-and-yellows' (Cambridge Greek and Latin Classics), my single-authored Plutarch's *Antony* (1988) and the Herodotus Book 6 co-written with Simon Hornblower (2017). Many notes too are keyed to the *Cambridge Grammar of Classical Greek* (van Emde Boas, Rijksbaron, Huitink and de Bakker 2019), and I hope that these too will be helpful. In many Thucydidean sentences the syntax is difficult or ambiguous while the meaning is clear, and not every native speaker may have heard that syntax in the same way. I have tried to keep this in mind throughout, along with the importance of oral delivery for texts that were designed for hearing as well as reading.

In line with the aims of the series, I have also given particular attention to literary aspects. This has often squeezed out historical material that would be relevant even for a literary critic, for one can hardly gauge what Thucydides has done with his material without an idea of what that material would have been. Still, brevity here may be forgiven because so much

---

[1] Macaulay, letter to Thomas Flower Ellis, 25 July 1836, Pinney 1974–81 iii: 181 (cited by Rood 2017: 20).

is readily accessible in the commentaries of Dover and Hornblower: 'cf. *HCT* and *CT*' could have been added much more frequently than it is, and can be taken for granted throughout. In particular, there are many topographical issues which cannot be gone into here, especially in the closing chapters of Book 6, and here the thorough work done by Dover and by Peter Green (Green 1970) is still as authoritative as ever. What I have tried to contribute is more attention to what listeners or readers without maps or local knowledge would make of the narrative and what sort of picture of the terrain they would build. Thucydides tried to tell them what they needed to know to make sense of his account, but that would not always have been easy and sometimes it is hard to think that it was possible. Still, even when bewildered those readers or listeners would carry away an impression of a writer thoroughly in command of his material, and that, perhaps, was enough.

Many debts have been accumulated. These commentaries were originally to be jointly written with John Marincola: that turned out to be impossible, but I have benefited from his advice and from an Oxford graduate seminar that he and I gave in summer 2017. A notable moment came when, after discussion of the debate of the generals at 6.47–50.1, a straw vote produced a majority for Nicias. They were a cautious group. Emily Baragwanath kindly agreed to expose some of her own graduate students to an early draft of the commentary on 6.1–31, and her reports and advice were invaluable. Edith Foster, busy with her own commentary on Book 4, found time to exchange materials and send very useful comments. I have also gained much from e-correspondence with Elisabetta Bianco, Bob Connor, Irene de Jong, Donald Lateiner, Christopher Mallan, Hunter Rawlings III, Jeff Rusten, Dan Tompkins, and Tony Woodman, and from conversations locally in Oxford with Richard Rutherford, Tim Rood, and Andreas Willi. The series editors, Richard Hunter and the late Neil Hopkinson, went through the drafts with their usual meticulous eyes for detail and for superfluity, and I am grateful. One final debt is to Simon Hornblower. I have not embarrassed him by asking him to read any of what I have written, but he has been supportive throughout and has lent books and expertise. After collaborating with him literally in our commentary on Herodotus Book 6, I have often found myself figuratively doing the same in these two volumes, with his commentary always on my desk.

This and its sister commentary on Book 7 should appear almost simultaneously. Each is complete in itself and some material appears in both introductions, but there are many cross-references to the other volume in the form, e.g. 'cf. 7.69.2 n.'. Where references are to other passages in Book 6, the chapter number is printed in **bold**.

ABBREVIATIONS

Where dates are given in the form 418/7 they refer to archon-years; when in the form 418–417 they refer to a period, normally the winter, spanning both calendar years.

I ANCIENT AUTHORS AND WORKS

Abbreviations for Greek and Latin authors usually follow those in *OCD*, except for the following:

D. H.	Dionysius of Halicarnassus
Diod.	Diodorus
Hdt.	Herodotus
Plut.	Plutarch
Th.	Thucydides
X.	Xenophon

Ar. is Aristophanes, Arist. is Aristotle.

II TEXTS, COMMENTARIES, AND SECONDARY WORKS

Alberti	G. B. Alberti, *Thucydidis historiae*, 3 vols. (Rome, 1972–2000)
APF	J. K. Davies, *Athenian propertied families 600-300 BC* (Oxford, 1971)
Barr.	R. Talbert (ed.), *Barrington atlas of the Greek and Roman world* (Princeton, 2000)
Bétant	E.-A. Bétant, *Lexicon Thucydideum*, 2 vols. (Geneva, 1843; repr. Hildesheim, 1969)
BNJ	I. Worthington (ed.), *Brill's new Jacoby* (Leiden, on-line)
BNP	H. Cancik, H. Schneider, and M. Landester (eds.), *Brill's new Pauly* (Leiden, Boston, and Cologne, in print and on-line, 1996–)
CAH	*Cambridge Ancient History*. Most references are to vol. iv², *Persia, Greece and the western Mediterranean c. 525 to 479 B.C.* (ed. J. Boardman, N. G. L. Hammond, D. M. Lewis, and M. Ostwald, Cambridge, 1988) and vol. v², *The fifth century B.C.* (ed. D. M. Lewis, J. Boardman, J. K. Davies, and M. Ostwald, Cambridge, 1992)

CGCG	E. van Emde Boas, A. Rijksbaron, L. Huitink, and M. de Bakker, *The Cambridge grammar of Classical Greek* (Cambridge, 2019)
CHGRW	P. Sabin, H. van Wees, and M. Whitby (eds.), *The Cambridge History of Greek and Roman warfare* i–ii (Cambridge, 2017)
C–S	J. Classen, *Thukydides. Sechster Band, Sechstes Buch*, bearbeitet von J. Steup (Berlin, 3rd ed., 1905)
CT	S. Hornblower, *A commentary on Thucydides*, 3 vols. (Oxford, 1991–2008); unless noted otherwise, references are to vol. III, and if no page number is given the reference is to the note on the passage discussed
EGM	R. L. Fowler, *Early Greek mythography*, 2 vols. (Oxford, 2000–13)
FGrH	F. Jacoby, et al., *Die Fragmente der griechischen Historiker* (Berlin and Leiden, 1923–58; Leiden, 1994–)
Fornara	C. W. Fornara, *Archaic times to the end of the Peloponnesian War* (*Translated documents of Greece & Rome* 1, Cambridge, 2nd ed., 1983)
GG	W. W. Goodwin, *A Greek grammar* (Basingstoke and London, new ed., 1930)
GP	J. D. Denniston, *The Greek particles* (Oxford, 2nd ed., 1954)
GSW	W. K. Pritchett, *The Greek state at war*, vols. I–V (Berkeley and London, 1971–91)
Hammond	M. Hammond, *Thucydides: the Peloponnesian War* (Oxford, 2009)
HCT	A. Andrewes, A. W. Gomme, and K. J. Dover, *A historical commentary on Thucydides*, 5 vols. (Oxford 1945–80); unless otherwise noted, references are to vol. IV, and if no page number is given the reference is to the note on the passage discussed
Hornblower–Pelling	S. Hornblower and C. Pelling, *Herodotus: Book 6* (Cambridge, 2017)
Huitink–Rood	L. Huitink and T. Rood, *Xenophon: Anabasis Book III* (Cambridge, 2019)
IACP	M. H. Hansen and T. H. Nielsen (eds.), *An inventory of archaic and classical Greek poleis* (Oxford, 2004)
IG	*Inscriptiones Graecae*, Berlin (1873–)
ILS	H. Dessau (ed.), *Inscriptiones Latinae selectae* (Berlin, 1892–1916)

K–A	R. Kassel and C. Austin, *Poetae comici Graeci* (Berlin, 1983–9)
Krüger	K. W. Krüger, Θουκυδίδου Συγγραφη *mit erklärenden Anmerkungen*, zweiten Bandes erstes Heft, fünftes und sechstes Buch (Berlin, 2nd ed., 1858)
LGPN	P. M. Fraser et al., *A lexicon of Greek personal names* (Oxford, 1987–)
LSJ	H. G. Liddell, R. Scott, and H. S. Jones, *A Greek–English lexicon* (Oxford, 9th ed. with rev. supplement, 1996)
M&T	W. W. Goodwin, *Syntax of the moods and tenses of the Greek verb* (Boston and London, 1890; reissued, 1965)
Marchant	E. C. Marchant, *Thucydides: Book VI* (London, 1906)
ML	R. Meiggs and D. Lewis, *A selection of Greek historical inscriptions to the end of the fifth century BC* (Oxford, revised ed., 1988)
OCD	S. Hornblower, A. J. S. Spawforth and E. Eidinow, eds., *The Oxford classical dictionary* (Oxford, 4th ed., 2012)
OCT	Oxford classical text
OR	R. Osborne and P. J. Rhodes, *Greek historical inscriptions 478–404 BC* (Oxford, 2017)
P. Oxy	Oxyrhynchus papyri
P–S	E. F. Poppo, *Thucydidis de bello Peloponnesiaco*, vol. III, sect. 1, rev. and aug. J. M. Stahl (Leipzig, 2nd ed., 1879)
RO	P. J. Rhodes and R. Osborne (eds.), *Greek historical inscriptions 404–323 BC* (Oxford, 2003)
Rusten	J. S. Rusten, *Thucydides: the Peloponnesian War book 2* (Cambridge, 1989)
Σ	Scholiast
SEG	*Supplementum epigraphicum Graecum* (Amsterdam, 1923–)
Walbank	M. Walbank, *Athenian proxenies of the fifth century BC* (Toronto, 1978)

MAPS

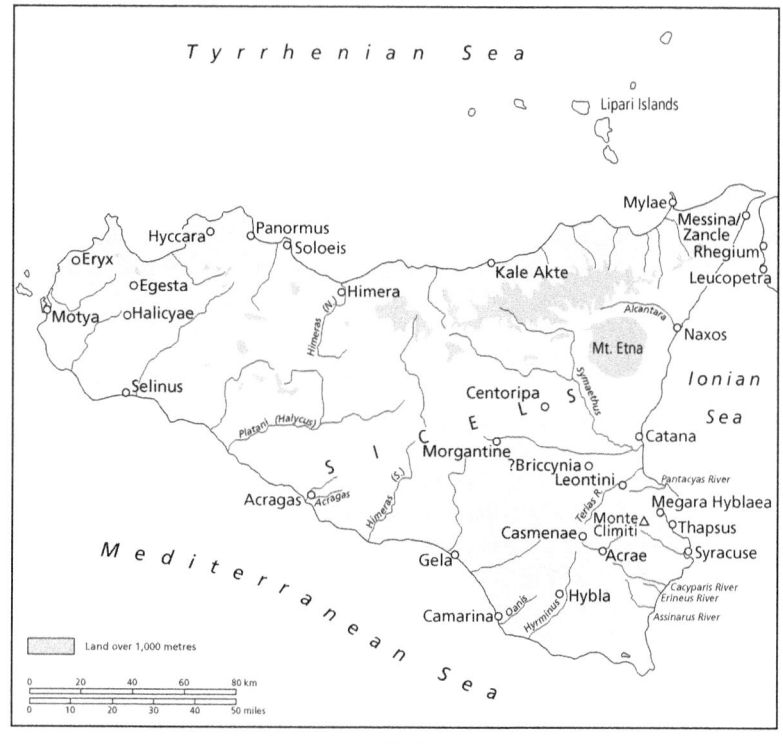

1 Sicily

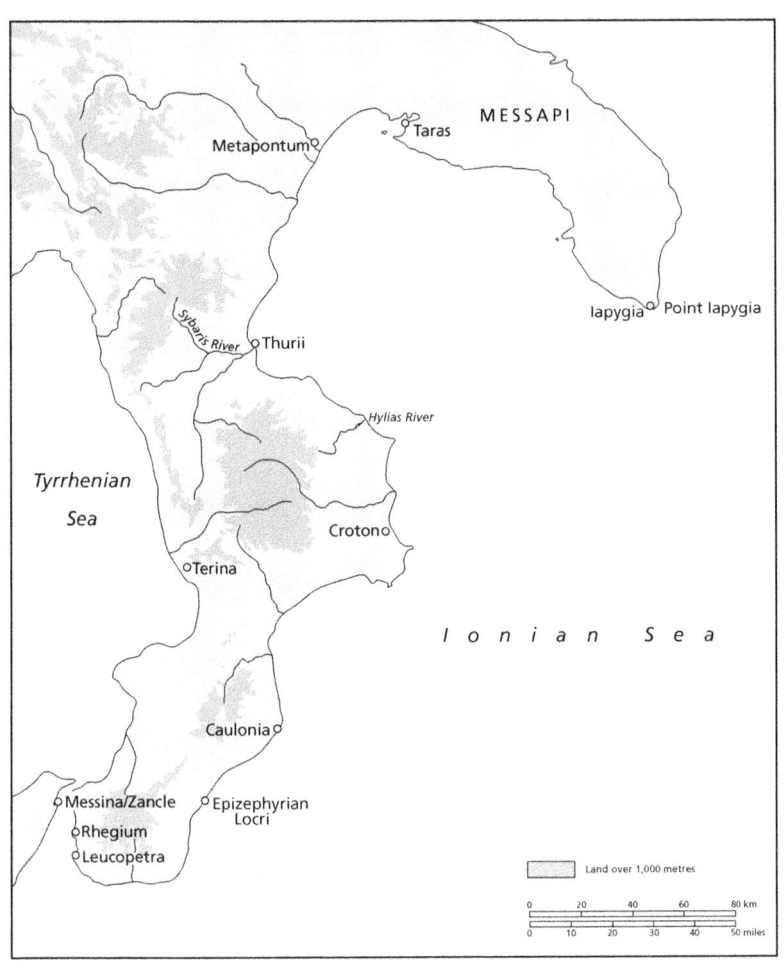

2 Southern Italy

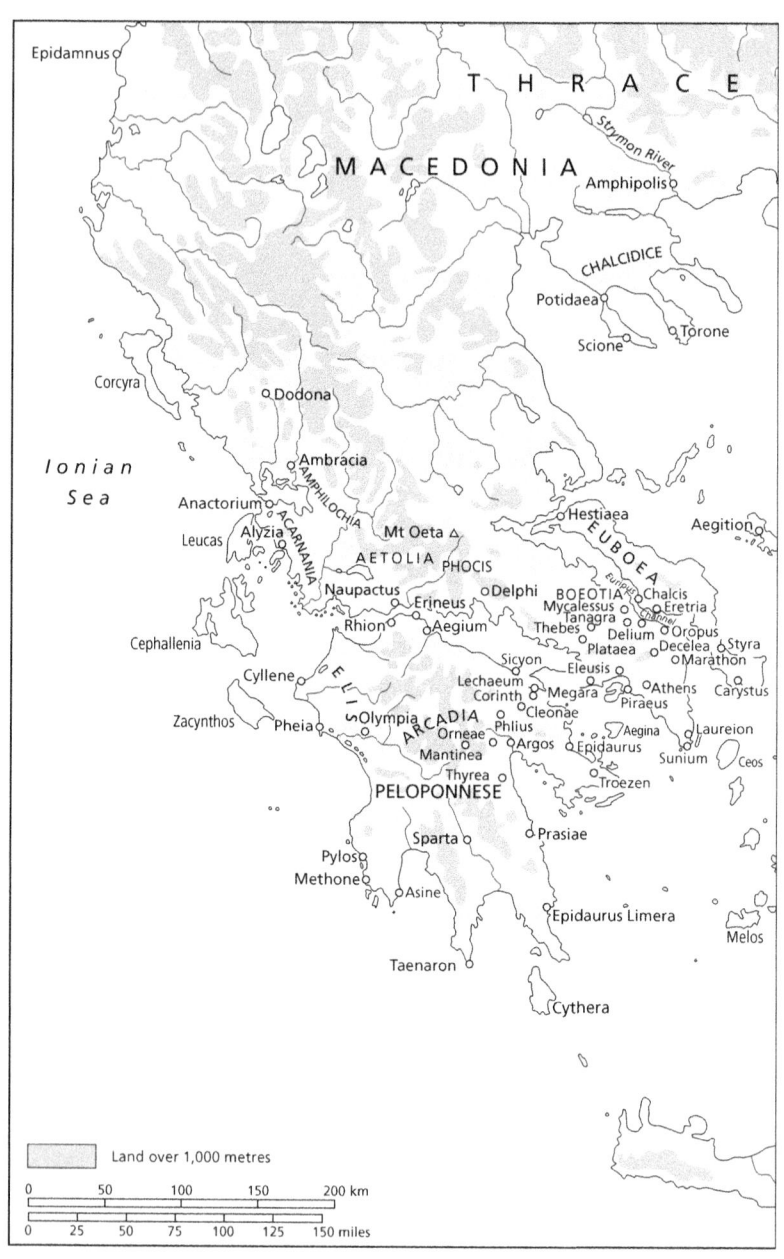

3a Greece

MAPS   xvii

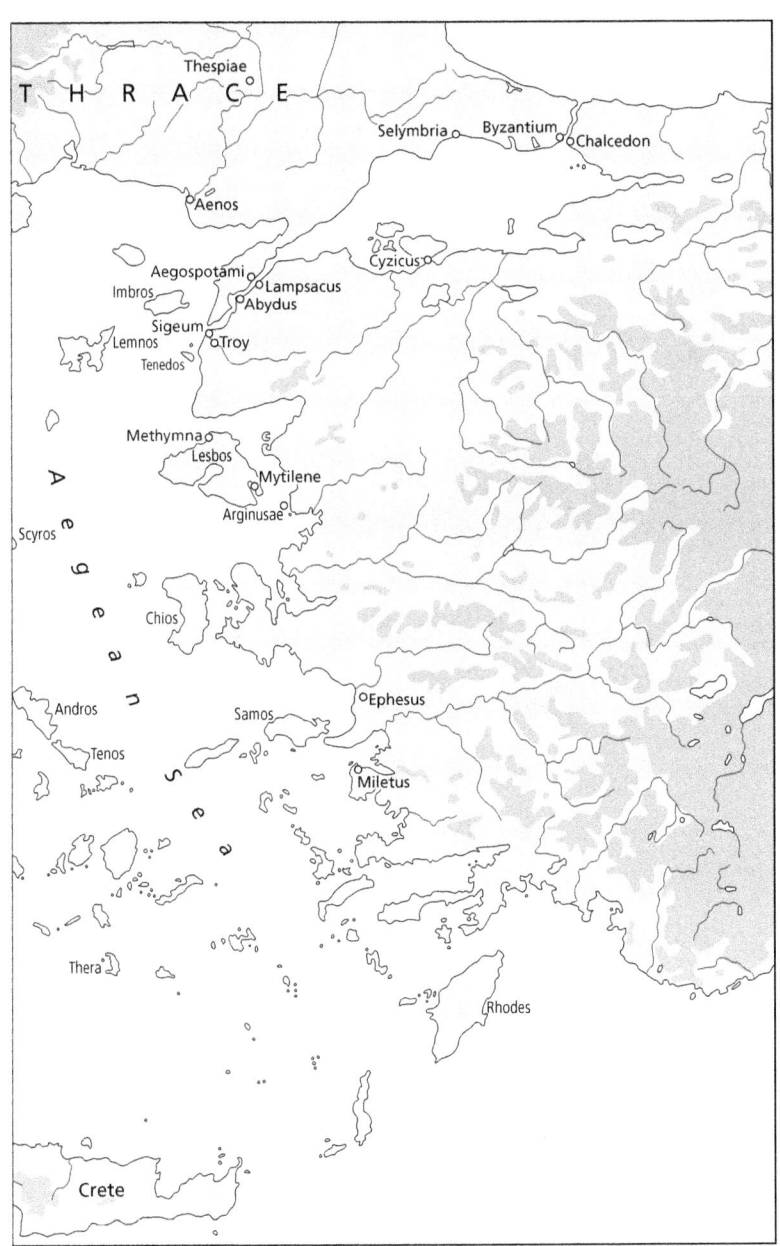

3b Greece

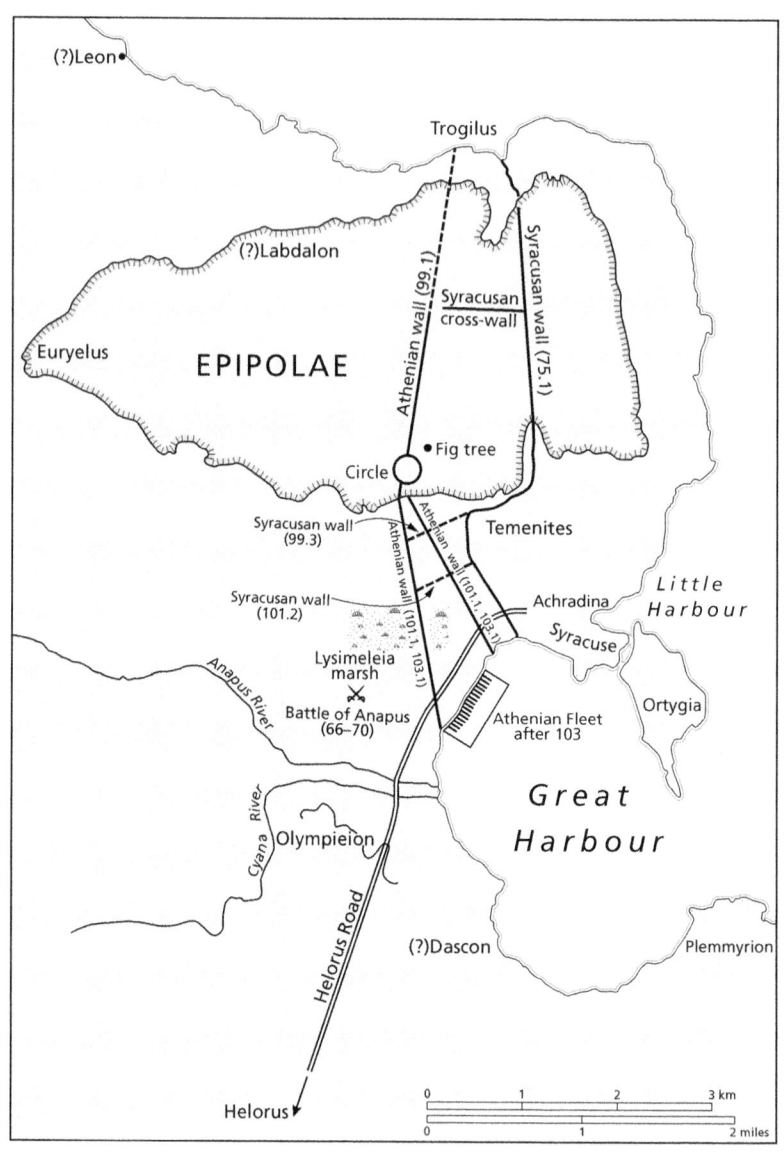

4 Syracuse

INTRODUCTION

1 THUCYDIDES AND THE SICILIAN EXPEDITION

In spring 415 BCE, Athens was an excited city. Ambassadors from the small Sicilian town of Egesta were in town (**6** n.).[1] In the assembly, and doubtless in private conversation, they were pressing the Athenians to help them against their local enemy Selinus and, much more significantly, the powerful city of Syracuse. The idea of an expedition had begun to take hold; commissioners had been sent to confirm that Egesta could really provide the funds it promised, and had returned with a positive report. Opinion was divided. Everyone knew that there were threats closer to home: a treaty had been agreed in 421 to end the open war with Sparta and her allies that had broken out in 431, but it had been an uneasy peace, punctuated by intermittent fighting including the major battle of Mantinea in 418 (**7**.1 n.). Would an ambitious overseas campaign really be wise? Some cautious heads doubted it, including Nicias. Yet it could equally be argued that it might even make Athens safer (**6**.2), and the mood of the moment was enthusiastic. Years earlier Pericles, at least in Thucydides' version,[2] had urged Athenians to become 'lovers of the city' (ἐρασταί, 2.43.1); now there was a new form of ἔρως, a passionate desire for the expedition itself, at least once the assembly had agreed to increase its scale to a point where it seemed certain to succeed (**24**.3 [nn.]). When the grand expedition set out, it was a spectacle such as nobody had seen before (**30–32**.2). What with camp-followers too – bakers, masons, carpenters, as well as the fighting force – it was as if a whole city was on the move, a new colonising expedition to match those of old.[3]

Not that Thucydides himself was there to see it. He had not been in the city since 424, in exile after his failure as general to prevent the loss of the northern city of Amphipolis. One can imagine him now settled in his estate in Thrace[4] and eagerly picking up what news he could get. He had begun assembling materials for his history as soon as the war had begun in 431, 'realising that this was going to be a great war and more worth recording than any before' (1.1.1). It is an easy guess that he had a

---

[1] References in **bold** type are to chapters within Book 6.
[2] And very likely in real life: Brock 2013c and 2013a: 115–16; Zaccarini 2018 brings out how arresting and provocative the phrase would be.
[3] **23**.2: cf. **1**.2–**5**.3 n., **44**.1, **63**.3 nn.; Avery 1973.
[4] He mentions this estate and his mining interests in the area at 4.105.1; cf. Marcellinus *Life of Thucydides* 14, 25 (the delightful and implausible detail that he wrote the history there 'under a plane tree') and 46–7.

presentiment in 421 that it was not over yet, and he will have continued to track events closely: when he came to look back after the war ended in 404, he was sure that it was a single twenty-seven-year conflict rather than two wars punctuated by a peace (5.26). What was still uncertain in 415 is whether this new initiative would be the trigger to set it off again. Nor was it clear that the expedition would fail, still less that it would end in the catastrophe that it did, and indeed it could easily have gone the other way (7.2.4, 7.42.3); by the end of Book 6 both the Syracusans and Gylippus are giving up hope (**103**.3, **104**.1). As a narrator Thucydides makes sure that his readers and listeners know that it will end badly (**1**.1 n.), but he allows a play in his narrative between causality and contingency, allowing the reader to sense the uncertainties of the time as events might develop in any of a number of ways:[5] some of the reasons why the enterprise failed could be explained, possibly even predicted, but that is not to say that it was predetermined that it would play out as it did. Nor was it certain that Sparta would become embroiled. Alcibiades had a lot to do with that, and his manoeuvrings were bizarrely unpredictable (**89–92** n.). Athens had sent forces to Sicily before, in 427–424 in considerable numbers and then again in 422 (section 5), yet these expeditions had had relatively little impact on the broader war. As the news of the Athenian decision came in, Thucydides might suspect that this was going to be momentous, but he could not be sure.

Gathering material was painstaking, and he needed as many versions as possible:

> As to the actions of the war, I have thought it right to record them not on the basis of chance informants nor according to my own impressions, but covering matters as accurately as possible, and this applies both to what I witnessed myself and to cases where I was reliant on others. It was a laborious business, because eye-witnesses would disagree about events, each according to their own partisanship or memory.   (1.22.2–3)

The difficulties, it should be noted, do not seem to include *finding* eye-witnesses;[6] weighing their evidence is the problem. Who might these informants be? Doubtless traders brought tales to Thrace, often gathered in harbour gossip (cf. **31**.6, **32**.3 n.), but he could get more reliable material too. Exile had one advantage, as it allowed him to become familiar with affairs on the side of 'the Peloponnesians' as well (5.26.5), and at

---

[5] Grethlein 2010: 248–52 and 2013: esp. ch. 2; Greenwood 2017: 170–2.
[6] Hunt 2006: 391 n. 35.

7.44.1 he also makes clear that he had questioned men who had fought for the Syracusans. Sometimes he may have talked to more prominent people too. It is not impossible that Alcibiades was one,[7] though if so it did not blind Thucydides to the man's dangers as well as his charms. Some have also wondered about Hermocrates, himself in exile from 411 or 410 to 408 (8.85.3, X. *Hell.* 1.1.27);[8] he might even have visited Thucydides in Thrace, especially if – and it is a big 'if' – Thucydides had already circulated a version of his 431–421 narrative (1–5.24) and was becoming known as an authoritative recorder of the war.[9] Letters doubtless came too, and Thucydides would have kept in touch with friends in Athens. Nor would he have stayed steadily at home. He had the means to travel, and those contacts with 'the Peloponnesians' show that he did. It is tempting to think that he would have visited Syracuse too, at least after the end of the war in 404:[10] he is certainly familiar with features of local topography and their names. Still, this remains unclear. He may just have heard the names so often and pondered so much that he could – or thought he could – visualise it all with great lucidity. Immersed as he was, he may sometimes have committed the human error of assuming that his readers had gathered a similar familiarity.[11]

All this will have taken time, with his knowledge and his notes gradually building as more information arrived. When he first began to shape a polished narrative can only be a matter of speculation. Even once he had done so, it might not preclude revision: that was a more cumbersome business with papyrus rolls than it is for a modern author, but it was still possible for a section to be snipped out and/or a new version stitched in. So if some passages are clearly written after 404 – **15**.4 (n.) and the passage at 2.65 discussed below – that does not mean that everything was. What is reasonably certain, given the extraordinary skill and finish of Books 6–7, is that these are now substantially in the form that Thucydides would have wished to pass them on to posterity.

He did not live to finish the history as a whole, though it is not known when he died. Book 8 terminates in late summer 411, and it was left to several writers – not just Xenophon in the surviving *Hellenica*, but also

---

[7] The thesis is most fully argued by Brunt 1952; Delebecque 1965: 231–3 even names the place and date, Thrace in 406–405. Nývlt 2014 thoughtfully revisits the question, and concludes in favour. Gribble 1999 is sceptical (162–3, 188, and 197 n. 102), and Andrewes very cautious (*HCT* v. 3).

[8] Hammond 1973: 52–3; Fauber 2001: 39–40; cf. *CT* on 7.73.2.

[9] Cf. also n. 75.

[10] So e.g. Golden 2015: 204.

[11] So *HCT* 467; cf. *CT* on **66**.2 and **98**.2.

Cratippus, Theopompus, and the *Hellenica Oxyrhynchia*[12] – to pick up where he left it.

By 404, and doubtless long before, it was clear that the Sicilian expedition had played a critical part in deciding the war's outcome. Many clearly expected it to end much sooner than it did; many at Athens feared as much when the news of the catastrophe first arrived (8.1.2). But the city gathered its strength, fought on for nine more years, and might well still have won. Thucydides shows his admiration for this resilience in a passage prompted by the death of Pericles and written after the war had ended (2.65.12, cf. 7.28.3 n.).

He also says something there about the Sicilian adventure itself. It showed a failure of leadership:

> This resulted in many mistakes (ἡμαρτήθη), as one might expect in a great city and one ruling an empire, including the voyage to Sicily. This was not so much an error of judgement with regard to the expedition's target (οὐ τοσοῦτον γνώμης ἁμάρτημα ἦν πρὸς οὓς ἐπῇισαν), but more a matter of those who despatched the force not making the follow-up decisions that would be advantageous for those in the field (οἱ ἐκπέμψαντες οὐ τὰ πρόσφορα τοῖς οἰχομένοις ἐπιγιγνώσκοντες). Instead, their own wranglings as they contended for popular leadership both blunted the edge of affairs in the camp and stimulated the first internal convulsions at home. (2.65.11)

How comfortably does this sit with the narrative of Books 6–7 itself? Not well, many have thought,[13] particularly given the implication early in Book 6 that the decision was indeed a serious error of judgement; furthermore, 'on each occasion that Nikias asked for them, supplies and reinforcements were sent, and in good measure, and, comparatively, with little or no delay' (cf. **96**.4, 7.16); in contrast the narrative of Books 6 and 7 suggests that the failure 'was due ... almost entirely to military blunders by the men on the spot' (both citations are from Gomme in *HCT* ii. 196).

---

[12] Marincola 1997: 289–90; Gray 2017.
[13] Esp. Gomme 1951: 72 and *HCT* ii. 195–6. Gomme concludes that 2.65.11 and the narrative of Books 6–7 were 'thought at a different time', with 2.65 presumably later; cf. *HCT* v. 368 (Andrewes) and v. 423–7 (Dover). The usual explanation of this presumed change of mind is that Alcibiades' military successes in 410–407 persuaded Thucydides that had he stayed Athens might after all have won; alternatively, Cawkwell 1997: 76 and 81–2 suggests that Thucydides came to think that Athenian ambitions were more limited and realistic than he had originally taken them to be.

Yet the verdict chimes well enough with the narrative, even if the emphasis and outlook are different:[14]

(1) At 2.65.11 Thucydides is not talking directly about the reason for the expedition's failure, as Gomme and many others have implied. He is simply gauging which were the biggest mistakes in political leadership, presaging the wranglings that he claims were a principal reason for Athens' eventual defeat. They 'blunted the edge of affairs in the camp', but this need not be 'the' or even the main explanation for the disastrous outcome. Those reasons can be left to emerge from the narrative, and on this see introduction to Book 7, pp. 26–32.

(2) 2.65.11 does not deny that the initial decision was wrong-headed; it clearly says it was a mistake (ἡμαρτήθη). It was simply not so big or consequential a mistake as the subsequent ones. Thucydides is fond of such formulations, which have antecedents in Herodotus and parallels in the Hippocratic corpus:[15] Agamemnon recruited his forces for Troy because of his power 'and not so much because Helen's suitors were bound by their oaths to Tyndareus' (1.9.1); the Spartans decided on war 'not so much persuaded by their allies' arguments as fearing that the Athenians should grow more powerful' (1.88); different cities sided with Athens or with Syracuse 'not more according to justice or kinship but as it fell out for each city through expediency or necessity' (7.57.1).[16] They should be taken literally: 'more X than Y' is not the same as 'X, not Y'.[17]

(3) Mistake or not, the expedition might well have succeeded (7.2.4 and 7.42.3, p. 2), and Thucydides even suggests some reasons why: doubtless he would have sided with Nicias in the initial debate, but his initial survey of Sicily provides some support for Alcibiades as well (**1.2–5**.3 [n.]). It was not a wholly irrational decision.

(4) 'Not making the follow-up decisions that would be advantageous for those in the field' need not exclude a willingness to send

---

[14] So Connor 1984: 158 n. 2; Rood 1998: 159–61, 177–9, 181–2; Gribble 1999: 178–82. Westlake 1958a had led the way; Hornblower 1994b: 157 = 2011: 88 takes 2.65.11 as a warning against being misled by the different perspectives: 'the Sicilian Expedition failed, not so much because of bad judgement – as you might think from reading my books 6 and 7 which you haven't got to yet – as because it was marred in the execution.'

[15] Pelling 2019: 100–2, 104–5.

[16] Cf. also 1.111.1, 1.127.2, and 8.45.2 (Westlake 1958a: 102–4 = 1969: 162–5).

[17] Cf. also **6**.1, **31**.4, **69**.3, 7.57.1 nn.

reinforcements.[18] The 'follow-up decision' most in point is surely the recall of Alcibiades (**61**), and his presence would have injected more imagination into diplomacy and tactics alike. Even with reinforcements, it is possible that the timing and quantity was not 'advantageous for those in the field'. More cavalry at an early stage would have been better, for this deficiency becomes crucial to the campaign;[19] and once the tide had turned in summer 414 it might have been better not to reinforce at all but to cut losses and withdraw, just as they had ten years earlier (section 5). Alternatively they might have replaced Nicias completely, as Nicias himself suggests at 7.16.2.

Why, then, is the emphasis at 2.65.11 so different from Books 6–7? Simply because that stress on leadership is so appropriate to its context, where Thucydides is highlighting the qualities of Pericles and the wisdom of his strategy by contrasting the deficiencies of his successors and the mistakes that ensued.[20] Pericles, he says, had the status and inspired the respect to be able to lead rather than follow the *dēmos*, restraining and reassuring according to the situation:

> those that came later were more on a level with one another and each wanted to be first, and so they turned to letting the *dēmos* do as it liked. (2.65.10)

It is a strong statement, and one that affects how the later books will be read: 'every successive leader at Athens should be measured against Pericles' standard.'[21] In the Sicilian books too the absence of a Pericles is often felt (esp. **8–26, 9–14, 15, 32.3–41, 33–4, 82–7**, 7.61–8, 7.72–4 nn.). It is reasonable to talk of decline, but it is not in the *dēmos* itself – at no stage has Thucydides conveyed confidence in the wisdom of crowds – but in those who carry the responsibility of guiding it. He is interested in 'democracy' as a concept, too; he allows the Syracusan Athenagoras to give an elaborate theory of democracy (**36–9**), and it certainly matters that Syracuse and Athens are ὁμοιότροποι, both democracies, so that Athens cannot exploit some of its usual subversive tricks (7.55.2, 8.96.5: pp. 33–4). He could doubtless see democracy's inspirational qualities,

---

[18] But for a different view see Kallet 2001: 115–18, arguing both that 2.65.11 does suggest that reinforcements were inadequate and that Thucydides was right.
[19] Cf. **21.1** n, **37**.1, **43**, **52**.2, **64**.1, **70**.3, **71**.2, **88**.6, and the Introduction to Book 7, p. 27; Stahl 1973: 66–9 = 2003: 178–80; Steiner 2005.
[20] Cf. esp. Gribble 1999: 169–75, emphasising the contrast of the successors' individualism with Pericles' position and goals. The wisdom of Thucydides' judgement on this is another question, and not one to be discussed here.
[21] Stadter 2017: 287.

for otherwise he could not have written Pericles' stirring praises in the Funeral Speech (2.35–46) – though the one system of which he expresses explicit approval is the constitution of the 5000 in 411 (8.97.2, **18**.6 n.). But whatever the system, it needs leaders, and these are not the right sort. Syracuse's Hermocrates is a different matter (pp. 28–9 below).

One reason is their self-seeking ambition. Pericles had sought to avoid unnecessary risks and argued against adding to Athens' empire during the war:

> Those who followed reversed this completely and pursued other aims apparently extraneous to the war according to their own personal ambitions and gains; this was bad for them and bad for the allies. If these initiatives went well, they brought honour and benefit more to private citizens; if badly, it was the city that suffered damage for the war. (2.65.7)

One naturally thinks of Alcibiades in particular, whose personal ambitions were so important for his urging of the expedition; that passage is echoed when Thucydides makes this clear (**15** nn.), and Alcibiades' own speech often adapts what Pericles said about the city and applies it to himself (**16–18** n.). But it is not just Alcibiades.[22] When peace was in the air in the late 420s, Thucydides makes it clear why:

> Nicias' concern was to protect his good fortune at this point where he had suffered no defeats and had a high reputation. In the short term he wished to get some respite for himself and for his fellow citizens, and for the future he wanted to leave behind a name as someone whose career included no reverses for the city; and he thought that the way to achieve this was to take no risks and to be the person who trusted as little as possible to fortune – and peace was the way to avoid risks. (5.16.1)

That is surely written with an eye to what would happen in Sicily, and the irony that Nicias would leave behind a very different 'name'. Nicias is not wholly selfish there: he wants respite for his fellow Athenians as well as for himself. But there is still a self-directedness that contrasts with Pericles' commended immersion of self in city (2.60.2–4) and concern for the city's 'name' rather than one's own (2.64.3–4). By late summer 413 it is evidently time to abandon the expedition; Nicias knows it. Yet he fears what will happen to him if he returns to Athens in such abject failure, and he prevaricates (7.48.4). That is understandable, given the way

---

[22] Cf. Gribble 2006: esp. 443, 458–64.

the city treated failed generals; Thucydides had good reason to know that himself. Nicias does not even feel the need to conceal that motive from his fellow generals. Still, if this is 'love of the city', it is very different from the Periclean version. If a free state, perhaps particularly a democracy, can pride itself on the scope it leaves for an individual to flourish,[23] it is also all too easy for individuality to become egotism.

2 AUTHOR, AUDIENCE, AND PERFORMANCE

Ancient texts were meant to be heard as well as read.[24] That is why the cumbersome 'reader or listener' will so often recur in this commentary. 'Publication' would often begin with reading versions to a listening audience; even when the book market had spread copies more widely, the experiencing of a book would often be more aural and less optic than we are used to. There is evidence for collective readings among small gatherings of friends;[25] even some solitary 'readers' might have passages read to them by a literate slave; others would read aloud, as seems to have been quite common even though it is no longer thought that silent reading was rare;[26] even silent readers usually 'hear' the words internally.[27] There might be public readings too, for such ἀκροάσεις of historical works are well attested from the fifth century onwards.[28] Between 424 and 404 Thucydides was in no position to give these in Athens, but any portions of his text that he was willing to release could reach there even if he could not. It seems quite likely, for instance, that Xenophon's *Anabasis* was first released anonymously or pseudonymously; whoever performed it in that case, it was not the self-confessing author himself.[29]

A reading might not always have involved a whole book or more, but it might often have done. A combined performance of both Book 6 and Book 7 has been said to take eight hours,[30] but this is almost certainly an

---

[23] Though the issues here are not straightforward: Pelling 2019: 204–10.
[24] See now esp. Vatri 2017, with careful discussion of the impact this has on an author's style. For this mix of oral and written reception see Morrison 2007, though his emphasis falls more heavily than mine would on the oral side; mine resembles that of Rawlings 2016 and 2017: 199. Crane 1996 and e.g. Bakker 2006 and Wiseman 2018: XVI by contrast focus almost exclusively on the written.
[25] Kelly 1996; Vatri 2017: 30–2.
[26] See McCutcheon 2015, esp. 10–11 on the way that even accomplished readers like Cicero would often read aloud. On silent reading, Knox 1968 was seminal.
[27] Vatri 2017: 29–30.
[28] Clarke 2008: 367–9; Chaniotis 2009: 259–62.
[29] Pelling 2013: 40–2. On such absent authors see Baragwanath and Foster 2017b: 6–7, Vatri 2017: 18.
[30] *CT* 11–12.

over-estimate. At 5.2 syllables per second (well below the range of speeds for modern native speakers given by Vatri 2017: 90–1) or 140 words per minute (roughly the speed of a modern lecturer), the 18,000 words or 40,000 syllables of Book 6 would take just over 2 hours and the 16,500 words or 37,000 syllables of Book 7 just under,[31] and this is roughly in line with the time taken by a modern audiobook of similar length. So Books 6 and 7 together would be no longer than a Wagner opera or an uncut *Hamlet*. Some passages, though, would be particularly suitable for extraction for shorter occasions, and anyone who has attended a live performance of the Melian Dialogue (5.84–116) knows how gripping the experience can be. Within Books 6–7, the debates in Athens (**8–26**), Syracuse (**32.3–40**), and Camarina (**75.3–88**.2) would be obvious candidates, along with the Peisistratid excursus (**54–59**) and the vivid narratives of the night battle on Epipolae (7.43–5) and the battle in the Great Harbour (7.57–71).[32] So would the splendour of the departure (**30–32**) and the harrowing scenes of the final retreat (7.75–86); the second at times echoes the first, and they could form a poignant performance pair – perhaps too poignant and distressing, indeed, for performance in Athens itself. Eighty years earlier the poet Phrynichus had been fined for his tragedy describing the fall of Miletus as coming 'too close to home' (H. 6.21.2). One wonders too what would have been the Athenians' reaction if they heard this version of Alcibiades' speech at Sparta (6.89–92): doubtless mixed, given the polarisation that the man provoked both during his lifetime and after his death, but even his enthusiasts would have found their sympathy strained.

Still, it was not just an Athenian audience that Thucydides would have in mind. There was an international book-trade (Xenophon mentions a cargo including books en route for the Black Sea, *Anab.* 7.5.14), and Thucydides could reasonably expect his work, whenever he chose to circulate it, to spread throughout the Greek world. Just as Athenian drama reached an enthusiastic public in Sicily and Southern Italy – many scenes are depicted on pottery,[33] and some Athenian survivors apparently owed their freedom to their knowledge of Euripides (Plut. *Nic.* 29, 7.87.4 n.) – so Books 6 and 7 in particular might find an intrigued audience in the Greek west. When Thucydides recorded details of Syracusan topography,

---

[31] Vatri 2017: 83 n. 57 gives good reasons for preferring phonemes-per-second as a more accurate guide to performance time; still, the conversion-rate for syllables into phonemes has to be speculative, and these rougher figures can suffice to give a reasonable idea. The syllable count was made using the method set out by Vatri 2017: 83 n. 57.

[32] *CT* 31 offers some further possibilities.

[33] Taplin 1993: 12–20, 98–9.

he will have known that some of his readers would be able to match them to the locale, though he could hardly think of these as his primary audience. His treatment of Syracusan politics may set the scene for Athens too, especially in view of the oligarchic coup that would come in 411 (**36–40** n.), but many of his readers would be just as interested in Syracuse itself.

Nor was it only, nor even principally, a contemporary audience that Thucydides has in mind. He proudly proclaims his work as a 'possession for ever more than a prize-composition for immediate hearing' (1.22.4): that is another of his 'more X than Y' formulations (p. 5) and need not exclude a concern for immediate hearing as well, but it does indicate a priority. There is nothing new about this. When Herodotus expressed his hope of saving great events from being 'erased by time' (proem), it is future time that he has in mind; Homer's great figures, not just the fighters but his Helen too (*Il.* 6.358–9), also eyed future memory, and Homer is the poet who gave them that fame. What is new is the explicitness with which Thucydides spells out why these future generations might find useful the knowledge that he gives:[34]

> It will be enough for me if people judge this useful who wish to gain a clear understanding of things that happened in the past and will some day happen again, the human condition being what it is, in the same and similar ways. (1.22.4)

> I shall describe what the plague was like, setting out the symptoms that might allow someone, if it ever strikes again, to have the foreknowledge to be able to recognise it; this is on the basis of my own experience of having the disease myself and of my observation of others. (2.48.3)

> Civil strife brought many hard things to the cities, things that happen and will always happen as long as human nature stays the same, but in more intense or gentler ways and in different forms according to the individual changes of circumstances. (3.82.2)

So similar events – not identical, but alike – will recur in the future. He hopes his work will be 'useful' and bring 'clarity' (ὠφέλιμα, σαφές, 1.22.4), both for the past and for these future recurrences. He might have been

---

[34] The explicitness, but not necessarily the thinking itself. Herodotus too develops patterns of past behaviour that have continued in the present and may continue in the future; his history gives his audience plenty of material that may help in their interpretation. I develop this further at Pelling 2019: 229–31.

gratified to know that his history would be studied in modern institutes of international relations and strategic studies,[35] even if he might have reservations about the implications that are often drawn. He puts it carefully: the value will be in 'understanding' and 'recognising' the patterns as they come back. That need not exclude the drawing of morals of what to do about it – how, say, to handle a reckless *dēmos* or fight a naval battle, or indeed how to avoid launching a disastrous overseas expedition in the first place. But it does not explicitly include such take-home lessons either.

These envisaged audiences, present and future, are clearly expected to be ready to think hard about what they read or hear; very possibly we should imagine 'an interactive social setting, somewhat on a par with the Athenian assembly, in which Athenian citizens would listen critically ... and then engage in serious oral debate on the difficult issues in hand',[36] and the same goes for citizens of other states too. That audience need not expect a comfortable ride, for Thucydides is frequently not an easy read and would be an even more difficult listen. That is partly for linguistic reasons: even the native speaker Dionysius of Halicarnassus confessed his trouble in understanding the most rebarbative passages (*On Thucydides* 49, 51), though there are generally reasons why, for instance, speakers come up with formulations that obfuscate as much as clarify (frankness might damage their case),[37] or why there are so many abstractions or impersonal verbs (these may suggest aspects that go beyond the context- or person-specific).[38] But the thinking is not easy either, and often for the same reasons as for making those linguistic choices. He frequently seeks to tease general implications out of the particular and individual, sometimes to indicate a type of encounter that will recur in the narrative and often to suggest a broader truth of human behaviour. Aristotle pointed out that 'poetry deals more with universals, history with particulars' (*Poetics* 1451b6–7), citing 'what Alcibiades did or what happened to

---

[35] Low 2007: 7–32. Harloe and Morley 2012 and Lee and Morley 2015 also contain several good overviews and critiques: see esp. Forde 2012, Lebow 2012, Hawthorn 2012, Hesk 2015, Keene 2015, Johnson 2015, Stradis 2015, and Sawyer 2015. For wise reservations about the lessons often drawn for international relations see Welch 2003.

[36] Morrison 2004: 113–14; cf. Morrison 2006: 175 and 2007: 220–1, extending the point to reception outside Athens. Similarly Rawlings 2016 and 2017: 199, Baragwanath and Foster 2017b: 6–7, and for Herodotus Thomas 1992: 125–6 and 2000: 258–60.

[37] Price 2013.

[38] See for instance Macleod's exemplary study (1979 =1983: 123–39) of the difficult language in the chapters on Corcyra, 3.82–3. For the taste for abstractions cf. **12.1**, **24.2**, **89–92**, 7.4.6, 7.34.6 n., Poschenrieder 2011, and the extended study of Joho, forthcoming.

him' as the stuff of history (1451b11). That is yet another of those 'more X than Y' examples that allows some room for both: history, especially Thucydidean history, can be allowed some universals too, even if the balance is different from that in, say, Sophocles' *Oedipus Tyrannus*. It is these universal insights, after all, that explain why those similar and parallel events can be expected to recur (1.22.4).

So we need to imagine audiences that are prepared to engage as well as receive; those audiences include us, readers and still listeners too (audiobooks sell well) of that 'possession for ever' in this very distant future. He has other expectations of his audience too, not all of which a modern reader or listener is as equipped to satisfy as a contemporary would have been. A. W. Gomme began his great commentary on Thucydides with an introductory section on 'what Thucydides takes for granted',[39] covering 'the work of his predecessors', 'general economic conditions', 'conditions of warfare', and 'constitutional practice' (*HCT* i. 1–25). The present volume is not that sort of historical commentary, though some related topics will crop up.[40] One of these aspects does need treatment here, though, and that is the work of his predecessors; for this raises questions of intertextuality, the ways in which knowledge of other texts affects one's response to Thucydides' own account.

Two earlier works are particularly important here, the epics of Homer, particularly the *Iliad*, and the histories of Herodotus. (Possibly the Attic tragedians should be mentioned too, but this raises particular issues which will be discussed in the Introduction to Book 7.) Specific cases will be discussed in the notes as they arise (**1.2–5.3, 70.1, 105.**1, and then esp. 7.43–5, 7.57–59.1, 7.69.3–71, 7.78–85, 7.87.6 nn.: see also the Introduction to Book 7, pp. 14–18), but it should be noted here that echoes are even stronger and more frequent in Book 7 than in Book 6: the battle in the Great Harbour often suggests Herodotus' battle of Salamis, and the miserable retreat and end has several Iliadic echoes, for instance of Achilles fighting the river (7.84.5 n.). The whole sequence seems to foreshadow the end of the Peloponnesian War just as Salamis prefigures the final Persian defeat in Herodotus Book 9 and as the death of Hector is a premature counterpart of the fall of Troy itself (7.69.3–71, 7.75, 7.87.5–6 nn.).

---

[39] On Gomme's idiosyncratic choice of introductory topics see Pelling 2021.
[40] E.g. p. 6 on cavalry; p. 34 on the Syracusan constitution; **8.**1, **31.**5, **62.**4, 7.16.1, 7.28.3–4 nn. on finance; **22, 44.**2, 7.24.2, 7.39.2 nn. on matters of supply; **26.**2, **31.**3, **43** nn. on recruitment; **31.**2 n. on hoplites; **31.**3, 7.13.2 nn. on crewing; **49.**3, **95.**1–2, 7.13.2, 7.49.2 nn. on plunder and ravaging; **69.**2 n. on battle tactics; 7.12.4, 7.34.5 nn. on ship technology; 7.78.2 n. on marching deployment.

It is not necessary to think that every reader would have picked up every suggestion. Not everyone will have had deep knowledge or total memory even of Homer; some might be familiar only with a 'highlights reel'.[41] Even connoisseurs will not always have been attuned with total alertness. Usually intertextuality does not fundamentally change or subvert the impression that the less sensitive would have received, but just deepens and strengthens that response. Still, the deepening matters, and in several ways. It can elevate, just as Simonides elevated the battle of Plataea by echoing Achilles (fr. 11 W²) and as the Stoa Poikile in Athens elevated Marathon by depicting scenes from that battle alongside those of the Trojan War.[42] These scenes are the modern-day equivalent, just as momentous as the great triumphs and disasters of long ago. It can add immediacy: one might have a strong visual image of classic scenes, possibly created by one's own imagination or possibly drawn from paintings on vases or walls, and the picture will transfer to these similar scenes now. It can add plausibility: if events like these had happened before, or could even be imagined as happening, they could happen again now. Modern studies of court behaviour confirm that juries are more likely to believe narratives that fit story-patterns familiar from the fiction that they know, though these days those patterns are drawn more from television and film. Again, none of these effects *relies* on intertextuality. It would be a dull reader who failed anyway to find the narrative momentous, immediate, and plausible. But those responses are reinforced and intensified for those who remember those other texts.

There are contributions to interpretation too. The idea of Athens as a 'tyrant city' is again in the text anyway; the Corinthians blame themselves and the other Peloponnesians for allowing this to develop in their midst (1.122.3); Pericles uses the figure as an analogy ('like a tyranny', 2.63.2); Cleon strengthens it to an identification ('is a tyranny', 3.37.2); and Euphemus too alludes to the idea (**85**.1 n.; cf. **9**.3 n.).[43] Now Athens can be seen as the new Herodotean Xerxes, behaving as he did and meeting with a similar fate (7.77.4 n.). That is more than negative colouring. 'Tyrant' brings with it a bundle of expectations. Those help a reader or listener to understand why Athens acts as it does, brutally and arrogantly driven on by its self-belief until its final over-reach and calamity, and to understand too how its enemies react, proudly fighting for freedom and

---

[41] As Kelly forthcoming puts it in the context of Hipponax, admittedly referring there to the earlier poetic landscape; cf. also Kelly 2015.
[42] Arafat 2013; Arrington 2015: 201–3. The Stoa seems to date from the 460s: Camp 2015: 476–94.
[43] Cf. Raaflaub 1979; Tuplin 1985; Pelling 2019: 86–7 and 144.

for glory. Pattern-building was an important technique in Herodotus' explanatory repertoire, showing king after king behaving in similar ways and allowing the reader to extrapolate what is recurrent and what is case-specific. Thucydides has a smaller canvas than Herodotus, concentrating as he does on his single test-case of the Peloponnesian War, but he can build on his predecessor's work to bring out how his own cases map on to his.[44] It is another way of suggesting what is universal: such things happened before, they happen again in Thucydides' story, and are therefore all the likelier to happen again, 'the human condition being what it is' (1.22.4, quoted above).

It is not only other authors' texts that Thucydides' audience is invited to recall but also his own: intratextuality matters as well as intertextuality. Those long-distance memories of Pericles made that clear (p. 6). So let us look more deeply at the part Book 6 plays in Thucydides' history.

3 BOOK 6 IN THE HISTORY

(a) Books 6–7

The eight-book division of the history is not the only one possible; we know of an alternative thirteen-book division in antiquity, and Diodorus twice refers to a nine-book version as well.[45] But whoever divided the text at 6.105.3 knew what they were doing. As the scholiast points out, Book 7 then begins with a turning-point ('this is where Syracuse's victory and Athens' defeat begins'), and Gylippus arrives just as Syracuse is in its greatest danger. The 'battle of the walls' (**96–103** n.) is at its height, and the Athenians come within a few feet of winning it (7.2.4). There are several echoes of the opening chapters in **104–5** (nn.), including Gylippus' storm-tossed journey at **104**.2 and its symmetry with that of the Trojan refugees at **2**.3, and then the quiet 'return' of the book's final words, ἀπῆλθον ἐπ' οἴκου, is not merely a regular closural motif but also presages the far more searing 'return' of only 'a few from many' that will end Book 7 (7.87.5–6 n.).

---

[44] Pelling 2019: 235.
[45] Thirteen books: Marcellinus, *Life of Thucydides* 58, also noting that the eight-book version was the more usual; he cites the authority of 'Asclepios', often amended to 'Asclepiades', who would be the fourth-century historian (*FGrH* 12). The thirteen-book division is also at times mentioned by the scholia (Hemmerdinger 1948: 108). Nine: Diod. 12.37.2, 13.42.5. Dionysius of Halicarnassus uses the eight-book division throughout *On Thucydides*. Cf. Bonner 1920.

Books 6–7 could as readily have fallen into three books out of thirteen[46] as two books out of eight or nine, but it is clear that they form a strongly demarcated unit together. It is not that they are wholly self-contained, as we shall see; Thucydides emphasises that this was one twenty-seven-year-long war (5.26, p. 2). But he also makes it clear that there is something special about this sequence. 1.1, along with the sketch of Sicily that follows at 1.2–5.3, is an emphatic opening, and already gives a strong hint that it will not end well (n.). That prognosis is shortly reinforced by the negativity of Nicias, even if he does not go so far as to prophesy total failure (9–14, 20–22). 7.87.5–6, quoted below, will be even more clear-cut an ending, with many closural features (nn., Fowler 2000: 254–5) and a pathetic echo of the Odyssean hints of the beginning (2.1 with 1.2–5.3 n.): it is almost as if the war is over (p. 12). The last stages recall the beginning in other ways too. The strong visuality of the description of the departure helps (30–32.2 n.), with its 'brilliance' (λαμπρότης, 31.6) fixing the scene in the reader/listener's imagination. It is explicitly recalled as they begin their dismal withdrawal:

> It was hard to bear, particularly as the brilliance and pride of the beginning has come to such an ignominious conclusion. This was the greatest reverse of fortunes ever to befall a Greek army. They had set out to enslave others; it now fell to them to depart more in fear of suffering this themselves. They had sailed to the sound of prayers and paeans, and now began to leave with the opposite in their ears, marching on foot rather than sailing, more like an army than a fleet. (7.75.6–7)

There had already been echoes of 30–32.2 during the battle in the Great Harbour, the clash that finally made certain that 'greatest reverse of fortune' (7.69.3–71 n.). Readers and listeners are encouraged to look forward at the beginning just as they will look back at the end. The dominant mood of the crowd at 30–32.2 is one of excitement and optimism, but there is an undercurrent of unease: there are 'wailings' as well as paeans and prayers (ὀλοφυρμοί, 30.2), just as there will be οἰμωγή at the end (7.71.6, 75.4). One can compare as well as contrast the method of Plutarch, who depicts the excited fascination as Athenians trace out the shape of Sicily in the gymnasium dust (Nic. 12.1, Alc. 17.4: 1.1 n.). But priests deliver warnings (Nic. 13.1), and anecdotes create an atmosphere of gloom: Socrates' internal

---

[46] Break-points at **62.5** or **74.2** and at 7.18.4 would give three blocks of more or less even length, but Bonner 1920: 77 preferred **93.4** and 7.41.4. Earlier treatments posited **62.5** and 7.18.4 (Krüger), and **93.4** and 7.18.4 (Kalinka and Festa): Hemmerdinger 1948: 109.

daimonion warns him that it will end badly; the astronomer Meton burns down his own house to win sympathy that might let him off going; the departure coincides with the laments that were part of the festival of the Adonia (*Alc.* 17.5–18.5). The manner could not be more different from that of Thucydides, and yet there is a certain similarity in the implications.

That shaping is made even stronger by the recurrent intertextual suggestions of Xerxes' invasion (pp. 12–13), itself moulded into a narrative unity by Herodotus in his Books 7–9. That like this begins with a long debate, weighing the arguments for and against and illuminating the aggressor's mindset (**8–26** n., Hdt. 7.8–19); such elaboration indicates the importance of what is to come. Both campaigns also end in defeat and débâcle: in Sicily's case,

> this was the greatest event of this war, and it seems to me the greatest of any Greek events that we know of from tradition, most brilliant for the victors and most catastrophic for the victims. For they were altogether defeated in every respect, and their suffering was unqualified in any way. It was what people call total annihilation – infantry, fleet, everything; and only a few returned home from the many who sailed. So much for what happened in Sicily. (7.87.5–6)

And 8.1 goes on to stress the shattering effect on the city. At first they could not believe it; when they realised the truth, they turned on the orators who had urged the expedition and the seers and oracle-mongers who had encouraged their hopes, and it is now the Spartans, not the Athenians, who are 'full of good hope' (εὐέλπιδες, 8.2.4 ~ 6.24.3):

> Everything pressed in on every side to cause the Athenians anguish and envelop them in the greatest fear and terror that they had ever known. For individuals and city alike had been stripped of many hoplites and cavalry and a generation of young men for which they could see no ready substitute; they could see too that there were not enough ships in the dockyards nor funds in the treasury nor crews to row. All hope of salvation was gone. (8.1.2)

So Thucydides has crafted a story with a beginning, a middle, and a catastrophic end, and that end is then used as the starting-point of the next phase. That shaping may affect how strongly his judgements are put. Two years later Athens loses the island of Euboea, so vital for the city's grain supply:

> When news reached the Athenians, there was terror such as there had never been before. Not the disaster in Sicily, even though it had seemed great at the time, nor anything else had ever yet so frightened them. (8.96.1)

'Even though it had seemed great at the time'? Perhaps this is 'progressive correction', a familiar technique in Greek narrative whereby an initial impression is overlaid by a more nuanced one;[47] or there may be some implicit focalisation or free indirect discourse here, what Irene de Jong calls a 'short "peep" into the minds of characters participating in those events',[48] with the narrator conveying the way people thought and talked now that the impact of Sicily was receding into the distance: 'well, that seemed terrifying enough, but this is even worse'. But the phrasing is still grudging. One could understand if, rather as Tycho von Wilamowitz argued long ago for Sophoclean tragedy,[49] Thucydides here allowed the impact of the individual scene to override strict consistency in the whole.

(b) Book 5 and Book 6

The firm narrative contours of Book 6 contrast with the disjointed narrative of Book 5. Many have suspected that Book 5 lacks Thucydides' final touch; it is probably better to see the narrative manner as reflecting the history itself, with all parties treading uncertainly and aware that anything might bring them back to total war.[50] Events could easily have taken that path after the major confrontation of Mantinea in 418 (p. 1, 7.1 n.). But the book had ended with a sequence that is not at all unpolished, the Melian dialogue (5.85–113). The Athenians there enter into secret conclave with the councillors of Melos, and urge them not to resist or insist on neutrality; otherwise Athens will be forced to reduce the island. Hope, they urge, is pointless; the Spartans will not help; why not save themselves and give in now? But the Melians do not give up their hopes; they fight and they lose; and the Athenians kill the men of military age and enslave the women and children (5.116).

The closeness of Melos to the Syracusan expedition is a matter of history, not of Thucydides' art: the Athenians went to one in 416, to the other in 415. And yet Thucydides did not need to elaborate Melos so much. It was not the only, nor the first, Athenian atrocity of this sort; yet there was no such treatment given to Scione (5.32.1) or Torone (5.3), two cases that would later be remembered with Melos in a catalogue of Athenian disgrace (X. *Hell.* 2.2.3, Isoc. 12.63, Ael. Arist. *On the peace with*

---

[47] So Rood 1998: 278 n. 82, but see also *CT* on 8.96.1. For the technique see Pelling 2019, index s.v. 'revision in stride'.
[48] De Jong 1987: 112–13, discussing instances in Homer.
[49] Wilamowitz-Moellendorff 1917.
[50] Rood 83–108 argues similarly.

Athens p. 404 J.). The elaboration is Thucydides' choice, and the juxtaposition must be suggestive. But of what?

There was an answer readily on offer in Greek thinking: Melos as an act of *hybris*, Syracuse as the come-uppance. Such a pattern would not be surprising in tragedy nor in Herodotus nor in Xenophon. It would generally involve the gods, though tragic poets and historians alike might incorporate a human and secular register as well, just as in Homer Troy falls both because the gods are punishing Paris and because the Greeks have the bigger battalions and the better fighters. In his provocatively titled *Thucydides Mythistoricus* of 1907, Francis Cornford related Thucydides' narrative to these ways of thinking: by the end of Book 7

> Tyche, Elpis, Apate, Hybris, Eros, Phthonos, Nemesis, Ate – all these have crossed the stage and the play is done. (Cornford 1907: 220)

Cornford himself was happy to accept that in Thucydides too there might be some theological implications. Most modern readers of Thucydides would find that harder to believe. It is not that religion is wholly absent: it plays a major part in Thucydides' treatment of the Herms and Mysteries outrage of 415 (**27–29** n.), and at 7.18 2 he stresses the importance of Spartan religious sentiment in comparing their mentality in 431 and in 413 (n.). He even allows his Nicias at the end to address something like the *hybris* view: 'if our campaign stirred any of the gods to envy, by now we have been punished enough' (7.77.4). But his focus is on religious anthropology, how humans thought about the gods and their likely anger, rather than on finding any divine force to be genuinely at work. It is more plausible to see Thucydides as suggesting some naturalistic equivalent,[51] but it would be all the more credible to an audience primed by those supernatural expectations to find familiar the underlying pattern in events.[52]

If the connection is nothing to do with the gods, what else might it be? A continuity of bullying can certainly be found: Athens first takes on a little state close to home, then thinks it can impose its will on a more distant

---

[51] So Herter 1954: 330 = 1968: 384–5; Macleod 1974: 395, 400 = 1983: 62, 67; Connor 1984: 167–8 n. 22; Orwin 1994: 111, 118; cf. Liebeschuetz 1968a: 76–7.
[52] For the approach cf. Kallet 2013 and Liotsakis 2015, though both argue that Thucydides leaves open the possibility of genuine divine intervention; so does Marinatos 1981.

one about which it knows far less and far too little (**1.1**). That may affect audience response:

> The Athenians will receive in Sicily what they gave in Melos. And they well deserve it. We assent; perhaps we even feel some pleasure in the foreknowledge of so just a punishment. (Connor 1984: 168)

Most would not go that far. Any such 'pleasure' would be short-lived, and it is hard to think that many readers or listeners respond with relish to the sufferings of the final retreat (7.78–85). But it is true that some feeling of justice may affect what Aristotle calls τὸ φιλάνθρωπον, that humane moral sensibility that becomes offended when suffering or prosperity bears no relation to desert (*Poetics* 1452b38b, 1453a2).

Still, that is not yet a naturalistic counterpart for a pattern involving divinity, for such traditional thinking would also offer an explanation: pride goes before a fall, because the gods ensure that it should. Can there be a human explanation for why Melos should be followed by disaster in Sicily?

The key lies in two emotions: hope and fear.[53] Hope drives the Melians to resistance and the Athenians to sail against Syracuse, and in each case hope turns sour. By the end the Athenian plight is as hopeless as the Melians', and now it is the Athenian Nicias who vainly looks to the gods (7.77.2–4, cf. the Melians at 5.104, 112). Thucydides' Diodotus knew that hope, so often ill-founded and damaging, is a universal human characteristic (3.45): just so.

Equally important is the Athenians' fear or, rather, a paradoxical combination of fearlessness and fear. At Melos their envoys parade their fearlessness: no fear of the Spartans, no fear of the gods (5.91, 105). Yet there is fear too. It may seem a paradox that a mighty eagle like Athens should be afraid of a sparrow like Melos, but there is a genuine fear that unless they act now, unless they use Melos to set an example to others, they may suffer badly later (5.91, 95, 97, 99). There is then a strand of fearful caution as well as recklessness in the decision to go to Sicily. It is prudent (σῶφρον), say the Egestaeans, to strike before Syracuse becomes powerful

---

[53] Pelling 2014: 74–81. On hope see e.g. Wassermann 1947: 30 and esp. Lateiner 2018. Orwin 1994: 97–141 emphasises Athens' entrusting of her fate to Alcibiades, almost an incarnation of her own optimistic qualities, and Nicias, embodying Melos-like piety and eventually empty hopes. Luginbill 1999: 65–81 and Ober and Perry 2014 bring hope and fear together, with Ober and Perry interestingly arguing that Thucydides sees the combination as generating 'excessive risk-aversion in the face of probable gains and excessive risk-seeking by decision-makers faced with high probability losses': this is in line with modern 'prospect theory'. They see this as the link between Melos and Sicily.

enough to aid its Peloponnesian kinsmen (**6.**2); Nicias' rebuttal is not very strong (**11.**2–3). Alcibiades adds that there are dangers to the empire itself unless it keeps pressing onwards (**18.**2). Both with Melos and with Sicily there is also a readiness to adopt uncompromising means, for it is a concern for safety (ἀσφάλεια) that convinces the Athenians to go in even greater numbers (**24–6**). These prove counterproductive, for they generate a corresponding fear in the Sicilian and Italian cities that might otherwise have been valuable allies (**33.**4–5, **44.**2 nn.). The numbers are so great that it is like a city on the move (p. 1), on a scale that will mean that the failure imperils the city at home (7.77 n.). Fear plays its part in the recall of Alcibiades as well (**15.**4, **29.**3, **53.**2–3, **60.**1 nn.). The fear that motivates the expedition, just as it motivated what happened at Melos, is also responsible for the vastness of the catastrophe.[54]

(c) *Book 6 in the Whole*

If fear is playing a part now, that is one way in which Book 6 recalls Book 1, for in Thucydides' mind it was fear that precipitated the war:

> The truest explanation (ἀληθεστάτην πρόφασιν), most unclear in what was said at the time, I regard as the Athenians becoming great, frightening the Spartans, and forcing them to war. As for the openly expressed reasons (or grievances, αἰτίαι) of each side, on the basis of which they broke the truce and began the war, those were the following. (1.23.6)

That passage is resonantly echoed at **6.**1 (n.): it is all beginning again. It is possible to find more elaborate symmetries too, with a new 'archaeology' (**1.**2–**5.**3) to match 1.1–23, a new large debate (**8–26**) about helping one's allies to mirror the Corcyrean debate of 1.31–44. and then a switch to the other side to discussion at Syracuse (**32.**3–**41**) or Sparta (1.67–88).[55] There will be a similar effect at the end of Book 7 when the collapse of the expedition seems to prefigure the fall of Athens and the end of the war (7.87.5–6; p. 12). The books together can seem a microcosm of the whole war, not unlike the way that the four days' action of the *Iliad* captures in miniature all ten years at Troy.

---

[54] For a related but different reading see Desmond 2006, who agrees about the importance of fear in Thucydides' thinking but puts more weight on Athens' 'fatal fearlessness' (366) at Melos, and sees this also as explaining their failure at Syracuse.

[55] Cf. Rawlings 1981: 58–125, arguing for a more intricate symmetry.

These books, then, look both backwards and forwards. There were moments too when the earlier books seemed to carry a forward glance to the expedition. That was most explicit at 2.65 (pp. 4–8), but there are less explicit touches as well: one of these has also already been noted, the irony to be found in Nicias' aspirations at 5.16 (p. 7). The treatment of the first Sicilian expedition of 427–424 will be discussed in section 5, but it showed no shortage of ambition: the motivation included 'making a preliminary trial to see if Sicilian affairs could be brought under their control' (3.86.4, quoted at p. 31), and by 425 the Syracusans are entertaining fears 'that the Athenians might one day use Messina as a base for attacking them in bigger force', μείζονι παρασκευῆι (4.1.2, cf. Hermocrates at 4.60.2). Whether or not the Syracusans were already looking ten years ahead, it is likely that Thucydides' readers and listeners would. That earlier expedition ends with a substantial speech of Hermocrates, pleading for pan-Sicilian unity to face the imperialist aggressor (4.59–64). That is too big to sit comfortably on the scattered notices of the first expedition that have preceded, and Thucydides must already have been thinking forward to the bigger one to come:[56] it then forms a useful point of reference several times in Books 6–7, not least for measuring the harder tone that Hermocrates will adopt at Camarina (**76–80** n., cf. also **33–34** n.). Finally there is the vindictiveness of the Athenian *dēmos* towards the generals who they thought were culpable for the failure, exiling two and fining the third (4.65.3–4, pp. 31–2). That prefigures what the generals now have to fear: that grim and unforgiving absent presence of the *dēmos* is as relevant for Alcibiades in Book 6 (**29**.2, **61**) as for Nicias in Book 7 (esp. 7.48.4).

So there are various ways in which the sparse narrative of the earlier expedition has acclimatised the audience to what will happen now. There has been a broader foretaste too that something like this will come: not perhaps catastrophe in Sicily, but catastrophe somehow and somewhere, and the qualities that built Athens will eventually bring her down. Pericles himself, at least Thucydides' Pericles, foresaw the danger. What was needed was a policy of calm restraint (ἡσυχία), not taking risks and not trying to expand the empire during the war (2.65.7):

> I could give you many other reasons why you should feel confident in ultimate victory, if only you will make up your minds not to add

---

[56] As Jebb pointed out long ago (1880: 288), Hermocrates says the Athenians are in Sicily 'with a few ships', 4.60.1, but in fact the number (a total of 60) was small only in comparison with the force eventually sent in 415 (**1.1** n.): cf. *HCT* v. 412, Rood 1998: 6–8. Hermocrates goes on at 4.60.1 to make explicit his fear that they may one day come in greater numbers (πλέονί ποτε στόλωι).

to the empire while the war is in progress, and not to go out of your way to add new perils to those you have already. What I fear is more our own mistakes than anything the enemy may devise. (1.144.1)

Well might he have that fear. For that strategy required the opposite qualities to the ones that had made Athens great, those so strongly (perhaps over-strongly) described by the Corinthians at Sparta at 1.70: the daring, the risk-taking, the self-belief, the irrepressible energy. ἡσυχία by contrast characterises the Spartans (1.69.4), so concerned to safeguard what they have (τὰ ὑπάρχοντα σώιζειν), so averse to any unnecessary hazard (1.70.3–4). Pericles had the leadership skills to keep the Athenian temperament in check – though only just, and even he was thrown out of office before the people thought better of it (2.65.2–4). His successors had no such stature (pp. 6–8). Now the inheritance is split (**8–26** n.). Alcibiades has something of Pericles' charisma, and abuses it (**16–18** n., **89–92** n.); Nicias echoes the policy, and several times sounds more Spartan than Athenian (**9–10** nn., p. 28). No wonder 'mistakes' followed that were worse 'than anything the enemy may devise'. Not that failure in Sicily was predetermined. It could easily have been otherwise (p. 2). But if it had not been Sicily, it might be somewhere else: Carthage, perhaps (**15**.2, **34**.2, **90**.2 nn.). One day the empire would fall, as all empires do. Pericles knew that too (2.64.3).

4 THE SPEECHES

Book 6 has more speeches[57] (ten, including the short speech of the general at **41**) than any other book, and they make up the largest proportion of the whole (about 38 per cent). Next after it are Book 1 (eight, comprising about 30 per cent of the book) and Book 3 (six, about 32 per cent). Book 7 is some way behind (four if we include Nicias' letter of 7.11–15; about 13 per cent). This density in Book 6 is not coincidence. Like Book 1 it deals with the onset of a conflict, and this involves exploring the mindset of the participants; like Book 3, it also investigates the relations of powerful states to those they can bully (or think they can), and that too

---

[57] Throughout this section 'speech' refers to those delivered in direct discourse. The narrative mentions many further speech-acts and at times important material is given in indirect speech, especially at **47–50** and 7.42. These could have just as big an impact on events. This section, though, is concerned with the particular effects that direct discourse can have. Much of the next few paragraphs draws on Pelling 2000: 112–22; a fuller bibliography is given there. For more recent treatments see esp. Marincola 2001: 77–85 and 2007b: 120–2; Vössing 2005; Porciani 2007; Schütrumpf 2011; Feddern 2016; Tsakmakis 2017: 272–4; Tosi 2018.

4 THE SPEECHES

invites interest in what and how both sides thought. Speeches do not give uncomplicated access to such thinking, for the words aim to persuade and can be wrapped in mendacity. They can often give sharper insight into the attitudes of their internal Athenian or Syracusan audiences, or what the speakers expect those attitudes to be, than those of the speakers themselves. But they are a good start.

Thucydides' readers and listeners would not be surprised to find speeches, and they would be under no illusion that these were verbatim reports. They were used to such speeches in Homer and Herodotus, and nobody would have thought that Herodotus knew the actual words of Solon to Croesus (1.30–2) or of Xerxes to his counsellors (7.8–18), still less of Atossa's pillow-talk with Darius (3.134). What would surprise them more is that Thucydides made a fuss about it:

> As for all that they said, either before the war or after its outbreak, it was difficult both for myself in the cases of the speeches I heard and for my various informants to remember the precise things that were said; but I have put this so as to capture how in my view each speaker might most have said what was required (τὰ δέοντα εἰπεῖν) about the issues at hand, keeping as close as possible to the overall line of thought of what was really said (ἐχομένωι ὅτι ἐγγύτατα τῆς ξυμπάσης γνώμης τῶν ἀληθῶς λεχθέντων).[58]   (1.22.1)

A fuss, then – but not a very clear fuss. A reader or listener might gather more from the context than from these words themselves. Thucydides has just expressed his conviction that impartial observers who 'base their views on the facts themselves' (ἀπ' αὐτῶν τῶν ἔργων σκοποῦσι) will decide that this war was the biggest ever fought (1.21.2): these 'facts themselves' are then subdivided into 'what they said' and τὰ δ' ἔργα τῶν πραχθέντων, an awkward way of putting 'the facts proper', the doings rather than the sayings, among αὐτὰ τὰ ἔργα. What he says about those doings has been discussed above (p. 2). So his procedure with words will not be the same as with actions, though with words too he has gathered informants; the words too will be a way of deepening insight into 'the facts themselves',

---

[58] 'Overall line of thought' or 'sentiment' is a better translation here than the usual 'general sense', as like γνώμη it directs more attention to the person who formulates that view, who γιγνώσκει: thus Badian 1992 suggested 'intention' and Vössing 2005 'Einschätzung' ('evaluation'). It is important though to retain an emphasis on the content of what is said, not just the mentality: the 'evaluation' of Nicias at **20–23** is that this is a bad idea and the 'intention' is that it will persuade the assembly to abandon it, but the sentiment of the speech is that they should send a bigger force. That is why Thucydides says 'the γνώμη of *what was said*', not 'of the speakers', τῶν λεχθέντων rather than τῶν λεγόντων (Vössing 2005: 215).

what made this war what it was and as big as it was, but will aim at a different type of accuracy.

What sort of accuracy, though, and what sort of procedure? The reader/listener would be impressed that Thucydides had thought about it, and notice that some respect was being paid to 'the overall line of thought of what was really said'. How much, though, is anything but clear.

(1) 'To say what was required': in what sense of 'required'? 'Required' if the speaker was to give the best advice? Clearly not, at least in those cases where two speakers give contradictory advice, like Nicias and Alcibiades in **8–18** or Hermocrates and Athenagoras at **32.3–41**: they could not both be right. 'Required' to make the best case possible for the course recommended? 'Required' to phrase in the best way whatever arguments were really used, good or bad? Or some mix of, or compromise among, all of these?

(2) 'The overall line of argument of what was really said': how overall is overall? Something as broad as 'we should go to Sicily' or 'you should support our side, not the enemy' or 'I, Alcibiades, am not that bad, so don't think too harshly of me'? Or does the 'sense' include the particular arguments that were used?

(3) 'Keeping as close as possible . . .': 'possible' in view of the hazy and conflicting memories of my informants? Or 'possible' given that, as I have just said, I have prioritised making the speeches as effective as I could, which might sometimes, but not always, coincide with the line that the speaker in fact took?

Thucydides' formulation has been much discussed, but nothing can iron out those ambiguities: they are there in the Greek. Perhaps he was deliberately giving himself an umbrella definition, one that would be consistent with different balances in different cases between historical authenticity and free composition;[59] after all, he must have had access to much better information in some cases – the Corcyrean debate, for instance, which he may have heard (1.31–44), or the arguments of Nicias and Alcibiades at **8–25**, ruefully picked over in retrospect by many who had been there – than in others, for example the Plataean debate of 3.52–68 or Nicias' final speech at 7.77. There were few survivors to tell the tale of either. And if speeches before battle were given (they probably were,

---

[59] So I argued in Pelling 2000: 112–22 = 2009: 176–87. Vössing 2005: 212 n. 12 reasonably asks why Thucydides might not in that case have preferred to say nothing at all. The answer is that he wanted to indicate *some* respect throughout for what was really said; as in many other aspects of 1.20–3 he is signalling some distance from, as well as respect for, his predecessors and especially Herodotus.

7.60.5 n.), not everyone would have heard every word, and what had been said to tribe A might be different from what would be said a few minutes later to tribe G.

Amid all the scholarly controversy, one or two points ought to be clear. Thucydides did take the trouble to find out what he could about what was really said, and he cross-examined his 'various informants' on this just as he did on the actions. He cared. He also meant the speeches to aid historical insight into what really happened (αὐτῶν τῶν ἔργων). That need not always mean strict faithfulness to every word or argument used, and sometimes the insight may be more into the general background than the events of one particular day:[60] for instance, the emphasis on expediency in the Mytilenean debate (3.37–48) may underplay the humane emotion of pity that motivated many of those present, but can still illuminate the way that Athenians were coming usually to think and argue. But it is hard to think that much insight would be given by arguments that were wholly anachronistic and could not possibly have been used. All this tells against free composition for the sake of it, on any occasion when he felt he had good information.

On the other hand, even in cases of the highest fidelity he had plenty of choices to make. It was up to him where to put speeches and which speakers to choose. In Sicily Lamachus and Demosthenes doubtless had things to say too, and indirect speech makes it clear that they were important (**49**, 7.42); but Nicias is the one given speeches, three on campaign (**68**, 7.61–4, 7.77), together with the letter of 7.11–15, and two in the assembly before they left (**9–14, 20–22**). The historian had to make selections too within speeches as well as among speakers. His major speeches are usually much of a length, though they would not have been in reality: those of Nicias (**9–14**), Alcibiades (**16–18**), Hermocrates (**33–34**), Athenagoras (**36–40**), Hermocrates again (**76–80**), Euphemus (**82–87**), and Alcibiades again (**89–92**) are all between 750 and 1000 words, perhaps five-and-a-half to seven minutes in performance. It is likely that all in real life were longer. Demosthenes' *Olynthiacs* and *Philippics* are all twice as long and sometimes a lot more, and in Attic court-cases between 15 and 30 minutes were allowed.[61] Even if Thucydides had had total and precise knowledge of what had been said, he would have had to decide what to cut and what to keep. Some candidates for cutting would be obvious: untendentious

---

[60] Cf. Kitto 1966: 341–50, taking a different example from the Mytilenean debate, the generalisation that unexpected prosperity leads states astray (3.39.4).

[61] Vatri 2017: 83. These speeches in Thucydides are symbouleutic rather than dicastic, but the court conventions still allow an idea of what was thought reasonable for making an important case.

narrative of material the reader or listener would know already; the sort of rhetorical throat-clearing that the best of speakers sometimes allow; the froth of indignation or exuberance once the point had been got across; any 'I am going to argue . . .' preliminaries or 'Thus we see . . .' summaries, especially when the general purpose could be inferred from the narrative scene-setting (e.g. **8.**4, **75.**3–4, **88.**10). Elsewhere he would keep what seemed to him most telling and thought-provoking; hence it is not surprising that there are so many generalisations about human nature or about the character of the empire. All such things might well have been said; perhaps he had good evidence to know that they were said; but they might not have been said quite like this, nor constituted so large a fraction of the whole.

This commentary will be concerned with what Thucydides does with his material and only rarely with what was said in the real-life equivalents. That is not because the reality would be irrelevant even for those who focus on Thucydides' literary techniques. If only we had verbatim transcripts there would be no better way of illustrating his technique, as we can do by comparing Tacitus' version of a speech of the emperor Claudius with the original that is preserved on stone (*Ann.* 11.24 and *ILS* 212). But too much of the reconstruction of the reality has to be speculative, and often relies on uncertain modern preconceptions of what would be comprehensible or acceptable to an audience. At least with Thucydides' versions we know what we are dealing with.

What, then, are the choices that Thucydides makes? Each speech will be discussed in its place, along with their individualising features of style and manner, but this is the place to discuss why Thucydides chose these as the ones to develop. These are not the only settings possible. Athenians, probably Alcibiades, would have made speeches at Rhegium (**44.**3), Messina (**50.**1), and elsewhere, but it is the Camarina debate that gets the space (**75.**3–**88.**2). There were many land-battles, but it is at **68** and 7.61–9 that there are pre-battle speeches. The Syracusans would have spoken at Carthage (**88.**6). The debate of the generals could have been put in direct speech (**47–50.**1). The Corinthians might have had just as much impact at Sparta as Alcibiades (**88.**10, **93.**1 n.), but it is Alcibiades who gets the words. One can usually see why Thucydides chose as he did. The Camarina debate was one where a Syracusan viewpoint can be presented as well as an Athenian, and can be taken as paradigmatic of the issues in people's minds elsewhere. Similarly Nicias' speech at **68** can indicate the sort of things said on other occasions too, while 7.61–9 is part of the build-up for the climactic battle. Carthage did not come to much: it is the dog that did not bark (see Introduction to Book 7, p. 35). At **47–50.**1 it is the content of the different generals' viewpoints that matters rather than the way they put it; in any case, Lamachus is a man of deeds rather than words while enough has already been done to characterise Nicias and Alcibiades. Or perhaps not quite enough in Alcibiades' case: the reader may already understand the pressure that Corinth might or might not exercise on Sparta (Book 1 has explored that question), but there is a good deal more interest in how this prince of twisters might twist when facing the solid and suspicious men of Sparta.

The speeches also illuminate their different locales, with one exchange in the Athenian assembly, one at Syracuse, one in Camarina, and one at Sparta. As for the speakers, there is a clear reason for favouring Nicias, Hermocrates, and Alcibiades, for these are the men who made a difference: Thucydides' belief in the force of personalities was already clear in his treatment of Pericles (pp. 4–8), and clear again when he explored the reasons for making peace in 421 (p. 7). As for the less prominent speakers, the Syracusan general at **41** is not given a name, perhaps because Thucydides did not know it, perhaps because his office matters more than his identity (**41**.1 n.). Athenagoras and Euphemus both have significant names, 'Athens-speaker' and 'Good Speaker'. That should not encourage doubts as to their existence – Euphemus happens to be independently attested at Athens in a Sicilian connection (**75**.4 n.) – but the names can still be found suggestive (**35**.2 n.): Athenagoras is indeed reminiscent of Athenian politics and especially Cleon (**35**.2 n.), and Euphemus is a good name for a diplomat who is expected to be persuasive. Both are also vehicles for ideas that go beyond their immediate context. Athenagoras' theoretical defence of democracy helps to prepare for the Athenian constitutional upheavals of 411 (**36–40** n.), while Euphemus expresses a view of the empire that many Athenians may have shared (**82–87** nn.). He is indeed a better mouthpiece for that than Alcibiades would have been: a speech on his lips at (say) Messina would have generated more interest in the maverick speaker than in his city (**75**.3–**88**.2 n.).

Speech and narrative must always be taken together, and readers and listeners weigh what speakers claim against what the narrative has already made clear. The initial survey of Sicily lends credence to some of Nicias' claims, but there is support there for Alcibiades too (**1**.2–**5**.3 n, **16–18**, **17**.2 nn.); it is not hard, though, to sense the hollowness of Alcibiades' claim for credit for his achievement at Mantinea (**16**.6 n.). It is already clear that Hermocrates is right and Athenagoras wrong about Athens' intentions (**36–40** n.); whether Hermocrates is right about the way to deal with them is another question (**34**.4–8 n.). Readers and listeners will already have formed opinions about the Athenian empire against which they can measure the claims of Euphemus (**82–87**), and they will certainly have views of their own about Alcibiades' 'patriotism' (**89–92**). In other cases it is the subsequent rather than preceding narrative that guides assessment. Whichever general's advice immediately seems shrewdest at **47–50**.1, the failure of diplomacy that follows and an increasing sense of Nicias' dithering may cement the awareness that Lamachus' up-and-at-them approach was best: that is then confirmed by Demosthenes' brisk professional judgement at 7.42.3 (n.). The audience may remember distant speeches too, especially those of Pericles (pp. 6–8) and the Melian dialogue (**9**.3, **10**.1, **13**.1, **80**.2, **83**.2, 7.66–8 nn.), and Euphemus' words at **82–87** also recall the rather different claims made by Athenians for their empire before the war (n.). These inter-speech links create a further 'narrative' of their own, showing how mindsets have changed under the pressure and tribulations of the war.

Thucydides stresses national character too. The powerful picture of innovative, risk-taking, irrepressible Athens has already been mentioned (p. 22); it is then important to the course of the war that Syracuse has something, perhaps an increasing amount, of the same, a democracy that is shaping to be the new Athens (pp. 33–4) just as Athens is something of a new Persia (p. 13). The relation of the great individuals to their cities is just as interesting, and it is usually the speeches that make it clear. Alcibiades is too much like Athens for the city's own good (**30–32**.2 n.); he was not the man to restrain Athenian instincts when Periclean restraint was needed (p. 6). Nicias on the other hand is out of tune with those instincts, often sounding rather Spartan (**9**.1, **9**.3, **10**.2 nn.).[62] The most Periclean figure is arguably Hermocrates, at least at this stage of his career (**33–4**, **72**.2, **77**.1–2, **78**.2, **78**.3 nn.);[63] at 4.61.1 he was already commending a strategy that echoed Periclean restraint.

Nor is that the only symmetry between Hermocrates and Athenian individuals. One that might have been developed in the later books was with Alcibiades, as Hermocrates too will be forced into exile under suspicion of tyranny and will then turn against his own city: Athens is not the only city to have trouble in coping with its great men (**33–4** n.; Introduction to Book 7, pp. 33–4). A particularly intriguing and paradoxical comparison is with Nicias. Hermocrates knows what Syracuse needs to do and Nicias knows where Athens is weak, but their insight is better than their timing. Hermocrates articulates his wisdom too soon (**72–3**, **76–80** nn.); Syracuse does what he urges and consequently loses those early encounters, and if the city had fully taken his advice there might

---

[62] 'An Athenian with a Spartan heart', Edmunds 1975: 109.
[63] Cf. Westlake 1958b: 265–7 = 1969: 199–201 and e.g. Shanske 2007: 56; Kremmydas 2017: 113. This is complicated but not undermined by his less Periclean future (Hinrichs 1981).

have been catastrophe even before the fighting began (**34**.4–8 n.). Nicias also articulates his too soon. The situation in late 415 does not justify the backs-to-the-wall rhetoric of **68** (n.); his despairing letter of 7.11–15 identifies the weaknesses of Athens' position, but things are not that bad yet (n.). Hermocrates is premature in optimism and Nicias in defeatism; the eager can-do of the one is compounded by the can't-do of the other; and Syracuse wins.

5 ATHENS AND SYRACUSE

Thucydides' Sicilian survey at **1**.2–**5**.3 ends with Syracuse on the move, strengthening its power still further by devastating and recolonising Camarina (**5**.3 n.): this is a useful way of highlighting not just Syracuse but Camarina too, the city that will be the centre of attention at **75**.3–**88**.2. In fact that Camarina resettlement had been nearly forty years earlier, perhaps around 461 (Diod. 11.76.5), soon after the tyranny of the Deinomenids at Syracuse had come to an end in 465 (**38**.3 n.). That was an anti-tyrannical time, and those at Acragas and Messina also disappeared within the decade 471–461. Syracuse had had its ups and downs since; during the 450s for instance the Sicel leader Ducetius had established a power base, only to be first defeated by an alliance of Syracuse and Acragas in 451/50 and then restored with Syracusan help to found a new city at Kale Akte in 446 (**7**.1.4 n.). But since then the ups had been greater than the downs, including a great victory over Acragas at the River Himeras in 446, and the city had shown no reluctance to exploit the civic strife that was so recurrent a feature in Sicily and S. Italy (p. 34). During the 440s it completed its subjugation of various Sicel settlements (**34**.1, **45**.1, **88**.3–5, **7**.1.4 nn.), and by the 420s its domination was clear.[64]

The city had long been powerful enough to impress (perhaps indeed over-impress[65]) the Greek world, and in 481–480 an embassy of Spartans and Athenians had come to plead for assistance against the Persian invader; the city's ruler Gelon was not tempted, nor did he like the way they set about it (Hdt. 7.157–62), and it came to nothing. In the 430s, with war anticipated, both Sparta and Athens again turned their eyes to the west. When Athens formed its alliance with Corcyra in 433, one of their reasons was that 'the island seemed to them well situated for the journey to Italy and Sicily' (1.44.3), a point that the Corcyreans themselves

---

[64] On Sicily between the Persian and Peloponnesian Wars see esp. Asheri 1992, an outstandingly clear summary, and Zahrnt 2006.
[65] Cf. Cawkwell 1997: 79; **17**.5 n.

had stressed (1.36.2);[66] in the same year it either made or, more likely, reconfirmed[67] alliances with Leontini and Rhegium (OR 149 = ML 63-4 = Fornara 124-5; **6**.2, **44**.2 nn.). There were relations with powerful individuals too: Archonides of Herbita (7.1.4 n.) and the Messapian Artas or Artos (7.33.4 n.) at some point became Athenian *proxenoi* (i.e. official 'friends', who would do what they could to help Athens). Athenian individuals too had their personal links, and Nicias himself may even have been a *proxenos* of Syracuse (Diod. 13.27.3: 7.48.2 n.).[68] Nor were Spartans inactive. Gylippus' father had some personal relationship with Thurii (**104**.2 n.), and in 431 the Spartans went so far as to fix a quota of ships and amount of money for each Sicilian and Italian ally (2.7.2). It seems that those contributions never came, but Athens had good reasons for concern. This was partly for economic reasons, as Athens imported Sicilian grain[69] and South Italian timber and pitch were needed for its ship-building,[70] but there was a real prospect of military intervention as well. Many of the Sicilian and Italian towns were Dorian, and several, Syracuse included, were colonies of Athens' enemies: it could readily be feared that 'Dorians might come to help their Dorian kinsmen, and colonies to help the cities that had sent them out' (**6**.2). When the Corcyreans made their point in 433 about 'the journey to Italy and Sicily', Thucydides represents them as adding '. . . so that it could stop a fleet (ναυτικόν) coming to the Peloponnesians and could escort movements from here to there' (1.36.2): ναυτικόν means a *military* fleet, not just trading vessels.

In fact the aggression during the Archidamian War came in the other direction, with twenty Athenian ships sent to Sicily in 427 (3.86), later reinforced by forty more (4.2.2) – a substantial force. Syracuse was then at war with Leontini; Syracuse was supported by Locri and the other Dorian states except for Camarina, Leontini by Rhegium, Naxos, Catana, and Camarina, and the Leontinians asked for Athenian help in view of 'old alliance'[71] and of their shared Ionian kinship (3.86.2: for these ethnic

---

[66] The argument aged well: Corcyreans argued in a similar way in 373/2 according to Xen. *Hell*. 6.2.9.

[67] The original prescripts, dating firmly to 433/2, have been erased and reinscribed. The usual view is that this points to reconfirmation of a decree dating from earlier, probably the 440s; the alternative is to think that 433/2 is the date of the original treaties (so e.g. Papazarkadas 2009: 75) and the prescripts were reinscribed either immediately to correct an error (Smart 1972: 144-6) or in the 420s (Mattingly 1963: 272). Cf. Low 2020: 243 and n. 71.

[68] Cf. Trevett 1995.

[69] Moreno 2007: 342 cites the evidence.

[70] Timber: **90**.3, 7.25.2 nn., with Meiggs 1982: 462-6. Pitch: *CT* on 5.5.2.

[71] The 433 alliance (**6**.2 n.) was hardly 'old', and this is one reason for regarding that as a reconfirmation; the original date has been the subject of much

5 ATHENS AND SYRACUSE

links cf. **1**.2–**5**.3 n., **6**.1, **34**.4, **88**.6 nn.). Athenian forces remained there till 424, operating mainly around Messina (**48** n.), Rhegium, and the northern coast;[72] there are sporadic references through Books 3–4 (3.86, 88, 90, 99, 103, 115; 4.1–2, 24–5), though important aspects such as the alliances with Camarina (**75**.3 n.) and perhaps Metapontum (7.33.5 n.) are mentioned only when they become relevant in Books 6–7. Much more could have been said, as we can tell from a papyrus fragment of another historian – probably Philistus, possibly Antiochus of Syracuse – dealing with some of the action.[73] 'A general feeling of littleness runs through everything.'[74] The one exception is the culminating conference at Gela in 424, with Hermocrates' powerful speech pleading for pan-Sicilian unity against the threat that Athens poses to them all (4.59–64). Thucydides may well have played that up in preparation for what is to come nine years later (p. 21); he may equally have played the earlier expedition itself down in order to make the 415 counterpart seem even bigger in comparison (**1**.1 n.) and more of a leap into the unknown, or at least treated the earlier campaign more briefly so as to leave the thunder for the more momentous one to come.[75]

That 'littleness', though, is combined with big ideas. When the expedition starts,

> ... the Athenians' explanation was in terms of kinship, but they wished to prevent the transport of corn to the Peloponnese and to make a preliminary trial to see if Sicilian affairs could be brought under their control. (3.86.4)

When it ends,

> ... the Athenians at home punished with exile two of the returning generals, Pythodorus and Sophocles, and fined the third, Eurymedon, on the grounds that they could have subdued Sicily but had been bribed to withdraw. (4.65.3)

---

discussion. Cf. e.g. Maddoli 2010, plumping for the late 450s. It is also possible that 'old alliance' is simply a grandiose way of referring to the traditional principle of Athens sticking by its kinsmen (Smart 1972: 145–6, followed hesitantly by *CT*).

[72] At least, the northern focus is what Thucydides' material would suggest; but Bosworth 1992 infers from the scanty remains of the papyrus (see n. 73) that a good deal more was happening in the south.

[73] *FGrH* 577 F 2; cf. *HCT* and *CT* on 3.88 and Bosworth 1992.

[74] Freeman 1891–4: iii. 30, cited by Westlake 1960: 387 n. 11 = 1969: 103 n. 11.

[75] So Raaflaub 2016: 613–5, comparing Herodotus' much briefer treatment of Marathon in comparison with Thermopylae, Salamis, and Plataea. If so, it tells against the notion that 1.1–5.24 might have circulated as a separate work (p. 3), but it remains possible that any such version could have been revised for integration into the whole.

That was very unjust, as Thucydides immediately makes clear: the Athenians were carried away by their unexpected run of fortune to believe that they could achieve anything, no matter how impractical or how deficient their preparation (4.65.4).

There had not been a complete lull between 424 and 415. At some point in the late 420s Syracuse had stepped in during *stasis* at Leontini, expelling the *dēmos* and offering the elite a home at Syracuse itself (**6.2** n.); such mass expulsions and wanderings had been a feature of Sicilian politics a few generations before (**3.**3 nn.), sufficiently well known for Thucydides' Alcibiades to make capital of them now (**17.**2-3), but they had rather gone out of fashion. In response, Athens had launched a diplomatic initiative in 422, with Phaeax and two colleagues seeing if they could drum up support for a campaign against Syracuse (5.4). That was not a total failure: Camarina and Acragas were interested, and it looks as if that Hermocratean ideal of pan-Sicilian unity against Athens was already crumbling. But this was not enough, and the diplomats returned home, taking the opportunity as they went to visit some S. Italian towns to discuss 'friendship with Athens' (5.5, cf. 7.33.4 n.). Rather remarkably, they even had some success in Locri, normally a resolute enemy (**44.**2 n.).

Nor were things in Sicily calm, nor Athenian eyes averted, after the peace of 421. The border-dispute of Egesta and Selinus, so momentous in its consequences, had clearly been simmering for some time (**6.**2 nn.); it was probably a factor in the Athenian–Egestaean alliance if this was made in 418/7 (**6** n.). How much these alliances really entitled one to expect from the other side is a further question, one that was given an airing in 415 (**13.**2, **18.**1 nn.). They could often be sabre-rattling, intended to show solidarity and intimidate potential allies (**6** n., cf. **46.**2 n., **75.**3-**88.**2 n.). That was one reason why there was point in reconfirming them (p. 30): 'yes, we still mean it' was the message. Alliance or not, it was clearly an open question whether Athens should do anything to help Egesta, and that was why a delegation was sent to investigate how far Egesta could pay for it (**6.**3, **8.**1, cf. **46.**1-2). But Athenians at least cared enough about Egesta to rattle that sabre, and in spring 415 Egestaean ambassadors were making the case for more tangible aid. Leontinian exiles were there too, and added to the noise level (**19.**1).

So thoughts of Sicily were nothing new. Yet **1.**1 is insistent that 'most were unacquainted with the size of the island and the numbers who lived there, both Greek and barbarian, and did not realise that they were taking on a war not much smaller than that against the Peloponnesians'. The survey that follows strengthens the feeling of a plunge into a distant world, one that invited Herodotean ethnography and echoes of Odysseus' adventures (**1.**2-**5.**3 n.). Plutarch leaves a similar impression in a different way, with those intrigued observers poring over maps in the dust to find out more about Sicily (*Nic.* 12.1, *Alc.* 17.4: p. 15). That earlier Athenian interest makes this seem odd, and yet these may not be over-statements.[76] Thucydides does not say that everyone was ignorant, only that 'most' (οἱ πολλοί) were 'unacquainted', without *personal* experience (ἄπειροι: **1.1** n.). Veterans of 427–424 would know more, of course, but may not have seen much more than the coastline and the few towns where they could buy provisions. These would be the ones sketching out those triangles in the dust. Thucydides' edgy comment on that treatment of the generals in 424 (p. 31) confirms his own view that the people had no real ideas of the practicalities that they had had to face, and not a great deal of thought need have been given to those alliances when they were agreed. It will not be coincidence that Aristophanes' *Birds*, staged in early 414, portrays another flight into the unknown, this time in the fantasy version of soaring upwards into the clouds to found a new and brighter city there. His protagonists are Peisetaerus, Mr Persuade-a-Friend, and Euelpides, Mr Full-of-Good-Hope. Thucydides' Athenians are εὐέλπιδες too: **24.3**.

When Aristophanes' heroes reach their destination they find it all too similar to home, in that case because of people coming from Athens itself (a sycophant, an oracle-monger, a tax-collector, and so on). Thucydides' Athenians find something similar, but the equivalents are home-grown in Syracuse, the Cleon-like Athenagoras, the more Periclean Hermocrates (p. 27). The whole people, indeed, are very like themselves:

> These were the only cities that resembled Athens in character (ὁμοιότροποι), democracies like themselves and possessing ships and horses and everything on a large scale; therefore the Athenians could not bring into play the prospect of constitutional change to encourage internal divisions, nor could they deploy much greater resources. (7.55.2)

The point comes back at a later retrospect. Athens continued to be very different from Sparta, swift, energetic, and daring, qualities especially valuable in a maritime empire:

> The Syracusans made the point clear. They were the most ὁμοιότροποι to Athens and the most effective of their adversaries. (8.96.5)

And they become all the more capable of out-Athenianing the Athenians as the campaign goes on, eventually deploying naval innovations to get

---

[76] *Pace* Smith 2004, who argues that Thucydides was here deliberately misleading in order to highlight how the *dēmos* would base decisions on vague rumour and popular misconceptions.

the better of them even in their own cherished maritime skills (**69–71** n.; Introduction to Book 7, pp. 31–2).

These similarities were not just a matter of the constitution: inventiveness, courage, and enterprise were important too, and so, it gradually emerges, was a readiness to turn on their leaders (**103**.4, 7.81.1 nn.). But the constitution mattered.[77] It was less radical a democracy than Athens; for instance, the Syracusan equivalent of ostracism, πεταλισμός, had been abandoned soon after its institution (Diod. 11.86–7). The assembly (ἐκκλησία, **32**.3; ξύλλογος, **41**.4) clearly took some decisions (**73**, **103**.4, 7.2.1, 7.21 and nn., and e.g. Diod. 11.92, 13.19.4–5, 33.1, 34.6), but it looks too as if the 15 Syracusan *stratēgoi* could do more on their own initiative than was usual in Athens (**41** n., **63**.2 n.; cf. 7.73). It is anyway not known who constituted 'the *dēmos*' forming the assembly, how regularly it met, or how free it was to set its own agenda. When a move to a more thoroughgoing democracy came in 412–411, Aristotle could describe it as a change from πολιτεία (for him a 'good' form of government, retaining some oligarchic features) to 'democracy' itself (*Pol.* 1304a27–9). Then the tyranny of Dionysius I began in 405. These later changes may have been known to Thucydides' first audience and have affected how they read or heard the narrative: cf. **33–4** n., **36–40** n., **38**.3 n., **72–3** n. and Introduction to Book 7, pp. 32–5.

There were other ways too in which Sicilian politics might not seem very different from those in mainland Greece. There were border disputes; Egesta's argument with Selinus may go back to the 450s, when Egesta was engaged in something similar with someone, very likely Selinus (a textual difficulty leaves this less than certain, Diod. 11.86.2). There was *stasis*, as was becoming ever more prevalent in Greece itself (3.82.1). In Sicily, this was relevant not just at Leontini (5.4.1–3) but also at Rhegium (4.1.3), Camarina (4.25.7), Catana (**50**.3 n.), Messina (**74**.1 n.), Thurii (7.33.5–6, 7.57.11), Acragas (7.46, 50), and Metapontum (7.57.11): cf. Berger 1992a. The Athenian commanders were prepared to believe that there were possibilities in Syracuse too (7.48.2, cf. **5**.1 n.): no wonder. Forced mass expulsions were not unknown in Greece either: Athens had done the same to Aegina (2.27). A less familiar feature was the ethnic mix in close proximity, with Greek *poleis*, themselves a mix of Dorian and Ionian, dominating the northern and eastern coasts, Phoenicians in the north-west, and Sicels in the interior, but even

---

[77] On the constitution see *IACP* 226–7; Rutter 2000; Robinson 2000 and 2011: 67–89.

5 ATHENS AND SYRACUSE

this should not be over-stated. Egesta was Elymian, but very Hellenised, with a fine late fifth-century Doric temple.[78] The Sicel leader Ducetius had established his base at Palice, and built up what looks like a very Hellenised city. The different peoples could co-operate, and the same goes for Dorian and Ionian Greeks: witness the cross-ethnic alliance against Syracuse in 466 of Gela, Acragas, Selinus, Himera, and Sicels (Diod. 11.68).

Had Thucydides so chosen, there was a lot more to say about Sicily and Greece. The Syracusan tyrants had been proud of their Greekness; Pindar and Bacchylides had written odes to commemorate Sicilian victories at the Panhellenic games, and the great charioteer at Delphi had been dedicated by Hieron's younger brother Polyzelos around 477. Thank-offerings for military successes were sent to Delphi by Gelon, commemorating his victory over Carthage in 480 (ML 28 = Fornara 54), and to Olympia by Hieron after he defeated the Etruscans in 474 (OR 101 = ML 29 = Fornara 64); Taras did the same for its own local victories (SIG^3 40; OR 140 = ML 57 = Fornara 112). Fifth-century Sicily and S. Italy produced philosophers and physicians in the Greek tradition like Acron and Empedocles of Acragas and Parmenides of Elea; Aeschylus put on his *Aetna* there and went back to Sicily to die; prolific vase-painting shows the local taste both for Greek art and Greek theatre.[79] There was comedy with Epicharmus, historiography with Antiochus of Syracuse, and rhetoric with Corax and Teisias; the rhetorical superstar Gorgias visited Athens as one of Leontini's ambassadors in 427 (p. 30).[80]

Thucydides the man was doubtless interested in such things. Traces of Gorgianic rhetoric are often visible, especially in Cleon's speech in the Mytilenean debate (3.37–40). But Thucydides the writer did not think such matters were the stuff of his sort of history, any more than he allowed Pericles to celebrate the magnificence of the Athenian theatre or the Parthenon in the Funeral Speech. Gorgias' role in 427 goes unmentioned (3.86). Yet culture could make a difference even in the military and political worlds that so absorbed the historian. Some of Athens' survivors even owed their lives to their knowledge of Euripides, if Plutarch's story is true (*Nic.* 29, p. 9). In choosing what to cover and what to exclude, Thucydides set the young Greek genre of historiography in a political and military direction that was to prove all too long-lasting.

---

[78] Fragoulaki 2013: 304–13.
[79] Above, p. 9.
[80] On all this cf. esp. Willi 2008.

6 THE TEXT

The best text is now that of Alberti (Rome 1972–2000). The preface to his vol. i contains an extensive discussion of the manuscript tradition, and this is updated in his prefaces to vols. ii and iii. The apparatus criticus in this volume is extremely selective, and uses Alberti's sigla. A list is appended on pp. 38–9 of the passages where this text diverges from Alberti.

Up to **92**.5 the manuscripts fall into two groups, the first consisting principally of CG and the second of ABEFHM; after **92**.5 B and H begin to import readings from a different source (see Introduction to Book 7, pp. 35–6). In the first group, C is closer than G to the hyparchetype (the original from which both manuscripts descend). In the second, M is closest to the group's hyparchetype and EFAB and H, in that order, are progressively further away. See the stemmata representing this diagrammatically at Alberti i, pp. li and cxlii, and with mild corrections at iii. xix; Dover 1965: xxviii gives a simpler version of the uncontroversial elements. Still, several of these manuscripts incorporate readings or note variants from sources other than their main exempla, so that readings of the first group are found in the second and vice versa; apparently correct readings sometimes crop up in late and unexpected places.

Occasionally papyri offer alternative readings. The most important one in Book 6 is P. Bodmer XXVII, of the third or fourth century CE, though this covers only the first two chapters. This is valuable at **1**.2 and **2**.5, and Alberti also prefers its reading at **2**.2.

There are also extensive citations from Thucydides in later authors, often clearly intended to be verbatim: Dionysius of Halicarnassus *On Thucydides* is particularly rich in these. They are naturally subject to the vagaries of their own manuscript traditions and it is sometimes impossible to be sure that the Thucydides text these authors knew was itself uncorrupted, but they still provide a valuable control.

The Latin translation of Lorenzo Valla (1448–52) seems occasionally to draw on a Greek text that diverges from ours, and the reading he knew can in some cases be reconstructed: this is (or may be) helpful especially at **36**.2 and **64**.1.

There are many times when conjectural emendation is tempting. It tempted the copyists themselves, and at least one later hand in H (marked here as H²) shows a scribe who was particularly inventive: he is often overbold, but is acute at noticing linguistic irregularities (**43**, **46**.2, **58**.2, **65**.3 nn.). Still, it is often difficult to know if a challenging passage is obscure because of copyists' mistakes or because of Thucydides' own style. His difficulty was notorious even in antiquity; when Dionysius of Halicarnassus commented on the problems (p. 11), he added that even those who can cope often need the aid of a linguistic commentary (*On Thucydides* 51). The Byzantine scholar Ioannes Tzetzes worked his way through his imperfect manuscript with increasing impatience, at one point complaining that 'here the copyist's shit really stinks' (ὄζει κόπρος κάκιστον ἡ βιβλιογράφου), but he knew that it was not always the fault of the scribe; by Book 8 he thought the best way of defending its Thucydidean authorship was to say that the style was too impenetrable to be the work of anyone else. He added an epigram at the end wishing that Athenians had cast the man and his book into a pit. The last word, however, should be given to a more generous epigram in the Palatine Anthology, found appended to several of our manuscripts:

Ὦ φίλος, εἰ σοφὸς εἶ, λάβε μ' ἐς χέρας· εἰ δέ γε πάμπαν
νῆις ἔφυς Μουσέων, ῥῖψον ἃ μὴ νοέεις.
εἰμὶ γὰρ οὐ πάντεσσι βατός, παῦροι δ' ἀγάσαντο
Θουκυδίδην Ὀλόρου, Κεκροπίδην τὸ γένος.

Friend, if you are wise, take me up; but if utterly untouched
By the Muses, throw away what you do not understand.
My path is not for everyone, though a few have admired
Thucydides son of Olorus, one of Cecrops' race.

(*Anth. Pal.* 9.583)

DEVIATIONS FROM ALBERTI

There are also some minor variations in punctuation, esp. in **89**, and paragraphing.

2.2   ἐκαλεῖτο for ἐκλήθη.
4.1   παραδόντος (Classen) rather than προδόντος.
4.2   <μετα>πέμψαντες (Marchant) and τῆς rather than τις.
6.1   προσγεγενημένοις rather than προ-.
6.2   ἐπαγόμενοι rather than ἐπαγαγόμενοι.
6.2   διαφθείροντες rather than διαφθείραντες.
8.2   ἤν τι περιγίγνηται rather than ἤν <τέ> τι περιγίγνηται.
10.1 ὑμᾶς rather than ἡμᾶς.
10.4 πολλῶν rather than πολλοῦ.
13.1 παρακελευστούς rather than παρακελεύστους.
18.2 ἡσυχάζοιεν πάντες ... φυλοκρινοῖεν rather than ἡσυχάζοιμεν πάντως ... φυλοκρινοῖμεν.
21.1 εἰ ξυστῶσιν rather than ἤν ξυστῶσιν.
21.2 καὶ ὅτε τοῖς rather than καὶ ὅτε ἐν τοῖς.
24.1 μάλιστα οὕτως rather than μάλιστ' <ἂν> οὕτως.
31.1 Ἑλληνικῆι rather than Ἑλληνικῆς.
31.3 κενάς rather than καινάς.
34.1 ξυμμαχίαν ποιώμεθα rather than ξυμμαχίδα ποιώμεθα.
34.4 περὶ τῆς Σικελίας rather than περὶ τῆι Σικελίαι.
37.2 οἰκίσαντες rather than οἰκήσαντες.
38.3 τυραννίδας δὲ rather than τυραννίδας τε.
38.4 τοὺς δὲ τὰ τοιαῦτα μηχανωμένους κολάζων rather than τοὺς [δὲ] τὰ τοιαῦτα μηχανωμένους κολάζειν.
40.1 γὰρ added between εἰ and μὴ μανθάνετε, and repunctuated accordingly.
41.3 τοῦ τε rather than τοῦ γε, and repunctuated accordingly.
41.4 οἴσομεν rather than ἐσοίσομεν.
43   ἑπτακόσιοι rather than ἑξακόσιοι.
46.2 πρῶτον rather than πρώτους.
58.2 ἀνεχώρησαν rather than ἀπεχώρησαν.
64.1 καί retained after δυνηθέντες.
65.3 ἐς τὸ κατὰ τὸ Ὀλυμπιεῖον rather than ἐς τὸν μέγαν λιμένα κατὰ τὸ Ὀλυμπιεῖον.
87.4 ἀδεεῖ rather than ἀδεές.
87.5 ἐξισώσαντες τοῖς ἄλλοις μεθ' ἡμῶν τοὺς Συρακοσίους rather than ἐξισώσαντες [τοῖς ἄλλοις] μεθ' ἡμῶν τοῖς Συρακοσίοις.

88.9 φορτηγικοῦ rather than φορτικοῦ.
89.6 ὅσωι καὶ λοιδορήσαιμι rather than ὅσωι καὶ <μέγιστ' ἠδίκημαι>, λοιδορήσαιμι.
92.5 οὖσαν rather than παροῦσαν.

SIGLA

A	=	Parisinus suppl. Gr. 255, early eleventh century
B	=	Vaticanus Gr. 126, late eleventh century
C	=	Laurentianus LXIX 2, middle of tenth century
E	=	Palatinus (Heidelbergensis) Gr. 252, early tenth century
F	=	Monacensis Gr. 430, late tenth century
G	=	Monacensis Gr. 228, late thirteenth century
H	=	Parisinus Gr. 1734, early fourteenth century
J	=	Basileensis E-III-4, fourteenth century
L	=	Laurentianus LXIX 30, fourteenth century
M	=	Britannicus Add. 11.727, eleventh century
Pl	=	Parisinus suppl. Gr. 256, early fourteenth century
Ud	=	Vaticinuus Urbinas Gr. 92, early fourteenth century
Z	=	membranae Mutinenses, late tenth century
Σ	=	reading cited or presupposed by (some) scholia

Papyrus:
P. Bodmer XXVII, third or fourth century, containing **1**.1–**2**.6

Superscript indicates correcting hands.

THUCYDIDES: BOOK VI

ΘΟΥΚΥΔΙΔΟΥ ΞΥΓΓΡΑΦΗΣ Ζ

Τοῦ δ' αὐτοῦ χειμῶνος Ἀθηναῖοι ἐβούλοντο αὖθις μείζονι παρασκευῆι 1 τῆς μετὰ Λάχητος καὶ Εὐρυμέδοντος ἐπὶ Σικελίαν πλεύσαντες καταστρέψασθαι, εἰ δύναιντο, ἄπειροι οἱ πολλοὶ ὄντες τοῦ μεγέθους τῆς νήσου καὶ τῶν ἐνοικούντων τοῦ πλήθους καὶ Ἑλλήνων καὶ βαρβάρων, καὶ ὅτι οὐ πολλῶι τινι ὑποδεέστερον πόλεμον ἀνηιροῦντο ἢ τὸν πρὸς Πελοποννησίους.

Σικελία γὰρ περίπλους μέν ἐστιν ὁλκάδι οὐ πολλῶι τινι ἔλασσον ἢ 2 ὀκτὼ ἡμερῶν, καὶ τοσαύτη οὖσα ἐν εἰκοσισταδίωι μάλιστα μέτρωι τῆς θαλάσσης διείργεται τὸ μὴ ἤπειρος εἶναι· ὠικίσθη δὲ ὧδε τὸ ἀρχαῖον, καὶ 2 τοσάδε ἔθνη ἔσχε τὰ ξύμπαντα. παλαίτατοι μὲν λέγονται ἐν μέρει τινὶ τῆς χώρας Κύκλωπες καὶ Λαιστρυγόνες οἰκῆσαι, ὧν ἐγὼ οὔτε γένος ἔχω εἰπεῖν οὔτε ὁπόθεν ἐσῆλθον ἢ ὅποι ἀπεχώρησαν· ἀρκείτω δὲ ὡς ποιηταῖς τε εἴρηται καὶ ὡς ἕκαστός πηι γιγνώσκει περὶ αὐτῶν. Σικανοὶ δὲ μετ' 2 αὐτοὺς πρῶτοι φαίνονται ἐνοικισάμενοι, ὡς μὲν αὐτοί φασι, καὶ πρότεροι διὰ τὸ αὐτόχθονες εἶναι, ὡς δὲ ἡ ἀλήθεια εὑρίσκεται, Ἴβηρες ὄντες καὶ ἀπὸ τοῦ Σικανοῦ ποταμοῦ τοῦ ἐν Ἰβηρίαι ὑπὸ Λιγύων ἀναστάντες, καὶ ἀπ' αὐτῶν Σικανία τότε ἡ νῆσος ἐκαλεῖτο, πρότερον Τρινακρία καλουμένη· οἰκοῦσι δὲ ἔτι καὶ νῦν τὰ πρὸς ἑσπέραν τῆς Σικελίας. Ἰλίου δὲ ἁλισκομένου 3 τῶν Τρώων τινὲς διαφυγόντες Ἀχαιοὺς πλοίοις ἀφικνοῦνται πρὸς τὴν Σικελίαν, καὶ ὅμοροι τοῖς Σικανοῖς οἰκήσαντες ξύμπαντες μὲν Ἔλυμοι ἐκλήθησαν, πόλεις δ' αὐτῶν Ἔρυξ τε καὶ Ἔγεστα. προσξυνώικησαν δὲ αὐτοῖς καὶ Φωκέων τινὲς τῶν ἀπὸ Τροίας τότε χειμῶνι ἐς Λιβύην πρῶτον, ἔπειτα ἐς Σικελίαν ἀπ' αὐτῆς κατενεχθέντες. Σικελοὶ δὲ ἐξ Ἰταλίας 4 (ἐνταῦθα γὰρ ὤικουν) διέβησαν ἐς Σικελίαν, φεύγοντες Ὀπικούς, ὡς μὲν εἰκὸς καὶ λέγεται, ἐπὶ σχεδιῶν, τηρήσαντες τὸν πορθμὸν κατιόντος τοῦ ἀνέμου, τάχα ἂν δὲ καὶ ἄλλως πως ἐσπλεύσαντες. εἰσὶ δὲ καὶ νῦν ἔτι ἐν τῆι Ἰταλίαι Σικελοί, καὶ ἡ χώρα ἀπὸ Ἰταλοῦ βασιλέως τινὸς Σικελῶν, τοὔνομα τοῦτο ἔχοντος, οὕτως Ἰταλία ἐπωνομάσθη. ἐλθόντες δὲ ἐς τὴν 5 Σικελίαν στρατὸς πολὺς τούς τε Σικανοὺς κρατοῦντες μάχηι ἀπέστειλαν πρὸς τὰ μεσημβρινὰ καὶ ἑσπέρια αὐτῆς καὶ ἀντὶ Σικανίας Σικελίαν τὴν νῆσον ἐποίησαν καλεῖσθαι, καὶ τὰ κράτιστα τῆς γῆς ὤικησαν ἔχοντες,

1.2 Σικελία P. Bodmer XXVII (coniecerat Krüger): Σικελίας codd.   2.2 ἐνοικισάμενοι CEG: ἐνοικησάμενοι ABFMZ   ἐκαλεῖτο codd.: ἐκλήθη P. Bodmer XXVII

ἐπεὶ διέβησαν, ἔτη ἐγγύτατα τριακόσια πρὶν Ἕλληνας ἐς Σικελίαν ἐλθεῖν·
6 ἔτι δὲ καὶ νῦν τὰ μέσα καὶ τὰ πρὸς βορρᾶν τῆς νήσου ἔχουσιν. ὤικουν δὲ καὶ Φοίνικες περὶ πᾶσαν μὲν τὴν Σικελίαν ἄκρας τε ἐπὶ τῆι θαλάσσηι ἀπολαβόντες καὶ τὰ ἐπικείμενα νησίδια ἐμπορίας ἕνεκα τῆς πρὸς τοὺς Σικελούς· ἐπειδὴ δὲ οἱ Ἕλληνες πολλοὶ κατὰ θάλασσαν ἐπεσέπλεον, ἐκλιπόντες τὰ πλείω Μοτύην καὶ Σολόεντα καὶ Πάνορμον ἐγγὺς τῶν Ἐλύμων ξυνοικήσαντες ἐνέμοντο, ξυμμαχίαι τε πίσυνοι τῆι τῶν Ἐλύμων, καὶ ὅτι ἐντεῦθεν ἐλάχιστον πλοῦν Καρχηδὼν Σικελίας ἀπέχει. βάρβαροι μὲν οὖν τοσοίδε Σικελίαν καὶ οὕτως ὤικησαν.

3 Ἑλλήνων δὲ πρῶτοι Χαλκιδῆς ἐξ Εὐβοίας πλεύσαντες μετὰ Θουκλέους οἰκιστοῦ Νάξον ὤικισαν, καὶ Ἀπόλλωνος Ἀρχηγέτου βωμὸν ὅστις νῦν ἔξω τῆς πόλεώς ἐστιν ἱδρύσαντο, ἐφ᾽ ὧι, ὅταν ἐκ Σικελίας θεωροὶ
2 πλέωσι, πρῶτον θύουσιν. Συρακούσας δὲ τοῦ ἐχομένου ἔτους Ἀρχίας τῶν Ἡρακλειδῶν ἐκ Κορίνθου ὤικισε, Σικελοὺς ἐξελάσας πρῶτον ἐκ τῆς νήσου ἐν ἧι νῦν οὐκέτι περικλυζομένηι ἡ πόλις ἡ ἐντός ἐστιν· ὕστερον δὲ
3 χρόνωι καὶ ἡ ἔξω προστειχισθεῖσα πολυάνθρωπος ἐγένετο. Θουκλῆς δὲ καὶ οἱ Χαλκιδῆς ἐκ Νάξου ὁρμηθέντες ἔτει πέμπτωι μετὰ Συρακούσας οἰκισθείσας Λεοντίνους τε πολέμωι τοὺς Σικελοὺς ἐξελάσαντες οἰκίζουσι καὶ μετ᾽ αὐτοὺς Κατάνην· οἰκιστὴν δὲ αὐτοὶ Καταναῖοι ἐποιήσαντο Εὔαρχον.
4 κατὰ δὲ τὸν αὐτὸν χρόνον καὶ Λάμις ἐκ Μεγάρων ἀποικίαν ἄγων ἐς Σικελίαν ἀφίκετο, καὶ ὑπὲρ Παντακύου τε ποταμοῦ Τρώτιλόν τι ὄνομα χωρίον οἰκίσας καὶ ὕστερον αὐτόθεν τοῖς Χαλκιδεῦσιν ἐς Λεοντίνους ὀλίγον χρόνον ξυμπολιτεύσας καὶ ὑπὸ αὐτῶν ἐκπεσὼν καὶ Θάψον οἰκίσας αὐτὸς μὲν ἀποθνήισκει, οἱ δ᾽ ἄλλοι ἐκ τῆς Θάψου ἀναστάντες Ὕβλωνος βασιλέως Σικελοῦ παραδόντος τὴν χώραν καὶ καθηγησαμένου, Μεγαρέας ὤικισαν
2 τοὺς Ὑβλαίους κληθέντας. καὶ ἔτη οἰκήσαντες πέντε καὶ τεσσαράκοντα καὶ διακόσια ὑπὸ Γέλωνος τυράννου Συρακοσίων ἀνέστησαν ἐκ τῆς πόλεως καὶ χώρας. πρὶν δὲ ἀναστῆναι, ἔτεσιν ὕστερον ἑκατὸν ἢ αὐτοὺς οἰκίσαι, Πάμμιλον ⟨μετα⟩πέμψαντες Σελινοῦντα κτίζουσι, καὶ ἐκ Μεγάρων τῆς
3 μητροπόλεως οὔσης αὐτοῖς ἐπελθὼν ξυγκατώικισεν. Γέλαν δὲ Ἀντίφημος ἐκ Ῥόδου καὶ Ἔντιμος ἐκ Κρήτης ἐποίκους ἀγαγόντες κοινῆι ἔκτισαν, ἔτει πέμπτωι καὶ τεσσαρακοστῶι μετὰ Συρακουσῶν οἴκισιν. καὶ τῆι μὲν πόλει ἀπὸ τοῦ Γέλα ποταμοῦ τοὔνομα ἐγένετο, τὸ δὲ χωρίον οὗ νῦν ἡ πόλις ἐστὶ καὶ ὃ πρῶτον ἐτειχίσθη Λίνδιοι καλεῖται· νόμιμα δὲ Δωρικὰ ἐτέθη

2.5 ἐγγύτατα P. Bodmer XXVII: ἐγγύς codd.   **4.1** παραδόντος Classen: προ δόντος F   προδόντος cett.   **4.2** ⟨μετα⟩πέμψαντες Marchant: πέμψαντες codd.   τῆς codd.: τις Weidgen; lacunam post Μεγάρων indicauit Stein

αὐτοῖς. ἔτεσι δὲ ἐγγύτατα ὀκτὼ καὶ ἑκατὸν μετὰ τὴν σφετέραν οἴκισιν 4
Γελῶιοι Ἀκράγαντα ὤικισαν, τὴν μὲν πόλιν ἀπὸ τοῦ Ἀκράγαντος ποταμοῦ
ὀνομάσαντες, οἰκιστὰς δὲ ποιήσαντες Ἀριστόνουν καὶ Πυστίλον, νόμιμα δὲ
τὰ Γελώιων δόντες. Ζάγκλη δὲ τὴν μὲν ἀρχὴν ἀπὸ Κύμης τῆς ἐν Ὀπικίαι 5
Χαλκιδικῆς πόλεως ληιστῶν ἀφικομένων ὠικίσθη, ὕστερον δὲ καὶ ἀπὸ
Χαλκίδος καὶ τῆς ἄλλης Εὐβοίας πλῆθος ἐλθὸν ξυγκατενείμαντο τὴν γῆν·
καὶ οἰκισταὶ Περιήρης καὶ Κραταιμένης ἐγένοντο αὐτῆς, ὁ μὲν ἀπὸ Κύμης,
ὁ δὲ ἀπὸ Χαλκίδος. ὄνομα δὲ τὸ μὲν πρῶτον Ζάγκλη ἦν ὑπὸ τῶν Σικελῶν
κληθεῖσα, ὅτι δρεπανοειδὲς τὴν ἰδέαν τὸ χωρίον ἐστί (τὸ δὲ δρέπανον οἱ
Σικελοὶ ζάγκλον καλοῦσιν), ὕστερον δ' αὐτοὶ μὲν ὑπὸ Σαμίων καὶ ἄλλων
Ἰώνων ἐκπίπτουσιν, οἳ Μήδους φεύγοντες προσέβαλον Σικελίαι, τοὺς δὲ 6
Σαμίους Ἀναξίλας Ῥηγίνων τύραννος οὐ πολλῶι ὕστερον ἐκβαλὼν καὶ τὴν
πόλιν αὐτὸς ξυμμείκτων ἀνθρώπων οἰκίσας Μεσσήνην ἀπὸ τῆς ἑαυτοῦ
τὸ ἀρχαῖον πατρίδος ἀντωνόμασεν. καὶ Ἱμέρα ἀπὸ Ζάγκλης ὠικίσθη ὑπὸ 5
Εὐκλείδου καὶ Σίμου καὶ Σάκωνος, καὶ Χαλκιδῆς μὲν οἱ πλεῖστοι ἦλθον ἐς
τὴν ἀποικίαν, ξυνώικισαν δὲ αὐτοῖς καὶ ἐκ Συρακουσῶν φυγάδες στάσει
νικηθέντες, οἱ Μυλητίδαι καλούμενοι· καὶ φωνὴ μὲν μεταξὺ τῆς τε Χαλκιδέων
καὶ Δωρίδος ἐκράθη, νόμιμα δὲ τὰ Χαλκιδικὰ ἐκράτησεν. Ἄκραι δὲ καὶ 2
Κασμέναι ὑπὸ Συρακοσίων ὠικίσθησαν, Ἄκραι μὲν ἑβδομήκοντα ἔτεσι
μετὰ Συρακούσας, Κασμέναι δ' ἐγγὺς εἴκοσι μετὰ Ἄκρας. καὶ Καμάρινα τὸ 3
πρῶτον ὑπὸ Συρακοσίων ὠικίσθη, ἔτεσιν ἐγγύτατα πέντε καὶ τριάκοντα
καὶ ἑκατὸν μετὰ Συρακουσῶν κτίσιν· οἰκισταὶ δὲ ἐγένοντο αὐτῆς Δάσκων
καὶ Μενέκωλος. ἀναστάτων δὲ Καμαριναίων γενομένων πολέμωι ὑπὸ
Συρακοσίων δι' ἀπόστασιν, χρόνωι Ἱπποκράτης ὕστερον Γέλας τύραννος,
λύτρα ἀνδρῶν Συρακοσίων αἰχμαλώτων λαβὼν τὴν γῆν τὴν Καμαριναίων,
αὐτὸς οἰκιστὴς γενόμενος κατώικισε Καμάριναν. καὶ αὖθις ὑπὸ Γέλωνος
ἀνάστατος γενομένη τὸ τρίτον κατωικίσθη ὑπὸ Γελώιων.

Τοσαῦτα ἔθνη Ἑλλήνων καὶ βαρβάρων Σικελίαν ὤικει, καὶ ἐπὶ 6
τοσήνδε οὖσαν αὐτὴν οἱ Ἀθηναῖοι στρατεύειν ὥρμηντο, ἐφιέμενοι μὲν
τῆι ἀληθεστάτηι προφάσει τῆς πάσης ἄρξαι, βοηθεῖν δὲ ἅμα εὐπρεπῶς
βουλόμενοι τοῖς ἑαυτῶν ξυγγενέσι καὶ τοῖς προσγεγενημένοις ξυμμάχοις.
μάλιστα δ' αὐτοὺς ἐξώρμησαν Ἐγεσταίων [τε] πρέσβεις παρόντες καὶ 2
προθυμότερον ἐπικαλούμενοι. ὅμοροι γὰρ ὄντες τοῖς Σελινουντίοις ἐς
πόλεμον καθέστασαν περί τε γαμικῶν τινῶν καὶ περὶ γῆς ἀμφισβητήτου,
καὶ οἱ Σελινούντιοι Συρακοσίους ἐπαγόμενοι ξυμμάχους κατεῖργον αὐτοὺς

6.1 προσγεγενημένοις ABCF: προγεγενημένοις EGMZ   6.2 τε del. Krüger

τῶι πολέμωι καὶ κατὰ γῆν καὶ κατὰ θάλασσαν· ὥστε τὴν γενομένην ἐπὶ
Λάχητος καὶ τοῦ προτέρου πολέμου Λεοντίνων οἱ Ἐγεσταῖοι ξυμμαχίαν
ἀναμιμνῄσκοντες τοὺς Ἀθηναίους ἐδέοντο σφίσι ναῦς πέμψαντας ἐπαμῦναι,
λέγοντες ἄλλα τε πολλὰ καὶ κεφάλαιον, εἰ Συρακόσιοι Λεοντίνους τε
ἀναστήσαντες ἀτιμώρητοι γενήσονται καὶ τοὺς λοιποὺς ἔτι ξυμμάχους
αὐτῶν διαφθείροντες αὐτοὶ τὴν ἅπασαν δύναμιν τῆς Σικελίας σχήσουσι,
κίνδυνον εἶναι μή ποτε μεγάληι παρασκευῆι Δωριῆς τε Δωριεῦσι
κατὰ τὸ ξυγγενὲς καὶ ἅμα ἄποικοι τοῖς ἐκπέμψασι Πελοποννησίοις
βοηθήσαντες καὶ τὴν ἐκείνων δύναμιν ξυγκαθέλωσιν· σῶφρον δ' εἶναι
μετὰ τῶν ὑπολοίπων ἔτι ξυμμάχων ἀντέχειν τοῖς Συρακοσίοις, ἄλλως

3 τε καὶ χρήματα σφῶν παρεξόντων ἐς τὸν πόλεμον ἱκανά. ὧν ἀκούοντες
οἱ Ἀθηναῖοι ἐν ταῖς ἐκκλησίαις τῶν τε Ἐγεσταίων πολλάκις λεγόντων
καὶ τῶν ξυναγορευόντων αὐτοῖς ἐψηφίσαντο πρέσβεις πέμψαι πρῶτον
ἐς τὴν Ἔγεσταν περί τε τῶν χρημάτων σκεψομένους εἰ ὑπάρχει, ὥσπερ
φασίν, ἐν τῶι κοινῶι καὶ ἐν τοῖς ἱεροῖς, καὶ τὰ τοῦ πολέμου ἅμα πρὸς
τοὺς Σελινουντίους ἐν ὅτωι ἐστὶν εἰσομένους.

7 Καὶ οἱ μὲν πρέσβεις τῶν Ἀθηναίων ἀπεστάλησαν ἐς τὴν Σικελίαν·
Λακεδαιμόνιοι δὲ τοῦ αὐτοῦ χειμῶνος καὶ οἱ ξύμμαχοι πλὴν Κορινθίων
στρατεύσαντες ἐς τὴν Ἀργείαν τῆς τε γῆς ἔτεμον οὐ πολλὴν καὶ σῖτον
ἀνεκομίσαντό τινα ζεύγη κομίσαντες, καὶ ἐς Ὀρνεὰς κατοικίσαντες τοὺς
Ἀργείων φυγάδας καὶ τῆς ἄλλης στρατιᾶς παρακαταλιπόντες αὐτοῖς
ὀλίγους, καὶ σπεισάμενοί τινα χρόνον ὥστε μὴ ἀδικεῖν Ὀρνεάτας καὶ
2 Ἀργείους τὴν ἀλλήλων, ἀπεχώρησαν τῶι στρατῶι ἐπ' οἴκου. ἐλθόντων δὲ
Ἀθηναίων οὐ πολλῶι ὕστερον ναυσὶ τριάκοντα καὶ ἑξακοσίοις ὁπλίταις, οἱ
Ἀργεῖοι μετὰ τῶν Ἀθηναίων πανστρατιᾶι ἐξελθόντες τοὺς μὲν ἐν Ὀρνεαῖς
μίαν ἡμέραν ἐπολιόρκουν· ὑπὸ δὲ νύκτα αὐλισαμένου τοῦ στρατεύματος
ἄπωθεν ἐκδιδράσκουσιν οἱ ἐκ τῶν Ὀρνεῶν. καὶ τῆι ὑστεραίαι οἱ Ἀργεῖοι
ὡς ᾔσθοντο, κατασκάψαντες τὰς Ὀρνεὰς ἀνεχώρησαν καὶ οἱ Ἀθηναῖοι
ὕστερον ταῖς ναυσὶν ἐπ' οἴκου.

3 Καὶ ἐς Μεθώνην τὴν ὅμορον Μακεδονίαι ἱππέας κατὰ θάλασσαν
κομίσαντες Ἀθηναῖοι σφῶν τε αὐτῶν καὶ Μακεδόνων τοὺς παρὰ σφίσι
4 φυγάδας ἐκακούργουν τὴν Περδίκκου. Λακεδαιμόνιοι δὲ πέμψαντες
παρὰ Χαλκιδέας τοὺς ἐπὶ Θράικης, ἄγοντας πρὸς Ἀθηναίους δεχημέρους
σπονδάς, ξυμπολεμεῖν ἐκέλευον Περδίκκαι· οἱ δ' οὐκ ἤθελον. καὶ ὁ χειμὼν
ἐτελεύτα, καὶ ἕκτον καὶ δέκατον ἔτος ἐτελεύτα τῶι πολέμωι τῶιδε ὃν
Θουκυδίδης ξυνέγραψεν.

8 Τοῦ δ' ἐπιγιγνομένου θέρους ἅμα ἦρι οἱ τῶν Ἀθηναίων πρέσβεις
ἧκον ἐκ τῆς Σικελίας καὶ οἱ Ἐγεσταῖοι μετ' αὐτῶν ἄγοντες ἑξήκοντα

6.2 διαφθείροντες codd.: διαφθείραντες H² Cn¹ (coniecerat Portus) τάλαντα ἀσήμου ἀργυρίου ὡς ἐς ἑξήκοντα ναῦς μηνὸς μισθόν, ἃς ἔμελλον δεήσεσθαι πέμπειν. καὶ οἱ Ἀθηναῖοι ἐκκλησίαν ποιήσαντες καὶ 2 ἀκούσαντες τῶν τε Ἐγεσταίων καὶ τῶν σφετέρων πρέσβεων τά τε ἄλλα ἐπαγωγὰ καὶ οὐκ ἀληθῆ καὶ περὶ τῶν χρημάτων ὡς εἴη ἑτοῖμα ἔν τε τοῖς ἱεροῖς πολλὰ καὶ ἐν τῶι κοινῶι, ἐψηφίσαντο ναῦς ἑξήκοντα πέμπειν ἐς Σικελίαν καὶ στρατηγοὺς αὐτοκράτορας Ἀλκιβιάδην τε τὸν Κλεινίου καὶ Νικίαν τὸν Νικηράτου καὶ Λάμαχον τὸν Ξενοφάνους, βοηθοὺς μὲν Ἐγεσταίοις πρὸς Σελινουντίους, ξυγκατοικίσαι δὲ καὶ Λεοντίνους, ἤν τι περιγίγνηται αὐτοῖς τοῦ πολέμου, καὶ τἆλλα τὰ ἐν τῆι Σικελίαι πρᾶξαι ὅπηι ἂν γιγνώσκωσιν ἄριστα Ἀθηναίοις. μετὰ δὲ τοῦτο ἡμέραι 3 πέμπτηι ἐκκλησία αὖθις ἐγίγνετο, καθ᾽ ὅ τι χρὴ τὴν παρασκευὴν ταῖς ναυσὶ τάχιστα γίγνεσθαι, καὶ τοῖς στρατηγοῖς, εἴ του προσδέοιντο, ψηφισθῆναι ἐς τὸν ἔκπλουν. καὶ ὁ Νικίας ἀκούσιος μὲν ἡιρημένος ἄρχειν, 4 νομίζων δὲ τὴν πόλιν οὐκ ὀρθῶς βεβουλεῦσθαι, ἀλλὰ προφάσει βραχείαι καὶ εὐπρεπεῖ τῆς Σικελίας ἁπάσης, μεγάλου ἔργου, ἐφίεσθαι, παρελθὼν ἀποτρέψαι ἐβούλετο καὶ παρήινει τοῖς Ἀθηναίοις τοιάδε.

"Ἡ μὲν ἐκκλησία περὶ παρασκευῆς τῆς ἡμετέρας ἥδε ξυνελέγη, καθ᾽ 9 ὅ τι χρὴ ἐς Σικελίαν ἐκπλεῖν· ἐμοὶ μέντοι δοκεῖ καὶ περὶ αὐτοῦ τούτου ἔτι χρῆναι σκέψασθαι, εἰ ἄμεινόν ἐστιν ἐκπέμπειν τὰς ναῦς, καὶ μὴ οὕτω βραχείαι βουλῆι περὶ μεγάλων πραγμάτων ἀνδράσιν ἀλλοφύλοις πειθομένους πόλεμον οὐ προσήκοντα ἄρασθαι. καίτοι ἔγωγε καὶ τιμῶμαι 2 ἐκ τοῦ τοιούτου καὶ ἧσσον ἑτέρων περὶ τῶι ἐμαυτοῦ σώματι ὀρρωδῶ, νομίζων ὁμοίως ἀγαθὸν πολίτην εἶναι ὃς ἂν καὶ τοῦ σώματός τι καὶ τῆς οὐσίας προνοῆται· μάλιστα γὰρ ἂν ὁ τοιοῦτος καὶ τὰ τῆς πόλεως δι᾽ ἑαυτὸν βούλοιτο ὀρθοῦσθαι. ὅμως δὲ οὔτε ἐν τῶι πρότερον χρόνωι διὰ τὸ προτιμᾶσθαι εἶπον παρὰ γνώμην οὔτε νῦν, ἀλλὰ ἧι ἂν γιγνώσκω βέλτιστα, ἐρῶ. καὶ πρὸς μὲν τοὺς τρόπους τοὺς ὑμετέρους ἀσθενὴς ἂν 3 μου ὁ λόγος εἴη, εἰ τά τε ὑπάρχοντα σώιζειν παραινοίην καὶ μὴ τοῖς ἑτοίμοις περὶ τῶν ἀφανῶν καὶ μελλόντων κινδυνεύειν· ὡς δὲ οὔτε ἐν καιρῶι σπεύδετε οὔτε ῥάιδιά ἐστι κατασχεῖν ἐφ᾽ ἃ ὥρμησθε, ταῦτα διδάξω.

Φημὶ γὰρ ὑμᾶς πολεμίους πολλοὺς ἐνθάδε ὑπολιπόντας καὶ ἑτέρους 10 ἐπιθυμεῖν ἐκεῖσε πλεύσαντας δεῦρο ἐπαγαγέσθαι. καὶ οἴεσθε ἴσως τὰς 2 γενομένας ὑμῖν σπονδὰς ἔχειν τι βέβαιον, αἳ ἡσυχαζόντων μὲν ὑμῶν ὀνόματι σπονδαὶ ἔσονται (οὕτω γὰρ ἐνθένδε τε ἄνδρες ἔπραξαν αὐτὰ καὶ ἐκ τῶν ἐναντίων), σφαλέντων δέ που ἀξιόχρεωι δυνάμει ταχεῖαν τὴν ἐπιχείρησιν ἡμῖν οἱ ἐχθροὶ ποιήσονται, οἷς πρῶτον μὲν διὰ ξυμφορῶν ἡ ξύμβασις καὶ ἐκ τοῦ αἰσχίονος ἢ ἡμῖν κατ᾽ ἀνάγκην ἐγένετο, ἔπειτα

10.1 ὑμᾶς KVm: ἡμᾶς cett.

3 ἐν αὐτῆι ταύτηι πολλὰ τὰ ἀμφισβητούμενα ἔχομεν. εἰσὶ δ' οἳ οὐδὲ ταύτην πω τὴν ὁμολογίαν ἐδέξαντο, καὶ οὐχ οἱ ἀσθενέστατοι· ἀλλ' οἱ μὲν ἄντικρυς πολεμοῦσιν, οἱ δὲ καὶ διὰ τὸ Λακεδαιμονίους ἔτι ἡσυχάζειν
4 δεχημέροις σπονδαῖς καὶ αὐτοὶ κατέχονται. τάχα δ' ἂν ἴσως, εἰ δίχα ἡμῶν τὴν δύναμιν λάβοιεν, ὅπερ νῦν σπεύδομεν, καὶ πάνυ ἂν ξυνεπιθοῖντο μετὰ Σικελιωτῶν, οὓς πρὸ πολλῶν ἂν ἐτιμήσαντο ξυμμάχους γενέσθαι
5 ἐν τῶι πρὶν χρόνωι. ὥστε χρὴ σκοπεῖν τινὰ αὐτὰ καὶ μὴ μετεώρωι τῆι πόλει ἀξιοῦν κινδυνεύειν καὶ ἀρχῆς ἄλλης ὀρέγεσθαι πρὶν ἣν ἔχομεν βεβαιωσώμεθα, εἰ Χαλκιδῆς γε οἱ ἐπὶ Θράικης ἔτη τοσαῦτα ἀφεστῶτες ἡμῶν ἔτι ἀχείρωτοί εἰσι καὶ ἄλλοι τινὲς κατὰ τὰς ἠπείρους ἐνδοιαστῶς ἀκροῶνται. ἡμεῖς δὲ Ἐγεσταίοις δὴ οὖσι ξυμμάχοις ὡς ἀδικουμένοις ὀξέως βοηθοῦμεν, ὑφ' ὧν δ' αὐτοὶ πάλαι ἀφεστώτων ἀδικούμεθα, ἔτι
11 μέλλομεν ἀμύνεσθαι. καίτοι τοὺς μὲν κατεργασάμενοι κἂν κατάσχοιμεν· τῶν δ' εἰ καὶ κρατήσαιμεν, διὰ πολλοῦ γε καὶ πολλῶν ὄντων χαλεπῶς ἂν ἄρχειν δυναίμεθα. ἀνόητον δ' ἐπὶ τοιούτους ἰέναι ὧν κρατήσας τε μὴ κατασχήσει τις καὶ μὴ κατορθώσας μὴ ἐν τῶι ὁμοίωι καὶ πρὶν ἐπιχειρῆσαι
2 ἔσται. Σικελιῶται δ' ἄν μοι δοκοῦσιν, ὥς γε νῦν ἔχουσι, καὶ ἔτι ἂν ἧσσον δεινοὶ ἡμῖν γενέσθαι, εἰ ἄρξειαν αὐτῶν Συρακόσιοι, ὅπερ οἱ Ἐγεσταῖοι
3 μάλιστα ἡμᾶς ἐκφοβοῦσιν. νῦν μὲν γὰρ κἂν ἔλθοιεν ἴσως Λακεδαιμονίων ἕκαστοι χάριτι, ἐκείνως δ' οὐκ εἰκὸς ἀρχὴν ἐπὶ ἀρχὴν στρατεῦσαι· ὧι γὰρ ἂν τρόπωι τὴν ἡμετέραν μετὰ Πελοποννησίων ἀφέλωνται, εἰκὸς
4 ὑπὸ τῶν αὐτῶν καὶ τὴν σφετέραν διὰ τοῦ αὐτοῦ καθαιρεθῆναι. ἡμᾶς δ' ἂν οἱ ἐκεῖ Ἕλληνες μάλιστα μὲν ἐκπεπληγμένοι εἶεν εἰ μὴ ἀφικοίμεθα, ἔπειτα δὲ καὶ εἰ δείξαντες τὴν δύναμιν δι' ὀλίγου ἀπέλθοιμεν· εἰ δὲ σφαλεῖμέν τι, τάχιστ' ἂν ὑπεριδόντες μετὰ τῶν ἐνθάδε ἐπιθοῖντο· τὰ γὰρ διὰ πλείστου πάντες ἴσμεν θαυμαζόμενα καὶ τὰ πεῖραν ἥκιστα τῆς
5 δόξης δόντα. ὅπερ νῦν ὑμεῖς, ὦ Ἀθηναῖοι, ἐς Λακεδαιμονίους καὶ τοὺς ξυμμάχους πεπόνθατε· διὰ τὸ παρὰ γνώμην αὐτῶν πρὸς ἃ ἐφοβεῖσθε τὸ πρῶτον περιγεγενῆσθαι, καταφρονήσαντες ἤδη καὶ Σικελίας ἐφίεσθε.
6 χρὴ δὲ μὴ πρὸς τὰς τύχας τῶν ἐναντίων ἐπαίρεσθαι, ἀλλὰ τὰς διανοίας κρατήσαντας θαρσεῖν, μηδὲ Λακεδαιμονίους ἄλλο τι ἡγήσασθαι ἢ διὰ τὸ αἰσχρὸν σκοπεῖν ὅτωι τρόπωι ἔτι καὶ νῦν, ἢν δύνωνται, σφήλαντες ἡμᾶς τὸ σφέτερον ἀπρεπὲς εὖ θήσονται, ὅσωι καὶ περὶ πλείστου καὶ
7 διὰ πλείστου δόξαν ἀρετῆς μελετῶσιν. ὥστε οὐ περὶ τῶν ἐν Σικελίαι

10.4 πολλῶν: πολλοῦ H² (coniecerat Herwerden)   10.5 ἡμῶν CM: ὑμῶν G ἀφ' ἡμῶν ABEFZ

Ἐγεσταίων ἡμῖν, ἀνδρῶν βαρβάρων, ὁ ἀγών, εἰ σωφρονοῦμεν, ἀλλ' ὅπως πόλιν δι' ὀλιγαρχίας ἐπιβουλεύουσαν ὀξέως φυλαξόμεθα.

Καὶ μεμνῆσθαι χρὴ ἡμᾶς ὅτι νεωστὶ ἀπὸ νόσου μεγάλης καὶ πολέμου 12 βραχύ τι λελωφήκαμεν, ὥστε καὶ χρήμασι καὶ τοῖς σώμασιν ηὐξῆσθαι· καὶ ταῦτα ὑπὲρ ἡμῶν δίκαιον ἐνθάδε ἀναλοῦν, καὶ μὴ ὑπὲρ ἀνδρῶν φυγάδων τῶνδε ἐπικουρίας δεομένων, οἷς τό τε ψεύσασθαι καλῶς χρήσιμον καὶ τῶι τοῦ πέλας κινδύνωι, αὐτοὺς λόγους μόνον παρασχομένους, ἢ κατορθώσαντας χάριν μὴ ἀξίαν εἰδέναι ἢ πταίσαντάς που τοὺς φίλους ξυναπολέσαι. εἴ τέ τις ἄρχειν ἄσμενος αἱρεθεὶς παραινεῖ ὑμῖν ἐκπλεῖν, τὸ 2 ἑαυτοῦ μόνον σκοπῶν, ἄλλως τε καὶ νεώτερος ὢν ἔτι ἐς τὸ ἄρχειν, ὅπως θαυμασθῆι μὲν ἀπὸ τῆς ἱπποτροφίας, διὰ δὲ πολυτέλειαν καὶ ὠφεληθῆι τι ἐκ τῆς ἀρχῆς, μηδὲ τούτωι ἐμπαράσχητε τῶι τῆς πόλεως κινδύνωι ἰδίαι ἐλλαμπρύνεσθαι, νομίσατε δὲ τοὺς τοιούτους τὰ μὲν δημόσια ἀδικεῖν, τὰ δὲ ἴδια ἀναλοῦν, καὶ τὸ πρᾶγμα μέγα εἶναι καὶ μὴ οἷον νεωτέρωι βουλεύσασθαί τε καὶ ὀξέως μεταχειρίσαι.

Οὓς ἐγὼ ὁρῶν νῦν ἐνθάδε τῶι αὐτῶι ἀνδρὶ παρακελευστοὺς 13 καθημένους φοβοῦμαι, καὶ τοῖς πρεσβυτέροις ἀντιπαρακελεύομαι μὴ καταισχυνθῆναι, εἴ τῳ τις παρακάθηται τῶνδε, ὅπως μὴ δόξει, ἐὰν μὴ ψηφίζηται πολεμεῖν, μαλακὸς εἶναι, μηδ', ὅπερ ἂν αὐτοὶ πάθοιεν, δυσέρωτας εἶναι τῶν ἀπόντων, γνόντας ὅτι ἐπιθυμίαι μὲν ἐλάχιστα κατορθοῦνται, προνοίαι δὲ πλεῖστα, ἀλλ' ὑπὲρ τῆς πατρίδος ὡς μέγιστον δὴ τῶν πρὶν κίνδυνον ἀναρριπτούσης ἀντιχειροτονεῖν καὶ ψηφίζεσθαι τοὺς μὲν Σικελιώτας οἷσπερ νῦν ὅροις χρωμένους πρὸς ἡμᾶς, οὐ μεμπτοῖς, τῶι τε Ἰονίωι κόλπωι παρὰ γῆν ἤν τις πλέηι, καὶ τῶι Σικελικῶι διὰ πελάγους, τὰ αὐτῶν νεμομένους καθ' αὑτοὺς καὶ ξυμφέρεσθαι· τοῖς 2 δ' Ἐγεσταίοις ἰδίαι εἰπεῖν, ἐπειδὴ ἄνευ Ἀθηναίων καὶ ξυνῆψαν πρὸς Σελινουντίους τὸ πρῶτον πόλεμον, μετὰ σφῶν αὐτῶν καὶ καταλύεσθαι· καὶ τὸ λοιπὸν ξυμμάχους μὴ ποιεῖσθαι ὥσπερ εἰώθαμεν, οἷς κακῶς μὲν πράξασιν ἀμυνοῦμεν, ὠφελίας δ' αὐτοὶ δεηθέντες οὐ τευξόμεθα.

Καὶ σύ, ὦ πρύτανι, ταῦτα, εἴπερ ἡγεῖ σοι προσήκειν κήδεσθαί τε 14 τῆς πόλεως καὶ βούλει γενέσθαι πολίτης ἀγαθός, ἐπιψήφιζε καὶ γνώμας προτίθει αὖθις Ἀθηναίοις, νομίσας, εἰ ὀρρωδεῖς τὸ ἀναψηφίσαι, τὸ μὲν λύειν τοὺς νόμους μὴ μετὰ τοσῶνδ' ἂν μαρτύρων αἰτίαν σχεῖν, τῆς δὲ πόλεως κακῶς βουλευσαμένης ἰατρὸς ἂν γενέσθαι, καὶ τὸ καλῶς ἄρξαι τοῦτ' εἶναι, ὃς ἂν τὴν πατρίδα ὠφελήσηι ὡς πλεῖστα ἢ ἑκὼν εἶναι μηδὲν βλάψηι.'

12.1 ἐνθάδε C Ud Pl¹: ἐνθάδε εἶναι cett.

15 Ὁ μὲν Νικίας τοιαῦτα εἶπε, τῶν δὲ Ἀθηναίων παριόντες οἱ μὲν πλεῖστοι στρατεύειν παρῄνουν καὶ τὰ ἐψηφισμένα μὴ λύειν, οἱ δέ
2 τινες καὶ ἀντέλεγον. ἐνῆγε δὲ προθυμότατα τὴν στρατείαν Ἀλκιβιάδης ὁ Κλεινίου, βουλόμενος τῶι τε Νικίαι ἐναντιοῦσθαι, ὢν καὶ ἐς τἆλλα διάφορος τὰ πολιτικὰ καὶ ὅτι αὐτοῦ διαβόλως ἐμνήσθη, καὶ μάλιστα στρατηγῆσαί τε ἐπιθυμῶν καὶ ἐλπίζων Σικελίαν τε δι' αὐτοῦ καὶ Καρχηδόνα λήψεσθαι καὶ τὰ ἴδια ἅμα εὐτυχήσας χρήμασί τε καὶ δόξηι
3 ὠφελήσειν. ὢν γὰρ ἐν ἀξιώματι ὑπὸ τῶν ἀστῶν, ταῖς ἐπιθυμίαις μείζοσιν ἢ κατὰ τὴν ὑπάρχουσαν οὐσίαν ἐχρῆτο ἔς τε τὰς ἱπποτροφίας καὶ τὰς ἄλλας δαπάνας· ὅπερ καὶ καθεῖλεν ὕστερον τὴν τῶν Ἀθηναίων πόλιν
4 οὐχ ἥκιστα. φοβηθέντες γὰρ αὐτοῦ οἱ πολλοὶ τὸ μέγεθος τῆς τε κατὰ τὸ ἑαυτοῦ σῶμα παρανομίας ἐς τὴν δίαιταν καὶ τῆς διανοίας ὧν καθ' ἓν ἕκαστον ἐν ὅτωι γίγνοιτο ἔπρασσεν, ὡς τυραννίδος ἐπιθυμοῦντι πολέμιοι καθέστασαν, καὶ δημοσίαι κράτιστα διαθέντι τὰ τοῦ πολέμου ἰδίαι ἕκαστοι τοῖς ἐπιτηδεύμασιν αὐτοῦ ἀχθεσθέντες, καὶ ἄλλοις ἐπιτρέψαντες,
5 οὐ διὰ μακροῦ ἔσφηλαν τὴν πόλιν. τότε δ' οὖν παρελθὼν τοῖς Ἀθηναίοις παρῄνει τοιάδε.

16 'Καὶ προσήκει μοι μᾶλλον ἑτέρων, ὦ Ἀθηναῖοι, ἄρχειν (ἀνάγκη γὰρ ἐντεῦθεν ἄρξασθαι, ἐπειδή μου Νικίας καθήψατο), καὶ ἄξιος ἅμα νομίζω εἶναι. ὧν γὰρ πέρι ἐπιβόητός εἰμι, τοῖς μὲν προγόνοις μου καὶ ἐμοὶ
2 δόξαν φέρει ταῦτα, τῆι δὲ πατρίδι καὶ ὠφελίαν. οἱ γὰρ Ἕλληνες καὶ ὑπὲρ δύναμιν μείζω ἡμῶν τὴν πόλιν ἐνόμισαν τῶι ἐμῶι διαπρεπεῖ τῆς Ὀλυμπίαζε θεωρίας, πρότερον ἐλπίζοντες αὐτὴν καταπεπολεμῆσθαι, διότι ἅρματα μὲν ἑπτὰ καθῆκα, ὅσα οὐδείς πω ἰδιώτης πρότερον, ἐνίκησα δὲ καὶ δεύτερος καὶ τέταρτος ἐγενόμην καὶ τἆλλα ἀξίως τῆς νίκης παρεσκευασάμην. νόμωι μὲν γὰρ τιμὴ τὰ τοιαῦτα, ἐκ δὲ τοῦ
3 δρωμένου καὶ δύναμις ἅμα ὑπονοεῖται. καὶ ὅσα αὖ ἐν τῆι πόλει χορηγίαις ἢ ἄλλωι τωι λαμπρύνομαι, τοῖς μὲν ἀστοῖς φθονεῖται φύσει, πρὸς δὲ τοὺς ξένους καὶ αὕτη ἰσχὺς φαίνεται. καὶ οὐκ ἄχρηστος ἥδ' ἡ ἄνοια, ὃς ἂν τοῖς ἰδίοις τέλεσι μὴ ἑαυτὸν μόνον, ἀλλὰ καὶ τὴν πόλιν
4 ὠφελῆι. οὐδέ γε ἄδικον ἐφ' ἑαυτῶι μέγα φρονοῦντα μὴ ἴσον εἶναι, ἐπεὶ καὶ ὁ κακῶς πράσσων πρὸς οὐδένα τῆς ξυμφορᾶς ἰσομοιρεῖ· ἀλλ' ὥσπερ δυστυχοῦντες οὐ προσαγορευόμεθα, ἐν τῶι ὁμοίωι τις ἀνεχέσθω καὶ ὑπὸ τῶν εὐπραγούντων ὑπερφρονούμενος, ἢ τὰ ἴσα νέμων τὰ ὁμοῖα
5 ἀνταξιούτω. οἶδα δὲ τοὺς τοιούτους, καὶ ὅσοι ἔν τινος λαμπρότητι προέσχον, ἐν μὲν τῶι καθ' αὑτοὺς βίωι λυπηροὺς ὄντας, τοῖς ὁμοίοις μὲν μάλιστα, ἔπειτα δὲ καὶ τοῖς ἄλλοις ξυνόντας, τῶν δὲ ἔπειτα ἀνθρώπων προσποίησίν τε ξυγγενείας τισὶ καὶ μὴ οὖσαν καταλιπόντας, καὶ ἧς ἂν

ὦσι πατρίδος, ταύτηι αὔχησιν ὡς οὐ περὶ ἀλλοτρίων οὐδ᾽ ἁμαρτόντων, ἀλλ᾽ ὡς περὶ σφετέρων τε καὶ καλὰ πραξάντων. ὧν ἐγὼ ὀρεγόμενος 6 καὶ διὰ ταῦτα τὰ ἴδια ἐπιβοώμενος τὰ δημόσια σκοπεῖτε εἴ του χεῖρον μεταχειρίζω. Πελοποννήσου γὰρ τὰ δυνατώτατα ξυστήσας ἄνευ μεγάλου ὑμῖν κινδύνου καὶ δαπάνης Λακεδαιμονίους ἐς μίαν ἡμέραν κατέστησα ἐν Μαντινείαι περὶ τῶν ἁπάντων ἀγωνίσασθαι· ἐξ οὗ καὶ περιγενόμενοι τῆι μάχηι οὐδέπω καὶ νῦν βεβαίως θαρσοῦσιν.

Καὶ ταῦτα ἡ ἐμὴ νεότης καὶ ἄνοια παρὰ φύσιν δοκοῦσα εἶναι ἐς 17 τὴν Πελοποννησίων δύναμιν λόγοις τε πρέπουσιν ὡμίλησε καὶ ὀργῆι πίστιν παρασχομένη ἔπεισεν. καὶ νῦν μὴ πεφόβησθε αὐτήν, ἀλλ᾽ ἕως ἐγώ τε ἔτι ἀκμάζω μετ᾽ αὐτῆς καὶ ὁ Νικίας εὐτυχὴς δοκεῖ εἶναι, ἀποχρήσασθε τῆι ἑκατέρου ἡμῶν ὠφελίαι. καὶ τὸν ἐς τὴν Σικελίαν πλοῦν 2 μὴ μεταγιγνώσκετε ὡς ἐπὶ μεγάλην δύναμιν ἐσόμενον. ὄχλοις τε γὰρ ξυμμείκτοις πολυανδροῦσιν αἱ πόλεις καὶ ῥαιδίας ἔχουσι τῶν πολιτῶν τὰς μεταβολὰς καὶ ἐπιδοχάς. καὶ οὐδεὶς δι᾽ αὐτὸ ὡς περὶ οἰκείας πατρίδος 3 οὔτε τὰ περὶ τὸ σῶμα ὅπλοις ἐξήρτυται οὔτε τὰ ἐν τῆι χώραι νομίμοις κατασκευαῖς· ὅ τι δὲ ἕκαστος ἢ ἐκ τοῦ λέγων πείθειν οἴεται ἢ στασιάζων ἀπὸ τοῦ κοινοῦ λαβὼν ἄλλην γῆν, μὴ κατορθώσας, οἰκήσειν, ταῦτα ἑτοιμάζεται. καὶ οὐκ εἰκὸς τὸν τοιοῦτον ὅμιλον οὔτε λόγου μιᾶι γνώμηι 4 ἀκροᾶσθαι οὔτε ἐς τὰ ἔργα κοινῶς τρέπεσθαι· ταχὺ δ᾽ ἂν ὡς ἕκαστοι, εἴ τι καθ᾽ ἡδονὴν λέγοιτο, προσχωροῖεν, ἄλλως τε καὶ εἰ στασιάζουσιν, ὥσπερ πυνθανόμεθα. καὶ μὴν οὐδ᾽ ὁπλῖται οὔτ᾽ ἐκείνοις ὅσοιπερ κομποῦνται, 5 οὔτε οἱ ἄλλοι Ἕλληνες διεφάνησαν τοσοῦτοι ὄντες ὅσους ἕκαστοι σφᾶς αὐτοὺς ἠρίθμουν, ἀλλὰ μέγιστον δὴ αὐτοὺς ἐψευσμένη ἡ Ἑλλὰς μόλις ἐν τῶιδε τῶι πολέμωι ἱκανῶς ὡπλίσθη. τά τε οὖν ἐκεῖ, ἐξ ὧν ἐγὼ ἀκοῆι 6 αἰσθάνομαι, τοιαῦτα καὶ ἔτι εὐπορώτερα ἔσται (βαρβάρους [τε] γὰρ πολλοὺς ἕξομεν οἳ Συρακοσίων μίσει ξυνεπιθήσονται αὐτοῖς) καὶ τὰ ἐνθάδε οὐκ ἐπικωλύσει, ἢν ὑμεῖς ὀρθῶς βουλεύσησθε. οἱ γὰρ πατέρες 7 ἡμῶν τοὺς αὐτοὺς τούτους οὕσπερ νῦν φασὶ πολεμίους ὑπολείποντας ἂν ἡμᾶς πλεῖν καὶ προσέτι τὸν Μῆδον ἐχθρὸν ἔχοντες τὴν ἀρχὴν ἐκτήσαντο, οὐκ ἄλλωι τινὶ ἢ τῆι περιουσίαι τοῦ ναυτικοῦ ἰσχύοντες. καὶ νῦν οὔτε 8 ἀνέλπιστοί πω μᾶλλον Πελοποννήσιοι ἐς ἡμᾶς ἐγένοντο, εἴ τε καὶ πάνυ ἔρρωνται, τὸ μὲν ἐς τὴν γῆν ἡμῶν ἐσβάλλειν, κἂν μὴ ἐκπλεύσωμεν, ἱκανοί εἰσι, τῶι δὲ ναυτικῶι οὐκ ἂν δύναιντο βλάπτειν· ὑπόλοιπον γὰρ ἡμῖν ἐστιν ἀντίπαλον ναυτικόν.

17.6 τε del. Haacke

18 Ὥστε τί ἂν λέγοντες εἰκὸς ἢ αὐτοὶ ἀποκνοῖμεν ἢ πρὸς τοὺς ἐκεῖ ξυμμάχους σκηπτόμενοι μὴ βοηθοῖμεν; οἷς χρεών, ἐπειδή γε καὶ ξυνωμόσαμεν, ἐπαμύνειν, καὶ μὴ ἀντιτιθέναι ὅτι οὐδὲ ἐκεῖνοι ἡμῖν. οὐ γὰρ ἵνα δεῦρο ἀντιβοηθῶσι προσεθέμεθα αὐτούς, ἀλλ᾽ ἵνα τοῖς ἐκεῖ ἐχθροῖς
2 ἡμῶν λυπηροὶ ὄντες δεῦρο κωλύωσιν αὐτοὺς ἐπιέναι. τήν τε ἀρχὴν οὕτως ἐκτησάμεθα καὶ ἡμεῖς καὶ ὅσοι δὴ ἄλλοι ἦρξαν, παραγιγνόμενοι προθύμως τοῖς αἰεὶ ἢ βαρβάροις ἢ Ἕλλησιν ἐπικαλουμένοις, ἐπεί, εἴ γε ἡσυχάζοιεν πάντες ἢ φυλοκρινοῖεν οἷς χρεὼν βοηθεῖν, βραχὺ ἄν τι προσκτώμενοι αὐτῇ περὶ αὐτῆς ἂν ταύτης μᾶλλον κινδυνεύοιμεν. τὸν γὰρ προύχοντα οὐ μόνον ἐπιόντα τις ἀμύνεται, ἀλλὰ καὶ ὅπως
3 μὴ ἔπεισι προκαταλαμβάνει. καὶ οὐκ ἔστιν ἡμῖν ταμιεύεσθαι ἐς ὅσον βουλόμεθα ἄρχειν, ἀλλ᾽ ἀνάγκη, ἐπειδήπερ ἐν τῷδε καθέσταμεν, τοῖς μὲν ἐπιβουλεύειν, τοὺς δὲ μὴ ἀνιέναι, διὰ τὸ ἀρχθῆναι ἂν ὑφ᾽ ἑτέρων αὐτοῖς κίνδυνον εἶναι, εἰ μὴ αὐτοὶ ἄλλων ἄρχοιμεν. καὶ οὐκ ἐκ τοῦ αὐτοῦ ἐπισκεπτέον ὑμῖν τοῖς ἄλλοις τὸ ἥσυχον, εἰ μὴ καὶ τὰ ἐπιτηδεύματα ἐς τὸ ὁμοῖον μεταλήψεσθε.
4 Λογισάμενοι οὖν τάδε μᾶλλον αὐξήσειν, ἐπ᾽ ἐκεῖνα ἢν ἴωμεν, ποιώμεθα τὸν πλοῦν, ἵνα Πελοποννησίων τε στορέσωμεν τὸ φρόνημα, εἰ δόξομεν ὑπεριδόντες τὴν ἐν τῷ παρόντι ἡσυχίαν καὶ ἐπὶ Σικελίαν πλεῦσαι· καὶ ἅμα ἢ τῆς Ἑλλάδος τῶν ἐκεῖ προσγενομένων πάσης τῷ εἰκότι ἄρξομεν, ἢ κακώσομέν γε Συρακοσίους, ἐν ᾧ καὶ αὐτοὶ καὶ οἱ ξύμμαχοι
5 ὠφελησόμεθα. τὸ δὲ ἀσφαλές, καὶ μένειν, ἤν τι προχωρῇ, καὶ ἀπελθεῖν, αἱ νῆες παρέξουσιν· ναυκράτορες γὰρ ἐσόμεθα καὶ ξυμπάντων Σικελιωτῶν.
6 καὶ μὴ ὑμᾶς ἡ Νικίου τῶν λόγων ἀπραγμοσύνη καὶ διάστασις τοῖς νέοις ἐς τοὺς πρεσβυτέρους ἀποτρέψῃ, τῷ δὲ εἰωθότι κόσμῳ, ὥσπερ καὶ οἱ πατέρες ἡμῶν ἅμα νέοι γεραιτέροις βουλεύοντες ἐς τάδε ἦραν αὐτά, καὶ νῦν τῷ αὐτῷ τρόπῳ πειρᾶσθε προαγαγεῖν τὴν πόλιν, καὶ νομίσατε νεότητα μὲν καὶ γῆρας ἄνευ ἀλλήλων μηδὲν δύνασθαι, ὁμοῦ δὲ τό τε φαῦλον καὶ τὸ μέσον καὶ τὸ πάνυ ἀκριβὲς ἂν ξυγκραθὲν μάλιστ᾽ ἂν ἰσχύειν, καὶ τὴν πόλιν, ἐὰν μὲν ἡσυχάζῃ, τρίψεσθαί τε αὐτὴν περὶ αὑτὴν ὥσπερ καὶ ἄλλο τι, καὶ πάντων τὴν ἐπιστήμην ἐγγηράσεσθαι, ἀγωνιζομένην δὲ αἰεὶ προσλήψεσθαί τε τὴν ἐμπειρίαν καὶ τὸ ἀμύνεσθαι οὐ λόγῳ ἀλλ᾽
7 ἔργῳ μᾶλλον ξύνηθες ἕξειν. παράπαν τε γιγνώσκω πόλιν μὴ ἀπράγμονα τάχιστ᾽ ἄν μοι δοκεῖν ἀπραγμοσύνης μεταβολῇ διαφθαρῆναι, καὶ τῶν

18.2 ἡσυχάζοιεν πάντες ... φυλοκρινοῖεν codd.: ἡσυχάζοιμεν πάντως ... φυλοκρινοῖμεν Hude ἀνθρώπων ἀσφαλέστατα τούτους οἰκεῖν οἳ ἂν τοῖς παροῦσιν ἤθεσι καὶ νόμοις, ἢν καὶ χείρω ἦι, ἥκιστα διαφόρως πολιτεύωσιν.'

Τοιαῦτα μὲν ὁ Ἀλκιβιάδης εἶπεν· οἱ δ' Ἀθηναῖοι ἀκούσαντες ἐκείνου 19 τε καὶ τῶν Ἐγεσταίων καὶ Λεοντίνων φυγάδων, οἳ παρελθόντες ἐδέοντό τε καὶ τῶν ὁρκίων ὑπομιμνήισκοντες ἱκέτευον βοηθῆσαι σφίσι, πολλῶι μᾶλλον ἢ πρότερον ὥρμηντο στρατεύειν. καὶ ὁ Νικίας γνοὺς ὅτι ἀπὸ 2 μὲν τῶν αὐτῶν λόγων οὐκ ἂν ἔτι ἀποτρέψειε, παρασκευῆς δὲ πλήθει, εἰ πολλὴν ἐπιτάξειε, τάχ' ἂν μεταστήσειεν αὐτούς, παρελθὼν αὐτοῖς αὖθις ἔλεγε τοιάδε.

'Ἐπειδὴ πάντως ὁρῶ ὑμᾶς, ὦ Ἀθηναῖοι, ὡρμημένους στρατεύειν, 20 ξυνενέγκοι μὲν ταῦτα ὡς βουλόμεθα, ἐπὶ δὲ τῶι παρόντι ἃ γιγνώσκω σημανῶ. ἐπὶ γὰρ πόλεις, ὡς ἐγὼ ἀκοῆι αἰσθάνομαι, μέλλομεν ἰέναι 2 μεγάλας καὶ οὔθ' ὑπηκόους ἀλλήλων οὔτε δεομένας μεταβολῆς, ἧι ἂν ἐκ βιαίου τις δουλείας ἄσμενος ἐς ῥάιω μετάστασιν χωροίη, οὐδ' ἂν τὴν ἀρχὴν τὴν ἡμετέραν εἰκότως ἀντ' ἐλευθερίας προσδεξαμένας, τό τε πλῆθος, ὡς ἐν μιᾶι νήσωι, πολλὰς τὰς Ἑλληνίδας. πλὴν γὰρ Νάξου καὶ 3 Κατάνης, ἃς ἐλπίζω ἡμῖν κατὰ τὸ Λεοντίνων ξυγγενὲς προσέσεσθαι, ἄλλαι εἰσὶν ἑπτά, καὶ παρεσκευασμέναι τοῖς πᾶσιν ὁμοιοτρόπως μάλιστα τῆι ἡμετέραι δυνάμει, καὶ οὐχ ἥκιστα ἐπὶ ἃς μᾶλλον πλέομεν, Σελινοῦς καὶ Συράκουσαι. πολλοὶ μὲν γὰρ ὁπλῖται ἔνεισι καὶ τοξόται καὶ ἀκοντισταί, 4 πολλαὶ δὲ τριήρεις καὶ ὄχλος ὁ πληρώσων αὐτάς. χρήματά τ' ἔχουσι τὰ μὲν ἴδια, τὰ δὲ καὶ ἐν τοῖς ἱεροῖς ἐστι Σελινουντίοις, Συρακοσίοις δὲ καὶ ἀπὸ βαρβάρων τινῶν ἀπαρχὴ φέρεται· ὧι δὲ μάλιστα ἡμῶν προύχουσιν, ἵππους τε πολλοὺς κέκτηνται καὶ σίτωι οἰκείωι καὶ οὐκ ἐπακτῶι χρῶνται.

'Πρὸς οὖν τοιαύτην δύναμιν οὐ ναυτικῆς καὶ φαύλου στρατιᾶς μόνον 21 δεῖ, ἀλλὰ καὶ πεζὸν πολὺν ξυμπλεῖν, εἴπερ βουλόμεθα ἄξιον τῆς διανοίας δρᾶν καὶ μὴ ὑπὸ ἱππέων πολλῶν εἴργεσθαι τῆς γῆς, ἄλλως τε καὶ εἰ ξυστῶσιν αἱ πόλεις φοβηθεῖσαι καὶ μὴ ἀντιπαράσχωσιν ἡμῖν φίλοι τινὲς γενόμενοι ἄλλοι ἢ Ἐγεσταῖοι ὧι ἀμυνούμεθα ἱππικόν (αἰσχρὸν δὲ 2 βιασθέντας ἀπελθεῖν ἢ ὕστερον ἐπιμεταπέμπεσθαι, τὸ πρῶτον ἀσκέπτως βουλευσαμένους)· αὐτόθεν δὲ παρασκευῆι ἀξιόχρεωι ἐπιέναι, γνόντας ὅτι πολύ τε ἀπὸ τῆς ἡμετέρας αὐτῶν μέλλομεν πλεῖν καὶ οὐκ ἐν τῶι ὁμοίωι στρατευσόμενοι καὶ ὅτε τοῖς τῆιδε ὑπηκόοις ξύμμαχοι ἤλθετε ἐπί τινα, ὅθεν ῥάιδιαι αἱ κομιδαὶ ἐκ τῆς φιλίας ὧν προσέδει, ἀλλ' ἐς ἀλλοτρίαν πᾶσαν ἀπαρτήσοντες, ἐξ ἧς μηνῶν οὐδὲ τεσσάρων τῶν χειμερινῶν

21.2 καὶ ὅτε τοῖς Badham: καὶ οὐκ ἐν τοῖς codd: καὶ ὅτε ἐν τοῖς Portus

22 ἄγγελον ῥᾴδιον ἐλθεῖν. ὁπλίτας τε οὖν πολλούς μοι δοκεῖ χρῆναι ἡμᾶς ἄγειν καὶ ἡμῶν αὐτῶν καὶ τῶν ξυμμάχων, τῶν τε ὑπηκόων καὶ ἤν τινα ἐκ Πελοποννήσου δυνώμεθα ἢ πεῖσαι ἢ μισθῶι προσαγαγέσθαι, καὶ τοξότας πολλοὺς καὶ σφενδονήτας, ὅπως πρὸς τὸ ἐκείνων ἱππικὸν ἀντέχωσι, ναυσί τε καὶ πολὺ περιεῖναι, ἵνα καὶ τὰ ἐπιτήδεια ῥᾷον ἐσκομιζώμεθα, τὸν δὲ καὶ αὐτόθεν σῖτον ἐν ὁλκάσι, πυροὺς καὶ πεφρυγμένας κριθάς, ἄγειν καὶ σιτοποιοὺς ἐκ τῶν μυλώνων πρὸς μέρος ἠναγκασμένους ἐμμίσθους, ἵνα, ἤν που ὑπὸ ἀπλοίας ἀπολαμβανώμεθα, ἔχῃ ἡ στρατιὰ τὰ ἐπιτήδεια (πολλὴ γὰρ οὖσα οὐ πάσης ἔσται πόλεως ὑποδέξασθαι), τά τε ἄλλα ὅσον δυνατὸν ἑτοιμάσασθαι, καὶ μὴ ἐπὶ ἑτέροις γίγνεσθαι, μάλιστα δὲ χρήματα αὐτόθεν ὡς πλεῖστα ἔχειν. τὰ δὲ παρ᾽ Ἐγεσταίων, ἃ λέγεται
23 ἐκεῖ ἑτοῖμα, νομίσατε καὶ λόγωι ἂν μάλιστα ἑτοῖμα εἶναι. ἢν γὰρ αὐτοὶ ἔλθωμεν ἐνθένδε μὴ ἀντίπαλον μόνον παρασκευασάμενοι, πλήν γε πρὸς τὸ μάχιμον αὐτῶν, τὸ ὁπλιτικόν, ἀλλὰ καὶ ὑπερβάλλοντες τοῖς πᾶσι,
2 μόλις οὕτως οἷοί τε ἐσόμεθα τῶν μὲν κρατεῖν, τὰ δὲ καὶ διασῶσαι. πόλιν τε νομίσαι χρὴ ἐν ἀλλοφύλοις καὶ πολεμίοις οἰκιοῦντας ἱέναι, οὓς πρέπει τῆι πρώτηι ἡμέραι ἧι ἂν κατάσχωσιν εὐθὺς κρατεῖν τῆς γῆς, ἢ εἰδέναι
3 ὅτι, ἢν σφάλλωνται, πάντα πολέμια ἕξουσιν. ὅπερ ἐγὼ φοβούμενος καὶ εἰδὼς πολλὰ μὲν ἡμᾶς δέον εὖ βουλεύσασθαι, ἔτι δὲ πλείω εὐτυχῆσαι – χαλεπὸν δὲ ἀνθρώπους ὄντας – ὅτι ἐλάχιστα τῆι τύχηι παραδοὺς ἐμαυτὸν βούλομαι ἐκπλεῖν, παρασκευῆι δὲ ἀπὸ τῶν εἰκότων ἀσφαλὴς
4 ἐκπλεῦσαι. ταῦτα γὰρ τῆι τε ξυμπάσηι πόλει βεβαιότατα ἡγοῦμαι καὶ ἡμῖν τοῖς στρατευσομένοις σωτήρια. εἰ δέ τωι ἄλλως δοκεῖ, παρίημι αὐτῶι τὴν ἀρχήν.᾽

24 Ὁ μὲν Νικίας τοσαῦτα εἶπε νομίζων τοὺς Ἀθηναίους τῶι πλήθει τῶν πραγμάτων ἢ ἀποτρέψειν ἤ, εἰ ἀναγκάζοιτο στρατεύεσθαι, μάλιστα
2 οὕτως ἀσφαλῶς ἐκπλεῦσαι· οἱ δὲ τὸ μὲν ἐπιθυμοῦν τοῦ πλοῦ οὐκ ἐξῃρέθησαν ὑπὸ τοῦ ὀχλώδους τῆς παρασκευῆς, πολὺ δὲ μᾶλλον ὥρμηντο, καὶ τοὐναντίον περιέστη αὐτῶι· εὖ τε γὰρ παραινέσαι ἔδοξε
3 καὶ ἀσφάλεια νῦν δὴ καὶ πολλὴ ἔσεσθαι. καὶ ἔρως ἐνέπεσε τοῖς πᾶσιν ὁμοίως ἐκπλεῦσαι· τοῖς μὲν γὰρ πρεσβυτέροις ὡς ἢ καταστρεψομένοις ἐφ᾽ ἃ ἔπλεον ἢ οὐδὲν ἂν σφαλεῖσαν μεγάλην δύναμιν, τοῖς δ᾽ ἐν τῆι ἡλικίαι τῆς τε ἀπούσης πόθωι ὄψεως καὶ θεωρίας, καὶ εὐέλπιδες ὄντες σωθήσεσθαι, ὁ δὲ πολὺς ὅμιλος καὶ στρατιώτης ἔν τε τῶι παρόντι ἀργύριον οἴσειν
4 καὶ προσκτήσεσθαι δύναμιν ὅθεν ἀίδιον μισθοφορὰν ὑπάρξειν. ὥστε διὰ

24.1 μάλιστα οὕτως codd.: μάλιστ᾽ <ἂν> οὕτως Bekker

τὴν ἄγαν τῶν πλεόνων ἐπιθυμίαν, εἴ τωι ἄρα καὶ μὴ ἤρεσκε, δεδιὼς μὴ ἀντιχειροτονῶν κακόνους δόξειεν εἶναι τῆι πόλει ἡσυχίαν ἦγεν. καὶ 25 τέλος παρελθών τις τῶν Ἀθηναίων καὶ παρακαλέσας τὸν Νικίαν οὐκ ἔφη χρῆναι προφασίζεσθαι οὐδὲ διαμέλλειν, ἀλλ' ἐναντίον ἁπάντων ἤδη λέγειν ἥντινα αὐτῶι παρασκευὴν Ἀθηναῖοι ψηφίσωνται. ὁ δὲ ἄκων μὲν εἶπεν 2 ὅτι καὶ μετὰ τῶν ξυναρχόντων καθ' ἡσυχίαν μᾶλλον βουλεύσοιτο, ὅσα μέντοι ἤδη δοκεῖν αὐτῶι, τριήρεσι μὲν οὐκ ἔλασσον ἢ ἑκατὸν πλευστέα εἶναι αὐτῶν Ἀθηναίων, ὧν ἔσεσθαι ὁπλιταγωγοὺς ὅσαι ἂν δοκῶσι, καὶ ἄλλας ἐκ τῶν ξυμμάχων μεταπεμπτέας εἶναι, ὁπλίταις δὲ τοῖς ξύμπασιν Ἀθηναίων καὶ τῶν ξυμμάχων πεντακισχιλίων μὲν οὐκ ἐλάσσοσιν, ἢν δέ τι δύνωνται, καὶ πλέοσιν· τὴν δὲ ἄλλην παρασκευὴν ὡς κατὰ λόγον, καὶ τοξοτῶν τῶν αὐτόθεν καὶ ἐκ Κρήτης καὶ σφενδονητῶν, καὶ ἤν τι ἄλλο πρέπον δοκῆι εἶναι, ἑτοιμασάμενοι ἄξειν. ἀκούσαντες δ' οἱ Ἀθηναῖοι 26 ἐψηφίσαντο εὐθὺς αὐτοκράτορας εἶναι καὶ περὶ στρατιᾶς πλήθους καὶ περὶ τοῦ παντὸς πλοῦ τοὺς στρατηγοὺς πράσσειν ἧι ἂν αὐτοῖς δοκῆι ἄριστα εἶναι Ἀθηναίοις. καὶ μετὰ ταῦτα ἡ παρασκευὴ ἐγίγνετο, καὶ ἔς 2 τε τοὺς ξυμμάχους ἔπεμπον καὶ αὐτόθεν καταλόγους ἐποιοῦντο. ἄρτι δ' ἀνειλήφει ἡ πόλις ἑαυτὴν ἀπὸ τῆς νόσου καὶ τοῦ ξυνεχοῦς πολέμου ἔς τε ἡλικίας πλῆθος ἐπιγεγενημένης καὶ ἐς χρημάτων ἄθροισιν διὰ τὴν ἐκεχειρίαν, ὥστε ῥᾶιον πάντα ἐπορίζετο. καὶ οἱ μὲν ἐν παρασκευῆι ἦσαν.

Ἐν δὲ τούτωι, ὅσοι Ἑρμαῖ ἦσαν λίθινοι ἐν τῆι πόλει τῆι Ἀθηναίων 27 (εἰσὶ δὲ κατὰ τὸ ἐπιχώριον, ἡ τετράγωνος ἐργασία, πολλοὶ καὶ ἐν ἰδίοις προθύροις καὶ ἐν ἱεροῖς), μιᾶι νυκτὶ οἱ πλεῖστοι περιεκόπησαν τὰ πρόσωπα. καὶ τοὺς δράσαντας ἤιδει οὐδείς, ἀλλὰ μεγάλοις μηνύτροις 2 δημοσίαι οὗτοί τε ἐζητοῦντο καὶ προσέτι ἐψηφίσαντο, καὶ εἴ τις ἄλλο τι οἶδεν ἀσέβημα γεγενημένον, μηνύειν ἀδεῶς τὸν βουλόμενον καὶ ἀστῶν καὶ ξένων καὶ δούλων. καὶ τὸ πρᾶγμα μειζόνως ἐλάμβανον· τοῦ 3 τε γὰρ ἔκπλου οἰωνὸς ἐδόκει εἶναι καὶ ἐπὶ ξυνωμοσίαι ἅμα νεωτέρων πραγμάτων καὶ δήμου καταλύσεως γεγενῆσθαι. μηνύεται οὖν ἀπὸ 28 μετοίκων τέ τινων καὶ ἀκολούθων περὶ μὲν τῶν Ἑρμῶν οὐδέν, ἄλλων δὲ ἀγαλμάτων περικοπαί τινες πρότερον ὑπὸ νεωτέρων μετὰ παιδιᾶς καὶ οἴνου γεγενημέναι, καὶ τὰ μυστήρια ἅμα ὡς ποιεῖται ἐν οἰκίαις ἐφ' ὕβρει· ὧν καὶ τὸν Ἀλκιβιάδην ἐπηιτιῶντο. καὶ αὐτὰ ὑπολαμβάνοντες 2 οἱ μάλιστα τῶι Ἀλκιβιάδηι ἀχθόμενοι ἐμποδὼν ὄντι σφίσι μὴ αὐτοῖς τοῦ δήμου βεβαίως προεστάναι, καὶ νομίσαντες, εἰ αὐτὸν ἐξελάσειαν, πρῶτοι ἂν εἶναι, ἐμεγάλυνον καὶ ἐβόων ὡς ἐπὶ δήμου καταλύσει τά τε μυστικὰ καὶ ἡ τῶν Ἑρμῶν περικοπὴ γένοιτο καὶ οὐδὲν εἴη αὐτῶν ὅ τι οὐ μετ' ἐκείνου ἐπράχθη, ἐπιλέγοντες τεκμήρια τὴν ἄλλην αὐτοῦ ἐς τὰ

29 ἐπιτηδεύματα οὐ δημοτικὴν παρανομίαν. ὁ δ᾽ ἔν τε τῶι παρόντι πρὸς τὰ μηνύματα ἀπελογεῖτο καὶ ἑτοῖμος ἦν πρὶν ἐκπλεῖν κρίνεσθαι εἴ τι τούτων εἰργασμένος ἦν (ἤδη γὰρ καὶ τὰ τῆς παρασκευῆς ἐπεπόριστο),
2 καὶ εἰ μὲν τούτων τι εἴργαστο, δίκην δοῦναι, εἰ δ᾽ ἀπολυθείη, ἄρχειν. καὶ ἐπεμαρτύρετο μὴ ἀπόντος πέρι αὐτοῦ διαβολὰς ἀποδέχεσθαι, ἀλλ᾽ ἤδη ἀποκτείνειν, εἰ ἀδικεῖ, καὶ ὅτι σωφρονέστερον εἴη μὴ μετὰ τοιαύτης αἰτίας,
3 πρὶν διαγνῶσι, πέμπειν αὐτὸν ἐπὶ τοσούτωι στρατεύματι. οἱ δ᾽ ἐχθροὶ δεδιότες τό τε στράτευμα μὴ εὔνουν ἔχηι, ἢν ἤδη ἀγωνίζηται, ὅ τε δῆμος μὴ μαλακίζηται, θεραπεύων ὅτι δι᾽ ἐκεῖνον οἵ τ᾽ Ἀργεῖοι ξυνεστράτευον καὶ τῶν Μαντινέων τινές, ἀπέτρεπον καὶ ἀπέσπευδον, ἄλλους ῥήτορας ἐνιέντες οἳ ἔλεγον νῦν μὲν πλεῖν αὐτὸν καὶ μὴ κατασχεῖν τὴν ἀναγωγήν, ἐλθόντα δὲ κρίνεσθαι ἐν ἡμέραις ῥηταῖς, βουλόμενοι ἐκ μείζονος διαβολῆς, ἣν ἔμελλον ῥᾶιον αὐτοῦ ἀπόντος ποριεῖν, μετάπεμπτον κομισθέντα αὐτὸν ἀγωνίσασθαι. καὶ ἔδοξε πλεῖν τὸν Ἀλκιβιάδην.

30 Μετὰ δὲ ταῦτα θέρους μεσοῦντος ἤδη ἡ ἀναγωγὴ ἐγίγνετο ἐς τὴν Σικελίαν. τῶν μὲν οὖν ξυμμάχων τοῖς πλείστοις καὶ ταῖς σιταγωγοῖς ὁλκάσι καὶ τοῖς πλοίοις καὶ ὅση ἄλλη παρασκευὴ ξυνείπετο πρότερον εἴρητο ἐς Κέρκυραν ξυλλέγεσθαι ὡς ἐκεῖθεν ἁθρόοις ἐπὶ ἄκραν Ἰαπυγίαν τὸν Ἰόνιον διαβαλοῦσιν· αὐτοὶ δ᾽ Ἀθηναῖοι καὶ εἴ τινες τῶν ξυμμάχων παρῆσαν ἐς τὸν Πειραιᾶ καταβάντες ἐν ἡμέραι ῥητῆι ἅμα ἕωι ἐπλήρουν
2 τὰς ναῦς ὡς ἀναξόμενοι. ξυγκατέβη δὲ καὶ ὁ ἄλλος ὅμιλος ἅπας ὡς εἰπεῖν ὁ ἐν τῆι πόλει καὶ ἀστῶν καὶ ξένων, οἱ μὲν ἐπιχώριοι τοὺς σφετέρους αὐτῶν ἕκαστοι προπέμποντες, οἱ μὲν ἑταίρους, οἱ δὲ ξυγγενεῖς, οἱ δὲ υἱεῖς, καὶ μετ᾽ ἐλπίδος τε ἅμα ἰόντες καὶ ὀλοφυρμῶν, τὰ μὲν ὡς κτήσοιντο, τοὺς δ᾽ εἴ ποτε ὄψοιντο, ἐνθυμούμενοι ὅσον πλοῦν ἐκ τῆς σφετέρας
31 ἀπεστέλλοντο. καὶ ἐν τῶι παρόντι καιρῶι, ὡς ἤδη ἔμελλον μετὰ κινδύνων ἀλλήλους ἀπολιπεῖν, μᾶλλον αὐτοὺς ἐσῄει τὰ δεινὰ ἢ ὅτε ἐψηφίζοντο πλεῖν· ὅμως δὲ τῆι παρούσηι ῥώμηι, διὰ τὸ πλῆθος ἑκάστων ὧν ἑώρων τῆι ὄψει, ἀνεθάρσουν. οἱ δὲ ξένοι καὶ ὁ ἄλλος ὄχλος κατὰ θέαν ἧκεν ὡς ἐπ᾽ ἀξιόχρεων καὶ ἄπιστον διάνοιαν. παρασκευὴ γὰρ αὕτη ⟨ἡ⟩ πρώτη ἐκπλεύσασα μιᾶς πόλεως δυνάμει Ἑλληνικῆι πολυτελεστάτη δὴ καὶ
2 εὐπρεπεστάτη τῶν ἐς ἐκεῖνον τὸν χρόνον ἐγένετο. ἀριθμῶι δὲ νεῶν καὶ ὁπλιτῶν καὶ ἡ ἐς Ἐπίδαυρον μετὰ Περικλέους καὶ ἡ αὐτὴ ἐς Ποτείδαιαν μετὰ Ἅγνωνος οὐκ ἐλάσσων ἦν· τετράκις γὰρ χίλιοι ὁπλῖται αὐτῶν Ἀθηναίων καὶ τριακόσιοι ἱππῆς καὶ τριήρεις ἑκατόν, καὶ Λεσβίων καὶ
3 Χίων πεντήκοντα, καὶ ξύμμαχοι ἔτι πολλοὶ ξυνέπλευσαν. ἀλλὰ ἐπί τε

βραχεῖ πλῶι ὡρμήθησαν καὶ παρασκευῆι φαύληι, οὗτος δὲ ὁ στόλος ὡς χρόνιός τε ἐσόμενος καὶ κατ' ἀμφότερα, οὗ ἂν δέηι, καὶ ναυσὶ καὶ πεζῶι ἅμα ἐξαρτυθείς, τὸ μὲν ναυτικὸν μεγάλαις δαπάναις τῶν τε τριηράρχων καὶ τῆς πόλεως ἐκπονηθέν, τοῦ μὲν δημοσίου δραχμὴν τῆς ἡμέρας τῶι ναύτηι ἑκάστωι διδόντος καὶ ναῦς παρασχόντος κενὰς ἑξήκοντα μὲν ταχείας, τεσσαράκοντα δὲ ὁπλιταγωγοὺς καὶ ὑπηρεσίας ταύταις τὰς κρατίστας, τῶν δὲ τριηράρχων ἐπιφοράς τε πρὸς τῶι ἐκ δημοσίου μισθῶι διδόντων τοῖς θρανίταις τῶν ναυτῶν καὶ ταῖς ὑπηρεσίαις καὶ τἆλλα σημείοις καὶ κατασκευαῖς πολυτελέσι χρησαμένων, καὶ ἐς τὰ μακρότατα προθυμηθέντος ἑνὸς ἑκάστου ὅπως αὐτῶι τινι εὐπρεπείαι τε ἡ ναῦς μάλιστα προέξει καὶ τῶι ταχυναυτεῖν, τὸ δὲ πεζὸν καταλόγοις τε χρηστοῖς ἐκκριθὲν καὶ ὅπλων καὶ τῶν περὶ τὸ σῶμα σκευῶν μεγάληι σπουδῆι πρὸς ἀλλήλους ἁμιλληθέν. ξυνέβη δὲ πρός τε σφᾶς αὐτοὺς ἅμα 4 ἔριν γενέσθαι, ὧι τις ἕκαστος προσετάχθη, καὶ ἐς τοὺς ἄλλους Ἕλληνας ἐπίδειξιν μᾶλλον εἰκασθῆναι τῆς δυνάμεως καὶ ἐξουσίας ἢ ἐπὶ πολεμίους παρασκευήν. εἰ γάρ τις ἐλογίσατο τήν τε τῆς πόλεως ἀνάλωσιν 5 δημοσίαν καὶ τῶν στρατευομένων τὴν ἰδίαν, τῆς μὲν πόλεως ὅσα τε ἤδη προετετελέκει καὶ ἃ ἔχοντας τοὺς στρατηγοὺς ἀπέστελλε, τῶν δὲ ἰδιωτῶν ἅ τε περὶ τὸ σῶμά τις καὶ τριήραρχος ἐς τὴν ναῦν ἀνηλώκει καὶ ὅσα ἔτι ἔμελλεν ἀναλώσειν, χωρὶς δ' ἃ εἰκὸς ἦν καὶ ἄνευ τοῦ ἐκ τοῦ δημοσίου μισθοῦ πάντα τινὰ παρασκευάσασθαι ἐφόδιον ὡς ἐπὶ χρόνιον στρατείαν, καὶ ὅσα ἐπὶ μεταβολῆι τις ἢ στρατιώτης ἢ ἔμπορος ἔχων ἔπλει, πολλὰ ἂν τάλαντα ηὑρέθη ἐκ τῆς πόλεως τὰ πάντα ἐξαγόμενα. καὶ 6 ὁ στόλος οὐχ ἧσσον τόλμης τε θάμβει καὶ ὄψεως λαμπρότητι περιβόητος ἐγένετο ἢ στρατιᾶς πρὸς οὓς ἐπῆισαν ὑπερβολῆι, καὶ ὅτι μέγιστος ἤδη διάπλους ἀπὸ τῆς οἰκείας καὶ ἐπὶ μεγίστηι ἐλπίδι τῶν μελλόντων πρὸς τὰ ὑπάρχοντα ἐπεχειρήθη.

Ἐπειδὴ δὲ αἱ νῆες πλήρεις ἦσαν καὶ ἐσέκειτο πάντα ἤδη ὅσα ἔχοντες 32 ἔμελλον ἀνάξεσθαι, τῆι μὲν σάλπιγγι σιωπὴ ὑπεσημάνθη, εὐχὰς δὲ τὰς νομιζομένας πρὸ τῆς ἀναγωγῆς οὐ κατὰ ναῦν ἑκάστην, ξύμπαντες δὲ ὑπὸ κήρυκος ἐποιοῦντο, κρατῆράς τε κεράσαντες παρ' ἅπαν τὸ στράτευμα καὶ ἐκπώμασι χρυσοῖς τε καὶ ἀργυροῖς οἵ τε ἐπιβάται καὶ οἱ ἄρχοντες σπένδοντες. ξυνεπηύχοντο δὲ καὶ ὁ ἄλλος ὅμιλος ὁ ἐκ τῆς 2 γῆς τῶν τε πολιτῶν καὶ εἴ τις ἄλλος εὔνους παρῆν σφίσιν. παιανίσαντες δὲ καὶ τελεώσαντες τὰς σπονδὰς ἀνήγοντο, καὶ ἐπὶ κέρως τὸ πρῶτον ἐκπλεύσαντες ἅμιλλαν ἤδη μέχρι Αἰγίνης ἐποιοῦντο. καὶ οἱ μὲν ἐς τὴν Κέρκυραν, ἔνθαπερ καὶ τὸ ἄλλο στράτευμα τῶν ξυμμάχων ξυνελέγετο, ἠπείγοντο ἀφικέσθαι.

31.3 κενὰς codd.: καινὰς Naber

3 Ἐς δὲ τὰς Συρακούσας ἠγγέλλετο μὲν πολλαχόθεν τὰ περὶ τοῦ ἐπίπλου, οὐ μέντοι ἐπιστεύετο ἐπὶ πολὺν χρόνον οὐδέν, ἀλλὰ καὶ γενομένης ἐκκλησίας ἐλέχθησαν τοιοίδε λόγοι ἀπό τε ἄλλων, τῶν μὲν πιστευόντων τὰ περὶ τῆς στρατείας τῆς τῶν Ἀθηναίων, τῶν δὲ τὰ ἐναντία λεγόντων, καὶ Ἑρμοκράτης ὁ Ἕρμωνος παρελθὼν αὐτοῖς, ὡς σαφῶς οἰόμενος εἰδέναι τὰ περὶ αὐτῶν, ἔλεγε καὶ παρῄνει τοιάδε.

33 "Ἄπιστα μὲν ἴσως, ὥσπερ καὶ ἄλλοι τινές, δόξω ὑμῖν περὶ τοῦ ἐπίπλου τῆς ἀληθείας λέγειν, καὶ γιγνώσκω ὅτι οἱ τὰ μὴ πιστὰ δοκοῦντα εἶναι ἢ λέγοντες ἢ ἀπαγγέλλοντες οὐ μόνον οὐ πείθουσιν, ἀλλὰ καὶ ἄφρονες δοκοῦσιν εἶναι· ὅμως δὲ οὐ καταφοβηθεὶς ἐπισχήσω κινδυνευούσης τῆς
2 πόλεως, πείθων γε ἐμαυτὸν σαφέστερόν τι ἑτέρου εἰδὼς λέγειν. Ἀθηναῖοι γὰρ ἐφ' ὑμᾶς, ὃ πάνυ θαυμάζετε, πολλῆι στρατιᾶι ὥρμηνται καὶ ναυτικῆι καὶ πεζῆι, πρόφασιν μὲν Ἐγεσταίων ξυμμαχίαι καὶ Λεοντίνων κατοικίσει, τὸ δὲ ἀληθὲς Σικελίας ἐπιθυμίαι, μάλιστα δὲ τῆς ἡμετέρας
3 πόλεως, ἡγούμενοι, εἰ ταύτην σχοῖεν, ῥαιδίως καὶ τἆλλα ἕξειν. ὡς οὖν ἐν τάχει παρεσομένων, ὁρᾶτε ἀπὸ τῶν ὑπαρχόντων ὅτωι τρόπωι κάλλιστα ἀμυνεῖσθε αὐτούς, καὶ μήτε καταφρονήσαντες ἄφαρκτοι ληφθήσεσθε μήτε
4 ἀπιστήσαντες τοῦ ξύμπαντος ἀμελήσετε. εἰ δέ τωι καὶ πιστά, τὴν τόλμαν αὐτῶν καὶ δύναμιν μὴ ἐκπλαγῆι. οὔτε γὰρ βλάπτειν ἡμᾶς πλείω οἷοί τ' ἔσονται ἢ πάσχειν, οὔθ' ὅτι μεγάλωι στόλωι ἐπέρχονται, ἀνωφελεῖς, ἀλλὰ πρός τε τοὺς ἄλλους Σικελιώτας πολὺ ἄμεινον (μᾶλλον γὰρ ἐθελήσουσιν ἐκπλαγέντες ἡμῖν ξυμμαχεῖν), καὶ ἢν ἄρα ἢ κατεργασώμεθα αὐτοὺς ἢ ἀπράκτους ὧν ἐφίενται ἀπώσωμεν (οὐ γὰρ δὴ μὴ τύχωσί γε ὧν προσδέχονται φοβοῦμαι), κάλλιστον δὴ ἔργων ἡμῖν ξυμβήσεται,
5 καὶ οὐκ ἀνέλπιστον ἔμοιγε. ὀλίγοι γὰρ δὴ στόλοι μεγάλοι ἢ Ἑλλήνων ἢ βαρβάρων πολὺ ἀπὸ τῆς ἑαυτῶν ἀπάραντες κατώρθωσαν. οὔτε γὰρ πλείους τῶν ἐνοικούντων καὶ ἀστυγειτόνων ἔρχονται (πάντα γὰρ ὑπὸ δέους ξυνίσταται), ἤν τε δι' ἀπορίαν τῶν ἐπιτηδείων ἐν ἀλλοτρίαι γῆι σφαλῶσι, τοῖς ἐπιβουλευθεῖσιν ὄνομα, κἂν περὶ σφίσιν αὐτοῖς τὰ πλείω
6 πταίσωσιν, ὅμως καταλείπουσιν. ὅπερ καὶ Ἀθηναῖοι αὐτοὶ οὗτοι, τοῦ Μήδου παρὰ λόγον πολλὰ σφαλέντος, ἐπὶ τῶι ὀνόματι ὡς ἐπὶ Ἀθήνας ἤιει ηὐξήθησαν, καὶ ἡμῖν οὐκ ἀνέλπιστον τὸ τοιοῦτον ξυμβῆναι.

34 Θαρσοῦντες οὖν τά τε αὐτοῦ παρασκευαζώμεθα καὶ ἐς τοὺς Σικελοὺς πέμποντες τοὺς μὲν μᾶλλον βεβαιωσώμεθα, τοῖς δὲ φιλίαν καὶ ξυμμαχίαν πειρώμεθα ποιεῖσθαι, ἔς τε τὴν ἄλλην Σικελίαν πέμπωμεν πρέσβεις

33.2 ὑμᾶς ABCEFM: ἡμᾶς G   33.4 ἀνωφελεῖς codd.: ἀνωφελὲς Dobree

δηλοῦντες ὡς κοινὸς ὁ κίνδυνος, καὶ ἐς τὴν Ἰταλίαν, ὅπως ἢ ξυμμαχίαν ποιώμεθα ἡμῖν ἢ μὴ δέχωνται Ἀθηναίους. δοκεῖ δέ μοι καὶ ἐς Καρχηδόνα 2 ἄμεινον εἶναι πέμψαι· οὐ γὰρ ἀνέλπιστον αὐτοῖς, ἀλλ' αἰεὶ διὰ φόβου εἰσὶ μή ποτε Ἀθηναῖοι αὐτοῖς ἐπὶ τὴν πόλιν ἔλθωσιν, ὥστε τάχ' ἂν ἴσως νομίσαντες, εἰ τάδε προήσονται, κἂν σφεῖς ἐν πόνωι εἶναι, ἐθελήσειαν ἡμῖν ἤτοι κρύφα γε ἢ φανερῶς ἢ ἐξ ἑνός γέ του τρόπου ἀμῦναι. δυνατοὶ δέ εἰσι μάλιστα τῶν νῦν βουληθέντες· χρυσὸν γὰρ καὶ ἄργυρον πλεῖστον κέκτηνται, ὅθεν ὅ τε πόλεμος καὶ τἆλλα εὐπορεῖ. πέμπωμεν δὲ καὶ ἐς τὴν 3 Λακεδαίμονα καὶ ἐς Κόρινθον δεόμενοι δεῦρο κατὰ τάχος βοηθεῖν καὶ τὸν ἐκεῖ πόλεμον κινεῖν.

"Ὃ δὲ μάλιστα ἐγώ τε νομίζω ἐπίκαιρον ὑμεῖς τε διὰ τὸ ξύνηθες ἥσυχον 4 ἥκιστ' ἂν ὀξέως πείθοισθε, ὅμως εἰρήσεται. Σικελιῶται γὰρ εἰ ἐθέλοιμεν ξύμπαντες, εἰ δὲ μή, ὅτι πλεῖστοι μεθ' ἡμῶν, καθελκύσαντες ἅπαν τὸ ὑπάρχον ναυτικὸν μετὰ δυοῖν μηνοῖν τροφῆς ἀπαντῆσαι Ἀθηναίοις ἐς Τάραντα καὶ ἄκραν Ἰαπυγίαν, καὶ δῆλον ποιῆσαι αὐτοῖς ὅτι οὐ περὶ τῆς Σικελίας πρότερον ἔσται ὁ ἀγὼν ἢ τοῦ ἐκείνους περαιωθῆναι τὸν Ἰόνιον, μάλιστ' ἂν αὐτοὺς ἐκπλήξαιμεν καὶ ἐς λογισμὸν καταστήσαιμεν ὅτι ὁρμώμεθα μὲν ἐκ φιλίας χώρας φύλακες (ὑποδέχεται γὰρ ἡμᾶς Τάρας), τὸ δὲ πέλαγος αὐτοῖς πολὺ περαιοῦσθαι μετὰ πάσης τῆς παρασκευῆς, χαλεπὸν δὲ διὰ πλοῦ μῆκος ἐν τάξει μεῖναι, καὶ ἡμῖν ἂν εὐεπίθετος εἴη, βραδεῖά τε καὶ κατ' ὀλίγον προσπίπτουσα. εἰ δ' αὖ τῶι ταχυναυτοῦντι 5 ἀθροωτέρωι κουφίσαντες προσβάλοιεν, εἰ μὲν κώπαις χρήσαιντο, ἐπιθοίμεθ' ἂν κεκμηκόσιν, εἰ δὲ μὴ δοκοίη, ἔστι καὶ ὑποχωρῆσαι ἡμῖν ἐς Τάραντα· οἱ δὲ μετ' ὀλίγων ἐφοδίων ὡς ἐπὶ ναυμαχίαι περαιωθέντες ἀποροῖεν ἂν κατὰ χωρία ἐρῆμα, καὶ ἢ μένοντες πολιορκοῖντο ἂν ἢ πειρώμενοι παραπλεῖν τήν τε ἄλλην παρασκευὴν ἀπολείποιεν ἂν καὶ τὰ τῶν πόλεων οὐκ ἂν βέβαια ἔχοντες, εἰ ὑποδέξοιντο, ἀθυμοῖεν. ὥστ' 6 ἔγωγε τούτωι τῶι λογισμῶι ἡγοῦμαι ἀποκληιομένους αὐτοὺς οὐδ' ἂν ἀπᾶραι ἀπὸ Κερκύρας, ἀλλ' ἢ διαβουλευσαμένους καὶ κατασκοπαῖς χρωμένους, ὁπόσοι τ' ἐσμὲν καὶ ἐν ὧι χωρίωι, ἐξωσθῆναι ἂν τῆι ὥραι ἐς χειμῶνα, ἢ καταπλαγέντας τῶι ἀδοκήτωι καταλῦσαι ἂν τὸν πλοῦν, ἄλλως τε καὶ τοῦ ἐμπειροτάτου τῶν στρατηγῶν, ὡς ἐγὼ ἀκούω, ἄκοντος ἡγουμένου καὶ ἀσμένου ἂν πρόφασιν λαβόντος, εἴ τι ἀξιόχρεων ἀφ' ἡμῶν ὀφθείη. ἀγγελλοίμεθα δ' ἂν εὖ οἶδ' ὅτι ἐπὶ τὸ πλέον· τῶν δ' ἀνθρώπων 7 πρὸς τὰ λεγόμενα καὶ αἱ γνῶμαι ἵστανται, καὶ τοὺς προεπιχειροῦντας ἢ τοῖς γε ἐπιχειροῦσι προδηλοῦντας ὅτι ἀμυνοῦνται μᾶλλον πεφόβηνται, ἰσοκινδύνους ἡγούμενοι. ὅπερ ἂν νῦν Ἀθηναῖοι πάθοιεν. ἐπέρχονται γὰρ 8 ἡμῖν ὡς οὐκ ἀμυνουμένοις, δικαίως κατεγνωκότες ὅτι αὐτοὺς οὐ μετὰ

Λακεδαιμονίων ἐφθείρομεν· εἰ δ' ἴδοιεν παρὰ γνώμην τολμήσαντας, τῶι ἀδοκήτωι μᾶλλον ἂν καταπλαγεῖεν ἢ τῆι ἀπὸ τοῦ ἀληθοῦς δυνάμει.

9 Πείθεσθε οὖν μάλιστα μὲν ταῦτα τολμήσαντες, εἰ δὲ μή, ὅτι τάχιστα τἆλλα ἐς τὸν πόλεμον ἑτοιμάζειν, καὶ παραστῆναι παντὶ τὸ μὲν καταφρονεῖν τοὺς ἐπιόντας ἐν τῶν ἔργων τῆι ἀλκῆι δείκνυσθαι, τὸ δ' ἤδη τὰς μετὰ φόβου παρασκευὰς ἀσφαλεστάτας νομίσαντας ὡς ἐπὶ κινδύνου πράσσειν χρησιμώτατον ἂν ξυμβῆναι. οἱ δὲ ἄνδρες καὶ ἐπέρχονται καὶ ἐν πλῶι εὖ οἶδ' ὅτι ἤδη εἰσὶ καὶ ὅσον οὔπω πάρεισιν.'

35 Καὶ ὁ μὲν Ἑρμοκράτης τοσαῦτα εἶπεν· τῶν δὲ Συρακοσίων ὁ δῆμος ἐν πολλῆι πρὸς ἀλλήλους ἔριδι ἦσαν, οἱ μὲν ὡς οὐδενὶ ἂν τρόπωι ἔλθοιεν οἱ Ἀθηναῖοι οὐδ' ἀληθῆ ἐστὶν ἃ λέγει, τοῖς δέ, εἰ καὶ ἔλθοιεν, τί ἂν δράσειαν αὐτοὺς ὅ τι οὐκ ἂν μεῖζον ἀντιπάθοιεν· ἄλλοι δὲ καὶ πάνυ καταφρονοῦντες ἐς γέλωτα ἔτρεπον τὸ πρᾶγμα. ὀλίγον δ' ἦν τὸ πιστεῦον τῶι Ἑρμοκράτει 2 καὶ φοβούμενον τὸ μέλλον. παρελθὼν δ' αὐτοῖς Ἀθηναγόρας, ὃς δήμου τε προστάτης ἦν καὶ ἐν τῶι παρόντι πιθανώτατος τοῖς πολλοῖς, ἔλεγε τοιάδε.

36 'Τοὺς μὲν Ἀθηναίους ὅστις μὴ βούλεται οὕτω κακῶς φρονῆσαι καὶ ὑποχειρίους ἡμῖν γενέσθαι ἐνθάδε ἐλθόντας, ἢ δειλός ἐστιν ἢ τῆι πόλει οὐκ εὔνους· τοὺς δὲ ἀγγέλλοντας τὰ τοιαῦτα καὶ περιφόβους ὑμᾶς ποιοῦντας τῆς μὲν τόλμης οὐ θαυμάζω, τῆς δὲ ἀξυνεσίας, εἰ μὴ οἴονται ἔνδηλοι εἶναι. 2 οἱ γὰρ δεδιότες ἰδίαι τι βούλονται τὴν πόλιν ἐς ἔκπληξιν καθιστάναι, ὅπως τῶι κοινῶι φόβωι τὸ σφέτερον ἐπηλυγάζωνται. καὶ νῦν αὗται αἱ ἀγγελίαι τοῦτο δύνανται· αἳ οὐκ ἀπὸ ταὐτομάτου, ἐκ δὲ ἀνδρῶν οἵπερ 3 αἰεὶ τάδε κινοῦσι ξύγκεινται. ὑμεῖς δὲ ἢν εὖ βουλεύησθε, οὐκ ἐξ ὧν οὗτοι ἀγγέλλουσι σκοποῦντες λογιεῖσθε τὰ εἰκότα, ἀλλ' ἐξ ὧν ἂν ἄνθρωποι 4 δεινοὶ καὶ πολλῶν ἔμπειροι, ὥσπερ ἐγὼ Ἀθηναίους ἀξιῶ, δράσειαν. οὐ γὰρ αὐτοὺς εἰκὸς Πελοποννησίους τε ὑπολιπόντας καὶ τὸν ἐκεῖ πόλεμον μήπω βεβαίως καταλελυμένους ἐπ' ἄλλον πόλεμον οὐκ ἐλάσσω ἑκόντας ἐλθεῖν, ἐπεὶ ἔγωγε ἀγαπᾶν οἴομαι αὐτοὺς ὅτι οὐχ ἡμεῖς ἐπ' ἐκείνους 37 ἐρχόμεθα, πόλεις τοσαῦται καὶ οὕτω μεγάλαι. εἰ δὲ δή, ὥσπερ λέγονται, ἔλθοιεν, ἱκανωτέραν ἡγοῦμαι Σικελίαν Πελοποννήσου διαπολεμῆσαι ὅσωι κατὰ πάντα ἄμεινον ἐξήρτυται, τὴν δὲ ἡμετέραν πόλιν αὐτὴν τῆς νῦν στρατιᾶς, ὥς φασιν, ἐπιούσης, καὶ εἰ δὶς τοσαύτη ἔλθοι, πολὺ κρείσσω εἶναι, οἷς γ' ἐπίσταμαι οὔθ' ἵππους ἀκολουθήσοντας, οὐδ' αὐτόθεν ποριζομένους εἰ μὴ ὀλίγους τινὰς παρ' Ἐγεσταίων, οὔθ' ὁπλίτας

---

35 λέγει, τοῖς δέ codd.: λέγεται, οἱ δέ Madvig: λέγοιτο, οἱ δέ Marchant 36.2 τό codd.: τόν fortasse Σ, Valla

ἰσοπλήθεις τοῖς ἡμετέροις ἐπὶ νεῶν γε ἐλθόντας (μέγα γὰρ τὸ καὶ αὐταῖς ταῖς ναυσὶ κούφαις τοσοῦτον πλοῦν δεῦρο κομισθῆναι), τήν τε ἄλλην παρασκευήν, ὅσην δεῖ ἐπὶ πόλιν τοσήνδε πορισθῆναι, οὐκ ὀλίγην οὖσαν. ὥστε, παρὰ τοσοῦτον γιγνώσκω, μόλις ἄν μοι δοκοῦσιν, εἰ πόλιν ἑτέραν 2 τοσαύτην ὅσαι Συράκουσαί εἰσιν ἔλθοιεν ἔχοντες καὶ ὅμορον οἰκίσαντες τὸν πόλεμον ποιοῖντο, οὐκ ἂν παντάπασι διαφθαρῆναι, ἦ πού γε δὴ ἐν πάσηι πολεμίαι Σικελίαι (ξυστήσεται γάρ) στρατοπέδωι τε ἐκ νεῶν ἱδρυθέντι καὶ ἐκ σκηνιδίων καὶ ἀναγκαίας παρασκευῆς οὐκ ἐπὶ πολὺ ὑπὸ τῶν ἡμετέρων ἱππέων ἐξιόντες. τό τε ξύμπαν οὐδ᾽ ἂν κρατῆσαι αὐτοὺς τῆς γῆς ἡγοῦμαι· τοσούτωι τὴν ἡμετέραν παρασκευὴν κρείσσω νομίζω.

Ἀλλὰ ταῦτα, ὥσπερ ἐγὼ λέγω, οἵ τε Ἀθηναῖοι γιγνώσκοντες τὰ 38 σφέτερα αὐτῶν εὖ οἶδ᾽ ὅτι σώιζουσι, καὶ ἐνθένδε ἄνδρες οὔτε ὄντα οὔτε ἂν γενόμενα λογοποιοῦσιν, οὓς ἐγὼ οὐ νῦν πρῶτον, ἀλλ᾽ αἰεὶ 2 ἐπίσταμαι ἤτοι λόγοις γε τοιοῖσδε καὶ ἔτι τούτων κακουργοτέροις ἢ ἔργοις βουλομένους καταπλήξαντας τὸ ὑμέτερον πλῆθος αὐτοὺς τῆς πόλεως ἄρχειν. καὶ δέδοικα μέντοι μήποτε πολλὰ πειρῶντες καὶ κατορθώσωσιν· ἡμεῖς δὲ κακοί, πρὶν ἐν τῶι παθεῖν ὦμεν, προφυλάξασθαί τε καὶ αἰσθόμενοι ἐπεξελθεῖν. τοιγάρτοι δι᾽ αὐτὰ ἡ πόλις ἡμῶν ὀλιγάκις 3 μὲν ἡσυχάζει, στάσεις δὲ πολλὰς καὶ ἀγῶνας οὐ πρὸς τοὺς πολεμίους πλέονας ἢ πρὸς αὑτὴν ἀναιρεῖται, τυραννίδας δὲ ἔστιν ὅτε καὶ δυναστείας ἀδίκους. ὧν ἐγὼ πειράσομαι, ἤν γε ὑμεῖς ἐθέλητε ἕπεσθαι, μήποτε ἐφ᾽ 4 ἡμῶν τι περιιδεῖν γενέσθαι, ὑμᾶς μὲν τοὺς πολλοὺς πείθων, τοὺς δὲ τὰ τοιαῦτα μηχανωμένους κολάζων μὴ μόνον αὐτοφώρους (χαλεπὸν γὰρ ἐπιτυγχάνειν) ἀλλὰ καὶ ὧν βούλονται μέν, δύνανται δ᾽ οὔ (τὸν γὰρ ἐχθρὸν οὐχ ὧν δρᾶι μόνον, ἀλλὰ καὶ τῆς διανοίας προαμύνεσθαι χρή, εἴπερ καὶ μὴ προφυλαξάμενός τις προπείσεται), τοὺς δ᾽ αὖ ὀλίγους τὰ μὲν ἐλέγχων, τὰ δὲ φυλάσσων, τὰ δὲ καὶ διδάσκων· μάλιστα γὰρ δοκῶ ἄν μοι οὕτως ἀποτρέπειν τῆς κακουργίας. καὶ δῆτα, ὃ πολλάκις ἐσκεψάμην, 5 τί καὶ βούλεσθε, ὦ νεώτεροι; πότερον ἄρχειν ἤδη; ἀλλ᾽ οὐκ ἔννομον· ὁ δὲ νόμος ἐκ τοῦ μὴ δύνασθαι ὑμᾶς μᾶλλον ἢ δυναμένους ἐτέθη ἀτιμάζειν. ἀλλὰ δὴ μὴ μετὰ πολλῶν ἰσονομεῖσθαι; καὶ πῶς δίκαιον τοὺς αὐτοὺς μὴ τῶν αὐτῶν ἀξιοῦσθαι; φήσει τις δημοκρατίαν οὔτε ξυνετὸν οὔτ᾽ ἴσον 39 εἶναι, τοὺς δ᾽ ἔχοντας τὰ χρήματα καὶ ἄρχειν ἄριστα βελτίστους. ἐγὼ δέ φημι πρῶτα μὲν δῆμον ξύμπαν ὠνομάσθαι, ὀλιγαρχίαν δὲ μέρος, ἔπειτα φύλακας μὲν ἀρίστους εἶναι χρημάτων τοὺς πλουσίους, βουλεῦσαι δ᾽ ἂν βέλτιστα τοὺς ξυνετούς, κρῖναι δ᾽ ἂν ἀκούσαντας ἄριστα τοὺς

38.4 δὲ ante τὰ τοιαῦτα del. Weil   κολάζων codd.: κολάζειν Weil

πολλούς, καὶ ταῦτα ὁμοίως καὶ κατὰ μέρη καὶ ξύμπαντα ἐν δημοκρατίαι
2 ἰσομοιρεῖν. ὀλιγαρχία δὲ τῶν μὲν κινδύνων τοῖς πολλοῖς μεταδίδωσι,
τῶν δ' ὠφελίμων οὐ πλεονεκτεῖ μόνον, ἀλλὰ καὶ ξύμπαντ' ἀφελομένη
ἔχει· ἃ ὑμῶν οἵ τε δυνάμενοι καὶ οἱ νέοι προθυμοῦνται, ἀδύνατα ἐν
40 μεγάληι πόλει κατασχεῖν. ἀλλ' ἔτι καὶ νῦν, ὦ πάντων ἀξυνετώτατοι –
εἰ ⟨γὰρ⟩ μὴ μανθάνετε κακὰ σπεύδοντες, ἢ ἀμαθέστατοί ἐστε ὧν ἐγὼ
οἶδα Ἑλλήνων, ἢ ἀδικώτατοι, εἰ εἰδότες τολμᾶτε – ἀλλ' ἤτοι μαθόντες
γε ἢ μεταγνόντες τὸ τῆς πόλεως ξύμπασι κοινὸν αὔξετε, ἡγησάμενοι
τοῦτο μὲν ἂν καὶ ἴσον καὶ πλέον οἱ ἀγαθοὶ ὑμῶν ὧνπερ τὸ τῆς πόλεως
πλῆθος μετασχεῖν, εἰ δ' ἄλλα βουλήσεσθε, κἂν τοῦ παντὸς κινδυνεῦσαι
στερηθῆναι· καὶ τῶν τοιῶνδε ἀγγελιῶν ὡς πρὸς αἰσθανομένους καὶ μὴ
2 ἐπιτρέψοντας ἀπαλλάγητε. ἡ γὰρ πόλις ἥδε, καὶ εἰ ἔρχονται Ἀθηναῖοι,
ἀμυνεῖται αὐτοὺς ἀξίως αὑτῆς, καὶ στρατηγοί εἰσιν ἡμῖν οἳ σκέψονται
αὐτά· καὶ εἰ μή τι αὐτῶν ἀληθές ἐστιν, ὥσπερ οὐκ οἴομαι, οὐ πρὸς τὰς
ὑμετέρας ἀγγελίας καταπλαγεῖσα καὶ ἑλομένη ὑμᾶς ἄρχοντας αὐθαίρετον
δουλείαν ἐπιβαλεῖται, αὐτὴ δ' ἐφ' αὑτῆς σκοποῦσα τούς τε λόγους ἀφ'
ὑμῶν ὡς ἔργα δυναμένους κρινεῖ καὶ τὴν ὑπάρχουσαν ἐλευθερίαν οὐχὶ ἐκ
τοῦ ἀκούειν ἀφαιρεθήσεται, ἐκ δὲ τοῦ ἔργωι φυλασσομένη μὴ ἐπιτρέπειν
πειράσεται σώιζειν.'

41 Τοιαῦτα δὲ Ἀθηναγόρας εἶπεν. τῶν δὲ στρατηγῶν εἷς ἀναστὰς
ἄλλον μὲν οὐδένα ἔτι εἴασε παρελθεῖν, αὐτὸς δὲ πρὸς τὰ παρόντα
2 ἔλεξε τοιάδε. 'διαβολὰς μὲν οὐ σῶφρον οὔτε λέγειν τινὰς ἐς ἀλλήλους
οὔτε τοὺς ἀκούοντας ἀποδέχεσθαι, πρὸς δὲ τὰ ἐσαγγελλόμενα μᾶλλον
ὁρᾶν, ὅπως εἷς τε ἕκαστος καὶ ἡ ξύμπασα πόλις καλῶς τοὺς ἐπιόντας
3 παρασκευασόμεθα ἀμύνεσθαι. καὶ ἢν ἄρα μηδὲν δεήσηι, οὐδεμία βλάβη
τοῦ τε τὸ κοινὸν κοσμηθῆναι καὶ ἵπποις καὶ ὅπλοις καὶ τοῖς ἄλλοις οἷς ὁ
4 πόλεμος ἀγάλλεται – τὴν δ' ἐπιμέλειαν καὶ ἐξέτασιν αὐτῶν ἡμεῖς ἕξομεν –
καὶ τῶν πρὸς τὰς πόλεις διαπομπῶν ἅμα ἔς τε κατασκοπὴν καὶ ἤν τι
ἄλλο φαίνηται ἐπιτήδειον. τὰ δὲ καὶ ἐπιμελήμεθα ἤδη, καὶ ὅ τι ἂν
αἰσθώμεθα ἐς ὑμᾶς οἴσομεν.' καὶ οἱ μὲν Συρακόσιοι τοσαῦτα εἰπόντος
τοῦ στρατηγοῦ διελύθησαν ἐκ τοῦ ξυλλόγου.

42 Οἱ δ' Ἀθηναῖοι ἤδη ἐν τῆι Κερκύραι αὐτοί τε καὶ οἱ ξύμμαχοι ἅπαντες
ἦσαν. καὶ πρῶτον μὲν ἐπεξέτασιν τοῦ στρατεύματος καὶ ξύνταξιν, ὥσπερ
ἔμελλον ὁρμιεῖσθαί τε καὶ στρατοπεδεύεσθαι, οἱ στρατηγοὶ ἐποιήσαντο,
καὶ τρία μέρη νείμαντες ἓν ἑκάστωι ἐκλήρωσαν, ἵνα μήτε ἅμα πλέοντες

40.1 ⟨γὰρ⟩ Gomme   ἢ ἀμαθέστατοί ἐστε secl. Madvig   ὧνπερ Dover: ἥπερ codd.

ἀπορῶσιν ὕδατος καὶ λιμένων καὶ τῶν ἐπιτηδείων ἐν ταῖς καταγωγαῖς, πρός τε τἆλλα εὐκοσμότεροι καὶ ῥάιους ἄρχειν ὦσι, κατὰ τέλη στρατηγῶι προστεταγμένοι· ἔπειτα δὲ προύπεμψαν καὶ ἐς τὴν Ἰταλίαν καὶ Σικελίαν 2 τρεῖς ναῦς εἰσομένας αἵτινες σφᾶς τῶν πόλεων δέξονται. καὶ εἴρητο αὐταῖς προαπαντᾶν, ὅπως ἐπιστάμενοι καταπλέωσιν. μετὰ δὲ ταῦτα 43 τοσῆιδε ἤδη τῆι παρασκευῆι Ἀθηναῖοι ἄραντες ἐκ τῆς Κερκύρας ἐς τὴν Σικελίαν ἐπεραιοῦντο, τριήρεσι μὲν ταῖς πάσαις τέσσαρσι καὶ τριάκοντα καὶ ἑκατόν, καὶ δυοῖν Ῥοδίοιν πεντηκοντόροιν (τούτων Ἀττικαὶ μὲν ἦσαν ἑκατόν, ὧν αἱ μὲν ἑξήκοντα ταχεῖαι, αἱ δ' ἄλλαι στρατιώτιδες, τὸ δὲ ἄλλο ναυτικὸν Χίων καὶ τῶν ἄλλων ξυμμάχων), ὁπλίταις δὲ τοῖς ξύμπασιν ἑκατὸν καὶ πεντακισχιλίοις (καὶ τούτων Ἀθηναίων μὲν αὐτῶν ἦσαν πεντακόσιοι μὲν καὶ χίλιοι ἐκ καταλόγου, ἑπτακόσιοι δὲ θῆτες ἐπιβάται τῶν νεῶν, ξύμμαχοι δὲ οἱ ἄλλοι ξυνεστράτευον, οἱ μὲν τῶν ὑπηκόων, οἱ δ' Ἀργείων πεντακόσιοι καὶ Μαντινέων καὶ μισθοφόρων πεντήκοντα καὶ διακόσιοι), τοξόταις δὲ τοῖς πᾶσιν ὀγδοήκοντα καὶ τετρακοσίοις (καὶ τούτων Κρῆτες οἱ ὀγδοήκοντα ἦσαν) καὶ σφενδονήταις Ῥοδίων ἑπτακοσίοις, καὶ Μεγαρεῦσι ψιλοῖς φυγάσιν εἴκοσι καὶ ἑκατόν, καὶ ἱππαγωγῶι μιᾶι τριάκοντα ἀγούσηι ἱππέας.

Τοσαύτη ἡ πρώτη παρασκευὴ πρὸς τὸν πόλεμον διέπλει, τούτοις 44 δὲ τὰ ἐπιτήδεια ἄγουσαι ὁλκάδες μὲν τριάκοντα σιταγωγοί, καὶ τοὺς σιτοποιοὺς ἔχουσαι καὶ λιθολόγους καὶ τέκτονας καὶ ὅσα ἐς τειχισμὸν ἐργαλεῖα, πλοῖα δὲ ἑκατόν, ἃ ἐξ ἀνάγκης μετὰ τῶν ὁλκάδων ξυνέπλει· πολλὰ δὲ καὶ ἄλλα πλοῖα καὶ ὁλκάδες ἑκούσιοι ξυνηκολούθουν τῆι στρατιᾶι ἐμπορίας ἕνεκα· ἃ τότε πάντα ἐκ τῆς Κερκύρας ξυνδιέβαλλε τὸν Ἰόνιον κόλπον. καὶ προσβαλοῦσα ἡ πᾶσα παρασκευὴ πρός τε ἄκραν 2 Ἰαπυγίαν καὶ πρὸς Τάραντα καὶ ὡς ἕκαστοι ηὐπόρησαν, παρεκομίζοντο τὴν Ἰταλίαν, τῶν μὲν πόλεων οὐ δεχομένων αὐτοὺς ἀγορᾶι οὐδὲ ἄστει, ὕδατι δὲ καὶ ὅρμωι, Τάραντος δὲ καὶ Λοκρῶν οὐδὲ τούτοις, ἕως ἀφίκοντο ἐς Ῥήγιον τῆς Ἰταλίας ἀκρωτήριον. καὶ ἐνταῦθα ἤδη ἠθροίζοντο, καὶ ἔξω τῆς 3 πόλεως, ὡς αὐτοὺς ἔσω οὐκ ἐδέχοντο, στρατόπεδόν τε κατεσκευάσαντο ἐν τῶι τῆς Ἀρτέμιδος ἱερῶι, οὗ αὐτοῖς καὶ ἀγορὰν παρεῖχον, καὶ τὰς ναῦς ἀνελκύσαντες ἡσύχασαν. καὶ πρός τε τοὺς Ῥηγίνους λόγους ἐποιήσαντο, ἀξιοῦντες Χαλκιδέας ὄντας Χαλκιδεῦσιν οὖσι Λεοντίνοις βοηθεῖν· οἱ δὲ οὐδὲ μεθ' ἑτέρων ἔφασαν ἔσεσθαι, ἀλλ' ὅ τι ἂν καὶ τοῖς ἄλλοις Ἰταλιώταις ξυνδοκῆι, τοῦτο ποιήσειν. οἱ δὲ πρὸς τὰ ἐν τῆι Σικελίαι πράγματα 4 ἐσκόπουν ὅτωι τρόπωι ἄριστα προσοίσονται· καὶ τὰς προπλους ναῦς ἐκ

---

43 ἑπτακόσιοι codd.: ἑξακόσιοι H²

τῆς Ἐγέστης ἅμα προσέμενον, βουλόμενοι εἰδέναι περὶ τῶν χρημάτων εἰ ἔστιν ἃ ἔλεγον ἐν ταῖς Ἀθήναις οἱ ἄγγελοι.

45 Τοῖς δὲ Συρακοσίοις ἐν τούτωι πολλαχόθεν τε ἤδη καὶ ἀπὸ τῶν κατασκόπων σαφῆ ἠγγέλλετο ὅτι ἐν Ῥηγίωι αἱ νῆές εἰσι, καὶ ὡς ἐπὶ τούτοις παρεσκευάζοντο πάσηι τῆι γνώμηι καὶ οὐκέτι ἠπίστουν. καὶ ἔς τε τοὺς Σικελοὺς περιέπεμπον, ἔνθα μὲν φύλακας, πρὸς δὲ τοὺς πρέσβεις, καὶ ἐς τὰ περιπόλια τὰ ἐν τῆι χώραι φρουρὰς ἐσεκόμιζον, τά τε ἐν τῆι πόλει ὅπλων ἐξετάσει καὶ ἵππων ἐσκόπουν εἰ ἐντελῆ ἐστί, καὶ τἆλλα ὡς ἐπὶ ταχεῖ πολέμωι καὶ ὅσον οὐ παρόντι καθίσταντο.

46 Αἱ δ' ἐκ τῆς Ἐγέστης τρεῖς νῆες αἱ πρόπλοι παραγίγνονται τοῖς Ἀθηναίοις ἐς τὸ Ῥήγιον, ἀγγέλλουσαι ὅτι τἆλλα μὲν οὐκ ἔστι χρήματα
2 ἃ ὑπέσχοντο, τριάκοντα δὲ τάλαντα μόνα φαίνεται. καὶ οἱ στρατηγοὶ εὐθὺς ἐν ἀθυμίαι ἦσαν, ὅτι αὐτοῖς τοῦτό τε πρῶτον ἀντεκεκρούκει καὶ οἱ Ῥηγῖνοι οὐκ ἐθελήσαντες ξυστρατεύειν, οὓς πρῶτον ἤρξαντο πείθειν καὶ εἰκὸς ἦν μάλιστα, Λεοντίνων τε ξυγγενεῖς ὄντας καὶ σφίσιν αἰεὶ ἐπιτηδείους. καὶ τῶι μὲν Νικίαι προσδεχομένωι ἦν τὰ παρὰ τῶν Ἐγεσταίων, τοῖν δὲ
3 ἑτέροιν καὶ ἀλογώτερα. οἱ δὲ Ἐγεσταῖοι τοιόνδε τι ἐξετεχνήσαντο τότε ὅτε οἱ πρῶτοι πρέσβεις τῶν Ἀθηναίων ἦλθον αὐτοῖς ἐς τὴν κατασκοπὴν τῶν χρημάτων. ἔς τε τὸ ἐν Ἔρυκι ἱερὸν τῆς Ἀφροδίτης ἀγαγόντες αὐτοὺς ἐπέδειξαν τὰ ἀναθήματα, φιάλας τε καὶ οἰνοχόας καὶ θυμιατήρια καὶ ἄλλην κατασκευὴν οὐκ ὀλίγην, ἃ ὄντα ἀργυρᾶ πολλῶι πλείω τὴν ὄψιν ἀπ' ὀλίγης δυνάμεως χρημάτων παρείχετο· καὶ ἰδίαι ξενίσεις ποιούμενοι τῶν τριηριτῶν τά τε ἐξ αὐτῆς Ἐγέστης ἐκπώματα καὶ χρυσᾶ καὶ ἀργυρᾶ ξυλλέξαντες καὶ τὰ ἐκ τῶν ἐγγὺς πόλεων καὶ Φοινικικῶν καὶ Ἑλληνίδων
4 αἰτησάμενοι ἐσέφερον ἐς τὰς ἑστιάσεις ὡς οἰκεῖα ἕκαστοι. καὶ πάντων ὡς ἐπὶ τὸ πολὺ τοῖς αὐτοῖς χρωμένων καὶ πανταχοῦ πολλῶν φαινομένων μεγάλην τὴν ἔκπληξιν τοῖς ἐκ τῶν τριήρων Ἀθηναίοις παρεῖχε, καὶ
5 ἀφικόμενοι ἐς τὰς Ἀθήνας διεθρόησαν ὡς χρήματα πολλὰ ἴδοιεν. καὶ οἱ μὲν αὐτοί τε ἀπατηθέντες καὶ τοὺς ἄλλους τότε πείσαντες, ἐπειδὴ διῆλθεν ὁ λόγος ὅτι οὐκ εἴη ἐν τῆι Ἐγέστηι τὰ χρήματα, πολλὴν τὴν αἰτίαν εἶχον ὑπὸ τῶν στρατιωτῶν· οἱ δὲ στρατηγοὶ πρὸς τὰ παρόντα ἐβουλεύοντο.

47 Καὶ Νικίου μὲν ἦν γνώμη πλεῖν ἐπὶ Σελινοῦντα πάσηι τῆι στρατιᾶι, ἐφ' ὅπερ μάλιστα ἐπέμφθησαν, καὶ ἢν μὲν παρέχωσι χρήματα παντὶ τῶι στρατεύματι Ἐγεσταῖοι, πρὸς ταῦτα βουλεύεσθαι, εἰ δὲ μή, ταῖς ἑξήκοντα ναυσίν, ὅσασπερ ἠιτήσαντο, ἀξιοῦν διδόναι αὐτοὺς τροφήν, καὶ παραμείναντας Σελινουντίους ἢ βίαι ἢ ξυμβάσει διαλλάξαι αὐτοῖς,

46.2 πρῶτον codd.: πρώτους H[2] (coni. Herwerden)

καὶ οὕτω παραπλεύσαντας τὰς ἄλλας πόλεις καὶ ἐπιδείξαντας μὲν τὴν δύναμιν τῆς Ἀθηναίων πόλεως, δηλώσαντας δὲ τὴν ἐς τοὺς φίλους καὶ ξυμμάχους προθυμίαν, ἀποπλεῖν οἴκαδε, ἢν μή τι δι' ὀλίγου καὶ ἀπὸ τοῦ ἀδοκήτου ἢ Λεοντίνους οἷοί τε ὦσιν ὠφελῆσαι ἢ τῶν ἄλλων τινὰ πόλεων προσαγαγέσθαι, καὶ τῆι πόλει δαπανῶντας τὰ οἰκεῖα μὴ κινδυνεύειν.

Ἀλκιβιάδης δὲ οὐκ ἔφη χρῆναι τοσαύτηι δυνάμει ἐκπλεύσαντας αἰσχρῶς **48** καὶ ἀπράκτους ἀπελθεῖν, ἀλλ' ἔς τε τὰς πόλεις ἐπικηρυκεύεσθαι πλὴν Σελινοῦντος καὶ Συρακουσῶν τὰς ἄλλας, καὶ πειρᾶσθαι καὶ τοὺς Σικελοὺς τοὺς μὲν ἀφιστάναι ἀπὸ τῶν Συρακοσίων, τοὺς δὲ φίλους ποιεῖσθαι, ἵνα σῖτον καὶ στρατιὰν παρέχωσι, πρῶτον δὲ πείθειν Μεσσηνίους (ἐν πόρωι γὰρ μάλιστα καὶ προσβολῆι εἶναι αὐτοὺς τῆς Σικελίας, καὶ λιμένα καὶ ἐφόρμησιν τῆι στρατιᾶι ἱκανωτάτην ἔσεσθαι)· προσαγαγομένους δὲ τὰς πόλεις, εἰδότας μεθ' ὧν τις πολεμήσει, οὕτως ἤδη Συρακούσαις καὶ Σελινοῦντι ἐπιχειρεῖν, ἢν μὴ οἱ μὲν Ἐγεσταίοις ξυμβαίνωσιν, οἱ δὲ Λεοντίνους ἐῶσι κατοικίζειν.

Λάμαχος δὲ ἄντικρυς ἔφη χρῆναι πλεῖν ἐπὶ Συρακούσας καὶ πρὸς τῆι πόλει **49** ὡς τάχιστα τὴν μάχην ποιεῖσθαι, ἕως ἔτι ἀπαράσκευοί τε εἰσὶ καὶ μάλιστα ἐκπεπληγμένοι. τὸ γὰρ πρῶτον πᾶν στράτευμα δεινότατον εἶναι· ἢν δὲ **2** χρονίσηι πρὶν ἐς ὄψιν ἐλθεῖν, τῆι γνώμηι ἀναθαρσοῦντας ἀνθρώπους καὶ τῆι ὄψει καταφρονεῖν μᾶλλον. αἰφνίδιοι δὲ ἢν προσπέσωσιν, ἕως ἔτι περιδεεῖς προσδέχονται, μάλιστ' ἂν σφᾶς περιγενέσθαι καὶ κατὰ πάντα ἂν αὐτοὺς ἐκφοβῆσαι, τῆι τε ὄψει (πλεῖστοι γὰρ ἂν νῦν φανῆναι) καὶ τῆι προσδοκίαι ὧν πείσονται, μάλιστα δ' ἂν τῶι αὐτίκα κινδύνωι τῆς μάχης. εἰκὸς δὲ εἶναι **3** καὶ ἐν τοῖς ἀγροῖς πολλοὺς ἀποληφθῆναι ἔξω διὰ τὸ ἀπιστεῖν σφᾶς μὴ ἥξειν, καὶ ἐσκομιζομένων αὐτῶν τὴν στρατιὰν οὐκ ἀπορήσειν χρημάτων, ἢν πρὸς τῆι πόλει κρατοῦσα καθέζηται. τούς τε ἄλλους Σικελιώτας οὕτως ἤδη μᾶλλον καὶ ἐκείνοις οὐ ξυμμαχήσειν καὶ σφίσι προσιέναι καὶ οὐ διαμελλήσειν περισκοποῦντας ὁπότεροι κρατήσουσιν. ναύσταθμον δὲ ἐπαναχωρήσαντας **4** καὶ ἐφόρμησιν τὰ Μέγαρα ἔφη χρῆναι ποιεῖσθαι, ἃ ἦν ἐρῆμα, ἀπέχοντα Συρακουσῶν οὔτε πλοῦν πολὺν οὔτε ὁδόν.

Λάμαχος μὲν ταῦτα εἰπὼν ὅμως προσέθετο καὶ αὐτὸς τῆι Ἀλκιβιάδου **50** γνώμηι. μετὰ δὲ τοῦτο Ἀλκιβιάδης τῆι αὐτοῦ νηὶ διαπλεύσας ἐς Μεσσήνην καὶ λόγους ποιησάμενος περὶ ξυμμαχίας πρὸς αὐτούς, ὡς οὐκ ἔπειθεν, ἀλλ' ἀπεκρίναντο πόλει μὲν ἂν οὐ δέξασθαι, ἀγορὰν δ' ἔξω παρέξειν, ἀπέπλει ἐς τὸ Ῥήγιον. καὶ εὐθὺς ξυμπληρώσαντες ἑξήκοντα **2** ναῦς ἐκ πασῶν οἱ στρατηγοὶ καὶ τὰ ἐπιτήδεια λαβόντες παρέπλεον ἐς Νάξον, τὴν ἄλλην στρατιὰν ἐν Ῥηγίωι καταλιπόντες καὶ ἕνα σφῶν αὐτῶν. Ναξίων δὲ δεξαμένων τῆι πόλει παρέπλεον ἐς Κατάνην. καὶ **3**

49.4 ἐφόρμησιν τὰ Boehme: ἐφορμηθέντας codd. (ἐφορμεῖν τὰ H²): ἐφορμισθέντας Schaefer ὡς αὐτοὺς οἱ Καταναῖοι οὐκ ἐδέχοντο (ἐνῆσαν γὰρ αὐτόθι ἄνδρες τὰ Συρακοσίων βουλόμενοι), ἐκομίσθησαν ἐπὶ τὸν Τηρίαν ποταμόν, καὶ αὐλισάμενοι τῆι ὑστεραίαι ἐπὶ Συρακούσας ἔπλεον ἐπὶ κέρως ἔχοντες τὰς

4 ἄλλας ναῦς· δέκα δὲ τῶν νεῶν προύπεμψαν ἐς τὸν μέγαν λιμένα πλεῦσαί τε καὶ κατασκέψασθαι εἴ τι ναυτικόν ἐστι καθειλκυσμένον, καὶ κηρῦξαι ἀπὸ τῶν νεῶν προσπλεύσαντας ὅτι Ἀθηναῖοι ἥκουσι Λεοντίνους ἐς τὴν ἑαυτῶν κατοικιοῦντες κατὰ ξυμμαχίαν καὶ ξυγγένειαν· τοὺς οὖν ὄντας ἐν Συρακούσαις Λεοντίνων ὡς παρὰ φίλους καὶ εὐεργέτας Ἀθηναίους

5 ἀδεῶς ἀπιέναι. ἐπεὶ δ' ἐκηρύχθη καὶ κατεσκέψαντο τήν τε πόλιν καὶ τοὺς λιμένας καὶ τὰ περὶ τὴν χώραν ἐξ ἧς αὐτοῖς ὁρμωμένοις πολεμητέα

51 ἦν, ἀπέπλευσαν πάλιν ἐς Κατάνην. καὶ ἐκκλησίας γενομένης τὴν μὲν στρατιὰν οὐκ ἐδέχοντο οἱ Καταναῖοι, τοὺς δὲ στρατηγοὺς ἐσελθόντας ἐκέλευον, εἴ τι βούλονται, εἰπεῖν. καὶ λέγοντος τοῦ Ἀλκιβιάδου, καὶ τῶν ἐν τῆι πόλει πρὸς τὴν ἐκκλησίαν τετραμμένων, οἱ στρατιῶται πυλίδα τινὰ ἐνωικοδομημένην κακῶς ἔλαθον διελόντες, καὶ ἐσελθόντες

2 ἐς τὴν πόλιν ἠγόραζον. τῶν δὲ Καταναίων οἱ μὲν τὰ τῶν Συρακοσίων φρονοῦντες, ὡς εἶδον τὸ στράτευμα ἔνδον, εὐθὺς περιδεεῖς γενόμενοι ὑπεξῆλθον οὐ πολλοί τινες, οἱ δὲ ἄλλοι ἐψηφίσαντό τε ξυμμαχίαν τοῖς Ἀθηναίοις καὶ τὸ ἄλλο στράτευμα ἐκέλευον ἐκ Ῥηγίου κομίζειν.

3 μετὰ δὲ τοῦτο πλεύσαντες οἱ Ἀθηναῖοι ἐς τὸ Ῥήγιον, πάσηι ἤδη τῆι στρατιᾶι ἄραντες ἐς τὴν Κατάνην, ἐπειδὴ ἀφίκοντο, κατεσκευάζοντο τὸ στρατόπεδον.

52 Ἐσηγγέλλετο δὲ αὐτοῖς ἔκ τε Καμαρίνης ὡς, εἰ ἔλθοιεν, προσχωροῖεν ἄν, καὶ ὅτι Συρακόσιοι πληροῦσι ναυτικόν. ἁπάσηι οὖν τῆι στρατιᾶι παρέπλευσαν πρῶτον μὲν ἐπὶ Συρακούσας· καὶ ὡς οὐδὲν ηὗρον ναυτικὸν πληρούμενον, παρεκομίζοντο αὖθις ἐπὶ Καμαρίνης, καὶ σχόντες ἐς τὸν αἰγιαλὸν ἐπεκηρυκεύοντο. οἱ δ' οὐκ ἐδέχοντο, λέγοντες σφίσι τὰ ὅρκια εἶναι μιᾶι νηὶ καταπλεόντων Ἀθηναίων δέχεσθαι, ἢν μὴ αὐτοὶ πλείους

2 μεταπέμπωσιν. ἄπρακτοι δὲ γενόμενοι ἀπέπλεον· καὶ ἀποβάντες κατά τι τῆς Συρακοσίας καὶ ἁρπαγὴν ποιησάμενοι, καὶ τῶν Συρακοσίων ἱππέων βοηθησάντων καὶ τῶν ψιλῶν τινὰς ἐσκεδασμένους διαφθειράντων,

53 ἀπεκομίσθησαν ἐς Κατάνην. καὶ καταλαμβάνουσι τὴν Σαλαμινίαν ναῦν ἐκ τῶν Ἀθηνῶν ἥκουσαν ἐπί τε Ἀλκιβιάδην ὡς κελεύσοντας ἀποπλεῖν ἐς

51.1 ἐς τὴν πόλιν ἠγόραζον Richards: ἠγόραζον ἐς τὴν πόλιν codd.: ἐς τὴν πόλιν del. Herwerden ἀπολογίαν ὧν ἡ πόλις ἐνεκάλει, καὶ ἐπ' ἄλλους τινὰς τῶν στρατιωτῶν τῶν μετ' αὐτοῦ μεμηνυμένων περὶ τῶν μυστηρίων ὡς ἀσεβούντων, τῶν δὲ καὶ περὶ τῶν Ἑρμῶν. οἱ γὰρ Ἀθηναῖοι, ἐπειδὴ ἡ στρατιὰ ἀπέπλευσεν, 2 οὐδὲν ἧσσον ζήτησιν ἐποιοῦντο τῶν περὶ τὰ μυστήρια καὶ τῶν περὶ τοὺς Ἑρμᾶς δρασθέντων, καὶ οὐ δοκιμάζοντες τοὺς μηνυτάς, ἀλλὰ πάντα ὑπόπτως ἀποδεχόμενοι, διὰ πονηρῶν ἀνθρώπων πίστιν πάνυ χρηστοὺς τῶν πολιτῶν ξυλλαμβάνοντες κατέδουν, χρησιμώτερον ἡγούμενοι εἶναι βασανίσαι τὸ πρᾶγμα καὶ εὑρεῖν ἢ διὰ μηνυτοῦ πονηρίαν τινὰ καὶ χρηστὸν δοκοῦντα εἶναι αἰτιαθέντα ἀνέλεγκτον διαφυγεῖν. ἐπιστάμενος 3 γὰρ ὁ δῆμος ἀκοῆι τὴν Πεισιστράτου καὶ τῶν παίδων τυραννίδα χαλεπὴν τελευτῶσαν γενομένην καὶ προσέτι οὐδ' ὑφ' ἑαυτῶν καὶ Ἁρμοδίου καταλυθεῖσαν, ἀλλ' ὑπὸ τῶν Λακεδαιμονίων, ἐφοβεῖτο αἰεὶ καὶ πάντα ὑπόπτως ἐλάμβανεν.

Τὸ γὰρ Ἀριστογείτονος καὶ Ἁρμοδίου τόλμημα δι' ἐρωτικὴν ξυντυχίαν 54 ἐπεχειρήθη, ἣν ἐγὼ ἐπὶ πλέον διηγησάμενος ἀποφανῶ οὔτε τοὺς ἄλλους οὔτε αὐτοὺς Ἀθηναίους περὶ τῶν σφετέρων τυράννων οὐδὲ περὶ τοῦ γενομένου ἀκριβὲς οὐδὲν λέγοντας. Πεισιστράτου γὰρ γηραιοῦ 2 τελευτήσαντος ἐν τῆι τυραννίδι οὐχ Ἵππαρχος, ὥσπερ οἱ πολλοὶ οἴονται, ἀλλ' Ἱππίας πρεσβύτατος ὢν ἔσχε τὴν ἀρχήν. γενομένου δὲ Ἁρμοδίου ὥραι ἡλικίας λαμπροῦ Ἀριστογείτων ἀνὴρ τῶν ἀστῶν, μέσος πολίτης, ἐραστὴς ὢν εἶχεν αὐτόν. πειραθεὶς δὲ ὁ Ἁρμόδιος ὑπὸ Ἱππάρχου τοῦ 3 Πεισιστράτου καὶ οὐ πεισθεὶς καταγορεύει τῶι Ἀριστογείτονι. ὁ δὲ ἐρωτικῶς περιαλγήσας καὶ φοβηθεὶς τὴν Ἱππάρχου δύναμιν μὴ βίαι προσαγάγηται αὐτόν, ἐπιβουλεύει εὐθὺς ὡς ἀπὸ τῆς ὑπαρχούσης ἀξιώσεως κατάλυσιν τῆι τυραννίδι. καὶ ἐν τούτωι ὁ Ἵππαρχος ὡς αὖθις 4 πειράσας οὐδὲν μᾶλλον ἔπειθε τὸν Ἁρμόδιον, βίαιον μὲν οὐδὲν ἐβούλετο δρᾶν, ἐν τρόπωι δέ τινι ἀφανεῖ ὡς οὐ διὰ τοῦτο δὴ παρεσκευάζετο προπηλακιῶν αὐτόν. οὐδὲ γὰρ τὴν ἄλλην ἀρχὴν ἐπαχθεῖς ἦσαν ἐς τοὺς 5 πολλούς, ἀλλ' ἀνεπιφθόνως κατεστήσαντο· καὶ ἐπετήδευσαν ἐπὶ πλεῖστον δὴ τύραννοι οὗτοι ἀρετὴν καὶ ξύνεσιν, καὶ Ἀθηναίους εἰκοστὴν μόνον πρασσόμενοι τῶν γιγνομένων τήν τε πόλιν αὐτῶν καλῶς διεκόσμησαν καὶ τοὺς πολέμους διέφερον καὶ ἐς τὰ ἱερὰ ἔθυον. τὰ δὲ ἄλλα αὐτὴ ἡ πόλις 6 τοῖς πρὶν κειμένοις νόμοις ἐχρῆτο, πλὴν καθ' ὅσον αἰεί τινα ἐπεμέλοντο σφῶν αὐτῶν ἐν ταῖς ἀρχαῖς εἶναι. καὶ ἄλλοι τε αὐτῶν ἦρξαν τὴν ἐνιαύσιον

54.5 ἐπαχθεῖς ἦσαν Hude: ἐπαχθὴς (-εἰς C²) ἦν codd.   κατεστήσαντο Pi³ (coni. Hude): κατεστήσατο codd.

Ἀθηναίοις ἀρχὴν καὶ Πεισίστρατος ὁ Ἱππίου τοῦ τυραννεύσαντος υἱός, τοῦ πάππου ἔχων τοὔνομα, ὃς τῶν δώδεκα θεῶν βωμὸν τὸν ἐν τῆι

7 ἀγορᾶι ἄρχων ἀνέθηκε καὶ τὸν τοῦ Ἀπόλλωνος ἐν Πυθίου. καὶ τῶι μὲν ἐν τῆι ἀγορᾶι προσοικοδομήσας ὕστερον ὁ δῆμος Ἀθηναίων μεῖζον μῆκος τοῦ βωμοῦ ἠφάνισε τοὐπίγραμμα· τοῦ δ᾽ ἐν Πυθίου ἔτι καὶ νῦν δῆλόν ἐστιν ἀμυδροῖς γράμμασι λέγον τάδε·

    μνῆμα τόδ᾽ ἧς ἀρχῆς Πεισίστρατος Ἱππίου υἱός
    θῆκεν Ἀπόλλωνος Πυθίου ἐν τεμένει.

55 Ὅτι δὲ πρεσβύτατος ὢν Ἱππίας ἦρξεν, εἰδὼς μὲν καὶ ἀκοῆι ἀκριβέστερον ἄλλων ἰσχυρίζομαι, γνοίη δ᾽ ἄν τις καὶ αὐτῶι τούτωι· παῖδες γὰρ αὐτῶι μόνωι φαίνονται τῶν γνησίων ἀδελφῶν γενόμενοι, ὡς ὅ τε βωμὸς σημαίνει καὶ ἡ στήλη ἡ περὶ τῆς τῶν τυράννων ἀδικίας ἡ ἐν τῆι Ἀθηναίων ἀκροπόλει σταθεῖσα, ἐν ἧι Θεσσαλοῦ μὲν οὐδ᾽ Ἱππάρχου οὐδεὶς παῖς γέγραπται, Ἱππίου δὲ πέντε, οἳ αὐτῶι ἐκ Μυρρίνης τῆς Καλλίου τοῦ Ὑπεροχίδου θυγατρὸς ἐγένοντο· εἰκὸς γὰρ

2 ἦν τὸν πρεσβύτατον πρῶτον γῆμαι. καὶ ἐν τῆι αὐτῆι στήληι πρῶτος γέγραπται μετὰ τὸν πατέρα, οὐδὲ τοῦτο ἀπεοικότως διὰ τὸ πρεσβεύειν

3 τε ἀπ᾽ αὐτοῦ καὶ τυραννεῦσαι. οὐ μὴν οὐδ᾽ ἂν κατασχεῖν μοι δοκεῖ ποτὲ Ἱππίας τὸ παραχρῆμα ῥαιδίως τὴν τυραννίδα, εἰ Ἵππαρχος μὲν ἐν τῆι ἀρχῆι ὢν ἀπέθανεν, αὐτὸς δὲ αὐθημερὸν καθίστατο· ἀλλὰ καὶ διὰ τὸ πρότερον ξύνηθες τοῖς μὲν πολίταις φοβερόν, ἐς δὲ τοὺς ἐπικούρους ἀκριβές, πολλῶι τῶι περιόντι τοῦ ἀσφαλοῦς κατεκράτησε, καὶ οὐχ ὡς ἀδελφὸς νεώτερος ὢν ἠπόρησεν, ἐν ὧι οὐ πρότερον ξυνεχῶς ὡμιλήκει τῆι

4 ἀρχῆι. Ἱππάρχωι δὲ ξυνέβη τοῦ πάθους τῆι δυστυχίαι ὀνομασθέντα καὶ τὴν δόξαν τῆς τυραννίδος ἐς τὰ ἔπειτα προσλαβεῖν.

56 Τὸν δ᾽ οὖν Ἁρμόδιον ἀπαρνηθέντα τὴν πείρασιν, ὥσπερ διενοεῖτο, προυπηλάκισεν· ἀδελφὴν γὰρ αὐτοῦ κόρην ἐπαγγείλαντες ἥκειν κανοῦν οἴσουσαν ἐν πομπῆι τινι, ἀπήλασαν λέγοντες οὐδὲ ἐπαγγεῖλαι τὴν ἀρχὴν

2 διὰ τὸ μὴ ἀξίαν εἶναι. χαλεπῶς δὲ ἐνεγκόντος τοῦ Ἁρμοδίου πολλῶι δὴ μᾶλλον δι᾽ ἐκεῖνον καὶ ὁ Ἀριστογείτων παρωξύνετο. καὶ αὐτοῖς τὰ μὲν ἄλλα πρὸς τοὺς ξυνεπιθησομένους τῶι ἔργωι ἐπέπρακτο, περιέμενον δὲ Παναθήναια τὰ μεγάλα, ἐν ἧι μόνον ἡμέραι οὐχ ὕποπτον ἐγίγνετο ἐν ὅπλοις τῶν πολιτῶν τοὺς τὴν πομπὴν πέμψοντας ἀθρόους γενέσθαι· καὶ ἔδει ἄρξαι μὲν αὐτούς, ξυνεπαμύνειν δὲ εὐθὺς τὰ πρὸς τοὺς δορυφόρους

3 ἐκείνους. ἦσαν δὲ οὐ πολλοὶ οἱ ξυνομωμοκότες ἀσφαλείας ἕνεκα· ἤλπιζον γὰρ καὶ τοὺς μὴ προειδότας, εἰ καὶ ὁποσοιοῦν τολμήσειαν, ἐκ τοῦ

57 παραχρῆμα ἔχοντάς γε ὅπλα ἐθελήσειν σφᾶς αὐτοὺς ξυνελευθεροῦν. καὶ

ὡς ἐπῆλθεν ἡ ἑορτή, Ἱππίας μὲν ἔξω ἐν τῶι Κεραμεικῶι καλουμένωι μετὰ τῶν δορυφόρων διεκόσμει ὡς ἕκαστα ἐχρῆν τῆς πομπῆς προϊέναι, ὁ δὲ Ἁρμόδιος καὶ ὁ Ἀριστογείτων ἔχοντες ἤδη τὰ ἐγχειρίδια ἐς τὸ ἔργον προῆισαν. καὶ ὡς εἶδόν τινα τῶν ξυνωμοτῶν σφίσι διαλεγόμενον οἰκείως 2 τῶι Ἱππίαι (ἦν δὲ πᾶσιν εὐπρόσοδος ὁ Ἱππίας), ἔδεισαν καὶ ἐνόμισαν μεμηνῦσθαί τε καὶ ὅσον οὐκ ἤδη ξυλληφθήσεσθαι. τὸν λυπήσαντα 3 οὖν σφᾶς καὶ δι' ὅνπερ πάντα ἐκινδύνευον ἐβούλοντο πρότερον, εἰ δύναιντο, προτιμωρήσασθαι, καὶ ὥσπερ εἶχον ὥρμησαν ἔσω τῶν πυλῶν, καὶ περιέτυχον τῶι Ἱππάρχωι παρὰ τὸ Λεωκόρειον καλούμενον, καὶ εὐθὺς ἀπερισκέπτως προσπεσόντες καὶ ὡς ἂν μάλιστα δι' ὀργῆς ὁ μὲν ἐρωτικῆς, ὁ δὲ ὑβρισμένος, ἔτυπτον καὶ ἀποκτείνουσιν αὐτόν. καὶ ὁ μὲν 4 τοὺς δορυφόρους τὸ αὐτίκα διαφεύγει ὁ Ἀριστογείτων, ξυνδραμόντος τοῦ ὄχλου, καὶ ὕστερον ληφθεὶς οὐ ῥαιδίως διετέθη· Ἁρμόδιος δὲ αὐτοῦ παραχρῆμα ἀπόλλυται. ἀγγελθέντος δὲ Ἱππίαι ἐς τὸν Κεραμεικόν, οὐκ 58 ἐπὶ τὸ γενόμενον, ἀλλ' ἐπὶ τοὺς πομπέας τοὺς ὁπλίτας, πρότερον ἢ αἰσθέσθαι αὐτοὺς ἄπωθεν ὄντας, εὐθὺς ἐχώρησε, καὶ ἀδήλως τῆι ὄψει πλασάμενος πρὸς τὴν ξυμφορὰν ἐκέλευσεν αὐτούς, δείξας τι χωρίον, ἀπελθεῖν ἐς αὐτὸ ἄνευ τῶν ὅπλων. καὶ οἱ μὲν ἀνεχώρησαν οἰόμενοί τι 2 ἐρεῖν αὐτόν, ὁ δὲ τοῖς ἐπικούροις φράσας τὰ ὅπλα ὑπολαβεῖν ἐξελέγετο εὐθὺς οὓς ἐπηιτιᾶτο καὶ εἴ τις ηὑρέθη ἐγχειρίδιον ἔχων· μετὰ γὰρ ἀσπίδος καὶ δόρατος εἰώθεσαν τὰς πομπὰς ποιεῖν.

Τοιούτωι μὲν τρόπωι δι' ἐρωτικὴν λύπην ἥ τε ἀρχὴ τῆς ἐπιβουλῆς 59 καὶ ἡ ἀλόγιστος τόλμα ἐκ τοῦ παραχρῆμα περιδεοῦς Ἁρμοδίωι καὶ Ἀριστογείτονι ἐγένετο. τοῖς δ' Ἀθηναίοις χαλεπωτέρα μετὰ τοῦτο 2 ἡ τυραννὶς κατέστη, καὶ ὁ Ἱππίας διὰ φόβου ἤδη μᾶλλον ὤν τῶν τε πολιτῶν πολλοὺς ἔκτεινε καὶ πρὸς τὰ ἔξω ἅμα διεσκοπεῖτο, εἴ ποθεν ἀσφάλειάν τινα ὁρώιη μεταβολῆς γενομένης ὑπάρχουσάν οἱ. Ἱππόκλου 3 γοῦν τοῦ Λαμψακηνοῦ τυράννου Αἰαντίδηι τῶι παιδὶ θυγατέρα ἑαυτοῦ μετὰ ταῦτα Ἀρχεδίκην Ἀθηναῖος ὢν Λαμψακηνῶι ἔδωκεν, αἰσθανόμενος αὐτοὺς μέγα παρὰ βασιλεῖ Δαρείωι δύνασθαι. καὶ αὐτῆς σῆμα ἐν Λαμψάκωι ἐστὶν ἐπίγραμμα ἔχον τόδε·

ἀνδρὸς ἀριστεύσαντος ἐν Ἑλλάδι τῶν ἐφ' ἑαυτοῦ
Ἱππίου Ἀρχεδίκην ἥδε κέκευθε κόνις,
ἣ πατρός τε καὶ ἀνδρὸς ἀδελφῶν τ' οὖσα τυράννων
παίδων τ' οὐκ ἤρθη νοῦν ἐς ἀτασθαλίην.

58.2 ἀνεχώρησαν codd.: ἀπεχώρησαν H² (coni. Poppo)

4 Τυραννεύσας δὲ ἔτη τρία Ἱππίας ἔτι Ἀθηναίων καὶ παυθεὶς ἐν τῶι τετάρτωι ὑπὸ Λακεδαιμονίων καὶ Ἀλκμεωνιδῶν τῶν φευγόντων, ἐχώρει ὑπόσπονδος ἔς τε Σίγειον καὶ παρ' Αἰαντίδην ἐς Λάμψακον, ἐκεῖθεν δὲ ὡς βασιλέα Δαρεῖον, ὅθεν καὶ ὁρμώμενος ἐς Μαραθῶνα ὕστερον ἔτει εἰκοστῶι ἤδη γέρων ὢν μετὰ Μήδων ἐστράτευσεν.

60 Ὧν ἐνθυμούμενος ὁ δῆμος ὁ τῶν Ἀθηναίων, καὶ μιμνηισκόμενος ὅσα ἀκοῆι περὶ αὐτῶν ἠπίστατο, χαλεπὸς ἦν τότε καὶ ὑπόπτης ἐς τοὺς περὶ τῶν μυστικῶν τὴν αἰτίαν λαβόντας, καὶ πάντα αὐτοῖς ἐδόκει ἐπὶ
2 ξυνωμοσίαι ὀλιγαρχικῆι καὶ τυραννικῆι πεπρᾶχθαι. καὶ ὡς αὐτῶν διὰ τὸ τοιοῦτον ὀργιζομένων πολλοί τε καὶ ἀξιόλογοι ἄνθρωποι ἤδη ἐν τῶι δεσμωτηρίωι ἦσαν καὶ οὐκ ἐν παύληι ἐφαίνετο, ἀλλὰ καθ' ἡμέραν ἐπεδίδοσαν μᾶλλον ἐς τὸ ἀγριώτερόν τε καὶ πλείους ἔτι ξυλλαμβάνειν, ἐνταῦθα ἀναπείθεται εἷς τῶν δεδεμένων, ὅσπερ ἐδόκει αἰτιώτατος εἶναι, ὑπὸ τῶν ξυνδεσμωτῶν τινος εἴτε ἄρα καὶ τὰ ὄντα μηνῦσαι εἴτε καὶ οὔ· ἐπ' ἀμφότερα γὰρ εἰκάζεται, τὸ δὲ σαφὲς οὐδεὶς οὔτε τότε οὔτε
3 ὕστερον ἔχει εἰπεῖν περὶ τῶν δρασάντων τὸ ἔργον. λέγων δὲ ἔπεισεν αὐτὸν ὡς χρή, εἰ μὴ καὶ δέδρακεν, αὑτόν τε ἄδειαν ποιησάμενον σῶσαι καὶ τὴν πόλιν τῆς παρούσης ὑποψίας παῦσαι· βεβαιοτέραν γὰρ αὐτῶι σωτηρίαν εἶναι ὁμολογήσαντι μετ' ἀδείας ἢ ἀρνηθέντι διὰ δίκης ἐλθεῖν.
4 καὶ ὁ μὲν αὐτός τε καθ' ἑαυτοῦ καὶ κατ' ἄλλων μηνύει τὸ τῶν Ἑρμῶν· ὁ δὲ δῆμος ὁ τῶν Ἀθηναίων ἄσμενος λαβών, ὡς ὤιετο, τὸ σαφὲς καὶ δεινὸν ποιούμενοι πρότερον εἰ τοὺς ἐπιβουλεύοντας σφῶν τῶι πλήθει μὴ εἴσονται, τὸν μὲν μηνυτὴν εὐθὺς καὶ τοὺς ἄλλους μετ' αὐτοῦ ὅσων μὴ κατηγορήκει ἔλυσαν, τοὺς δὲ καταιτιαθέντας κρίσεις ποιήσαντες τοὺς μὲν ἀπέκτειναν, ὅσοι ξυνελήφθησαν, τῶν δὲ διαφυγόντων θάνατον
5 καταγνόντες ἐπανεῖπον ἀργύριον τῶι ἀποκτείναντι. κἀν τούτωι οἱ μὲν παθόντες ἄδηλον ἦν εἰ ἀδίκως ἐτετιμώρηντο, ἡ μέντοι ἄλλη πόλις ἐν τῶι
61 παρόντι περιφανῶς ὠφέλητο. περὶ δὲ τοῦ Ἀλκιβιάδου ἐναγόντων τῶν ἐχθρῶν, οἵπερ καὶ πρὶν ἐκπλεῖν αὐτὸν ἐπέθεντο, χαλεπῶς οἱ Ἀθηναῖοι ἐλάμβανον· καὶ ἐπειδὴ τὸ τῶν Ἑρμῶν ὤιοντο σαφὲς ἔχειν, πολὺ δὴ μᾶλλον καὶ τὰ μυστικά, ὧν ἐπαίτιος ἦν, μετὰ τοῦ αὐτοῦ λόγου καὶ τῆς
2 ξυνωμοσίας ἐπὶ τῶι δήμωι ἀπ' ἐκείνου ἐδόκει πραχθῆναι. καὶ γάρ τις καὶ στρατιὰ Λακεδαιμονίων οὐ πολλὴ ἔτυχε κατὰ τὸν καιρὸν τοῦτον ἐν ὧι περὶ ταῦτα ἐθορυβοῦντο μέχρι Ἰσθμοῦ παρελθοῦσα, πρὸς Βοιωτούς τι πράσσοντες. ἐδόκει οὖν ἐκείνου πράξαντος καὶ οὐ Βοιωτῶν ἕνεκα ἀπὸ ξυνθήματος ἥκειν, καὶ εἰ μὴ ἔφθασαν δὴ αὐτοὶ κατὰ τὸ μήνυμα ξυλλαβόντες τοὺς ἄνδρας, προδοθῆναι ἂν ἡ πόλις. καί τινα μίαν νύκτα
3 καὶ κατέδαρθον ἐν Θησείωι τῶι ἐν πόλει ἐν ὅπλοις. οἵ τε ξένοι τοῦ

Ἀλκιβιάδου οἱ ἐν Ἄργει κατὰ τὸν αὐτὸν χρόνον ὑπωπτεύθησαν τῶι δήμωι ἐπιτίθεσθαι, καὶ τοὺς ὁμήρους τῶν Ἀργείων τοὺς ἐν ταῖς νήσοις κειμένους οἱ Ἀθηναῖοι τότε παρέδοσαν τῶι Ἀργείων δήμωι διὰ ταῦτα διαχρήσασθαι. πανταχόθεν τε περιειστήκει ὑποψία ἐς τὸν Ἀλκιβιάδην. 4 ὥστε βουλόμενοι αὐτὸν ἐς κρίσιν ἀγαγόντες ἀποκτεῖναι, πέμπουσιν οὕτω τὴν Σαλαμινίαν ναῦν ἐς τὴν Σικελίαν ἐπί τε ἐκεῖνον καὶ ὧν πέρι ἄλλων ἐμεμήνυτο. εἴρητο δὲ προειπεῖν αὐτῶι ἀπολογησομένωι 5 ἀκολουθεῖν, ξυλλαμβάνειν δὲ μή, θεραπεύοντες τό τε πρὸς τοὺς ἐν τῆι Σικελίαι στρατιώτας τε σφετέρους καὶ πολεμίους μὴ θορυβεῖν καὶ οὐχ ἥκιστα τοὺς Μαντινέας καὶ Ἀργείους βουλόμενοι παραμεῖναι, δι' ἐκείνου νομίζοντες πεισθῆναι σφίσι ξυστρατεύειν. καὶ ὁ μὲν ἔχων τὴν ἑαυτοῦ 6 ναῦν καὶ οἱ ξυνδιαβεβλημένοι ἀπέπλεον μετὰ τῆς Σαλαμινίας ἐκ τῆς Σικελίας ὡς ἐς τὰς Ἀθήνας· καὶ ἐπειδὴ ἐγένοντο ἐν Θουρίοις, οὐκέτι ξυνείποντο, ἀλλ' ἀπελθόντες ἀπὸ τῆς νεὼς οὐ φανεροὶ ἦσαν, δείσαντες τὸ ἐπὶ διαβολῆι ἐς δίκην καταπλεῦσαι. οἱ δ' ἐκ τῆς Σαλαμινίας τέως μὲν 7 ἐζήτουν τὸν Ἀλκιβιάδην καὶ τοὺς μετ' αὐτοῦ· ὡς δ' οὐδαμοῦ φανεροὶ ἦσαν, ὤιχοντο ἀποπλέοντες. ὁ δὲ Ἀλκιβιάδης ἤδη φυγὰς ὢν οὐ πολὺ ὕστερον ἐπὶ πλοίου ἐπεραιώθη ἐς Πελοπόννησον ἐκ τῆς Θουρίας· οἱ δ' Ἀθηναῖοι ἐρήμηι δίκηι θάνατον κατέγνωσαν αὐτοῦ τε καὶ τῶν μετ' ἐκείνου.

Μετὰ δὲ ταῦτα οἱ λοιποὶ τῶν Ἀθηναίων στρατηγοὶ ἐν τῆι Σικελίαι, 62 δύο μέρη ποιήσαντες τοῦ στρατεύματος καὶ λαχὼν ἑκάτερος, ἔπλεον ξύμπαντι ἐπὶ Σελινοῦντος καὶ Ἐγέστης, βουλόμενοι μὲν εἰδέναι τὰ χρήματα εἰ δώσουσιν οἱ Ἐγεσταῖοι, κατασκέψασθαι δὲ καὶ τῶν Σελινουντίων τὰ πράγματα καὶ τὰ διάφορα μαθεῖν τὰ πρὸς Ἐγεσταίους. παραπλέοντες 2 δ' ἐν ἀριστερᾶι τὴν Σικελίαν, τὸ μέρος τὸ πρὸς τὸν Τυρσηνικὸν κόλπον, ἔσχον ἐς Ἱμέραν, ἥπερ μόνη ἐν τούτωι τῶι μέρει τῆς Σικελίας Ἑλλὰς πόλις ἐστίν· καὶ ὡς οὐκ ἐδέχοντο αὐτούς, παρεκομίζοντο. καὶ ἐν τῶι 3 παράπλωι αἱροῦσιν Ὕκκαρα, πόλισμα Σικανικὸν μέν, Ἐγεσταίοις δὲ πολέμιον· ἦν δὲ παραθαλασσίδιον. καὶ ἀνδραποδίσαντες τὴν πόλιν παρέδοσαν Ἐγεσταίοις (παρεγένοντο γὰρ αὐτῶν ἱππῆς), αὐτοὶ δὲ πάλιν τῶι μὲν πεζῶι ἐχώρουν διὰ τῶν Σικελῶν ἕως ἀφίκοντο ἐς Κατάνην, αἱ δὲ νῆες περιέπλευσαν τὰ ἀνδράποδα ἄγουσαι. Νικίας δὲ εὐθὺς ἐξ Ὑκκάρων 4 ἐπὶ Ἐγέστης παραπλεύσας, καὶ τἆλλα χρηματίσας καὶ λαβὼν τάλαντα τριάκοντα παρῆν ἐς τὸ στράτευμα· καὶ τἀνδράποδα ἀπέδοσαν, καὶ

61.5 σφίσι Lindau: σφᾶς codd.

5 ἐγένοντο ἐξ αὐτῶν εἴκοσι καὶ ἑκατὸν τάλαντα. καὶ ἐς τοὺς τῶν Σικελῶν ξυμμάχους περιέπεμψαν, στρατιὰν κελεύοντες πέμπειν· τῆι τε ἡμισείαι τῆς ἑαυτῶν ἦλθον ἐπὶ Ὕβλαν τὴν Γελεᾶτιν πολεμίαν οὖσαν, καὶ οὐχ εἷλον. καὶ τὸ θέρος ἐτελεύτα.

63 Τοῦ δ' ἐπιγιγνομένου χειμῶνος εὐθὺς τὴν ἔφοδον οἱ Ἀθηναῖοι ἐπὶ Συρακούσας παρεσκευάζοντο, οἱ δὲ Συρακόσιοι καὶ αὐτοὶ ὡς ἐπ' ἐκείνους 2 ἰόντες. ἐπειδὴ γὰρ αὐτοῖς πρὸς τὸν πρῶτον φόβον καὶ τὴν προσδοκίαν οἱ Ἀθηναῖοι οὐκ εὐθὺς ἐπέκειντο, κατά τε τὴν ἡμέραν ἑκάστην προϊοῦσαν ἀνεθάρσουν μᾶλλον καὶ ἐπειδὴ πλέοντές τε τὰ ἐπ' ἐκεῖνα τῆς Σικελίας πολὺ ἀπὸ σφῶν ἐφαίνοντο καὶ πρὸς τὴν Ὕβλαν ἐλθόντες καὶ πειράσαντες οὐχ εἷλον βίαι, ἔτι πλέον κατεφρόνησαν καὶ ἠξίουν τοὺς στρατηγούς, οἷον δὴ ὄχλος φιλεῖ θαρσήσας ποιεῖν, ἄγειν σφᾶς ἐπὶ Κατάνην, ἐπειδή γε οὐκ 3 ἐκεῖνοι ἐφ' ἑαυτοὺς ἔρχονται. ἱππῆς τε προσελαύνοντες αἰεὶ κατάσκοποι τῶν Συρακοσίων πρὸς τὸ στράτευμα τῶν Ἀθηναίων ἐφύβριζον ἄλλα τε καὶ εἰ ξυνοικήσοντες σφίσιν αὐτοὶ μᾶλλον ἥκοιεν ἐν τῆι ἀλλοτρίαι ἢ 64 Λεοντίνους ἐς τὴν οἰκείαν κατοικιοῦντες. ἃ γιγνώσκοντες οἱ στρατηγοὶ τῶν Ἀθηναίων καὶ βουλόμενοι αὐτοὺς ἄγειν πανδημεὶ ἐκ τῆς πόλεως ὅτι πλεῖστον, αὐτοὶ δὲ ταῖς ναυσὶν ἐν τοσούτωι ὑπὸ νύκτα παραπλεύσαντες στρατόπεδον καταλαμβάνειν ἐν ἐπιτηδείωι καθ' ἡσυχίαν, εἰδότες οὐκ ἂν ὁμοίως δυνηθέντες καὶ εἰ ἐκ τῶν νεῶν πρὸς παρεσκευασμένους ἐκβιβάζοιεν ἢ κατὰ γῆν ἰόντες γνωσθεῖεν (τοὺς γὰρ ἂν ψιλοὺς τοὺς σφῶν καὶ τὸν ὄχλον τῶν Συρακοσίων τοὺς ἱππέας πολλοὺς ὄντας, σφίσι δ' οὐ παρόντων ἱππέων, βλάπτειν ἂν μεγάλα, οὕτω δὲ λήψεσθαι χωρίον ὅθεν ὑπὸ τῶν ἱππέων οὐ βλάψονται ἄξια λόγου· ἐδίδασκον δ' αὐτοὺς περὶ τοῦ πρὸς τῶι Ὀλυμπιείωι χωρίου, ὅπερ καὶ κατέλαβον, Συρακοσίων φυγάδες, οἳ ξυνείποντο), τοιόνδε τι οὖν πρὸς ἃ ἐβούλοντο οἱ στρατηγοὶ μηχανῶνται. 2 πέμπουσιν ἄνδρα σφίσι μὲν πιστόν, τοῖς δὲ τῶν Συρακοσίων στρατηγοῖς τῆι δοκήσει οὐχ ἧσσον ἐπιτήδειον· ἦν δὲ Καταναῖος ὁ ἀνήρ, καὶ ἀπ' ἀνδρῶν ἐκ τῆς Κατάνης ἥκειν ἔφη ὧν ἐκεῖνοι τὰ ὀνόματα ἐγίγνωσκον καὶ 3 ἠπίσταντο ἐν τῆι πόλει ἔτι ὑπολοίπους ὄντας τῶν σφίσιν εὔνων. ἔλεγε δὲ τοὺς Ἀθηναίους αὐλίζεσθαι ἀπὸ τῶν ὅπλων ἐν τῆι πόλει, καὶ εἰ βούλονται ἐκεῖνοι πανδημεὶ ἐν ἡμέραι ῥητῆι ἅμα ἕωι ἐπὶ τὸ στράτευμα ἐλθεῖν, αὐτοὶ μὲν ἀποκλήισειν τοὺς παρὰ σφίσι καὶ τὰς ναῦς ἐμπρήσειν, ἐκείνους δὲ ῥαιδίως τὸ στράτευμα προσβαλόντας τῶι σταυρώματι αἱρήσειν· εἶναι δὲ ταῦτα τοὺς ξυνδράσοντας πολλοὺς Καταναίων καὶ ἡτοιμάσθαι ἤδη, ἀφ'

62.5 περιέπεμψαν H² (coni. Stahl): περιέπλευσαν codd.   63.3 ἐπειδή γε M: γε om. cett.   64.1 καὶ post δυνηθέντες secl. Reiske, fort. non legit Σ aut Valla

ὧν αὐτὸς ἥκειν. οἱ δὲ στρατηγοὶ τῶν Συρακοσίων, μετὰ τοῦ καὶ ἐς τὰ 65
ἄλλα θαρσεῖν καὶ εἶναι ἐν διανοίαι καὶ ἄνευ τούτων ἰέναι [παρεσκευάσθαι]
ἐπὶ Κατάνην, ἐπίστευσάν τε τῶι ἀνθρώπωι πολλῶι ἀπερισκεπτότερον
καὶ εὐθὺς ἡμέραν ξυνθέμενοι ἧι παρέσονται ἀπέστειλαν αὐτόν, καὶ αὐτοί
(ἤδη γὰρ καὶ τῶν ξυμμάχων Σελινούντιοι καὶ ἄλλοι τινὲς παρῆσαν)
προεῖπον πανδημεὶ πᾶσιν ἐξιέναι Συρακοσίοις. ἐπεὶ δὲ ἑτοῖμα αὐτοῖς καὶ
τὰ τῆς παρασκευῆς ἦν καὶ αἱ ἡμέραι ἐν αἷς ξυνέθεντο ἥξειν ἐγγὺς ἦσαν,
πορευόμενοι ἐπὶ Κατάνης ηὐλίσαντο ἐπὶ τῶι Συμαίθωι ποταμῶι ἐν τῆι
Λεοντίνηι. οἱ δ᾽ Ἀθηναῖοι ὡς ἤισθοντο αὐτοὺς προσιόντας, ἀναλαβόντες 2
τό τε στράτευμα ἅπαν τὸ ἑαυτῶν καὶ ὅσοι Σικελῶν αὐτοῖς ἢ ἄλλος τις
προσεληλύθει καὶ ἐπιβιβάσαντες ἐπὶ τὰς ναῦς καὶ τὰ πλοῖα, ὑπὸ νύκτα
ἔπλεον ἐπὶ τὰς Συρακούσας. καὶ οἵ τε Ἀθηναῖοι ἅμα ἕωι ἐξέβαινον ἐς τὸ 3
κατὰ τὸ Ὀλυμπιεῖον ὡς τὸ στρατόπεδον καταληψόμενοι, καὶ οἱ ἱππῆς οἱ
Συρακοσίων πρῶτοι προσελάσαντες ἐς τὴν Κατάνην καὶ αἰσθόμενοι ὅτι
τὸ στράτευμα ἅπαν ἀνῆκται, ἀποστρέψαντες ἀγγέλλουσι τοῖς πεζοῖς,
καὶ ξύμπαντες ἤδη ἀποτρεπόμενοι ἐβοήθουν ἐπὶ τὴν πόλιν. ἐν τούτωι 66
δ᾽ οἱ Ἀθηναῖοι, μακρᾶς οὔσης τῆς ὁδοῦ αὐτοῖς, καθ᾽ ἡσυχίαν καθῖσαν
τὸ στράτευμα ἐς χωρίον ἐπιτήδειον, καὶ ἐν ὧι μάχης τε ἄρξειν ἔμελλον
ὁπότε βούλοιντο καὶ οἱ ἱππῆς τῶν Συρακοσίων ἥκιστ᾽ ἂν αὐτοὺς
καὶ ἐν τῶι ἔργωι καὶ πρὸ αὐτοῦ λυπήσειν· τῆι μὲν γὰρ τειχία τε καὶ
οἰκίαι εἶργον καὶ δένδρα καὶ λίμνη, παρὰ δὲ τὸ κρημνοί. καὶ τὰ ἐγγὺς 2
δένδρα κόψαντες καὶ κατενεγκόντες ἐπὶ τὴν θάλασσαν παρά τε τὰς
ναῦς σταύρωμα ἔπηξαν καὶ ἐπὶ τῶι Δάσκωνι ἐρυμά τε, ἧι εὐεφοδώτατον
ἦν τοῖς πολεμίοις, λίθοις λογάδην καὶ ξύλοις διὰ ταχέων ὤρθωσαν,
καὶ τὴν τοῦ Ἀνάπου γέφυραν ἔλυσαν. παρασκευαζομένων δὲ ἐκ μὲν 3
τῆς πόλεως οὐδεὶς ἐξιὼν ἐκώλυε, πρῶτοι δὲ οἱ ἱππῆς τῶν Συρακοσίων
προσεβοήθησαν, ἔπειτα δὲ ὕστερον καὶ τὸ πεζὸν ἅπαν ξυνελέγη. καὶ
προσῆλθον μὲν ἐγγὺς τοῦ στρατεύματος τῶν Ἀθηναίων τὸ πρῶτον,
ἔπειτα δέ, ὡς οὐκ ἀντιπροῆισαν αὐτοῖς, ἀναχωρήσαντες καὶ διαβάντες
τὴν Ἑλωρίνην ὁδὸν ηὐλίσαντο.

Τῆι δ᾽ ὑστεραίαι οἱ Ἀθηναῖοι καὶ οἱ ξύμμαχοι παρεσκευάζοντο ὡς 67
ἐς μάχην καὶ ξυνετάξαντο ὧδε. δεξιὸν μὲν κέρας Ἀργεῖοι εἶχον καὶ
Μαντινῆς, Ἀθηναῖοι δὲ τὸ μέσον, τὸ δὲ ἄλλο οἱ ξύμμαχοι οἱ ἄλλοι. καὶ

65.1 παρεσκευάσθαι del. Duker   65.3 ἐς τὸ E: ἐς τὸν ABCFGM μέγαν λιμένα post κατὰ τὸ Ὀλυμπιεῖον add. H²   66.2 ἔρυμά τε vett., lemma Σ: ἔρυμά τι recc. (coni. Krüger)

τὸ μὲν ἥμισυ αὐτοῖς τοῦ στρατεύματος ἐν τῶι πρόσθεν ἦν τεταγμένον ἐπὶ ὀκτώ, τὸ δὲ ἥμισυ ἐπὶ ταῖς εὐναῖς ἐν πλαισίωι, ἐπὶ ὀκτὼ καὶ τοῦτο τεταγμένον· οἷς εἴρητο, ἧι ἂν τοῦ στρατεύματός τι πονῆι μάλιστα, ἐφορῶντας παραγίγνεσθαι. καὶ τοὺς σκευοφόρους ἐντὸς τούτων τῶν
2 ἐπιτάκτων ἐποιήσαντο. οἱ δὲ Συρακόσιοι ἔταξαν τοὺς μὲν ὁπλίτας πάντας ἐφ' ἑκκαίδεκα, ὄντας πανδημεὶ Συρακοσίους καὶ ὅσοι ξύμμαχοι παρῆσαν (ἐβοήθησαν δὲ αὐτοῖς Σελινούντιοι μὲν μάλιστα, ἔπειτα δὲ καὶ Γελώιων ἱππῆς, τὸ ξύμπαν ἐς διακοσίους, καὶ Καμαριναίων ἱππῆς ὅσον εἴκοσι καὶ τοξόται ὡς πεντήκοντα), τοὺς δὲ ἱππέας ἐπετάξαντο ἐπὶ τῶι δεξιῶι, οὐκ ἔλασσον ὄντας ἢ διακοσίους καὶ χιλίους, παρὰ δ'
3 αὐτοὺς καὶ τοὺς ἀκοντιστάς. μέλλουσι δὲ τοῖς Ἀθηναίοις προτέροις ἐπιχειρήσειν ὁ Νικίας κατά τε ἔθνη ἐπιπαριὼν ἕκαστα καὶ ξύμπασι τοιάδε παρεκελεύετο.

68 'Πολλῆι μὲν παραινέσει, ὦ ἄνδρες, τί δεῖ χρῆσθαι, οἳ πάρεσμεν ἐπὶ τὸν αὐτὸν ἀγῶνα; αὐτὴ γὰρ ἡ παρασκευὴ ἱκανωτέρα μοι δοκεῖ εἶναι θάρσος παρασχεῖν ἢ καλῶς λεχθέντες λόγοι μετὰ ἀσθενοῦς στρατοπέδου.
2 ὅπου γὰρ Ἀργεῖοι καὶ Μαντινῆς καὶ Ἀθηναῖοι καὶ νησιωτῶν οἱ πρῶτοί ἐσμεν, πῶς οὐ χρὴ μετὰ τοιῶνδε καὶ τοσῶνδε ξυμμάχων πάντα τινὰ μεγάλην τὴν ἐλπίδα τῆς νίκης ἔχειν, ἄλλως τε καὶ πρὸς ἄνδρας πανδημεί τε ἀμυνομένους καὶ οὐκ ἀπολέκτους ὥσπερ καὶ ἡμᾶς, καὶ προσέτι Σικελιώτας, οἳ ὑπερφρονοῦσι μὲν ἡμᾶς, ὑπομενοῦσι δὲ οὔ, διὰ τὸ τὴν
3 ἐπιστήμην τῆς τόλμης ἥσσω ἔχειν. παραστήτω δέ τινι καὶ τόδε, πολύ τε ἀπὸ τῆς ἡμετέρας αὐτῶν εἶναι καὶ πρὸς γῆι οὐδεμιᾶι φιλίαι, ἥντινα μὴ αὐτοὶ μαχόμενοι κτήσεσθε. καὶ τοὐναντίον ὑπομιμνήισκω ὑμᾶς ἢ οἱ πολέμιοι σφίσιν αὐτοῖς εὖ οἶδ' ὅτι παρακελεύονται· οἱ μὲν γὰρ ὅτι περὶ πατρίδος ἔσται ὁ ἀγών, ἐγὼ δὲ ὅτι οὐκ ἐν πατρίδι, ἐξ ἧς κρατεῖν
4 δεῖ ἢ μὴ ῥαιδίως ἀποχωρεῖν· οἱ γὰρ ἱππῆς πολλοὶ ἐπικείσονται. τῆς τε οὖν ὑμετέρας αὐτῶν ἀξίας μνησθέντες ἐπέλθετε τοῖς ἐναντίοις προθύμως, καὶ τὴν παροῦσαν ἀνάγκην καὶ ἀπορίαν φοβερωτέραν ἡγησάμενοι τῶν πολεμίων.'

69 Ὁ μὲν Νικίας τοιαῦτα παρακελευσάμενος ἐπῆγε τὸ στρατόπεδον εὐθύς. οἱ δὲ Συρακόσιοι ἀπροσδόκητοι μὲν ἐν τῶι καιρῶι τούτωι ἦσαν ὡς ἤδη μαχούμενοι, καί τινες αὐτοῖς ἐγγὺς τῆς πόλεως οὔσης καὶ ἀπεληλύθεσαν· οἱ δὲ καὶ διὰ σπουδῆς προσβοηθοῦντες δρόμωι ὑστέριζον μέν, ὡς δὲ ἕκαστός πηι τοῖς πλέοσι προσμείξειε καθίσταντο. οὐ γὰρ δὴ προθυμίαι ἐλλιπεῖς ἦσαν οὐδὲ τόλμηι οὔτ' ἐν ταύτηι τῆι μάχηι οὔτ' ἐν ταῖς ἄλλαις, ἀλλὰ τῆι μὲν ἀνδρείαι οὐχ ἥσσους ἐς ὅσον ἡ ἐπιστήμη ἀντέχοι, τῶι δὲ ἐλλείποντι αὐτῆς καὶ τὴν βούλησιν ἄκοντες προυδίδοσαν. ὅμως δὲ οὐκ

ἂν οἰόμενοι σφίσι τοὺς Ἀθηναίους προτέρους ἐπελθεῖν καὶ διὰ τάχους ἀναγκαζόμενοι ἀμύνασθαι, ἀναλαβόντες τὰ ὅπλα εὐθὺς ἀντεπῇσαν. καὶ πρῶτον μὲν αὐτῶν ἑκατέρων οἵ τε λιθοβόλοι καὶ σφενδονῆται καὶ 2 τοξόται προυμάχοντο καὶ τροπάς, οἵας εἰκὸς ψιλούς, ἀλλήλων ἐποίουν· ἔπειτα δὲ μάντεις τε σφάγια προύφερον τὰ νομιζόμενα καὶ σαλπικταὶ ξύνοδον ἐπώτρυνον τοῖς ὁπλίταις, οἱ δ' ἐχώρουν, Συρακόσιοι μὲν περί τε 3 πατρίδος μαχούμενοι καὶ τῆς ἰδίας ἕκαστος τὸ μὲν αὐτίκα σωτηρίας, τὸ δὲ μέλλον ἐλευθερίας, τῶν δ' ἐναντίων Ἀθηναῖοι μὲν περί τε τῆς ἀλλοτρίας οἰκείαν σχεῖν καὶ τὴν οἰκείαν μὴ βλάψαι ἡσσώμενοι, Ἀργεῖοι δὲ καὶ τῶν ξυμμάχων οἱ αὐτόνομοι ξυγκτήσασθαί τε ἐκείνοις ἐφ' ἃ ἦλθον καὶ τὴν ὑπάρχουσαν σφίσι πατρίδα νικήσαντες πάλιν ἐπιδεῖν· τὸ δ' ὑπήκοον τῶν ξυμμάχων μέγιστον μὲν περὶ τῆς αὐτίκα ἀνελπίστου σωτηρίας, ἢν μὴ κρατῶσι, τὸ πρόθυμον εἶχον, ἔπειτα δὲ ἐν παρέργωι καὶ εἴ τι ἄλλο ξυγκαταστρεψαμένοι ῥᾶιον αὐτοῖς ὑπακούσονται. γενομένης δ' ἐν χερσὶ 70 τῆς μάχης ἐπὶ πολὺ ἀντεῖχον ἀλλήλοις, καὶ ξυνέβη βροντάς τε ἅμα τινὰς γενέσθαι καὶ ἀστραπὰς καὶ ὕδωρ πολύ, ὥστε τοῖς μὲν πρῶτον μαχομένοις καὶ ἐλάχιστα πολέμωι ὡμιληκόσι καὶ τοῦτο ξυνεπιλαβέσθαι τοῦ φόβου, τοῖς δ' ἐμπειροτέροις τὰ μὲν γιγνόμενα καὶ ὥραι ἔτους περαίνεσθαι δοκεῖν, τοὺς δὲ ἀνθεστῶτας πολὺ μείζω ἔκπληξιν μὴ νικωμένους παρέχειν. ὠσαμένων δὲ τῶν Ἀργείων πρῶτον τὸ εὐώνυμον κέρας τῶν Συρακοσίων 2 καὶ μετ' αὐτοὺς τῶν Ἀθηναίων τὸ κατὰ σφᾶς αὐτούς, παρερρήγνυτο ἤδη καὶ τὸ ἄλλο στράτευμα τῶν Συρακοσίων καὶ ἐς φυγὴν κατέστη. καὶ 3 ἐπὶ πολὺ μὲν οὐκ ἐδίωξαν οἱ Ἀθηναῖοι (οἱ γὰρ ἱππῆς τῶν Συρακοσίων πολλοὶ ὄντες καὶ ἀήσσητοι εἶργον, καὶ ἐσβαλόντες ἐς τοὺς ὁπλίτας αὐτῶν, εἴ τινας προδιώκοντας ἴδοιεν, ἀνέστελλον), ἐπακολουθήσαντες δὲ ἁθρόοι ὅσον ἀσφαλῶς εἶχε πάλιν ἐπανεχώρουν καὶ τροπαῖον ἵστασαν. οἱ δὲ 4 Συρακόσιοι ἁθροισθέντες ἐς τὴν Ἑλωρίνην ὁδὸν καὶ ὡς ἐκ τῶν παρόντων ξυνταξάμενοι ἔς τε τὸ Ὀλυμπιεῖον ὅμως σφῶν αὐτῶν παρέπεμψαν φυλακήν, δείσαντες μὴ οἱ Ἀθηναῖοι τῶν χρημάτων ἃ ἦν αὐτόθι κινήσωσι, καὶ οἱ λοιποὶ ἐπανεχώρησαν ἐς τὴν πόλιν. οἱ δὲ Ἀθηναῖοι πρὸς μὲν τὸ 71 ἱερὸν οὐκ ἦλθον, ξυγκομίσαντες δὲ τοὺς ἑαυτῶν νεκροὺς καὶ ἐπὶ πυρὰν ἐπιθέντες ηὐλίσαντο αὐτοῦ. τῆι δ' ὑστεραίαι τοῖς μὲν Συρακοσίοις ἀπέδοσαν ὑποσπόνδους τοὺς νεκρούς (ἀπέθανον δὲ αὐτῶν καὶ τῶν ξυμμάχων περὶ ἑξήκοντα καὶ διακοσίους), τῶν δὲ σφετέρων τὰ ὀστᾶ ἀνέλεξαν (ἀπέθανον δὲ αὐτῶν καὶ τῶν ξυμμάχων ὡς πεντήκοντα), καὶ τὰ

69.3 ξυγκαταστρεψάμενοι... ὑπακούσονται H² Σ (coni. Haacke): -οι... ὑπακούσεται E; -οις... ὑπακούσεται cett.

2 τῶν πολεμίων σκῦλα ἔχοντες ἀπέπλευσαν ἐς Κατάνην· χειμών τε γὰρ ἦν καὶ τὸν πόλεμον αὐτόθεν ποιεῖσθαι οὔπω ἐδόκει δυνατὸν εἶναι, πρὶν ἂν ἱππέας τε μεταπέμψωσιν ἐκ τῶν Ἀθηνῶν καὶ ἐκ τῶν αὐτόθεν ξυμμάχων ἀγείρωσιν, ὅπως μὴ παντάπασιν ἱπποκρατῶνται, καὶ χρήματα δὲ ἅμα αὐτόθεν τε ξυλλέξωνται καὶ παρ' Ἀθηναίων ἔλθηι, τῶν τε πόλεών τινας προσαγάγωνται, ἃς ἤλπιζον μετὰ τὴν μάχην μᾶλλον σφῶν ὑπακούσεσθαι, τά τε ἄλλα καὶ σῖτον καὶ ὅσων δέοι παρασκευάσωνται ὡς ἐς τὸ ἔαρ ἐπιχειρήσοντες ταῖς Συρακούσαις.

72 Καὶ οἱ μὲν ταύτηι τῆι γνώμηι ἀπέπλευσαν ἐς τὴν Νάξον καὶ Κατάνην διαχειμάσοντες, Συρακόσιοι δὲ τοὺς σφετέρους αὐτῶν νεκροὺς θάψαντες
2 ἐκκλησίαν ἐποίουν. καὶ παρελθὼν αὐτοῖς Ἑρμοκράτης ὁ Ἕρμωνος, ἀνὴρ καὶ ἐς τἆλλα ξύνεσιν οὐδενὸς λειπόμενος καὶ κατὰ τὸν πόλεμον ἐμπειρίαι τε ἱκανὸς γενόμενος καὶ ἀνδρείαι ἐπιφανής, ἐθάρσυνέ τε καὶ οὐκ εἴα τῶι
3 γεγενημένωι ἐνδιδόναι· τὴν μὲν γὰρ γνώμην αὐτῶν οὐχ ἡσσῆσθαι, τὴν δὲ ἀταξίαν βλάψαι. οὐ μέντοι τοσοῦτόν γε λειφθῆναι ὅσον εἰκὸς εἶναι, ἄλλως τε καὶ τοῖς πρώτοις τῶν Ἑλλήνων ἐμπειρίαι ἰδιώτας ὡς
4 εἰπεῖν χειροτέχναις ἀνταγωνισαμένους. μέγα δὲ βλάψαι καὶ τὸ πλῆθος τῶν στρατηγῶν καὶ τὴν πολυαρχίαν (ἦσαν γὰρ πεντεκαίδεκα οἱ στρατηγοὶ αὐτοῖς) τῶν τε πολλῶν τὴν ἀξύντακτον ἀναρχίαν. ἢν δὲ ὀλίγοι τε στρατηγοὶ γένωνται ἔμπειροι καὶ ἐν τῶι χειμῶνι τούτωι παρασκευάσωσι τὸ ὁπλιτικόν, οἷς τε ὅπλα μὴ ἔστιν ἐκπορίζοντες, ὅπως ὡς πλεῖστοι ἔσονται, καὶ τῆι ἄλληι μελέτηι προσαναγκάζοντες, ἔφη κατὰ τὸ εἰκὸς κρατήσειν σφᾶς τῶν ἐναντίων, ἀνδρείας μὲν σφίσιν ὑπαρχούσης, εὐταξίας δ' ἐς τὰ ἔργα προσγενομένης· ἐπιδώσειν γὰρ ἀμφότερα αὐτά, τὴν μὲν μετὰ κινδύνων μελετωμένην, τὴν δ' εὐψυχίαν αὐτὴν ἑαυτῆς μετὰ τοῦ πιστοῦ τῆς ἐπιστήμης θαρσαλεωτέραν ἔσεσθαι.
5 τούς τε στρατηγοὺς καὶ ὀλίγους καὶ αὐτοκράτορας χρῆναι ἑλέσθαι καὶ ὀμόσαι αὐτοῖς τὸ ὅρκιον ἦ μὴν ἐάσειν ἄρχειν ὅπηι ἂν ἐπίστωνται· οὕτω γὰρ ἅ τε κρύπτεσθαι δεῖ μᾶλλον ἂν στέγεσθαι καὶ τἆλλα κατὰ
73 κόσμον καὶ ἀπροφασίστως παρασκευασθῆναι. καὶ οἱ Συρακόσιοι αὐτοῦ ἀκούσαντες ἐψηφίσαντό τε πάντα ὡς ἐκέλευε καὶ στρατηγὸν αὐτόν τε εἵλοντο τὸν Ἑρμοκράτη καὶ Ἡρακλείδην τὸν Λυσιμάχου
2 καὶ Σικανὸν τὸν Ἐξηκέστου, τούτους τρεῖς, καὶ ἐς τὴν Κόρινθον καὶ ἐς τὴν Λακεδαίμονα πρέσβεις ἀπέστειλαν, ὅπως ξυμμαχία τε αὐτοῖς παραγένηται καὶ τὸν πρὸς Ἀθηναίους πόλεμον βεβαιότερον πείθωσι ποιεῖσθαι ἐκ τοῦ προφανοῦς ὑπὲρ σφῶν τοὺς Λακεδαιμονίους, ἵνα ἢ ἀπὸ τῆς Σικελίας ἀπαγάγωσιν αὐτοὺς ἢ πρὸς τὸ ἐν Σικελίαι στράτευμα ἧσσον ὠφελίαν ἄλλην ἐπιπέμπωσιν.

Τὸ δ' ἐν τῆι Κατάνηι στράτευμα τῶν Ἀθηναίων ἔπλευσεν εὐθὺς ἐπὶ 74 Μεσσήνην ὡς προδοθησομένην. καὶ ἃ μὲν ἐπράσσετο οὐκ ἐγένετο· Ἀλκιβιάδης γὰρ ὅτ' ἀπῆιει ἐκ τῆς ἀρχῆς ἤδη μετάπεμπτος, ἐπιστάμενος ὅτι φεύξοιτο, μηνύει τοῖς τῶν Συρακοσίων φίλοις τοῖς ἐν τῆι Μεσσήνηι ξυνειδὼς τὸ μέλλον· οἱ δὲ τούς τε ἄνδρας διέφθειραν πρότερον καὶ τότε στασιάζοντες καὶ ἐν ὅπλοις ὄντες ἐπεκράτουν μὴ δέχεσθαι τοὺς Ἀθηναίους οἱ ταῦτα βουλόμενοι. ἡμέρας δὲ μείναντες περὶ τρεῖς καὶ δέκα οἱ Ἀθηναῖοι 2 ὡς ἐχειμάζοντο καὶ τὰ ἐπιτήδεια οὐκ εἶχον καὶ προυχώρει οὐδέν, ἀπελθόντες ἐς Νάξον καὶ ὅρια καὶ σταυρώματα περὶ τὸ στρατόπεδον ποιησάμενοι αὐτοῦ διεχείμαζον· καὶ τριήρη ἀπέστειλαν ἐς τὰς Ἀθήνας ἐπί τε χρήματα καὶ ἱππέας, ὅπως ἅμα τῶι ἦρι παραγένωνται.

Ἐτείχιζον δὲ καὶ οἱ Συρακόσιοι ἐν τῶι χειμῶνι πρός τε τῆι πόλει, 75 τὸν Τεμενίτην ἐντὸς ποιησάμενοι, τεῖχος παρὰ πᾶν τὸ πρὸς τὰς Ἐπιπολὰς ὁρῶν, ὅπως μὴ δι' ἐλάσσονος εὐαποτείχιστοι ὦσιν, ἢν ἄρα σφάλλωνται, καὶ τὰ Μέγαρα φρούριον, καὶ ἐν τῶι Ὀλυμπιείωι ἄλλο· καὶ τὴν θάλασσαν προυσταύρωσαν πανταχῆι ἧι ἀποβάσεις ἦσαν. καὶ τοὺς 2 Ἀθηναίους εἰδότες ἐν τῆι Νάξωι χειμάζοντας ἐστράτευσαν πανδημεὶ ἐπὶ τὴν Κατάνην, καὶ τῆς τε γῆς αὐτῶν ἔτεμον καὶ τὰς τῶν Ἀθηναίων σκηνὰς καὶ τὸ στρατόπεδον ἐμπρήσαντες ἀνεχώρησαν ἐπ' οἴκου. καὶ 3 πυνθανόμενοι τοὺς Ἀθηναίους ἐς τὴν Καμάριναν κατὰ τὴν ἐπὶ Λάχητος γενομένην ξυμμαχίαν πρεσβεύεσθαι, εἴ πως προσαγάγοιντο αὐτούς, ἀντεπρεσβεύοντο καὶ αὐτοί· ἦσαν γὰρ ὕποπτοι αὐτοῖς οἱ Καμαριναῖοι μὴ προθύμως σφίσι μήτ' ἐπὶ τὴν πρώτην μάχην πέμψαι ἃ ἔπεμψαν, ἔς τε τὸ λοιπὸν μὴ οὐκέτι βούλωνται ἀμύνειν, ὁρῶντες τοὺς Ἀθηναίους ἐν τῆι μάχηι εὖ πράξαντας, προσχωρῶσι δ' αὐτοῖς κατὰ τὴν προτέραν φιλίαν πεισθέντες. ἀφικομένων οὖν ἐκ μὲν Συρακουσῶν Ἑρμοκράτους καὶ 4 ἄλλων ἐς τὴν Καμάριναν, ἀπὸ δὲ τῶν Ἀθηναίων Εὐφήμου μεθ' ἑτέρων, ὁ Ἑρμοκράτης ξυλλόγου γενομένου τῶν Καμαριναίων βουλόμενος προδιαβάλλειν τοὺς Ἀθηναίους ἔλεγε τοιάδε.

Οὐ τὴν παροῦσαν δύναμιν τῶν Ἀθηναίων, ὦ Καμαριναῖοι, μὴ αὐτὴν 76 καταπλαγῆτε δείσαντες ἐπρεσβευσάμεθα, ἀλλὰ μᾶλλον τοὺς μέλλοντας ἀπ' αὐτῶν λόγους, πρίν τι καὶ ἡμῶν ἀκοῦσαι, μὴ ὑμᾶς πείσωσιν. ἥκουσι 2 γὰρ ἐς τὴν Σικελίαν προφάσει μὲν ἧι πυνθάνεσθε, διανοίαι δὲ ἣν πάντες ὑπονοοῦμεν· καί μοι δοκοῦσιν οὐ Λεοντίνους βούλεσθαι κατοικίσαι, ἀλλ' ἡμᾶς μᾶλλον ἐξοικίσαι. οὐ γὰρ δὴ εὔλογον τὰς μὲν ἐκεῖ πόλεις ἀναστάτους

74.2 ὅρια καὶ pler. edd.: ὅρα καὶ Σ γρ. ὅρια in marg. C³FΣM¹ Θρᾶικας uel Θρᾶκας (uar. acc.) codd. (eras. H²): χάρακας Portus, qui tamen deleuit ut glossema

ποιεῖν, τὰς δὲ ἐνθάδε κατοικίζειν, καὶ Λεοντίνων μὲν Χαλκιδέων ὄντων κατὰ τὸ ξυγγενὲς κήδεσθαι, Χαλκιδέας δὲ τοὺς ἐν Εὐβοίαι, ὧν οἵδε
3 ἄποικοί εἰσι, δουλωσαμένους ἔχειν. τῆι δὲ αὐτῆι ἰδέαι ἐκεῖνά τε ἔσχον καὶ τὰ ἐνθάδε νῦν πειρῶνται· ἡγεμόνες γὰρ γενόμενοι ἑκόντων τῶν τε Ἰώνων καὶ ὅσοι ἀπὸ σφῶν ἦσαν ξύμμαχοι ὡς ἐπὶ τοῦ Μήδου τιμωρίαι, τοὺς μὲν λιποστρατίαν, τοὺς δὲ ἐπ' ἀλλήλους στρατεύειν, τοῖς δ' ὡς
4 ἑκάστοις τινὰ εἶχον αἰτίαν εὐπρεπῆ ἐπενεγκόντες κατεστρέψαντο. καὶ οὐ περὶ τῆς ἐλευθερίας ἄρα οὔτε οὗτοι τῶν Ἑλλήνων οὔθ' οἱ Ἕλληνες τῆς ἑαυτῶν τῶι Μήδωι ἀντέστησαν, περὶ δὲ οἱ μὲν σφίσιν ἀλλὰ μὴ ἐκείνωι καταδουλώσεως, οἱ δ' ἐπὶ δεσπότου μεταβολῆι οὐκ ἀξυνετωτέρου, κακοξυνετωτέρου δέ.

77 Ἀλλ' οὐ γὰρ δὴ τὴν τῶν Ἀθηναίων εὐκατηγόρητον οὖσαν πόλιν νῦν ἥκομεν ἀποφανοῦντες ἐν εἰδόσιν ὅσα ἀδικεῖ, πολὺ δὲ μᾶλλον ἡμᾶς αὐτοὺς αἰτιασόμενοι ὅτι ἔχοντες παραδείγματα τῶν τ' ἐκεῖ Ἑλλήνων ὡς ἐδουλώθησαν οὐκ ἀμύνοντες σφίσιν αὐτοῖς, καὶ νῦν ἐφ' ἡμᾶς ταὐτὰ παρόντα σοφίσματα, Λεοντίνων τε ξυγγενῶν κατοικίσεις καὶ Ἐγεσταίων ξυμμάχων ἐπικουρίας, οὐ ξυστραφέντες βουλόμεθα προθυμότερον δεῖξαι αὐτοῖς ὅτι οὐκ Ἴωνες τάδε εἰσὶν οὐδ' Ἑλλησπόντιοι καὶ νησιῶται, οἳ δεσπότην ἢ Μῆδον ἢ ἕνα γέ τινα αἰεὶ μεταβάλλοντες δουλοῦνται, ἀλλὰ Δωριῆς ἐλεύθεροι ἀπ' αὐτονόμου τῆς Πελοποννήσου τὴν Σικελίαν
2 οἰκοῦντες. ἢ μένομεν ἕως ἂν ἕκαστοι κατὰ πόλεις ληφθῶμεν, εἰδότες ὅτι ταύτηι μόνον ἁλωτοί ἐσμεν καὶ ὁρῶντες αὐτοὺς ἐπὶ τοῦτο τὸ εἶδος τρεπομένους ὥστε τοὺς μὲν λόγοις ἡμῶν διιστάναι, τοὺς δὲ ξυμμάχων ἐλπίδι ἐκπολεμοῦν πρὸς ἀλλήλους, τοὺς δὲ ὡς ἑκάστοις τι προσηνὲς λέγοντες δύνανται κακουργεῖν; καὶ οἰόμεθα τοῦ ἄπωθεν ξυνοίκου προαπολλυμένου οὐ καὶ ἐς αὐτόν τινα ἥξειν τὸ δεινόν, πρὸ δὲ αὐτοῦ
78 μᾶλλον τὸν πάσχοντα καθ' ἑαυτὸν δυστυχεῖν; καὶ εἴ τωι ἄρα παρέστηκε τὸν μὲν Συρακόσιον, ἑαυτὸν δ' οὒ πολέμιον εἶναι τῶι Ἀθηναίωι, καὶ δεινὸν ἡγεῖται ὑπέρ γε τῆς ἐμῆς κινδυνεύειν, ἐνθυμηθήτω οὐ περὶ τῆς ἐμῆς μᾶλλον, ἐν ἴσωι δὲ καὶ τῆς ἑαυτοῦ ἅμα ἐν τῆι ἐμῆι μαχούμενος, τοσούτωι δὲ καὶ ἀσφαλέστερον ὅσωι οὐ προδιεφθαρμένου ἐμοῦ, ἔχων δὲ ξύμμαχον ἐμὲ καὶ οὐκ ἔρημος ἀγωνιεῖται, τόν τε Ἀθηναῖον μὴ τὴν τοῦ Συρακοσίου ἔχθραν κολάσασθαι, τῆι δ' ἐμῆι προφάσει τὴν ἐκείνου φιλίαν
2 οὐχ ἧσσον βεβαιώσασθαι βούλεσθαι. εἴ τέ τις φθονεῖ μὲν ἢ καὶ φοβεῖται (ἀμφότερα γὰρ τάδε πάσχει τὰ μείζω), διὰ δὲ αὐτὰ τὰς Συρακούσας

77.2 τοὺς δὲ ante ὡς ἑκάστοις Badham: τοῖς δὲ codd.

κακωθῆναι μὲν ἵνα σωφρονισθῶμεν βούλεται, περιγενέσθαι δὲ ἕνεκα τῆς αὑτοῦ ἀσφαλείας, οὐκ ἀνθρωπίνης δυνάμεως βούλησιν ἐλπίζει· οὐ γὰρ οἷόν τε ἅμα τῆς τε ἐπιθυμίας καὶ τῆς τύχης τὸν αὐτὸν ὁμοίως ταμίαν γενέσθαι. καὶ εἰ γνώμηι ἁμάρτοι, τοῖς αὑτοῦ κακοῖς ὀλοφυρθεὶς τάχ᾽ ἂν 3 ἴσως καὶ τοῖς ἐμοῖς ἀγαθοῖς ποτὲ βουληθείη αὖθις φθονῆσαι. ἀδύνατον δὲ προεμένωι καὶ μὴ τοὺς αὐτοὺς κινδύνους οὐ περὶ τῶν ὀνομάτων, ἀλλὰ περὶ τῶν ἔργων, ἐθελήσαντι προσλαβεῖν· λόγωι μὲν γὰρ τὴν ἡμετέραν δύναμιν σώιζοι ἄν τις, ἔργωι δὲ τὴν αὑτοῦ σωτηρίαν. καὶ μάλιστα εἰκὸς 4 ἦν ὑμᾶς, ὦ Καμαριναῖοι, ὁμόρους ὄντας καὶ τὰ δεύτερα κινδυνεύσοντας προορᾶσθαι αὐτὰ καὶ μὴ μαλακῶς ὥσπερ νῦν ξυμμαχεῖν, αὐτοὺς δὲ πρὸς ἡμᾶς μᾶλλον ἰόντας, ἅπερ ἂν εἰ ἐς τὴν Καμαριναίαν πρῶτον ἀφίκοντο οἱ Ἀθηναῖοι δεόμενοι ἂν ἐπεκαλεῖσθε, ταῦτα ἐκ τοῦ ὁμοίου καὶ νῦν παρακελευομένους ὅπως μηδὲν ἐνδώσομεν φαίνεσθαι. ἀλλ᾽ οὔθ᾽ ὑμεῖς νῦν γέ πω οὔθ᾽ οἱ ἄλλοι ἐπὶ ταῦτα ὥρμησθε.

'Δειλίαι δὲ ἴσως τὸ δίκαιον πρός τε ἡμᾶς καὶ πρὸς τοὺς ἐπιόντας 79 θεραπεύσετε, λέγοντες ξυμμαχίαν εἶναι ὑμῖν πρὸς Ἀθηναίους· ἥν γε οὐκ ἐπὶ τοῖς φίλοις ἐποιήσασθε, τῶν δὲ ἐχθρῶν ἤν τις ἐφ᾽ ὑμᾶς ἴηι, καὶ τοῖς γε Ἀθηναίοις βοηθεῖν, ὅταν ὑπ᾽ ἄλλων καὶ μὴ αὐτοὶ ὥσπερ νῦν τοὺς πέλας ἀδικῶσιν, ἐπεὶ οὐδ᾽ οἱ Ῥηγῖνοι ὄντες Χαλκιδῆς Χαλκιδέας ὄντας Λεοντίνους ἐθέλουσι ξυγκατοικίζειν. καὶ δεινὸν εἰ ἐκεῖνοι μὲν τὸ ἔργον 2 τοῦ καλοῦ δικαιώματος ὑποπτεύοντες ἀλόγως σωφρονοῦσιν, ὑμεῖς δ᾽ εὐλόγωι προφάσει τοὺς μὲν φύσει πολεμίους βούλεσθε ὠφελεῖν, τοὺς δὲ ἔτι μᾶλλον φύσει ξυγγενεῖς μετὰ τῶν ἐχθίστων διαφθεῖραι. ἀλλ᾽ οὐ 3 δίκαιον, ἀμύνειν δὲ καὶ μὴ φοβεῖσθαι τὴν παρασκευὴν αὐτῶν· οὐ γὰρ ἢν ἡμεῖς ξυστῶμεν πάντες δεινή ἐστιν, ἀλλ᾽ ἤν, ὅπερ οὗτοι σπεύδουσι, τἀναντία διαστῶμεν, ἐπεὶ οὐδὲ πρὸς ἡμᾶς μόνους ἐλθόντες καὶ μάχηι περιγενόμενοι ἔπραξαν ἃ ἐβούλοντο, ἀπῆλθον δὲ διὰ τάχους. ὥστε οὐχ 80 ἀθρόους γε ὄντας εἰκὸς ἀθυμεῖν, ἰέναι δὲ ἐς τὴν ξυμμαχίαν προθυμότερον, ἄλλως τε καὶ ἀπὸ Πελοποννήσου παρεσομένης ὠφελίας, οἳ τῶνδε κρείσσους εἰσὶ τὸ παράπαν τὰ πολέμια· καὶ μὴ ἐκείνην τὴν προμηθίαν δοκεῖν τωι ἡμῖν μὲν ἴσην εἶναι, ὑμῖν δὲ ἀσφαλῆ, τὸ μηδετέροις δὴ ὡς καὶ ἀμφοτέρων ὄντας ξυμμάχους βοηθεῖν. οὐ γὰρ ἔργωι ἴσον ὥσπερ 2 τῶι δικαιώματί ἐστιν. εἰ γὰρ δι᾽ ὑμᾶς μὴ ξυμμαχήσαντας ὅ τε παθὼν σφαλήσεται καὶ ὁ κρατῶν περιέσται, τί ἄλλο ἢ τῆι αὐτῆι ἀπουσίαι τοῖς μὲν οὐκ ἠμύνατε σωθῆναι, τοὺς δὲ οὐκ ἐκωλύσατε κακοὺς γενέσθαι; καίτοι κάλλιον τοῖς ἀδικουμένοις καὶ ἅμα ξυγγενέσι προσθεμένους τήν τε κοινὴν ὠφελίαν τῆι Σικελίαι φυλάξαι καὶ τοὺς Ἀθηναίους φίλους δὴ ὄντας μὴ ἐᾶσαι ἁμαρτεῖν.

3 Ξυνελόντες τε λέγομεν οἱ Συρακόσιοι ἐκδιδάσκειν μὲν οὐδὲν ἔργον εἶναι σαφῶς οὔτε ὑμᾶς οὔτε τοὺς ἄλλους περὶ ὧν αὐτοὶ οὐδὲν χεῖρον γιγνώσκετε· δεόμεθα δὲ καὶ μαρτυρόμεθα ἅμα, εἰ μὴ πείσομεν, ὅτι ἐπιβουλευόμεθα μὲν ὑπὸ Ἰώνων αἰεὶ πολεμίων, προδιδόμεθα δὲ ὑφ' ὑμῶν
4 Δωριῆς Δωριῶν. καὶ εἰ καταστρέψονται ἡμᾶς Ἀθηναῖοι, ταῖς μὲν ὑμετέραις γνώμαις κρατήσουσι, τῶι δ' αὑτῶν ὀνόματι τιμηθήσονται, καὶ τῆς νίκης οὐκ ἄλλον τινὰ ἆθλον ἢ τὸν τὴν νίκην παρασχόντα λήψονται· καὶ εἰ αὖ ἡμεῖς περιεσόμεθα, τῆς αἰτίας τῶν κινδύνων οἱ αὐτοὶ τὴν τιμωρίαν
5 ὑφέξετε. σκοπεῖτε οὖν καὶ αἱρεῖσθε ἤδη ἢ τὴν αὐτίκα ἀκινδύνως δουλείαν ἢ κἂν περιγενόμενοι μεθ' ἡμῶν τούσδε τε μὴ αἰσχρῶς δεσπότας λαβεῖν καὶ τὴν πρὸς ἡμᾶς ἔχθραν μὴ ἂν βραχεῖαν γενομένην διαφυγεῖν.'
81 Τοιαῦτα μὲν ὁ Ἑρμοκράτης εἶπεν, ὁ δ' Εὔφημος ὁ τῶν Ἀθηναίων πρεσβευτὴς μετ' αὐτὸν τοιάδε.
82 'Ἀφικόμεθα μὲν ἐπὶ τῆς πρότερον οὔσης ξυμμαχίας ἀνανεώσει, τοῦ δὲ Συρακοσίου καθαψαμένου ἀνάγκη καὶ περὶ τῆς ἀρχῆς εἰπεῖν ὡς
2 εἰκότως ἔχομεν. τὸ μὲν οὖν μέγιστον μαρτύριον αὐτὸς εἶπεν, ὅτι οἱ Ἴωνες αἰεί ποτε πολέμιοι τοῖς Δωριεῦσιν εἰσίν. ἔχει δὲ καὶ οὕτως· ἡμεῖς γὰρ Ἴωνες ὄντες Πελοποννησίοις Δωριεῦσι καὶ πλέοσιν οὖσι καὶ παροικοῦσιν
3 ἐσκεψάμεθα ὅτωι τρόπωι ἥκιστα [αὐτῶν] ὑπακουσόμεθα, καὶ μετὰ τὰ Μηδικὰ ναῦς κτησάμενοι τῆς μὲν Λακεδαιμονίων ἀρχῆς καὶ ἡγεμονίας ἀπηλλάγημεν, οὐδὲν προσῆκον μᾶλλόν τι ἐκείνους ἡμῖν ἢ καὶ ἡμᾶς ἐκείνοις ἐπιτάσσειν, πλὴν καθ' ὅσον ἐν τῶι παρόντι μεῖζον ἴσχυον, αὐτοὶ δὲ τῶν ὑπὸ βασιλεῖ πρότερον ὄντων ἡγεμόνες καταστάντες οἰκοῦμεν, νομίσαντες ἥκιστ' ἂν ὑπὸ Πελοποννησίοις οὕτως εἶναι, δύναμιν ἔχοντες ἧι ἀμυνούμεθα, καὶ ἐς τὸ ἀκριβὲς εἰπεῖν οὐδὲ ἀδίκως καταστρεψάμενοι τούς τε Ἴωνας καὶ νησιώτας, οὓς ξυγγενεῖς φασὶν ὄντας ἡμᾶς Συρακόσιοι
4 δεδουλῶσθαι. ἦλθον γὰρ ἐπὶ τὴν μητρόπολιν ἐφ' ἡμᾶς μετὰ τοῦ Μήδου καὶ οὐκ ἐτόλμησαν ἀποστάντες τὰ οἰκεῖα φθεῖραι, ὥσπερ ἡμεῖς ἐκλιπόντες τὴν πόλιν, δουλείαν δὲ αὐτοί τε ἐβούλοντο καὶ ἡμῖν τὸ αὐτὸ ἐπενεγκεῖν.
83 ἀνθ' ὧν ἄξιοί τε ὄντες ἅμα ἄρχομεν, ὅτι τε ναυτικὸν πλεῖστόν τε καὶ προθυμίαν ἀπροφάσιστον παρεσχόμεθα ἐς τοὺς Ἕλληνας, καὶ διότι καὶ τῶι Μήδωι ἑτοίμως τοῦτο δρῶντες οὗτοι ἡμᾶς ἔβλαπτον, ἅμα δὲ τῆς
2 πρὸς Πελοποννησίους ἰσχύος ὀρεγόμενοι. καὶ οὐ καλλιεπούμεθα ὡς ἢ τὸν βάρβαρον μόνοι καθελόντες εἰκότως ἄρχομεν ἢ ἐπ' ἐλευθερίαι τῆι τῶνδε μᾶλλον ἢ τῶν ξυμπάντων τε καὶ τῆι ἡμετέραι αὐτῶν κινδυνεύσαντες. πᾶσι δὲ ἀνεπίφθονον τὴν προσήκουσαν σωτηρίαν ἐκπορίζεσθαι. καὶ

82.2 αὐτῶν del. Herwerden

νῦν τῆς ἡμετέρας ἀσφαλείας ἕνεκα καὶ ἐνθάδε παρόντες ὁρῶμεν καὶ ὑμῖν ταὐτὰ ξυμφέροντα. ἀποφαίνομεν δὲ ἐξ ὧν οἵδε τε διαβάλλουσι 3 καὶ ὑμεῖς μάλιστα ἐπὶ τὸ φοβερώτερον ὑπονοεῖτε, εἰδότες τοὺς περιδεῶς ὑποπτεύοντάς τι λόγου μὲν ἡδονῆι τὸ παραυτίκα τερπομένους, τῆι δ' ἐγχειρήσει ὕστερον τὰ ξυμφέροντα πράσσοντας. τήν τε γὰρ ἐκεῖ ἀρχὴν 4 εἰρήκαμεν διὰ δέος ἔχειν καὶ τὰ ἐνθάδε διὰ τὸ αὐτὸ ἥκειν μετὰ τῶν φίλων ἀσφαλῶς καταστησόμενοι, καὶ οὐ δουλωσόμενοι, μὴ παθεῖν δὲ μᾶλλον τοῦτο κωλύσοντες.

Ὑπολάβηι δὲ μηδεὶς ὡς οὐδὲν προσῆκον ὑμῶν κηδόμεθα, γνοὺς 84 ὅτι σωιζομένων ὑμῶν καὶ διὰ τὸ μὴ ἀσθενεῖς ὑμᾶς ὄντας ἀντέχειν Συρακοσίοις ἧσσον ἂν τούτων πεμψάντων τινὰ δύναμιν Πελοποννησίοις ἡμεῖς βλαπτοίμεθα. καὶ ἐν τούτωι προσήκετε ἤδη ἡμῖν τὰ μέγιστα. δι' 2 ὅπερ καὶ τοὺς Λεοντίνους εὔλογον κατοικίζειν μὴ ὑπηκόους ὥσπερ τοὺς ξυγγενεῖς αὐτῶν τοὺς ἐν Εὐβοίαι, ἀλλ' ὡς δυνατωτάτους, ἵνα ἐκ τῆς σφετέρας ὅμοροι ὄντες τοῖσδε ὑπὲρ ἡμῶν λυπηροὶ ὦσιν. τὰ μὲν 3 γὰρ ἐκεῖ καὶ αὐτοὶ ἀρκοῦμεν πρὸς τοὺς πολεμίους, καὶ ὁ Χαλκιδεύς, ὃν ἀλόγως ἡμᾶς φησὶ δουλωσαμένους τοὺς ἐνθάδε ἐλευθεροῦν, ξύμφορος ἡμῖν ἀπαράσκευος ὢν καὶ χρήματα μόνον φέρων, τὰ δὲ ἐνθάδε καὶ Λεοντῖνοι καὶ οἱ ἄλλοι φίλοι ὅτι μάλιστα αὐτονομούμενοι. ἀνδρὶ δὲ 85 τυράννωι ἢ πόλει ἀρχὴν ἐχούσηι οὐδὲν ἄλογον ὅ τι ξυμφέρον οὐδ' οἰκεῖον ὅ τι μὴ πιστόν· πρὸς ἕκαστα δὲ δεῖ ἢ ἐχθρὸν ἢ φίλον μετὰ καιροῦ γίγνεσθαι. καὶ ἡμᾶς τοῦτο ὠφελεῖ ἐνθάδε, οὐκ ἢν τοὺς φίλους κακώσωμεν, ἀλλ' ἢν οἱ ἐχθροὶ διὰ τὴν τῶν φίλων ῥώμην ἀδύνατοι ὦσιν. ἀπιστεῖν δὲ οὐ χρή· καὶ γὰρ τοὺς ἐκεῖ ξυμμάχους ὡς ἕκαστοι χρήσιμοι 2 ἐξηγούμεθα, Χίους μὲν καὶ Μηθυμναίους νεῶν παροκωχῆι αὐτονόμους, τοὺς δὲ πολλοὺς χρημάτων βιαιότερον φορᾶι, ἄλλους δὲ καὶ πάνυ ἐλευθέρως ξυμμαχοῦντας, καίπερ νησιώτας ὄντας καὶ εὐλήπτους, διότι ἐν χωρίοις ἐπικαίροις εἰσὶ περὶ τὴν Πελοπόννησον. ὥστε καὶ τἀνθάδε εἰκὸς 3 πρὸς τὸ λυσιτελοῦν καὶ, ὃ λέγομεν, ἐς Συρακοσίους δέος καθίστασθαι. ἀρχῆς γὰρ ἐφίενται ὑμῶν καὶ βούλονται ἐπὶ τῶι ἡμετέρωι ξυστήσαντες ὑμᾶς ὑπόπτωι, βίαι ἢ καὶ κατ' ἐρημίαν, ἀπράκτων ἡμῶν ἀπελθόντων, αὐτοὶ ἄρξαι τῆς Σικελίας. ἀνάγκη δέ, ἢν ξυστῆτε πρὸς αὐτούς· οὔτε γὰρ ἡμῖν ἔτι ἔσται ἰσχὺς τοσαύτη ἐς ἓν ξυστᾶσα εὐμεταχείριστος, οὔθ' οἵδ' ἀσθενεῖς ἂν ἡμῶν μὴ παρόντων πρὸς ὑμᾶς εἶεν. καὶ ὅτωι ταῦτα 86 μὴ δοκεῖ, αὐτὸ τὸ ἔργον ἐλέγχει. τὸ γὰρ πρότερον ἡμᾶς ἐπηγάγεσθε οὐκ ἄλλον τινὰ προσείοντες φόβον ἢ, εἰ περιοψόμεθα ὑμᾶς ὑπὸ Συρακοσίοις γενέσθαι, ὅτι καὶ αὐτοὶ κινδυνεύσομεν. καὶ νῦν οὐ δίκαιον, 2 ὧιπερ καὶ ἡμᾶς ἠξιοῦτε λόγωι πείθειν, τῶι αὐτῶι ἀπιστεῖν, οὐδ' ὅτι δυνάμει μείζονι πρὸς τὴν τῶνδε ἰσχὺν πάρεσμεν ὑποπτεύεσθαι, πολὺ

3 δὲ μᾶλλον τοῖσδε ἀπιστεῖν. ἡμεῖς μέν γε οὔτε ἐμμεῖναι δυνατοὶ μὴ μεθ' ὑμῶν, εἴ τε καὶ γενόμενοι κακοὶ κατεργασαίμεθα, ἀδύνατοι κατασχεῖν διὰ μῆκός τε πλοῦ καὶ ἀπορίαι φυλακῆς πόλεων μεγάλων καὶ τῆι παρασκευῆι ἠπειρωτίδων· οἵδε δὲ οὐ στρατοπέδωι, πόλει δὲ μείζονι τῆς ἡμετέρας παρουσίας ἐποικοῦντες ὑμῖν αἰεί τε ἐπιβουλεύουσι καί, ὅταν καιρὸν λάβωσιν ἑκάστου, οὐκ ἀνιᾶσιν (ἔδειξαν δὲ καὶ ἄλλα ἤδη
4 καὶ τὰ ἐς Λεοντίνους), καὶ νῦν τολμῶσιν ἐπὶ τοὺς ταῦτα κωλύοντας καὶ ἀνέχοντας τὴν Σικελίαν μέχρι τοῦδε μὴ ὑπ' αὐτοὺς εἶναι παρακαλεῖν
5 ὑμᾶς ὡς ἀναισθήτους. πολὺ δὲ ἐπὶ ἀληθεστέραν γε σωτηρίαν ἡμεῖς ἀντιπαρακαλοῦμεν, δεόμενοι τὴν ὑπάρχουσαν ἀπ' ἀλλήλων ἀμφοτέροις μὴ προδιδόναι, νομίσαι δὲ τοῖσδε μὲν καὶ ἄνευ ξυμμάχων αἰεὶ ἐφ' ὑμᾶς ἑτοίμην διὰ τὸ πλῆθος εἶναι ὁδόν, ὑμῖν δ' οὐ πολλάκις παρασχήσειν μετὰ τοσῆσδε ἐπικουρίας ἀμύνασθαι· ἣν εἰ τῶι ὑπόπτωι ἢ ἄπρακτον ἐάσετε ἀπελθεῖν ἢ καὶ σφαλεῖσαν, ἔτι βουλήσεσθε καὶ πολλοστημόριον αὐτῆς ἰδεῖν, ὅτε οὐδὲν ἔτι περανεῖ παραγενόμενον ὑμῖν.

87 Ἀλλὰ μήτε ὑμεῖς, ὦ Καμαριναῖοι, ταῖς τῶνδε διαβολαῖς ἀναπείθεσθε μήτε οἱ ἄλλοι· εἰρήκαμεν δ' ὑμῖν πᾶσαν τὴν ἀλήθειαν περὶ ὧν ὑποπτευόμεθα,
2 καὶ ἔτι ἐν κεφαλαίοις ὑπομνήσαντες ἀξιώσομεν πείθειν. φαμὲν γὰρ ἄρχειν μὲν τῶν ἐκεῖ, ἵνα μὴ ὑπακούωμεν ἄλλου, ἐλευθεροῦν δὲ τὰ ἐνθάδε, ὅπως μὴ ὑπ' αὐτῶν βλαπτώμεθα, πολλὰ δ' ἀναγκάζεσθαι πράσσειν, διότι καὶ πολλὰ φυλασσόμεθα, ξύμμαχοι δὲ καὶ νῦν καὶ πρότερον τοῖς ἐνθάδε
3 ὑμῶν ἀδικουμένοις οὐκ ἄκλητοι, παρακληθέντες δὲ ἥκειν. καὶ ὑμεῖς μήθ' ὡς δικασταὶ γενόμενοι τῶν ἡμῖν ποιουμένων μήθ' ὡς σωφρονισταί, ὃ χαλεπὸν ἤδη, ἀποτρέπειν πειρᾶσθε, καθ' ὅσον δέ τι ὑμῖν τῆς ἡμετέρας πολυπραγμοσύνης καὶ τρόπου τὸ αὐτὸ ξυμφέρει, τούτωι ἀπολαβόντες χρήσασθε, καὶ νομίσατε μὴ πάντας ἐν ἴσωι βλάπτειν αὐτά, πολὺ δὲ
4 πλείους τῶν Ἑλλήνων καὶ ὠφελεῖν· ἐν παντὶ γὰρ πᾶς χωρίωι, καὶ ὧι μὴ ὑπάρχομεν, ὅ τε οἰόμενος ἀδικήσεσθαι καὶ ὁ ἐπιβουλεύων διὰ τὸ ἑτοίμην ὑπεῖναι ἐλπίδα τῶι μὲν ἂν τι τυχεῖν ἐπικουρίας ἀφ' ἡμῶν, τῶι δὲ εἰ ἥξομεν, μὴ ἀδεεῖ εἶναι κινδυνεύειν, ἀμφότεροι ἀναγκάζονται ὁ μὲν ἄκων σωφρονεῖν,
5 ὁ δ' ἀπραγμόνως σώιζεσθαι. ταύτην οὖν τὴν κοινὴν τῶι τε δεομένωι καὶ ὑμῖν νῦν παροῦσαν ἀσφάλειαν μὴ ἀπώσησθε, ἀλλ' ἐξισώσαντες τοῖς ἄλλοις μεθ' ἡμῶν τοὺς Συρακοσίους, ἀντὶ τοῦ αἰεὶ φυλάσσεσθαι αὐτούς, καὶ ἀντεπιβουλεῦσαί ποτε ἐκ τοῦ ὁμοίου μεταλάβετε.'

87.4 ἄν τι τυχεῖν J² L²: ἀντιτυχεῖν codd.   87.4 ἀδεεῖ Krüger: ἀδεεῖς codd.; ἀδεὲς Reiske   87.5 τοὺς Συρακοσίους Camps: τοῖς Συρακοσίοις codd.; τοῖς ἄλλοις del. Dover, Alberti

Τοιαῦτα δὲ ὁ Εὔφημος εἶπεν. οἱ δὲ Καμαριναῖοι ἐπεπόνθεσαν τοιόνδε 88
τι· τοῖς μὲν Ἀθηναίοις εὖνοι ἦσαν, πλὴν καθ' ὅσον [εἰ] τὴν Σικελίαν
ὤιοντο αὐτοὺς δουλώσεσθαι, τοῖς δὲ Συρακοσίοις αἰεὶ κατὰ τὸ ὅμορον
διάφοροι· δεδιότες δ' οὐχ ἧσσον τοὺς Συρακοσίους ἐγγὺς ὄντας μὴ καὶ
ἄνευ σφῶν περιγένωνται, τό τε πρῶτον αὐτοῖς τοὺς ὀλίγους ἱππέας
ἔπεμψαν καὶ τὸ λοιπὸν ἐδόκει αὐτοῖς ὑπουργεῖν μὲν τοῖς Συρακοσίοις
μᾶλλον ἔργωι, ὡς ἂν δύνωνται μετριώτατα, ἐν δὲ τῶι παρόντι, ἵνα
μηδὲ τοῖς Ἀθηναίοις ἔλασσον δοκῶσι νεῖμαι, ἐπειδὴ καὶ ἐπικρατέστεροι
τῆι μάχηι ἐγένοντο, λόγωι ἀποκρίνασθαι ἴσα ἀμφοτέροις. καὶ οὕτω 2
βουλευσάμενοι ἀπεκρίναντο, ἐπειδὴ τυγχάνει ἀμφοτέροις οὖσι ξυμμάχοις
σφῶν πρὸς ἀλλήλους πόλεμος ὤν, εὔορκον δοκεῖν εἶναι σφίσιν ἐν τῶι
παρόντι μηδετέροις ἀμύνειν. καὶ οἱ πρέσβεις ἑκατέρων ἀπῆλθον.

Καὶ οἱ μὲν Συρακόσιοι τὰ καθ' ἑαυτοὺς ἐξηρτύοντο ἐς τὸν πόλεμον, 3
οἱ δ' Ἀθηναῖοι ἐν τῆι Νάξωι ἐστρατοπεδευμένοι τὰ πρὸς τοὺς Σικελοὺς
ἔπρασσον ὅπως αὐτοῖς ὡς πλεῖστοι προσχωρήσονται. καὶ οἱ μὲν πρὸς 4
τὰ πεδία μᾶλλον τῶν Σικελῶν ὑπήκοοι ὄντες τῶν Συρακοσίων οὐ
πολλοὶ ἀφειστήκεσαν· τῶν δὲ τὴν μεσόγειαν ἐχόντων αὐτόνομοι οὖσαι
καὶ πρότερον αἰεὶ αἱ οἰκήσεις εὐθὺς πλὴν ὀλίγοι μετὰ τῶν Ἀθηναίων
ἦσαν, καὶ σῖτόν τε κατεκόμιζον τῶι στρατεύματι καὶ εἰσὶν οἳ καὶ
χρήματα. ἐπὶ δὲ τοὺς μὴ προσχωροῦντας οἱ Ἀθηναῖοι στρατεύοντες 5
τοὺς μὲν προσηνάγκαζον, τοὺς δὲ καὶ ὑπὸ τῶν Συρακοσίων φρουρούς
τ' ἐσπεμπόντων καὶ βοηθούντων ἀπεκωλύοντο. τόν τε χειμῶνα
μεθορμισάμενοι ἐκ τῆς Νάξου ἐς τὴν Κατάνην καὶ τὸ στρατόπεδον ὃ
κατεκαύθη ὑπὸ τῶν Συρακοσίων αὖθις ἀνορθώσαντες διεχείμαζον. καὶ 6
ἔπεμψαν μὲν ἐς Καρχηδόνα τριήρη περὶ φιλίας, εἰ δύναιντό τι ὠφελεῖσθαι,
ἔπεμψαν δὲ καὶ ἐς Τυρσηνίαν, ἔστιν ὧν πόλεων ἐπαγγελλομένων καὶ
αὐτῶν ξυμπολεμεῖν. περιήγγελλον δὲ καὶ τοῖς Σικελοῖς καὶ ἐς τὴν
Ἔγεσταν πέμψαντες ἐκέλευον ἵππους σφίσιν ὡς πλείστους πέμπειν, καὶ
τἆλλα ἐς τὸν περιτειχισμόν, πλινθεῖα καὶ σίδηρον, ἡτοίμαζοντο, καὶ ὅσα
ἔδει, ὡς ἅμα τῶι ἦρι ἑξόμενοι τοῦ πολέμου.

Οἱ δ' ἐς τὴν Κόρινθον καὶ Λακεδαίμονα τῶν Συρακοσίων ἀποσταλέντες 7
πρέσβεις τούς τε Ἰταλιώτας ἅμα παραπλέοντες ἐπειρῶντο πείθειν μὴ
περιορᾶν τὰ γιγνόμενα ὑπὸ τῶν Ἀθηναίων, ὡς καὶ ἐκείνοις ὁμοίως
ἐπιβουλευόμενα, καὶ ἐπειδὴ ἐν τῆι Κορίνθωι ἐγένοντο, λόγους ἐποιοῦντο

88.1 εἰ del. Reiske   88.1 δοκῶσι νεῖμαι Valckenaer: δοκῶσιν εἶναι codd.   88.3
οὐ πολλοί Canter: οἱ πολλοί codd.   88.5 ἀπεκωλύοντο Döderlein: ἀπεκώλυον
codd.   88.6 πλινθεῖα Σ: πλινθία codd.

8 ἀξιοῦντες σφίσι κατὰ τὸ ξυγγενὲς βοηθεῖν. καὶ οἱ Κορίνθιοι εὐθὺς ψηφισάμενοι αὐτοὶ πρῶτοι ὥστε πάσηι προθυμίαι ἀμύνειν, καὶ ἐς τὴν Λακεδαίμονα ξυναπέστελλον αὐτοῖς πρέσβεις, ὅπως καὶ ἐκείνους ξυναναπείθοιεν τόν τε αὐτοῦ πόλεμον σαφέστερον ποιεῖσθαι πρὸς τοὺς
9 Ἀθηναίους καὶ ἐς τὴν Σικελίαν ὠφελίαν τινὰ πέμπειν. καὶ οἵ τε ἐκ τῆς Κορίνθου πρέσβεις παρῆσαν ἐς τὴν Λακεδαίμονα καὶ Ἀλκιβιάδης μετὰ τῶν ξυμφυγάδων περαιωθεὶς τότ' εὐθὺς ἐπὶ πλοίου φορτηγικοῦ ἐκ τῆς Θουρίας ἐς Κυλλήνην τῆς Ἠλείας πρῶτον, ἔπειτα ὕστερον ἐς τὴν Λακεδαίμονα αὐτῶν τῶν Λακεδαιμονίων μεταπεμψάντων ὑπόσπονδος
10 ἐλθών· ἐφοβεῖτο γὰρ αὐτοὺς διὰ τὴν περὶ τῶν Μαντινικῶν πρᾶξιν. καὶ ξυνέβη ἐν τῆι ἐκκλησίαι τῶν Λακεδαιμονίων τούς τε Κορινθίους καὶ τοὺς Συρακοσίους τὰ αὐτὰ καὶ τὸν Ἀλκιβιάδην δεομένους πείθειν τοὺς Λακεδαιμονίους. καὶ διανοουμένων τῶν τε ἐφόρων καὶ τῶν ἐν τέλει ὄντων πρέσβεις πέμπειν ἐς Συρακούσας κωλύοντας μὴ ξυμβαίνειν Ἀθηναίοις, βοηθεῖν δὲ οὐ προθύμων ὄντων, παρελθὼν ὁ Ἀλκιβιάδης παρώξυνέ τε τοὺς Λακεδαιμονίους καὶ ἐξώρμησε λέγων τοιάδε.

89 Ἀναγκαῖον περὶ τῆς ἐμῆς διαβολῆς πρῶτον ἐς ὑμᾶς εἰπεῖν, ἵνα μὴ
2 χεῖρον τὰ κοινὰ τῶι ὑπόπτωι μου ἀκροάσησθε. τῶν δ' ἐμῶν προγόνων τὴν προξενίαν ὑμῶν κατά τι ἔγκλημα ἀπειπόντων αὐτὸς ἐγὼ πάλιν ἀναλαμβάνων ἐθεράπευον ὑμᾶς ἄλλα τε καὶ περὶ τὴν ἐκ Πύλου ξυμφοράν. καὶ διατελοῦντός μου προθύμου ὑμεῖς πρὸς Ἀθηναίους καταλλασσόμενοι τοῖς μὲν ἐμοῖς ἐχθροῖς δύναμιν δι' ἐκείνων πράξαντες,
3 ἐμοὶ δὲ ἀτιμίαν περιέθετε. καὶ διὰ ταῦτα δικαίως ὑπ' ἐμοῦ πρός τε τὰ Μαντινέων καὶ Ἀργείων τραπομένου καὶ ὅσα ἄλλα ἠναντιούμην ὑμῖν ἐβλάπτεσθε· καὶ νῦν, εἴ τις καὶ τότε ἐν τῶι πάσχειν οὐκ εἰκότως ὠργίζετό μοι, μετὰ τοῦ ἀληθοῦς σκοπῶν ἀναπειθέσθω. ἢ εἴ τις, διότι καὶ τῶι δήμωι προσεκείμην μᾶλλον, χείρω με ἐνόμιζε, μηδ' οὕτως ἡγήσηται
4 ὀρθῶς ἄχθεσθαι. τοῖς γὰρ τυράννοις αἰεί ποτε διάφοροί ἐσμεν (πᾶν δὲ τὸ ἐναντιούμενον τῶι δυναστεύοντι δῆμος ὠνόμασται), καὶ ἀπ' ἐκείνου ξυμπαρέμεινεν ἡ προστασία ἡμῖν τοῦ πλήθους. ἅμα δὲ καὶ τῆς πόλεως
5 δημοκρατουμένης τὰ πολλὰ ἀνάγκη ἦν τοῖς παροῦσιν ἕπεσθαι· τῆς δὲ ὑπαρχούσης ἀκολασίας ἐπειρώμεθα μετριώτεροι ἐς τὰ πολιτικὰ εἶναι. ἄλλοι δ' ἦσαν καὶ ἐπὶ τῶν πάλαι καὶ νῦν οἳ ἐπὶ τὰ πονηρότερα ἐξῆγον
6 τὸν ὄχλον· οἵπερ καὶ ἐμὲ ἐξήλασαν. ἡμεῖς δὲ τοῦ ξύμπαντος προέστημεν, δικαιοῦντες ἐν ὧι σχήματι μεγίστη ἡ πόλις ἐτύγχανε καὶ ἐλευθερωτάτη

89.2 ἐμῶν H[2] (coni. Haacke): ἡμῶν codd.

οὖσα καὶ ὅπερ ἐδέξατό τις, τοῦτο ξυνδιασώιζειν, ἐπεὶ δημοκρατίαν γε καὶ ἐγιγνώσκομεν οἱ φρονοῦντές τι, καὶ αὐτὸς οὐδενὸς ἂν χεῖρον, ὅσωι καὶ λοιδορήσαιμι· ἀλλὰ περὶ ὁμολογουμένης ἀνοίας οὐδὲν ἂν καινὸν λέγοιτο. καὶ τὸ μεθιστάναι αὐτὴν οὐκ ἐδόκει ἡμῖν ἀσφαλὲς εἶναι ὑμῶν πολεμίων προσκαθημένων.

'Καὶ τὰ μὲν ἐς τὰς ἐμὰς διαβολὰς τοιαῦτα ξυνέβη· περὶ δὲ ὧν ὑμῖν τε 90 βουλευτέον καὶ ἐμοί, εἴ τι πλέον οἶδα, ἐσηγητέον, μάθετε ἤδη. ἐπλεύσαμεν 2 ἐς Σικελίαν πρῶτον μέν, εἰ δυναίμεθα, Σικελιώτας καταστρεψόμενοι, μετὰ δ' ἐκείνους αὖθις καὶ Ἰταλιώτας, ἔπειτα καὶ τῆς Καρχηδονίων ἀρχῆς καὶ αὐτῶν ἀποπειράσοντες. εἰ δὲ προχωρήσειε ταῦτα ἢ πάντα ἢ καὶ 3 τὰ πλείω, ἤδη τῆι Πελοποννήσωι ἐμέλλομεν ἐπιχειρήσειν, κομίσαντες ξύμπασαν μὲν τὴν ἐκεῖθεν προσγενομένην δύναμιν τῶν Ἑλλήνων, πολλοὺς δὲ βαρβάρους μισθωσάμενοι καὶ Ἴβηρας καὶ ἄλλους τῶν ἐκεῖ ὁμολογουμένως νῦν βαρβάρων μαχιμωτάτους, τριήρεις τε πρὸς ταῖς ἡμετέραις πολλὰς ναυπηγησάμενοι, ἐχούσης τῆς Ἰταλίας ξύλα ἄφθονα, αἷς τὴν Πελοπόννησον πέριξ πολιορκοῦντες καὶ τῶι πεζῶι ἅμα ἐκ γῆς ἐφορμαῖς τῶν πόλεων τὰς μὲν βίαι λαβόντες, τὰς δ' ἐντειχισάμενοι, ῥαιδίως ἠλπίζομεν καταπολεμήσειν καὶ μετὰ ταῦτα καὶ τοῦ ξύμπαντος Ἑλληνικοῦ ἄρξειν. χρήματα δὲ καὶ σῖτον, ὥστε εὐπορώτερον γίγνεσθαί τι αὐτῶν, 4 αὐτὰ τὰ προσγενόμενα ἐκεῖθεν χωρία ἔμελλε διαρκῆ ἄνευ τῆς ἐνθένδε προσόδου παρέξειν. τοιαῦτα μὲν περὶ τοῦ νῦν οἰχομένου στόλου παρὰ 91 τοῦ τὰ ἀκριβέστατα εἰδότος ὡς διενοήθημεν ἀκηκόατε· καὶ ὅσοι ὑπόλοιποι στρατηγοί, ἢν δύνωνται, ὁμοίως αὐτὰ πράξουσιν. ὡς δέ, εἰ μὴ βοηθήσετε οὐ περιέσται τἀκεῖ, μάθετε ἤδη. Σικελιῶται γὰρ ἀπειρότεροι μέν εἰσιν, 2 ὅμως δ' ἂν ξυστραφέντες ἀθρόοι καὶ νῦν ἔτι περιγένοιντο· Συρακόσιοι δὲ μόνοι μάχηι τε ἤδη πανδημεὶ ἡσσημένοι καὶ ναυσὶν ἅμα κατειργόμενοι ἀδύνατοι ἔσονται τῆι νῦν Ἀθηναίων ἐκεῖ παρασκευῆι ἀντίσχειν. καὶ εἰ 3 αὕτη ἡ πόλις ληφθήσεται, ἔχεται καὶ ἡ πᾶσα Σικελία, καὶ εὐθὺς καὶ Ἰταλία· καὶ ὃν ἄρτι κίνδυνον ἐκεῖθεν προεῖπον, οὐκ ἂν διὰ μακροῦ ὑμῖν ἐπιπέσοι. ὥστε μὴ περὶ τῆς Σικελίας τις οἰέσθω μόνον βουλεύειν, ἀλλὰ 4 καὶ περὶ τῆς Πελοποννήσου, εἰ μὴ ποιήσετε τάδε ἐν τάχει, στρατιάν τε ἐπὶ νεῶν πέμψετε τοιαύτην ἐκεῖσε οἵτινες αὐτερέται κομισθέντες καὶ ὁπλιτεύσουσιν εὐθύς, καὶ ὃ τῆς στρατιᾶς ἔτι χρησιμώτερον εἶναι νομίζω, ἄνδρα Σπαρτιάτην ἄρχοντα, ὡς ἂν τούς τε παρόντας ξυντάξηι καὶ τοὺς μὴ 'θέλοντας προσαναγκάσηι· οὕτω γὰρ οἵ τε ὑπάρχοντες ὑμῖν φίλοι θαρσήσουσι μᾶλλον καὶ οἱ ἐνδοιάζοντες ἀδεέστερον προσίασιν. καὶ τὰ 5 ἐνθάδε χρὴ ἅμα φανερώτερον ἐκπολεμεῖν, ἵνα Συρακόσιοί τε νομίζοντες ὑμᾶς ἐπιμέλεσθαι μᾶλλον ἀντέχωσι καὶ Ἀθηναῖοι τοῖς ἑαυτῶν ἧσσον

89.6 <μέγιστ' ἠδίκημαι> ante λοιδορήσαιμι add. Steup

6 ἄλλην ἐπικουρίαν πέμπωσιν. τειχίζειν τε χρὴ Δεκέλειαν τῆς Ἀττικῆς, ὅπερ Ἀθηναῖοι μάλιστα αἰεὶ φοβοῦνται καὶ μόνου αὐτοῦ νομίζουσι τῶν ἐν τῶι πολέμωι οὐ διαπεπειρᾶσθαι. βεβαιότατα δ' ἄν τις οὕτω τοὺς πολεμίους βλάπτοι, εἰ ἃ μάλιστα δεδιότας αὐτοὺς αἰσθάνοιτο, ταῦτα σαφῶς πυνθανόμενος ἐπιφέροι· εἰκὸς γὰρ αὐτοὺς ἀκριβέστατα ἑκάστους
7 τὰ σφέτερα αὐτῶν δεινὰ ἐπισταμένους φοβεῖσθαι. ἃ δ' ἐν τῆι ἐπιτειχίσει αὐτοὶ ὠφελούμενοι τοὺς ἐναντίους κωλύσετε, πολλὰ παρεὶς τὰ μέγιστα κεφαλαιώσω. οἷς τε γὰρ ἡ χώρα κατεσκεύασται, τὰ πολλὰ πρὸς ὑμᾶς τὰ μὲν ληφθέντα, τὰ δ' αὐτόματα ἥξει· καὶ τὰς τοῦ Λαυρείου τῶν ἀργυρείων μετάλλων προσόδους καὶ ὅσα ἀπὸ γῆς καὶ δικαστηρίων νῦν ὠφελοῦνται εὐθὺς ἀποστερήσονται, μάλιστα δὲ τῆς ἀπὸ τῶν ξυμμάχων προσόδου ἧσσον διαφορουμένης, οἳ τὰ παρ' ὑμῶν νομίσαντες ἤδη κατὰ κράτος
92 πολεμεῖσθαι ὀλιγωρήσουσιν. γίγνεσθαι δέ τι αὐτῶν καὶ ἐν τάχει καὶ προθυμότερον ἐν ὑμῖν ἐστίν, ὦ Λακεδαιμόνιοι, ἐπεὶ ὥς γε δυνατά (καὶ οὐχ ἁμαρτήσεσθαι οἶμαι γνώμης) πάνυ θαρσῶ.
2 'Καὶ χείρων οὐδενὶ ἀξιῶ δοκεῖν ὑμῶν εἶναι, εἰ τῆι ἐμαυτοῦ μετὰ τῶν πολεμιωτάτων φιλόπολίς ποτε δοκῶν εἶναι νῦν ἐγκρατῶς ἐπέρχομαι,
3 οὐδὲ ὑποπτεύεσθαί μου ἐς τὴν φυγαδικὴν προθυμίαν τὸν λόγον. φυγάς τε γάρ εἰμι τῆς τῶν ἐξελασάντων πονηρίας, καὶ οὐ τῆς ὑμετέρας, ἢν πείθησθέ μοι, ὠφελίας· καὶ πολεμιώτεροι οὐχ οἱ τοὺς πολεμίους που
4 βλάψαντες ὑμεῖς ἢ οἱ τοὺς φίλους ἀναγκάσαντες πολεμίους γενέσθαι. τό τε φιλόπολι οὐκ ἐν ὧι ἀδικοῦμαι ἔχω, ἀλλ' ἐν ὧι ἀσφαλῶς ἐπολιτεύθην. οὐδ' ἐπὶ πατρίδα οὖσαν ἔτι ἡγοῦμαι νῦν ἰέναι, πολὺ δὲ μᾶλλον τὴν οὐκ οὖσαν ἀνακτᾶσθαι. καὶ φιλόπολις οὗτος ὀρθῶς, οὐχ ὃς ἂν τὴν ἑαυτοῦ ἀδίκως ἀπολέσας μὴ ἐπίηι, ἀλλ' ὃς ἂν ἐκ παντὸς τρόπου διὰ
5 τὸ ἐπιθυμεῖν πειραθῆι αὐτὴν ἀναλαβεῖν. οὕτως ἐμοί τε ἀξιῶ ὑμᾶς καὶ ἐς κίνδυνον καὶ ἐς ταλαιπωρίαν πᾶσαν ἀδεῶς χρῆσθαι, ὦ Λακεδαιμόνιοι, γνόντας τοῦτον δὴ τὸν ὑφ' ἁπάντων προβαλλόμενον λόγον, ὡς εἰ πολέμιός γε ὢν σφόδρα ἔβλαπτον, κἂν φίλος ὢν ἱκανῶς ὠφελοίην, ὅσωι τὰ μὲν Ἀθηναίων οἶδα, τὰ δ' ὑμέτερα ἥικαζον· καὶ αὐτοὺς νῦν νομίσαντας περὶ μεγίστων δὴ τῶν διαφερόντων βουλεύεσθαι μὴ ἀποκνεῖν τὴν ἐς τὴν Σικελίαν τε καὶ ἐς τὴν Ἀττικὴν στρατείαν, ἵνα τά τε ἐκεῖ βραχεῖ μορίωι ξυμπαραγενόμενοι μεγάλα σώσητε καὶ Ἀθηναίων τήν τε οὖσαν καὶ τὴν μέλλουσαν δύναμιν καθέλητε, καὶ μετὰ ταῦτα αὐτοί τε ἀσφαλῶς οἰκῆτε καὶ τῆς ἁπάσης Ἑλλάδος ἑκούσης καὶ οὐ βίαι, κατ' εὔνοιαν δὲ ἡγῆσθε.'
93 Ὁ μὲν Ἀλκιβιάδης τοσαῦτα εἶπεν, οἱ δὲ Λακεδαιμόνιοι διανοούμενοι μὲν καὶ αὐτοὶ πρότερον στρατεύειν ἐπὶ τὰς Ἀθήνας, μέλλοντες δ' ἔτι καὶ

περιορώμενοι, πολλῶι μᾶλλον ἐπερρώσθησαν διδάξαντος ταῦτα ἕκαστα αὐτοῦ καὶ νομίσαντες παρὰ τοῦ σαφέστατα εἰδότος ἀκηκοέναι· ὥστε τῆι 2 ἐπιτειχίσει τῆς Δεκελείας προσεῖχον ἤδη τὸν νοῦν καὶ τὸ παραυτίκα καὶ τοῖς ἐν τῆι Σικελίαι πέμπειν τινὰ τιμωρίαν. καὶ Γύλιππον τὸν Κλεανδρίδου προστάξαντες ἄρχοντα τοῖς Συρακοσίοις ἐκέλευον μετ᾽ ἐκείνων καὶ τῶν Κορινθίων βουλευόμενον ποιεῖν ὅπηι ἐκ τῶν παρόντων μάλιστα καὶ τάχιστά τις ὠφελία ἥξει τοῖς ἐκεῖ. ὁ δὲ δύο μὲν ναῦς τοὺς Κορινθίους 3 ἤδη ἐκέλευέν οἱ πέμπειν ἐς Ἀσίνην, τὰς δὲ λοιπὰς παρασκευάζεσθαι ὅσας διανοοῦνται πέμπειν καί, ὅταν καιρὸς ἦι, ἑτοίμας εἶναι πλεῖν. ταῦτα δὲ ξυνθέμενοι ἀνεχώρουν ἐκ τῆς Λακεδαίμονος.

Ἀφίκετο δὲ καὶ ἡ ἐκ τῆς Σικελίας τριήρης τῶν Ἀθηναίων, ἣν ἀπέστειλαν 4 οἱ στρατηγοὶ ἐπί τε χρήματα καὶ ἱππέας. καὶ οἱ Ἀθηναῖοι ἀκούσαντες ἐψηφίσαντο τήν τε τροφὴν πέμπειν τῆι στρατιᾶι καὶ τοὺς ἱππέας. καὶ ὁ χειμὼν ἐτελεύτα, καὶ ἕβδομον καὶ δέκατον ἔτος τῶι πολέμωι ἐτελεύτα τῶιδε ὃν Θουκυδίδης ξυνέγραψεν.

Ἅμα δὲ τῶι ἦρι εὐθὺς ἀρχομένωι τοῦ ἐπιγιγνομένου θέρους οἱ ἐν τῆι 94 Σικελίαι Ἀθηναῖοι ἄραντες ἐκ τῆς Κατάνης παρέπλευσαν ἐπὶ Μεγάρων τῶν ἐν τῆι Σικελίαι, οὓς ἐπὶ Γέλωνος τοῦ τυράννου, ὥσπερ καὶ πρότερόν μοι εἴρηται, ἀναστήσαντες Συρακόσιοι αὐτοὶ ἔχουσι τὴν γῆν. ἀποβάντες 2 δὲ ἐδήιωσαν τοὺς ἀγροὺς καὶ ἐλθόντες ἐπὶ ἔρυμά τι τῶν Συρακοσίων καὶ οὐχ ἑλόντες αὖθις καὶ πεζῆι καὶ ναυσὶ παρακομισθέντες ἐπὶ τὸν Τηρίαν ποταμὸν τό τε πεδίον ἀναβάντες ἐδήιουν καὶ τὸν σῖτον ἐνεπίμπρασαν, καὶ τῶν Συρακοσίων περιτυχόντες τισὶν οὐ πολλοῖς καὶ ἀποκτείναντές τέ τινας καὶ τροπαῖον στήσαντες ἀνεχώρησαν ἐπὶ τὰς ναῦς. καὶ ἀποπλεύσαντες 3 ἐς Κατάνην, ἐκεῖθεν δὲ ἐπισιτισάμενοι πάσηι τῆι στρατιᾶι ἐχώρουν ἐπὶ Κεντόριπα, Σικελικὸν πόλισμα, καὶ προσαγαγόμενοι ὁμολογίαι ἀπῆισαν, ἐμπιμπράντες ἅμα τὸν σῖτον τῶν τε Ἰνησσαίων καὶ τῶν Ὑβλαίων. καὶ 4 ἀφικόμενοι ἐς Κατάνην καταλαμβάνουσι τούς τε ἱππέας ἥκοντας ἐκ τῶν Ἀθηνῶν πεντήκοντα καὶ διακοσίους ἄνευ τῶν ἵππων μετὰ σκευῆς, ὡς αὐτόθεν ἵππων πορισθησομένων, καὶ ἱπποτοξότας τριάκοντα καὶ τάλαντα ἀργυρίου τριακόσια.

Τοῦ δ᾽ αὐτοῦ ἦρος καὶ ἐπ᾽ Ἄργος στρατεύσαντες Λακεδαιμόνιοι μέχρι 95 μὲν Κλεωνῶν ἦλθον, σεισμοῦ δὲ γενομένου ἀπεχώρησαν. καὶ Ἀργεῖοι μετὰ ταῦτα ἐσβαλόντες ἐς τὴν Θυρεᾶτιν ὅμορον οὖσαν λείαν τῶν Λακεδαιμονίων πολλὴν ἔλαβον, ἣ ἐπράθη ταλάντων οὐκ ἔλασσον πέντε καὶ εἴκοσι. καὶ ὁ Θεσπιῶν δῆμος ἐν τῶι αὐτῶι θέρει οὐ πολὺ ὕστερον 2 ἐπιθέμενος τοῖς τὰς ἀρχὰς ἔχουσιν οὐ κατέσχεν, ἀλλὰ βοηθησάντων Θηβαίων οἱ μὲν ξυνελήφθησαν, οἱ δ᾽ ἐξέπεσον Ἀθήναζε.

96 Καὶ οἱ Συρακόσιοι τοῦ αὐτοῦ θέρους, ὡς ἐπύθοντο τούς τε ἱππέας ἥκοντας τοῖς Ἀθηναίοις καὶ μέλλοντας ἤδη ἐπὶ σφᾶς ἰέναι, νομίσαντες, ἐὰν μὴ τῶν Ἐπιπολῶν κρατήσωσιν οἱ Ἀθηναῖοι, χωρίου ἀποκρήμνου τε καὶ ὑπὲρ τῆς πόλεως εὐθὺς κειμένου, οὐκ ἂν ῥαιδίως σφᾶς, οὐδ' εἰ κρατοῖντο μάχηι, ἀποτειχισθῆναι, διενοοῦντο τὰς προσβάσεις αὐτῶν φυλάσσειν,
2 ὅπως μὴ κατὰ ταύτας λάθωσι σφᾶς ἀναβάντες οἱ πολέμιοι· οὐ γὰρ ἂν ἄλληι γε αὐτοὺς δυνηθῆναι. ἐξήρτηται γὰρ τὸ ἄλλο χωρίον, καὶ μέχρι τῆς πόλεως ἐπικλινές τέ ἐστι καὶ ἐπιφανὲς πᾶν ἔσω· καὶ ὠνόμασται ὑπὸ
3 τῶν Συρακοσίων διὰ τὸ ἐπιπολῆς τοῦ ἄλλου εἶναι Ἐπιπολαί. καὶ οἱ μὲν ἐξελθόντες πανδημεὶ ἐς τὸν λειμῶνα παρὰ τὸν Ἄναπον ποταμὸν ἅμα τῆι ἡμέραι (ἐτύγχανον γὰρ αὐτοῖς καὶ οἱ περὶ τὸν Ἑρμοκράτη στρατηγοὶ ἄρτι παρειληφότες τὴν ἀρχήν) ἐξέτασίν τε ὅπλων ἐποιοῦντο καὶ ἑξακοσίους λογάδας τῶν ὁπλιτῶν ἐξέκριναν πρότερον, ὧν ἦρχε Διόμιλος φυγὰς ἐξ Ἄνδρου, ὅπως τῶν τε Ἐπιπολῶν εἶεν φύλακες καί, ἢν ἐς ἄλλο τι δέηι, ταχὺ
97 ξυνεστῶτες παραγίγνωνται. οἱ δὲ Ἀθηναῖοι ταύτης τῆς νυκτός, ⟨ἧι⟩ τῆι ἐπιγιγνομένηι ἡμέραι ἐξητάζοντο ἐκεῖνοι, ἔλαθον αὐτοὺς παντὶ ἤδη τῶι στρατεύματι ἐκ τῆς Κατάνης σχόντες κατὰ τὸν Λέοντα καλούμενον, ὃς ἀπέχει τῶν Ἐπιπολῶν ἓξ ἢ ἑπτὰ σταδίους, καὶ τοὺς πεζοὺς ἀποβιβάσαντες, ταῖς τε ναυσὶν ἐς τὴν Θάψον καθορμισάμενοι· ἔστι δὲ χερσόνησος μὲν ἐν στενῶι ἰσθμῶι προύχουσα ἐς τὸ πέλαγος, τῆς δὲ Συρακοσίων πόλεως οὔτε
2 πλοῦν οὔτε ὁδὸν πολλὴν ἀπέχει. καὶ ὁ μὲν ναυτικὸς στρατὸς τῶν Ἀθηναίων ἐν τῆι Θάψωι διασταυρωσάμενος τὸν ἰσθμὸν ἡσύχαζεν· ὁ δὲ πεζὸς ἐχώρει εὐθὺς δρόμωι πρὸς τὰς Ἐπιπολὰς καὶ φθάνει ἀναβὰς κατὰ τὸν Εὐρύηλον πρὶν τοὺς Συρακοσίους αἰσθομένους ἐκ τοῦ λειμῶνος καὶ τῆς ἐξετάσεως
3 παραγενέσθαι. ἐβοήθουν δὲ οἵ τε ἄλλοι, ὡς ἕκαστος τάχους εἶχε, καὶ οἱ περὶ τὸν Διόμιλον ἑξακόσιοι· στάδιοι δὲ πρὶν προσμεῖξαι ἐκ τοῦ λειμῶνος
4 ἐγίγνοντο αὐτοῖς οὐκ ἔλασσον ἢ πέντε καὶ εἴκοσι. προσπεσόντες οὖν αὐτοῖς τοιούτωι τρόπωι ἀτακτότερον καὶ μάχηι νικηθέντες οἱ Συρακόσιοι ἐπὶ ταῖς Ἐπιπολαῖς ἀνεχώρησαν ἐς τὴν πόλιν· καὶ ὅ τε Διόμιλος ἀποθνήισκει
5 καὶ τῶν ἄλλων ὡς τριακόσιοι. καὶ μετὰ τοῦτο οἱ Ἀθηναῖοι τροπαῖόν τε στήσαντες καὶ τοὺς νεκροὺς ὑποσπόνδους ἀποδόντες τοῖς Συρακοσίοις, πρὸς τὴν πόλιν αὐτὴν τῆι ὑστεραίαι ἐπικαταβάντες, ὡς οὐκ ἐπεξῆισαν αὐτοῖς, ἐπαναχωρήσαντες φρούριον ἐπὶ τῶι Λαβδάλωι ὠικοδόμησαν, ἐπ' ἄκροις τοῖς κρημνοῖς τῶν Ἐπιπολῶν, ὁρῶν πρὸς τὰ Μέγαρα, ὅπως εἴη αὐτοῖς, ὁπότε προΐοιεν ἢ μαχούμενοι ἢ τειχιοῦντες, τοῖς τε σκεύεσι καὶ τοῖς

97.1 ⟨ἧι⟩ add. Classen   ἐκεῖνοι Classen: καὶ codd.
97.5 προΐοιεν Portus (*prodirent* Valla): προσίοιεν codd.

χρήμασιν ἀποθήκη. καὶ οὐ πολλῶι ὕστερον αὐτοῖς ἦλθον ἔκ τε Ἐγέστης 98 ἱππῆς τριακόσιοι καὶ Σικελῶν καὶ Ναξίων καὶ ἄλλων τινῶν ὡς ἑκατόν· καὶ Ἀθηναίων ὑπῆρχον πεντήκοντα καὶ διακόσιοι, οἷς ἵππους τοὺς μὲν παρ' Ἐγεσταίων καὶ Καταναίων ἔλαβον, τοὺς δ' ἐπρίαντο, καὶ ξύμπαντες πεντήκοντα καὶ ἑξακόσιοι ἱππῆς ξυνελέγησαν. καὶ καταστήσαντες ἐν 2 τῶι Λαβδάλωι φυλακὴν ἐχώρουν πρὸς τὴν Συκῆν οἱ Ἀθηναῖοι, ἵναπερ καθεζόμενοι ἐτείχισαν τὸν κύκλον διὰ τάχους. καὶ ἔκπληξιν τοῖς Συρακοσίοις παρέσχον τῶι τάχει τῆς οἰκοδομίας· καὶ ἐπεξελθόντες μάχην διενοοῦντο ποιεῖσθαι καὶ μὴ περιορᾶν. καὶ ἤδη ἀντιπαρατασσομένων ἀλλήλοις οἱ 3 τῶν Συρακοσίων στρατηγοὶ ὡς ἑώρων σφίσι τὸ στράτευμα διεσπασμένον τε καὶ οὐ ῥαιδίως ξυντασσόμενον, ἀνήγαγον πάλιν ἐς τὴν πόλιν πλὴν μέρους τινὸς τῶν ἱππέων· οὗτοι δὲ ὑπομένοντες ἐκώλυον τοὺς Ἀθηναίους λιθοφορεῖν τε καὶ ἀποσκίδνασθαι μακροτέραν. καὶ τῶν Ἀθηναίων φυλὴ 4 μία τῶν ὁπλιτῶν καὶ οἱ ἱππῆς μετ' αὐτῶν πάντες ἔτρεψαντο τοὺς τῶν Συρακοσίων ἱππέας προσβαλόντες, καὶ ἀπέκτεινάν τέ τινας καὶ τροπαῖον τῆς ἱππομαχίας ἔστησαν.

Καὶ τῆι ὑστεραίαι οἱ μὲν ἐτείχιζον τῶν Ἀθηναίων τὸ πρὸς βορέαν τοῦ 99 κύκλου τεῖχος, οἱ δὲ λίθους καὶ ξύλα ξυμφοροῦντες παρέβαλλον ἐπὶ τὸν Τρωγίλον καλούμενον αἰεί, ἧιπερ βραχύτατον ἐγίγνετο αὐτοῖς ἐκ τοῦ μεγάλου λιμένος ἐπὶ τὴν ἑτέραν θάλασσαν τὸ ἀποτείχισμα. οἱ δὲ Συρακόσιοι 2 οὐχ ἥκιστα Ἑρμοκράτους τῶν στρατηγῶν ἐσηγησαμένου μάχαις μὲν πανδημεὶ πρὸς Ἀθηναίους οὐκέτι ἐβούλοντο διακινδυνεύειν, ὑποτειχίζειν δὲ ἄμεινον ἐδόκει εἶναι, ἧι ἐκεῖνοι ἔμελλον ἄξειν τὸ τεῖχος, καί, εἰ φθάσειαν, ἀποκλήισεις γίγνεσθαι, καὶ ἅμα καὶ ἐν τούτωι εἰ ἐπιβοηθοῖεν, μέρος ἀντιπέμπειν αὐτοῖς τῆς στρατιᾶς καὶ φθάνειν αὐτοὶ προκαταλαμβάνοντες τοῖς σταυροῖς τὰς ἐφόδους, ἐκείνους δὲ ἂν παυομένους τοῦ ἔργου πάντας ἂν πρὸς σφᾶς τρέπεσθαι. ἐτείχιζον οὖν ἐξελθόντες ἀπὸ τῆς σφετέρας 3 πόλεως ἀρξάμενοι, κάτωθεν τοῦ κύκλου τῶν Ἀθηναίων ἐγκάρσιον τεῖχος ἄγοντες, τάς τε ἐλάας ἐκκόπτοντες τοῦ τεμένους καὶ πύργους ξυλίνους καθιστάντες. αἱ δὲ νῆες τῶν Ἀθηναίων οὔπω ἐκ τῆς Θάψου 4 περιεπεπλεύκεσαν ἐς τὸν μέγαν λιμένα, ἀλλ' ἔτι οἱ Συρακόσιοι ἐκράτουν τῶν περὶ τὴν θάλασσαν, κατὰ γῆν δ' ἐκ τῆς Θάψου οἱ Ἀθηναῖοι τὰ ἐπιτήδεια ἐπήγοντο. ἐπειδὴ δὲ τοῖς Συρακοσίοις ἀρκούντως ἐδόκει ἔχειν 100 ὅσα τε ἐσταυρώθη καὶ ὠικοδομήθη τοῦ ὑποτειχίσματος, καὶ οἱ Ἀθηναῖοι αὐτοὺς οὐκ ἦλθον κωλύσοντες, φοβούμενοι μὴ σφίσι δίχα γιγνομένοις

99.2 αὐτοῖς Bekker: αὐτοὺς codd.   ἂν παυομένους ACEFGM in marg. B¹: ἀναπαυομένους B   ἂν post πάντας om. B

ῥᾶιον μάχωνται, καὶ ἅμα τὴν καθ' αὑτοὺς περιτείχισιν ἐπειγόμενοι, οἱ μὲν Συρακόσιοι φυλὴν μίαν καταλιπόντες φύλακα τοῦ οἰκοδομήματος ἀνεχώρησαν ἐς τὴν πόλιν, οἱ δὲ Ἀθηναῖοι τούς τε ὀχετοὺς αὐτῶν, οἳ ἐς τὴν πόλιν ὑπονομηδὸν ποτοῦ ὕδατος ἠγμένοι ἦσαν, διέφθειραν, καὶ τηρήσαντες τούς τε ἄλλους Συρακοσίους κατὰ σκηνὰς ὄντας ἐν μεσημβρίαι καί τινας καὶ ἐς τὴν πόλιν ἀποκεχωρηκότας καὶ τοὺς ἐν τῶι σταυρώματι ἀμελῶς φυλάσσοντας, τριακοσίους μὲν σφῶν αὐτῶν λογάδας καὶ τῶν ψιλῶν τινὰς ἐκλεκτοὺς ὡπλισμένους προύταξαν θεῖν δρόμωι ἐξαπιναίως πρὸς τὸ ὑποτείχισμα, ἡ δ' ἄλλη στρατιὰ δίχα, ἡ μὲν μετὰ τοῦ ἑτέρου στρατηγοῦ πρὸς τὴν πόλιν, εἰ ἐπιβοηθοῖεν, ἐχώρουν, ἡ δὲ μετὰ τοῦ ἑτέρου
2 πρὸς τὸ σταύρωμα τὸ παρὰ τὴν πυλίδα. καὶ προσβαλόντες οἱ τριακόσιοι αἱροῦσι τὸ σταύρωμα· καὶ οἱ φύλακες αὐτὸ ἐκλιπόντες κατέφυγον ἐς τὸ προτείχισμα τὸ περὶ τὸν Τεμενίτην. καὶ αὐτοῖς ξυνεσέπεσον οἱ διώκοντες, καὶ ἐντὸς γενόμενοι βίαι ἐξεκρούσθησαν πάλιν ὑπὸ τῶν Συρακοσίων, καὶ
3 τῶν Ἀργείων τινὲς αὐτόθι καὶ τῶν Ἀθηναίων οὐ πολλοὶ διεφθάρησαν. καὶ ἐπαναχωρήσασα ἡ πᾶσα στρατιὰ τήν τε ὑποτείχισιν καθεῖλον καὶ τὸ σταύρωμα ἀνέσπασαν καὶ διεφόρησαν τοὺς σταυροὺς παρ' ἑαυτοὺς καὶ τροπαῖον ἔστησαν.

101 Τῆι δ' ὑστεραίαι ἀπὸ τοῦ κύκλου ἐτείχιζον οἱ Ἀθηναῖοι τὸν κρημνὸν τὸν ὑπὲρ τοῦ ἕλους, ὃς τῶν Ἐπιπολῶν ταύτηι πρὸς τὸν μέγαν λιμένα ὁρᾶι, καὶ ἧιπερ αὐτοῖς βραχύτατον ἐγίγνετο καταβᾶσι διὰ τοῦ ὁμαλοῦ
2 καὶ τοῦ ἕλους ἐς τὸν λιμένα τὸ περιτείχισμα. καὶ οἱ Συρακόσιοι ἐν τούτωι ἐξελθόντες καὶ αὐτοὶ ἀπεσταύρουν αὖθις ἀρξάμενοι ἀπὸ τῆς πόλεως διὰ μέσου τοῦ ἕλους, καὶ τάφρον ἅμα παρώρυσσον, ὅπως μὴ οἷόν τε ἦι
3 τοῖς Ἀθηναίοις μέχρι τῆς θαλάσσης ἀποτειχίσαι. οἱ δ', ἐπειδὴ τὸ πρὸς τὸν κρημνὸν αὐτοῖς ἐξείργαστο, ἐπιχειροῦσιν αὖθις τῶι τῶν Συρακοσίων σταυρώματι καὶ τάφρωι, τὰς μὲν ναῦς κελεύσαντες περιπλεῦσαι ἐκ τῆς Θάψου ἐς τὸν μέγαν λιμένα τὸν τῶν Συρακοσίων, αὐτοὶ δὲ περὶ ὄρθρον καταβάντες ἀπὸ τῶν Ἐπιπολῶν ἐς τὸ ὁμαλὸν καὶ διὰ τοῦ ἕλους, ἧι πηλῶδες ἦν καὶ στεριφώτατον, θύρας καὶ ξύλα πλατέα ἐπιθέντες καὶ ἐπ' αὐτῶν διαβαδίσαντες, αἱροῦσιν ἅμα ἕωι τό τε σταύρωμα πλὴν ὀλίγου
4 καὶ τὴν τάφρον, καὶ ὕστερον καὶ τὸ ὑπολειφθὲν εἷλον. καὶ μάχη ἐγένετο, καὶ ἐν αὐτῆι ἐνίκων οἱ Ἀθηναῖοι. καὶ τῶν Συρακοσίων οἱ μὲν τὸ δεξιὸν κέρας ἔχοντες πρὸς τὴν πόλιν ἔφευγον, οἱ δ' ἐπὶ τῶι εὐωνύμωι παρὰ τὸν ποταμόν. καὶ αὐτοὺς βουλόμενοι ἀποκλῃσασθαι τῆς διαβάσεως οἱ τῶν Ἀθηναίων τριακόσιοι λογάδες δρόμωι ἠπείγοντο πρὸς τὴν γέφυραν.
5 δείσαντες δὲ οἱ Συρακόσιοι (ἦσαν γὰρ καὶ τῶν ἱππέων αὐτοῖς οἱ πολλοὶ ἐνταῦθα) ὁμόσε χωροῦσι τοῖς τριακοσίοις τούτοις, καὶ τρέπουσί τε αὐτοὺς καὶ ἐσβάλλουσιν ἐς τὸ δεξιὸν κέρας τῶν Ἀθηναίων· καὶ προσπεσόντων

αὐτῶν ξυνεφοβήθη καὶ ἡ πρώτη φυλὴ τοῦ κέρως. ἰδὼν δὲ ὁ Λάμαχος 6 παρεβοήθει ἀπὸ τοῦ εὐωνύμου τοῦ ἑαυτῶν μετὰ τοξοτῶν τε οὐ πολλῶν καὶ τοὺς Ἀργείους παραλαβών, καὶ ἐπιδιαβὰς τάφρον τινὰ καὶ μονωθεὶς μετ' ὀλίγων τῶν ξυνδιαβάντων ἀποθνήισκει αὐτός τε καὶ πέντε ἢ ἓξ τῶν μετ' αὐτοῦ. καὶ τούτους μὲν οἱ Συρακόσιοι εὐθὺς κατὰ τάχος φθάνουσιν ἁρπάσαντες πέραν τοῦ ποταμοῦ ἐς τὸ ἀσφαλές, αὐτοὶ δὲ ἐπιόντος ἤδη καὶ τοῦ ἄλλου στρατεύματος τῶν Ἀθηναίων ἀπεχώρουν. ἐν τούτωι δὲ 102 οἱ πρὸς τὴν πόλιν αὐτῶν τὸ πρῶτον καταφυγόντες ὡς ἑώρων ταῦτα γιγνόμενα, αὐτοί τε πάλιν ἀπὸ τῆς πόλεως ἀναθαρσήσαντες ἀντετάξαντο πρὸς τοὺς κατὰ σφᾶς Ἀθηναίους, καὶ μέρος τι αὑτῶν πέμπουσιν ἐπὶ τὸν κύκλον τὸν ἐπὶ ταῖς Ἐπιπολαῖς, ἡγούμενοι ἐρῆμον αἱρήσειν. καὶ τὸ 2 μὲν δεκάπλεθρον προτείχισμα αὐτῶν αἱροῦσι καὶ διεπόρθησαν, αὐτὸν δὲ τὸν κύκλον Νικίας διεκώλυσεν· ἔτυχε γὰρ ἐν αὐτῶι δι' ἀσθένειαν ὑπολελειμμένος. τὰς γὰρ μηχανὰς καὶ ξύλα ὅσα πρὸ τοῦ τείχους ἦν καταβεβλημένα, ἐμπρῆσαι τοὺς ὑπηρέτας ἐκέλευσεν, ὡς ἔγνω ἀδυνάτους ἐσομένους ἐρημίαι ἀνδρῶν ἄλλωι τρόπωι περιγενέσθαι. καὶ ξυνέβη οὕτως· 3 οὐ γὰρ ἔτι προσῆλθον οἱ Συρακόσιοι διὰ τὸ πῦρ, ἀλλὰ ἀπεχώρουν πάλιν. καὶ γὰρ πρός τε τὸν κύκλον βοήθεια ἤδη κάτωθεν τῶν Ἀθηναίων ἀποδιωξάντων τοὺς ἐκεῖ ἐπανήιει, καὶ αἱ νῆες ἅμα αὐτῶν ἐκ τῆς Θάψου, ὥσπερ εἴρητο, κατέπλεον ἐς τὸν μέγαν λιμένα. ἃ ὁρῶντες οἱ ἄνωθεν κατὰ 4 τάχος ἀπῆισαν καὶ ἡ ξύμπασα στρατιὰ τῶν Συρακοσίων ἐς τὴν πόλιν, νομίσαντες μὴ ἂν ἔτι ἀπὸ τῆς παρούσης σφίσι δυνάμεως ἱκανοὶ γενέσθαι κωλῦσαι τὸν ἐπὶ τὴν θάλασσαν τειχισμόν.

Μετὰ δὲ τοῦτο οἱ Ἀθηναῖοι τροπαῖον ἔστησαν καὶ τοὺς νεκροὺς 103 ὑποσπόνδους ἀπέδοσαν τοῖς Συρακοσίοις καὶ τοὺς μετὰ Λαμάχου καὶ αὐτὸν ἐκομίσαντο· καὶ παρόντος ἤδη σφίσι παντὸς τοῦ στρατεύματος καὶ τοῦ ναυτικοῦ καὶ τοῦ πεζοῦ, ἀπὸ τῶν Ἐπιπολῶν καὶ τοῦ κρημνώδους ἀρξάμενοι ἀπετείχιζον μέχρι τῆς θαλάσσης τείχει διπλῶι τοὺς Συρακοσίους. τὰ δ' ἐπιτήδεια τῆι στρατιᾶι ἐσήγετο ἐκ τῆς Ἰταλίας πανταχόθεν. 2 ἦλθον δὲ καὶ τῶν Σικελῶν πολλοὶ ξύμμαχοι τοῖς Ἀθηναίοις, οἳ πρότερον περιεωρῶντο, καὶ ἐκ τῆς Τυρσηνίας νῆες πεντηκόντοροι τρεῖς, καὶ τἆλλα προυχώρει αὐτοῖς ἐς ἐλπίδας. καὶ γὰρ οἱ Συρακόσιοι πολέμωι μὲν οὐκέτι 3 ἐνόμιζον ἂν περιγενέσθαι, ὡς αὐτοῖς οὐδὲ ἀπὸ τῆς Πελοποννήσου ὠφελία οὐδεμία ἧκε, τοὺς δὲ λόγους ἔν τε σφίσιν αὐτοῖς ἐποιοῦντο ξυμβατικοὺς καὶ πρὸς τὸν Νικίαν· οὗτος γὰρ ἤδη μόνος εἶχε Λαμάχου τεθνεῶτος τὴν ἀρχήν. καὶ κύρωσις μὲν οὐδεμία ἐγίγνετο, οἷα δὲ εἰκὸς ἀνθρώπων 4 ἀπορούντων καὶ μᾶλλον ἢ πρὶν πολιορκουμένων, πολλὰ ἐλέγετο πρός τε ἐκεῖνον καὶ πλείω ἔτι κατὰ τὴν πόλιν. καὶ γάρ τινα καὶ ὑποψίαν ὑπὸ τῶν παρόντων κακῶν ἐς ἀλλήλους εἶχον, καὶ τοὺς στρατηγούς τε ἐφ' ὧν αὐτοῖς ταῦτα ξυνέβη ἔπαυσαν, ὡς ἢ δυστυχίαι ἢ προδοσίαι τῆι ἐκείνων βλαπτόμενοι, καὶ ἄλλους ἀνθείλοντο, Ἡρακλείδην καὶ Εὐκλέα καὶ Τελλίαν.

104 Ἐν δὲ τούτωι Γύλιππος ὁ Λακεδαιμόνιος καὶ αἱ ἀπὸ τῆς Κορίνθου νῆες περὶ Λευκάδα ἤδη ἦσαν, βουλόμενοι ἐς τὴν Σικελίαν διὰ τάχους βοηθῆσαι. καὶ ὡς αὐτοῖς αἱ ἀγγελίαι ἐφοίτων δειναὶ καὶ πᾶσαι ἐπὶ τὸ αὐτὸ ἐψευσμέναι ὡς ἤδη παντελῶς ἀποτετειχισμέναι αἱ Συράκουσαί εἰσι, τῆς μὲν Σικελίας οὐκέτι ἐλπίδα οὐδεμίαν εἶχεν ὁ Γύλιππος, τὴν δὲ Ἰταλίαν βουλόμενος περιποιῆσαι αὐτὸς μὲν καὶ Πυθὴν ὁ Κορίνθιος ναυσὶ δυοῖν μὲν Λακωνικαῖν, δυοῖν δὲ Κορινθίαιν ὅτι τάχιστα ἐπεραιώθησαν τὸν Ἰόνιον ἐς Τάραντα, οἱ δὲ Κορίνθιοι πρὸς ταῖς σφετέραις δέκα Λευκαδίας δύο καὶ Ἀμπρακιώτιδας 2 τρεῖς προσπληρώσαντες ὕστερον ἔμελλον πλεύσεσθαι. καὶ ὁ μὲν Γύλιππος ἐκ τοῦ Τάραντος ἐς τὴν Θουρίαν πρῶτον πρεσβευσάμενος κατὰ τὴν τοῦ πατρός ποτε πολιτείαν καὶ οὐ δυνάμενος αὐτοὺς προσαγαγέσθαι, ἄρας παρέπλει τὴν Ἰταλίαν, καὶ ἁρπασθεὶς ὑπ' ἀνέμου κατὰ τὸν Τεριναῖον κόλπον, ὃς ἐκπνεῖ ταύτηι μέγας κατὰ βορέαν ἑστηκώς, ἀποφέρεται ἐς τὸ πέλαγος, καὶ πάλιν χειμασθεὶς ἐς τὰ μάλιστα τῶι Τάραντι προσμίσγει· καὶ τὰς ναῦς, ὅσαι μάλιστα ἐπόνησαν ὑπὸ τοῦ χειμῶνος, ἀνελκύσας 3 ἐπεσκεύαζεν. ὁ δὲ Νικίας πυθόμενος αὐτὸν προσπλέοντα ὑπερεῖδε τὸ πλῆθος τῶν νεῶν, ὅπερ καὶ οἱ Θούριοι ἔπαθον, καὶ ληιστικώτερον ἔδοξε παρεσκευασμένους πλεῖν καὶ οὐδεμίαν φυλακήν πω ἐποιεῖτο.

105 Κατὰ δὲ τοὺς αὐτοὺς χρόνους τούτου τοῦ θέρους καὶ Λακεδαιμόνιοι ἐς τὸ Ἄργος ἐσέβαλον αὐτοί τε καὶ οἱ ξύμμαχοι καὶ τῆς γῆς τὴν πολλὴν ἐδήιωσαν, καὶ Ἀθηναῖοι Ἀργείοις τριάκοντα ναυσὶν ἐβοήθησαν· αἵπερ τὰς σπονδὰς φανερώτατα τὰς πρὸς τοὺς Λακεδαιμονίους αὐτοῖς ἔλυσαν. 2 πρότερον μὲν γὰρ ληιστείαις ἐκ Πύλου καὶ περὶ τὴν ἄλλην Πελοπόννησον μᾶλλον ἢ ἐς τὴν Λακωνικὴν ἀποβαίνοντες μετά τε Ἀργείων καὶ Μαντινέων ξυνεπολέμουν, καὶ πολλάκις Ἀργείων κελευόντων ὅσον σχόντας μόνον ξὺν ὅπλοις ἐς τὴν Λακωνικὴν καὶ τὸ ἐλάχιστον μετὰ σφῶν δηιώσαντας ἀπελθεῖν οὐκ ἤθελον. τότε δὲ Πυθοδώρου καὶ Λαισποδίου καὶ Δημαράτου ἀρχόντων ἀποβάντες ἐς Ἐπίδαυρον τὴν Λιμηρὰν καὶ Πρασιὰς καὶ ὅσα ἄλλα ἐδήιωσαν τῆς γῆς, καὶ τοῖς Λακεδαιμονίοις ἤδη εὐπροφάσιστον μᾶλλον τὴν αἰτίαν ἐς τοὺς Ἀθηναίους τοῦ ἀμύνεσθαι 3 ἐποίησαν. ἀναχωρησάντων δὲ τῶν Ἀθηναίων ἐκ τοῦ Ἄργους ταῖς ναυσὶ καὶ τῶν Λακεδαιμονίων οἱ Ἀργεῖοι ἐσβαλόντες ἐς τὴν Φλειασίαν τῆς τε γῆς αὐτῶν ἔτεμον καὶ ἀπέκτεινάν τινας, καὶ ἀπῆλθον ἐπ' οἴκου.

104.2 κατὰ τὴν τοῦ πατρός ποτε πολιτείαν ACEFGM: καὶ τὴν τοῦ πατρὸς ἀνανεωσάμενος πολιτείαν B   Τεριναῖον codd.: Ταραντῖνον Poppo Θουριναῖον Peronaci

COMMENTARY

1–5: INTRODUCTORY

1.1 *Athenian Interest in Sicily*

Th. will later emphasise that the expedition might have succeeded (Intr., 2); **8–26** will illuminate not just Nicias' reasons for caution but also the reasons why the *dēmos* decided the way it did (p. 122). This first sentence, however, leaves no doubt that the decision was ill-considered, and at several points he overstates the case (nn.). His first audience would know the expedition's outcome; even those future readers that he has in mind (1.22.3–4) have learned at 2.65.11–12 that it ended in disaster. This is not the way one would introduce an enterprise that would end in success.

Several phrases here are accordingly echoed in Nicias' first speech. On the scale of the project cf. **8.**4 μεγάλου ἔργου, **9.**1 μεγάλων πραγμάτων, **12.**2 τὸ πρᾶγμα μέγα εἶναι; with the comparison to the war with the Peloponnesians cf. **10.**1–3; on barbarians cf. **9.**1 ἀνδράσιν ἀλλοφύλοις (though here their numbers and presence make Sicily more formidable while Nicias' tone is dismissive). The stress on conquest (καταστρέψασθαι, εἰ δύναιντο), repeated at **6.**1 (τῆς πάσης ἄρξαι), also exposes the mealy-mouthed phrasing of the decree at **8.**2 (n.) ('if the war left them any further possibility, to settle other Sicilian affairs in whichever way they thought in Athens' best interests').

1.1 Τοῦ δ᾽ αὐτοῦ χειμῶνος: 416–415 BCE; arrangement 'by summers and winters' (2.1.1, 5.26.1) is a hallmark of Th.'s narrative. The final event recorded in Bk. 5 was the treatment of Melos, together with the notice that Athens later sent out 500 colonists (thus showing themselves a colonising power along with the others of **2–5**: Avery 1973: 10). On the juxtaposition of Melos and Sicily see Intr., 17–20. **ἐβούλοντο:** the imperfect may be 'inceptive' ('began to want') but if so it also marks the continuation of that wanting: see *CGCG* 33.52 n.1. The eagerness therefore pre-existed the debate of **8–24** (spring 415) and was there already during winter 416–415 as they completed the defeat of Melos. Th. does not yet mention the 'oracle-mongers, seers, and those who in any way used divination to give them hope of success' (8.1.1): they illuminate the popular mood more tellingly then, as the target of recriminations after the catastrophe. For the moment, the Athenians do not need much egging on.

αὖθις μείζονι παρασκευῆι τῆς μετὰ Λάχητος καὶ Εὐρυμέδοντος: αὖθις is placed early for emphasis, and works closely with μείζονι: to go again, but this time with a bigger force. For the first expedition of 427–424 BCE see Intr., 30–2. Laches was sent with the first detachment in 427 (3.86.1); Eurymedon followed in winter 426–425 (3.115.5). The total of ships sent then was 20 + 40 (3.86.1, 3.115.4, 4.2.2), though doubtless some of the first 20 ships of 3.86.1 were no longer seaworthy by the time the 40 arrived. Now the first proposal is for 60 (**8.2**), later upgraded to 100 (**25.2**), or 100 + 34 allied triremes + 2 Rhodian penteconters (**31.3, 43**). That initial proposal is therefore not for a detachment much 'bigger' than the 20 + 40 of 427–424 (cf. Intr., 31), but the imperfect tense of ἐβούλοντο may be taken as extending also to and beyond the debate itself. παρασκευή = 'resources' held in preparation for (especially military) action. This is a Thucydidean preoccupation: his first sentence observes that both sides began the Peloponnesian War at the peak of their παρασκευή (1.1.1, cf. 1.19.1), and, as here, that prepares for the greatness of what is to come. The noun occurs more frequently in Bk. 6 (31x) than in any other, with a particular concentration in **1–44** (Allison 1989: 66): the theme culminates at **31.1** (n.).   καταστρέψασθαι: in Th.'s view, similar thoughts had been in play as early as 427, when the Athenians launched that expedition 'on the πρόφασις of kinship but wanting to prevent the transport of corn to the Peloponnese and to make a preliminary trial (πρόπειραν) to see if Sicilian affairs could be brought under their control (ὑποχείρια γενέσθαι)', 3.86.4. That need not imply any delusion in 427 that the initial 20 ships might be enough, only that these might explore the potential for later activity. Then in 424 the Athenian *dēmos* punished the returning generals for abandoning the expedition 'when it was possible to καταστρέψασθαι Sicilian affairs' (4.65.3). If Th. is right about such thinking, his Hermocrates has some reason to denounce Athenian 'plotting' against 'all Sicily' and their thoughts of one day coming in larger numbers, 4.60. See Intr., 21, 31.   ἄπειροι οἱ πολλοὶ ὄντες: in 'partial apposition' to Ἀθηναῖοι, 'unacquainted, most of them, . . .'. The qualification is necessary, as some 5000 Athenians would have seen Sicilian service in 427–424 (Kagan 1981: 165), though not all would still be alive. Plutarch describes how the better informed would draw the outline of Sicily in the dust and tell of the sea, the harbours, and the topography (*Nic.* 12.1, *Alc.* 17.4): that sounds like the sort of knowledge that veterans would bring back. In their different ways both writers are bringing out the blend of fascination and ignorance (Intr., 15, 33). On ἄπειροι see also on ἀνηιροῦντο below.   καὶ Ἑλλήνων καὶ βαρβάρων: a 'seed' for several passages where the Greek–barbarian distinction becomes important. It is an organising principle in **1.2–5** (nn.); Nicias then tries to stir up racial prejudice at **9**.1 (n.), and ethnic differences are important in the catalogues of 7.57–8 (cf. esp. 7.58.3 n.), even though self-interest matters more (7.57.1). The impact of the war on barbarians as well as Greeks was stressed at the outset (1.1.2), but despite Peloponnesian approaches to non-Greeks (2.7.1, cf. 1.82.1, 4.50) their role has so far been small. Bks. 6–7 will change that, and Persian involvement is important in Bk. 8. οὐ πολλῶι τινὶ ὑποδεέστερον 'not smaller to any great degree'; cf. Athenagoras at **36**.4. Here and at **1**.2 τινι adds as little as 'any' in the difference between 'not to any great degree' and 'not to a great degree', and Th. elsewhere uses just οὐ πολλῶι in such phrases (5.59.2, 7.19.2): Hdt. too favours the phrase οὐ πολλῶι τεωι, particularly in geographical and ethnographic passages (Hdt. 1.181.1, 2.48.2, 2.67.2, 4.47.1, etc.), and so this may be the first of the Herodoteanisms (**1**.2–**5** n.). Such phrases as οὐ πολλοί τινες (**51**.2), τισὶν οὐ πολλοῖς (**94**.2), and τινὲς . . . οὐ πολλοί (**100**.2) have a different effect, with τινες felt in stronger apposition: 'some – not many'. ἀνηιροῦντο 'they were taking up' or 'on'. Strictly this is proleptic, as the 'taking up' would only come with the decision to go, not the 'wanting'; Spratt and Marchant therefore take it as 'imperfect of intention' (a questionable category, but cf. *M&T* 38). It also extends ἄπειροι from its narrower meaning 'not having experience' (LSJ 1) to a broader 'not knowing' (LSJ 2). But the shorthand is easy enough. τὸν πρὸς Πελοποννησίους 'the one against the Peloponnesians'. The phrase leaves it open whether this implies 'the one they were already fighting', thus agreeing with Nicias at **10**.1–2 and Th. himself at 5.26.2 that the war had not stopped, or 'the [Archidamian] war that they had fought', or 'the war that would shortly resume'.

1.2–5.3 *Sicily and its Peoples*

The Athenians were ignorant of Sicily's size and the number of its inhabitants, both Greek and barbarian (**1**.1): this survey accordingly treats first size (**1**.2) and then population, both barbarian (**2**) and Greek (**3–5**). As at 1.1–21 Th. delves back into the distant past (hence this is sometimes known as the 'Sicilian Archaeology' just as 1.1–21 is the 'Archaeology'). The structural parallel with Bk. 1 (Rawlings 1981: 65–7) underlines that it is all beginning again, and for similar reasons (**6**.1 n.). The echoes of 1.1.1–2 in the first sentence may already have suggested as much (nn. above on παρασκευή and on καὶ Ἑλλήνων καὶ βαρβάρων). The length of the panel is itself a pointer to the momentousness of what is to come.

The Bk. 1 equivalent had a clear argumentative thrust: this was the greatest war yet (1.1, 21.2). Here Th. does not underline a single thesis in the same way. He does not elaborate on Sicilian manpower or wealth, though he had mentioned these briefly at 1.17 (Kallet 2001: 24–5: cf. Hdt. 7.158.4), or on the terrain in which they would be operating. Nor does he indicate the Greek cities' geographical relation to one another, though he does with the barbarians (**2**.4–6). The chapters do provide some knowledge to contrast with that Athenian ignorance, but much is left to the reader to piece together as the narrative unfolds, for instance Athens' various alliances (Intr., 29–32) and a clearer idea of the geography, esp. in 7.58 (Rood 2012: 142, Fantasia 2012: 13–14). Still, just as 1.1–21 also insinuated other themes – sea-power, wealth, the different sorts of imperial control – so here Th. introduces ideas: the mobility and instability of Sicilian populations, the links to their mother-cities (Fragoulaki 2013: 91–2), the ethnic mix, the 'destructions' of cities by their neighbours, the gathering power of Syracuse. Past migrations and colonisations are presented as largely successful, and the Athenian enterprise will come to resemble a colonisation itself, a whole city on the move (**23**.2, **44**.1, 7.77.7 nn.; Avery 1973, Kallet 2001: 25–7). Just as **1**.1 might support Nicias' caution, so this material gives some support to Alcibiades: this 'colonisation' might be successful too, and the power of Syracuse is a threat that needs to be met. Alcibiades duly echoes these themes at **17** (nn.) just as Nicias echoes **1**.1 (n.).

It is generally thought that Th. draws much of his information here from the *Sikelika* of his older contemporary Antiochus of Syracuse (*FGrH* 555), who carried the story down to 424/3 BCE. Our fragments of the *Sikelika* are sparse, but this may well be right: the case was argued in detail by Dover (1953 and in *HCT*), though it is more likely than Dover allows that Th. supplemented this from other reading and general knowledge. See *EGM* ii. 503–11 and 633–6, Luraghi 1991, 1992, 2002, and in *BNJ*, and *CT* 272–4.

Th. combines two chronological schemes, relating the pre-Greek phase (**2**) to the Trojan War, then giving intervals of years for Greek colonisation (**3–5**): the initial anchor is the founding of Syracuse (**3**.2 n.). The two schemes need not reflect a change of source; an earlier author might have combined them as Th. does. But they may ultimately depend on different types of local tradition, one concerned with legendary ancestors and one giving chronicles or lists (not necessarily authentic ones) of magistrates or eras (*CT* 273, 276, cf. Morakis 2011: 463–7), or possibly a list of cities' annual sacrifices at the shrine of Apollo Archegetes (**3**.1 n.: so Murray 2014).

The only indication of the absolute distance from the present is given not for Syracuse but for Megara Hyblaea (**4**.2), and then only indirectly by giving the time between foundation and destruction (483/2 BCE). Th. knew from Hdt. 7.156.2 when that destruction took place; he could have done the calculation, and dated the foundation of Syracuse to, for instance, 'about 320 years before the Athenians attacked' in the manner that he used at 1.13.3–4. His readers might have welcomed the help. His focus on Megara is the odder because it imports uncertainty over the earlier dates, as the interval between the takeover of Leontini, four years after Syracuse, and the foundation of Megara Hyblaea (**4.**1 n.) is left unspecified: as in *HCT* the symbol '*x*' will represent that interval in the nn. here. Th.'s choice may reflect a geographical habit of specifying a city's life-span (e.g. Diod. 13.59.4 and 13.62.4, 242 years from Selinus' foundation and 240 years from Himera's to their destruction in 409/8 BCE; cf. Luraghi 1992: 51 n. 44); it may also strike a Herodotean note, emphasising the transience of a city's good fortune (Hdt. 1.5.3–4). Cf. Th. 3.68.5: 'such was the end of Plataea, in the ninety-third year after they became allies of the Athenians'. Cities come and go.

D. H. *Ad Pomp.* 3.12 noted the change in style from the usual narrative, and thought such variation a 'pleasant thing' (ἡδὺ χρῆμα). But the survey is crowded with too many facts for easy digestion, in contrast to the slower-paced 1.1–21. That has its own effect, conveying instability and complexity. These chapters also show some distinctive quirks of style, often Ionic rather than Attic, that have parallels in Herodotus, especially in his more ethnographic passages (nn.: Fowler 1996: 76 n. 106 = 2013: 67 n. 106 and *EGM* ii. 634–6), and these may be more general features of ethnographic writing; some may be taken over directly from Antiochus. There are Herodoteanisms in the excursus on Pausanias and Themistocles too (1.128–38: Munson 2012), and they are felt appropriate for a world that is distant in time (Pausanias and Themistocles) or, as here, in both time and place.

That feeling of difference is reinforced by the gestures to Homer and 'the poets' at **2.**1 (cf. 'Charybdis' during the first Sicilian expedition, 4.24.5; Rood 2012: 154), and the admissions of uncertainty in **2.**1–4. Athenians are voyaging into the unknown, a distant, Homeric world (Mackie 1996), but one from which most will enjoy no Odyssean νόστος (ὀλίγοι ἀπὸ πολλῶν ἐπ' οἴκου ἀπενόστησαν, 7.87.6: Frangoulidis 1993). Cf. Intr., 33.

On the role of the survey within the history and its relation to the archaeological evidence see Pothou 2009: 134–41 and Congiu, Miccichè, and Modeo 2012, both with full bibliography up to those dates. Th.'s dates for the Greek foundations stand up fairly well, though there is a case for pushing the dates of the earliest colonies some twenty years earlier (la Torre 2012).

1.2 Σικελία γὰρ περίπλους . . . ἡμερῶν 'Sicily can be circumnavigated in a merchant ship in not much less than eight days'. γάρ explains the massiveness of what they were taking on. All MSS have the genitive Σικελίας, which is certainly easier Greek. Σικελία though is the reading of P. Bodmer XXVII (Intr., 36) and is probably right: cf. 2.97.1, again in a geographical excursus: 'this land [that of the Odrysae] is περίπλους . . . τεσσάρων ἡμερῶν καὶ ἴσων νυκτῶν in a merchant ship'. It is less clear whether περίπλους would be heard as an adj., 'circumnavigable', as LSJ takes 2.97.1 and the scholiast there suggests (δυνατὴ περιπλευσθῆναι), or as a noun (Rusten on 2.97.1). The rare adjectival use is easier with ἐστιν but more difficult with ἡμερῶν, which would then be 'best explained as depending on the substantive implied' in the adj. (*GG* 1145). Some analogy for a noun is offered by Hdt. 2.29.3 τὸ δὲ χωρίον τοῦτό ἐστι ἐπ' ἡμέρας τέσσερας πλόος, but that is easier as χωρίον is there an expanse covered in a journey. On balance, it is preferable to take it as an adj., but not all may have heard the syntax in the same way: cf. p. ix.   **μέν** picks up the first aspect of Athenian ignorance, size (**1.1**); the second, the inhabitants, is taken up at **2.1** (δέ). **οὐ πολλῶι τινι: 1.1** n.   **ἔλασσον:** ἐλάσσων might be expected, but neuter or adverbial ἔλασσον is regular with numerals: cf. e.g. **25**.2, **67**.2, **95**.1, **97**.3; with πλέον, 7.19.2, 7.27.5.   **ὀκτὼ ἡμερῶν:** Ephorus, *FGrH* 70 F 135 (= Strabo 6.2.1) says 'five days and nights'. Th. is assuming that the crew would rest at night.   **ἐν εἰκοσισταδίωι . . . εἶναι** 'is prevented in a twenty-stade expanse of sea from being mainland'. This is an odd way of describing the Straits of Messina, but it has a point: this island that is almost mainland is now being attacked by the mainland power, Athens, that would be almost impregnable were it an island (1.143.5, cf. Ps.-Xen. ['Old Oligarch'] *Ath. Pol.* 2.14–16: Connor 1984: 160, Kopp 2016: 92–3; cf. **3**.2 n.). Crushing the small island Melos was one thing; this big one would be different. Sicily's closeness to the mainland also means, as Th. had earlier noted (4.24.4–5), that 'the Athenians would not be able to blockade and control the strait'. Engl. would say that the island was separated 'by' a particular distance; it is just as logical to say that the separation is 'in' an area. A 'stade' most often approximates to 150–200 metres (see *CT* and 7.19.2 n.), and so this is 3–4 km. The minimum distance today is 3.1 km (approx. 2 miles). Other authors give distances between 6 and 12 stades, the most usual being 12 stades or 1.5 'miles' (Plb. 1.42.5, Pliny, *NH* 3.73, 86). On land one can count paces; judging distances over water is more difficult.   **τὸ μὴ ἤπειρος εἶναι:** for τὸ μή + inf. after verbs of hindrance and prevention see *CGCG* 51.36. Demetrius *On Style* 72 cites the words μὴ ἤπειρος εἶναι as an example of elevated style because of the concurrence of long vowels.

2.1 ὠικίσθη δέ: answering περίπλους μέν above. In fact the 'colonisation' aspect is left to the Greek phase of **3–5** (see **2**.2 n.), but τοσάδε ἔθνη ἔσχε τὰ ξύμπαντα is capacious enough to include barbarians (**2**) as well; so the relation between this introductory sentence and the exposition is chiastic (A-B-B-A). **τὸ ἀρχαῖον** 'in ancient times', adverbial as at 4.6 (*GG* 1060): it is a Herodotean phrase (e.g. 1.56.2, 7.155.1), but perhaps not distinctively so (e.g. Aesch. *Supp.* 326, Plato, *Crat.* 411e, X. *Hell.* 5.2.7). **τοσάδε ἔθνη ἔσχε τὰ ξύμπαντα:** it is easier to take 'Sicily' as still the subject and ἔθνη as object (cf. 2.68.4, Soph. *Phil.* 1147) rather than the other way round (cf. 1.12.3), but different native speakers may have 'heard' the syntax in different ways. **ἐν μέρει τινὶ τῆς χώρας:** the vagueness signals the caution appropriate for the very early material. **Κύκλωπες καὶ Λαιστρυγόνες ... ἀρκείτω δὲ ὡς ποιηταῖς τε εἴρηται:** the *Odyssey* does not give the Cyclopes (Bk. 9) or the Laestrygonians (10.80–132) an identifiable location, though the Laestrygonians' 'short nights' (if that is what *Od.* 10.85–6 means) suggest the far N. Hesiod's *Catalogue* placed the Laestrygonians in Sicily (F 150), and Theopompus later specifically in Leontini (*FGrH* 115 F 225a). By the fifth century the Cyclopes were also associated with the island: Eur. *Cycl.* (408 BCE?) 20–2, etc. **ἐγώ:** first-person statements and other 'narrator interventions' become more frequent in Th.'s later books (Gribble 1998: esp. 47–9), but they are also characteristic of ethnographic writing: there are many in Hdt. 2. The phrase οὐκ ἔχω εἰπεῖν or οὐκ ἔχω ἀτρεκέως εἰπεῖν is a particular Herodotean favourite (some 20x): here cf. esp. Hdt. 2.130.2 οὐκ ἔχω εἰπεῖν πλὴν ἢ τὰ λεγόμενα. **καὶ ὡς ἕκαστός πηι γιγνώσκει περὶ αὐτῶν:** the tone is dismissive: you might as well think what you like. Th. is more respectful of Homer at 1.9–11. Th. does not spell out that these creatures of Odysseus' world would have been there, presumably co-existing with the Sicans, when the Trojans arrived (**2.3**).

2.2 πρῶτοι φαίνονται ἐνοικισάμενοι 'are clearly the first to have settled there': not 'appear to have been the first...', which would require the inf. ἐνοικίσασθαι rather than the participle: LSJ φαίνω B.II.1. **ἐνοικισάμενοι** 'settled', from ἐνοικίζεσθαι. Th. elsewhere prefers οἰκεῖν ('dwell') and its compounds in **2** (8 x), leaving to **3** οἰκίζειν language with its connotations of Greek colonisation (**2.6, 3.1** nn.); but he probably preferred ἐνοικίζεσθαι here (though ἐνοικησάμενοι is a MS variant) as the word rejects the claim to autochthony. They 'settled' rather than having always been there. **ὡς μὲν αὐτοί φασι:** the Sicans' claim is recorded and endorsed by Timaeus, *FGrH* 566 FF 38, 164. The citing of local tradition and the recording of alternative versions are both more characteristic of Hdt. than of Th. elsewhere (Luraghi 1992: 43). **καὶ πρότεροι** 'being even earlier' dwellers there than the Cyclopes and Laestrygonians. **ὡς δὲ ἡ ἀλήθεια εὑρίσκεται:** 'discovered': by Th. himself or by a predecessor? And on what grounds? Th. does not say, but scepticism about autochthony claims was not unusual: cf. e.g. Hdt. 1.171.2, Diod. 3.20.2, Pelling 2009, Fragoulaki 2013: 220–8. Antiochus, if he is the source and chose the same way, may have given fuller reasons; so may Philistus (see next n.). **Ἴβηρες ὄντες . . . ἀναστάντες:** this was also the version given by Philistus, *FGrH* 556 F 45, and he was roundly criticised for it by Timaeus (Diod. 5.6.1). The dynamic mirrors early Greece in general ('migrations . . . and people readily leaving their territory under pressure from more powerful invaders', 1.2.1). **τοῦ Σικανοῦ ποταμοῦ:** probably the river later called the Sucro, the modern Segre. **Λιγύων:** 'Liguria' was for Romans and is today the coastal region around Genoa, but ps.-Scylax *Periplous* 3–4 says that the 'Ligyes' extended along the French coast from Antion (? Antibes) as far as the Rhône, then mingled with the Iberians as far as Emporion in Catalonia. Cf. Shipley 2011: 92–3: 'Ligyes' and 'Ligurians' may not be an exact match, 'and both may be more construct than reality'. This expulsion of the Sicans is envisaged as happening at the extreme W of the Ligyes' activity. **ἐκαλεῖτο** 'began and continued to be called', 'inceptive' imperf. (cf. **1.**1 n. on ἐβούλοντο). This is the reading of all the MSS; ἐκλήθη (P. Bodmer XXVII) would suggest a once-for-all change of name. That is not impossible, as **2.**2 (ἐκλήθησαν) and **2.**4 (ἐπωνομάσθη) show, but a gradual shift makes better sense. **Τρινακρία:** unlike e.g. Hellanicus, *FGrH* 4 F 79b, Timaeus, *FGrH* 566 F 164.2, and Strabo 6.2.1, Th. does not explain that the old name reflected the triangular shape: he takes for granted that readers know that much. Contrast his explanation of 'sickle-shaped' Zancle, **4.**5 (n.). **ἔτι καὶ νῦν:** a natural enough phrase when current artefacts or behaviour reflect the past (cf. e.g. **54.**7), and predictably found in Hdt. (e.g. 1.173. 3, 2.135.3, 7.178.2). It recurs twice more before the end of this chapter.

2.3 Ἰλίου δὲ ἁλισκομένου: to be taken with διαφυγόντες rather than ἀφικνοῦνται. They fled 'as Troy was falling', but arrived much later. **ξύμπαντες μὲν Ἔλυμοι ἐκλήθησαν** 'the people as a whole were called Elymi', as opposed to the individual cities in the δέ clause. But Hellanicus (*FGrH* 4 F 79b) said that the Elymi were Italians who reached Sicily four years before the Sicels or, as he calls them, Ausoni (**2.**4 n.), and archaeological finds seem to support ultimate Italic descent: see *BNP* 'Elymi' (G. Falco). **ἐκλήθησαν:** 2.2 n. The passive leaves it open whether this naming was their own choice, as presumably in the case of the cities Eryx and Egesta, or that of the Sicans. **Ἔρυξ τε καὶ Ἔγεστα:** see **46.**3 and Fragoulaki 2013: 298–316. Egesta will be important in 415 (**6** nn.), and fittingly features early in the book. In Virgil Aeneas founds the temple of Venus Erycina (**46.**3 n.) and the city of 'Acesta' for the Trojans left in Sicily (*Aen.* 5.746–61): cf. Cic. *Verr.* 2.4.72. This may be what Th. refers to here, but this aspect of the myth may be later (Galinsky

1969: 110; Casali 2010: 44); a vaguer tradition of 'Trojan' settlement was probably sharpened, perhaps by Sicilians themselves, as the Aeneas legend became more popular with the rise of Rome. προσξυνῴκησαν δὲ αὐτοῖς 'also (προσ-) joined in living with (ξυν-)them'. Φωκέων: 'Phocians' do briefly figure in the *Iliad* (2.517–26), and their leader Schedius seems to be killed by Hector not once but twice (15.515–6, 17.307–11). They are still unexpected because, despite indications of a 'hybrid Greek-and-Sicilian self' (Fragoulaki 2013: 308), Egesta is unequivocally seen as 'barbarian' not just by Nicias (**9.**1, **11.**7) but by Th. himself (7.57.11), and at **2.**6 these are all the foundations of βάρβαροι: cf. Sammartano 2012. Emendation to Φρυγῶν has been suggested (Ridgeway 1888; Rigsby 1987), but a distinction between Phrygians and Trojans would seem hair-splitting. Paus. 5.25.3 mentions a Phocian settlement in Sicily, and at **2.**6 it is best to assume that any vestige of that Greekness is regarded as by now washed away by time and miscegenation.   χειμῶνι ἐς Λιβύην πρῶτον . . . κατενεχθέντες: again like Aeneas (see on Ἔρυξ τε καὶ Ἔγεστα above), but now it is Greeks who are storm-tossed and 'driven ashore'. Gylippus' similar weatherbeaten arrival will symmetrically end (what is now, Intr., 14) Bk. 6, **104.**2.

2.4 Σικελοὶ δὲ . . . ἐς Σικελίαν: similarly but more fully Hellanicus, *FGrH* 4 F 79a, 'led by Sicelus, the Ausoni [cf. Virgil's 'Ausonia'] were displaced from Italy by the Iapyges and crossed to the island, which was then called Sicania; they settled there around Etna under the rule of Sicelus, who established a monarchy. Using this as his base, Sicelus established control of the whole island, and it took its name from the king.' Ausoni are 'a shadowy prehistoric people, available for various reconstructions' (*EGM* ii. 510); for Antiochus, they were synonymous with the Opici (see next n.: *FGrH* 555 F 11). Th. does not say that this crossing came after the Trojan War, but his sequence implies it and that is what D. H. *A.R.* 1.22 takes him as meaning. D. H. there cites Hellanicus as dating it to the third generation *before* the Trojan War (= *FGrH* 4 F 79a) and Philistus to the eightieth year before the war (= *FGrH* 556 F 46), adding that Antiochus 'does not make the timing clear' (= *FGrH* 555 F 4). This need not be seen as a serious deviation of Th. from Antiochus, requiring explanation in terms of a second source (though this is possible) or of D. H. using only Antiochus' *On Italy* whereas his *On Sicily* would have made the date clear (e.g. Dover 1953: 11–12 = 1968: 357–8 and *HCT*; Luraghi 1992: 60–1 and on *BNJ* 555 F 4; Murray 2014: 461). Th. too does not 'make the timing clear' with the precision that D. H. cites for Hellanicus and Philistus.   Ὀπικούς: a people based in Campania, predecessors of the Oscans: see *OCD*[1]. Antiochus said 'Oenotrians and Opici', *FGrH* 555 F 4 = D. H. *A.R.* 1.22.5; the Oenotrians extended S of the Opici as far as

Calabria (*EGM* ii. 504–6). Hellanicus (above) specifies the Iapyges, whose homeland was Apulia; D. H. *A.R.* 1.22.1 has 'Aborigines and Pelasgians', neither name pointing to any very specific location.   ὡς μὲν εἰκὸς καὶ λέγεται, ἐπὶ σχεδιῶν: on 'rafts' in contrast to the πλοίοις of **2**.3: so also D. H. *A.R.* 1.22.1. Th. again (cf. **2**.2 n.) does not say why he prefers this version, as nothing would preclude a people in the toe of Italy from becoming more maritime than to rely on rafts. Such a manoeuvre would be perilous even with a favourable wind (κατιόντος τοῦ ἀνέμου, cf. 2.84.3), for the water flows deep and fast (4.24.5), but migrants are driven to desperate measures. In 250 BCE L. Caecilius Metellus was said to have transported 140 elephants across the straits on giant rafts constructed from amphorae lashed together (Frontin. *Strat.* 1.7.1).   τηρήσαντες τὸν πορθμόν: πορθμός is probably here an abstract 'passage', the act of crossing water, as at Eur. *Cycl.* 108 where Silenus is shocked by Odysseus' arrival in Sicily: 'How could that be? Did you not know the πορθμός to your homeland?' τηρεῖν will then be 'look out for' the opportunity to cross, as in ἄνεμον τηρεῖν, 1.65.1. Less likely, 'keep an eye on the [physical] crossing itself', i.e. the Straits.   τάχα ἄν δὲ ... 'but perhaps they might have ...'. Th. is again cautious.   ἐν τῆι Ἰταλίαι Σικελοί: it is not known where.   ἡ χώρα ... Ἰταλία ἐπωνομάσθη: 'this was his name' makes it clear that Ἰταλοῦ is not just 'an Italian'. Antiochus made Italus a king of the Oenotrians a generation before the crossing (*FGrH* 555 F 2), ruling over much of S. Italy (FF 3a, 5: *EGM* ii. 508). His kingdom would therefore include the Italian Sicels, and Th. may be abbreviating rather than disagreeing. Hellanicus, *FGrH* 4 F 111 took a different approach, deriving 'Italia' from *uitulus* ('calf'): cf. *EGM* ii. 302–3.

2.5 στρατὸς πολύς 'as a large army', in apposition with the plural ἐλθόντες.   τούς τε Σικανοὺς ... ἑσπέρια αὐτῆς: if this is later than **2**.3, the Sicels would have had to deal with the Trojans (now 'Elymi') and Phocians as well as the Sicans, but Eryx and Egesta were not affected by the migration and Th. focuses on the defeat that led to the change of name.   ἐπεὶ διέβησαν 'from the time that they crossed'. The use is mainly poetic and archaic (LSJ ἐπεί A.I.2).   ἔτη ἐγγύτατα τριακόσια πρὶν Ἕλληνας ἐς Σικελίαν ἐλθεῖν: acc. of the period during which they held the best land. ἐγγύτατα is read by P. Bodmer XXVII; the codd. have ἐγγύς. Either is possible: for ἐγγύς cf. **5**.2, for ἐγγύτατα **4**.4 and **5**.3. Th. usually prefers μάλιστα when qualifying numerals (**1**.2, 7.1.5, 19.2, 29.3, etc.), and ἐγγύς/ἐγγύτατα again looks like an ethnographic (though not in this case Herodotean) mannerism. This dating pushes the arrival of the Sicels back to c. 1035 BCE. D. H. *A.R.* 1.22.5 infers that Th. is placing it 'many years' after the Trojan War, which would be true if Th. accepted a date for the fall of Troy similar to that of Herodotus ('eight hundred years before my time', 2.145.4) or even Ephorus (1135 BCE, *FGrH* 70 F 223). Th. does not commit himself, leaving the cluster around the Trojan War (**2.3**) in a separate chronological category from the Greek colonisations (**3–5**; cf. **1.2–5**.3 n.). τὰ μέσα καὶ τὰ πρὸς βορρᾶν τῆς νήσου ἔχουσιν: as one would expect if they came from the Italian N. But this can hardly be taken as evidence for their origin: the Phoenicians could have driven them northwards (**2.6** n.). Th. notes it as a corollary rather than as an argument.

2.6 ᾤκουν δὲ καὶ Φοίνικες   'Phoenicians too were dwelling' or 'began to dwell', which need not suggest anything on the scale of the later colonisation (which would be ᾤκισαν, **3.1**): see Moscati 1985. Th. leaves it vague when they arrived, though 'Sicels' suggests it was later than **2.5**. Archaeology has not confirmed such an early Phoenician presence, and it looks as if they arrived at more or less the same time as the Greeks (*IACP* 173; Leighton 1999: 255–32). It is not clear whether 'Phoenicians' around the Mediterranean yet thought of themselves as a coherent whole; perhaps the name was at this stage a catch-all used by Greek and later by Roman observers. On this see Quinn 2018.   περὶ πᾶσαν μὲν τὴν Σικελίαν 'around all Sicily', on the coast rather than diffused throughout the island: μέν … δέ … contrasts the later phase when they concentrated in the NW.   ἀπολαβόντες 'occupying', 'separating off' the promontories and adjacent islands from inland Sicily: 'occupying enclaves on' (Hammond) captures the sense. It need not imply formidable barriers: the trade with the Sicels suggests easy coming and going.   πολλοί 'in great numbers'.   κατὰ θάλασσαν 'by sea' – apparently redundant with ἐπεσέπλεον, but the point may be to contrast the open sea with the earlier arrivals over the straits (**2.4**).   ἐπεσέπλεον: the ἐπ- conveys 'in addition' to the peoples already settled there. Malkin 2005: 250 = 2011: 134 translates the imperfect as inceptive, 'began arriving by sea', and comments that this puts the NW settlements too early. The fortification of Motye for instance seems to be c. 580, and if Th. is right that proximity to Carthage was a factor, that becomes plausible only with the city's rise c. 600: thus 'Thucydides implies resistance and conflict right from the start between the two ethnicities Phoenicians and Greeks, whereas in fact the initial situation in Sicily had been fluid, reciprocal, and transitory'. So also Quinn 2018: 52, and it does seem that early peaceful interactions worsened only in the sixth century: *IACP* 175–6, de Angelis 2016: 49–50. But the 'inceptive' imperfect typically suggests 'began *and continued*' (*CGCG* 33.52 n.1), and can point to a gradual process, with Th. summing up the 'barbarian' aspects over a longer period before jumping back to the arrival of the Greeks. He need not then be implying that any conflict began 'right from the start'. **Μοτύην καὶ Σολόεντα καὶ Πάνορμον:** the modern San Pantaleo, Solanto, and Palermo, in and off the NW of the island: see Map 1. **βάρβαροι μὲν οὖν . . .:** summing up and preparing for the transition ('Ελλήνων δὲ . . .). βάρβαροι ignores the Greek Phocians (**2.3** n.); it is also the earliest case we have where the Phoenicians are counted as barbarians (Quinn 2018: 51–2). The point is to distinguish this phase from that of Greek colonisation ('Ελλήνων δὲ . . ., **3.1**), and this explains the simplification. It should not be taken to indicate an unresolved contradiction of different sources (Luraghi 1992: 48–9). **τοσοίδε** 'so many': the point is less 'so many in total', as only στρατὸς πολύς (**2.5**) has suggested great numbers, than 'so many different' as at **6.1**. Sicilians are a mixed bunch.

3.1 Ἑλλήνων δὲ πρῶτοι Χαλκιδῆς . . . Νάξον ᾤκισαν: for Naxos see *IACP* 218–20. For Th.'s dates see **1.2–5.3** n.; this foundation will be 733 + *x* BCE (where *x* = the interval between Leontini and Megara Hyblaea, **3.3–4.1**). That is reasonably close to the date of the earliest ceramic finds at Naxos (*IACP* 173, 218, de Angelis 2016: 69), though the true foundation date may be c. 750 (la Torre 2012). Naxos will have been one of the Chalcidian cities backing Leontini against Syracuse in 427 (3.86.2), and it supported Athens in 415–413. **μετὰ Θουκλέους οἰκιστοῦ:** Ephorus, *FGrH* 70 F 137 made 'Theocles' an Athenian who led a party including 'many Euboean Chalcidians, some Ionians, and some Dorians, mainly from Megara': the Chalcideans founded Naxos and the Dorians Megara 'that was previously called Hybla'. Ephorus put this in the tenth generation after the Trojan War. He also seems to imply near-simultaneity of the Naxos and Megara foundations against Th.'s interval of over five years (**3.2–4.1**), but our citations of the fragment may have omitted an interval of racial harmony before the Dorians split away. Still, Ephorus' description of the foundation of Megara is different anyway (**4.1** n.), and we should not try too hard to reconcile the versions. **οἰκιστοῦ Νάξον ᾤκισαν:** the first of 31 (apparently, though in some cases the MSS differ) οἰκίζειν, οἰκιστής, ἀποικία, and κτίζειν words in **3–5**, picking up ᾠκίσθη δὲ ὧδε at **2.1**. Colonisation, with all its Greek connotations – founders and founder-cult, links to mother-city – is the refrain of this Greek phase, whereas **2** talked less technically of 'dwelling', οἰκεῖν: **2.2, 2.6** nn.

Mother-cities' relations with their colonies could vary, sometimes coming close to 'control' and sometimes being much looser. Colonies could also come about in different ways, sometimes perhaps launched by the enterprise of the οἰκισταί rather than on a state initiative (Osborne 1998, but see also Malkin 2002, 2003, Murray 2014: 469, Figueira 2015:

318–19). Osborne also argued that archaeology sometimes points to some continuity before and after the claimed foundation-date, so that 'becoming a Greek settlement . . . may often have been a gradual process' (Osborne 1998: 264–5). Yet the material finds in most cases, not all, fit the traditional dates pretty well, and these dates will usually reflect an important turning-point, not just an invented past. 'For most Greek colonies the foundation was an "event" in concrete and sometimes traumatic ways: conquest, violent destruction, and appropriation' (Malkin 2002: 201, cf. Dougherty 1993). Ἀπόλλωνος Ἀρχηγέτου: 'Apollo who leads and guides' is appropriate for colonisation projects (cf. Pind. *P.* 5.60 and the Cyrene foundation inscription, ML 5 = Fornara 18 ll. 10–11), especially if Delphian Apollo had given them oracular approval. The altar was still in place in 36 BCE (App. *BC* 5.109.454–5). βωμὸν ὅστις νῦν ἔξω τῆς πόλεώς ἐστιν: again Herodotean/ethnographic in manner. In particular, Th. elsewhere uses ὅς rather than ὅστις in such formulations, but for the Ionic ὅστις as a simple relative (LSJ s.v. II.1 fin.) cf. e.g. Hdt. 2.99 πόλιν . . . ἥτις νῦν Μέμφις καλεῖται; *EGM* ii. 634 and n.7. It is also found in Antiochus of Syracuse, *FGrH* 555 F 2 τὴν γῆν ταύτην, ἥτις νῦν Ἰταλία καλεῖται, but that need not imply that the phrasing here is taken over directly from Antiochus. The wording may suggest that originally the altar was inside rather than outside the city (Sammartano 2018); if so, it will be the city that moved. ἐφ' ὧι . . . θύουσιν: an odd detail in so compressed an account. It is no surprise that θεωροί – members of a religious delegation, often to Delphi – should sacrifice to Apollo before sailing; but there is point in noting (a) that such θεωρίαι are a regular feature, reflecting the close contact with Greece, and (b) that apparently all Sicilian θεωροί do this. There already exists some sense of a 'Sikeliote–Hellenic identity' (Malkin 2011: ch. 3). Th. is not yet following through the threads of the individual cities (4.2 n.), and hence does not mention the Naxians' 'enslavement' by Hippocrates of Gela in the 480s (Hdt. 7.154) or Hieron's transplantation of its population to Leontini in 476 (3.3 n.). The expatriates presumably returned after Hieron's death (*IACP* 218); the city was repopulated by 415 (50.2–3, etc.).

3.2 τοῦ ἐχομένου ἔτους 'in the next year' (LSJ ἔχω C.a.3), i.e. 732 + *x*. Th. never uses ἐχομένου in this sense elsewhere, preferring τοῦ δ' ἐπιγιγνομένου ἦρος / χειμῶνος / θέρους. This might be another ethnographic mannerism, though parallels seem to be lacking: Hdt. 2.12.1 τῆς ἐχομένης γῆς, is local rather than temporal. With words like 'year', 'night', or 'summer', it is often possible to phrase either as 'in' (dat.) or 'during' (gen.). With ἔτος Th. usually prefers the dat., as at 3.3, 4.3, 59.4, and 7.28.3 (16x as opposed to 2x gen., George 2014: 77). Here the preference for the gen.

may be because it is the 'next' year rather than a more distant one as in the other instances (George 2014: 86).

These short intervals bring out the speed of Greek infiltration. This date for the foundation of Syracuse fits the archaeological finds (*IACP* 173, 228), though the exact date is much debated. There is also evidence both for Euboeans playing a part in the Syracusan settlement along with Corinthians, or even being there already (Braccesi and Millino 2000: 24–5), and for native Sicilians continuing to live there along with the Greeks (de Angelis 2016: 70–1). **Ἀρχίας:** ps.-Plut. *Love Stories* 772e–773b has a story of Archias leaving Corinth under a cloud: he had been rejected by a boy, Actaeon, whom he was courting, tried to abduct him, and in the struggle the boy was torn to pieces. Delphi ordered that Archias should be punished, and he did not dare to return to Corinth but sailed off to found Syracuse. Paus. 5.7.3 quotes three lines of an oracle delivered to Archias; Strabo 6.2.4 has a variant version. The items exemplify the sort of Herodotean material that typically figured in colonisation stories – the Actaeon story fits a pattern of colonisations originating in blood-guilt (Dougherty 1993) – and that Th. has here excised. Contrast the more expansive 2.102.5–6 (Fragoulaki 2013: 89–93) and **54–59**, where the love story is presented as carrying historical point. **τῶν Ἡρακλειδῶν:** Th. similarly introduces the οἰκιστής of Epidamnus (Φάλιος . . . Κορίνθιος γένος ἀφ' Ἡρακλέους, 1.24.2). Heracles, the great western journeyer, was an appropriate forebear for οἰκισταί. He was also notionally the ancestor of the Bacchiad dynasty, who would have ruled Corinth at the time of the colonisation. It is duly Heracles whom the Syracusans honour at the time of their victory (7.73.2). **τῆς νήσου . . . ἐστιν:** Ortygia. So Syracuse too has its own microhistory in which there is a play between being and not being an island (**1.2** n.). The island was joined to the mainland by a mole: see Map 4. **καὶ ἡ ἔξω προστειχισθεῖσα πολυάνθρωπος ἐγένετο** 'the outer city too' (as well as the inner) 'was included within the walls and became heavily populated': i.e. Achradina (Map 4). Syracuse is immediately signalled as a centre of growth and population: its importance is also marked by the use of its foundation as the anchoring date for the later colonisations, parallel to the use of the Trojan War in **2**.

3.3 καὶ οἱ Χαλκιδῆς: Th. continues to note the original mother-city, as later with the Megarian foundations. **ἔτει πέμπτωι μετὰ Συρακούσας οἰκισθείσας** 'in the fifth year after' (not 'five years after') 'the foundation of Syracuse', hence 728 + *x*. This 'dominant' use of the participle (*CGCG* 52.45) is more common in Latin (e.g. *ab urbe condita*) than in Greek, but cf. e.g. Hdt. 1.34.1 μετὰ δὲ Σόλωνα οἰχόμενον, and see **80.2** n. Th. then varies the phrasing at **4.3**, μετὰ Συρακουσῶν οἴκησιν. **Λεοντίνους . . . οἰκίζουσι:** for

Leontini see *IACP* 209–11.   καὶ μετ' αὐτοὺς Κατάνην: i.e. after Leontini (= αὐτούς), not necessarily in the same year. For Catana see *IACP* 206–7. Th. is not yet presenting in separate threads (4.2 n.), and hence does not follow through Catana's tumultuous fifth-century history: in 476 Hieron had moved its population along with that of Naxos to Leontini, renamed Catana Αἴτνη, and settled it with 10,000 colonists (Diod. 11.49.1–2). The Catanians returned in 461 and expelled the Aetneans (Diod. 11.76.3, Strabo 6.2.3). For *stasis* in the city now cf. 50.3 n., 51.2.   οἰκιστὴν δὲ αὐτοὶ Καταναῖοι ἐποιήσαντο Εὔαρχον: middle because the Catanians chose Euarchos for themselves, as αὐτοί too emphasises; the active ποιήσαντες at 4.4 is because the Geloans appointed Acragas' οἰκισταί. This implies that Catana 'obtained autonomous status soon after its foundation' (*IACP* 206), or rather that the new colonists made a point of claiming this (Malkin 1987: 257).

4.1 κατὰ δὲ τὸν αὐτὸν χρόνον: as in the preceding καὶ μετ' αὐτούς, the following καὶ ὕστερον . . . ὀλίγον χρόνον, and the participles with Lamis, Th. does not pretend to precision when he does not know the intervals. Thus the time elapsed between the settlement of Leontini and that of Megara Hyblaea (= *x*, 1.2–5.3 n.) is the total of these unspecified intervals (Leontini → Catana and 'around the same time' Trotilus → Lamis at Leontini → Thapsus → Megara Hyblaea).   Λάμις ἐκ Μεγάρων ἀποικίαν ἄγων ἐς Σικελίαν ἀφίκετο: whereas Ephorus has Megara Hyblaea a foundation of those Dorians who had arrived with Theocles, *FGrH* 70 F 137 (3.1 n.).   ὑπὲρ Παντακύου τε ποταμοῦ Τρώτιλόν τι ὄνομα χωρίον οἰκίσας: we say 'on' a river; ὑπέρ, 'above', is more exact. Trotilus is not firmly identified; the R. Pantacyas flows S. and E. of Leontini (*Barr.* 47 G 4).   ἐς Λεοντίνους ὀλίγον χρόνον ξυμπολιτεύσας 'he [went] to Leontini [and] joined the settlement for a short time'.   ὑπὸ αὐτῶν ἐκπεσών: relations between the city-groups, here Megarians and Chalcidians, are already full of hostility. Th. has presented the pre-Greek phase of **2** as having moments of violence, but on the whole more placid.   παραδόντος τὴν χώραν 'handing over the territory'. The MSS have προδόντος, 'betraying', which would be oddly succinct even in so compressed a treatment. χώραν, rather than πόλιν, suggests that it is land for development, and it would be strange too to talk of 'betraying' such a plot. Such friendliness contrasts with the violent clashes elsewhere. Malkin 2002: 220–1 explores the reason: 'Greeks were flooding the shores of eastern Sicily . . . Hyblon probably felt threatened and wished to use some Greeks against others'; similarly Graham 2001: 164, Fragoulaki 2013: 55–7. Th. does not speculate. Ephorus' account is again different, with a pre-existing town called Hybla (3.1 n.).   Μεγαρέας ᾤκισαν τοὺς Ὑβλαίους κληθέντας: οἰκίζω can be used either of 'colonising' a place or of 'settling' people, and the place-name is usually Μέγαρα but occasionally Μεγαρεῖς, the same as the people (*IACP* 216): here and at **4.2** (αὐτοὺς οἰκίσαι) it is probably better to take it as the people, already called (κληθέντας) 'the Hyblaean Megarians' even before they founded their eponymous city. For Megara Hyblaea see *IACP* 213–15, *CT*, and Malkin 1987: 164–74 and 2002. Archaeology points to a Greek presence there from the middle of the eighth century or earlier.

4.2 καὶ ἔτη οἰκήσαντες πέντε καὶ τεσσαράκοντα καὶ διακόσια ... ἀνέστησαν: in 483/2 BCE (Hdt. 7.156.2), and so the foundation is dated to 728/7. This is the absolute date from which the others are calculated (**1.2–5.3** n.).   **ὑπὸ Γέλωνος ... χώρας:** so Megara's history began with a friendly barbarian king, Hyblon, and ends at the hands of a hostile Greek tyrant, Gelon. Hdt. 7.156.2 gives details. A siege was ended by negotiation; Gelon made the rich or 'fat cats' (τοὺς παχέας) citizens of Syracuse, but sold the *dēmos* as slaves. By 415 the city's site lay abandoned (**49.4**, cf. **75.1** n.).   **ἔτεσιν ὕστερον ἑκατὸν ἢ αὐτοὺς οἰκίσαι ... Σελινοῦντα κτίζουσι:** so 628 BCE or thereabouts ('100' may be a round number). Diod. 13.59.4 and Euseb. *Chron.* 163F. = 93b H. put it in 651/0 and the earlier date is consistent with the archaeology (*IACP* 172–4, 220–4; Morakis 2011: 479–80), but maybe there were two stages (de Angelis 2016: 73; Braccesi and Millino 2000: 35). If οἰκίσαι is the right reading it must be transitive: Th. writes as if 'the Megarians' in Sicily are an overarching grouping that settled first the 'Hyblaean Megarians' and now Selinus. At this point the arrangement shifts from linear chronology to chains of primary and secondary foundations.   **Πάμμιλον <μετα>πέμψαντες ... ξυγκατῴκισεν** 'they founded Selinus after sending for Pammilus, and he came from the mother-city Megara and joined them in founding the colony'. Without the addition of <μετα-> we simply have 'they sent Pammilus ... and he came from Megara ...', and it is odd to talk of 'sending' an absentee who had to be summoned first. Alternatively Alberti prints τις for τῆς, 'and someone came ...', but we should expect such a co-founder to be remembered and Th. to name him. It would be better to assume that a name has fallen out before τῆς μητροπόλεως (Stein). See 1.24.2 and Malkin 1987: 132–3, 256 for the 'ancestral custom' of inviting an οἰκιστής from the mother-city when founding a secondary colony. The spelling of the man's name is uncertain: Pammilus or Pamillus? Despite *LGPN* III.A 348, probably Πάμμιλον: the grammarian Herodian twice links it with other -ιλος words.

4.3 Γέλαν ... ἔτει πέμπτωι καὶ τεσσαρακοστῶι μετὰ Συρακουσῶν οἴκισιν: so 688 + *x* BCE. Here the archaeological evidence suggests a Greek presence before the end of the eighth century: perhaps the city was founded in two waves (*IACP* 173), or perhaps this is one case of gradual development from trading post to colony (p. 105). Cf. Morakis 2011: 471–3. **Ἀντίφημος ἐκ Ῥόδου καὶ Ἔντιμος ἐκ Κρήτης:** Diod. 8.23.1 records the Delphic oracle that they were said to have received; Antiphemus was a recipient of cult (*IACP* 192), as only a single οἰκιστής would be honoured in this way (Malkin 1987: 254–60). Hdt. 7.153.1 makes it a foundation just of Rhodians and Antiphemus, and it does look as if Rhodes came to be the dominant partner (Malkin 1987: 52–4, 259–60). **οὖ νῦν ἡ πόλις ἐστί:** apparently referring to the old city, as the city as a whole was of course now known just as 'Gela'. **Λίνδιοι καλεῖται:** after Lindos on Rhodes, the settlers' hometown (Hdt. 7.153.1). **νόμιμα δὲ Δωρικὰ ἐτέθη αὐτοῖς:** both Cretans and Rhodians were Dorians, though presumably their institutions were not identical. It is the complication of a joint foundation that makes this worth specifying, here and with the secondary settlement of Acragas (**4.4**). In the other cases it is assumed that the institutions would initially be based on the pattern of mother-cities (Graham 1964: 14). Th. implies that the institutions were imposed at a definite moment; *CT* contrasts **5.1**, where at Gela and Acragas Chalcidian νόμιμα 'prevailed', suggesting a drawn-out wrangling.

4.4 ἔτεσι δὲ ἐγγύτατα ὀκτὼ καὶ ἑκατὸν ... Ἀκράγαντα ᾤκισαν: so around 580 + *x*. Other sources indicate that a Rhodian contingent also participated (*IACP* 186), and possibly some Cretans too (*CT* 292, 297).

4.5 Ζάγκλη δὲ τὴν μὲν ἀρχὴν ... ὕστερον δὲ ... : Th. does not date either phase in relation to another foundation, nor does he date later events concerning Zancle (**4.6, 5.1** nn.): he is unlikely to be less informed, but may be more sceptical, about numbers with this city than the others. In fact Zancle's foundation was c. 730 BCE (*IACP* 172, 234; de Angelis 2016: 68) or possibly earlier. This therefore pre-dates the Gela thread of **4.3–4**, but if Th. was aware of this he may have displaced it to allow the end of the Zancle thread to give the transition back to Syracuse at **5.1–2**. **τὴν μὲν ἀρχὴν** 'in the beginning', adverbial acc. (*GG* 226). **Κύμης τῆς ἐν Ὀπικίαι Χαλκιδικῆς πόλεως:** for 'Opicia' cf. **2.4** n.; Chalcis, possibly together with its Euboean neighbour Eretria, founded Cyme c. 750–725 BCE (*IACP* 271). **πλῆθος ... ξυγκατενείμαντο:** 'a singular collective noun denoting persons *may* take a plural verb', *GG* 900; cf. **53.3** (ἑαυτῶν), **61.2** (πράσσοντες), and *CGCG* 27.6. **καὶ οἰκισταὶ Περιήρης καὶ Κραταιμένης ἐγένοντο αὐτῆς:** Th. has again passed over juicy foundation stories. Paus. 4.23.7 puts Perieres and Crataimenes among those original ληισταί, and these two are also named by Call. *Aet.* 2 fr. 43.58–82, who says that they ignored a bad omen and went on to quarrel: at Delphi the god told them that neither should be the founder, and 'still the land does not call on the οἰκιστής by name', inviting to the feast 'whoever it was that built the city'. ὄνομα δὲ τὸ μὲν πρῶτον Ζάγκλη ἦν ὑπὸ τῶν Σικελῶν κληθεῖσα: ὄνομα may be either nom., 'the name was at first "Zancle" . . .', with κληθεῖσα constructed according to sense with the fem. Zancle (so Marchant), or acc. of respect, 'in name it was at first called "Zancle", called that by the Sicilians' (so C–S). Th.'s listeners or readers would grasp the sense without needing mentally to parse it. ὅτι δρεπανοειδὲς τὴν ἰδέαν τὸ χωρίον ἐστί: so Th. does here give the sort of explanation of a name that he did not with Trinacria (**2**.2 n.), presumably because readers needed telling what the Sicilian term was for a 'sickle'. It appears on Zanclean coin-types, and probably refers to its crescent-shaped promontory, though Call. *Aet.* 2 fr. 43.69–72 tells how the founders built the city around the sickle that Cronus had used to castrate his father. Cf. Antonelli 1996. ὕστερον: Th. does not give an interval, but the mention of flight from the Medes gives a chronological pointer. It was after the battle of Lade, 494 BCE. The story also involved double dealing by Hippocrates, tyrant of Gela (Hdt. 6.23–4, with Hornblower–Pelling ad loc.), which Th. here omits. This was later than the foundation of Himera (**5**.1 n.): as with Megara Hyblaea, Th. is following through the city's fortunes before jumping back to another foundation.

4.6 τοὺς δὲ Σαμίους Ἀναξίλας Ῥηγίνων τύραννος οὐ πολλῶι ὕστερον ἐκβαλών: around 490 BCE. Hdt.'s version (6.23.2–3) is different: Anaxilas persuades the Samians to help him take Zancle, and so is the Samians' ally rather than their foe; a few years later it is not Anaxilas but Cadmus, son of the deposed Zanclean ruler Scythes, who apparently 'takes the city from' the Samians (7.164.1, but the text is not certain). A further alternative tradition attributes the renaming to Messenians migrating from the Peloponnese (Strabo 6.2.3, cf. 6.1.6), again perhaps around 490 (*CT*). Th. does not mention that Rhegium had itself been a secondary foundation, with Zancle inviting colonists from Chalcis and nominating the οἰκιστής Antimnestus (Antiochus, *FGrH* 555 F 9). Despite the importance that S. Italy and especially Rhegium will have in the campaign, Th. limits this introductory sketch to Sicily itself. τὴν πόλιν αὐτὸς ξυμμείκτων ἀνθρώπων οἰκίσας: proleptic, 'founded it himself as a city of mixed peoples'. Cf. Alcibiades' contempt for the racial mix, **17**.2. ἀπὸ τῆς ἑαυτοῦ τὸ ἀρχαῖον πατρίδος 'from his own ancestral fatherland', i.e. Messenia. For adverbial τὸ ἀρχαῖον cf. **2**.1 n.

5.1 καὶ Ἱμέρα ἀπὸ Ζάγκλης ὠικίσθη: again Th. does not give a date (**4**.5 n.), but this was much earlier than the events of **4**.6: Diod. 13.62.4 implies a date of 648 BCE, and this fits the archaeological record (*IACP* 198–201, de Angelis 2016: 71–3). Χαλκιδῆς μὲν οἱ πλεῖστοι 'Chalcidians formed the majority' of those founding Himera, outnumbering the Syracusan exiles. Not all the Chalcidians need be from Zancle, for some may have come from the mother-city or other foundations. Later inscriptions confirm the mixed community, including also native Sicilians (de Angelis 2016: 73, 166). καὶ ἐκ Συρακουσῶν φυγάδες στάσει νικηθέντες: Th. skilfully brings the discussion back to Syracuse, allowing a transition to its other secondary colonies. This also introduces στάσις as a recurrent Syracusan phenomenon (IACP 226–7; Berger 1992a: 34–53, observing that 'its staseis constitute one-third of all those recorded in the Greek West'). That theme is already familiar from the earlier Sicilian narrative (Intr., 34), and will be important for Alcibiades, **17**.3 (n.) and Athenagoras, **38**.3. Athens will benefit from one group of exiles (**64**.1 n.). οἱ Μυλητίδαι καλούμενοι: Strabo 6.2.6 briefly mentions 'the Zancleans who lived in Mylae' (a dependent city: IACP 216–7), rather than Syracusan Myletidae, as Himera's founders; but he may not have known any better than Th. νόμιμα δὲ τὰ Χαλκιδικὰ ἐκράτησεν: 4.3 n.

5.2 Ἄκραι μὲν ἑβδομήκοντα ἔτεσι μετὰ Συρακούσας: so 662 + x BCE. For Acrae see IACP 189–90: it was some 40 km W of Syracuse, perhaps a military outpost for the city. Κασμέναι δ' ἐγγὺς εἴκοσι μετὰ Ἄκρας: so around 642 + x BCE. Its site is tentatively identified some 12 km W of Acrae: IACP 205–6.

5.3 Καμάρινα ... μετὰ Συρακουσῶν κτίσιν: so around 597 + x BCE, a date that again fits the archaeology: IACP 202–5. οἰκισταὶ δὲ ἐγένοντο αὐτῆς Δάσκων καὶ Μενέκωλος: 'Dascon' was also the name of a locality in Syracuse (**66**.2): Cordano 1987: 121 speculates that Dascon was therefore a Syracusan, and in that case Menecolus may have been Corinthian. ἀναστάτων δὲ Καμαριναίων γενομένων: 552–549 BCE according to the scholiast on Pind. O. 5.16, but the city continued to be populated (IACP 203). δι' ἀπόστασιν 'because they had revolted'. Th. leaves no doubt of what Syracuse expected by way of fealty. Philistus, FGrH 556 F 5 seems to refer to this war with Syracuse: in it Camarina allied with Sicels, Gela, and others. λύτρα ... τὴν γῆν τὴν Καμαριναίων: 492 BCE. This was part of a peace-deal after a battle in which Syracuse and other cities were crushed by Hippocrates of Gela (Hdt. 7.154.3). αὐτὸς οἰκιστὴς γενόμενος κατῴκισε Καμάριναν: probably just by settling new inhabitants in the old buildings (IACP 203). Philistus, FGrH 555 F 15 and Timaeus, FGrH 566 F 19 use συνοικίζω, which suggests that other cities were also involved. καὶ αὖθις ὑπὸ Γέλωνος ἀνάστατος γενομένη: 483/2 BCE. Hdt. again gives more detail (7.156.2). Gelon had by now become tyrant first of Gela and then of Syracuse: he moved all the Camarinaeans to Syracuse and gave them citizenship, and did the same with half the people of Gela as well as the 'fat cats' of 'the Euboeans in Sicily' (presumably Chalcidians) and those of Megara Hyblaea (**4**.2 n.).   τὸ τρίτον κατωικίσθη ὑπὸ Γελώιων: around 461 BCE according to Diod. 11.76.5. There is archaeological evidence for some rebuilding around then: Zuchtriegel 2018: 35, 124, 212–4.

The excursus ends with the Syracusans on the move, and a threat to all including her own foundations. That will be no surprise to a reader who recalls the ease with which Acragas and Camarina were persuaded of the Syracusan threat at 5.5–6. Despite the precise chronology at various points, it would be easy for a reader to overlook that these mass destructions and migrations happened some time ago: Th.'s presentation makes it sound as if Alcibiades is talking some sense at **17**.2–3, as indeed he may be – but, for instance, we hear of no Syracusan *stasis* in the forty years after 454/3 (Berger 1992a: 39), a notable gap given the many cases at other times. There are other aspects too of more recent Sicilian history that Th. might have included, e.g. the alliances in place (Intr., 29–32) or the internal divisions within cities. These will emerge as the narrative progresses.

6–26: THE DECISION TO SAIL

6 *The Background*

1.1 has made it clear that the Athenians were underinformed but enthusiastic. **6** sets out the first stages whereby that mindset transformed into action, first explaining the enthusiasm (**6**.1), then how this was worked on by the Egestaean ambassadors (**6**.2), and finally the steps taken to get better information (**6**.3). Despite the feeling of a jump into the dark in **1**.2–**5**.3 (p. 97), the Athenians are not totally impetuous. The Egestaeans have to repeat their arguments 'many times' (**6**.3), and argue in terms of prudence (σῶφρον δ' εἶναι, **6**.2): they emphasise rather than ignore the dangers facing Athens at home, and this is the way for the Athenians to *reduce* risk – or so they claim. The Athenians themselves feel the need to find out more, and send their fact-finding delegation to Egesta.

The internal sequence within **6** is clear, though the absolute chronology is not. The Egestaean ambassadors are in town: Egesta is already at war with Selinus. They emphasise the threat of Syracuse now that Leontini has been destroyed (that was between 424 and 421, **6**.2 n.): better for Athens to pre-empt that threat now, and they remind the assembly of 'the Leontini alliance' contracted in 427–424 (**6**.2 n.). After hearing frequent rehearsals of the argument, the assembly sends its delegation.

It is 'the Leontini alliance' that the Egestaeans appeal to: the word order of **6**.2 emphasises the point (n.). Yet by 415 the Egestaeans had an Athenian alliance of their own, OR 166 = ML 37 = Fornara 81, dated to the archonship of a certain . . .]ον; it is presumably this alliance to which Nicias (**10**.5 [n.], **13**.2) and Hermocrates (**33**.2, **77**.1) allude. Only two -ον (i.e. -ων) eponymous archons have names that might fit the inscription, Habron (458–7) and Antiphon (418/7). As long as a date of the 450s was regarded as likely (as in both ML and Fornara), it was understandable that the Egestaeans should now appeal to the much more recent 'Leontini alliance': the circumstances of the 420s were more akin to the threat of now. But in 1990 Chambers, Gannucci, and Spanos presented new arguments for preferring the 418/7 date: laser technology and image enhancement identified what was claimed to be an ι and a φ – i.e. Ἀντ]ιφον. See images at http://www.csad.ox.ac.uk/CSAD/Images/00/Image67.html. Not everyone has been convinced: see esp. Henry 1992, 1995. But expert opinion now strongly favours the 418/7 date (see the discussions in *CT* and OR), and this will be assumed here.

Why, then, should the Egestaeans not appeal to their own alliance? Much depends on the pluperfect tense of ὥρμηντο, **6**.1 (n.): the Athenians *had been* eager already before winter 416–415, and Th. then moves back to that earlier time when the Egestaeans spurred them on (ἐξώρμησαν, **6**.2). This process was clearly drawn out: they had to make the arguments many times before the ambassadors were sent (aorist ἀπεστάλησαν, **7**.1). With their despatch we return from the flashback to 'the same winter' 416–415 (τοῦ αὐτοῦ χειμῶνος, **7**.1) and the despatch of the ambassadors. The Egestaeans' pressure may therefore have begun as early as Antiphon's archon-year (Smart 1972: 136), ending in mid-summer 417. The *dēmos* will first have reacted with the alliance, hoping that this would scare the Selinuntines off; then, when it did not, moved on to consider sending military aid. In that case the Leontini alliance might initially be the best the Egestaeans could initially appeal to.

This however just moves the difficulty to a different stage: if the Athenians responded to the Egestaean pressure in two phases, first the alliance then the fact-finding mission, why does Th. not mention that first phase at **6**.3? Part of the answer may be that such alliances were just sabre-rattling (Intr., 32): the significant question was whether to do anything as a consequence. Still, the obligations of such an alliance become a flashpoint in the debate (**13**.2, **18**.1), and Nicias himself speaks of the Egestaeans as already allies (**10**.5 n.); at **19**.1 it seems that both Egestaeans and Leontinians have 'oaths' that they can point to. Th. can hardly be acquitted of over-compression, though it is unlikely that he is trying to mislead. If for instance he had been over-egging Athenian irresponsibility by concealing the moral obligation, he would not have retained those passages in the debate. It is more likely that his silence is to make the decision to sail a once-for-all dramatic moment, not the end of a trickling process.

Other explanations fail to convince, e.g. that Th., deep in Thracian exile, did not know of the alliance (Chambers, Gannucci, and Spanos 1990: 53–4); or that the inscription does not record an alliance at all, but a preliminary negotiation (Bolmarcich 2014); or that the inscription records a reaffirmation of an alliance from the 427–424 fighting, which Th. would here be calling 'the Leontini war' (Matthaiou 2004 and 2011: 57–70, cf. Papazarkadas 2009: 75–6, OR p. 397; but see **6**.2 n.).

6.1 Τοσαῦτα ἔθνη Ἑλλήνων καὶ βαρβάρων . . . καὶ ἐπὶ τοσήνδε οὖσαν: this chiastically rounds off the survey, first echoing τοσάδε ἔθνη at **2**.1 and βάρβαροι μὲν οὖν τοσοίδε . . . Ἑλλήνων δέ at **3**.1, then going back to τοσαύτη οὖσα at **1**.2.   ὥρμηντο 'they had been eager', pluperfect, giving a flashback to earlier events: this too is part of the chiastic rounding off, echoing ἐβούλοντο at **1**.1. It will in turn be echoed by Nicias (**9**.3, **20**.1) and at **19**.1 (n.) and **24**.2. On the pluperfect see introductory n. above. It is true that the pluperfect sense does not always imply delay, when the emphasis falls on the action that follows immediately after the ὁρμή: thus at those echoes at **19**.1 and **24**.2. But it can always imply a longer backstory where relevant (2.59.2, 4.48.6, 4.74.2, 8.47.2), and here ἐβούλοντο at **1**.1 (n.) has already made clear that the Athenians' pre-existing wishes were relevant.   ἐφιέμενοι μὲν τῆι ἀληθεστάτηι προφάσει . . . βοηθεῖν δὲ ἅμα εὐπρεπῶς βουλόμενοι: this may recall the blend of motives at 3.86.4 (**1.1** n., Intr., 31), but is an even more resonant echo of 1.23.6 τὴν μὲν γὰρ ἀληθεστάτην πρόφασιν . . . αἱ δὲ ἐς τὸ φανερὸν λεγόμεναι αἰτίαι. The echo 'aligns this initiative with the fundamental power politics of the whole Peloponnesian War' (Brock 2013b: 51): it is all beginning again. Both here and at 1.23.6 Th. reverses usual language, as αἰτία rather than πρόφασις is more regular for a deeper underlying cause (Pelling 2019: 5–11). This disruption of expectation makes both passages more memorable and more readily related to each other (Heubeck 1980: 233–4). Elsewhere too Th. weights one explanation more heavily than another, as at 3.86.4 (above) and e.g. 7.57.1 (n.) and 2.65.11 (Intr., 5). In such cases the lesser explanation is not worthless: that is made clear here by ἅμα – the Athenians really did wish 'at the same time to aid their allies in a way that would look good' – and both here and at 1.23.6 ἀληθεστάτη conveys 'the truest', the one that explains most, not the only one that is true.

In 1.23.6 the 'truest explanation' is one more of self-defence than, as here, aggression: the Spartans were alarmed by the growth of Athens.

Still, in both passages Athenian power is crucial, as an object there of fear and here of aspiration, and here too another city's increasing power – there Athens, here Syracuse (**5**) – is felt as a threat that must be met. The lesser arguments focus on moral points that are aired in public: at 1.23.6 the 'openly expressed αἰτίαι' – Corcyra and Potidaea – focus on the sense of 'grievance' in αἰτία (Pelling 2019: 7–8), whereas here the claim that will 'look good' (εὐπρεπῶς) is an obligation to help kinsfolk and allies.   **προφάσει** 'explanation'. The word is often used as at **76**.2 of 'pretexts', explanations that are not true or not the whole truth, but the word can also extend, as here, to explanations that carry some truth. See Rawlings 1975 and Pelling 2019: 8–9.   **τῆς πάσης ἄρξαι:** conquest has already been signalled as an Athenian aspiration (**1**.1 n.). How Athenians would exercise that rule is left unclear, and may have been unclear to the assembly in 415. Nicias points out the problem at **9**.3 and **11**.1, and it becomes an issue in Euphemus' speech, **86**.3. Cf. Brock 2013b.   **εὐπρεπῶς** 'in a way that would look good'. Like ἐφιέμενοι, the word is picked up in the introduction to Nicias' speech, **8**.4. Cf. Hermocrates at **76**.3 and already at 4.60.1: 'parading the legalistic name of "alliance", they turn a state of embedded enmity εὐπρεπῶς to their own advantage'.   **τοῖς ἑαυτῶν ξυγγενέσι:** the Melian Dialogue and the Sicilian books 'form a unit where the kinship theme really takes off' (Fragoulaki 2013: 33), with 17 of Th.'s 28 cases of inter-city ξυγγένεια. At 3.86.3 Chalcidian Leontini appealed to Athens 'both in view of ancient alliance and because they were Ionians'. Hermocrates too assumes at **76**.2 that Chalcidian kinship is in point. Still, the other Chalcidian cities of **3–5** – Naxos, Catana, Zancle/Messina, and in part Himera – are not the ones asking for aid, and by 415 Leontini no longer exists (5.4.3) and Egesta itself is felt as barbarian (**2**.3 n., 7.57.11). So kinship comes into it only for the 'Leontinian exiles' of **19**.1. A lot of weight therefore falls on those 'additional allies': see next n.   **καὶ τοῖς προσγεγενημένοις ξυμμάχοις** 'and the additional allies that had accrued'. The MSS are, as often with these two prefixes, divided between προσ- and προ-: if προ-, the meaning would be 'the allies that had accrued before this', but in that case Th. might have left it as τοῖς ξυγγενέσι καὶ τοῖς ξυμμάχοις. The προσ- adds the important point that Athens had acquired further alliances with non-kin; in 427–424 Camarina (3.86.2) and the Siculi (3.103.1, etc.) had fought on the Athenian side, and Acragas had been sympathetic in 421 (5.4.6). τοῖς προσγεγενημένοις might also include possible further alliances: the Athenians could think in the future perfect, 'those who will have accrued . . .'.

6.2 μάλιστα δ' αὐτοὺς ἐξώρμησαν: picking up ὥρμηντο, and explaining how the envoys had provided the further urge (ὁρμ-) that stirred the Athenians into action (ἐξ-): cf. **88**.10 (n.). Doubtless the envoys talked to anyone who would listen, but they would seek official audiences as well. They would approach the βουλή first (Rhodes 1972: 20, 43, 57–8), who could then grant access to the 'assemblies' of the *dēmos* that they addressed 'many times' (**6**.3), as the Persian envoys are brought before the assembly in the first scene of Aristophanes' *Acharnians*. **Ἐγεσταίων [τε] πρέσβεις παρόντες:** some 'Leontinian exiles' also played a part (**19**.1): see on Λεοντίνους ἀναστήσαντες below. Those Leontinians are given more prominence by Diod. 12.83 and Plut. *Nic.* 12.1. It is possible that a mention of those exiles or of the Egestaeans' Athenian supporters (**6**.3) has fallen out of the text here and that τε was followed by <καὶ . . . >, but Krüger was more likely right to delete τε. It is uncertain when the Egestaeans arrived. Diod. 12.83 narrates this under the year 416 but has already moved out of his year-by-year register at 12.82.1 ('Around the same time . . .) to include the Egesta–Selinus backstory. It may well therefore be earlier: see p. 113. Syracuse will presumably also have sent envoys to put their side of the argument (Piccirilli 2000), though the only indications of this are [Plato], *Eryx.* 392a–d and probably Andoc. 3.30: cf. Cawkwell 1997: 88 and n. 39. **προθυμότερον** 'more enthusiastically': the word, especially in its comparative form, becomes something of a refrain as the ups and downs of morale become important (**77**.1, **80**.1, **88**.8, **92**.1, 7.1.4). But 'more enthusiastically' than when, or than whom? Perhaps than they themselves had done at first, which would again suggest a prolonged stay; or than those who had persuaded the Athenians into their intervention in 427 (3.86). **ἐπικαλούμενοι:** the word is especially used of calling upon a powerful ally to intervene: **18**.2, **78**.4, 1.33.2, etc. **καθέστασαν:** pluperfect again; the imperfect κατεῖργον then reverts to the current state of the border conflict. **περί τε γαμικῶν τινῶν καὶ περὶ γῆς ἀμφισβητήτου:** γαμικά would concern intermarriage and the status of offspring. These are typical reasons for neighbourly friction, and Th. sees no reason to give details. (Diod. 12.82.3–7 fills in more; cf. **13**.2 n.) What was unusual was the escalation, started by the Selinuntines when they brought in Syracuse. Nor does Th. explain the Syracusan decision to intervene: Syracusan expansionism has been sufficiently emphasised in **5**. **ἐπαγόμενοι** 'bringing in': like ἐπικαλούμενοι above (n.), the word is again especially used of involving powerful allies. Cf. 5.4.3, cited below on Λεοντίνους τε ἀναστήσαντες. **κατεῖργον** 'were pressing them hard': cf. **91**.2, 7.57.7. **καὶ κατὰ γῆν καὶ κατὰ θάλασσαν:** so the Syracusans were not just a force on land, as **5** had already made clear, but also on sea. This explains why the Egestaean request stressed ships in particular (ναῦς πέμψαντας ἐπαμῦναι). **τὴν γενομένην ἐπὶ Λάχητος . . . ἀναμιμνῄσκοντες τοὺς Ἀθηναίους:** 'Laches' and 'the earlier war' are taken as familiar, as in the similarly succinct references at **6**.1 and **75**.3 (nn.): for this war see Intr., 30–2. Λεοντίνων here should be taken with ξυμμαχίαν rather than with πολέμου: 'the Leontini war' would be an odd way to refer to 427–424, especially once 'Laches' and 'the earlier war' have already left no doubt what is being referred to, and if Th. had meant this he could have avoided ambiguity by inserting a further <τοῦ> before Λεοντίνων (cf. 8.18.2). The interlaced word order of Λεοντίνων . . . ξυμμαχίαν moves Leontini forward for emphasis: it was a *Leontini* alliance that the *Egestaeans* put forward. Th. is not glossing over the oddity but highlighting it, and he has made it seem odder by failing to mention the Leontinians who were present (**19**.1: see above on Ἐγεσταίων . . . πρέσβεις).

It is normally assumed that 'the Leontini alliance' is one of *Athens* with Leontini during the 427–424 fighting; this will be a further reaffirmation of the earlier alliance made or (more likely) renewed in 433/2 (OR 149 = ML 64 = Fornara 125; Intr., 30). It is not mentioned in the narrative of 427–424, but nor is the alliance with Camarina (**75**.3 and n.). This is probably right, but it is also possible that the reference is to an alliance of *Egesta* with Leontini (C–S 249–51; Roos 1962): no such alliance is attested elsewhere, but that Camarina alliance shows that there were diplomatic manoeuvres in 427–424 that Th. passed over in his sparse narrative. Either way, Th. leaves gaps in the argument for the reader to fill in: if the first, 'you were prepared to get involved with Leontini in 427–424, and similar arguments should lead you to get involved now'; if the second, 'you and we were both on the same side then because of the ties we both had with Leontini, and we should still be on the same side now'. **ἀναμιμνῄσκοντες** 'making mention of', taking a double accusative here as at Hdt. 6.140.1, Soph. *OT* 1133. This need not mean 'reminding' the Athenians of something they might have forgotten (cf. Hornblower–Pelling on Hdt. 6.21.2), and so no inferences can be drawn as to the date of whatever alliance is meant. **λέγοντες ἄλλα τε πολλὰ καὶ κεφάλαιον:** Athens prided itself on its tradition of helping the poor and vulnerable (e.g. Hdt. 9.27.2–3, Eur. *Hcld.* 329–32, Soph. *OC* 261–2; Loraux 1986: 67); 'pity' too was paraded as an Athenian virtue (Lys. 2.14, Dem. 24.171, 25.81; Low 2007: 178–83). It would have been odd if the envoys had failed to appeal to those traditions, but Th. gives them no space beyond 'many other things'. For him the 'nub' or, literally, 'head argument' (κεφάλαιον) focuses on self-interest, just as it had in the way the Athenians argued at Melos (Intr., 17–20). **εἰ . . . γενήσονται . . . σχήσουσι:** εἰ + fut. indic. (rather than ἐάν + subj. or, in indirect speech, εἰ + opt.) is favoured when the fulfilment of the condition is unwelcome, especially in threats or warnings: *CGCG* 49.5, Wakker 1994: 167–8. Cf. **80**.2 and 4, **86**.1, **91**.1, 3, and 4.

Λεοντίνους τε ἀναστήσαντες: between 424 and 422 (Intr., 32). 5.4.2–4 explains what happened: the men of power had brought in (ἐπάγονται) the Syracusans to expel the *dēmos*; they themselves moved to Syracuse, leaving the city empty (ἐρημώσαντες), though some of the powerful later moved back to a fortress in Leontinian territory. Fighting then followed when the *dēmos* regathered. Th. describes in similar terms the Syracusans' treatment of Megara Hyblaea, 4.2 and 94.1, and Camarina, 5.3 (ἀναστάτων); Camarina survived for resettlement, but not much of Megara Hyblaea seems to have been left (4.2 n., *IACP* 214). The envoys' warning of further cities' 'destruction' (διαφθείροντες) did not exaggerate by much. τοὺς λοιποὺς ἔτι ξυμμάχους αὐτῶν διαφθείροντες 'destroying the rest of their allies as well'. The present tense is to be preferred to the variant διαφθείραντες: the Syracusans would carry on continuously destroying and continuously seizing and holding (σχήσουσι) power, with the destruction both supporting and made possible by that power. αὐτῶν = 'the Athenians' rather than 'the Egestaeans' (which would be σφῶν) or 'the Leontinians', just as μετὰ τῶν ὑπολοίπων ἔτι ξυμμάχων below refers to Athens' allies. ἔτι is here more likely 'as well' (Bétant's category 'd: *praeterea, insuper*') than 'still' (as Bétant himself takes it, 'a: *adhuc*'), though in μετὰ τῶν ὑπολοίπων ἔτι ξυμμάχων it has shifted to 'still', 'those allies that still remained'. The tone grows more desperate as well as more portentous as the long sentence goes on and the reasons for fear and for intervention pile up. τὴν ἅπασαν δύναμιν τῆς Σικελίας: the article conveys 'all the power that there might be' over Sicily, 'total domination'. The scaremongering assumes that the Syracusans would have the same aspiration as the Athenians themselves, 6.1. κίνδυνον εἶναι μή ποτε . . .: the tone is almost oracular, but here as at 34.2 and e.g. 3.11.6 the fears are based on purely human considerations. The argument of the Corcyreans in Bk. 1 is similar: if you do not help us now, there is a danger that our forces will end up fighting on the enemy's side (1.36.3, cf. 1.44.2), here by adding to their παρασκευή (1.1 n.). Δωριῆς τε Δωριεῦσι κατὰ τὸ ξυγγενές: emphasised by the repetition of the same noun in different cases ('polyptoton'). There is again a symmetry, with kinship playing a role for both sides. καὶ ἅμα 'and besides' (Rusten on 2.42.1). τοῖς ἐκπέμψασι Πελοποννησίοις: i.e. the Corinthians (3.2), but put more generally because the whole Peloponnesian alliance would be 'helped'. καὶ τὴν ἐκείνων δύναμιν ξυγκαθέλωσιν 'they might join in destroying their [the Athenians'] power as well (καί)' as those powers in Sicily that they had already dealt with. σῶφρον δ' εἶναι: see intr. n. to 6. The note of caution and moderation is continued with ἀντέχειν: it is represented as a matter of 'resistance', not – despite the Athenian mood of 6.1 – of conquest. μετὰ τῶν ὑπολοίπων ἔτι ξυμμάχων: see on τοὺς λοιπούς ἔτι ξυμμάχους above. **σφῶν:** referring back to the subject of the sentence, i.e. the Egestaeans. **ἱκανά:** in emphatic final position.

6.3 ὧν ἀκούοντες . . . τῶν τε Ἐγεσταίων . . . καὶ τῶν ξυναγορευόντων αὐτοῖς: ὧν is neuter plural, genitive of the thing heard as at Soph. *OC* 1187 λόγων δ' ἀκοῦσαι, then τῶν τε Ἐγεσταίων . . . is gen. absolute. Th. does not specify who these 'supporters' were: they may well have included Alcibiades (**12**.2 n.). **ἐν ταῖς ἐκκλησίαις . . . πολλάκις:** see intr. n. to **6**. The Egestaeans would not have addressed the assembly 'often' unless the βουλή, or rather its rotating presidencies, had repeatedly granted permission, a stage about which Th. is, as so often, silent. **περί τε τῶν χρημάτων . . . εἰ ὑπάρχει . . . καὶ τὰ τοῦ πολέμου . . . ἐν ὅτωι ἐστίν:** variants of the 'I know thee who thou art' construction, where the content is first stated generally and then more closely defined by an indirect question: cf. **9**.1, **16**.6, and Sommerstein 2013 on Men. *Samia* 391 ὄψει σεαυτὴν νῦν ἀκριβῶς ἥτις εἶ. **ἐν τῶι κοινῶι καὶ ἐν τοῖς ἱεροῖς:** Pericles similarly enumerated Athens' own assets at the beginning of the war (2.13.3–5), including artefacts in the temples. That passage may well be recalled here, with a further suggestion of it all beginning again (**1**.3–5 n., **6**.1n.): cf. 8.1 n., Kallet 2001: 28–31. **καὶ τὰ τοῦ πολέμου:** acc. after εἰσομένους, with the indirect question to follow.

At least one further mission probably took place around this time, to Delphi to consult the oracle on the wisdom of any expedition: cf. Plut. *On the Pythian Oracles* 403b, *Nic*. 13.5–6. The Athenians may also have consulted Dodona, Paus. 8.11.12, and even Siwah too, Plut. *Nic*. 13.2, though it is uncertain how far these accounts should be believed. Th.'s religious reticence (Intr., 18) may therefore leave an incomplete impression of popular thinking (cf. Powell 1979: 17–18; Flower 2009: 9–10). He also misses an opportunity to point to another parallel with the war's outset, for in 432 the Spartans sent to Delphi with a similar question (1.118.3); cf. **9**.1 n.

7 *Back in Greece: Further Events, Winter 416–415*

This end-of-year interlude, besides injecting some narrative suspense while the Athenian envoys are away, also reminds the reader that fighting in Greece is continuing: that supports Nicias in the debate (**10**.2–3). Still, it is desultory, with emphasis on its smallness, at least on the Peloponnesian side – οὐ πολλήν, σῖτον . . . τινα, ὀλίγους, μίαν ἡμέραν, though the Athenians and Argives respond in strength – and on unsuccessful initiatives. There is not much here to worry the Athenians. Greek events also resemble Sicilian: a frontier land dispute (**7**.1), with powerful allies intervening; the bigger forces resettling exiles (7.1, 7.3) and destroying a small city (7.2) when foiled.

7.1 Λακεδαιμόνιοι δὲ ... στρατεύσαντες ἐς τὴν Ἀργείαν: hostilities between Sparta and Argos had continued during the years of the Peace, culminating in the battle of Mantinea (418). That was followed by a peace treaty (5.77), but then Argive *stasis* – first an oligarchic revolution encouraged by Sparta, then a democratic counter-revolution – led to resumed hostilities in 417–416, with Sparta invading the Argolid and Argos attacking Phlius, where most of the oligarchs had found refuge (5.82–3). There was further fighting in Phlius in 416 (5.115.1). **τοῦ αὐτοῦ χειμῶνος:** 416–415. Th. need not be implying that these events happened after the envoys departed, nor that this Peloponnesian incursion was earlier than the Athenian initiative of 7.3. All these operations would take some time and would overlap. **πλὴν Κορινθίων:** similarly in winter 417–416 the Spartans were accompanied by 'their allies except for the Corinthians' when they invaded the Argolid (5.83.1). No reason is given in either passage for the Corinthians' failure to participate (for plausible speculation cf. Salmon 1984: 330–1 and *CT*), but their relations with Sparta had not been good since 421 (5.25.1), even though they fought on Sparta's side at Mantinea in 418. During summer 416 too Corinth had followed an independent anti-Athenian line, but Th. gives no details (5.115.3). **σῖτον ἀνεκομίσαντό τινα ζεύγη κομίσαντες** 'they brought wagons and removed some corn' – i.e. stored grain, as it was winter. τινα should be taken with σῖτον rather than with ζεύγη. **Ὀρνεάς:** in the W Argolid, and repeatedly claimed by Sparta (*IACP* 612–3). At Mantinea it had fought on the Argive side (5.72.4, 74.2); perhaps it had then passed under Spartan domination, but maybe this was Sparta's half-hearted attempt to achieve that result. Aristophanes puns on the campaign at *Birds* 395, where the joke works best if the fighting had been a damp squib (Dunbar 1995: 289). **κατοικίσαντες:** 3.1 n. **τοὺς Ἀργείων φυγάδας:** the definite article because they are taken as familiar from Bk. 5, i.e. those that had taken refuge in Phlius (n. on Λακεδαιμόνιοι δέ above). **παρακαταλιπόντες** 'leaving them there along with' the returning exiles. **σπεισάμενοί τινα χρόνον ... τὴν ἀλλήλων:** understand γῆν, as also with τὴν Περδίκκου, 7.3. The cities' mutual hostility is taken for granted. σπένδομαι here takes an acc. of the time-period agreed as at e.g. 2.73.1 and 5.60.1. Oaths and treaties are nearly always broken in Th. (Lateiner 2012), and so it proves here (7.2).

7.2 ὑπὸ δὲ νύκτα: Th. might equally have said νυκτός (3.2 n.), but ὑπὸ νύκτα is a favourite phrase (e.g. 64.1, 65.2, 7.22.1), perhaps implying a local as well as temporal sense: the besieged slink out 'beneath the canopy of the sky', as George puts it (2014: 109–11). οἱ ἐκ τῶν Ὀρνεῶν 'those coming from Orneae', with the 'from' already assuming the 'running away': cf. **32**.2 and e.g. 1.8.2 οἱ γὰρ ἐκ τῶν νήσων κακοῦργοι ἀνέστησαν. κατασκάψαντες: a strong word, often conveying a severe punishment for serious crimes – murder, treason, tyranny (Connor 1985: esp. 97). It is used of the Spartan dismantling of Athens' walls in 404, X. *Hell.* 2.2.23 and Plut. *Lys.* 15.3. The depth of feeling between these neighbours is clear.

7.3 Καὶ ἐς Μεθώνην τὴν ὅμορον Μακεδονίαι . . . τὴν Περδίκκου: 'the one neighbouring Macedonia' (see Map 3a; *IACP* 804) to distinguish it from Methone in the SW Peloponnese (2.25.1). After Mantinea Sparta had tried to mobilise Perdiccas, king of Macedonia and a man of many changes of side, against Athens (5.80); they exchanged oaths, but he had preferred to bide his time. In winter 417–416 Athens blockaded the Macedonian coast, annoyed by his dealings with the Peloponnesians and his failure to help them in a planned campaign against Chalcidice (**7.4** n.). ἱππέας . . . σφῶν τε αὐτῶν καὶ Μακεδόνων τοὺς παρὰ σφίσι φυγάδας: the placing of τε might imply that the 'cavalry' are subdivided into Athenians and the Macedonian exiles and that therefore these Macedonians were all horsemen, but probably that is over-strict and the exiles included infantrymen.

7.4 Χαλκιδέας τοὺς ἐπὶ Θράικης: the cities of Chalcidice (Map 3a) had revolted from Athens in 433–432 (1.57–65) and had remained hostile during the Archidamian War. They had been approached by the Spartans after Mantinea (5.80.2), and Dion on the Athos peninsula had left the Athenian alliance (5.82.1). An Athenian campaign was planned under Nicias' command, but this fizzled out when Perdiccas failed to give support (5.83.4, **7.3** n.). δεχημέρους σπονδάς: ones that required renewal every ten days or (less likely, *CT* 47–8) ones that could be terminated at ten days' notice. Like those between Athens and Boeotia (5.26.2, 32.5–7), they were presumably part of the peace terms in 421. οἱ δ' οὐκ ἤθελον: as with the Corinthians (**7.1** n.), Th. does not explain why. These cities had no love for Athens, but they certainly had no reason to trust Perdiccas. καὶ ὁ χειμὼν . . . ὃν Θουκυδίδης ξυνέγραψεν: Th. had adopted this signing-off formula for the end of each year throughout the Archidamian War (2.70.4, 103.2, etc.), and without the 'which Thucydides described' (dropped already at 2.47.1 and 4.116.3) through the Peace (5.39.1, etc.); that is true to his insistence that the twenty-seven years should be seen as a single conflict (5.26). He now resumes the full formula: cf. **93**.4, 7.18.4. Cf. Rood 2006: 228–9.

8–26 *The Debate at Athens*

For Th. as for Hdt., aggressive imperialism often needs no explanation (Pelling 2019: 136–7); when motivation is explored, it is as much a sign of the momentousness of the decision as of any difficulty in understanding it. This decision, like Xerxes' resolve to invade Greece (Hdt. 7.8–19), is momentous indeed: that Herodotean grand set-piece debate may be recalled here (Rood 1999: 154 = 2009: 161; Raaflaub 2002: 23–6). This, clearly, is the start of something big – big in its thinking, and, as the audience already sensed at **1**.1 (n.), big in its ultimate catastrophe. Nicias may also prompt the reader to another Herodotean reminiscence, that of 'Warner' figures like Bias/Pittacus (Hdt. 1.27), Sandanis (1.71), and Artabanus (7.10), who argue against an enterprise that they see is rash (Marinatos 1980). The wisdom of such figures is not always unimpeachable, but they are more right than wrong.

One function of the debate is to explore the Athenian mindset, both the enthusiasm – Nicias acknowledges that his audience is against him (**9**.3) – and the caution that ensures a welcome for his disingenuous upscaling (**24**). Both themes have already been hinted in the narrative, which has also included material lending support to each speaker (**1**.1, **5**.3, **6**, **7** nn.). Still, as with the Mytilenean Debate (3.36–49, Intr., 25), it elucidates not merely this one decision but also the whole texture of politics – the rancour of Nicias' personal attack (**12**.1), the self-centredness of Alcibiades' reply (**16**), the divisiveness (**13**.1), the importance of personal enmity (**15**.2). That focus helps to explain Th.'s omission of another major development some time in 417–415, the ostracism of, as it turned out, Hyperbolus (Plut. *Nic.* 11, *Alc.* 13, *Arist.* 7). There too the central players were Nicias and Alcibiades, and one such confrontation was enough.

In some ways the democracy does not come out of this debate too badly. Nicias' divisiveness misfires, and the old are as enthusiastic as the young (**24**.3); Alcibiades' slippery rhetoric intensifies the enthusiasm, but the Egestaean and Leontinian envoys and considerations of sworn oaths are important too (**19**.1). Yet the whole debate also takes place under the shadow of Pericles, with memories of what impressive leadership used to be like (Intr., 22). Nicias echoes mantras of Periclean strategy: keep safe what you have, do not take unnecessary risks (**9**.3 and n.). Such was not the Athenian way – it was risk-taking that made the city great (1.70) – but Pericles had the charisma, the record, and the rhetorical power to make Athenians trust his advice. Alcibiades at least has the charisma, and his own echoes of Periclean oratory focus on Athenian greatness (**16–18** n.). Athenians might now hope to reunite these strands by combining the strengths of both (as Alcibiades says, **17**.1), with a further admixture of Lamachus; but it will not turn out to be so easy. Readers and hearers may also recall Th.'s survey of Pericles' successors and their self-seeking ambitions (2.65.7–11). It does not take much to suspect that similar motives are in play here, more obviously with Alcibiades (**15**.2, cf. **16–18** n.) but arguably with Nicias too (**9–14** n.). See Intr., 7–8.

Another uneasy feature is that the important debate happens at the second assembly rather than the first (Rawlings 1981: 73–6). Other great Athenian set-pieces too involve two debates, Corcyra and Corinth (1.30–44) and Mytilene (3.36–49). With Corcyra Th. focuses on the first debate, but the Athenians cautiously decide to sleep on it; on the second day opinion has shifted and a force is despatched (1.44.1). With Mytilene Th. focuses on the second debate, with the assembly feeling its initial decision had been 'harsh and excessive' (3.36.5) and changing its mind (3.49): that makes a point about these democratic Athenians, ταχύβουλοι and μετάβουλοι as they are ('swift to decide' and 'prone to rethink', Ar. *Ach.* 630, 632). Here too the focus falls on the second debate, and Nicias' argument implies that this is another case of rash over-hastiness (**8**.4). Yet the Athenians are cautious too (**6** nn.), and that is why Nicias finds a ready ear for his upscaling (**20–23**).

For detailed analysis see esp. Tompkins 1972, Kohl 1977, Canevaro 2019: 371–80, and *HCT* and *CT*.

8 *First and Second Assemblies*

A series of inscriptions (OR 171 = ML 78 = Fornara 146) is usually taken to relate to these debates, though Kallet 2001: 184–93 has some good reasons for feeling doubts. The inscriptions present problems that cannot be discussed here: see *HCT*, *CT*, OR, and Kallet. It appears that the question was raised (presumably at the first assembly) whether to send a single general, though later there are 'generals'; the proposed instructions include doing 'as much [damage?] to the enemies as possible'; there is mention of 'the allies' being involved 'in whatever way' [they may wish]; ten days are mentioned, apparently as a (maximum?) interval between assemblies (cf. on ἡμέραι πέμπτηι, **8**.3 n.); the number of ships appears first as 60 and then as 100; there is provision for 'peltasts' and 'archers'; '3,000' of something, possibly talents or possibly troops, should not be used 'for any other purpose or expedition'; other arrangements concern 'tribute', and a possible *eisphora* (an exceptional property tax) 'whenever necessary'. If these do relate to 415, it follows that Th.'s account is selective, and not just in **8**; the provisions for state financing contrast with the focus of both Nicias (**47**) and Alcibiades (**90**.4) on avoiding expenditure from home resources.

The proposer of at least one decree may have been Demostratus, together with a rider about recruiting Zacynthian hoplites (Ar. *Lys*. 387–98, cf. 'allies' in the inscription): cf. **26**.1 n.

8.1 τοῦ δ' ἐπιγιγνομένου θέρους: 415 BCE. **ἑξήκοντα τάλαντα ἀσήμου ἀργυρίου:** Kallet 2001: 28–9 notes the echo of Pericles' reassuring speech at 2.13.3, mentioning both their minted silver and not less than 500 talents of unminted (ἄσημον) gold and silver. For further echoing of 2.13 see **6**.3, **8**.2 nn. But, as Kallet says, there the unminted metals are only a last resort; here unminted is better, for Egestaean coinage would be usable only in the local city. **ὡς ἐς ἑξήκοντα ναῦς μηνὸς μισθόν:** so 200 drachmas per ship per day. A rower's regular rate of state pay on campaign was one drachma a day, topped up by trierarchs (**31**.3 n.), but captains and helmsmen would be paid more, marines and archers too might have a different rate, and there may have been differentials among classes of rowers (Jordan 2000b: 82; Kallet 2001: 53 n. 115). So this assumes a crew of rather fewer than 200 men per ship. 60 ships was a regular size for a squadron: cf. **50**.2 n. **ἃς ἔμελλον δεήσεσθαι πέμπειν** 'that they were going to ask [the Athenians] to send'.

8.2 τά τε ἄλλα ἐπαγωγὰ καὶ οὐκ ἀληθῆ καὶ περὶ τῶν χρημάτων: as usual in ἄλλοι τε καί constructions, here the second καί = 'and in particular': the claim about 'the money' ('the' because familiar from **6**.2–3) is included in the things that are 'attractive and false' (not 'attractive but false': the attractiveness and the falsehood are closely connected). τά τε ἄλλα also adds a different nuance from just ἄλλα τε ἐπαγωγά . . .: 'the rest of what they said too' was attractive and false, or possibly even 'the [usual] other attractive and false things'. As with ἄλλα τε πολλά at **6**.2 (n.), Th. leaves it to the reader to reconstruct what these 'other things' might have been. **ὡς εἴη ἑτοῖμα ἔν τε τοῖς ἱεροῖς πολλὰ καὶ ἐν τῶι κοινῶι:** echoing **6**.3. The most significant 'sacred place' was the temple of Aphrodite at Eryx, but that is again left until **46**.3. This too echoes Pericles at 2.13.4–5 (**8**.1 n.) – but what Pericles said had been true.

The Athenian envoys too, not just the Egestaeans, delivered these arguments: they had evidently been taken in, but how they were misled is delayed to **46**, the more dramatic moment of the discovery. **στρατηγοὺς αὐτοκράτορας:** these 'full powers' did not yet (ctr. **26**.1 n.) extend to defining the scale, as a further assembly would be needed to vote them 'anything they might need', **8**.3; but once on campaign they were empowered to make decisions without always referring them back to Athens. That would not protect them from scrutiny and possible prosecution after the campaign, as Nicias feared (7.48.3–4). OR 171 frag. *b* (p. 123) suggests that it was discussed whether to send one general or three. If it had been one, it would probably have been Alcibiades.   Ἀλκιβιάδην . . . καὶ Νικίαν . . . καὶ Λάμαχον: probably all three were members of the regular board of ten and were duly re-elected for 415/4. The formal introduction with patronymics is not because the men are unfamiliar, but marks the solemnity of what is at stake (cf. Griffiths 1961: 21–3): thus 'Pericles son of Xanthippus' at 1.139.4 and 2.34.8, even though he first appeared at 1.111.2. As usual, Th. does not say why generals were chosen: his Syracusan proxeny, if this is historical, may have influenced the choice of Nicias (7.48.2 n.). Plut. fills the gap in a different way, with voters given confidence 'by the addition of Nicias' caution to the audacity of Alcibiades and the fieriness of Lamachus' (Plut. *Nic.* 12.5, cf. *Alc.* 18.1). That might be Plut.'s own inference, but he may have got it right.   βοηθοὺς μὲν . . . ξυγκατοικίσαι δὲ . . . καὶ τἆλλα πρᾶξαι: the variation in construction is typical of Th., with βοηθούς in apposition to ναῦς . . . καὶ στρατηγούς, then ξυγκατοικίσαι and πρᾶξαι as infinitives of purpose (*CGCG* 51.16).   ἤν τι περιγίγνηται αὐτοῖς τοῦ πολέμου 'if the course of the war left them any opportunity', literally 'if there was any of the war left over for them'. Alberti adds <τέ> (Hude) before τι, which would attach this qualification to what follows rather than what precedes. That would leave the first two elements, helping Egesta and resettling Leontini, as war-aims of equal status, and this is how they are later regarded both by Athenians (**44**.3, **48**, **50**.4) and in Hermocrates' counter-invective (**33**.2, **76**.2, **77**.1). This later emphasis though is better explained in terms of rhetoric, as (a) those Athenian claims will appeal to Leontini's fellow Ionians and (b) Hermocrates makes Athenian aspirations as unqualified as he can. Or perhaps it was simply mission-creep.   ξυγκατοικίσαι δὲ καὶ Λεοντίνους 'to join in the settlement of Leontini': ξυν- = 'together with' the returning Leontinians and any other Sicilians who wished. One can 'settle' either a people or a town (**4**.1 n.), and Λεοντῖνοι too can be either 'Leontinians' or 'Leontini'; at **50**.4, **63**.2, and **79**.2 it is the people, but this is another case (**2**.1 n.) where different readers/listeners might hear the syntax differently.   πρᾶξαι ὅπῃ ἂν γιγνώσκωσιν ἄριστα Ἀθηναίοις: a vaguer and gentler brief than was explicitly stated in 427 (3.86.4, ' . . . make a preliminary trial to see whether Sicilian affairs could be brought under their control'), and what Th. suggests that the Athenians then had in mind (4.65.3, 'to subdue Sicily'): cf. Intr., 31. Stronger language too was in the air – 'to do the enemy as much [damage] as possible' (OR 171 frag. *b*, above p. 123).

8.3 ἡμέραι πέμπτηι: Th. doubtless had good information for this, but it is also in the style of a good Herodotean story: cf. Hdt. 1.1.3, 1.30.1, 3.52.3, etc.

8.4 προφάσει βραχείαι καὶ εὐπρεπεῖ . . . μεγάλου ἔργου: echoing the authorial voice at **1**.1 and **6**.1. πρόφασις, used at **6**.1 of total conquest, has now reverted to its usual sense of a lesser or openly paraded explanation (**6**.1 n.). Still, here too both factors play a part: in his speech Nicias sees the need to counter the argument concerning allies. A schol. notes the Homeric texture of μεγάλου ἔργου ἐφίεσθαι, comparing *Il.* 10.401 μεγάλων δώρων ἐπεμαίετο θυμός; for μέγα ἔργον cf. e.g. *Il.* 5.303 and 13.366. **παρελθὼν . . . παρήινει τοῖς Ἀθηναίοις τοιάδε:** it need not follow that Nicias had not spoken at the first meeting as well.

9–14 *The First Speech of Nicias*

Nicias is by now familiar, both as a successful general (3.51, 91; 4.43.1, 53–4, 130–2, cf. **7**.4 n.), though mainly in minor operations, and as a performer in the assembly. At 4.28 he read the *dēmos* better than Cleon, though Cleon was eventually vindicated, but then at 5.43–6 he was in his turn outsmarted by Alcibiades. He was much trusted, as his frequent re-election as *stratēgos* shows. He was also the major Athenian player in bringing about the Peace of 421 (though Th., unlike Plut. *Nic.* 9.9 and modern scholars, never calls it 'the Peace of Nicias'). At 5.16.1 Th. dwells on his motives, 'to leave behind a name as someone whose career included no reverses for the city, and he thought that the way to achieve this was to take no risks . . .': see Intr., 7.

The Hellenistic historian Callisthenes insisted that a historian's speeches should fit the speaker (*FGrH* 124 F 44), and Nicias here fits the character that we already know, cautious, uncertain in his touch with the assembly, anxious to avoid leading the expedition himself just as he passed over his command to Cleon at 4.28. The style also fits the man (Tompkins 1972), full of sidetracks and concessions, with long sentences lacking in punchiness; even his good points suffer through overstatement and circumlocution (nn.). He talks less about himself than Alcibiades will, but there is still too much, and that distracts and delays the argument at **9**.2. He knows he is out of tune with the Athenian character (**9**.3), and he does not have the stature of a Pericles to browbeat his audience (2.65.8). He will then fail in his second speech to realise that he is saying things that will chime with them all too well (**20–23** n.). He has an uphill task, as the decision is already taken. It never sounds as if he is likely to succeed.

On self-characterisation in both speakers see Kremmydas 2017: 108–10.

9.1 περὶ παρασκευῆς ... καθ' ὅ τι χρὴ ἐς Σικελίαν ἐκπλεῖν: cf. 6.3 n. for the construction, with the topic first outlined and then sharpened by an indirect question. καθ' ὅ τι χρή ... echoes the (official?) language of the meeting's agenda, 8.3.   εἰ ἄμεινόν ἐστιν ἐκπέμπειν τὰς ναῦς: Nicias' way of phrasing the question is almost oracular (e.g. Hdt. 4.156.2, 7.169.1, X. *Anab.* 6.2.15): cf. 1.118.3, where the Spartans ask Delphi whether it will be better for them if they wage war (εἰ πολεμοῦσιν ἄμεινον ἔσται). But the Athenians now will be working that out for themselves, with no oracle mentioned to help them (though cf. 6.3 n.).   μὴ οὕτω βραχείαι βουλῆι ... ἄρασθαι: the four balanced cola, given extra weight by the alliteration of β and π and the assonance of α, each make an important point, supported by the echoes of the narratorial voice. The decision has been too quick (cf. προφάσει βραχείαι, 8.4, echoing 6.1); the matter is big (1.1, 8.4); the Egestaeans are non-Greek (1.1, 2.3 – this ignores the Leontinians, 6.2 n. and 19.1 n.); the war is not our own. There are longer echoes too. Hermocrates rallied *Sicily* to resist the ἀλλόφυλοι *Athenians* (4.64.4); the *Spartan* Archidamus was proud that his city took time to decide (1.84.1), especially over a big war (1.80–1) undertaken precipitately for the sake of allies (1.82.5–6). Cf. 9.3 n. for Nicias' Spartan resonance.   πόλεμον οὐ προσήκοντα: the war is 'not befitting' (LSJ προσήκω III.2) because it 'does not belong to us', is not our war (LSJ II.2). Cf. 83.2.

9.2 καίτοι ἔγωγε ... ὀρθοῦσθαι: a long and complicated sentence. Nicias first talks about himself. This is not rhetorically pointless: if an honoured and experienced general is against the expedition, then other older people too should not fear the charge of cowardice (13.1), even if they risk only possessions, οὐσία, rather than life. Personal attacks are anyway the stuff of assembly exchanges (cf. 3.42.2–3), and Nicias gives as good as he expects to get, 12.2; honour demands that he responds, here preemptively. But the diffident style lacks impact, with its concessions and complications, and the logic is not easy to follow. It seems to be (a) war has brought me honour, and I have less fear than others; (b) not that there is anything wrong in concern for one's safety or [a new point, but again with some self-reference] one's wealth; (c) for self-protection gives the citizen a selfish reason for wanting the city to be safe too. (d) Still [why 'still'? See n.], I have never allowed that honour to speak against my convictions, and will not do so now. 'Honour' does link (a) and (d), but (b) and (c) have developed (a) in a different direction. There is a lot of throat-clearing here.   ἐκ τοῦ τοιούτου: i.e. from military campaigns.   ἧσσον ἑτέρων περὶ τῶι ἐμαυτοῦ σώματι ὀρρωδῶ: Nicias does not explain why. Maybe this is just a flat assertion that he is no coward, but it may assume that a general runs less risk than others: at 7.77.2 he notes that by then he 'is in the same danger as the humblest of you', but the point is that this is irregular. Yet the mortality rate among generals was high; Paul 1987: 308 calculates that 23 commanders die in Th.'s 83 or so land-battles.

Th.'s readers may already know enough of the outcome to sense the ironies: Nicias' bodily suffering will eventually be a major theme (7.15.1, 77.2), and he will be intensely fearful – but of the danger from his fellow citizens, those to whom he is talking here (7.48.3–4). νομίζων 'even though I think': concessive. ὁμοίως ἀγαθὸν πολίτην εἶναι 'to be just as good a citizen' as the person who feels no fear. ὃς ἂν καὶ τοῦ σώματός τι καὶ τῆς οὐσίας προνοῆται 'whoever takes some thought both for his bodily safety and for his property': οὐσία can indicate possessions on some scale, e.g. Lys. 24.11, 'if I had been a man of property, I would have ridden on a mule with a cushioned saddle'. It is particularly the older citizens, most of whom would not share the physical dangers, that Nicias will urge not to fear the charge of cowardice (**13**.1). Once more, too, there is some self-direction, as Nicias was rich (7.86.4 n.). καὶ τὰ τῆς πόλεως δι' ἑαυτὸν βούλοιτο ὀρθοῦσθαι 'for his own sake would wish the affairs of the city as well [as his own] to be guided aright': ὀρθοῦσθαι suggests both good decision-making and success, as at 3.37.4 and 42.4. An echo of Pericles may also be heard: more benefit comes when the city as a whole is ὀρθουμένη than when private citizens do well and the state does not (2.60.2). But Pericles' conclusion is that everyone should do what the state requires; Nicias' emphasis – that one has selfish reasons for wanting the state to succeed – is different. We are some way from the idealistic portrayal of the Athenians at 1.70.6: 'on behalf of the state they use their bodies as if they belonged to someone else completely, but they use their mind as something totally their own to do something for the city'. ὅμως δὲ ... : the preceding point would suggest rather 'And therefore...', but Nicias is resuming his train of thought from τιμῶμαι ἐκ τοῦ τοιούτου. The logic is still opaque. Is it (1) that his military honour might make him likely to press for more of the same, 'but still' he will not? But such honour is not likely to make him back warfare *against* his true beliefs (παρὰ γνώμην); it would make him more sincerely bellicose. Or (2) that he might not be expected to endanger that honour by giving unpopular advice (cf. 3.42.6), 'but still' he will speak out? That gives a better transition into **9**.3, where he acknowledges that he will be speaking against the popular grain; it also fits Th.'s picture of post-Periclean leaders telling the people what they want to hear (2.65.10, Intr., 7–8). But the point takes some excavating, and Nicias is not making things easy for his listeners. οὔτε ἐν τῶι πρότερον χρόνωι ... οὔτε νῦν: claims of consistency (cf. Pericles at 1.140.1 and 2.62.1, Cleon at 3.37.1, and e.g. Dem. 15.1) and statements of intention to express unpopular views frankly (cf. **33**.1 and e.g. Dem. 3.3, 9.1–3) are both characteristic opening gambits, but speakers rarely put them in such resigned terms. ἧι ἂν γιγνώσκω βέλτιστα 'in whatever way I judge best'. βέλτιστα is probably an adv. (Marchant); were it direct object, one would expect <τὰ> βέλτιστα. There may be an echo of καὶ τἄλλα τὰ ἐν τῆι Σικελίαι πρᾶξαι ὅπηι ἂν γιγνώσκωσιν ἄριστα Ἀθηναίοις at 8.2: Nicias is only following instructions, even though not yet in Sicily.

9.3 τοὺς τρόπους τοὺς ὑμετέρους: i.e. the energetic and risk-taking ways sketched by the Corinthians at 1.70. ἂν ... εἴη, εἰ ... παραινοίην 'would be ... if I were to advise'. Nicias is again unassertive, for that is exactly what he is going to advise, but he shies from saying so in the future tense as in ἐρῶ and διδάξω. The optative construction is typical of his diffidence: he uses it more frequently than any other speaker except Hermocrates (Tompkins 1972: 185). τά τε ὑπάρχοντα σώιζειν ... κινδυνεύειν 'to keep safe what you have already, and not to risk what is at hand in the hope of uncertain future prospects'. Those are watchwords not of Athenians but of Spartans: as the Corinthians put it at 1.70, you Spartans like τὰ ὑπάρχοντα ... σώιζειν and think that any enterprise might harm τὰ ἑτοῖμα. Yet Pericles too had to persuade the Athenians to practise a Spartan-like restraint: they should seek no new imperial possessions and avoid risks whenever they could (1.144.1, 2.65.7) – in fact, adopt a strategy of ἡσυχία (2.65.7), another Spartan characteristic (**10**.2 n). See Intr., 28. **περὶ τῶν ἀφανῶν καὶ μελλόντων:** the Athenians had warned the Melians too not to rate τὰ μέλλοντα higher than what was before their eyes nor rely on τὰ ἀφανῆ, 5.113. Diodotus pointed out that the Athenians tended to do the same, 3.45.5. Nicias returns to the point at **13**.1, τῶν ἀπόντων. **οὔτε ἐν καιρῶι σπεύδετε:** Athenians' trademark swiftness and enthusiasm are all very well, but this is not the time. Pericles was able to restrain the Athenians when he saw them παρὰ καιρὸν ὕβρει θαρσοῦντας, 2.65.9. **κατασχεῖν ἐφ' ἃ ὥρμησθε:** ὥρμησθε echoes **6**.1 (n.), and is here perfect rather than pluperfect (in form it could be either), conveying the ὁρμή that is still continuing after beginning in the past. κατασχεῖν introduces the difficulty of 'holding down' Sicily even if it can be defeated (**6**.1 n.): cf. **11**.1, **86**.3. The word can be used of various sorts of 'control', including good sorts: Pericles κατεῖχε τὸ πλῆθος ἐλευθέρως, 'in a way appropriate for free people', 2.65.8. But the word is often uglier (3.45.4, 107.2) and is appropriate for tyrants (1.17, Hdt. 1.59.1, 5.78, etc.) or near-tyrants (3.62.4): Forsdyke 2001: 332–41. Athens may not find it so easy to play the tyrant city (Intr., 13) in Sicily, whether or not the assembly would have put it to itself in those terms. **διδάξω:** the word is less condescending than 'teach' sounds to a modern ear: cf. 5.9.2 and e.g. Hdt. 7.16β.2, Dem. 18.26 with Yunis' 2001 n., Aeschin. 3.18.

10.1 φημί: strongly marking off his own view as different from his hearers' (οἴεσθε, **10**.2): cf. **39**.1, **87**.2. It is a regular oratorical ploy (e.g. Dem. 2.11, 4.8). πολεμίους πολλοὺς ἐνθάδε ὑπολιπόντας . . . ἐπαγαγέσθαι: this warning receives only scant support from 7 (n.) but more from what happens later, at least once Alcibiades has stirred the Spartans into action (**89–93**): cf. **10**.4 n. The Melians had warned similarly: you are strengthening your existing enemies and bringing in (ἐπάγεσθε) new ones who had no previous intention of fighting, 5.98. There as here the verb is paradoxical, as it is generally used of bringing in *allies*, **6**.2 n.

10.2 τὰς γενομένας ὑμῖν σπονδάς: those of 421. Nicias varies between 'you' and 'we' through this speech (in some cases the MSS offer both as variants) and at **21**.2: the initial 'you' continues to mark some distance between him and his audience. Nicias' claim again gets some support from the narratorial voice, for at 5.26.2 Th. had insisted that the peace was so fragile that it should be counted as part of the continuous war. There is still irony in Nicias' questioning the peace that he did so much to bring about (**9–14** n.). βέβαιον: a favourite word and preoccupation of Nicias (βεβαιωσώμεθα, **10**.5; cf. **23**.3 [n.]). His thinking here may be recalled at **73**.2 (n.). ἡσυχαζόντων: another Spartan (1.69.4, cf. **10**.3 below) rather than Athenian (1.70.8) watchword: **9**.3 n. Alcibiades picks up the word at **18**.2 and 6, pointing out that this is not the Athenian way. ὀνόματι: emphatic, 'in name [alone]'. οὕτω γὰρ ἐνθένδε τε ἄνδρες ἔπραξαν αὐτὰ καὶ ἐκ τῶν ἐναντίων 'that was the mindset in which men both from here and from the other side managed them'. ἔπραξαν and αὐτά are vague enough to embrace not just the making of the peace but also the wrangling about it afterwards, especially (as a schol. observes) the activities of the Spartan ephors Cleobulus and Xenares (5.36–8, 46.4) and of Alcibiades (5.43–8). As at **11**.6 (n.), Nicias affects to know the Spartan mindset as well as the Athenian. σφαλέντων δέ που ἀξιόχρεωι δυνάμει 'once you [or 'we'] have suffered a reverse anywhere in substantial strength'. Nicias returns to the theme of ἀξιόχρεως strength at **21**.2 (n.). ταχεῖαν τὴν ἐπιχείρησιν . . . ποιήσονται 'will make their attack quickly' – Athenian-style (**9**.3 n.). The definite article implies that 'the' attack can be expected some time; it is just a question of when. Cf. n. on τάχιστ' ἄν, **11**.4. διὰ ξυμφορῶν . . . ἐγένετο 'was forced upon them in disastrous circumstances' (LSJ διά A.III.c) 'and less honourably' (LSJ ἐκ III.8) 'than for us', particularly because the Spartans were so keen to get back the men captured on Pylos (4.1–41.1, 5.15). ξυμφορά is a favourite word for that reverse (**89**.2, 4.15.1, 5.14.3 etc.); for the 'dishonour' or 'shame' cf. **11**.6. At 5.28.2 (cf. 5.75.3) Th. comments that Spartan prestige had indeed suffered διὰ τὰς ξυμφοράς. Still, κατ' ἀνάγκην puts the contrast very strongly: at 5.15–17 Th. stressed the enthusiasm on both sides for peace. πολλὰ τὰ ἀμφισβητούμενα ἔχομεν: the disputes started immediately after the conclusion of the Peace, as Sparta's allies refused to comply (5.22, 25–6, 30.2, etc.) and the Spartans failed to give back Amphipolis (5.21); Athens in turn did not restore Pylos.

10.3 εἰσὶ δ' οἳ οὐδὲ ταύτην πω τὴν ὁμολογίαν ἐδέξαντο,: especially Corinth (5.25–32, 48, 115.3), but also Elis and Megara (5.17.2, cf. 22.1–2, 30.2) and Boeotia with its separate 'ten-day truces' (below). οἱ μὲν ἄντικρυς πολεμοῦσιν: especially the Corinthians (5.115.3), but also in 416 'the Spartans made war' upon the Athenians in Pylos 'though even so they did not renounce the peace' (5.115.2–3). δεχημέροις σπονδαῖς: 7.4 n. These are the cities of Boeotia (5.26.2, 32.5–7) and Thracian Chalcidice (7.4).

10.4 τάχα δ' ἂν ἴσως, εἰ . . . λάβοιεν . . . πάνυ ἂν ξυνεπιθοῖντο: more of Nicias' optatives (9.3 n.). For repeated ἄν see *CGCG* 60.12 and e.g. **11**.2, **18**.2, **35**.1, **49**.1, **78**.4, **99**.2. It is especially useful in 'if . . . then . . .' conditional sentences when they become long and complicated: cf. the parenthesis at **64**.1 and 2.41.1 with Rusten's n. Nicias speculates on uncertain futures after taking the Athenians to task for doing just that (9.3), but his point is that those uncertainties might be bad rather than good. Something like this does turn out to happen: at 7.18.2 Th. comments on the boost to Peloponnesian morale by having Athens fight a war on two fronts, and after their victory the Syracusans send a force E to help the Peloponnesians (8.26). In any case there is no reason to doubt that the fear was real. ὅπερ νῦν σπεύδομεν: echoing οὔτε ἐν καιρῶι σπεύδετε at 9.3, though now Nicias has moved into 'we' mode (**10**.2 n.). Σικελιωτῶν: Sicilian Greeks: see Malkin 2011: 107. οὓς πρὸ πολλῶν ἂν ἐτιμήσαντο: another remote conditional, this time an unreal one in the past: 'would have valued it highly to have them as their allies'. This takes πολλῶν as neuter, lit. 'valued it ahead of many things': cf. 1.33.2, 'a force you would have rated ahead of much money and gratitude to acquire', and Isoc. 15.176. But some may have heard it as masculine, 'valued these allies ahead of many others'.

10.5 χρὴ σκοπεῖν τινὰ αὐτά: not just 'someone must think about these things' but 'every individual must . . .': cf. **68**.3, **91**.4 (n.) and e.g. Hom. *Il.* 16.200 and 209, 'now let τις put courage in his heart . . .', and Hornblower–Pelling on Hdt. 6.9.3. μετεώρωι τῆι πόλει . . . κινδυνεύειν 'take risks with the city at sea' or 'up in the air'. μετέωρος conveys a lack of contact with firm land, either upwards or away from shore: the Athenians should keep their feet on the ground. But the metaphorical use may carry several suggestions and *CT* rightly says that it should not be pinned down: cf. 2.8.1, 'all the rest of Greece was μετέωρος', where the main sense is 'in suspense', 'agog', Dem. 19.122, of affairs that are hazardous, [Hipp.] e.g. *Epid.* 1 case 8 of bodily organs in a delicate condition. The word is often used of ships at sea, and the schol. saw that this gives the metaphor especial bite for a sea-borne operation. Cf. Dougherty 2014: 156–7, and see also nn. on ἀπαρτήσοντες, **21**.2, and αἰωροῦμαι, 7.77.2.   **μή . . . ἀρχῆς ἄλλης ὀρέγεσθαι πρὶν ἣν ἔχομεν βεβαιωσώμεθα:** another echo of Periclean strategy (2.65.7), and ὀρέγεσθαι further recalls the Athenians rejecting peace-offers because 'they were greedy for more' (μειζόνων . . . ὠρέγοντο, 4.41.4). βεβαιωσώμεθα also picks up ἔχειν τι βέβαιον at **10**.2 – more security is needed, as those σπονδαί offer none – and begins a rounding-off reprise of these dangers. For πρίν + subj. without ἄν cf. **29**.2, **38**.2, *CGCG* 47.16.   **εἰ:** not indicating any doubt, but 'citing a fact as a ground of argument or appeal' (LSJ B VI).   **Χαλκιδῆς γε οἱ ἐπὶ Θράικης . . . ἔτι ἀχείρωτοί εἰσι:** 7.3–4, **10**.3 nn.   **ἔτη τοσαῦτα ἀφεστῶτες ἡμῶν:** since the late 430s (7.4 n.).   **καὶ ἄλλοι τινὲς κατὰ τὰς ἠπείρους ἐνδοιαστῶς ἀκροῶνται:** Nicias leaves this vague, and κατὰ τὰς ἠπείρους is an unexpected emphasis. The defections highlighted by Th. are those of islands, Mytilene, Melos, and Chios. The point may be the contrast with the island Sicily (**1**.2 n.): mainland concerns should come first. But such a priority was not likely to appeal to the maritime Athenians.   **ἡμεῖς δὲ Ἐγεσταίοις δὴ οὖσι ξυμμάχοις . . . ἀμύνεσθαι:** ὀξύτης was an Athenian characteristic (ἐπινοῆσαι ὀξεῖς, 1.70.2), but one that Nicias now claims is being misapplied (**11**.7, **12**.2). Here 'δή does not throw doubt on the facts, but suggests that they constitute an unworthy or inadequate cause or motive' (*GP* 230): Nicias is not questioning that the Egestaeans are indeed allies (cf. **6** n.), as ὡς ξυμμάχοις δή would have done. Then the antitheses make many points in a few words: we, not they, are the victims of injustice; we attend more to allies than to rebels; we are slow in our interests but quick in theirs; we help others, but do not defend ourselves.   **μέλλομεν:** with a strong suggestion of delay, as when the Corinthians deride the Spartans as slow to act, οὐ τῆι δυνάμει τινά, ἀλλὰ τῆι μελλήσει ἀμυνόμενοι (1.69.3). Given the other echoes of 1.69–70, that passage may be recalled here: Nicias' own strategy may be Spartan-like ἡσυχία, but he also derides the Athenians for being over-Spartan. On campaign he will prove an arch-delayer himself (intr. to Bk. 7): a character in Aristophanes' *Birds* (414 BCE) urges the company not to μελλονικιᾶν, translated by Dunbar 1995 as 'suffer from the Nikias-dithers'.

11.1 καίτοι τοὺς μὲν κατεργασάμενοι κἂν κατάσχοιμεν 'in the case of the one group [the Thracian Chalcidians, etc.], if we subdued them we would be able to hold them down as well'. Cf. **86**.3 and for κατέχειν **9**.3 n. The alliteration of κ adds emphasis.   διὰ πολλοῦ γε καὶ πολλῶν ὄντων: the polyptoton (repetition of the same word in different cases) emphasises the point. διὰ πολλοῦ may convey 'separated from one another' by long distances (cf. 3.94.4) as well as being a long way away (**21**.2, cf. Euphemus at **86**.3). Both factors contribute to the difficulty.   ἀνόητον: **16**.3 n.   μὴ κατορθώσας μὴ ἐν τῶι ὁμοίωι καὶ πρὶν ἐπιχειρῆσαι ἔσται 'and if one does not succeed one will not be in the same position as one was before making the attack': for this use of καί expressing comparison see CGCG 32.14 and e.g. **21**.2, **88**.10, 7.28.4; cf. also **64**.1 n. Nicias does not rule out such aggression in the future, and this continues the idea of this not being 'the right time', **9**.3.

11.2 Σικελιῶται: **10**.4 n.   ὥς γε νῦν ἔχουσι 'at least in their current state', i.e. one of ethnic divisions and different loyalties.   καὶ ἔτι ἂν ἧσσον δεινοὶ ἡμῖν γενέσθαι, εἰ ἄρξειαν αὐτῶν Συρακόσιοι: more of Nicias' optatives (**9**.3 n.), and more speculation on uncertain futures, intensifying the point of **10**.4 (n.). But it is a dangerous rhetorical move to bring the possibility of Syracusan rule into play, especially as the supporting argument is so weak (**11**.3 n.).   ὅπερ . . . ἐκφοβοῦσιν: ὅπερ is internal acc., conveying the content of the scaremongering.

11.3 οὐκ εἰκὸς ἀρχὴν ἐπὶ ἀρχὴν στρατεῦσαι: an odd thing to claim, particularly in view of the succession of empires plotted early in Hdt.'s history (Medes replacing Assyrians, 1.95.2, and Cimmerians, 1.103.3, then Persians taking over the Lydian empire, 1.46–94). The Peloponnesian War could itself be seen as a counter-example, even if the way the Spartans controlled their league made it an atypical ἀρχή (1.19).   ὧι γὰρ ἂν τρόπωι . . . καθαιρεθῆναι 'for in the way that they might take away our empire in partnership with the Peloponnesians, it is reasonable to expect that their own empire might be destroyed by the same people in the same manner'. A second τρόπου is understood with διὰ τοῦ αὐτοῦ. This argument is not nonsensical – if the Syracusans really grew to rival Athens and Sparta, they might leave the other two to fight and weaken one another – but is inconsistent: Peloponnesians going on to attack a Sicily under Syracusan control would itself be a case of one ἀρχή taking on another.

11.4 ἡμᾶς δ᾽: placed first for emphasis, switching from (a) we have no reason to fear them to (b) this is how they might most fear us.   οἱ ἐκεῖ Ἕλληνες: just the Greeks, partly to reinforce Nicias' dismissiveness about barbarians (**9**.1, **11**.7), partly because only the Greeks might be expected to intervene in a Greek war.   ἡμᾶς δ᾽ ἄν . . . μάλιστα μὲν ἐκπεπληγμένοι εἶεν εἰ μὴ ἀφικοίμεθα: ἐκπλήσσω is a strong word, 'strike out of one's senses by a sudden shock' (LSJ, cf. 33.4 n.), and weakens the case: masterful inaction might impress, but not with such sudden intensity. For its passive use with acc., as if it were a stronger equivalent of φοβοῦμαι, cf. e.g. 33.4, 3.82.5. ἔκπληξις/κατάπληξις becomes important in Bk. 7: see intr. to that book, p. 31.   καὶ εἰ δείξαντες τὴν δύναμιν δι' ὀλίγου ἀπέλθοιμεν: this will be Nicias' strategy on campaign as well (47, with echoes of this passage). καί suggests that the Syracusans would 'also' be ἐκπεπληγμένοι by such a display, only less so than by their not going at all. Nicias' argument is not getting any more convincing.   εἰ δὲ σφαλεῖμέν τι: σφάλλω is a recurrent word: cf. 10.2, 11.6, 15.4, 24.3 n.   τάχιστ' ἄν: perhaps just 'very quickly', but Nicias' mindset suggests that the superlative force may be felt, 'most quickly of all', continuing the implication of ταχεῖαν τὴν ἐπιχείρησιν (10.2 [n.]) that such an attack is bound to come some time.   τὰ γὰρ διὰ πλείστου . . . δόντα: διὰ πλείστου – 'the things furthest away' – may pick up διὰ πολλοῦ at 11.1, with distance there a negative reason against going, here a positive reason for staying at home. The 'truth universally acknowledged' ploy is a rhetorical favourite (e.g. 7.68.2, Isoc. 7.15, Dem. 21.64), often for 'truths' that are highly questionable: Pelling 2000: 28, Maltagliati 2020: 90–2. This one sounds proverbial: cf. Tac. *Ann.* 1.47.2 *maior e longinquo reuerentia* ('respect is increased by distance').

11.5 ὅπερ: i.e. by experiencing the enemy at close quarters you have lost respect for them. Past battles are often used to encourage hope of victory (7.63.4 n.); Nicias makes them a reason to fear defeat.   διὰ τό . . . περιγεγενῆσθαι: αὐτῶν goes chiastically with περιγεγενῆσθαι and τὸ πρῶτον with ἐφοβεῖσθε; πρός = 'in relation to', 'in comparison with', LSJ C.III.4. Nicias extends his own negative mindset backwards to 431 and assumes that his audience shared it. Yet Pericles had given the Athenians rational reasons to expect that they would περιέσεσθαι (2.65.7, cf. 2.13.3), and Th. had stressed the widespread enthusiasm for the war (2.8.1).   καταφρονήσαντες ἤδη καὶ Σικελίας ἐφίεσθε: 'contempt' for the enemy can be dangerous (1.122.4, 2.11.4, 3.83.4), as Hermocrates knows (33.3, 34.9, cf. 35), but Pericles had found a place for it in urging Athenians to close with the enemy μὴ φρονήματι μόνον ἀλλὰ καὶ καταφρονήματι, 'looking down' on them through confidence in the Athenians' own superior γνώμῃ (2.62.3–4).

11.6 μὴ πρὸς τὰς τύχας τῶν ἐναντίων ἐπαίρεσθαι 'not to be buoyed up in response to one's enemy's fortunes'.   τὰς διανοίας κρατήσαντας: lit. 'overcoming them in respect of the mental processes': you must out-think them.   ἄλλο τι: to be taken with σκοπεῖν: 'you should think that the Spartans have nothing else in mind but . . .'. The hyperbaton – two words distant from one another but to be taken together – further complicates a sentence that is already long and packed.   τὸ αἰσχρόν... τὸ σφέτερον ἀπρεπές: see on ἐκ τοῦ αἰσχίονος, 10.2 n. Nicias had worked closely with Spartans in 421 and again, unsuccessfully, in 420 (5.43–6). His claims about Spartan thinking would carry authority, or so he hopes.   ὅσωι καὶ... μελετῶσιν 'the more so because' [lit. 'to the degree that'] 'they attach the greatest importance – and have done so for the greatest time – to their pursuit of a reputation for excellence'. μελετᾶν is particularly used of military training (72.4, 1.18, 1.142.2, etc.), and that suits Sparta where competition for honour was central to education (X. *Lac. Pol.* 4.2, Plut. *Lyc.* 14, *Ages.* 2, etc.). At 5.28.2 and 5.75.3 Th. had noted the blow to Sparta's prestige in others' eyes; Nicias focuses on how the Spartans have internalised the humiliation.

11.7 τῶν ἐν Σικελίαι Ἐγεσταίων..., ἀνδρῶν βαρβάρων: the points pile up, each making the prospect more remote from Athenian interests: Sicilians, mere Egestaeans, barbarians (2.3 n.). βαρβάρων is stronger than ἀλλοφύλοις, 9.1, and 'the temperature of Nicias' rhetoric has risen' (*CT*). Nicias' argument mirrors Hermocrates' in 424 (Intr., 21), though there the plotting enemy was Athens itself: 'we must realise that, if we are wise (εἰ σωφρονοῦμεν), the clash will not be about our local concerns, but to see if we can save all Sicily now that it is the object of a plot (ἐπιβουλευομένην), as I see it, by the Athenians' (4.60.1, with both εἰ σωφρονοῦμεν and ἐπιβουλευόμεθα again at 4.61.1).   ὁ ἀγών: see 7.56.2 n. and intr. to Bk. 7, p. 30.   εἰ σωφρονοῦμεν: countering the claim that it was σῶφρον to intervene (**6.2**).   πόλιν δι' ὀλιγαρχίας ἐπιβουλεύουσαν 'a city that is oligarchically plotting': διά + gen. conveys 'through oligarchy', using oligarchy as their means and manner. Does Nicias mean that Spartans are working underhand with oligarchic sympathisers in Athens, or that such plotting is what a democracy should expect from an oligarchy, or both? The vagueness adds to the sinister quality, triggering democratic prejudice.   ὀξέως φυλαξόμεθα: for ὅπως + fut. ind. after verbs of striving see *CGCG* 44.2. The phrase here is an oxymoron, as ὀξύς normally conveys quick movement as at **12.2** rather than 'being on one's guard': it echoes ὀξέως βοηθοῦμεν at **10.5** (n.) – this, not that, is the right sort of 'sharpness'. The Corinthians saw the Athenians as ὀξεῖς at 1.70.2, but sharp there to move into action and get things done.

12.1 νόσου μεγάλης: the great plague of 430–427 (2.48–57, 3.87): cf. **26.2**. It is a bad move for Nicias to dwell on the recovery, however 'recent' and 'slight': **26.2**, echoing this passage, will make it clear that this recovery helped rather than hindered the case for the expedition.   πολέμου 'from war' or 'from fighting': not τοῦ πολέμου, for 'the war' would suggest that it was over.   λελωφήκαμεν: particularly used of 'abatement' of physical illness or pain (2.49.5, Plato, *Phdr.* 251c, [Hipp.] *Aff.* 29, 49), and so appropriate for the plague and preparing for the 'physician' figure of **14**. καὶ χρήμασι καὶ τοῖς σώμασιν ηὐξῆσθαι: χρήματα and σώματα are often linked or contrasted (e.g. 1.121.3, 1.141.5, Dem 4.3); here the plague gives particular point to σώμασιν. καὶ ταῦτα . . . ξυναπολέσαι: another complicated sentence, especially as Nicias turns to the personal abuse of the 'fugitives': the 'temperature of the rhetoric' (**11.**7 n.) remains high. That then gives an easy transition to the invective against the self-seeker closer to home (**12.**2). καὶ ταῦτα ὑπὲρ ἡμῶν δίκαιον ἐνθάδε ἀναλοῦν: not merely prudent but also 'just', a strong claim but one necessary to counter the moral argument of duty to allies. ὑπὲρ ἀνδρῶν φυγάδων τῶνδε ἐπικουρίας δεομένων: Nicias presumably means the Leontinians (**19.**1, cf. **6.**2 n.): he now ignores the Egestaeans, who were offering cash as well as λόγοι, just as he ignored the Leontinians at **10.**5 and **11.**7. One can imagine the sneer of τῶνδε and the accompanying gesture: 'these fugitives here'. οἷς τό τε ψεύσασθαι . . . ξυναπολέσαι 'people to whom elegant lying is useful, and – with their neighbour taking the risk, and themselves providing only words – either winning and showing insufficient gratitude or suffering defeat somewhere and destroying their friends along with themselves'. All the rest of the sentence depends on οἷς . . . χρήσιμον. Th. is fond of verbal abstractions with τό (Intr., 11 and n. 38), but this is an unusually elaborate example, fully in Nicias' intricate style. τῶι τοῦ πέλας κινδύνωι qualifies the participles as well as the eventual inf. ξυναπολέσαι, another hyperbaton (**11.**6 n.). 'Only words' prepares for Nicias' scepticism about Egesta's promises at **22** and **46.**2. τοῦ πέλας: the singular as Nicias' language becomes gnomic, just as 'love thy neighbour' does not mean only one of them: cf. τοῦ ξυνοίκου, **77.**2. πέλας may seem odd after Nicias' stress on 'far away', but ὁ/οἱ πέλας is often just 'other people': cf. e.g. **79.**1 and 1.32.4 μὴ ἐν ἀλλοτρίαι ξυμμαχίαι τῆι τοῦ πέλας γνώμηι ξυγκινδυνεύειν.

12.2 εἴ τέ τις: τε marks a new topic as Nicias turns to Alcibiades – possibly, in a reader's or hearer's imagination, even turns physically. The non-naming may convey contempt: cf. **60.**2 n. For connective τε see **18.**7 n. ἄρχειν ἄσμενος αἱρεθείς: in contrast to Nicias, ἀκούσιος . . . ἡιρημένος ἄρχειν (**8.**4). παραινεῖ ὑμῖν ἐκπλεῖν: present rather than future, partly as the debate is under way (as a barrister might say in anticipation 'the defendant claims . . .'), partly perhaps because Alcibiades already urged this in the first debate (**8.**2) or even earlier (**6.**3 n.). τὸ ἑαυτοῦ μόνον σκοπῶν: an easy transition after the stress on the selfish Leontinians, **12.**1. For the emphasis on self-seeking see Intr., 7–8. ἄλλως τε καὶ νεώτερος ὢν ἔτι ἐς τὸ ἄρχειν 'particularly as he is still young for a command', lit. 'younger [than he ought to be or than one would expect] with regard to the commanding'. This explains τὸ ἑαυτοῦ μόνον σκοπῶν – he has particular reasons not to let the opportunity slip – but also insinuates that he was a poor choice anyway. In fact Alcibiades was at least 36, had been στρατηγός three times (420/19, 419/8, 416/5), and had commanded at least two missions (5.52.2, 84.1, Plut. *Alc.* 15). **ὅπως θαυμασθῆι . . . τῆς ἀρχῆς** 'so that he can reap the admiration from his horse-breeding and then, because of the extravagance, get some benefit from his command': cf. **15**.2–3. The μέν and δέ clauses go closely together: those horse-breeding successes (**16**.2 n.) have brought him fame, but this expensive habit has cost so much that he now needs to recoup. It is assumed that office-holding gives a chance to fill one's own pocket: Isoc. 7.24–7 laments this in his own day. Cf. Hansen 1980; Kallet 2001: 33. **μηδὲ τούτωι . . . ἐλλαμπρύνεσθαι** 'do not allow him either [any more than Egesta] the chance to win splendour for himself at the risk of the city'. ἰδίαι then becomes a key-word, repeated in the next line and echoed at **15**.4; ἐλλαμπρύνεσθαι is countered by Alcibiades at **16**.3 and **16**.5; there is a λαμπρότης of the whole expedition at **31**.6. This all echoes Th.'s judgement on Pericles' successors who pursued their ἰδίας φιλοτιμίας καὶ ἴδια κέρδη in ways that would bring honour and benefit to private citizens (ἰδιώταις) if successful but damage to the city if they failed (2.65.7): Intr., 7. The language is also echoed at 7.56.2–3, where the Syracusans anticipate 'admiration' (θαυμασθήσεσθαι) for 'providing their city' (ἐμπαρασχόντες) to bear the prime danger (προκινδυνεῦσαι) on behalf of others. But the Syracusans think civically; Alcibiades, according to Nicias, is more self-directed. **τοὺς τοιούτους** 'people like that', a dismissive touch. The individualistic Alcibiades would have been mortified at being reduced to a well-known type: cf. **16**.5 n. **τὰ μὲν δημόσια ἀδικεῖν, τὰ δὲ ἴδια ἀναλοῦν**: in Sicily Alcibiades will be spending public money rather than his own, but the point is that such people first 'spend' their own money and then 'wrong' the state in order to cover their losses. **καὶ τὸ πρᾶγμα . . . μεταχειρίσαι**: Nicias reprises to round off this part of the argument: for τὸ πρᾶγμα μέγα and βουλή/βουλεύσασθαι cf. **8**.4 and **9**.1; for νεωτέρωι, **12**.1; for ὀξέως **10**.5 and **11**.7.

13.1 Οὓς ἐγὼ ὁρῶ . . . ξυμφέρεσθαι: a beast of a sentence. The main verb is ἀντιπαρακελεύομαι: Nicias does his own 'telling' (-παρακελεύομαι) to counter (ἀντι-) those whom Alcibiades has 'told what to do' (παρακελευστούς). The older generation should not feel shamed (μὴ καταισχυνθῆναι, the first of four infs. dependent on ἀντιπαρακελεύομαι) by Alcibiades' supporters into voting for war; nor should they fall badly in love (δυσέρωτας εἶναι) with ideas of far away; but they should counter-vote (ἀντιχειροτονεῖν καὶ ψηφίζεσθαι, the third and fourth dependent infs.) to leave the Sicilians to their own devices. The final inf. ξυμφέρεσθαι is then dependent on ψηφίζεσθαι, what the assembly should vote for the Sicilians to do, and the participles χρωμένους and νεμομένους go with ξυμφέρεσθαι in summarising how the Sicilians should behave. On the further infs. εἰπεῖν and μὴ ποιεῖσθαι see **13**.2 n. Οὓς ἐγὼ ὁρῶν . . . φοβοῦμαι = 'the people whom I am now alarmed to see sitting here and told by the same man what to do . . .'. : the sitting was on the ground, or with a cushion if one was lucky or luxurious (Ar. *Knights* 784–5). οὕς is obj. of both ὁρῶν and φοβοῦμαι. παρακελευστός like ἀντιπαρακελεύομαι need not be as strong as 'ordered', but does suggest organised lobbying; that could include encouragement to turn up as well as to vote Alcibiades' way, and to that extent talk of a 'packed assembly' (LSJ παρακελευστός, Rhodes 1994: 93) is only a mild overstatement. **καὶ τοῖς πρεσβυτέροις:** καί because the older men are now to receive some παρακέλευσις 'too'. τοῖς πρεσβυτέροις picks up νεώτερος by insinuating that not just Alcibiades but all his supporters are junior. Th. corrects that impression at **24**.3. **μὴ καταισχυνθῆναι . . . μαλακὸς εἶναι** 'not to feel shamed by them, if anyone is sitting next to one of them (τωι = τινί), into wishing not to seem soft if he does not vote for war'. The triple negative does not make for stylistic clarity. For ὅπως + fut. ind. in a purpose clause see *M&T* 324: the thinking is again convoluted, for this is the 'purpose' that the older men might have had if they had felt such shame – but Nicias is telling them not to. μαλακός may not just = 'cowardly' but also carry a sexual tinge, as it is often used of an unmasculine passivity (Wohl 1999: 364–5). For Nicias it is the younger men who are erotically askew (δυσέρωτας). **εἴ τώι τις παρακάθηται τῶνδε:** so supporters were not sitting together as a group like football supporters, though there may have been some huddling (Plut. *Per.* 11.2): cf. Hansen 1987: 40–1. Theophrastus' 'oligarchic man' is discomfited when 'some scrawny and unkempt fellow comes and sits beside him' (*Char.* 26.4). **ὅπερ ἂν αὐτοὶ πάθοιεν** 'such as they (Alcibiades' supporters) might feel themselves'. **δυσέρωτας εἶναι τῶν ἀπόντων** 'badly in love with things that are not here': δυσέρως can convey both intensity and misjudgement, typically of romantic love and with trouble to come. This fits Nicias' antiyouth rhetoric, but that impression is again (cf. on καὶ τοῖς πρεσβυτέροις above) corrected at **24**.3 (n.). where old and young alike feel an ἔρως to sail. On the fascination of the far-away cf. esp. Pind. *P.* 3.20, (Coronis) ἤρατο τῶν ἀπόντων: Ludwig 2002: 130 and 142. **γνόντας ὅτι ἐπιθυμίαι μὲν ἐλάχιστα κατορθοῦνται, προνοίαι δὲ πλεῖστα** 'realising that very few successes are won by desire and most by forethought': ἐπιθυμίαι and προνοίαι are dat. singular. κατορθοῦται would be expected and perhaps should be read, but this may be an extension of the use of a plural verb when a neut. plural includes a numeral or 'many', as at **62**.4. Th. prizes πρόνοια (2.65.5–6, cf. 1.138.3), and his Pericles warns of the danger that it can be overwhelmed by hope and desire (2.62.5, cf. 4.108.4). Nicias ignores the forethought that inspired the investigative mission at **6**.3, but he is anyway sceptical about their report (**22, 46**.2). ὑπὲρ τῆς πατρίδος ... ἀντιχειροτονεῖν καὶ ψηφίζεσθαι 'put our hands up for our country against this and vote that . . .'. ὑπὲρ τῆς πατρίδος (cf. **14**.1 n.) strikes a contrast with self-centred Alcibiades (**12**.2); ἀντι- reinforces ἀντιπαρακελεύομαι – it is time to fight back – and the pleonastic ἀντιχειροτονεῖν καὶ ψηφίζεσθαι adds emphasis, with the first verb more visual and the second introducing the content of the proposal. ὡς μέγιστον δὴ τῶν πρὶν κίνδυνον ἀναρριπτούσης 'as taking a more dangerous risk than ever before', lit. 'the most dangerous of those that had preceded': for the apparent illogicality cf. e.g. 1.1.1, the war as 'the most memorable of those that had preceded', and 7.70.2. The metaphor is of 'throwing high' the dice, as with the proverbial ἀνερρίφθω κύβος of Caesar at the Rubicon: Plut. *Caes.* 32.8 with Pelling 2011: 317–18. The Athenian envoys had used it when warning the Melians, 5.103.1. οἷσπερ νῦν ὅροις χρωμένους πρὸς ἡμᾶς, οὐ μεμπτοῖς 'keeping the same boundaries with us as they have now, not bad ones'. The litotes οὐ μεμπτός conveys quite a strong positive; cf. e.g. Eur. *IA* 712 (Achilles 'not bad' as a potential husband for Iphigeneia), X. *Mem.* 3.5.3, Plato, *Laws* 4.716b. Nicias assumes the broader imperialist aims (**8**.2 n.): helping Egesta and Leontini and then returning would not broach those natural boundaries. τῶι τε Ἰονίωι . . . διὰ πελάγους: see Maps 2 and 3a. Even a coastal route would not hug the shore throughout, but would involve the short hop across from Corcyra (cf. 1.36.2, 44.3). The more direct route would be from the Corinthian Gulf across open sea. τὰ αὑτῶν νεμομένους καθ' αὑτοὺς καὶ ξυμφέρεσθαι 'take care of their own lands and reach their own agreements too (καί)'. Th. had similarly described what the Sicilians had done in 424 on the urging of Hermocrates: cf. 4.64.5 καθ' ἡμᾶς . . . νεμούμεθα, and 4.65.1 κατὰ σφᾶς αὐτοὺς ξυνηνέχθησαν.

13.2 τοῖς δ' Ἐγεσταίοις ἰδίαι εἰπεῖν 'and give the Egestaeans this separate reply'. ἰδίαι need not imply privacy, but reinforces the contrast with τοὺς μὲν Σικελιώτας, 'the Sicilians' in general. εἰπεῖν ... μὴ ποιεῖσθαι: not all the audience may have heard this difficult syntax in the same way. εἰπεῖν could be taken as a further inf. dependent on ψηφίζεσθαι, and καταλύεσθαι as dependent on εἰπεῖν: they should vote to tell the Egestaeans to come to terms. But μὴ ποιεῖσθαι must be a mental resolution that the Athenians should take, not a formal proposal for the present vote. This could still be dependent on ἀντιπαρακελεύομαι and parallel to ψηφίζεσθαι, and in that case some might have taken εἰπεῖν the same way, 'I urge you to tell them';

or Nicias may just have let his syntax run away with him.   ἐπειδὴ ἄνευ Ἀθηναίων . . . καταλύεσθαι: they started the war 'without the Athenians' and now must similarly finish it 'with [nobody but] themselves'. **6**.2 left it unclear whether the Egestaeans had started it, and it is unwise to take Nicias' word for it. Diod. 12.82.3 says it was the Selinuntines.   ξυμμάχους μὴ ποιεῖσθαι ὥσπερ εἰώθαμεν: Nicias again does not deny that the Egestaeans were allies (**10**.5 n.), though the Leontinians may also by now be included (cf. on φυγάδων, **12**.1 n.).   οἷς κακῶς . . . οὐ τευξόμεθα 'whom we shall defend when they are in trouble, but get no help when we need it ourselves'. Something like παρ' ὧν, 'from whom', is understood with ὠφελίας. So these allies are international counterparts of Alcibiades, people who reap all the benefits while the Athenian *dēmos* takes the risks.

14 Καὶ σύ, ὦ πρύτανι: Nicias now is to be imagined as turning to the *prytanis*, or more precisely the ἐπιστάτης τῶν πρυτανέων, the member of the duty *prytanis* whose turn to preside had come in the daily rotation: see *OCD*[1] s.v. *prytaneis*. As nobody could do this more than once in a lifetime, it is understandable that the citizen might feel overawed; but Nicias himself may also be projecting on the president his own apprehensiveness about a vindictive *dēmos* (7.48.3).   εἴπερ ἡγεῖ . . . πολίτης ἀγαθός: on the placing of τε see **15**.2 n. It is a regular rhetorical trick to claim that only one's own side are the patriots: Nicias has already exploited it at **13**.1, ὑπὲρ τῆς πατρίδος. Cf. Isoc. 8.34, Dem. 18.228, 266; Aeschin. 2.8 ridicules Demosthenes for such posturing.   ἐπιψήφιζε . . . ἀναψηφίσαι: ἐπιψηφίζειν is 'put to the vote'. It is uncertain whether ἀναψηφίζειν means 'put to the vote again' (LSJ, Bétant) or 'repeal', 'reverse the decision' as apparently at Pherecrates fr. 52 K–A, RO 49.19, and Dio Cass. 39.39.3: the president obviously could not reverse the decision on his own, but might be nervous of being held responsible if that was the result. Even though revisiting an issue was not illegal (see next nn.), a president might be reluctant to do this without authority from the *boulē*.   τὸ μὲν λύειν . . . σχεῖν (thinking that) 'as for breaking the laws, you would not be blamed given that so many witnesses are here': τὸ . . . λύειν is best taken as an acc. of respect. In fact there seems no doubt that the *dēmos* – prone to undecide (μετάβουλοι) as well as swift to decide (ταχύβουλοι, Ar. *Ach.* 630–2) – was free to rethink its earlier resolutions (Dover 1955), just as it had over Mytilene (3.36, 49); what was illegal here was putting a proposal which was not on the agenda and had not come to the *boulē* first (Harris 2014). μαρτύρων also gives a forensic twist in anticipation of a trial: the point is that 'all these witnesses will testify that the Assembly is genuinely divided, and you will not be accused of acting frivolously or maliciously' (Dover 1965: 22).   τῆς δὲ πόλεως κακῶς βουλευσαμένης ἰατρὸς ἂν γενέσθαι: still after νομίσας, 'thinking that you could become the healer of the city after its bad decision'. The notion of a 'sick state' that needed 'healing' was very familiar: cf. Brock 2013a: 69–76, 117. It becomes a favourite of Plato, whose philosopher-king is like a doctor who knows best; but in a democracy this treads on difficult ground. Many of Th.'s audience would already know that Nicias' own disease will be important in hampering the expedition's success (7.15.1, 77.2). καὶ τὸ καλῶς ἄρξαι τοῦτ' εἶναι, ὃς ἂν . . . βλάψηι: for the construction, with a definition given by a relative clause specifying who fits, cf. **16**.3, 7.68.1, and e.g. Pericles' definition of good fortune as 'the people who meet with the most honourable of deaths', οἳ ἂν τῆς εὐπρεπεστάτης λάχωσιν . . . τελευτῆς, 2.44.1. Tompkins 2013: 452–3 notes such loosely attached relative clauses as a feature of Periclean style: cf. also 2.44.2.   ὃς ἂν τὴν πατρίδα ὠφελήσηι ὡς πλεῖστα ἢ ἑκὼν εἶναι μηδὲν βλάψηι: the formulation suits Nicias' uninspiring rhetoric, but also fits a medical principle: cf. [Hipp.] *Epid.* 1.11 p. 164 J, 'the two things for a physician to practise are doing good or not doing harm' (ὠφελέειν ἢ μὴ βλάπτειν). Alcibiades strikes his own medical note in reply, **18**.6–7 (nn.).   ἑκὼν εἶναι: the εἶναι is apparently superfluous, but is particularly used with a verb where a negative is stated or implied (LSJ, *GG* 1535).

It is not clear that Nicias got what he wanted from the *prytanis* (Kohl 1977: 82): the debate continued along the lines Nicias had started (**15**.1), but that does not mean that the *prytanis* was yet committed to putting it to the vote, and when the vote does come it is not on this issue (**26**.1).

15 *Alcibiades*

Alcibiades was introduced at 5.43.2 as 'Alcibiades son of Cleinias, a man who would still be considered young in any other city but one honoured because of the prestige (ἀξιώματι, cf. **15**.3 [n.]) of his ancestors'. For Th.'s thumbnail character-sketches when figures are about to play key roles see **8**.2 and **72**.2 nn., but this one is unusually elaborate. The technique picks out the qualities about to come to the surface (**72**.2 n.) and 'lend[s] formality to his narrative while also marking off discrete discourse units' (Rood 2018: 157). **1**.1 had hinted that the expedition would end in failure (n.), and so had marked out Bks. 6–7 as a distinct 'discourse unit'; that unit is now expanded by extending the gaze to the end of the war (οὐ διὰ μακροῦ ἔσφηλαν τὴν πόλιν, **15**.4). The two perspectives of 415–413 and 415–404 overlap, as many of the later factors are already in play: the fears and distaste he inspired will be central to Alcibiades' removal from the Sicilian command as well as his later exile, and in both cases 'entrusting control to others' will not go well. The seed is sown here for the suggestion developed in 7.87, though already qualified at 7.28, that defeat in Sicily foreshadowed and eventually led to the overall outcome of the war. Cf. Intr., 12.

Th. also picks up ideas from 2.65, his earlier foresnap of the end of the war, and the reasons why the Athenians lost (Intr., 4–8). That was prompted by the death of Pericles; the departure of the one marked the end of the beginning of the war, and this (re-)entry of the other marks the beginning of the end. At 2.65 Th. had stressed how 'personal ambitions and personal gain' (τὰς ἰδίας φιλοτιμίας καὶ ἴδια κέρδη) drove Pericles' successors, and here too ἴδιος becomes a key-word. There are other echoes too (nn.). The narrative has already shown self-seeking in other politicians, including Nicias (**9–14** n., Intr., 7–8). This now both narrows the focus to Alcibiades and widens it to the general Athenian public, who were 'each personally pained' (ἰδίαι ἕκαστοι . . . ἀχθεσθέντες, **15**.4) by Alcibiades' ways. His ἐπιθυμίαι are stressed, both the expensive desires (**15**.3) leading to this overwhelming desire for this command (**15**.2) and also the desire for tyranny that others suspect (**15**.4). Nicias has already warned against disastrous ἐπιθυμίαι (**13**.1), but the Athenian people will respond with an even more intense emotion, ἔρως (**24**.3), itself a word with Alcibiadean resonance (Wohl 1999): a flamboyant picture of ἔρως decorated his shield, Plut. *Alc.* 16.1–2. Cf. Kallet 2001: 36–7.

Nicias' speech had already shown the bad feeling between the two men (**12.2–13** nn.), and 5.43–6 had described Alcibiades' outsmarting of Nicias and the Spartan envoys in 420. Jealousy there played a part, as Alcibiades resented the envoys' choice to act through Nicias rather than himself (5.43.2). Th. omits another recent clash, when – so the story goes – the two were front runners in an ostracism vote; their supporters struck a clandestine deal, and Hyperbolus was chosen (Plut. *Alc.* 13, *Nic.* 11, *Arist.* 7, with Pelling 2000: 49–52 and esp. Rhodes 1994). For a possible reason for the omission see **8–26** n.

15.1 τὰ ἐψηφισμένα μὴ λύειν: cf. on τὸ μὲν λύειν τοὺς νόμους, **14** n.

15.2 ἐνῆγε δὲ . . . τὴν στρατείαν 'pressed the case for the expedition', cf. 1.67.2, ἐνῆγον τὸν πόλεμον. Soon the pressure will be coming in the opposite direction, the work of Alcibiades' enemies, **61**.1. **προθυμότατα: 6**.2 n. **βουλόμενος τῶι τε Νικίαι ἐναντιοῦσθαι . . . καὶ μάλιστα:** the placing of τε gives a slight anacoluthon, as if στρατηγῆσαι were to be a second inf. dependent on βουλόμενος rather than on ἐπιθυμῶν. Such displacement is not unusual: cf. **14, 61**.5. **ὧν καὶ ἐς τἆλλα . . . ἐμνήσθη** 'as he was his political enemy in other respects as well and particularly because he had made a disparaging mention of him', **12**.2. τὰ πολιτικά is best taken as acc. of respect with διάφορος; the variety of construction, with ἐς τἆλλα balanced by a ὅτι-clause, is typical. διαβόλως leaves open the question of the truth of what Nicias had said: cf. Pelling 2007: 183–4.   **καὶ μάλιστα . . . ὠφελήσειν:** so Th. gives authorial support to some of Nicias' claims, especially the prospect of complete conquest (see on τούς μὲν Σικελιώτας . . ., **13**.1) and the allegation that Alcibiades was after money and reputation (**12**.2); ἐπιθυμῶν . . . ἐπιθυμίαις (**15**.3) picks up Nicias' warnings against untimely ἐπιθυμίαι, **13**.1. 'Carthage' introduces a new idea; Hermocrates speaks of Carthaginian fears of Athens at **34**.2 (n.), and at Sparta Alcibiades himself alleges such Athenian ambitions (**90**.2). Ar. *Knights* 1303–4 (424 BCE) has Hyperbolus propose '100 ships to sail for Carthage', and it is hard to tell whether that is Aristophanic fantasy or a reflection of genuine talk (Pelling 2000: 125). See **88**.6 and **90**.2 nn. and Intr. to Bk. 7, p. 35.   **δι' αὐτοῦ:** i.e. διὰ τοῦ στρατηγῆσαι.   **καὶ τὰ ἴδια ἅμα εὐτυχήσας χρήμασί τε καὶ δόξηι ὠφελήσειν:** Th. partly backs up Nicias' criticism of **12**.2 (n.), but ἅμα leaves the possibility that Alcibiades thought the expedition in the public interest as well, just as at 5.43.2 he genuinely thought an Argive alliance was the right course.

15.3 ὧν γὰρ ἐν ἀξιώματι ὑπὸ τῶν ἀστῶν 'enjoying prestige in the eyes of the citizens': for the construction cf. 1.130.1, Pausanias ἐν μεγάλωι ἀξιώματι ὑπὸ τῶν Ἑλλήνων. At 5.43.2 Alcibiades 'enjoyed prestige because of his ancestors'; it may be implied that in the intervening five years he had also won prestige on his own account, partly through those ἱπποτροφίαι. Pericles' great ἀξίωμα was acquired and exploited in rather different ways (2.65.8).   **ταῖς ἐπιθυμίαις μείζοσιν ἢ κατὰ τὴν ὑπάρχουσαν οὐσίαν** 'desires that were bigger than his existing wealth could support'. That wealth was considerable (some said more than 100 talents, Lys. 19.52) and so were the outgoings, especially in 421–416: see *APF* 20–1, concluding that he was then 'drawing heavily on his capital resources' and that 'severe financial embarrassment' threatened.   **ἔς τε τὰς ἱπποτροφίας καὶ τὰς ἄλλας δαπάνας:** for the ἱπποτροφίαι cf. **12**.2, **16**.2 and nn. The other expenses included his private ship, **50**.1 and **61**.6. His extravagances continued to capture the imagination centuries later: cf. Athen. 5.220c, 12.534b–535e, 13.574d–e; Plut. *Alc.* 11–12.

15.3–4 ὅπερ καὶ καθεῖλεν . . . ἔσφηλαν τὴν πόλιν: these phrases frame the summary of φοβηθέντες . . . ἐπιτρέψαντες, and make it clear that their primary reference is to later events beyond the limits of the text (narratologically, a 'heterodiegetic prolepsis', though Th. himself presumably intended them to be 'homodiegetic', i.e. included in the narrative that he did not live to complete). That is confirmed by καθεῖλεν, 'destroyed', too strong for anything short of the final defeat, and by κράτιστα διαθέντι τὰ τοῦ πολέμου, which can fit 411–406 but not anything achieved in Sicily.

But the language here is also picked up within the Sicilian narrative, esp. at **28**.2 (ἀχθόμενοι . . . τὴν ἄλλην αὐτοῦ ἐς τὰ ἐπιτηδεύματα οὐ δημοτικὴν παρανομίαν), with the fears of tyranny at **53–60**.1, and with the 'entrusting of the command to others' that followed Alcibiades' recall. What happens now prefigures the future, and the two timescales blur: cf. Gribble 1998: 61 and 1999: 182–4.

15.4 οἱ πολλοί . . . ἔσφηλαν τὴν πόλιν: so, despite all his attention to individual self-seeking (Intr., 7–8), Th. is unequivocal that responsibility for the city's fall lay with οἱ πολλοί. **τὸ μέγεθος . . . ἔπρασσεν** 'the greatness of his transgressiveness in his everyday pursuit of bodily pleasures [lit. 'transgressiveness with regard to his own body in lifestyle'] and of his thinking with which he did whatever particular thing [lit. 'one by one'] he might be engaged in'. Everything about him was big. Here and at **28**.2 παρανομία indicates unconventionality rather than illegality, going beyond the considerable licence allowed a young aristocrat; δίαιτα narrows that to everyday lifestyle, and κατὰ τὸ ἑαυτοῦ σῶμα makes explicit what sort of transgressiveness was involved. [Andoc.] 4.13–23 and Plut. *Alc.* 16 collect some good stories. **ὡς τυραννίδος ἐπιθυμοῦντι:** these suspicions become important at **53**.2–**60**.1. Tyranny might seem an unlikely option in late fifth-century Athens, but such talk and fears were real enough: Seaford 2000: 34–5. Aristophanes has fun with such suspicion at *Wasps* 486–502. It was Alcibiades' behaviour, rather than any indication of specific plans for a coup, that encouraged the suspicions (Seager 1967): thinking big and putting on airs could easily suggest tyrannical aspiration, as earlier with Pausanias, 1.132.2, and Cylon, 1.126 and Hdt. 5.71. **πολέμιοι καθέστασαν** 'had become his foes', pluperfect pointing to a time before the people turned decisively against him. Strong words: not just ἐχθροί, the usual word for personal enemies (**29**.3), but πολέμιοι. They are at war with him rather than with Sparta. Sophocles' Menelaus speaks in the same way about Ajax and his Philoctetes about Odysseus (*Ajax* 1132, immediately challenged there by Teucer, and *Phil.* 1302 with Schein 2013 ad loc.). **κράτιστα διαθέντι τὰ τοῦ πολέμου:** διαθέντι is dat. with ἄχθομαι as at **28**.2, and τοῖς ἐπιτηδεύμασιν adds a causal dat.; the profusion of different sorts of dative seems ugly, but cf. e.g. 3.82.1, 4.87.3, 4.126.6. Th. praises Alcibiades at 8.86.4–5 for restraining the fleet from sailing against the Four Hundred at Athens, and hints there at further services to come ('this seems the first time, and as important as any, when he brought benefit to the city'): Gribble 1999: 186–7. Alcibiades then won important victories in 411–406 at Abydus, Cyzicus, Selymbria, Chalcedon, and Byzantium. **ἰδίαι ἕκαστοι**

τοῖς ἐπιτηδεύμασιν αὐτοῦ ἀχθεσθέντες: again strong language: each individual feels personally affronted and pained. Plut. *Alc.* 36 expands, perhaps imaginatively, on the lubricious talk. ἄχθος becomes a key-word for Alcibiades' fortunes, here and at **28**.2, **89**.3 of the pain he causes in others; but by Bk. 8 his manoeuvres are causing ἄχθος between Tissaphernes and Sparta (8.87), and Alcibiades himself exploits the Athenians' ἄχθος with the oligarchy (8.89.1). ἄλλοις ἐπιτρέψαντες: understand τὰ τοῦ πολέμου again (schol.) or τὴν πόλιν or vaguely 'things' (Dover 1965): all come to much the same thing. This was in 407–406 (X. *Hell.* 1.5.16–17), after a naval defeat at Notium suffered in Alcibiades' absence. οὐ διὰ μακροῦ 'not much later', i.e. in 404. ἔσφηλαν τὴν πόλιν 'brought the city down': σφάλλω again (**11**.4 n). At 2.65.12 Th. used the word both of the Sicilian disaster and of the city's final defeat, perhaps already adumbrating the connection between the two.

15.5 δ' οὖν: resumptive, as Th. picks up the main thread (*GP* 463–4): cf. e.g. **56**.1, 7.59.2. παρελθών ... παρῄνει: the echo of **15**.1 rounds off the analysis.

16–18 *The Speech of Alcibiades*

15.4 had introduced Alcibiades as a big thinker; he now encourages the Athenians to think big too, with a large perspective both in geography – yes, they can handle Sicily as well as the threats at home – and in time. There is a good deal here on ancestors, both the Athenians' 'fathers' and, first, Alcibiades' own πρόγονοι. Readers/listeners too may look back in time and particularly to Pericles, already such a background presence, as Alcibiades applies to himself what Pericles said about the city (Macleod 1983: 75). It is now he who is 'worthy' to ἄρχειν (**16**.1), and it is his fame that arouses envy (**16**.5) but deserves respect (**16**.4) and will evoke pride in later generations (**16**.5). He turns on its head the accusation of Nicias (**12**.2) that he has prioritised τὰ ἴδια: his own λαμπρότης, he claims, has brought lustre to the city too (**16**.1–3), making others 'infer' or 'suspect' its power (**16**.2). Some of this is uncomfortable – 'he deals above all in semblances', Macleod 1983: 73 – but he is not the only politician to have claimed that private self-seeking can be advantageous for the state. Even his argument that empire requires constant reinforcement if it is not to be lost (**18**.3) has a Periclean ancestry, though it is again uneasily expressed (n.). Still, this cannot mask the fact that Nicias' strategy is more in line with Pericles' advice to avoid risk-taking (1.144.1, p. 129 above); nor that Pericles argued that one's personal concerns are as nothing if the city goes down (2.60.2–4, p. 7).

Alcibiades' style is much punchier than Nicias': cf. Tompkins 2013: 347–8 on the 'cascading metaphors' of **18**.3 and esp. 1972: 204–14 on the use of parataxis rather than Nicias' complex subordination: in **17** sentence after sentence begins with καί, as point piles upon point. He has a taste for potential optatives (cf. esp. **17**.8–**18**.2), fitting for a speaker and a *dēmos* eager for visions of hope. Nor are all Alcibiades' arguments bad. His analysis of Sicilian politics at **17**.2–6 echoes some of **1**.2–**5**, though several points are exaggerated (nn.); and the hope of acquiring more allies was not unreasonable, even if the outcome proved disappointing. He may overstate the obligation to help allies (**18**.1), but his view there of the reasons for contracting such alliances is probably one his audience would share (Cawkwell 1997: 78–9): that moral emphasis may appeal to those who put more weight on the narrower aims of **6**.1, while much is also geared to those sharing Alcibiades' own more imperialist perspective (Mader 1993a). Even that initial concentration on himself might not be too offputting: he needs to reply to Nicias' personal attack, and Athenian democracy was used to its big men. Still, the stress on his own haughty behaviour and consequential unpopularity seems less well judged (**16**.4–5), echoing **15**.3–4 more than anything Nicias had said, and his claim about the Mantinea campaign is over-inflated (**16**.6 n.). Most importantly, he is telling his audience what they want to hear. His appeals to Athenian tradition would strike a chord, and his appeal for cross-generational harmony has some nobility (**18**.6). It is not surprising that Nicias' divisive rhetoric on this front falls flat (**24**.3).

See esp. Macleod 1983: 68–87; Kurke 1999: 171–82; Kallet 2001: 37–42; Harris 2016, observing that boasting of one's ancestors and one's expenditure for the state is not found in real-life assembly speeches; and for a more positive view of Alcibiades' relation to Pericles Fulkerson 2012.

16.1 Καὶ προσήκει μοι . . . καὶ ἄξιος ἅμα νομίζω εἶναι: προσήκει refers more to expectations based on his birth and status, ἄξιος to his personal qualities. Alcibiades understandably begins with himself after Nicias' personal attack (**12**.2): he does the same at **89**.1, and this is what rhetoricians called a λύσις διαβολῆς (Arist. *Rhet.* 1415a28–34, *Rhet. ad Alex.* 1437b38–41, cf. Macleod 1983: 70). Euphemus begins similarly at **82**.1 (n.). Strikingly, the disparagement on which he first focuses concerns his suitability to command (**12**.2), not the wisdom of his advice. ἄρχειν and ἀρχή become key-words, returning at **17**.4–**18**.2 to apply to the city and by then referring to 'rule' rather than just this 'command'; the language here already veers towards the tyrannical, and the Olympic flamboyance recalls past tyrants (Kurke 1991: 176; Smith 2009, finding echoes of Pindaric epinician odes for Sicilian tyrants). The suspicions of **15**.4 become all the more understandable.   ἄρχειν ... ἄρξασθαι: the wordplay on the two senses 'command' and 'begin' may be felt, but it is less pointed than at Hdt. 6.67.2–3 or the ambiguities of Hdt. 8.142.2, on which see respectively the nn. of Hornblower–Pelling and Bowie 2007.   ἄξιος ἅμα νομίζω εἶναι: a similar claim was made by the Athenians at 1.75.1 and 76.2 and by Pericles at 2.41.3, but about the city. Euphemus reapplies such language in that direction at 82–3: cf. 82.1 n.   ὧν γὰρ πέρι ἐπιβόητός εἰμι 'the things that make me notorious': this is more than casual egotism, for it is important to the argument that people talk about him throughout Greece. ἐπιβοώμενος at **16.**6 confirms the pejorative nuance, and as at **16.**2–3 Alcibiades is appropriating the words his enemies would use and glorifying in them.   τοῖς μὲν προγόνοις μου καὶ ἐμοί: perhaps a reply to an implied criticism that he owes everything to family background, for at 5.43.2 his πρόγονοι were giving Alcibiades his prestige (ἀξίωμα). Alcibiades now reverses that: it is his achievements that add lustre to them. Cf. Isoc. 16.29; **15.**3 n.   ὠφελίαν: again picking up a thread of Nicias' speech, **12.**2, **13.**2, **14.**

16.2 οἱ γὰρ Ἕλληνες ... τῆς Ὀλυμπίαζε θεωρίας 'for my magnificence in the Olympic delegation made the Greeks rate the city higher [than they had before, or than they would otherwise], even (καί) to the extent of exaggerating its power'. These were the Olympics of 416 BCE: cf. esp. Gribble 2012. θεωρία is a delegation to the festival (hence 'to the Olympics', -αζε), normally a state affair (3.1 n.), but here Alcibiades makes its conspicuousness (διαπρεπεῖ) 'mine'. An Olympic victory carried international prestige, and it mattered which city was announced as the victor's: there had been a row about that in 420 (5.49–50). καὶ ὑπὲρ δύναμιν indicates that there is something fake about this projection of greatness, but often in diplomacy appearance drives reality, and modern politicians too are proud when a state 'punches above its weight'.   πρότερον ἐλπίζοντες αὐτὴν καταπεπολεμῆσθαι: as often, ἐλπίζω combines 'expect' and 'hope'. Alcibiades wisely leaves unspecified why Athens might have been thought defeated: in 416 the biggest recent blow had been the battle of Mantinea (**16.**6 n.), and that was largely his own doing. But the vagueness could easily be taken as a slur on the Peace of 421, closely associated with Nicias.   ἅρματα μὲν ἑπτὰ καθῆκα 'I sent down seven chariots' to the arena, LSJ καθίημι 2: cf. Hdt. 5.22.2, Alexander of Macedon 'going down' (καταβάντος) to compete. On the immense expense involved see Gribble 2012: 55–9.   ἰδιώτης: as at **16.**3 and 6, Alcibiades appropriates the ἰδι- language Nicias had used against him (**12.**2) and Th. had largely endorsed (**15.**2). The implied contrast is not just with states but also with kings and tyrants, the only individuals who might afford such displays.

Alcibiades again treads on delicate ground. ἐνίκησα δὲ καὶ δεύτερος καὶ τέταρτος ἐγενόμην: this presumably is correct, though the celebratory ode attributed to Euripides said first, second, and third (*PMG* 755–6, Plut. *Alc.* 11: cf. Bowra 1960; Smith 2009; Gribble 2012: 65); so also Isoc. 16.34. Th. may be silently correcting that ode here. Here too there was scandal, as it was said that Alcibiades entered under his own name at least one team that belonged to another Athenian (the details differ in our sources, [Andoc.] 4.26–7, Diod. 13.74, and Plut. *Alc.* 12: Gribble 1999: 98–100). A long-running wrangle followed, including a lawsuit for which Isoc. 16 (*On the Team of Horses*) was written for Alcibiades' son. Alcibiades' charioteering was celebrated in art as well: two pictures were attributed to Aglaophon or perhaps his son Aristophon, one representing the 'Olympian and Pythian festivals' and the other showing Nemea (Athen. 12. 535d, cf. Plut. *Alc.* 16.7), which suggests victories in those other festivals as well. There was also a sculpture by Pyromachus representing Alcibiades and his chariot (Pliny, *NH* 34.80). Cf. Bowra 1960: 72–3 = 1970: 139–40; Gribble 2012: 67–8. **καὶ τἆλλα ἀξίως τῆς νίκης παρεσκευασάμην:** further details and allegations concerning the magnificent pavilion and entertainment are given by [Andoc.] 4.29–31, Plut. *Alc.* 12.1, and Athen. 1.3e: cf. Gribble 2012: 59–67. [Andoc.] 4.29 tells of Alcibiades passing off as his own the ceremonial vessels of the Athenian delegation; when they were seen in the Athenian procession as well, it was assumed that Athens was borrowing his vessels rather than the other way round. The story is suspiciously similar to **46**.3. **νόμωι μὲν γὰρ τιμὴ τὰ τοιαῦτα ... ὑπονοεῖται** 'for such things are acknowledged to bring honour, and action brings with it also an inference of power'. νόμωι picks up ἐνόμισαν: pre-existing mindsets guide the conclusions that observers draw. Given the familiar distinction between νόμος and φύσις, the contrast with φθονεῖται φύσει (**16**.3) may also be felt; if so, the point is not that his international honour is 'less real than the envy he incurs at home' (Macleod 1983: 72), but that the first balances the second and may be more important. The idea that action is needed to convey power comes back in Alcibiades' scepticism about Nicias' proposal at **47–8**.

16.3 ὅσα: internal acc. with λαμπρύνομαι.   **χορηγίαις:** Alcibiades slips in these public services (*OCD*[4] *chorēgia*) that also have involved heavy expenditure. Normally assembly speeches, unlike court speeches, avoided mention of these (Harris 2016), but if he is going to include them at all he might be expected to make more of them, as does Isoc. 16.35; perhaps he did, but Th. regarded this as less interesting than the Olympic extravagance.   **λαμπρύνομαι:** again appropriating Nicias' language (ἐλλαμπρύνεσθαι, **12**.2 n.).   **τοῖς μὲν ἀστοῖς** 'in the eyes of one's fellow citizens'.   **φθονεῖται φύσει:** Pericles too had accepted the inevitability of φθόνος, but for the state as a whole (2.64.4–5, cf. 1.75.1); he had deprecated it among fellow citizens (2.35.2–3). Alcibiades again fits a tradition of tyrannical athletic victors: 'better to be envied than pitied', said Pindar (*P.* 1.85; cf. Hdt. 3.52.5), where Kurke comments that the sentiment 'would be unimaginable in a poem commissioned by a private citizen'; such individuals are advised to defuse envy rather than flaunt it (1991: 221–4).   **καὶ αὕτη ἰσχὺς φαίνεται**   'this too appears as strength': appearances again. 'This' is attracted into the case of ἰσχύς. It strains belief that foreigners would be so impressed by Athenian liturgies; maybe he is thinking of the Great Dionysia (*CT*, cf. Ar. *Ach.* 504–5), or maybe this is just egotism.   **καὶ οὐκ ἄχρηστος ἥδ' ἡ ἄνοια:** again an appropriation of his enemies' language: for Nicias the whole Sicilian project is ἀνόητον, **11.1**. Alcibiades will re-use the word himself at **89**.6, but of democracy.   **ὃς ἄν ... ὠφελῆι:** for the construction cf. **14** n.

16.4 μὴ ἴσον εἶναι ... ἰσομοιρεῖ: μὴ ἴσον εἶναι = 'not to behave in an egalitarian way'. Some of this recalls Aristotle's μεγαλόψυχος (*EN* 4.1123a33–25a35) who does not conceal his own superiority, but Alcibiades puts it in ways that grate against democratic ideology. ἰσο- compounds – ἰσότης, ἰσονομία, ἰσηγορία – were proud slogans, pity was an Athenian virtue (**6**.2 n.), and reproaching a fellow citizen for misfortune was unacceptable (Dover 1974: 240). 'Looking down on' the *dēmos* or its institutions (cf. ὑπερφρονούμενος) could be an impressive element on an orator's charge-sheet (Isoc. 20.21, Aeschin. 1.114, 141; cf. Xen *Mem.* 1.2.9); Pericles found room for contempt, but against the enemy when well-founded on reason (2.62.3–4, cf. **11**.5 n.). *Rhet. ad Alex.* 1437a2–5 recommends that an orator under attack should say that he will rebut the criticisms, but Alcibiades does not pretend that his behaviour has been misinterpreted: ctr. e.g. Isoc. 15.151.   **πρὸς οὐδένα τῆς ξυμφορᾶς ἰσομοιρεῖ** 'does not share his ill fortune with anyone'.   **οὐ προσαγορευόμεθα** 'we are not spoken to'. This echoes a gloomy insight that may well be proverbial: cf. Eur. *Phoen.* 403 τὰ φίλων δ' οὐδέν, ἤν τις δυστυχῆι, and e.g. *Med.* 561, Democr. DK 68 B 106.   **τὰ ἴσα νέμων τὰ ὁμοῖα ἀνταξιούτω** 'dole out an equal treatment and claim an equivalent response'. τὰ ἴσα serves a double purpose, picking up μὴ ἴσον εἶναι – I may not practise ἰσότης, but they show a lack of ἰσότης too – and as a synonym for τὰ ὁμοῖα, the consistency that he claims they lack.

16.5 τοὺς τοιούτους, καὶ ὅσοι ἔν τινος λαμπρότητι προέσχον: appropriating Nicias' ἐλλαμπρύνεσθαι, and perhaps his τοὺς τοιούτους too (**12.2**); the real 'people like that' are the great figures of previous generations. Rawlings

1981: 97 suggests that Themistocles is particularly in mind, exiled and disgraced but now claimed as a hero (1.74.1). ἔν τινος λαμπρότητι 'in brilliance of any sort'. τινος is gen. of material or description, underlining that brilliance comes in different types: even as Alcibiades assimilates himself to a class, he emphasises its variety. ἐν μὲν τῶι καθ' αὑτοὺς βίωι ... τῶν δὲ ἔπειτα ἀνθρώπων: whereas Pericles balanced the *city*'s present unpopularity and the pain it causes against the λαμπρότης that will be its legacy (2.64.5). λυπηρούς: different from Pericles' picture of tolerant Athenian life (2.37.2), where one avoids those 'annoyances that carry no penalty but cause pain (λυπηράς) at the sight'. τοῖς ὁμοίοις μὲν μάλιστα, ἔπειτα δὲ καὶ τοῖς ἄλλοις ξυνόντας 'especially to their peers, but then also to others when they keep company with them'. τῶν δὲ ἔπειτα ... καταλιπόντας 'but to some among later generations they leave a legacy of pretending to kinship even when it does not exist': οὖσαν logically goes with ξυγγενείας but is transferred to προσποίησιν ('hypallage'). The historian Duris of Samos (c. 340–260 BCE) claimed to be Alcibiades' descendant (Plut. *Alc.* 32.2). ἧς ἂν ὦσι πατρίδος: this shifts back from 'some' individuals (τισί) to the city, closing a small ring with **16**.1, linking family (πρόγονοι at **16**.1, [fake] descendants here) and πατρίς. αὔχησις offers a further resonance of Pericles, who deprecated baseless αὔχημα, 2.62.4.

16.6 ἐπιβοώμενος: **16**.1 n. τὰ δημόσια σκοπεῖτε εἴ του χεῖρον μεταχειρίζω: the 'I know thee who thou art' construction, **6**.3 n. μεταχειρίζω again echoes Nicias, **12**.2, and to an extent this is in line with Th.'s own view, κράτιστα διαθέντι τὰ τοῦ πολέμου (**15**.4), though that mainly refers to a later period (n.). Πελοποννήσου γὰρ τὰ δυνατώτατα ... ἀγωνίσασθαι: an extremely rosy view of the Mantinea campaign (418), ignoring the fact that it was a Spartan victory. Πελοποννήσου ... τὰ δυνατώτατα also overstates: Mantinea and Elis supported Argos, while Tegea and much of Arcadia supported Sparta. But it is true that the Argive alliance that was its precursor was largely Alcibiades' doing (5.43–7, cf. 56.3), and Alcibiades played an important part in rekindling the hostilities after the enemy had initially withdrawn (5.61.2). ἄνευ μεγάλου ὑμῖν κινδύνου: in fact the Athenian contingent had been in great danger during the battle (5.73.1–2). ἐς μίαν ἡμέραν: the notion of the 'single day' on which everything turns is familiar from tragedy (Soph. *Ajax* 748–53 with Finglass 2011 ad loc., Eur. *Her.* 510, *Or.* 48) and elsewhere (Pelling 2011: 469–70 on Plut. *Caes.* 63.5, the Ides of March). ἀγωνίσασθαι 'to contend', 'an athletic metaphor ... at the end of this notably "athletic" chapter', *CT.* ἐξ οὗ: not just 'after' (LSJ ἐκ II) but 'as a result of' (LSJ III.6). καὶ περιγενόμενοι τῆι μάχηι οὐδέπω καὶ νῦν βεβαίως θαρσοῦσιν: each καί is important: 'even though' they won, 'even now' they are not yet fully confident. But Th. has stressed the value of the victory to Spartan prestige (5.75.3), and there was no shortage of Spartan initiatives after it (76.1, 82.1, 82.3, 83.1, 115.2).

17.1 Καὶ ταῦτα ἡ ἐμὴ νεότης . . . ἔπεισεν 'And in these matters my unnatural-seeming youth and folly dealt in appropriate arguments with regard to the Peloponnesian power, and proved persuasive because it gave the confidence to go with the emotion.' The language is more contrived than is usual for Alcibiades, largely because of double meanings and constructive vagueness. ταῦτα is internal acc. with ὡμίλησε and ἔπεισεν; the direct object of ἔπεισεν is left unexpressed, but embraces both the Athenian assembly and the Peloponnesian allies, and perhaps even (though he is too tactful to say so) the Spartan ambassadors whom he duped at 5.43–6. 'Youth and folly' are put together as a single concept (ἡ . . . εἶναι, then αὐτήν and αὐτῆς in the next sentence); Andoc. 2.7 does the same but in an affectation of humility rather than Alcibiades' sarcasm. 'Unnatural-seeming' responds to Nicias' claim that the qualities are inappropriate for the needs of this command (**12.2**). ἐς τὴν Πελοποννησίων δύναμιν picks up Πελοποννήσου . . . τὰ δυνατώτατα of **16**.6, but the singular also points to the power structure of the Peloponnese 'with relation to' (ἐς) which the diplomacy dealt, in particular the power of Sparta. λόγοις τε πρέπουσιν ὡμίλησε covers the 'keeping company with' (ὁμιλία) the other side in diplomatic hob-nobbing, with λόγοις τε πρέπουσιν a dative of instrument or manner (Spratt); but the dative could also be taken as governed by ὡμίλησε, 'associating' with the appropriate words and arguments (Marchant), as one might keep company with war (1.122.1) or gymnastics (Plato, *Rep.* 3.410c). ὀργῆι finally leaves it open whether this 'emotion' or 'anger' is his own ('providing confidence through my emotion') or his listeners' ('adding confidence to/for their emotion') or both.   **πεφόβησθε:** the perf. subj. is unexpected but seems more emphatic than the usual pres. imperative or aor. subj. in such prohibitions (*M&T* 107). It suggests a continuing fear that has been injected in the past, here by Nicias: cf. 2.89.1, whereas here the injection is quite recent (Phormio's men are πεφοβημένοι by the numbers they see before them).   **ἀκμάζω μετ' αὐτῆς:** 'I am at my peak' (ἀκμάζω) goes readily with 'youth' (2.20.2, X. *Ages.* 11.15), and this allows the suggestion that the 'folly' of the expedition (**11**.1) links inextricably with such youthful vigour: they come as a package. Alcibiades is turning against Nicias his own divisiveness (**12.2–13**.1): if the generations are so different, why not use the qualities of both?   **καὶ ὁ Νικίας εὐτυχὴς δοκεῖ εἶναι:** for Nicias' εὐτυχία cf. 5.16.1, quoted at Intr., 7, and 7.77.2 (n.). There may be a barb in δοκεῖ, but this will not be to suggest that Nicias' εὐτυχία is appearance rather than reality: that would undermine the point.

It is more to balance παρὰ φύσιν δοκοῦσα εἶναι – exploit what you see in each of us, even if in my case it is paradoxical. The blending notion is developed at **18.6** (n.).

17.2 ὄχλοις τε γὰρ ξυμμείκτοις πολυανδροῦσιν αἱ πόλεις: populousness is normally a sign of prosperity and strength (**3**.2, **1**.24.3, X. *Hell.* 5.2.16, *Anab.* 2.4.13), but ὄχλοις (**63**.2 n.) and ξυμμείκτοις pejoratively qualify this: Alcibiades treats mixed ethnic origin dismissively (cf. 3.61.2), over-generalising from the displacements of **1**.2–**5**.3 (nn.) and recently of Leontini (**6**.2 n.). The rhetoric would appeal to Athenians, proud of their autochthony. Cf. the pride Euripides' Praxithea takes in Athens 'where first the people is not imported from elsewhere but we are autochthonous . . . The person who moves to a new city is like a square peg in a round hole, a citizen in name only' (*Erechth.* frag. 360 K.). Cf. Rosivach 1987: 302–3; Pelling 2009; Fragoulaki 2013: 220–8. **ῥαιδίας ἔχουσι τῶν πολιτῶν τὰς μεταβολὰς καὶ ἐπιδοχάς** 'readily change citizens and receive new ones'.

17.3 καὶ οὐδείς . . . κατασκευαῖς 'and for that reason nobody has equipped himself, as they would if it were for their own country, either with arms for physical combat or with the usual establishments in the country'. τὰ περὶ τὸ σῶμα and τὰ ἐν τῆι χώραι are accus. of respect; νομίμοις indicates the sorts of farms and estates one would conventionally expect. Alcibiades' overstatement grows worse, and here receives no support from **1**.2–**5**. He is beginning to emerge as himself one of those ἄπειροι Athenians (**1**.1) – or perhaps is playing on the ἀπειρία of his audience. **ὅ τι δὲ . . . ἑτοιμάζεται** 'whatever each person thinks he can take from the common purse either by persuasive talk (lit. 'from persuading people while speaking') or while playing a part in civic faction and then, if he does not succeed, go and live in another land – these things are what he sets about preparing'. ὅ τι depends on the participle λαβών, which like μὴ κατορθώσας is dependent on οἰκήσειν: the 'taking' comes first, then 'if he does not succeed' he thinks he will move away. The singular ὅ τι is loosely the antecedent of the plural ταῦτα, but by then 'these things' embraces the whole of the disreputable strategy. Alcibiades exploits what his audience may find easy to believe: Sicily was renowned for its orators, notably Gorgias of Leontini and earlier Corax and Teisias (see *OCD*[4]), and it did have a history of στάσις (**5**.1 n.): cf. Cawkwell 1997: 83–7. Nicias had been rude about empty Egestaean talk and 'exiles' (**12**.1); Alcibiades now turns rhetoric and στάσις into reasons for optimism.

'The words are painfully applicable to himself' (Macleod 1983: 79). He is the persuasive orator; he is pursuing his own financial gain (**12**.2, **15**.2); and he will give up his country and make for Sparta (**88**.10–**93**).

17.4 τὸν τοιοῦτον ὅμιλον 'such a collection'. ὅμιλος is sometimes pejorative (cf. 2.65.4, Hdt. 3.81.1), though less so than ὄχλος (**63**.2 n.), and probably has such a negative tinge here; the word often connotes a throng's gathering, as at **30**.2, **32**.2, and 7.58.4, and that is appropriate here for the ethnic mix. Cf. Hunter 1988–9: 19–20; Saïd 2013: 202–4. **οὔτε λόγου μιᾶι γνώμηι ἀκροᾶσθαι οὔτε ἐς τὰ ἔργα κοινῶς τρέπεσθαι:** Sicilian lack of cohesion fits the argument, but 'not listening with a single opinion' focuses the point on a democratic assembly. That is appropriate for democratic Syracuse (Intr., 34), and there may also be a foretaste of his contempt for democracy at **89**.6. **εἴ τι καθ' ἡδονὴν λέγοιτο** 'if anything were said that they wanted to hear', lit. 'according to [a criterion of] pleasure': the mark of the demagogue, applied to the leaders of post-Periclean Athens at 2.65.8 and 10, where Alcibiades himself is much in mind (Intr., 7–8). At Athens the typical danger is that the *dēmos* may be persuaded in a single wrong direction: cf. Cleon on ἡδονὴ λόγων, 3.40.2. Alcibiades turns it into the likelihood of Sicilian fragmentation, as each orator attracts a distinct following (ὡς ἕκαστοι). Part of the point is that different cities may take different decisions, but εἰ στασιάζουσιν then focuses on discord within a single city, and Syracuse, marked for στάσις (**5**.1 n.), is again in his sights. **προσχωροῖεν** 'would go over to'. This covers both individuals 'joining the faction' of a local leader and whole cities 'coming over' to Athens' side when won over by a visiting speaker, Alcibiades' strategy at **48**. In the second case Alcibiades would be the person to make the speeches: telling an audience what they want to hear is what he does best, and what he is doing now.

17.5 καὶ μὴν οὐδ' ὁπλῖται ... ὡπλίσθη: καὶ μήν moves on to a new point, and is especially appropriate when the speaker puts forward 'a point of which he as it were personally guarantees the truth' and 'is actually contradicting the addressee or his supposed expectations or wishes' (Wakker 1997: 215, 217–18, cf. van Emde Boas 2017: 419). οὐδέ then conveys 'not even hoplites ...', the one area in which a ship-bound force might expect to be outmatched: cf. **23**.1 n., **37**.1. The train of thought is complex: as for hoplites, neither (οὔτε) are there so many in Sicily nor (οὔτε) have other Greeks materialised in the numbers initially estimated (presumably 'during the Archidamian war'), but Greece was particularly deluded as to Sicilian numbers and so was under-equipped (ὡπλίσθη picks up ὁπλῖται). The shift of focus back to the Greek war prepares the transition to τὰ ἐνθάδε in **17**.6. Alcibiades is made (1) to share Th.'s conviction of a single war (τῶιδε τῶι πολέμωι) continuous since 431 (5.26.2, **10**.2 n.), and (2) to imply that expectation of Sicilian involvement had figured in the principal states' calculations. This may be right. Sparta had asked for ships from Sicily and Italy in 431 (2.7.2), though they do not seem to have materialised; and the value of Corcyra as a staging-post to Sicily had played a part in Athenian calculations in 433 (1.44.3, Intr., 29–30). Athenians tended to over-estimate what Syracuse might be able to do: Cawkwell 1997: 78–80. κομποῦνται 'are boasted of', presumably by the Sicilian Greeks ('the other Greeks' shows that only Greeks are in point) and especially the Syracusans. But the most relevant exaggeration will be that perpetrated by the non-Greek Egestaeans, and concern wealth rather than manpower (46.2). διεφάνησαν τοσοῦτοι ὄντες ὅσους ἕκαστοι σφᾶς αὐτοὺς ἠρίθμουν 'turned out not to exist in such numbers as each state counted itself as possessing'. The point is not just how many showed up but also each state's exaggeration of its strength. αὐτοὺς ἐψευσμένη 'deceived as to them', i.e. the numbers of Sicilians.

17.6 ἐξ ὧν ἐγὼ ἀκοῆι αἰσθάνομαι: as in ὥσπερ πυνθανόμεθα at **17**.4, Alcibiades lays claim to superior information and confidence in its accuracy: not just 'as I hear' but 'as I perceive on the basis of what I hear'. But he gives no further evidence and has not seen for himself; eyes were proverbially more reliable than ears (Hdt. 1.8.2). τοιαῦτα καὶ ἔτι εὐπορώτερα: but, as usual in the historians, what is claimed to be 'easy' will turn out to be very difficult (Rood 1998a: 34 n. 30; Pelling 2007: 180). βαρβάρους [τε] γὰρ πολλούς: a shift of focus away from 'the Greeks' of **17**.5. Nicias had used the Egestaeans' 'barbarian' ethnicity negatively (**9**.1, **11**.7); Alcibiades turns the theme positively – other barbarians too may take our side. Events prove him partly right, for most of the Sicels supported Athens, together with some Tyrrhenians and Iapygian mercenaries (7.57.11): cf. **62**.5, **88**.3–4, **98**.1, **103**.2, etc.

17.7 οἱ γὰρ πατέρες . . . ἰσχύοντες: cf. **18**.6. Alcibiades again channels Pericles, who appealed to 'our fathers' as the greatest generation (1.144.4, 2.36.2–4, 62.3) and pointed to the fleet as Athens' decisive advantage (1.141.3–4, 143.3–5, 2.62.1–2, 65.7), but he is using that insight to support an unPericlean adventure (**16–18** n.). Other speakers in Th. who appeal to fathers and forefathers do so to encourage virtue or resolve (Pericles, Archidamus at 2.11, Pagondas at 4.92.7, Hippocrates at 4.95.3); Alcibiades alone uses them as a paradigm for a particular policy (Jost 1935: 61, 73), and he tendentiously rewrites history. 'Having the Mede as our enemy' goes back to 478–449, but for the first part of that period Athens and Sparta were allies and the states that later constituted the ἀρχή were partners in a willing anti-Persian coalition (1.96–7). The description is fairer for 460–449. τοὺς αὐτοὺς . . . πλεῖν 'the same people as they [people like Nicias] say that we would now be leaving behind as enemies as we sailed'. τῆι περιουσίαι τοῦ ναυτικοῦ 'the superiority of the fleet'.

17.8 ἀνέλπιστοι 'lacking in hope', in an active sense, as at 3.30.2 and 8.1.2; passive, 'unexpected', at **33**.6 and **34**.2. **εἴ τε καὶ πάνυ ἔρρωνται:** ἔρρωνται (perf. pass. of ῥώννυμι, 'strengthen') is here a matter of morale, as at 2.8.1 and 4, 4.72.1 and 8.78.1: see Intr. to Bk. 7, p. 30. **τὸ μὲν... ἱκανοί εἰσι** 'as for invading our land, they can do it even if we do not sail'. For τό + inf. in such phrases cf. 2.53.3 καὶ τὸ μὲν προσταλαιπωρεῖν... οὐδεὶς πρόθυμος ἦν, and Soph. *Ant.* 78–9: *GG* 1545. It is technically acc. of respect, but differs from the simple ἱκανοὶ ἐσβάλλειν mainly in emphasis. Alcibiades is too sanguine about a double war: by 7.28.2 the dangers are clear, not least thanks to Alcibiades himself once at Sparta (**88**.9–**93**; Macleod 1983: 80–1).

18.1 **ὥστε τί ἂν λέγοντες... μὴ βοηθοῖμεν;** 'So – what could we say that was reasonable in either shrinking from engagement ourselves or in putting excuses to our allies there and not helping them?' For ὥστε introducing a sentence, esp. a question, see *CGCG* 46.6. μή is used because there is a sense of avoiding (*M&T* 292) – how could we not help? **ἐπειδή γε καὶ ξυνωμόσαμεν:** ἐπειδή is causal, and γε makes the logical link more emphatic (LSJ ἐπεί B.5): 'since indeed'. Cf. 7.55.2. Like **10**.5 and **13**.2 (nn.), the language seems to assume an alliance with Egesta as well as Leontini: cf. **6** n. **καὶ μὴ ἀντιτιθέναι ὅτι οὐδὲ ἐκεῖνοι ἡμῖν** 'and not set in the balance against them that they did not help us either'. ἀντιτίθημι is sharper than 'retort, rejoin' (LSJ): it points to balancing arguments for and against as at 3.56.5, Hdt. 1.207.4 and Eur. *Or.* 551. But even Nicias at **13**.2 did not reproach the Sicilian allies for not intervening in the Archidamian War; his point was that no help could be expected even in the direst need. **ἵνα... δεῦρο κωλύωσιν αὐτοὺς ἐπιέναι:** Euphemus makes the same point at **84**.1. For such fears of Sicilian intervention cf. **6**.2, **11**.2–3 and nn.

18.2 **τήν τε ἀρχὴν... ἐπικαλουμένοις:** Athenians were proud of helping the needy (**6**.2 n. on λέγοντες... κεφάλαιον), but Alcibiades (1) makes this self-interested imperialism rather than altruism – Hermocrates makes a similar charge at 4.61.4–5 and cf. **85**.1–2 n. – and thereby he makes it (2) less distinctively Athenian by extending it to other imperialists and (3) more extreme by including barbarians among those aided: that answers Nicias' slurs on the Egestaeans (**9**.1, **11**.7). For intervention to aid the weak as a path to imperial power cf. X. *Hell.* 3.5.10 and 14, Low 2007: 202–5; for the importance normally attached to Greek blood cf. e.g. Aesch. *Supp.*, where Greek ancestry is central to the Egyptian Danaids' claim for Argive assistance. **καὶ ἡμεῖς καὶ ὅσοι δὴ ἄλλοι ἦρξαν:** the Athenians at Sparta similarly relate the city's behaviour to other imperialists at 1.76.2–4, but add that they have behaved better than most. **τοῖς αἰεὶ ἢ βαρβάροις ἢ Ἕλλησιν ἐπικαλουμένοις** 'to whichever barbarians or Greeks called on them from time to time', αἰεί as at e.g. 2.37.3 τῶν αἰεὶ ἐν ἀρχῆι ὄντων and 7.57.9.   ἐπεί . . . κινδυνεύοιμεν   'if all were to remain quiet or pick and choose on ethnic grounds the people whom they should help, we would add to it only a little and would risk this very empire itself'. 'All' probably = 'all Athenians', though possibly = 'all empires', in which case Alcibiades is still subsuming Athens' behaviour to a general pattern; either way, the switch from third to first persons conveys the implications for 'us'. ἡσυχία echoes **10**.2 (n.). On the argument from empire see on **18**.3.   **φυλοκρινοῖεν:** a very rare word in literary sources before imperial Greek, though it may have been proverbial in speech: *Ath. pol.* 21.2 says that '"don't φυλοκρινεῖν", applied to those who want to look closely at γένη' originated in Cleisthenes' creation of ten new tribes to undermine loyalties to the previous four. The word was later used of 'nice (or over-nice) distinctions about sorts of people' (Rhodes 1981: 250), but in both Th. and *Ath. pol.* discrimination by blood, if not precisely by tribes, is still in point.   **ἄν . . . ἄν: 10**.4 n. Here the first goes closely with the προσκτώμενοι and the second with κινδυνεύοιμεν, emphasising the conditionality of both: cf. 5.9.5.   **τὸν γὰρ προύχοντα . . . προκαταλαμβάνει:** the generalisation recalls Th.'s analysis of the war's origins at 1.23.6 and Croesus' thinking at Hdt. 1.46.1. Other pre-emptive strikes have figured in Th., though as much by the stronger against the weaker as the other way round: 1.33.2–3, 1.57.6, 2.2.2, 3.2.3.

18.3 ταμιεύεσθαι ἐς ὅσον βουλόμεθα ἄρχειν 'to be stewards of how far we wish to be rulers': the striking metaphor is of a ταμίας who measures out supplies within a city or household. Cf. **78**.2, and for the financial connotation Kallet 2001: 40, observing that this continues in the idea of calculation (λογισάμενοι) and increase (αὐξήσειν), **18**.4. X. uses 'ταμιεύεσθαι how many people to fight against' of shrewd generals who pick off small enemy detachments (*Anab.* 2.5.18, *Cyr.* 3.3.47, 4.1.18): if that is proverbial, Alcibiades may be echoing the phrase here.   **ἀνάγκη** 'we must . . .': not a fatalistic necessity, but a human choice that realistically can only be made one way. Alcibiades' language is hardening from χρεών, **18**.1 and 2, the moral responsibility that they 'should' help allies.   **ἐπειδήπερ . . . ἄρχοιμεν** 'given that we are in this position, [we must] plot against some and hold tight to others, because of the danger that we might ourselves (αὐτοῖς) be ruled by others if we were not ourselves the rulers of others'. The language recurs in the Camarina debate (**80**.3, **86**.3 nn.). Pericles too had stressed the exigencies of empire ('like a tyranny') and the need to be active, 2.63.2–3, echoed by Cleon at 3.37.2. But Pericles' war-strategy was one of ἡσυχία (2.65.7), the quality disparaged by Alcibiades; and Pericles, the man of γνώμη and λογισμός, would not have accepted that 'they could not steward how far they should rule'. With this cf. Xerxes at Hdt. 7.11 and 7.50.2–3, passages that may be in Th.'s mind here (Rood 1999: 157 = 2009: 164; Raaflaub 2002: 25–6). καὶ οὐκ . . . μεταλήψεσθε 'you cannot consider a policy of inactivity on the same basis as others, unless you change your way of life too to be like theirs'. These 'ways of life' are those sketched at 1.71.2 and celebrated by Pericles at 2.37.2, but ἐπιτηδεύματα becomes a key-word for Alcibiades' own lifestyle too (**15.**4, **28.**2).

18.4 τάδε: the empire in Greece. **ἵνα Πελοποννησίων τε στορέσωμεν τὸ φρόνημα** 'so that we might both lay low the spirit of the Peloponnesians . . .': τε is then picked up with a slight anacoluthon by καὶ ἅμα . . . + future indicatives. This 'is the harshest figure in Thucydides, but in Alcibiades' style' (schol.). στόρνυμι is literally 'spread smooth' or 'strew': for the metaphor cf. [Aesch.] *Prom.* 190 (ὀργήν), Eur. *Hcld.* 702 (λῆμα). It was probably heard as one of 'levelling to the floor' rather than 'casting to the winds'. **εἰ δόξομεν ὑπεριδόντες . . . πλεῦσαι** 'if we give the impression of scorning the current inaction and sailing against Sicily as well (καί)'. This dismisses Nicias' warning against scorn, **11.**5. **τῆς Ἑλλάδος τῶν ἐκεῖ προσγενομένων πάσης τῶι εἰκότι ἄρξομεν:** τῶν ἐκεῖ might be heard as either masculine or neuter. Alcibiades does not conceal the ambition not just to rule all Sicily (cf. **1.**1, **6.**1) but also to make this a stepping-stone to even greater things: cf. **15.**2.

18.5 μένειν . . . ἀπελθεῖν: epexegetic infinitives after τὸ δ' ἀσφαλές. **ναυκράτορες γὰρ ἐσόμεθα καὶ ξυμπάντων Σικελιωτῶν:** cf. Hdt. 5.36.2, Hecataeus urging the Ionians to become ναυκρατέες τῆς θαλάσσης – but Alcibiades talks of mastery over the people, not just the element. In the Melian Dialogue the Athenians took naval dominance for granted (5.97, 109); in Sicily it will be crucial when it is lost. See Intr. to Bk. 7, pp. 31–2.

18.6 ἡ Νικίου . . . πρεσβυτέρους 'that inaction and divisiveness of young against old of Nicias' speech'. As at **17.**1, the combination of two nouns with the single ἡ links the concepts closely, as if such quietism inevitably divides young and old. Pericles is again echoed: 'a taste for inaction (τὸ ἄπραγμον) cannot survive unless it is accompanied by a talent for action, and it suits a subject city, not one leading an empire, to live a life of safe enslavement' (2.63.3). **ὥσπερ καὶ . . . αὐτά: 17.**7 n. Again echoing Pericles (1.144.4 οἱ γοῦν πατέρες ἡμῶν . . . ἐς τάδε προήγαγον αὐτά, cf. 2.36.2), but focusing on generational harmony; Pericles too found a role for each generation, 2.45–6. **ὁμοῦ δὲ . . . ἰσχύειν** 'but a mix of the common, the middling, and the very exacting would have the greatest strength'. The value of a mixture or blending of contrary elements was a commonplace of both medical and constitutional thinking (Pelling 2019: 84–8); it recurs when Th. praises the constitution of the 5,000 as 'a reasonable commingling (ξύγκρασις), respecting the interests both of the few and of the many' at 8.97.2. The medical analogy, already in the debate (**14**), must be felt (cf. Jouanna 1980: 301–4 = 2012: 23–5; Brock 2013a: 75). φαῦλος is normally derogatory, as at **31**.3, but can also convey unaffectedness: a Euripidean character praised Heracles as φαῦλον, ἄκομψον ('unsmart'), τὰ μέγιστ᾽ ἀγαθόν (fr. 473 K.), and a Platonic speaker is criticised for not answering φαύλως καὶ βραχέως (*Tht.* 147c). ἀκριβής should mean 'precise' or 'exact', and can be used of the strictness of empires or judges (1.99.1, 3.46.4). If φαῦλος is derogatory, the point may be that a mixture of pure and impure elements could be healthier than undiluted pure (Arist. *Pol.* 3. 1281b35–8, *De gen. anim.* 725a16–17: so de Romilly 1976 and *CT*); but it may simply be that both φαῦλος ([Hipp.] *Reg. acut. morb.* 9) and ἀκριβής (*Aph.* 1.4–5, *Fract.* 8, 26) can be used when, respectively, 'simple' and 'strict' diets are being recommended. Alcibiades is wise not to spell out what he means by each term, as to do so might alienate those who did not relish the box in which they were put: Athenagoras is more detailed at **39**.1 (n.).   **τρίψεσθαί τε αὐτὴν περὶ αὑτὴν ὥσπερ καὶ ἄλλο τι** 'will wear itself out just as everything else does': not necessarily 'by internal struggles' (LSJ τρίβω III.1), but for the reasons Alcibiades goes on to give. ὥσπερ καὶ ἄλλο τι is perhaps felt as a Periclean phrase (1.142.9). The idea that every organism may be programmed to flourish and then decay is again a commonplace in, but not confined to, medical thinking (Pelling 2019: esp. 18, 80–4), and ἐγγηράσεσθαι continues the implied comparison with human physiology. τρίβω also suggests the phrase τρίβειν βίον, 'disparagingly used of a dragging life which is wearisome, miserable, purposeless, etc.' (Fraenkel 1950: 236 on Aesch. *Ag.* 465): cf. e.g. Soph. *El.* 602, Eur. *Hcld.* 804). An Athens that gave up its restlessness would bore itself to death.   **πάντων τὴν ἐπιστήμην ἐγγηράσεσθαι:** πάντων is probably 'of everything', objective genitive, rather than 'everyone's knowledge'. The overall construction of the sentence then reasserts itself, and τὴν πόλιν resumes as the subject of ἀγωνιζομένην ... ἕξειν.   **ἀγωνιζομένην ... ἕξειν** 'but if it keeps contending it will keep gaining additional experience and will be more accustomed to defending itself not just in word but also in action'. The Corinthians had made a similar point (1.71.3): 'Innovation always wins, just as it does in a skill: unchanging customs suit a city that keeps quiet (ἡσυχαζούσηι πόλει), but a city that has to take a lot on must make technical advances (ἐπιτέχνησις)'. The appeal to the Athenian character then becomes explicit, **18**.7. The ἀγών imagery sits comfortably in the mouth of the Olympic victor.

18.7 παράπαν τε γιγνώσκω ... διαφθαρῆναι 'my overall verdict is that a city that is not given to inaction would, so it seems to me, be most swiftly destroyed by a change to inactivity'. The use of τε as a sentence-connective is a mannerism of Th. (some 9x in Bk. 6), esp. when, as here, summarising what has preceded (*GP* 499–500, Rusten 1989: 23). γιγνώσκω introduces that summing up, almost 'I propose' (cf. Lat. *censeo*): cf. Nicias at **20.1**. μή rather than οὐ is used because, as with the οἱ ἄν + subj. clause, he is generalising about any city or people who behave similarly. The idea that μεταβολαί are unhealthy is again medical, and so is the acceptance that an inferior but habitual regime may be less hazardous than a new one (*Reg. Acut. Morb.* 36 and *Aph.* 2.50 with Jouanna 1980: 305–6 = 2012: 26–7) – but *Aph.* 2.50 adds that change can still be necessary. Pericles too had deprecated ἀπραγμοσύνη as unAthenian (2.40.2, 64.4), but ἦν καὶ χείρω ἦι is closer to Cleon at 3.37.3.

19 Nicias Tries Something Different

19.1 τῶν Ἐγεσταίων καὶ Λεοντίνων φυγάδων perhaps 'the Egestaeans and ['the' or 'some'] Leontinian exiles', as the Egestaean diplomats were not exiles, though in that case <τῶν> Λεοντίνων or Λεοντίνων <τινῶν> (Stahl) would be expected: or perhaps Th. is writing loosely. For these Leontinians cf. **6.2** n.: their presence has not so far been made explicit, despite hints at **6.1** and **12.1** (nn.). Nicias ignored them at **9.1, 10.5**, and **11.7**. **οἳ παρελθόντες ἐδέοντό ... βοηθῆσαι σφίσι:** presumably the antecedent of οἵ is both Egestaeans and Leontinians, and this seems to confirm that Egesta too had a sworn alliance (**6** n., **6.2** n.). Th. characteristically does not say whether the supplication took place in βουλή or assembly (*CT*): presumably the assembly, as the impression is of one continuous session. They need not be pictured as falling to their knees, but they may have extended hands pleadingly to the *dēmos* (cf. 3.58.3, 3.66.2, 4.38.1, Hdt. 7.233.1; Naiden 2006: 51). **πολλῶι μᾶλλον ἢ πρότερον:** echoing στρατεύειν ὥρμηντο, **6.1**, and echoed at **20.1** and **24.2**: a sort of refrain, as every step encourages the enthusiasm still more. This is a case where the pluperfect tense of ὥρμηντο is not strongly felt (**6.1** n.), though the sense may be 'had been stirred up' while listening to the speeches and pleas.

19.2 παρασκευῆς δὲ πλήθει ... αὐτούς 'but that he might change their mind through the scale of the resources required, if he told them that this had to be large'. For παρασκευή cf. **1.1** n.: this was what the assembly was supposed to be about, **8.2**.

20–23 *The Second Speech of Nicias*

Nicias, intent on making the Sicilian prospect seem 'as cumbersome and complicated as possible', presents 'a confusing jumble of information that is as conspicuous for its ultimate vagueness as for its detail' (Kallet 2001: 42), but proves all too persuasive. His misjudged tactics turn out counter-productive for the whole expedition, not just for himself: the immense scale (for the numbers eventually sent in the various categories, see **43**) inspired fear rather than confidence in potential allies such as Rhegium (**44**.2), and this intensified the difficulties of supply that he foresees. See Intr., 20.

Th. does not say why he is so sure about Nicias' motivation, rejecting the possibility that he genuinely thought this the second-best option. Th. had no opportunity to speak to Nicias himself, though he might have met some of his confidants; but individuals are anyway not the most reliable sources on their motives, and are not always clear about them even to themselves. Most likely Th. simply thought his explanation the most cogent, taking into account Nicias' desperation to stop the expedition and his earlier more successful attempt to play the assembly (4.28).

20.1 πάντως ... ὡρμημένους στρατεύειν: echoing ὥρμηντο, **19**.1. πάντως conveys 'no matter how powerful the arguments against': cf. Artabanus at Hdt. 7.10θ.1 'if it is necessary to campaign πάντως, let the king at least stay at home', and 3, 'if you (Mardonius) lead an army πάντως against Greece . . .'. **ξυνενέγκοι μὲν ταῦτα ὡς βουλόμεθα:** again cf. Artabanus, hoping that a threatening dream 'might end as we both wish' (ὡς βουλόμεθα ἀμφότεροι τελευτήσειε, Hdt. 7.47.2). **ἃ γιγνώσκω σημανῶ:** as he was proud of always doing, **9**.2.

20.2 ὡς ἐγὼ ἀκοῆι αἰσθάνομαι: echoing **17**.6: Nicias replies to Alcibiades' didacticism with some generalisations of his own. His reputation for inside knowledge will turn out disastrously both for the army (7.48.2, 49.4) and for himself (7.86.4). **οὔθ' ὑπηκόους ἀλλήλων ... χωροίη** 'neither one subject to another nor eager for a revolution, circumstances in which someone might willingly move from a state of forced slavery towards a change for the better'. The 'slavery' might be either to another city ('one subject to another') or to an internal tyrant or oligarchy ('eager for a revolution'). Nicias was proved right, at least concerning the democratic states (7.55.2), though he underestimates the possibility of mobilising other cities' fears of Syracuse. **οὐδ' ἂν ... προσδεξαμένας** 'and which would not welcome', with the participle corresponding to οὐδ' ἂν προσδέξαιντο. **τό τε πλῆθος** 'and as to numbers', acc. of respect. **ὡς ἐν μιᾶι νήσωι** 'considering that they are all in a single island'.

20.3 Νάξου καὶ Κατάνης . . . κατὰ τὸ Λεοντίνων ξυγγενές: i.e. Chalcidian. Nicias ignores the Chalcidian elements in Messina and Himera (**4**.5 –**5**.1). Naxos and Catana did prove important allies, but in Catana's case not voluntarily: **50**.3–**51**.2. **ἄλλαι εἰσὶν ἑπτά:** presumably Syracuse, Selinus, Gela, Acragas, Messina, Himera, and Camarina (schol.). Nicias is wise to concentrate on Syracuse and Selinus: Acragas, Messina, and Camarina had mixed feelings and there was a good prospect of winning them over, and Gela and Himera were not significant players (Berger 1992b). **ὁμοιοτρόπως:** this becomes a key-word for the crucial 'similarities' at 7.55.2 and 8.96.5, passages which stress character and constitution (**20**.2) as well as resources (παρεσκευασμέναι here). Cf. Intr., 33–4. **ἐπὶ ἃς μᾶλλον πλέομεν:** they are 'more' the target, but not exclusively so: as at **9**.3 and **11**.1, Nicias assumes the aim of total conquest (**6**.1) as well.

20.4 πολλοὶ μὲν . . . αὐτάς: this turned out to be right: cf. 7.58.4, adding that Syracuse provided more than the rest put together. For ὄχλος cf. **63**.2 n.: not here pejorative. **χρήματά τ' ἔχουσι . . . φέρεται:** the division between private (τὰ μὲν ἴδια) and public (τὰ δὲ . . .) is introduced by ἔχουσι, then the public wealth is subdivided into Selinuntine and Syracusan. With both cities καί implies that these sources of wealth are there as well as other more predictable ones, presumably money already in hand. The temple treasure at Selinus might include both state reserves and private dedications that could be melted down (cf. Davies 2007: 185–8): similarly Pericles included sacred dedications at 2.13.3–5 and the Corinthians talked of 'borrowing' from Delphi and Olympia at 1.121.3, and at **6**.3 and **46**.3 it is assumed that sacred treasure at Egesta might be used. The votive material that has been found in Selinus' temples is 'very rich' (*IACP* 223–4). Nicias has so far concentrated only on Greek cities; the mention of 'barbarians' also qualifies the claim that cities are not subject to one another (**20**.2), for the distinction between 'subject' and 'paying an ἀπαρχή' – literally 'first fruits', a levy on a state's produce or income – would not seem a strong one for those used to Athens' own empire. At **88**.4 Th. unequivocally describes the plain-dwelling Sicels as Syracusan ὑπήκοοι. **ἵππους . . . χρῶνται:** for cavalry see **21**.1 n. and Intr., 6; for Sicilian corn, 3.86.4 and **28**.1 n. The implied contrast is with Athens itself, dependent on imported corn (Moreno 2007): Sicilians' self-sufficiency would make them less vulnerable to a purely naval blockade. **ὧι δὲ μάλιστα ἡμῶν προύχουσιν** 'the area in which they are particularly better off than us', i.e. than we shall be *on campaign*. Athens at home had a lot of cavalry.

21.1 οὐ ναυτικῆς καὶ φαύλου στρατιᾶς μόνον δεῖ: for φαῦλος see **18**.6 (n.), which Nicias may be echoing but to convey 'inadequate' as well as 'ordinary'. The assembly had been called to determine 'the παρασκευή for the ships' (8.3), a formulation that includes marines and sailors, and Nicias now calls for land-troops as well. His language is bold before an Athenian audience used to assuming the primacy of their naval power: Kallet 2001: 43 n. 78 compares Archidamus warning the Spartans that their hoplites might not be enough, 1.80–5.   δεῖ here takes first the gen., then πεζὸν πολὺν ξυμπλεῖν, and, after the colon, ἐπιέναι.   ἄξιον τῆς διανοίας δρᾶν 'to achieve a result on the same level as our thinking'. Nicias again (cf. **20**.3 n.) assumes the larger purpose of the expedition (**6**.1), and φοβηθεῖσαι implies that the Sicilians will see it the same way.   ὑπὸ ἱππέων πολλῶν εἴργεσθαι τῆς γῆς: this does not mean 'prevent their landing' – cavalry are not particularly suited to that – but 'prevent their going out to forage': this is the first hint that cavalry will play an important role. Cf. Athenagoras at **37**.2 and then 7.4.6 and 7.11.4 when this fear proved well founded: Intr., 6.   εἰ ξυστῶσιν: the regular construction would require ἐάν, but εἰ + subj. is found in verse (e.g. Soph. *OT* 198 with Finglass 2018: 231) and it is rash to exclude its possibility in prose: cf. LSJ εἰ B.II.   ἄλλοι ἢ Ἐγεσταῖοι: despite his scepticism about their promises (**22**, **46**.2), he accepts that at least the Egestaeans will provide these; so does Athenagoras, **37**.2. They are right: **62**.3, **98**.1. Despite his pressure to upscale, Nicias does not even consider shipping sufficient cavalry from Athens.   φίλοι τινὲς γενόμενοι: an understated reminder that such friendship is not to be relied upon (despite e.g. the Rhegium alliance, Intr., 30): cities would 'become' friends. Some cavalry did materialise from other cities (**98**.1 n.), but not enough.   ἀμυνούμεθα: he hopes only for enough to mount a defence. It is not his way to think about attack.

21.2 ἐπιμεταπέμπεσθαι 'to send for (μεταπέμπ-) others in addition (ἐπι-)'. The verb recurs at 7.7.3 when the Athenians do exactly that.   αὐτόθεν: a mix of 'from here' (LSJ I) rather than relying on supplies on the spot and 'right away' (LSJ II), now rather than later. Nicias repeats the word twice in **22**.   παρασκευῆι ἀξιόχρεωι: at **10**.2 Nicias stressed how bad *failure* would be with an ἀξιόχρεωι δυνάμει: that brings out what a dangerous game he is now playing.   ἀπὸ τῆς ἡμετέρας αὐτῶν 'from our own country', with αὐτῶν dependent on the ἡμῶν implicit in ἡμετέρας.   μέλλομεν πλεῖν: μέλλω tends to take the present rather than future inf. when preparations are already under way (Huitink–Rood on X. *Anab.* 3.1.8).   οὐκ ἐν τῶι ὁμοίωι στρατευσόμενοι καὶ ὅτε 'not going to be campaigning in the same way as when'. The MSS text is impossible; Badham's conjecture is the most elegant solution. For the construction see **11**.1 n.; for the insight, **44**.2 n.   ὅτε τοῖς τῆιδε ὑπηκόοις ξύμμαχοι ἤλθετε ἐπί τινα 'when you went against anyone in alliance with your subjects here'. Euphemistic: the Athenians were often fighting against their own 'allies' rather than together with them against others. For the switch from 'we' to 'you', **10.2** n. ὅθεν ῥάιδιαι αἱ κομιδαὶ ἐκ τῆς φιλίας ὧν προσέδει 'whence it was easy to transport from friendly territory anything that was additionally needed'. ὅθεν refers back to τοῖς τῆιδε ὑπηκόοις. ἐς ἀλλοτρίαν πᾶσαν ἀπαρτήσοντες: 'about to launch off to a land that is all alien': the tone has now hardened, and Nicias wholly discounts the possibility entertained at **21**.1 of gaining friends on the spot. This intransitive and metaphorical use of ἀπαρτάω builds on its sense '*detach, separate*' (LSJ II), but there may also be a hint of '*hang up*' or suspend (LSJ I), as with μετεώρωι at **10**.5 (n.). μηνῶν ... ῥάιδιον ἐλθεῖν 'from which it is not easy for a messenger to come even within four months in winter'; the word order excludes taking 'not even a messenger... during the four winter months'. The point is partly that by the time bad news arrived it might be too late to send help, and partly that if it is hard for a messenger it would be much harder for substantial reinforcements (O'Connor 2011: 24–5 n. 32). Nicias envisages a worst-case scenario, but even four centuries later crossing the Adriatic in winter was hazardous: Plut. *Caes.* 38 with Pelling 2011: 344–5.

22 ὁπλίτας τε ... προσαγαγέσθαι: first 'hoplites' are divided into our own and our allies', then the allies subdivided into 'subjects' who would have no choice and Peloponnesians who would need to be won over. Some Peloponnesian help did come, notably from Argos and Mantinea (**43**), and the mercenaries included some from Arcadia: 7.57.9. τοξότας... καὶ σφενδονήτας: often mentioned together (e.g. **25**.2, **43**, **69**.2). Athenian expeditions did not normally include these (O'Connor 2011: 28–9, 55–6 n. 98), but it was unusual to have to plan for a deficiency in cavalry. ὅπως πρὸς τὸ ἐκείνων ἱππικὸν ἀντέχωσι: little is then heard of them in this role, but day-to-day foraging does not make it into the narrative, and Lamachus does take archers against a predominantly cavalry force at **101**.6. They do more than this anyway: their skirmishing begins the land battle at **69**.2, and they serve as sharp-shooters in the naval battle, 7.60.4, 62.2. ναυσί: these 'ships' are probably 'triremes', as at **8**.2 and elsewhere (**1**.1 n.): cf. **25**.2 and πλοῖα at **44**.1 (n.). Their use for supplies would be to protect, and perhaps (Morrison and Williams 1968: 244–5) to tow, the merchantmen. τὸν δὲ καὶ αὐτόθεν σῖτον 'and the additional' (καί, i.e. in addition to the supplies that we can continue to ἐσκομίζεσθαι) 'grain transported from here and now': 'the' grain, because the need to transport and create a food-reserve is already implied by the argument about κομιδαί at **21**.2. αὐτόθεν is Nicias' key-word, **21**.2 n., and is repeated later in the sentence. O'Connor 2011 shows that there was nothing unusual in the transportation of grain to accompany an overseas expedition; what was abnormal was the form in which it was to be transported. See next n. πυροὺς καὶ πεφρυγμένας κριθάς 'wheat and parched barley': this defines the form the σῖτος should take. Wheat and milled barley flour (ἄλφιτα) were the normal forms in which grain was transported, but these may degrade more quickly than these whole-grain equivalents, roasted ready for milling; but that also created the need for bakers (O'Connor 2011: 34–41). σιτοποιοὺς ἐκ τῶν μυλώνων πρὸς μέρος ἠναγκασμένους ἐμμίσθους 'paid bread-makers from the mills, compulsorily enlisted on a proportionate basis'. This suggestion was taken up, **44**.1. πρὸς μέρος probably means that a specific 'part' of each mill's workforce would be requisitioned. Like the wheat and barley, such words are rare in elevated historiographic narrative (Kallet 2001: 43), and their jarring quality underlines Nicias' point: mundane details, not airy speculation, are what require attention. πολλὴ γὰρ οὖσα οὐ πάσης ἔσται πόλεως ὑποδέξασθαι 'its size will mean that not every city will be able to accommodate it', lit. 'being big it will not be for every city to receive it': cf. Soph. *OT* 393–4 τό γ' αἴνιγμ' οὐχὶ τοὐπιόντος ἦν | ἀνδρὸς διειπεῖν. Cities indeed proved reluctant to receive the army (**44**.2–3), and not just through lack of capacity: its size made it more fearsome as well as more cumbersome (Intr., 20). καὶ μὴ ἐπὶ ἑτέροις γίγνεσθαι 'and not become dependent on others'. ἑτοῖμα ... ἑτοῖμα: echoing ἑτοιμάσασθαι. Nothing is to be expected from Egesta: you need to do the 'readying' yourselves. νομίσατε καὶ λόγωι ἂν μάλιστα ἑτοῖμα εἶναι 'assume that it would indeed be in word that it would mainly be ready': λόγωι echoes λέγεται. And so it proved: **46**.

23.1 ἦν γὰρ αὐτοὶ ... διασῶσαι 'for unless we go ourselves from here in numbers that are not merely a match for them – with the exception of that against their fighting force, i.e. the hoplites – but that are also greater than theirs in all respects, we will barely in that way be able to conquer them and save our own forces'. This difficult sentence shows Nicias at his most convoluted, especially in πλήν γε πρὸς τὸ μάχιμον αὐτῶν, τὸ ὁπλιτικόν. He cannot be saying that a bare equality with the enemy hoplite force would suffice: he needs to state the requirement in gargantuan terms. So he will be characterising the alternative that he is rejecting as inadequate, either (a) as proposing '[no more than] a match in all respects except for hoplites [where of course we need to be superior]' – unlikely, as he sees that rejected alternative as understating the need on all fronts; or (b) characterising a force of 60 ships (**8**.2) as no more than 'a match for them – except, mind you, not for those forces which really do the *fighting*, their hoplites' (*HCT*), and therefore defective. A further implication may be (c) an acknowledgement that 'in that respect equality is impossible'

(Jowett's gloss, cf. Murray 1961: 36–41), which may be a qualification not just of the rejected alternative but also of his own proposal; he will still be recommending that the hoplites, as all the other forces, should outnumber the enemy (ὑπερβάλλοντες τοῖς πᾶσι), but conceding that other factors would still give the Syracusans a home advantage. That negativity would be typically Nician. It may be that Nicias' tone or gesture (or Th.'s in performance) would have helped to make his meaning clear, but it is still hard to be sure that all Nicias' or Th.'s audience would have taken this important point the same way.

23.2 πόλιν τε ... ἕξουσιν 'it is necessary to think of ourselves as people going to found a city among foreigners and enemies, who have to gain control of the land immediately on the first day they put to shore or know that, if they do not achieve this, they will find everything hostile'. Nicias now extends his stress on 'foreigners' (**9.1, 11.7**) to the Sicilians in general, with ἀλλοφύλοις embracing both 'non-Greek' and 'non-Ionian' (Fragoulaki 2013: 51); he again ignores the possibility of finding friends as well as enemies (**21.2 n.**). For this as almost a colonising expedition cf. Intr., 1. At 7.42.3 Demosthenes echoes the need for success 'on the first day', ironically in criticism of Nicias himself. Cf. Intr. to Bk. 7, p. 28.

23.3 εἰδὼς πολλὰ μὲν ἡμᾶς δέον εὖ βουλεύσασθαι, ἔτι δὲ πλείω εὐτυχῆσαι: this echoes Alcibiades' plea to 'make use of' Nicias' good fortune as well as his own youthful energy (**17.1**), but emphasises that everything has to go right for the expedition to succeed. For the construction with impersonal participle after a verb of knowledge see *M&T* 906; for Nicias' taste for impersonal verbs, Tompkins 1972: 192–3.   **χαλεπὸν δὲ ἀνθρώπους ὄντας** 'and that is a hard thing for humans to achieve', syntactically parenthetical, but central to the argument: this is why he wishes to trust to luck as little as possible. The fragility of good fortune is conventional wisdom (cf. esp. Hdt. 1.31), but this compounds the impression of Nicias' negativity. 'No other Athenian commander has so long a string of good fortune, but no other dwells so continuously on the dangers of τύχη' (Tompkins 2017: 108, cf. 7.61.3, 63.4, 77.2–3).   **ὅτι ἐλάχιστα τῆι τύχηι παραδοὺς ἐμαυτὸν βούλομαι ἐκπλεῖν:** a similar principle to that which in Th.'s view led Nicias to promote peace in 421, βουλόμενος ἐν ὧι ἀπαθὴς ἦν καὶ ἠξιοῦτο διασώσασθαι τὴν εὐτυχίαν, 5.16.1. There as here he is concerned for the city as well as himself (Intr., 7); but the emphasis on self might still seem excessive, and may presage the concern for his own safety that proves disastrous (7.48.3–4).   **ἐκπλεῖν ... ἐκπλεῦσαι:** it is unclear whether the change of aspect conveys any change in sense.   **ἀπὸ τῶν εἰκότων ἀσφαλής** 'secure, as far as one can reasonably judge'.

23.4 βεβαιότατα ... σωτήρια: 10.2 n. Even now Nicias cannot bring himself to speak in terms of 'victory': 'in Nicias' argument there is no place for Athenian victory, in Alcibiades' for Athenian defeat' (Kohl 1977: 169).   εἰ δέ τωι ἄλλως δοκεῖ, παρίημι αὐτῶι τὴν ἀρχήν: the same trick as he tried with Cleon at 4.28. Now it is given extra bite by Nicias' reluctance to serve in the first place, 8.4. He again offers to stand down at 7.15, but by then it is because of illness. We know of no other Athenian commander during the history of the democracy who offered to relinquish a command (Tompkins 2017: 109).

24–26 *Nicias' Ploy Misfires*

24.1 Ὁ μὲν Νικίας ... ἀσφαλῶς ἐκπλεῦσαι: the summary echoes **19**.2, but adds the second-best alternative of securing safety if still forced to sail: ἀσφαλῶς ἐκπλεῦσαι echoes **23**.3 and is picked up by ἀσφάλεια and οὐδὲν ἂν σφαλεῖσαν (n.) in **24**.2–3 as the *dēmos* comes to think in the same way.   **μάλιστα οὕτως ... ἀσφαλῶς ἐκπλεῦσαι:** verbs of hoping and expecting can take an aorist inf. (*M&T* 136), especially when, as here, the consequence is dependent on some specified condition (C–S on 2.3.2 ἐνόμισαν ἐπιθέμενοι ῥαιδίως κρατῆσαι): hence Bekker's <ἂν> is unnecessary.

24.2 οἱ δὲ τὸ μὲν ἐπιθυμοῦν τοῦ πλοῦ οὐκ ἐξηιρέθησαν 'but they did not have their desire for the voyage removed ...'. The middle of ἐξαιρέω can take a double acc. of (a) the person deprived and (b) what is removed (LSJ III.3): in the passive the first acc. moves into the nom. while the second acc. is retained. Cf. e.g. 2.41.5 and Hdt. 3.137.4 ἐξαιρεθέντες ... τὸν Δημοκήδεα. τὸ ἐπιθυμοῦν is one of Th.'s characteristic verbal abstractions: Intr., 11 and n. 38.   **ὥρμηντο: 19**.1 n.   **ἀσφάλεια νῦν δὴ καὶ πολλὴ ἔσεσθαι: 24**.1 n. δή emphasises the νῦν – *now*, at least, everything will be fine – and καί emphasises πολλή, not just safety but lots of it.

24.3 καὶ ἔρως ἐνέπεσε τοῖς πᾶσιν ὁμοίως ἐκπλεῦσαι: so Nicias' attempt to divide the generations fails, as does his dismissive rejection of being δυσέρωτας τῶν ἀπόντων, **13**.1 n.   **ἐνέπεσε** 'fell upon them', as a disease strikes (2.48.2, cf. 7.29.7 n., Winkler 1990: 82–3; Kallet 2001: 44–7) and as 'many hard things' fell upon (ἐπ-) cities during *stasis* (3.82.2). Clytemnestra, with relish, expresses a fear 'that some ἔρως may fall upon the army to destroy what they should not' once Troy has fallen (Aesch. *Agam.* 341–2): some find an echo of that passage here (Cornford 1907: 214–15; Connor 1984: 167–8: cf. *CT*), but the metaphor may be a cliché (cf. Soph. *Ant.* 782), and Ludwig 2002: 141–53 makes a good case for thinking it a favourite of contemporary political orators. Also comparable is the δεινὸς ἵμερος to take Athens that had 'dripped into' Mardonius (Hdt. 9.3.1): cf. Rogkotis 2006: 63–4. **τοῖς μὲν γὰρ πρεσβυτέροις . . . σωθήσεσθαι:** the construction carries over from καὶ ἔρως ἐνέπεσε τοῖς πᾶσιν ὁμοίως ἐκπλεῦσαι, but then switches with καὶ εὐέλπιδες . . . as if ἠράσθησαν had preceded: cf. 7.42.2 τοῖς Συρακοσίοις . . . ὁρῶντες, and 2.53.4 νόμος οὐδεὶς ἀπεῖργε [understand αὐτούς], τὸ μὲν κρίνοντες . . . That nom. construction then continues into ὁ δὲ πολὺς ὅμιλος καὶ στρατιώτης. The outcomes considered correspond to Nicias' final stress on reliability (βεβαιότατα) or at least safety (σωτήρια): **23**.3; the emphasis of the older fits their greater caution (οὐδὲν ἂν σφαλεῖσαν), of the younger their greater emotions (πόθωι . . . εὐέλπιδες σωθήσεσθαι). That chimes with Nicias' own stereotyping at **13**.1, but it has all gone wrong. **ἢ οὐδὲν ἂν σφαλεῖσαν μεγάλην δύναμιν** 'or [on the assumption] that a great force could not come to grief'. σφαλεῖσαν would be opt. σφαλείη in direct discourse, and picks up the root of ἀσφαλής, **23**.2. σφάλλω often recurs at narrative 'hinges' (**11**.4, **15**.4 nn.), especially in Bk. 7 when the irony of the present confidence becomes clear (7.55.2, 61.2 [n.], 66.3, 68.3). **τῆς τε ἀπούσης πόθωι ὄψεως καὶ θεωρίας:** brachylogy for τῆς τῶν ἀπόντων πόθωι ὄψεως καὶ θεωρίας, 'desire for the sight and spectacle of distant things'. ὄψις captures the perception itself, θεωρία the mental reaction to it. This echoes **13**.1, δυσέρωτας τῶν ἀπόντων, as πόθος too is often erotic, a yearning for what is not at hand (Eur. *Hipp.* 526, Soph. *Trach.* 103–7, etc.). Particularly close is Pind. *P.* 4.184, the Argonauts' πόθος for the adventure before them; cf. also Rood 1998a: 177 n. 68. It becomes a key-word for Arrian's Alexander, driving him ever onwards (*Anab.* 1.3.5, 2.3.1, etc.). For the importance of visuality see Intr., 15. This yearning for τὰ ἀφανῆ may already carry a hint of the Eleusinian Mysteries, shortly to be so important (**27–29**): so Joho 2020. **εὐέλπιδες ὄντες σωθήσεσθαι:** to be εὐέλπιδες in danger is identified by the Corinthians as an Athenian characteristic (1.70.3), and Euelpides is a character in Aristophanes' *Birds* of 414 BCE: Intr., 33. After Sicily these high hopes transfer to the other side, 8.2.4: cf. Avery 1973: 1–6. **ὁ δὲ πολὺς ὅμιλος καὶ στρατιώτης . . . ὑπάρξειν:** best taken as 'the mass of the people, those who served on campaign' (any στρατεία, so not just soldiers but sailors too): understand again εὔελπις ὤν. This is not a separate group but will include many ἐν ἡλικίαι and some πρεσβύτεροι: what is distinctive is their motive, conditioned by their economic status. **ἔν τε τῶι . . . μισθοφοράν:** ἀργύριον refers to the state-pay and possibly plunder on campaign, ἀίδιον μισθοφοράν to the prospect of more of the same, perhaps from the further campaigning that imperial power would involve (cf. Alcibiades on incessant expansionism, **18**.3) and perhaps from extra tribute to fund other citizen duties and benefits. Again the aim of full conquest (**6**.1) is assumed.

24.4 ὥστε... ἡσυχίαν ἦγεν: very much what Nicias warned against, **13**.1, but now it is not just charges of cowardice that are feared but of lack of patriotism, even treachery. ἄγαν makes Th.'s disapproval as clear here as when the *dēmos* τοῦ . . . πλέονος ὠρέγοντο and rejected peace at 4.21.3: here πλεόνων is more likely to be heard as 'the enthusiasm of the majority' rather than as obj. gen. as in πλέονος there, though both renderings are possible (Connor 1984: 168 n. 25).   **εἴ τωι ἄρα καὶ μὴ ἤρεσκε** 'even if, after all, anyone actually disapproved . . .': τωι = τινι, and for εἰ . . . ἄρα see **75**.1 n.   **ἡσυχίαν ἦγεν:** Nicias commended ἡσυχία (**10**.2 n.) – but not of this kind.

25.1 τις τῶν Ἀθηναίων: unnamed, giving symmetry with the unnamed Syracusan general at the end of the Syracusan debate, **41**. This is not necessarily the same man (? Demostratus) as proposed the decree, **26**.1 n.   **παρακαλέσας:** a mix of 'summon to the dais' (LSJ II.3), 'encourage' (LSJ III), and 'demand, require' (LSJ IV).   **προφασίζεσθαι** 'make excuses': echoed by Plut. *Nic.* 12.6 when he makes 'Demostratus' (**26**.1 n.) promise to 'stop Nicias uttering προφάσεις', but Plut. is telescoping the narrative and it need not follow that he took Th.'s τις to be Demostratus.   **ψηφίσωνται:** deliberative (or 'dubitative') subjunctive (*CGCG* 34.8), retained in this indirect question in historic sequence (*CGCG* 42.8).

25.2 ἄκων: just as he was reluctant (ἀκούσιος) to command, **8**.4.   **καὶ μετὰ τῶν ξυναρχόντων καθ' ἡσυχίαν μᾶλλον βουλεύσοιτο:** μᾶλλον goes closely with καθ' ἡσυχίαν, 'in greater peace and quiet': Nicias is not saying simply that he would prefer to do this, but that he will do this as well (καί). ἡσυχία is again his watchword, **24**.4 n. Given that the generals' requirements formed the agenda (**8**.3), listeners might well think that he had already had ample time to consult.   **ὅσα μέντοι ἤδη δοκεῖν αὐτῶι** 'but as far as his present thinking went': inf. δοκεῖν as in οὐχ ὅσον γ' ἔμ' εἰδέναι, 'no, not as far as I know' (Ar. *Clouds* 1252, Plato, *Theaet.* 145a; *M&T* 778).   **ἔλασσον: 1.2** n.   **ἑκατὸν ... ὧν ἔσεσθαι ὁπλιταγωγοὺς ὅσαι ἂν δοκῶσι:** in the event 40 of the 100 Athenian triremes were troop-carriers, **31**.3, **43**.   **ὅσαι ἂν δοκῶσι:** 'as many as seems appropriate' – but 'seems' to whom, to the assembly or to the generals? The assembly leaves it to the generals, **26**.1.   **καὶ ἄλλας ἐκ τῶν ξυμμάχων μεταπεμπτέας εἶναι:** 34 allied ships came, **43**. The acc. + inf. is parenthetic, and ὁπλίταις resumes the construction with πλευστέα.   **ὁπλίταις δὲ ... πλέοσιν:** the final number was 5,100: **43**.   **τὴν δὲ ἄλλην παρασκευὴν ὡς κατὰ λόγον:** i.e. proportionately to their contribution of manpower.   **καὶ τοξοτῶν τῶν αὐτόθεν καὶ ἐκ Κρήτης:** in fact 480, including 80 Cretan mercenaries (**43** with *HCT*). αὐτόθεν echoes Nicias' keyword of **21**.2 (n.)–**22**. Crete was famous for its archers: see Huitink–Rood on

X. *Anab.* 3.3.7. **καὶ σφενδονητῶν**: in the event 700 Rhodians, **43**. **καὶ ἤν τι ἄλλο πρέπον δοκῆι εἶναι**: **43** adds at the end 120 light troops from Megarian exiles and – importantly, Intr., 6 – a horse-carrying ship bearing 300 horses. **ἑτοιμασάμενοι ἄξειν**: still dependent on εἶπεν, but now plural as he includes the other generals.

26.1 οἱ Ἀθηναῖοι ἐψηφίσαντο: Plut. *Nic.* 12.6 and *Alc.* 18.3 names Demostratus, 'the most vigorous of the demagogues in stirring the Athenians up to fight' (*Nic.*) as the proposer. *Alc.* goes on to mention bad omens during the Adonia, 'which fell within the days' when everything was ready; *Nic.* tells the Adonia story a little later (13.10–11). For the date of the Adonia see Dillon 2003: the other evidence is consistent with the spring, though in that case Plut. is wrong to synchronise the festival with the final stages of preparation. Plut. likes to add items from elsewhere to Th.'s material (Pelling 1992: 11 = 2002: 117–18), and may well be inferring from Ar. *Lys.* 391–7 (411 BCE), where Demostratus proposes to 'sail to Sicily' and 'to levy hoplites from Zacynthus' at a time when women at the festival are crying 'woe for Adonis': cf. **8** n. Still, it cannot be excluded that Plut. had independent evidence for the proposer, possibly Craterus' collection of Athenian decrees (Sommerstein 1990: 173), which he certainly knew (Stadter 1989: lxix–lxx; Piccirilli 2000: 849–52). It is not even certain that the *Lys.* passage refers to 415 at all: it may be the debate about reinforcements two years later (7.8–16, 20). **αὐτοκράτορας . . . . τοῦ παντὸς πλοῦ**: thus extending the independent authority already granted four days' earlier (**8.2** n.). The *boulē* may still have worked closely with the generals until their departure (*CT*). περὶ τοῦ παντὸς πλοῦ is presumably 'about all the [arrangements for] the sailing', i.e. extending to other elements of the παρασκευή as well as the number of troops, rather than 'and the whole expedition', including decisions on campaign. The second had already been granted at **8.2**.

26.2 καταλόγους: lists of those to be drafted for this campaign. For the procedure see Christ 2001: 399–409; van Wees 2004: 102–4: commanders of the ten tribes worked with the generals to select troops, then posted call-up lists on boards before the statues of the eponymous heroes. Cf. **31**.3 n.   **τοῦ ξυνεχοῦς πολέμου**: for Th. the whole war was 'continuous' (5.26.2, **10**.2 n.), but here he means the continuous *fighting* of the Archidamian War.   **ἀπὸ τῆς νόσου**: **12**.1 n.   **ἔς τε ἡλικίας πλῆθος ἐπιγεγενημένης** 'with regard to the numbers of young men that had grown up', lit. 'accrued': cf. Hdt. 6.83.1. These would have been children during the plague: perhaps this is an argument for seeing the plague as pathogenetically related to typhus, from which children usually recover (cf. Mitchel 1964: 103–4) and might survive in greater number than those of military age, or perhaps relief 'from the continuous war' was the bigger factor. χρημάτων ἄθροισιν 'the gathering of money': -σις formations were a fad of intellectual discourse (Handley 1953) and favoured by Th. (Tompkins 1993: 102; Allison 1997: 20–1), though he does not use ἄθροισις elsewhere. Andoc. *On the Peace* 8 says that 7,000 talents had been replaced in the treasury during the peace: that is doubtless exaggerated, but a healthy reserve will have built up.

27–29: HERMS AND MYSTERIES

Herms – stone columns sporting an erect phallus and topped by a bust of a bearded Hermes – were symbols of fertility and good luck: 'the doorstep herm, that cheerfully shameless figure, must have been much the most familiar divine presence in the streets of Athens' (Parker 1996: 81). Any sacrilege would be taken seriously with such an expedition looming (cf. Ar. *Lys.* and Plut. on the bad omens during the Adonia, **26**.1 n.), and Hermes would be particularly dangerous to offend as the god of travellers, the god who mediated communication to other divinities, and the god who oversaw the journey of the dead to the underworld. The Eleusinian Mysteries, fundamental to Athenian religion, honoured Persephone and Demeter: Persephone's cult was especially associated with Sicily, where she had been abducted, and Sicily was a source of grain, Demeter's preserve. It would be hard to find more perilous gods to offend. It was in the same year 415/4 that Diagoras of Melos, who had himself earlier divulged Eleusinian and other mysteries, was prosecuted in Athens for atheism (Janko 1997: 87–92; Whitmarsh 2016: 112–13, 120–2).

The mutilation of the Herms and the profanation of the Mysteries are unlikely to have been part of a single plan, even though a few men (but not many – perhaps five out of the 65 names we know, Furley 1996: 46) were accused of both. Th. keeps the two separate throughout, while stressing that Alcibiades' enemies blurred the distinction (**28**.2, **61**.1). His language conveys the way that the scare spread, with more people and aspects drawn in (Tsakmakis 1995: 181–3): προσέτι (**27**.2), καί ... ἅμα (**27**.3, **28**.1), καί ... ἐπῃτιῶντο (**28**.1) ἐπιλέγοντες ... τὴν ἄλλην ... παρανομίαν (**28**.2). Alcibiades himself was unlikely to be involved in anything that might delay or compromise the expedition, and he was not initially suspected of the mutilation: his name came up as the investigation spread to the Mysteries, and then his critics claimed that he was involved with the Herms as well (**28**.2). Th. makes his own views less clear here than at **53**.2 and **60** (though μειζόνως may hint at them, **27**.3 n.); but the space given both to Alcibiades' reasonable-sounding protestations (**29**.1–2) and to his enemies' disingenuousness (**28**.2, **29**.3) prepares for those later opinions.

The motives of the mutilators have been much discussed. There may have been rumours that Corinthian infiltrators into Athens were behind it (Plut. *Alc.* 18.7, Philochorus, *FGrH* 328 F 133, Cratippus, *FGrH* 64 F 3), but such suspicions are not surprising in the panicky atmosphere. A 'Hell-Fire Club' mentality is more likely to have been in play, with young aristocrats delighting in the affront to conventional morality and even to the gods. Murray 1990: 157–60 and Gribble forthcoming cite parallels from later cultures for such behaviour and for extreme reactions to it. Thus far the two outrages may reflect a similar mindset. Still, the mimicking of the Mysteries may have been cases of private drunkenness, and would probably not have been made public or taken so seriously but for the Herms affair. That was too extensive and orchestrated to be an impromptu escapade (cf. Furley 1996: 28–30), and it was easy to see it as a prelude to something bolder (**27**.3 n.), a threat to democracy itself. Whether the perpetrators counted on that reaction and hoped not just 'to shock and irritate' (Rubel 2013: 85) but to intimidate ('a calculated act of terrorism', Fornara 1980: 45) is another question.

The sequence of denunciations has largely to be reconstructed from Andocides' *On the Mysteries*. This vividly describes (11–12) an assembly when the expedition was about to leave: a certain Pythonicus denounced Alcibiades for his part in the Mysteries profanation, and Alcibiades' slave Andromachus gave damaging evidence. A second μήνυσις came from Teucer, a metic: by then the fleet had presumably sailed. His information concerned both Herms and Mysteries, but there is no indication that he implicated Alcibiades (Andoc. 15, 34). Two more μηνύσεις concerned the Mysteries, one naming Alcibiades (Andoc. 16–18). Finally Diocleides delivered an elaborate account of the mutilation and of a subsequent cover-up, claiming that up to 300 were involved (Andoc. 37–45). Diocleides later admitted to lying and was executed, but 42 were arrested or fled. Andocides' own testimony followed (**60** nn.). By then some had been executed; most fled into exile.

An important epigraphic record survives of the property confiscated from those found guilty (ML 79 = Fornara 147 = OR 172): see *HCT* and OR. The names include many of those named by Andocides: see Furley 1996: 45–8.

Besides the full treatments in *HCT* and (especially excellent on religious aspects) *CT*, see Osborne 1985, Murray 1990, Furley 1996, Pelling 2000: 18–43, Graf 2000, Rubel 2013: 74–98, and Gribble forthcoming.

27.1 Ἐν δὲ τούτωι: Th. does not give any more exact indication of the date of the mutilation. There was time for one denunciation before the expedition left (above). *HCT* decides for a night around 25 May: that dating is as likely as any. εἰσὶ δὲ κατὰ τὸ ἐπιχώριον . . . ἐν ἱεροῖς 'they are in line with local custom, the squared-off style of workmanship, in large numbers before the entrances of both private houses and sacred buildings': προθύροις is to be understood with ἱεροῖς as well as ἰδίοις. ἡ . . . ἐργασία and πολλοί explain what is distinctive: 'the' workmanship indicates that that squared-off style is taken as familiar. οἱ πλεῖστοι: according to Andocides the bust in front of his house was the only one left untouched (*Myst.* 62). περιεκόπησαν τὰ πρόσωπα 'had their faces mutilated'. Cf. Fig. 1, a vase representation of a satyr attacking the face of a toppled Herm with an axe (c. 470 BCE). The choice of a satyr fits the idea of a drunken revelry. But the obvious way to mutilate a Herm was to knock off the phallus, and it looks as if this was done as well: at Ar. *Lys.* 1093–4 erect males are warned to 'make sure the Herm-choppers don't see you'. Perhaps some Herms had lost their phalloi already through wear and tear (Dover 1965), and/or it was felt important to destroy the interaction of gaze of viewer and Herm (Osborne 1985), but Th. also follows his view of historiographic propriety in mentioning only the faces. Phrynichus fr. 38 K–A, a warning to Hermes 'not to fall over and do yourself a mischief, giving some new Diocleides an opportunity for more bad-mouthing', indicates that some were also toppled: again cf. Fig. 1.

27.2 μηνύτροις: rewards for informing. Andromachus and Teucer (**27–9** n.) received respectively 10,000 and 1,000 drachmas (Andoc. *Myst.* 27). οὗτοί τε ἐζητοῦντο καὶ προσέτι ἐψηφίσαντο: the awkward change of subject from οὗτοι (οἱ δράσαντες) to an understood 'the people' marks the shift from one distinct target to the move against the other, those responsible for any other ἀσέβημα. On the assembly's instructions the *boulē* appointed investigators (ζητηταί). μηνύειν ἀδεῶς τὸν βουλόμενον: the official terminology of decrees, and probably therefore the wording of the announcement. ἀδεῶς: 'fear' would naturally be felt by the third group of possible informants, slaves denouncing their masters; but the ἀστοί and ξένοι most likely to know the truth would be those who were themselves involved, and this was also an offer of immunity from prosecution, one first taken up by the metic Teucer: Andoc. *Myst.* 15. This immunity becomes important with Andocides (**60.**3 n.).

27.3 μειζόνως ἐλάμβανον 'they took it more seriously' – than they would have done otherwise (the earlier ἀγαλμάτων περικοπαί had clearly not been followed up so vigorously, **28.**1 n.), with a hint of 'than they should have done'; also 'more extensively' than limiting the inquiry to just the Herms. For λαμβάνω cf. **53.**3, **61.**1. οἰωνός 'a [bad] omen', portending failure: largely because the gods, especially Hermes, were so likely

1 Vase of satyr attacking Herm

to take offence. ἐπὶ ξυνωμοσίαι ἅμα νεωτέρων πραγμάτων καὶ δήμου καταλύσεως 'it was also a matter of a conspiracy to mount a revolution and overthrow the democracy': cf. **28**.2 and **61**.1. ἐπί + dat. combines 'occasion or cause' (LSJ ἐπί B.III.1) and 'end or purpose' (B.III.2): cf. **83**.2. Andoc. *Myst.* 36 attributes this claim to the ζητηταί Peisander and

Charicles. A group might commit such an outrage as a mutual 'pledge', so that they would each have enough damaging information on the others to ensure that they stuck together for the bolder plot that would follow: cf. 3.82.6 and 8.73.3; Pelling 2000: 39–42. For the nervousness about anti-democratic revolution see **60**.1 and **60–61** n.

28.1 μηνύεται: Rijksbaron 2011 observes that four of the six historic presents in the Herms and Mysteries episodes relate to Alcibiades (here, **53**.1, **61**.4, and **74**.1), marking these as the critical moments. **μετοίκων τέ τινων καὶ ἀκολούθων:** corresponding respectively to ξένων and δούλων at **27**.2. **περὶ μὲν τῶν Ἑρμῶν οὐδέν:** the second informer, Teucer, did give information about Herms as well as Mysteries (**27–29** n.), but Th. may refer just to the denunciations made before the expedition sailed (*HCT* 274). **ἄλλων δὲ ἀγαλμάτων περικοπαί:** presumably these mutilations had really happened – the statues would have been incontrovertible evidence – even if the culprits were hard to identify. It sounds as if they had been taken as routine youthful high spirits and not thoroughly investigated, even though these ἀγάλματα would be offerings to the gods (Graf 2000: 123). **τὰ μυστήρια ἅμα ὡς ποιεῖται ἐν οἰκίαις ἐφ' ὕβρει:** ἅμα need not mean that the Mysteries performances were 'at the same time' as the mutilations, just that the informants also denounced these now. The bibliography on the Eleusinian Mysteries is vast: see conveniently *OCD*[1] 'Eleusis' and Parker 1996: 97–101; 2005: 327–68. The rites were known only to initiates; some of those involved had doubtless been initiated, but Lys. *Against Andocides* 51 explicitly claims that some had not – which doubtless did not prevent them from producing a version of their own. **ποιεῖται:** the present tense indicates a claim that these were happening repeatedly: similarly Andoc. *Myst.* 11–12, 16–17 has ποιοῦντα and γιγνοῖτο for the first denunciation and ποιεῖν and γίγνεσθαι for the later ones (**27–9** n.). ποιεῖν = 'perform' the rites (Murray 1990: 155–6; Graf 2000: 123–4), but to do so privately and in a non-regular way was itself a contemptuous insult to the gods (ἐφ' ὕβρει), and doubtless those 'showing contempt' in this way were not careful to get the details right (Wallace 1992: 328–9 n. 2). Plut. *Alc.* 22.4, apparently quoting Thessalus' charge (**61**.1 n.), and Lys. *Against Andocides* 51 say 'mimicking', and Gribble forthcoming gives cross-cultural parallels for such 'pararitual'. Talk of 'parody' is not unreasonable (cf. Bremmer 1995: 77), and after several cups of wine it doubtless seemed good fun. Thessalus' charge also included the roles that individuals played, in Alcibiades' case ἱεροφάντης (the one who revealed the sacred objects). **ἐν οἰκίαις:** Thessalus (**61**.1 n.) specified Alcibiades' own house. **ὧν καὶ τὸν Ἀλκιβιάδην ἐπῃτιῶντο** 'they additionally (ἐπ–) accused Alcibiades as well (καί) of these things'; perhaps καί focuses more on 'as well as other people' and ἐπ- on 'as well as the Herms', but that distinction may be too sharp.

28.2 οἱ μάλιστα . . . παρανομίαν: echoing **15**.4 (nn.) τῆς κατὰ τὸ ἑαυτοῦ σῶμα παρανομίας . . . ὡς τυραννίδος ἐπιθυμοῦντι . . . τοῖς ἐπιτηδεύμασιν αὐτοῦ ἀχθεσθέντες; Alcibiades' capacity to make enemies can therefore be taken as familiar. There οἱ πολλοί were offended; here the focus has sharpened to his rivals. Plut. *Alc.* 19.1–3 singles out 'Androcles the demagogue', presumably drawing on 8.65.2, where Androcles is murdered in 411 as 'a prominent leader of the δῆμος' and 'especially responsible for Alcibiades' exile'. The official charge (**61**.1 n.) was laid by Thessalus, who as Cimon's son was unlikely to see politics in the same way as Androcles. Hostility to Alcibiades could bring together people of very different persuasions. **ἐμποδὼν ὄντι σφίσι μὴ αὐτοῖς τοῦ δήμου βεβαίως προεστάναι** 'because he stood in the way of their establishing their own firm leadership of the people'. For μή + inf. after expressions of hindrance see *CGCG* 51.35, 37. At 2.65.10–11 Th. had stressed the contention of Pericles' successors περὶ τῆς τοῦ δήμου προστασίας, with disastrous results including the compromising of the expedition (Intr., 4–8). If that echo is felt, it is a reminder of the massive consequences of such rivalry, including not just the expedition's failure but also the outcome of the whole war. **ἐμεγάλυνον** 'they made more of' this, just as the *dēmos* had done with the Herms outrage (μειζόνως, **27**.3 n.). The politicians are following the people's lead. **ἐβόων:** popular agitators conventionally shout, as do the people they agitate: 4.28.3, 7.48.3, 8.86.2, and cf. **16**.1 n. and Pelling 2002: 224 and 392. Alcibiades' enemies are still shouting at 8.53.2. **οὐδὲν εἴη αὐτῶν ὅ τι οὐ μετ' ἐκείνου ἐπράχθη:** only now does Alcibiades become drawn by his enemies into the Herms' controversy. The phrasing may anyway mean that Alcibiades was '"behind" or in sympathy with the mutilation' (*HCT* 280) rather than an active mutilator himself. Nothing on the Herms figured in the formal charge (**61**.1 n.). **ἐπιλέγοντες . . . παρανομίαν** 'adding [to the evidence already given] the rest of his undemocratic transgressiveness in behaviour as further pointers to his guilt': cf. **15**.4 nn. A τεκμήριον is something that invites an inference: they have no more direct evidence of their own.

29.1 κρίνεσθαι εἴ τι τούτων εἰργασμένος ἦν 'and be put on trial to see whether he had done any of these things': for εἰ + indic. in indirect questions see *CGCG* 42.3. **εἰ μὲν τούτων τι εἴργαστο, δίκην δοῦναι, εἰ δ' ἀπολυθείη, ἄρχειν:** the two εἰ clauses do not quite match, as ἀπολυθείη refers to the trial-proceeding (opt., 'if he were to be acquitted') and εἴργαστο to what the trial would determine to be the facts of the case (indic., 'if he had done').

29.2 ἐπεμαρτύρετο 'he bore witness', first with an inf. as at Hdt. 5.93.2, then with a ὅτι clause for what he is claiming. **σωφρονέστερον:** again appealing to the sense of caution that was strong before the debate (σῶφρον, **6**.2 n.) and played its part in persuading the assembly to upscale. **πρίν** + subj. without ἄν: *M&T* 648. **διαγνῶσι** 'reach a verdict', in a court case as at Aesch. *Eum.* 709: cf. 3.53.4, where the Plataeans plead with the Spartans not to bring them ἐπὶ διεγνωσμένην κρίσιν. **ἐπὶ τοσούτωι στρατεύματι** 'with authority over so large a force', LSJ ἐπί B.III.6.

29.3 τό τε στράτευμα ... ὅ τε δῆμος: these overlapped, as the δῆμος would include many who would be part of the στράτευμα. **ἀγωνίζηται:** for the ἀγών language see Intr. to Bk. 7, p. 30. **ὅ τε δῆμος μὴ μαλακίζηται:** Nicias warned against the fear of seeming μαλακός, **13**.2; Alcibiades' other ἐχθροί are now afraid that the *dēmos* will turn genuinely soft. **θεραπεύων** 'taking care of' Alcibiades, making sure he was protected. **οἵ τ' Ἀργεῖοι ... καὶ τῶν Μαντινέων τινές:** these two groups are often mentioned together: **43**, **61**.5, **67**.1, **105**.2. At **61**.5 there are renewed fears that they might leave if Alcibiades were no longer in command, but they stay and more Argives are recruited at 7.20 and 26: Th. explains in terms of their hatred of Sparta, 7.57.9. The Mantineans were largely mercenaries (7.57.9): '*some* of the Mantineans' indicates that the Alcibiades factor was not important to all. Alcibiades' links with both cities were important in Bk. 5, as he implicitly boasted at **16**.6 (n.) and will explicitly say at **89**.3: knowledge of his Argive connections adds to Athenian suspicions at **61**.3. **ἀπέτρεπον καὶ ἀπέσπευδον** 'were deflecting and urging them away from this': the second verb is stronger than the first. **ἄλλους ῥήτορας ἐνιέντες** 'sending in other speakers': the phrasing suggests some devious masterminds behind the scenes. **ἔλεγον** + inf., 'say that he should', as at 1.78.4, 2.5.5, and Soph. *Phil.* 101 λέγω σ' ἐγώ δόλωι Φιλοκτήτην λαβεῖν. **ἐλθόντα:** = 'once he had come *home*'. **ἐν ἡμέραις ῥηταῖς** 'within a specified number of days'. **διαβολῆς ... ποριεῖν ... μετάπεμπτον ... ἀγωνίσασθαι:** echoing important words: the διαβολή that Alcibiades warned against in his absence (ἀπόντος), **29**.2; the 'providing' of slander now that provision (ἐπεπόριστο, **29**.1) for the expedition is completed; Alcibiades to be 'sent for' after pleading not to be sent out (πέμπειν, **29**.2) under such a cloud; the 'contending' that will come later rather than ἤδη (**29**.3). **καὶ ἔδοξε πλεῖν τὸν Ἀλκιβιάδην:** a brief phrase for a momentous decision. The effect is similar to the abrupt οἱ δὲ πεισθέντες at 1.135.3, 'the Athenians were persuaded' of Themistocles' guilt. Plut. *Alc.* 19.5–6 reconstructs the arguments that would have been used on both sides.

30–32.2: DEPARTURE

The description is 'brilliantly vivid' (Kallet 2001: 48; cf. Jordan 2000a: 68–9), and the central panel of **31** is highly visual (ἑώρων... ὄψει... θέαν... εὐπρεπεστάτη, **31**.1; σημείοις καὶ κατασκευαῖς πολυτελέσι... εὐπρεπείαι, **31**.3; ἐπίδειξιν, **31**.5; τόλμης τε θάμβει καὶ ὄψεως λαμπρότητι, **31**.6 [n.]). That is flanked by passages which are more audial, as the ὀλοφυρμοί of **30**.2 give way first to the strident σάλπιγξ and then to the σιωπή it commands, **32**.1, followed by the call of the κῆρυξ, the prayers shared by the crowd, then finally the paeans, **32**.1–2. The complex sentences at **31**.3 and **31**.5 come in a 'lumbering roll' (Cornford 1907: 217), as sight after sight crowds in and expense after expense has accumulated. The confidence, even ἔρως, of **24** initially falters, but is soon reinforced by such sights (**31**.1) – and seeing, after all, is so often basic to ἔρως (Sappho fr. 16.1–4, etc.). The excitement is felt by onlookers and combatants alike; the racing to Aegina (**32**.2) reflects the mood. But the reader will be less carried away than the internal audience, given those earlier hints that this will all fail (**1**.1 n.). The moment will be recalled as the vanquished Athenians begin their trudge away (7.75.6–7, quoted at Intr., 15); the Great Battle in the Harbour also echoes several phrases (7.69.3–71, cf. **31**.1, **31**.4, **32**.2 nn.: Jordan 2000a: 76–9); the bleak closure at 7.87.5–6 will then echo a keyword here when the outcome is τοῖς... κρατήσασι λαμπρότατον – glittering indeed, but for the Syracusan victors. The sight at Athens will then be one of empty shipyards and treasury (8.1.2), and a very different mindset will be required (8.1.3–4). Some might also have thought even further ahead, to the scene of Lysander sailing in triumph into the Piraeus in 404 ((X. *Hell*. 2.2.23, Diod. 13.107.2, Plut. *Lys*. 14.5).

This description also recalls Xerxes' invading force in 480 (**31**.1, **31**.4, **31**.6, **32**.2 nn.): that too was magnificent, put together in a spirit of competitive rivalry, and Hdt. too dwelt on the effect on the spectator, in that case Xerxes himself. Cf. Rood 1999: 153 = 2009: 161. The outcome of the two invasions will be similar too, not least because these vast numbers can be counterproductive: cf. Intr., 20, and for Xerxes Pelling 1991: 136–9.

Jordan 2000a and Kallet 2001: 48–66 emphasise the misleading impression the spectacle may give of the power behind it, and Harman 2018: 281–2 presents this metahistorically as a prompt to readers to reflect on the difficulty of reading events. For Kallet Th. is representing the display as 'wasteful' and 'extravagant'; Jordan even calls this a 'Potemkin fleet', like the fake façades put up to deceive Catherine the Great in 1787 into thinking the countryside prosperous. That goes too far: as Kallet stresses (2001: 55), Th. does not exclude this from being an effective war-machine *as well* (**31**.4 n. on καὶ ἐς τοὺς ἄλλους Ἕλληνας... παρασκευήν), and it might easily have won (Intr., 2). The narrative has shown that Athens was concerned with conquest, not with showing off. But whatever the intention, display can give an exaggerated impression of power: at 1.10 Th. comments that future observers comparing the remains of Athens and Sparta might reach the wrong inference (εἰκάζεσθαι, the same word as at **31**.4) about the cities' relative strength. Several aspects – the concern for appearance, the λαμπρότης, the competitiveness, the expense, the blurring of public and private – also recall Alcibiades, who was proud of making the city's power seem greater than it was 'before the Greeks' (**16**.2, cf. **31**.4). Alcibiades' style is infectious; or perhaps he and his city always had a lot in common. That is not reassuring.

30.1 θέρους μεσοῦντος ἤδη: ἤδη emphasises that some time has elapsed since the springtime (**8**.1) debate, not surprisingly in view of the scale. The date is probably early to mid June.   **ἡ ἀναγωγὴ ἐγίγνετο:** the imperfect, here as in the rounding-off ἀνήγοντο at **32**.2, may be inceptive, 'began to happen', but also signals that it took some time (*CGCG* 33.52 n.1).   **τῶν μὲν οὖν ξυμμάχων . . . ξυνείπετο:** not merely τοῖς πλείστοις but also ὁλκάσι, πλοίοις and παρασκευή are to be taken with τῶν ξυμμάχων.   **τοῖς πλοίοις:** here warships, as opposed to the cargo ships (ὁλκάδες).   **ἐς Κέρκυραν ξυλλέγεσθαι:** in 433 the Athenians were already seeing Corcyra as a good staging post for the voyage to Italy and Sicily (1.44.3, Intr., 30).   **ἐπὶ ἄκραν Ἰαπυγίαν** 'Point Iapygia', in the heel of S. Italy (Map 2), the modern Santa Maria di Leuca: cf. **34**.4, **44**.2, 7.33.3. ἄκρα seems to have become part of its name, not just a description.   **εἴ τινες τῶν ξυμμάχων παρῆσαν:** simply 'those of the allies that were present', as the phrasing, unlike 'if . . .' in Engl., need not imply any doubt or that the numbers were small. The Argives and Mantineans (**43**) and many of the Aegean and Euboean allies (7.57.2–7) will have found it easier to join here than in Corcyra.   **ἀναξόμενοι:** echoing the initial ἀναγωγή to round off the setting of the scene.

30.2 ὅμιλος: **17**.4 n. Not pejorative here.   **ὡς εἰπεῖν:** the absolute inf. 'limits a sweeping statement' (Rusten on 2.51.2): so 'virtually everyone'.   **τὰ μὲν ὡς κτήσοιντο, τοὺς δ' εἴ ποτε ὄψοιντο:** compressed language. τὰ μέν = the objects in Sicily of those 'hopes', implying those of conquest (**1**.1 n.). E.g. 'wondering' is understood before εἴ ποτε ὄψοιντο. For ὁρᾶν implying 'set eyes on again' cf. Soph. *OT* 824, quoted in next n.   **ὄψοιντο:** but such well-grounded fears for any future 'seeing' are soon crowded out by the immediate 'sight'. Cf. the more obvious irony at Soph. *OT* 824, where the soon-to-be-blinded Oedipus laments that exile from what he takes to be his native Corinth means that 'I cannot ἰδεῖν my own people', with ἰδεῖν twice more at 831 ('may I never see that day') and

832. ἐκ τῆς σφετέρας should refer back to the subj. of the sentence, so 'their own land' = that of the spectators, though of course this is the Athenian combatants' land too.   **ὅσον πλοῦν:** better taken as internal acc. with ἀπεστέλλοντο than acc. of space traversed, but it comes to the same thing.

31.1 μᾶλλον αὐτούς . . . ἢ ὅτε ἐψηφίζοντο πλεῖν: as the preceding ἀλλήλους shows, αὐτούς here includes the combatants as well as the spectators. Many would have been citizen voters: cf. **24**.   **ἐσήιει τὰ δεινά:** a stronger metaphor than cases where a pain (Aesch. *Pers.* 845) or a desire (Eur. *IA* 1410) or a reflective fear (Plato, *Rep.* 1.330d) enters one's mind. Now it is the fearful things themselves that 'get into them'. Bakker 1997 observes that the imperfect tends to be used of internal points of view, focalising through the agents, whereas aorists more regularly convey a narratorial viewpoint: cf. ἀνεθάρσουν.   **τῆι παρούσηι ῥώμηι, διὰ τὸ πλῆθος ἑκάστων ὧν ἑώρων τῆι ὄψει:** ῥώμη is a matter both of morale and of resources: see Intr. to Bk. 7, p. 30. Emphasis falls both on πλῆθος and on the pleonastic ἑώρων τῆι ὄψει: there is strength here, but they are (over?)-impressed by the pure numbers that they see. Cf. the displays that so move Xerxes as he advances on Greece, Hdt. 7.44–52, 100–5 (and cf. Konstan 1987: 63–5 for the Persian preoccupation with counting): those passages may be in mind here (**30–32**.2 n.).   **ἑκάστων ὧν:** ὧν replaces ἅ by relative attraction, *CGCG* 50.13.   **ἑώρων τῆι ὄψει:** the redundancy puts even more weight on the visuality (**30–32**.2 n.).   **οἱ δὲ ξένοι καὶ ὁ ἄλλος ὄχλος:** δέ contrasts with οἱ μὲν ἐπιχώριοι (**30**.2), but ὁ ἄλλος ὄχλος would also be mainly native Athenians; there is also a contrast with those who had relatives on board. As usual with ὄχλος (**63**.2 n.), a pejorative tinge may be felt, though here only slight: they were just there to sight-see.   **κατὰ θέαν:** the emphasis on visuality returns with the observers watching the great sea-battle at 7.71.3, the episode that will finally reverse all these hopes.   **ὡς ἐπ' ἀξιόχρεων καὶ ἄπιστον διάνοιαν:** paradoxical, as one cannot literally gaze upon (κατὰ θέαν) a διάνοια; but it was the big thinking behind the spectacle that made it so 'worthwhile and incredible'. ἀξιόχρεων and διάνοιαν both echo Nicias (**21**): he has got what he asked for. The question whether it is literally unbelievable then divides Hermocrates and Athenagoras: ἄπιστα is Hermocrates' first word, **33**.1.   **παρασκευή . . . ἐγένετο** 'this first force was the most lavishly equipped in Greek forces and the most impressive to look upon of any mounted by a single city up till that time'. 'First force' distinguishes it, as at **44**.1, from the later reinforcements of **93**.4 and esp. 7.16.1. The qualifications μιᾶς πόλεως and δυνάμει Ἑλληνικῆι are given to exclude the one expedition that was obviously greater, that of Xerxes in 480. For παρασκευή, see **1**.1 n.; for the apparent illogicality cf. on μέγιστον δὴ τῶν πρίν, **13**.1 n.

31.2 ὁπλιτῶν: despite their mention here, there is surprisingly little on hoplites in the rest of **30–32**.2, though e.g. the expenditure on personal equipment (**31**.3) would have affected hoplites most. Steiner 2005 sees this, along with the absence of cavalry (see on τριακόσιοι ἱππῆς), as reflecting a shift towards a more egalitarian version of the 'Athenian civic ideal'. Numbers are then given at **43** (n.).   ἡ ἐς Ἐπίδαυρον . . . καὶ ἡ αὐτὴ ἐς Ποτείδαιαν . . .: in 430 BCE, 2.56 and 58: 'the same', because Hagnon took over Pericles' force, 2.58.1.   τετράκις . . . ξυνέπλευσαν: the same figures are given at 2.56.2.   καὶ τριακόσιοι ἱππῆς: whereas no cavalry form part of the current force (Stahl 1973: 73–4 = 2003: 184; Steiner 2005). That will prove important (Intr., 6), but for the moment Th. leaves the point muted.

31.3 ἀλλὰ ἐπί τε βραχεῖ πλῶι . . . ἀμιλληθέν: the main verb ὡρμήθησαν goes with both the initial 'they', i.e. the combatants of 430 BCE, and οὗτος . . . ὁ στόλος; clauses then accumulate to describe this στόλος, subdivided into τὸ μὲν ναυτικόν and τὸ δὲ πεζόν, with the ναυτικόν part itself including a subdivision (μὲν . . . δὲ . . . καί) within a long gen. absolute to explain how it was 'worked up . . . at great expense'. On the stylistic effect of such overcrowding of detail see intr. n. to **30–32**.2.   ἐπί τε βραχεῖ πλῶι ὡρμήθησαν καὶ παρασκευῆι φαύληι: for ἐπί + dat. cf. **27**.3 n. and LSJ ἐπί B.III.3, 'condition upon which': 'for' a short voyage and 'with' not much equipment. Nicias at **21**.1 warned against sending such a φαύλη force now.   κατ᾿ ἀμφότερα . . . ἐξαρτυθείς 'equipped in both ways', with ships and infantry.   οὗ ἂν δέηι: οὗ may be heard either as local, '[for action] wherever it might be necessary', or as gen. with δεῖ, 'in both ways, [for] whichever should be necessary'.   τριηράρχων: the 'trierarchy' was one of the 'liturgies' whereby wealthy citizens were called upon to fund a public service for a year. The state provided the crew's basic pay and the ship, but the trierarch was responsible for keeping it in good repair.   δραχμὴν τῆς ἡμέρας τῶι ναύτηι ἑκάστωι διδόντος: this is also the rate for overseas service at 3.17.4 and 7.27.2, though at 8.45.2 Alcibiades (not always a reliable informant) tells Tissaphernes that the Athenians pay only half that rate. Cf. 8.1 n., *GSW* i. 14–24, and esp. Loomis 1998: 32–61. *GSW* argued that the drachma rate was above the norm, but Loomis 1998: 55–6 and esp. O'Connor 2016 have good arguments against this.   ναῦς παρασχόντος κενάς: elsewhere in Th. 'empty ships' = 'empty of men': cf. e.g. 4.14.1, 'they towed a few empty ships, their men having taken to flight'. Specifying that here seems odd, as it is clear from δραχμήν . . . διδόντος and from ὑπηρεσίας that the state took some responsibility for crews as well. If taken closely with that ὑπηρεσίας – not just the ships but the men to crew them – the point is feeble. Perhaps the implication is that the levies should be the trierarchs' responsibility (cf. on καταλόγοις τε χρηστοῖς ἐκκριθέν below), or perhaps κενάς = 'empty of fitments', and the point is that the trierarchs needed to provide them. Alberti prints Naber's καινάς, but it is unlikely that all the ships would be new or that so many could be built in so short a time.   **ἑξήκοντα μὲν ταχείας, τεσσαράκοντα δὲ ὁπλιταγωγούς:** following Nicias' recommendation of 100 including 'as many troop-carriers as seems appropriate', **25**.2. The same numbers are given at **43**.   **τοῖς θρανίταις τῶν ναυτῶν καὶ ταῖς ὑπηρεσίαις:** a difficult passage. θρανῖται technically = the 'rower[s] on the topmost of the three' [or possibly two, Jordan 2000b: 86–9] 'benches of a trireme' (LSJ). Elsewhere in Th. ὑπηρεσία seems best taken as a general word for 'crew', as in ὑπηρεσίας ταύταις τὰς κρατίστας in this sentence and at 1.143.1, where Pericles takes pride in them, and 8.1.2, where their absence causes despair: in each case the best sense is given if whole crews are meant, including the more skilled – the helmsman, the *keleustēs*, the *aulētēs* whose playing marked the rhythm and so on. Morrison 1984 and Morrison and Williams 1968: 206–8 however argued that the word regularly means these 'petty officers' alone, and that does fit some contexts elsewhere, notably passages in [Dem.] 50 where it is contrasted with ναῦται (10, 30, 32, 35–6: cf. Trevett 1992: 40). Here it is usually assumed that the θρανῖται were singled out for the bonus because their work was hardest or most perilous, and that ὑπηρεσίαι is to be taken in the narrower sense of more skilled personnel. This is probably right, though Jordan 2000b: 90 reasonably questions the effect on morale of leaving the lower rank(s) of rowers out of the bonuses when their musclepower was vital for speed (τῶι ταχυναυτεῖν below). These lower rowers had the worst of it in more ways than one: Ar. *Frogs* 1074 gets a joke out of their vulnerability to farting from the backsides just above.   **τἆλλα** 'in the other respects': 'the' suggests that these were familiar ways of putting one's trierarchic generosity on display.   **σημείοις** 'insignia' or 'signs', the equivalents of modern figureheads but carried on the stern: Eur. *IA* 231–302 lavishly describes those on the fleet at Aulis, and cf. Ar. *Frogs* 933.   **ἑνὸς ἑκάστου:** i.e. of the trierarchs.   **καὶ τῶι ταχυναυτεῖν:** so their competitiveness was not without some martial benefit. This, like ἁμιλληθέν below, prepares for the racing ἅμιλλα of **32**.2.   **καταλόγοις τε χρηστοῖς ἐκκριθέν** 'picked out in high-quality levies': cf. **26**.2 n. The call-ups needed to keep a balance between picking the best men and spreading the burden around (van Wees 2004: 102–4): the emphasis this time was on quality, though χρηστοῖς may also imply concern to avoid draft-dodging.   **καὶ ὅπλων ... ἁμιλληθέν:** thus showing the sort of pride in bodily equipment that Alcibiades claimed was lacking in Sicily, **17**.3. For the passive aor. form of the deponent ἁμιλλάομαι cf. Eur. *Supp.* 195, *Her.* 1255, Plato, *Laws* 12.968b.

31.4 ἔριν: there has been ἔρις at Athens already, with the wrangling of Nicias and Alcibiades, and the Syracusan equivalent will be seen at **32**.3–41; but ἔρις can be good as well as bad (Hes. *WD* 11–26), and this is potentially the good, productive kind. It recalls the prize that Xerxes offered for the best-equipped and smartest army (Hdt. 7.8δ.1), and the eager competition this provoked (Hdt. 7.19.2). In Th. there will be competition among the crews again at 7.70.3, but by then in a desperate situation: this may be recalled there (n.). **ὧι τις ἕκαστος προσετάχθη** 'in whatever area each individual had been assigned to'. **καὶ ἐς τοὺς ἄλλους Ἕλληνας ... παρασκευήν** 'and for the other Greeks a display for their power and authority to be gauged more than a preparation to fight the enemy'; the Athenians are picking up the manner of Alcibiades, **16**.2. εἰκασθῆναι is best taken as explanatory inf. after ἐπίδειξιν, lit. 'a display of their power and strength for these to be inferred'. μᾶλλον, as often in Th. (cf. **31**.6 οὐχ ἧσσον, and Intr., 5 on 2.65.11), does not exclude the lesser alternative – this was evidently a preparation against the enemy *as well*: it simply suggests that for the other Greeks the display of power was the more significant factor. They would be less alarmed by the prospect of Athens' conquering Sicily than by the thought that the city was clearly so wealthy: what else, in that case, might they be able to do? The sentence has been much discussed: *HCT* and *CT* both take εἰκασθῆναι as 'represent'; Kallet 2001: 54–9 defends 'infer' and takes this as an echo of 1.10.3 (cf. **30–32**.2 n.).

31.5 εἰ γάρ τις ἐλογίσατο ... πολλὰ ἂν τάλαντα ηὑρέθη: unreal conditional in the past, unreal because these observers are hypothetical. For Kallet 2001: 60 this is part of the point – someone really ought to have done the sums. Th. goes on to explain (γάρ) what the reasoning would have been, with ἐκ τῆς πόλεως ... ἐξαγόμενα adding a sting in the tail (just 'to have been spent' might be expected): the city felt able to send such wealth away. For the accumulative style see intr. n. to **30–32**.2. Some of it picks up points from **31**.3 (the previous expenditure of state, trierarchs, and combatants), but more is added: the war-chest for the generals to administer; the further private expenses to be expected; the prospects of trading. **ἅ τε ... ἀναλώσειν** 'what each person had spent on his bodily equipment and, in the case of a trierarch, on his ship, and the amount they would continue to spend in the future'. **καὶ ἄνευ τοῦ ἐκ τοῦ δημοσίου μισθοῦ ... ἐφόδιον:** i.e. the pay might not be enough to cover expenses; troops would have to buy their own food in whatever market a town would allow (**44**.2 n.). **πάντα τινά** 'everyone', as at **68**.2 and 7.60.2. **ὡς ἐπὶ χρόνιον στρατείαν** 'thinking that it would be a lengthy campaign'. On a shorter campaign they might make do, eking out their pay, living off the land, or just plundering the locals. ἐπὶ μεταβολῆι 'with a view to trading'. This might involve not just money but also goods for barter with the locals or for sale. ἔμπορος: there were quite a few of these camp-following traders, 44. πολλὰ ἂν τάλαντα . . . τὰ πάντα 'many talents in all', if one totalled them up. The conclusion is less bathetic in Greek than it sounds in translation: cf. Ar. *Clouds* 1065–6, 'Hyperbolus has taken πλεῖν ἢ τάλαντα πολλά'. The absence of a total figure is still notable, contrasting with Pericles' exact numbers at 2.13. Maybe nobody knew, or maybe Th. is recreating the thoughts and words of onlookers: there was so much that one could not even guess at the total, one just knew that it was a lot.

31.6 οὐχ ἧσσον: see on καὶ ἐς τοὺς ἄλλους Ἕλληνας . . . παρασκευήν, 31.4 n. θάμβει 'wonder', 'amazement', a strong and esp. poetic word, used e.g. when Athena appears to Achilles at *Il.* 1.199 or (twice) when Priam enters Achilles' tent, *Il.* 24.483–4. It is especially appropriate for such a visual surprise. The phrase is echoed at Plut. *Caes.* 32.2 as Caesar crosses the Rubicon. περιβόητος ἐγένετο 'became much talked about', and not just in retrospect: **32**.3 gives an idea of the gossip around the trading ports (n.), and this impressive combination of τόλμα, δύναμις, and distance of voyage was what Hermocrates sensed and feared at Syracuse (**33**.4–5). ἢ στρατιᾶς πρὸς οὓς ἐπῆισαν ὑπερβολῆι 'than for the exceedingly great size of the expedition in comparison with those they were attacking': πρὸς οὓς ἐπῆισαν = πρός ('in relation to, in comparison with'‚ LSJ C.III.4) ἐκείνους πρὸς ('against') οὓς ἐπῆισαν. ὑπερβολῆι suggests 'more than was necessary to outmatch Syracuse' (cf. **86**.2 and n.); there may also be a hint of 'more than there should have been'. μέγιστος ἤδη διάπλους 'the biggest crossing yet', biggest in a combination of distance and scale (not distance alone, as the first Sicilian expedition of 427 was the same, and the Egyptian campaign of 460 and Pericles' mid 430s expedition to the Black Sea both involved a longer crossing than that to Point Iapygia): the comparison forms a ring with **31**.1, πολυτελεστάτη δὴ καὶ εὐπρεπεστάτη τῶν ἐς ἐκεῖνον τὸν χρόνον. Xerxes' expedition is not an exception here (so there is no need, as at **31**.1, for the qualification 'Greek'): they came by land. ἐπὶ μεγίστηι ἐλπίδι τῶν μελλόντων πρὸς τὰ ὑπάρχοντα: Nicias in contrast had warned them to keep hold of τὰ ὑπάρχοντα and avoid risks for τὰ ἀφανῆ καὶ μέλλοντα, **9**.3.

32.1–2 Ἐπειδὴ δὲ αἱ νῆες πλήρεις ἦσαν . . . εὐχὰς δὲ τὰς νομιζομένας . . . σπένδοντες . . . παιανίσαντες: there was nothing extraordinary in such rituals before an expedition or a moment of danger, but the detail here marks the momentousness of this particular departure. What was unusual was the presence of so many well-wishers to share the prayer. The wording of **32.1** suggests that it was unusual for prayers to be delivered altogether rather than ship by ship, and this too may have been to allow the crowd to join in. The city as a whole is engaged. ἐσέκειτο: κεῖμαι verbs often function as equivalent to a past passive form of τίθημι, so here effectively 'had been loaded'. ξύμπαντες δὲ ὑπὸ κήρυκος ἐποιοῦντο 'they made them as a whole, prompted by a herald': see Pulleyn 1997: 173–8, concluding (1997: 176) that probably the herald led and 'the crews chimed in'. The herald perhaps shouted out the words for the crews to repeat, or perhaps gave a signal and all spoke together a familiar prayer. Less likely, 'one herald spoke for all of them' (*HCT*), i.e. the crews stayed silent. χρυσοῖς τε καὶ ἀργυροῖς: an extra touch of visual sumptuousness even as the emphasis has moved to the audial (**30–32.**2 n.). Like the ἅμιλλα of **32.**2 (n), this may recall Herodotus' Xerxes at Abydus (7.54.2), and this passage may itself be recalled at **46.**3 (n.). οἵ τε ἐπιβάται 'marines'; but not the rowers, already at their oars.

32.2 ξυνεπηύχοντο ... παιανίσαντες: these prayers and paeans are recalled at 7.75.7 (Intr., 15). ὁ ἄλλος ὅμιλος ὁ ἐκ τῆς γῆς: ἐκ is transferred from the prayers coming 'from the land' to the crowd itself: cf. **7.**2 n. καὶ εἴ τις ἄλλος: echoing καὶ εἴ τινες τῶν ξυμμάχων at **30.**1 and again not suggesting that the number was small. ἀνήγοντο: **30.**1 n. ἐπὶ κέρως 'in line ahead'. ἅμιλλαν ἤδη μέχρι Αἰγίνης ἐποιοῦντο: see on καὶ τῶι ταχυναυτεῖν, **31.**3 n.: Xerxes was eager to see a contest of ships at Abydus (νεῶν ἅμιλλαν, Hdt. 7.44) before making a libation with golden goblets (Hdt. 7.54.2). ἤδη captures the excitement: 'look, they're already racing ...'. Athenians were proud of their naval speed and expertise (cf. esp. Phormio at 2.89 and the sequel at 2.91–2), and as in the contests of *Il.* 23 and Virg. *Aen.* 5 those playful accomplishments will be needed soon enough in warfare. But when the crucial ἅμιλλα comes (the word recurs at 7.71.3), the cramped waters in the Great Harbour will mean that speed is of little avail. ἐς τὴν Κέρκυραν ... ξυνελέγετο: rounding off the description by echoing the initial ἐς Κέρκυραν ξυλλέγεσθαι, **30.**1.

32.3–41: DEBATE AT SYRACUSE

The narrative leaves Athens as debate turns to action, with the leaders' contention giving way to a more positive ἅμιλλα as the fleet sets sail, **32.**2. It now moves to a mirroring debate in Syracuse, and here too the arguments illuminate not only the immediate decision but the texture of politics. ('Texture' rather than formal workings: Th. says little of that – a democracy, 7.55.2, but less radical than at Athens. See Intr,

34.) Athenians were vague about Sicily's geography (**1**.1); Syracusans are vague about Athens' plan. Their reluctance to believe it (**32**.3) will be strangely mirrored in Athens two years later, but then it will be the scale of the disaster that seems incredible (8.1.1: Cusumano 2011: 44). The echoes of the Athenian debate (nn.) do not imply that either speaker is presented as knowing what was said – Athenagoras clearly has no inkling of what had been decided, though gossip was clearly flooding in (**32**.3 n.) and Hermocrates knows of Nicias' reluctance (**34**.6) – but only that the same factors play a part in both deliberations. The pieces come down in a different jumble here. Both speakers are often in tune with Nicias and therefore, ironically, with each other, agreeing that the Athenians would be taking a massive risk and the Syracusans can hope to build a winning alliance; but Hermocrates is more alert to those Athenian characteristics that make them take that risk. Each speaker echoes other Athenian speeches too, with Hermocrates recalling Pericles and Athenagoras Cleon (nn., Intr., pp. 27, 28). There are again similarities with Ar. *Birds*: far from home, the Athenians will come upon a world not too different from their own. Cf. **24**.3 n., Intr., 33).

The Athenian preparations were clearly under way: that was why people were talking about it (**32**.3), and **42**.1 suggests that the Athenians were already in Corcyra at the time of the debate. The μέν . . . δέ transition at **32**.3–4 does not however imply that the Athenian fleet had already sailed before rumours arrived, for **32**.2 has continued the story at Athens to its end-point before switching to Sicily. At **34**.9 Hermocrates claims that the ships are on their way (presumably from Athens rather than from Corcyra), but it is not clear that he can really be so sure: his suggested strategy at least implies that they have time to rethink (**34**.4, **34**.6 nn.).

On the debate, see esp. *CT*, Hunter 1973: ch. 9, Connor 1984: 168–76, Mader 1993b and esp. 2013, Bloedow 1993 and 1996, Stahl 2003: 121–2 and 194–9, and Andrews 2009.

32.3 ἠγγέλλετο πολλαχόθεν conveys both the ready traffic of gossip along trading routes and the hotness of the topic: everyone was talking about it.   ἐπὶ πολὺν χρόνον: ἐπί gives a different nuance from just πολὺν χρόνον, which would have been an acc. of duration of time: the news was not believed *until* a long time had passed. It is not obvious why it should be found incredible, for Athenians had been in Sicily in force only ten years before when they had many more commitments close to home. Probably it was the scale that was hard to believe (Connor 1984: 169 n. 26): this was what was περιβόητος at **31**.6. Or maybe there had been fake news before: **35**.1 n.   τοιοίδε λόγοι ἀπό τε ἄλλων . . . καὶ Ἑρμοκράτης ὁ Ἕρμωνος . . .: τοιοίδε need not imply that the speeches were *very* like those of Hermocrates or Athenagoras, given how strongly Th. characterises both, only that the others similarly took either a believing or an unbelieving line. For Hermocrates see **33–4** n.   ὡς σαφῶς οἰόμενος εἰδέναι τὰ περὶ αὐτῶν 'as someone who thought he had a clear knowledge of the truth'. οἰόμενος conveys his own confidence rather than others' in him, and this is his own stress too (**33.**1 σαφέστερόν τι ἑτέρου εἰδώς). Ctr. e.g. Archidamus, ἀνὴρ καὶ ξυνετὸς δοκῶν εἶναι καὶ σώφρων, 1.79.2, or Pericles, 1.139.4. Still, his audience too may have wanted to know why he was so confident.

33–34 *The Speech of Hermocrates*

Hermocrates is familiar from Bk. 4, where his speech (4.59–64) played a particularly persuasive role (ἔπεισε μάλιστα) in uniting the Sicilians against the earlier Athenian threat. That lends force to his conviction that Syracuse could do the same again (**33.**4), and his language several times recalls that earlier speech. This speech and that at **76–80** reinforce the impression left by 4.59–64 of 'a sharp and clear-thinking man, energetic and decisive, patriotic and boldly enterprising' (Steup on 4.58). His rhetoric suits his characterisation. His style is distinctive (Tompkins 2015), with several verbal mannerisms (nn.). His sentences are often long and may seem straggly (e.g. **33.**4 [n.], **34.**2, **34.**4), but the accumulation has a point, bringing out how the considerations knit together: the same goes for the repeated γάρ (6x in **33.**4–6), as he makes clear the logical steps that underpin his reasoning (Hunter 1973: 161–3). **34** moves confidently through many hypotheticals (ἄν 18x): whatever may happen the Syracusans will have options. Like Nicias at **9–14** he acknowledges that many of his audience will not like what he says (**33.**1, **34.**4 nn.), but his punchiness, combining pressure for action with reasoned optimism, is more in the style of Pericles (Intr., 28). He calls on the Syracusans too to be more like the Athenians (**34.**4 n.), with a corresponding hope that they may emulate Athens' own rise to glory after repulsing their foreign invader (**33.**6).

Th.'s early audiences may have known that Hermocrates had an uneasy future before him after his glories of Bks. 6 and 7. After serving in the Aegean (8.29.2, 45.3), he was exiled in 411 or 410 (8.85.3 with *CT*). He raised an army and returned, seizing Selinus and ravaging the Carthaginian parts of the island, then tried to seize Syracuse itself with the aid of supporters within its walls, including the later tyrant Dionysius I, and he was killed (408). It was understandably supposed that he was aiming for tyranny himself (Diod. 13.75.5). These ambitions may affect the reading of 4.59–64, **72**, **76–80** (cf. **78.**1 n.), and of Athenagoras' suspicions of conspiratorial plotting now (**38**.3 n.); this speech however is appropriate to any strong democratic leader, and nothing can be inferred about his own politics. See also Intr. to Bk. 7, pp. 33–4.

33.1 Ἄπιστα μὲν ἴσως...: this is less defeatist than Nicias' similar acknowledgement at **9**.3, as he stresses that he is not alone (ὥσπερ καὶ ἄλλοι τινές, echoing **32**.3) and ending on a note of conviction (σαφέστερόν τι ἑτέρου εἰδώς). The μέν indicates that a correction or complication is to come; it arrives at **33**.4, εἰ δέ τωι καὶ πιστά.   **περὶ τοῦ ἐπίπλου τῆς ἀληθείας** 'about the truth of their sailing against us'. τοῦ ἐπίπλου is advanced for emphasis: cf. **55**.4 n., **40**.2, **49**.2, *CGCG* 28.15 n.1.   **πείθων γε ἐμαυτὸν σαφέστερόν τι ἑτέρου εἰδὼς λέγειν** = πείθων γε ἐμαυτὸν ὅτι σαφέστερόν τι ἑτέρου εἰδὼς λέγω. 'As I persuade myself' became a rhetorical cliché (e.g. Andoc. 1.70, Plato, *Gorg.* 453b, Dem. 23.19, Aeschin. 1.45), but as Σ Dem. 24.18d acidly comments, the business of orators is to persuade not just themselves but others. The self-confidence here and at **32**.3 may recall Pericles' claim to be οὐδενὸς ἥσσων ... γνῶναί τε τὰ δέοντα καὶ ἑρμηνεῦσαι ταῦτα, 2.60.5.   **ἑτέρου:** singular, as in τοῦ πέλας (**12**.1 n.) and Engl. 'than the next person'.

33.2 ἐφ' ὑμᾶς: against 'you' rather than 'us' (though one MS reads ἡμᾶς): the distance between speaker and audience, re-emphasised in θαυμάζετε, marks the didactic tone, but by **33**.4 Hermocrates has changed to 'we'. Cf. **10**.2 n.   **πρόφασιν ... τὸ δὲ ἀληθές:** accs. of respect, 'in what they say' and 'in truth'. He had argued similarly at Gela, 4.60.1 and 4.61.3. The phrasing also echoes Th.'s narratorial comments at **6**.1 and (ἐπιθυμίαι) **24**.2–3: Hermocrates is right.

33.3 κάλλιστα: one might expect e.g. 'most safely' or 'most effectively', but this, like κάλλιστον δὴ ἔργων at **33**.4, already prepares for the καλὸς ὁ ἀγών theme of Bk. 7: see 7.56.2 n.   **μήτε καταφρονήσαντες ... ἀμελήσετε:** either scorn or disbelief will endanger 'everything', in the first case through taking inadequate steps and in the second through taking none. καταφρονήσαντες is picked up in his peroration at **34**.9 (n.); ἀπιστήσαντες rounds off this first section by echoing ἄπιστα.

33.4 εἰ δέ τωι καὶ πιστά 'but if someone does finds it credible ...': τωι = τινι. Like 'someone' but unlike 'anyone' in Engl., this does not suggest that such people are few in number. πιστά might be taken as acc. parallel to ἄπιστα in **33**.1, but most would probably hear it as nom. agreeing with an understood subject 'the news'.   **τὴν τόλμαν αὐτῶν καὶ δύναμιν μὴ ἐκπλαγῆι:** echoing **31**.6 (nn.), the qualities for which the expedition became περιβόητος. For ἐκπλήσσομαι see below.   **οὔθ' ... ἀνωφελεῖς** 'nor are they disadvantageous to us ...', i.e. they are playing into our hands.

ἀνωφελές (Dobree) would bring the phrase into closer parallel with πολὺ ἄμεινον, and may be right. **μᾶλλον γὰρ ἐθελήσουσιν ἐκπλαγέντες ἡμῖν ξυμμαχεῖν:** as Nicias feared, **21.1**. ἐκπλαγέντες echoes μὴ ἐκπλαγῆι: 'fear' – others' fear, here that felt by the other Sicilian cities and at **34**.2 by Carthage – paradoxically becomes a reason why the Syracusans should not be afraid (Mader 2013: 240). ἔκπληξις / κατάπληξις is an important theme of this debate, on both sides: **34**.4, **34**.6, **34**.8, **36**.2, **38**.2, **40**.2 (nn.); Cusumano 2011: 43–6. **ἀπράκτους ὧν ἐφίενται ἀπώσωμεν** 'repulse them without their achieving what they desire'. Hermocrates used similar language at 4.61.7: the Athenians ἄπρακτοι ἀπίασιν if only the Sicilians can unite. **κάλλιστον δὴ ἔργων:** slightly stronger than κάλλιστον ἔργον, rather as 'the most glorious of deeds' is stronger than 'a most glorious deed': cf. 2.42.4, 'judging this the κάλλιστον of dangers'. **καὶ οὐκ ἀνέλπιστον ἔμοιγε:** the style is less inelegant than it appears on the page. After the climax of κάλλιστον δὴ ἔργων, the speaker would pause before moving on to pragmatics: not just glorious, but also to be expected.

33.5 στόλοι μεγάλοι . . . πολὺ ἀπὸ τῆς ἑαυτῶν ἀπάραντες: again echoing **31**.6, there the impressiveness, here the difficulties. **ἢ Ἑλλήνων ἢ βαρβάρων:** Th. could have left it as simply ὀλίγοι . . . στόλοι, but the extra words hint at the Persian invasions: **33**.6 will make this explicit. Xerxes was in the background at **30–32.2** (nn.), but for the expedition's magnificence. Now the focus switches to its eventual débâcle. **τῶν ἐνοικούντων καὶ ἀστυγειτόνων:** 'neighbours' prepares the next point, that fear will lead them to join in. **πάντα γὰρ ὑπὸ δέους ξυνίσταται . . . δι' ἀπορίαν τῶν ἐπιτηδείων:** Th. tends to use δέος more of a reflective concern for one's security (cf. **83**.4, **85**.3), φόβος more of sudden terror or consternation (e.g. **63**.2, **68**.4, 7.42.3, 7.80.3: de Romilly 1956), but there are many exceptions and cross-overs (e.g. **34**.2, **91**.6: Desmond 2006: 360–4), not least 1.23.6 and 1.88 on the φόβος of Athenian expansion that drove the Spartans into war. Here Hermocrates' thinking again mirrors that of Nicias (**21**.1, fear will generate unity; **21**.2, difficulties of supply). It is odd that Hermocrates makes no mention of his success in producing such unity in 424, or even of the Athenians' failure then: 'you have beaten this enemy before' is a staple of pre-battle rhetoric (7.63.4 n.). Still, Th. finds other ways of recalling 424 (**33–34** n.), and even if Hermocrates did say anything along those lines Th. may have dropped it as too predictably routine: Intr., 25–6. **δι' ἀπορίαν τῶν ἐπιτηδείων:** Cawkwell 2005: 100–3 and 112 explores the implied judgement here on Xerxes' difficulties in 480, and persuasively argues (a) that Hermocrates here reflects Th.'s own judgement and (b) that he is likely to be right. **ἐπιβουλευθεῖσιν:** again a word used in Hermocrates' Gela speech, 4.64.5.

33.5–33.6 ὄνομα ... ἐπὶ τῶι ὀνόματι ...: the first ὄνομα is 'fame' or 'repute', the second more 'the claim' that Athens was the Persians' target, as put forward by the Persians (Hdt. 5.105. 6.94 etc.) and then trumpeted by the Athenians themselves. **κἂν περὶ σφίσιν αὐτοῖς τὰ πλείω πταίσωσιν ... πολλὰ σφαλέντος**: as Th.'s Corinthians claim was the case with Xerxes, αὐτὸν περὶ αὑτῶι τὰ πλείω σφαλέντα (1.69.5).

33.6 ὅπερ: acc. of respect, 'in this same way'. **καὶ Ἀθηναῖοι αὐτοὶ οὗτοι ...**: for 'Syracuse being like Athens' see Intr., 33–4. **ηὐξήθησαν**: used also at 1.89.1 of the rise of Athens after the Persian Wars. **οὐκ ἀνέλπιστον**: echoing 33.4 fin. to round off this important point.

34.1 τά τε αὐτοῦ 'matters here'. **ἐς τοὺς Σικελοὺς πέμποντες**: the Syracusans take this advice (**45**), 'sending guards to some' (= τοὺς μέν here) 'and envoys to others' (= τοῖς δέ). **τοὺς μὲν μᾶλλον βεβαιωσώμεθα**: the tribute-bearing subjects (**20**.4 n.), typically those living in the coastal plain (**88**.4). **ἔς τε τὴν ἄλλην Σικελίαν πέμποντες**: Hermocrates here mirrors Alcibiades (**48**). The Syracusans send such embassies at **45** and **75**.3. **ὡς κοινὸς ὁ κίνδυνος**: as Hermocrates had successfully argued at Gela, stressing τὸ κοινῶς φοβερόν (4.61.6) of Athenian presence in Sicily and calling on the Sicilian cities to act κοινῆι (4.61.2–3) in response. **ἡμῖν**: apparently superfluous, but the point is 'get them to make an alliance with *us*' rather than the Athenians. **ἢ μὴ δέχωνται Ἀθηναίους**: second-best to an alliance in Hermocrates' eyes, but it was such refusals to 'receive' the Athenians – i.e. to grant access to a market, and in some cases to allow even anchorage and watering – that proved Athens' first serious setback (**44**.2–3). For Hermocrates and second-bests, see on εἰ δὲ μή, **34**.4 n., and on τοὺς προεπιχειροῦντας, **34**.7 n.

34.2 ἐς Καρχηδόνα: for Carthage cf. **15**.2 n. There is no sign that the Syracusans did make any such approach. Hermocrates' proposal to look to Carthage and to Sparta and Corinth (**34**.3) does not sit well with his 'Sicily for the Sicilians' line in 424 (4.59–64), but politicians tend to adjust principle to circumstances. **ἄμεινον**: cf. 9.1 n. **οὐ γὰρ ἀνέλπιστον αὐτοῖς**: a Hermocratean refrain (**33**.4, **33**.6): this is all to be expected. But what would the Carthaginians be expecting, the Athenian attack or a Syracusan approach? Probably both. **ἀλλ' αἰεὶ διὰ φόβου εἰσί**: Hermocrates may over-state, but not by much: a possible Athenian attack was being talked about (**15**.2 n.). For διὰ φόβου cf. **59**.2, LSJ διά A.IV.a. **ὥστε τάχ' ἂν ... ἐθελήσειαν**: ὥστε + opt. is rare, but see *M&T* 602, *CGCG* 46.5. **εἰ τάδε προήσονται**: τὰ καθ' ἡμᾶς, clarifies the schol., or perhaps more generally τὰ κατὰ τὴν Σικελίαν. προήσονται is middle fut. of προΐημι. **ἐν πόνωι** 'in trouble', euphemistically: cf. 5.110.2, where the Melians try to persuade the Athenians that they may face the πόνος of a threat to their own land and alliance. **ἤτοι κρύφα γε ἢ φανερῶς ἢ ἐξ ἑνός γέ του τρόπου** 'either secretly or openly or somehow or other'. This is not strictly logical, as 'secretly' and 'openly' seem to exhaust the alternatives, but the rhetoric is effective: the Carthaginians can find a way. On ἤτοι . . . ἤ see **38**.2 n. **βουληθέντες** 'if they wish'. **ὅθεν ὅ τε πόλεμος καὶ τἆλλα εὐπορεῖ**: as the wise Spartan Archidamus realised, 1.83.2, and as Pericles implicitly agreed, 1.141.4–5, 2.13.3–5.

34.3 καὶ ἐς τὴν Λακεδαίμονα καὶ ἐς Κόρινθον: Sparta as leader of the coalition and Corinth as Syracuse's mother-city. This proposal was taken up, but not till **75**.3. **δεόμενοι δεῦρο κατὰ τάχος βοηθεῖν:** again (**34**.1 n.) mirroring Alcibiades, but this time after his defection: **91**.1–4. **καὶ τὸν ἐκεῖ πόλεμον κινεῖν:** like Nicias (**10**), he assumes that 'the' war in Greece is merely dormant.

34.4–8: Hermocrates' advice to sail out and meet the Athenians on their way. Th. leaves his readers and listeners to make up their own minds on the wisdom of this suggestion, though it is unlikely that he expected them to dismiss it out of hand. As with Lamachus at **49**, he will at least have thought well of Hermocrates' mindset and approach: the psychological generalisations on e.g. daring and surprise chime with incidents in the earlier narrative (e.g. 2.84.3, 5.9–10), and Hermocrates draws appropriate conclusions too from past armadas, especially that of Xerxes. The praise of his military intelligence at **72**.2 (n.) would be odd if this scheme was thought simply wrong-headed, and neither Athenagoras nor the Syracusans as a whole (**35**.1) criticise the strategy as unrealistic. Still, even if Hermocrates is thinking along the right lines, he may well come over as over-confident too soon: the Syracusan navy is not yet skilled enough or large enough to take on such an Athenian armada, and it is unlikely that there was time to put a coalition fleet together. This would chime with other cases where Hermocrates is alert to the right approach but presses for it before the time is right (Intr., 28–9). It is possible too to see this as a ploy to shock the audience out of complacency (Westlake 1958b: 247–8 = 1969: 182–3), along the lines of Pericles' more far-fetched 'if I thought I would persuade you, I'd urge you to go out and ravage your fields yourselves . . .' (1.143.5). For discussion cf. *HCT* and Kagan 1981: 220–1, both highly critical of the proposal; Stahl 2003: 195–8 (**34**.5 n.) and Bloedow 1993, defending it; and Hunter 1973: 157–9, concentrating on whether Th. *thought* it was a good idea.

This suggestion takes up nearly half of the speech. It may not have bulked so large in the original (Intr., 25–6), but it clearly interested Th. There may be various reasons that go beyond its relevance for the debate or the question of its immediate wisdom. It further explores why large-scale maritime invasions can be vulnerable, especially the difficulties of supply (**33.**5); this will be relevant at **42.**1, where the Athenians split their fleet into three squadrons, at 7.14.2, and particularly in the final retreat (7.78.6, 80.1, 83.4). The Syracusans' lack of interest may also illustrate their character: they are, for the moment, naturally ἥσυχοι (**34.**4). Still, that will change, and the shock value of unexpected daring (**34.**6, **34.**8) prefigures later features (**46.**4 n., 7.21.4, 55.1, 66.3) even though it is not what is done now. It becomes clear, too, that Hermocrates, even if he grasps the Athenians' risk-taking spirit better than Athenagoras, still under-rates it if he thinks they might be so easily deterred (**34.**6–7). He also underestimates Athenian superiority in naval skill, just as he goes on to do on land (**72**). But he will prove a good learner.   ὑμεῖς τε διὰ τὸ ξύνηθες ἥσυχον ἥκιστ' ἂν ὀξέως πείθοισθε: ἥκιστ' ἄν . . . πείθοισθε recalls Nicias' resigned awareness that his audience will be against him (**9.**3), but there is none of Nicias' slow circumlocution, and while Nicias was trying to shift his audience's risk-taking in a downbeat direction, Hermocrates urges his to cast caution aside and become more Athenian. ἡσυχία was not the Athenian way (**18.**2–4, 6; cf. **9.**3, **10.**2 nn); for Athenian ὀξύτης cf. 1.70.2 and **10.**5 n.; for the speed with which they can be persuaded, **26.**1 n.   Σικελιῶται . . . ξύμπαντες, εἰ δὲ μή, ὅτι πλεῖστοι μεθ' ἡμῶν: Hermocrates' signature tune, now as at Gela in 424. Such a coalition would take time to organise even with just the 'existing' ships, and it is hard to think how they could engage the Athenians in time if the fleet was really on its way (**34.**9, cf. **42.**1). εἰ δὲ μή is a favourite Hermocrates locution as he carefully enumerates options: **34.**5, **34.**9, 4.63.1. Even this second-best (**34.**1, **34.**7 nn.), he thinks, would be good enough.   ἅπαν τὸ ὑπάρχον ναυτικόν 'all the existing fleet': Hermocrates implies that more might be newly built or come later, presumably from Sparta, Corinth, or Carthage. In the earlier war the greatest number of ships mustered by the allies was a little over thirty (4.25.1).   ἐς Τάραντα καὶ ἄκραν Ἰαπυγίαν: for Point Iapygia see **30.**1 n. The big port of Taras lay about 120 km = 75 miles NW: see Map 2.   οὐ περὶ τῆς Σικελίας . . . τὸν Ἰόνιον 'that the contest for Sicily will not come before the one that they will have to cross the Ionian sea'.   φύλακες 'as guards'.   ὑποδέχεται γὰρ ἡμᾶς Τάρας: Taras as a Spartan colony could be expected to be anti-Athenian (**34.**5), and so it was (**44.**2, **104.**1–2, 7.1.1): Fragoulaki 2013: 180–2. For the present tense in such lively predictions of the future cf. Hermocrates again at **80.**3 (προδιδόμεθα) and e.g. **91.**3, 1.121.4: it is as good as happening already. Cf. *CGCG* 33.56, Wakker 1994: 168.   τὸ δὲ πέλαγος αὐτοῖς πολὺ περαιοῦσθαι μετὰ πάσης τῆς παρασκευῆς: the alliteration would be powerful in Hermocrates' (or Th.'s) delivery.   ἡμῖν ἂν εὐεπίθετος εἴη: the implied subject is ἡ παρασκευή.   προσπίπτουσα 'running up against us'.

34.5 τῶι ταχυναυτοῦντι ἀθροωτέρωι κουφίσαντες προσβάλοιεν '. . . they were to attack with their fast ships in closer formation after lightening their load', leaving their baggage and non-combatants behind for the ὁλκάδες (**30**.1) to bring later.   ἄν . . . ἄν . . . ἄν . . . ἄν . . . ἄν: see **33–34** n. εἰ δὲ μὴ δοκοίη: after εἰ μὲν κώπαις χρήσαιντο something like 'but if they arrive under sail' is expected, but Hermocrates passes on quickly to the likely consequence in that case, 'but if we decide not to'. Stahl 2003: 196 sees the whole plan as bluff, designed as a ploy to deter Athens, and thinks that he never envisages a real fight: in that case, they would certainly 'decide not to' if the Athenian fleet did materialise.   κατὰ χωρία ἐρῆμα: strongly phrased, but it is true that between Point Iapygia and Taras there were no cities large enough to offer a market.   τὰ τῶν πόλεων οὐκ ἂν βέβαια ἔχοντες, εἰ ὑποδέξοιντο 'not being certain of the attitude of the cities, whether or not they would receive them'. εἰ ὑποδέξοιντο is indirect question.

34.6 οὐδ' ἂν ἀπᾶραι ἀπὸ Κερκύρας: again an implausible time-scale (**34**.4 n.), implying that news of all this, or at least of the Syracusan decision, could reach Corcyra before the Athenians sailed.   ὁπόσοι τ' ἐσμὲν καὶ ἐν ὧι χωρίωι: indirect question after κατασκοπαῖς, 'scouting missions [to find out]'.   τῆι ὥραι: Hermocrates is pushing his case hard here. In fact there would prove to be time for a lot of activity before winter.   τοῦ ἐμπειροτάτου . . . ἡγουμένου: Hermocrates is well informed; cf. **8**.4. Nicias is not named, perhaps 'to give the slightly grand impression that the speaker is in possession of high-level information, not all of which he chooses to disclose' (*CT*), or perhaps the name would not yet mean much to most Syracusans.   ἀσμένου ἂν πρόφασιν λαβόντος: the participial equivalent of ἄσμενος ἂν πρόφασιν λάβοι. This goes beyond Th.'s earlier narrative but is not unreasonable, especially in view of εἰ δέ τωι ἄλλως δοκεῖ, παρίημι αὐτῶι τὴν ἀρχήν (**23**.4 [n.]). Hermocrates is a better reader of Nicias than he is of the Athenians as a whole, if he thinks that the city might so readily desist.

34.7 εὖ οἶδ' ὅτι: the phrasing recurs at **34**.9: he is as confident in his judgement as in his knowledge (**32**.3 n., **33**.1). Athenagoras throws the phrase back at him at **38**.1. Here the words are inserted parenthetically, as at **68**.2 and e.g. X. *Cyr.* 3.1.22 φοβεῖταί γε μέντοι εὖ οἶδ' ὅτι μὴ πάντα τὰ ἔσχατα πάθηι.   ἐπὶ τὸ πλέον 'in exaggerated numbers'.   τοὺς προεπιχειροῦντας . . . ὅτι ἀμυνοῦνται 'those who attack them first, or at least make it clear to the attackers that they will put up a fight'. As at **34**.1

and in his εἰ δὲ μή formulations (**34**.4 n.), Hermocrates stresses that even second-bests are good enough. ἰσοκινδύνους ἡγούμενοι 'thinking that their opponents face dangers on an equal scale', rather than dangers that are much greater. Engl. would probably say e.g. 'that the dangers were the same on both sides'.

34.8 ὅτι αὐτοὺς οὐ μετὰ Λακεδαιμονίων ἐφθείρομεν: strongly put, not just 'that we did not fight against them' but 'that we did not destroy them'. There is no need to take the imperfect as conative (C–S, Spratt): Hermocrates throws in the point that the Syracusans would have made a decisive difference, and (so he says) the Athenians know it. **παρὰ γνώμην τολμήσαντας** 'that we have been bolder than they expected', i.e. contrary to the opinion (γνώμη) that the Athenians had formed. This echoes the Corinthians' view of the Athenians, παρὰ δύναμιν τολμηταὶ καὶ παρὰ γνώμην κινδυνευταί, 1.70.2, but there the γνώμη was that of the risk-takers, 'against their better judgement'; here too there is perhaps a secondary sense that such boldness would be contrary to the Syracusans' own gauging of realities, but the primary reference of γνώμη must be the judgement of the observing Athenians. **τῶι ἀδοκήτωι μᾶλλον ἂν καταπλαγεῖεν ἢ τῆι ἀπὸ τοῦ ἀληθοῦς δυνάμει:** thus a counterpart of the expedition's splendour, where appearance was no less effective than the actual resources (**31**.6). Here as there this does not preclude 'the power based on the truth of the matter' from being effective as well.

34.9 Πείθεσθε οὖν μάλιστα μὲν ταῦτα τολμήσαντες: picking up and reversing ἥκιστ' ἄν . . . πείθοισθε, **34**.4, to round off. τολμήσαντες also reverses that opening: decide this daringly, not resisting persuasion through habitual caution. **εἰ δὲ μή:** **34**.4 n. **καὶ παραστῆναι παντί:** 'and that everyone should have firmly in mind that . . .'. παραστῆναι is impersonal as at **68**.3, and comes rather awkwardly after the personal ἑτοιμάζειν. The phrasing is a favourite of Hermocrates: cf. **78**.1 and 4.61.3. **τὸ μὲν καταφρονεῖν τοὺς ἐπιόντας:** echoing **33**.3, καταφρονήσαντες, but this is now the good sort of καταφρόνησις in the battle-line. Pericles knew its value (**11**.5 and **16**.4 nn.). For καταφρονεῖν + acc. cf. 8.82.1 and Eur. *Ba.* 503 καταφρονεῖ με καὶ Θήβας ὅδε. **δείκνυσθαι:** passive, 'is (best) shown'. **τὸ δ' ἤδη . . . ἂν ξυμβῆναι** 'but the most helpful course of action would be to make preparations right away as if in the presence of danger, thinking that those made in fear are the safest'. Hermocrates has been arguing that there is no need to panic, but this is the right sort of fear (Mader 2013: 241–3): the wise Archidamus too urged the value of preparing in a fearful mindset (2.11.5). **ἐν πλῶι εὖ οἶδ' ὅτι ἤδη εἰσὶ καὶ ὅσον οὔπω πάρεισιν:** for the problematic chronology and for doubts on whether Hermocrates can really be so sure, see **32**.3–**41** n., **34**.4 n., **34**.6 n; for εὖ οἶδ' ὅτι, **34**.7 n.

35 *The Syracusan Response to Hermocrates*

35.1 τοσαῦτα here, whereas τοιαῦτα after Athenagoras (**41**.1): τοιαῦτα is more usual (**15**.1, **19**.1, **81**, **88**.1). Sometimes τοσαῦτα may convey 'so much and no more' after a short speech, as perhaps at **24**.1, **41**.4, and 7.49.1, but it is hard to find that nuance at **93**.1 or here, for Hermocrates' speech is the same length as Athenagoras'. **ἔριδι:** a strong word, not just 'disagreement' but 'strife': cf. **31.4**n. and 2.21.3, the Athenians ἐν πολλῆι ἔριδι ἦσαν on whether to go out and fight the ravaging Peloponnesians. **οἱ μὲν ... τοῖς δέ:** understand 'saying' after οἱ μέν and perhaps ἔρις ἦν with τοῖς δέ (cf. 2.54.3 ἐγένετο ... ἔρις τοῖς ἀνθρώποις μὴ λοιμὸν ὠνομάσθαι ... ἀλλὰ λιμόν), or something vaguer like 'the question in their mind being'. The shift from nom. to dat. is harsher than the reverse equivalent at **24**.3 (n.), and perhaps we should emend: see app. crit. **καὶ πάνυ καταφρονοῦντες** 'in addition (καί) were altogether contemptuous . . .'. 'In addition', because each of these counted as one of either the οἱ μέν or the τοῖς δέ. καταφρονοῦντες picks up **33**.3 and **34**.9: Hermocrates himself, they implied, was the one that really deserved contempt. **ἐς γέλωτα ἔτρεπον τὸ πρᾶγμα:** often a bad sign, as when Xerxes laughs at what Demaratus says about Sparta at Hdt. 7.105 or when the Athenians laugh at Cleon at 4.28.5 (Foster 2017: 146). 'Thucydidean laughter is vicious and derisive' (Lateiner 1977: 175 n. 6). **ὀλίγον δ' ἦν τὸ πιστεῦον τῶι Ἑρμοκράτει:** this again (**32**.3 n.) raises the question why they found an Athenian invasion so incredible. Perhaps Athenagoras' οὐ νῦν πρῶτον at **38**.2 (n.) gives a clue: had there been scaremongering before? So Green 1970: 135–6.

35.2 Ἀθηναγόρας: he appears in Th.'s narrative only here and is otherwise unknown, but his existence should not be doubted. Even historical characters' names can be suggestive: Ceccarelli 2019 cites the persuasive Peithias at 3.70.5–6 and the excellent helmsman Ariston at 7.39.2 (n.), both cases where Th.'s language underlines the pun (πείθει ... ἀναπείσειν and ἄριστος ὢν κυβερνήτης). Here the echo of Cleon (below) serves a similar purpose: this is indeed an 'Athens-type speaker'. **ὃς δήμου ... πιθανώτατος τοῖς πολλοῖς:** a resounding echo of Cleon's introduction at 3.36.6 ὢν καὶ ἐς τὰ ἄλλα βιαιότατος τῶν πολιτῶν τῶι τε δήμωι παρὰ πολὺ ἐν τῶι τότε πιθανώτατος, and 4.21.2 ἀνὴρ δημαγωγὸς κατ᾽ ἐκεῖνον τὸν χρόνον καὶ τῶι πλήθει πιθανώτατος. Th.'s audience will recognise the type.

36–40 *The speech of Athenagoras*

The speech has little effect (cf. **41**), but serves broader purposes. It emphasises the risk that Athens is taking if the rumours are true: here he often echoes Nicias, as does Hermocrates, but Athenagoras thinks that Athens would therefore not do it. The reader already knows that he is wrong. It also illuminates the rancorous political atmosphere (**32.3–41** n.), so reminiscent of Athens. This prepares for the distrust felt of Hermocrates at **103**.4 (n.). Th. may also have intended to build on these suspicions in his planned narrative of later events, especially Hermocrates' own failed coup of 408 BCE (**33–34** n.) and the subsequent tyranny of Dionysius I from 405; for all we know, Athenagoras may himself have played a role in those events. But we can only speculate.

Why does Th. gives this defence of democracy to the non-Athenian Athenagoras rather than, say, Pericles, whose Funeral Speech (echoed here, but only a little) is more focused on the Athenian way of life than on the constitution? It may be partly because Athenian democracy stood in no need of defence during Pericles' lifetime, whereas constitutional issues will feature prominently from now on. That would have been true with Syracuse (Intr., 34) had Th. completed that narrative; it will also be the case within Athens when Bk. 8 reaches the reforms of 411 BCE. The issues can be aired now so that they need not be revisited in Athens; there may be added clarity in analysing them outside Athens, where circumstances were complicated and the outcome was mixed rather than a clear partisan victory (8.97) and anyway did not last.

Th.'s first listeners and readers would have had mixed responses. Th. himself was no democrat (8.97.2), and hardly intended the defence to be self-evidently cogent; unlike the Funeral Speech, it is not delivered by an impressive character.

36.1 Τοὺς μὲν Ἀθηναίους ὅστις μὴ βούλεται οὕτω: a hexameter, though not an elegant one. Hexameters that are presumably accidental are found in Th. (e.g. 1.38.2 with *CT*, 4.57.4) as in other prose authors (Page 1959: 211–12 n. 73 collects cases from Demosthenes), but some cases look expressive, e.g. the near-hexameter rhythm of the climactic 1.21.2, δηλώσει ὅμως μείζων γεγενημένος αὐτῶν (of the scale of the Peloponnesian War), and perhaps 4.85.5. The same can be said of Herodotus, esp. Syagrus at 7.159. Coincidence is especially unlikely here in an opening, just as it is in the first sentences of Tacitus' *Annals* and of Livy's history. The effect is hard to gauge, as neither character nor topic is especially poetic or heroic. Perhaps the impression is one of pretentiousness. Cf. Moles 1993: 103; Hornblower 1994a: 66; Boedeker 2001: 123–4; Grethlein 2010: 162.   **ἢ τῆι πόλει οὐκ εὔνους:** denigration of an opponent's motives is a regular demagogic trick (e.g. Cleon at 3.38.2 with Macleod 1978: 69 = 1983: 93; Diodotus replies in kind, 3.42.2); cf. **12.2**. Here it prepares for the more elaborate attack of **38**.   **τῆς μὲν τόλμης:** echoing Hermocrates' peroration, **34**.8 and 9. The point is that there is τόλμα around already – but not of a good sort.   τῆς δὲ ἀξυνεσίας: the ξυνετοί will be important at **39**.1 (nn.), and the antagonists ἀξυνετώτατοι again at **40**.1. But for Th. Hermocrates will be the man of ξύνεσις (**72**.2), and that is high praise (**54**.5 n.).

36.2 οἱ γὰρ δεδιότες ἰδίᾳ τι 'the people who have something to fear on their own account', i.e. Hermagoras and his supporters. This could be taken as a statement about humans in general (P–S), but does not need to be.   **ἔκπληξιν:** like καταπλήξαντας at **38**.2 and καταπλαγεῖσα at **40**.2, this again picks up Hermocrates' language: Hermocrates claimed that there is no need to be terrified (**33**.4) and hoped to terrify the Athenians instead (**34**.4, **34**.6), but – says Athenagoras – he still has ἔκπληξις in mind, and its target is yourselves.   **τὸ σφέτερον** 'their own business', what they are up to – anti-democratic plotting (**38**). τό is the MSS reading. The schol. and Valla (Intr., 36) possibly read τόν, i.e. 'their own φόβος', and this is preferred by many editors; but the vaguer the language, the more sinister the suggestion.   **ἐπηλυγάζωνται** 'mask', put up a barrier to sight as one might shade one's eyes (Arist. *GA* 780b19, 781b12) or lurk behind others (Plato, *Lys.* 207b). Ar. *Ach.* 684 uses ἠλύγη of speakers in the law-courts, casting 'fog' over the truth.   **ἀπὸ ταὐτομάτου** 'spontaneously'.   **τάδε κινοῦσι** 'agitating in this way'.   **ξύγκεινται:** serving as the passive of ξυντίθημι (**32**.2 n.), 'are put together'.

36.3 λογιεῖσθε τὰ εἰκότα 'you will work out what is likely to be true': picked up in εἰκός, **36**.4. Reasoning on the basis of εἰκός had been refined in fifth-century rhetorical theory and practice; it was particularly associated with the Sicilians Corax and Teisias, but there is no need to find a Sicilian tinge in its use here. Nicias tried something of the same at **11**.3 and **20**.1.   **δεινοὶ καὶ πολλῶν ἔμπειροι:** yet ἄπειροι concerning Sicily (**1**.1).   **ἀξιῶ** 'think it right' to see them as, 'rate' them.

36.4 Πελοποννησίους . . . ἐρχόμεθα: closely echoing Nicias: with ὑπολιπόντας cf. **10**.1; with τὸν ἐκεῖ πόλεμον μήπω βεβαίως καταλελυμένους cf. **10**.2–3 (n.) and **10**.5 (and also Hermocrates, τὸν ἐκεῖ πόλεμον at **34**.3); with ἐπ' ἄλλον πόλεμον οὐκ ἐλάσσω, cf. **20–3** and Th.'s authorial comment at **1**.1; with ἀγαπᾶν . . . ἐρχόμεθα, cf. **10**.2 and **11**.2–3.   **ἀγαπᾶν** 'to be content'.   **πόλεις τοσαῦται καὶ οὕτω μεγάλαι:** as at **37**.1 (Σικελίαν) and **37**.2 (ξυστήσεται γάρ), Athenagoras, unlike Hermocrates, takes a degree of Sicilian unity for granted.

37.1 διαπολεμῆσαι 'to carry the war through' to its end, as at 7.14.3 and Hdt. 7.158.5. This goes with the emphasis on Sicily's depth of resources: those are what are needed to see through a long war. Cf. Pericles at

2.13.2–9 on the strengths giving confidence that Athens would περιέσεσθαι, as much 'come through' as 'be superior'. ὥς φασιν 'so they say' or 'as they describe it': Athenagoras of course does not believe it is coming at all. ἐπίσταμαι 'I am quite certain': this is often a better translation than 'I know' (Hornblower 2004: 110 n. 94). Athenagoras is not claiming superior information, but drawing inferences (εἰκός again): there is only so much one can pack on a ship and only so many horses they can expect to collect on the spot. ἀκολουθήσοντας . . . πορισθησομένους: for the sake of argument, Athenagoras for the moment treats the rumours as true. οὔθ' . . . οὐδ' . . . οὔθ' . . . τε . . .: οὔθ' . . . οὔθ' give two categories, horses and hoplites, that cannot be transported in numbers, with the οὐδέ clause added parenthetically within the first to deal with a possible extra source; then τε . . . adds a further point in coordination with οὔθ' . . . οὔθ'. εἰ μὴ ὀλίγους τινὰς παρ' Ἐγεσταίων: Athenagoras is on the whole right about this (just 300 from Egesta, **98**.1, cf. **62**.3), though a few other cities provided some to make up 650 (**98**.1) with the 30 + 250 from Athens (**43**, **94**.4). It was not enough: Intr., 6. Nicias already had forebodings, **21**.1 n. οὔθ' ὁπλίτας ἰσοπληθεῖς τοῖς ἡμετέροις: cf. **23**.1 n. ἐπὶ νεῶν γε ἐλθόντας 'given that they would have come on ships'. μέγα γὰρ . . . κομισθῆναι 'for it is a big thing to complete a voyage here of that length even with the ships themselves, unladen', and so there is even more constraint on how many hoplites can be shipped. τοσοῦτον πλοῦν is acc. of space traversed. τήν τε ἄλλην παρασκευήν . . . οὐκ ὀλίγην οὖσαν: still dependent on ἐπίσταμαι.

37.2 παρὰ τοσοῦτον γιγνώσκω 'I even express this opinion', lit. 'to such an extent do I think . . .': inserted parenthetically, like εὖ οἶδ' ὅτι at **34**.7 (n.). εἰ πόλιν ἑτέραν . . . ἔχοντες: again echoing Nicias, **23**.2 n. The analogy with a city on the move is important (**44**.1 n., Intr., 1), but Athenagoras dismisses it as a ridiculous fantasy. ἦ πού γε δή 'far less', lit. 'surely I think . . . at least', an idiomatic way to introduce the punchline of an *a fortiori* argument (*GP* 281–2): cf. 1.142.3, it is hard enough to construct a military fortification in peacetime, ἦ που δή at war in hostile territory. σκηνιδίων 'little tents': Athenagoras speaks dismissively. The word is not found again until Cassius Dio (43.32.7, 60.33.3c), doubtless echoing Th. ἀναγκαίας 'basic'. οὐκ ἐπὶ πολὺ ὑπὸ τῶν ἡμετέρων ἱππέων ἐξιόντες 'not going far' from their makeshift camp 'under pressure from our cavalry'. This was what Nicias feared, **21**.1, and he was right, 7.4.6. τό τε ξύμπαν 'and to sum it all up': cf. Hermocrates at 4.63.2. κρατῆσαι . . . τῆς γῆς 'establish themselves on the land', again echoing Nicias, **23**.2. κρείσσω νομίζω: echoing **37**.1 to round off the point.

38.1 ταῦτα: perhaps just the obj. of γιγνώσκοντες, with the Athenians 'recognising' those strategic realities, but a different aspect of 'these things' may extend to λογοποιοῦσιν, his Syracusan antagonists 'making up' these false reports. **εὖ οἶδ' ὅτι:** Athenagoras is as certain as Hermocrates (**34**.7, **34**.9 nn.), though with a different sort of reasoning (**36**.3 n.). **λογοποιοῦσιν:** 'λογοποιία is the fabrication of false words and deeds', Theophr. *Char.* 8.1.

38.2 οὐ νῦν πρῶτον: cf. ὃ πολλάκις ἐσκεψάμην, **38**.5. Cleon similarly has 'πολλάκις . . . ἤδη thought the same thing' as he does over Mytilene (3.37.1). It is a conventional way of underlining the speaker's insight as well as giving a reason for thinking that the same is true again (Macleod 1978: 68 = 1983: 92). Maybe there had indeed been false reports before: **35**.1 n. **ἤτοι . . . ἤ:** also at **34**.2 and **40**.1. In other authors this seems little different from ἤ . . . ἤ, but Th. uses it only in speeches and 'this suggests that he felt τοι as vivid in the combination' (*GP* 553). If so, it is probably to emphasise the disjunction rather than put extra weight on one or the other. These plotters are always up to something, in word or in deed. **κακουργοτέροις:** the mild wordplay within the λόγοι/ἔργα distinction – these λόγοι themselves produce, or have the effect of, κακὰ ἔργα – may prepare for the peroration of **40**.2 (n.), τούς τε λόγους . . . ὡς ἔργα δυναμένους. **βουλομένους καταπλήξαντας . . . ἄρχειν:** καταπλήξαντας (**36**.2 n.) goes closely with ἄρχειν to define how they wish to achieve it. **κακοί:** with the two infs., 'we are bad at . . .'.

38.3 ὀλιγάκις μὲν ἡσυχάζει: perhaps again a barbed echo of Hermocrates (τὸ ξύνηθες ἥσυχον, **34.4**): there is less ἡσυχία here than he claimed, and it is his cronies' fault. **στάσεις δὲ πολλάς . . . ἀναιρεῖται:** 5.1 n. **τυραννίδας δὲ ἔστιν ὅτε καὶ δυναστείας ἀδίκους:** especially the tyranny of the Deinomenids (Gelon, Hieron, and Thrasybulus) from 485 to 465. It is harder to identify a phase of δυναστεῖαι, which probably means a narrow oligarchy (3.62.3, 4.78.3); this does not really fit the 'old' citizens who after the tyranny clashed with the 'new' ones that Gelon had enfranchised (Diod. 11.72–3, 76). In 454/3 Tyndarides was executed for, according to Diod. 11.86.4, 'aspiring to a δυναστεία', but there it probably = 'tyranny'. Still, it is not unusual for politicians to claim that the elite has enjoyed too much control, whatever the constitution, and they are often right. Th.'s first audiences may have known that a further tyranny was soon to come, that of Dionysius I, and so Athenagoras' scaremongering was not baseless: see introductory nn. to **33–34** and **36–40**.

38.4 μήποτε ἐφ' ἡμῶν τι περιιδεῖν γενέσθαι: περιορᾶν + inf. = to allow something to happen by turning a blind eye; + participle would = to turn a blind eye while it is happening (*M&T* 903.6). Cleon seems to have styled himself the people's watchdog (Ar. *Wasps* 902, *Knights* 1017–19, 1024–5), and later demagogues adopted the image: Dem. 25.40, Theophr. *Char.* 29.5, Plut. *Dem.* 23.5; cf. Brock 2013a: 156. ὑμᾶς μὲν τοὺς πολλοὺς πείθων . . . τοὺς δὲ τὰ τοιαῦτα μηχανωμένους . . . τοὺς δ' αὖ ὀλίγους: there are three groups, 'the many', 'the plotters', and 'the few', i.e. those among the elite who were non-plotters but had oligarchic sympathies. *HCT* and Alberti delete the first δέ and emend κολάζων to κολάζειν: that makes Athenagoras persuade the people to 'punish' the plotters rather than claim in advance the credit for himself, but such an anticipatory brag seems in character for Athenagoras. μέν . . . δέ . . . δ' αὖ is not found elsewhere in Th., but cf. e.g. Hdt. 7.23.1, Ar. *Frogs* 290, X. *Hell.* 4.8.28, Plato, *Gorg.* 491c, *Rep.* 4.436a. Here it eases the rhythm of the complicated sentence, introducing a third group as well as the more expected 'many' and 'plotters'. Engl. too might say 'and those, again, . . .'. ἐπιτυγχάνειν 'catch them' in action, '*deprehendere*' (Bétant): not just 'meet with' (LSJ), as frighteningly one meets these people every day without sensing what they are up to. The meaning here may come from ἐπιτυγχάνειν as 'get what one wants', as at 3.42.6 (ὁ μὴ ἐπιτυχών contrasted with ὁ κατορθῶν), and/or from understanding <αὐτῶν μηχανωμένων>. ὧν: gen. 'denoting the crime', *GG* 1121, really a subclass of gen. of cause, *GG* 1126. προαμύνεσθαι . . . προφυλαξάμενος . . . προπείσεται: the προ- prefixes recall how in *stasis* 'the person earned praise who got in first against someone else planning harm . . .', 3.82.5. Even as he attacks his opponents for generating *stasis* Athenagoras plays the στασιώτης. τὰ μὲν ἐλέγχων, τὰ δὲ φυλάσσων, τὰ δὲ καὶ διδάσκων: different approaches for people who might be more or less sympathetic to oligarchic ideas. ἀποτρέπειν: the equivalent of an opt. in direct speech.

38.5 ὃ πολλάκις ἐσκεψάμην: **38**.2 n. τί καὶ βούλεσθε . . . ; the sharp question would be even more striking in delivery, as Athenagoras is imagined as turning to face his adversaries. The technical term for the imagined suggestions is 'hypophora' ('putting forward'), and the repeated ἀλλά is typical: cf. 1.80.4: how are we to fight? πότερον ταῖς ναυσίν; ἀλλ' ἥσσους ἐσμέν. ἀλλὰ τοῖς χρήμασιν; ἀλλὰ πολλῶι πλέον ἔτι τούτου ἐλλείπομεν; Dem. 18.24 with Yunis' n.; *GP* 10–11. ὦ νεώτεροι: Hermocrates himself was no longer young, for he was senior enough to be entrusted with delicate diplomacy at Gela nine years earlier, but he may have been a figurehead for a younger generation: οἵ τε δυνάμενοι καὶ οἱ νέοι suggests as much (**39**.2). Still, the emphasis fits the stereotype of the young, well-born and rich as prone to anti-democratic plotting (Forrest 1975; Ostwald 1986: 232–4, cf. **15**.4). This also recalls Nicias' generational divisiveness (**13**.1 n.). πότερον ἄρχειν ἤδη; ἀλλ' οὐκ ἔννομον: little is known of the Syracusan constitution

(Intr., 34), but lower age-limits on office were not unusual. ὁ δὲ νόμος
... ἀτιμάζειν: 'the law was passed as a result of your incapacity to rule, not to dishonour people who were capable of it'. ἀλλὰ δὴ μὴ μετὰ πολλῶν ἰσονομεῖσθαι; 'Or (do you wish) not to be governed along with many others under laws applying equally to everyone?' ἰσονομία, a democratic catchword, is not quite 'equality before the law', as even in Athens ζευγῖται were only admitted to the archonship in 457/6 and θῆτες not even then, but the principle is that the laws embrace everyone (2.37.1, cf. Hdt. 3.80.6, 83.1): Pelling 2019: 191 and 291 nn. 7–8.

39.1 φήσει τις δημοκρατίαν οὔτε ξυνετὸν οὔτ' ἴσον εἶναι: the 'someone will say' trope (e.g. Hdt. 4.97.5, Dem. 3.34, 21.89) is given an ironic twist, for this is what 'someone' will indeed soon say, Alcibiades at Sparta: democracy is 'acknowledged folly' (89.6). 'Not an intelligent thing' is an unsurprising claim: in Hdt.'s constitutions debate Megabyxus says 'nothing is ἀξυνετώτερον or more violent than a useless mob', and asks 'how *could* a *dēmos* have any understanding, when it has had no education nor any familiarity with anything fine . . .?' (Hdt. 3.81.1–2); cf. e.g. Eur. *Suppl.* 417–25 and 481–5. To attack democracy as 'not an equal thing' is more striking, as ἰσότης, ἰσονομία, ἰσηγορία, ἰσοκρατία, and here ἰσομοιρεῖν were democratic slogans (Pelling 2019: 193–5). The argument of this 'someone' would be that there is no equality in denying a superior individual the rights to match his qualities. Thus Isoc. 7.21 distinguishes two sorts of equality, one giving the same to everyone and the other giving everyone their due; Plato's 'geometric equality' (*Gorg.* 507a, *Laws* 6.757b--c) is based on a similar principle, whereas for him democracy 'awards some sort of equality to equal and unequal alike' (*Rep.* 8.558c). καὶ ἄρχειν ἄριστα βελτίστους: the odd phrasing relies on the familiarity of βέλτιστοι as an oligarchic slogan (ps.-Xen. *Ath. pol.* 1.5, 3.10–11, Arist. *Pol.* 2. 1273a33, etc.): 'the "best", indeed – at ruling best'. The principle is captured in the story of Hdt. 5.29, where the Parian arbitrators note down the names of those with the best-kept estates and appoint them to control the state, 'thinking that these would take the same care of public business as they did of their own'. Athenagoras partly concedes the point in φύλακας μὲν ἀρίστους εἶναι χρημάτων τοὺς πλουσίους (n.). δῆμον ξύμπαν ὠνομάσθαι '"people" is the name for the whole'. Athenagoras gives a rather feeble twist to the sonorous commonplace 'in name it is called democracy' (2.37.1 with *CT*; Loraux 1986: ch. IV). The point is normally that this is the 'fairest of names': thus Otanes at Hdt. 3.80.6, though the 'name' is ἰσονομίη there and at Th. 3.82.8. Athenagoras is less celebratory, though he can take the resonance for granted; his point may be that a whole is greater than a part, or along the lines that we call this a democracy, and that means everyone. He exploits the ambiguity in δῆμος, which can mean either, as he presents it here, the whole civic community or, as at **35**.2, the commons as opposed to the elite: Moggi 2005: esp. 17–19; Saïd 2013: 201. **ὀλιγαρχίαν:** here = the ὀλίγοι who would then rule.   **φύλακας μὲν . . . τοὺς πολλούς:** the first clause has no ἄν, because it partly concedes the antagonists' claim about the abilities of the wealthy; the second and third do, as they qualify this by insisting that this is not enough to cope with each issue as it might come up (cf. Andrews 1992: 8). Engl. might capture this by translating the first clause 'Whereas . . .'. The argument becomes more interesting, and can even be seen as a prefiguring of later justifications for a 'mixed constitution' as combining the best of each constituent, though constitutionally the 'mix' is usually monarchy, oligarchy, and democracy: Athenagoras says that democracy itself gives room for each group to do what they do best. There are similarities too to Alcibiades' argument that a city does best when it allows a mixture of τό τε φαῦλον καὶ τὸ μέσον καὶ τὸ πάνυ ἀκριβές (**18**.6), though Alcibiades – wisely (n.) – did not specify what each of his categories means or what role they should fulfil.   **βουλεῦσαι δ' ἂν βέλτιστα τοὺς ξυνετούς:** picking up ξυνετόν: a δῆμος needs its intelligent δημαγωγοί, and Athenagoras would not diminish the role he would play himself. He is less extreme than Cleon, who argued that οἱ φαυλότεροι run their cities better than οἱ ξυνετώτεροι and deprecated any competition in ξύνεσις (3.37.3–5; see next n.).   **κρῖναι δ' ἂν ἀκούσαντας ἄριστα τοὺς πολλούς:** cf. the views on the people as κριταί voiced by Pericles, 'we judge . . . not by thinking words any impediment to action, but prefer to be instructed in advance' (2.40.2), and by Cleon, people 'get more things right when they judge on an equal basis rather than in a spirit of competition' (that is, after evaluating the rival arguments of clever speakers), 3.37.4. Athenagoras' ἀκούσαντας aligns more with Pericles than with Cleon, but Athenagoras' divisive factionalism embodies a very different style of leadership (Yunis 1991: 188–90; Mader 2013: 253–4). The pros and cons of entrusting decisions to a non-expert majority are weighed by Arist. *Pol.* 1281b39–1282a23: cf. Hansen 1991: 306–7, and more generally on this and other defences of democracy Raaflaub 1989. Recent discussion has been coloured by evidence that a diverse large group can make better decisions than a smaller number of more able people (the 'Diversity trumps ability' thesis: Hong and Page 2004): the implications for democracy are discussed by e.g. Landemore 2013: esp. chs. 4 and 6 and Allen 2018: 80–6.   **καὶ ταῦτα ὁμοίως . . . ἰσομοιρεῖν** 'and in a democracy these (three groups? three capacities?) have an equal share, both in the parts and in the whole'. For ἰσομοιρεῖν cf. **16**.4, where Alcibiades has a different idea of equality. κατὰ μέρη καὶ ξύμπαντα picks up ξύμπαν and μέρος, but it is hard to catch the point. Probably it is just 'politician's verbiage' (*CT*).

39.2 οὐ πλεονεκτεῖ... ἔχει: an oligarch would reply that it is the *dēmos* that takes away what is, or should be, the property of the rich (ps.-Xen. *Ath. pol. passim*). **ἃ ὑμῶν... κατασχεῖν:** ἃ is internal acc. with προθυμοῦνται, then ἔστιν is understood with ἀδύνατα, 'these are impossible to achieve'. κατασχεῖν conveys both the 'obtaining' of power (LSJ κατέχω II) and the subsequent 'holding it down' (LSJ I). For the combination of 'the men of power' and 'the young' see **38**.5 n.

40.1 (Some texts, including the OCT, have the words down to τολμᾶτε as still part of **39**.2) **ὦ πάντων ἀξυνετώτατοι:** picking up ξυνετόν and ξυνετούς from **39**.1. The imagined objector there was clearly thinking of himself as one of the 'intelligent': Athenagoras retorts that his antagonists have shown themselves unworthy of the term. **εἰ <γὰρ>... τολμᾶτε** 'for you are either the worst learners of any Greeks I know, if you are not learning that your objectives are evil, or the most unjust, if you know that but boldly go ahead anyway'. εἰ... σπεύδοντες is advanced before the first ἢ to give a chiastic structure. For the play with derogatory alternatives cf. Diodotus at 3.42.2–3, anyone who disagrees is either ἀξύνετος, if A, or out for his own interests, if B. <γὰρ> and a parenthesis, as proposed by Gomme 1920: 84–5, elegantly restores logic to the ἀξυνετώτατοι... ἢ ἀμαθέστατοι... ἢ ἀδικώτατοι string. **ἀλλ' ἤτοι μαθόντες γε ἢ μεταγνόντες** 'either learning your lesson [if you are ἀμαθέστατοι] or changing your ways [if ἀδικώτατοι]'. ἀλλ' resumes the construction of ἀλλ' ἔτι καὶ νῦν... On ἤτοι... ἢ see **38**.2 n. **τὸ τῆς πόλεως ξύμπασι κοινόν** 'the city's interest that is common to everyone'. **ἡγησάμενοι... μετασχεῖν** 'thinking that in this way [internal acc.] the good among you will get your fair share and more than your fair share of what the mass of the city obtains'; or, if οἱ ἀγαθοί goes more specifically with πλέον, 'you will get your fair share, and the good among you more than your fair share...'.

40.2 στρατηγοί εἰσιν ἡμῖν οἳ σκέψονται αὐτά: in fact fifteen of them, **72**.4. This prepares for the interjection of the στρατηγός at **41**, but Athenagoras' own point goes with what follows: do not think that *you* will be appointed to deal with the emergency. **ὥσπερ οὐκ οἴομαι:** Engl. would say 'as I think' rather than 'do not think', though in Engl. too a fuller expression might be 'as I do not think any of it to be true'. **οὐ... ἐπιβαλεῖται:** Athenagoras spells out more closely the plot, as he sees it (**36**.1–2, **38**.1–2) – to be given emergency powers for the crisis, then to hang on to them once it fails to materialise. Something like the first step does in fact happen at **73**.1 (**72–73** n.), with Hermocrates appointed as one of three στρατηγοί

to replace the fifteen. For καταπλαγεῖσα see **36**.2 n.   **αὐτὴ δ' ἐφ' αὑτῆς
... σώιζειν:** the peroration echoes several words from earlier: for 'words having the same effect as deeds' cf. λόγοις . . . κακουργοτέροις, **38**.1 n.; for κρινεῖ and ἀκούειν, **39**.1, though this ἀκούειν is listening to rumours rather than counsel; for φυλασσομένη, **38**.4; for μὴ ἐπιτρέπειν, **40**.1.   **τούς τε λόγους ἀφ' ὑμῶν:** for the omission of a second τούς see **33**.1 n.   **τὴν ὑπάρχουσαν ἐλευθερίαν οὐχὶ ἐκ τοῦ ἀκούειν ἀφαιρεθήσεται** 'will not be robbed of its existing liberty on the basis of hearsay'. ἀφαιρέομαι (middle) can take a double acc. of the thing taken and the person it is taken from; in the passive, the person becomes nom. and the acc. is retained for the thing (LSJ III, *CGCG* 30.9). Cf. **24**.2n.   **ἐκ δὲ τοῦ ἔργωι φυλασσομένη μὴ ἐπιτρέπειν** 'through prevention by taking measures to protect itself ', lit. 'through not allowing (you to get away with it), guarding itself through action'. φυλασσομένη is middle.

41 *The Speech of the Unnamed General*

This is a reminder 'that this is not quite Athens after all' (*CT*), for the general can stifle popular debate; still, even at Athens Pericles could refuse to convene an assembly when he expected it to reach the wrong conclusion (2.22.1). Without naming Athenagoras, the speaker clearly rebukes him for his partisan attack but also echoes him (**40**.2) in saying that the generals will take care of it all. They have indeed already taken measures (**41**.4), apparently without telling the assembly, for neither Hermocrates nor Athenagoras has shown any knowledge of these. Hermocrates' advice is taken, but only to a degree: delegations will be sent around, but 'to scout things out' (cf. **45**). That is weaker than Hermocrates' quest for firm alliances: ἤν τι ἄλλο φαίνηται ἐπιτήδειον is much vaguer. Embassies are sent to Corinth and Sparta (**34**.3) only at **73**.2 and not sent to Carthage (**34**.2) at all. The grand plan of **34**.4–8 is simply ignored. It is all 'decidedly half-hearted' (Hunter 1973: 155). More energy will be injected at **45**.

41.1 τῶν δὲ στρατηγῶν εἷς: one of the fifteen (**72**.4, **40**.2 nn.), probably presiding over the assembly, though it is also possible that οὐκ ἐᾶν is here used in the sense of 'urged not to' rather than 'forbade'. Why is he unnamed? Perhaps it indicates that his authority comes by dint of the office: the 'primadonnas' (*CT* ii. 137 n. 35) have had their say, and now the no-nonsense general speaks 'for Syracuse'. Or maybe Th. just did not know.   **αὐτὸς δέ:** i.e. he spoke 'himself' rather than leaving the floor to other speakers.   **πρὸς τὰ παρόντα** 'in response to the situation'. Not superfluous, because the general's emphasis will be that the situation does indeed require some response.

41.2 τοὺς ἐπιόντας: thus accepting at least provisionally that the Athenians will come, though **41.3** allows for the alternative possibility too.

41.3 οἷς ὁ πόλεμος ἀγάλλεται 'glorifies' or 'exults', almost 'preens itself': like κοσμηθῆναι the powerful word suggests display, continuing the emphasis in the Athenian preparations of **30–31**. For the personification of war cf. 1.122.1, 3.82.2, 4.18.4. In language, the general is not so down-to-earth as all that. **τὴν δ' ἐπιμέλειαν . . . ἡμεῖς ἕξομεν:** the parenthesis qualifies the first of the two measures, not because the generals are taking no 'care' for the second but because 'review' (ἐξέτασιν) is more appropriate to equipment than to delegations: cf. **45**.

41.4 τῶν πρὸς τὰς πόλεις διαπομπῶν: 'the' delegations, i.e. the ones Hermocrates proposed, **34**.1. **τὰ δὲ καί** 'other things too . . .', not necessarily anything that either Hermocrates or Athenagoras has urged. **οἴσομεν** 'we will bring before you'. The verb leaves it unclear whether for decision or just for report.

42–46: ARRIVAL

The narrative turns from Syracusan talk to Athenian action: the repeated ἤδη (3x in **42–44**) underlines that the moment has come. The account of the crossing reflects earlier points, the massive παρασκευή (**30–32**.2, **43** nn.), the feel of a city on the move (**1**.2–**5**.3, **23**.2, **37**.2 nn.), the difficulties of finding anchorage for so large a force (**21**.1, **23**.2, **33**.5, **37**.2 nn.); it also shows the Athenians facing the problems with experienced caution (**42**). The Syracusans too are moved to urgency (**45**, ἤδη again). But things also begin to go wrong for Athens: they do not find the friendly ports they had hoped for (**44**.2–3), perhaps because of those vast numbers, and disappointing news arrives from Egesta (**46**.1–3). It will not be easy to know how to respond: **47–50**.1.

42.1 Οἱ δ' Ἀθηναῖοι . . . ἦσαν: the crisp sentence, esp. ἤδη, quickly gives the lie to Athenagoras' scepticism. On the chronology see **32**.3–**41** n. **ἐπεξέτασιν** 'an additional review', now that 'the other allies' (**30**.1, **32**.2 nn.) had joined them. **ὁρμιεῖσθαί τε καὶ στρατοπεδεύεσθαι:** the combination of future and present infs. is odd, but such variation is a feature of Th.'s style. It may reflect the way that 'coming into anchor' is a single future act, but 'being in camp' will be a longer process. **ἐκλήρωσαν** 'allotted', though with a stronger literal sense of the lot than in Engl.: cf. **62**.1 (λαχών) and 8.30.1. **ἐν ταῖς καταγωγαῖς:** regular practice would be to go ashore each night when practicable. **κατὰ τέλη** 'in divisions' or 'squadrons', ones worked out *ad hoc* as at 1.48.3.

42.2 εἴρητο 'they had been instructed' before their despatch. προαπαντᾶν 'come to meet them in advance', while the fleet was still out to sea.

43 *The Size of the Athenian Force*

30–32.2 had stressed the massiveness, but with more emphasis on the spectacle and on the ships: land forces were mentioned, but their numbers are given here, now that all have coalesced. 'Catalogues' had been used to presage fighting from *Il.* 2 on (7.57–59.1 n.), and this reinforces the notion that the action is about to start. The numbers here and later pose intricate problems: cf. 7.42.1 nn. and see *CT* 1061–6 for detailed discussion. τοσῇδε ἤδη τῇ παρασκευῇ: ἤδη goes closely with τοσῇδε (**45** n.): the gathering forces had swollen to such numbers. For παρασκευή cf. **1.1** n. ἐπεραιοῦντο: the imperfect, like those at **44**.1, is often used of journeys preliminary to the main action (Huitink–Rood on X. *Anab.* 3.3.6). It is both inceptive ('set off') and one of process ('were on their way'), *CGCG* 33.52 n. 1. δυοῖν Ῥοδίοιν πεντηκοντόροιν: Rhodes was Dorian; 7.57.6 and 9 note the paradox of the support for Athens. Unlike Chios and Lesbos (**85**.2 n.), Rhodes also paid tribute, so the further contribution of ships and slingers (below) may suggest either particular enthusiasm or private initiative. The island went over to Sparta in 412/11 (8.44). Cf. *IACP* 1205–6. αἱ μὲν ἑξήκοντα ταχεῖαι, αἱ δ' ἄλλαι στρατιώτιδες: as at **31**.3 (n.), cf. **25**.2. The στρατιώτιδες here = the ὁπλιταγωγοί of **25**.2 and **31**.3. On the logistics of their crewing see Wallinga 1993: 174–7 and *CT* 1063–5: to make room for the hoplites there were presumably many fewer rowers than in a trireme, for it was exceptional for hoplites themselves to row (3.18.4). Χίων καὶ τῶν ἄλλων ξυμμάχων: esp. Methymna, the other city still contributing ships rather than money (**85**.2 n., 7.57.5); also Corcyra and Cephallenia, 7.57.7. Some of these ships too may have been troop-carriers or at least dual-purpose. ἐκ καταλόγου: **31**.3 n. ἑπτακόσιοι δὲ θῆτες ἐπιβάται τῶν νεῶν: contrasting (μὲν . . . δέ) with ἐκ καταλόγου, so these were volunteers: ctr. 8.24.2, where the marines too have been conscripted ἐκ καταλόγου. This is Th.'s only reference to *thētes*, the lowest property class as defined in Solon's constitution (*Ath. pol.* 7.3–4): that was probably still relevant in making service compulsory for the higher classes but voluntary for the *thētes* (van Wees 2006: 371–6), though Rosivach 2012 argues that the word here refers less technically to poor casual labourers. In any case, these *thētes* were not too poor to afford hoplite equipment, though the anticipated rewards (**24**.3) may have made this seem a big but good investment. Alberti prints ἑξακόσιοι (H²), presumably assuming 10 marines for each of the 60 Athenian triremes, but that assumption seems over-rigorous (Jordan 1975: 184–95) and it is unlikely that any fit and equipped *thētes* were turned away. **Ἀργείων... καὶ Μαντινέων: 29**.3 n. Not all would be mercenaries: Nicias had talked of recruiting Peloponnesians 'either by persuasion or by pay' (**22**), and at 7.57.9 some of the Argives are driven by anti-Spartan animosity. But 7.57.9 also implies that the Mantineans at least were largely or wholly mercenaries; and καί before μισθοφόρων effectively = 'and more generally' (Verdenius 1954), as at Plato, *Theaet.* 145a, καὶ ἀστρονομικὸς καὶ λογιστικός τε καὶ μουσικὸς καὶ ὅσα παιδείας δεῖται. **τοξόταις ... Κρῆτες:** as with Rhodes, Crete had been involved in the foundation of Gela (**4**.3), so they too were fighting against kin (7.57.9). **Μεγαρεῦσι ψιλοῖς φυγάσιν:** they had taken refuge in Athens after domestic *stasis* in 424 (4.74.2): cf. 7.57.8. **σφενδονήταις Ῥοδίων:** Rhodes was as renowned for its slingers (Huitink–Rood on X. *Anab.* 3.3.16) as Crete for its archers (**25**.2 n.). **ἱππαγωγῶι μιᾶι τριάκοντα ἀγούσηι ἱππέας:** but only one and only thirty: for this important deficiency see **21**.2, **31**.2, **37**.2 nn. and Intr., 6. Even these thirty are not present in battle at **64**.1, and Bugh 1989 suggests that their function was mainly to act as 'couriers and scouts'.

44.1 ἡ πρώτη παρασκευή: 30.1 n. **διέπλει... ξυνέπλει... ξυνηκολούθουν ... ξυνδιέβαλλε:** for the imperfects see **43**.1 n. **τοὺς σιτοποιούς:** 'the' bakers, as already familiar from Nicias' proposal at **22**. **λιθολόγους καὶ τέκτονας:** mentioned together again at 7.43.2 and X. *Hell.* 4.8.10: so siegecraft and circumvallation were anticipated from the outset. τέκτονες, 'carpenters', work mainly with wood, while λιθολόγοι are 'stone-gatherers', a skilled job when stones need to fit tightly together (cf. **66**.2, **98**.3, 4.31.2): 'λιθολόγοι say that without the small stones the big ones do not sit solidly' (Plato, *Laws* 10.902e). The 'stone-workers' (λιθουργοι) mentioned at 4.69.2 and, again with τέκτονες, at 5.82.6 are probably the same people, as collecting and fitting were part of the same job. Several late lexica gloss λιθολόγος simply by 'builder'. **ὅσα ἐς τειχισμὸν ἐργαλεῖα:** the tools that were lacking in the early stages of the Sphacteria exchanges, 4.4.2. Even in this campaign more were needed: 7.18.4. **πλοῖα ... ἃ ἐξ ἀνάγκης μετὰ τῶν ὁλκάδων ξυνέπλει:** triremes who 'had to' (ἐξ ἀνάγκης) escort the convoy as a matter of military necessity: see on ναυσί ... ἐσκομιζώμεθα, **22** n. This need not imply compulsory requisitioning. **ἑκούσιοι:** contrasting with ἐξ ἀνάγκης, and masc. by sense-construction for the men in them: cf. 1.110.4 τριήρεις ... οὐκ εἰδότες τῶν γεγονότων οὐδέν and **53**.1. Such traders were mentioned briefly at **31**.5.

44.2 ἄκραν Ἰαπυγίαν: 30.1 n. **καὶ ὡς ἕκαστοι ηὐπόρησαν:** i.e. they stopped wherever there looked to be a good chance of purchasing food. τῶν μὲν πόλεων 'some cities', contrasting with Taras and Locri (δέ). Th. moves briskly; Diod. 13.3.4 adds that they were received warmly by Thurii and granted an *agora* by Croton. This may be right. οὐ δεχομένων αὐτοὺς ἀγορᾶι οὐδὲ ἄστει, ὕδατι δὲ καὶ ὅρμωι 'not granting them access to a market or entry to the city but allowing them to get water and to anchor'. It would be surprising if this were true of Metapontum, later an important ally, but see 7.33.5 n.: Diod. 13.3.4 is explicit that they sailed past the town. O'Connor 2011 demonstrates the importance of such markets for provisioning; granting this need not compromise a city's neutrality. Nicias at **21**.2 was right – this will be very different from actions in the Aegean, where Athens could rely on support from subject-allies. **Λοκρῶν:** Epizephyrian Locri: *IACP* 273–8. In the 420s the Locrians were firmly anti-Athenian and they alone did not come to terms in 424, though Phaeax remarkably won them over in 422 (5.5.3). In 415–413 they reverted to hostility (7.1.1–2, 4.7, 25.3, 35.2; Fragoulaki 2013: 200–1). The city's enmity towards Athens-favouring Rhegium (4.1.2, 4.24.2) doubtless played a part. **Ῥήγιον: 4**.6 n. The Athens–Rhegium alliance perhaps originated in the 440s and was reaffirmed in 433–432 (Intr., 30); in the 420s the city often served as Athens' base (3.88.4, etc.). The lukewarm reception now was a serious disappointment. At some point they contributed more than 50 talents to Athens (*IG* i[3] 291 b col. 2.19–20 = *SEG* 17.7.11–12), but the view taken here is that this was in 427–424 (Ampolo 1987; Bauslaugh 1990: 147–50; Pope 2017) rather than 415–413 (Meritt 1957: 198–200, *HCT, CT* 458–9).

44.3 ἤδη ἠθροίζοντο: i.e. the three detachments (**42.**1) now reunited. στρατόπεδόν τε κατεσκευάσαντο ἐν τῶι τῆς Ἀρτέμιδος ἱερῶι: on this sanctuary see *IACP* 292. This is a disconcerting use for sacred ground, but if there is a story behind this Th. chooses not to tell it. Were the nervous locals placing their unwelcome visitors there in the hope of sacred protection? **Χαλκιδέας ὄντας Χαλκιδεῦσιν ... βοηθεῖν: 4**.6 n. 3.86.2 implies that kinship played a part in Rhegium's support of Leontini in 427, but at 7.57.1 Th. emphasises that in 415–413 expediency could trump kinship. οὐδὲ μεθ' ἑτέρων 'neutral', as at 7.33.2, 2.67.4, and 2.72.1. ὅ τι ἂν καὶ τοῖς ἄλλοις Ἰταλιώταις ξυνδοκῆι, τοῦτο ποιήσειν: despite ξυν-, this need not imply a convened meeting to decide a common policy; one city would go along with the line that others took, doubtless with some inter-city conversations. In fact only Thurii and Metapontum of the S. Italian cities took sides (7.57.11). The jump from Ἰταλιώταις to τὰ ἐν τῆι Σικελίαι πράγματα suggests that 'Italy' does not here include 'Sicily': cf. Ἰταλιωτῶν ... Σικελιωτῶν at 7.57.11 and ctr. **2.**4 n. on ἡ χώρα.

44.4 καὶ τὰς προπλους ναῦς: three in number (**46**.1), presumably the three ships sent in advance at **42**.2. They had probably been sent on to Egesta after they had first reported back (C–S). **ἃ ἔλεγον ἐν ταῖς Ἀθήναις οἱ ἄγγελοι:** 'messengers', not 'ambassadors', so this refers to the Athenians of **6**.3 and **8**.1–2 rather than the Egestaeans, **6**.2–3. Presumably they were now not only to investigate but also to bring the promised money, though Nicias at least (**22**) will have been prepared for a virtually null return.

45 πολλαχόθεν τε ἤδη ... ἠγγέλλετο: echoing the earlier flood of reports (**32**.3) and thus bookending the debate. But this time the facts are clear (σαφῆ). For ἤδη cf. **41–45** n.: here as often (**11**.5, **30**.1, **38**.5, **43**, **51**.3, **65**.3, etc.) it goes closely with the preceding word(s) – not just one, but by now many independent reports. **τῶν κατασκόπων: 41**.4. **ὡς ἐπὶ τούτοις** 'on these assumptions'. **ἔνθα μὲν φύλακας, πρὸς δὲ τοὺς πρέσβεις:** along the lines of Hermocrates' advice, **34**.1. The φύλακες would go to the subject states, the πρέσβεις to the allies. **τὰ περιπόλια** 'outposts' within their own territory: cf. 7.48.5. **ὅπλων ἐξετάσει καὶ ἵππων:** as the general had undertaken to do (**41**.4 ἐξέτασιν). **ἐντελῆ** 'up to strength'. **ἐπὶ ταχεῖ πολέμωι** 'for a war that was coming quickly': cf. 4.55.1. **ὅσον οὐ παρόντι:** echoing Hermocrates' final words, **34**.9: the Syracusans now accept that he was right.

46 *Disappointing News from Egesta*

The expedition begins, as it will end (7.87.6 n.), with a Herodotean flavour (Kallet 2001: 72–5): cf. esp. Hdt. 1.22, where Thrasybulus fools Astyages into thinking Miletus richer than it is by collecting all public and private supplies into the *agora* and having a noisy party, and 3.123, where Oroetes fools Polycrates' envoy by filling chests with stones and topping with a shallow layer of gold. That need not mean that the story here is untrue (Egestaeans could read Herodotus too, and anyway tricksters are found everywhere), but Th. makes the most of it, and one detail at least may be imaginative: see on τῶν ἐγγὺς πόλεων, **46**.3 n.

46.1 Αἱ δ' ἐκ τῆς Ἐγέστης τρεῖς νῆες: 44.4 n. **ὑπέσχοντο:** i.e. 'the Egestaeans', the ambassadors in Athens (**6**.2–3). **φαίνεται** 'are apparent': ὄντα is understood, not εἶναι. Cf. **2**.2 n.

46.2 τοῦτο ... ξυστρατεύειν 'this had been their first thing to set them back on their heels – this, and the unwillingness of the Rhegians to join in the campaign'. In fact the Rhegian reluctance came first, but the two are here linked as the early reverses. ἀντικρούειν is a strong metaphor: cf. Dem.'s impassioned *On the Crown* 198 and Phaedrus' mock-solemnity at Plato, *Phdr.* 228e ἐκκέκρουκάς με ἐλπίδος, ὦ Σώκρατες. **οὓς πρῶτον ἤρξαντο πείθειν** 'whom they had set about persuading as their first step': cf. **48**. Alberti prints πρώτους (H²), 'the first people' they had set about persuading: that is easier Greek, but is not necessary. **καὶ εἰκὸς ἦν μάλιστα** 'and who were especially likely' to be persuadable. **Λεοντίνων τε ξυγγενεῖς ὄντας:** the reprise of **44**.3 (n.) reinforces that those were not just words: the Athenians really thought that kinship would make a difference. **καὶ σφίσιν αἰεὶ ἐπιτηδείους:** so much so that they had a formal alliance, though Th. does not think this worth mentioning here. It presumably mattered less than the supportive record (Intr., 32). **τῶι μὲν Νικίαι προσδεχομένωι ἦν τὰ παρὰ τῶν Ἐγεσταίων: 22** n. For the construction cf. 2.60.1 καὶ προσδεχομένωι μοι τὰ τῆς ὀργῆς ὑμῶν ἐς με γεγένηται. **ἀλογώτερα** 'it made less sense' (than it did to Nicias), or – more tortuous, but giving more sense to καί – 'it was even less what they had counted on than it was expected by Nicias'. But Mader 1993a: 192–3 reasonably doubts whether the Egestaean contribution had really figured large in at least Alcibiades' thinking.

46.3 τὸ ἐν Ἔρυκι ἱερὸν τῆς Ἀφροδίτης: a mountaintop landmark, traditionally founded by Aeneas: cf. **2**.3 n. So this is why the Athenian delegation had specified great wealth ἔν τε τοῖς ἱεροῖς . . . καὶ ἐν τῶι κοινῶι (**8**.2 n.). **πολλῶι πλείω τὴν ὄψιν . . . παρείχετο** 'on the basis of a small financial capacity presented a much more impressive appearance', not 'more impressive' than the artefacts' real worth but giving an inflated idea of the wealth of the city (Kallet 2001: 74–7). It was easy to be impressed: Plb. 1.55.8 describes this as 'agreed to be the finest of the Sicilian temples in wealth and in general magnificence '. There is no suggestion of deceit here, unlike in the entertainments that followed and in the Herodotean story of Polycrates (3.123, **46** n.). These Athenian commissioners simply got it wrong. Polyaenus 6.21 makes the Egestaeans use the borrowed gold and silver to adorn the temple as well, but he is probably just misremembering Th. **τῶν τριηριτῶν:** so the generosity extended not just to the πρέσβεις but to the ordinary rowers. It is all part of the show. **ἐκπώματα καὶ χρυσᾶ καὶ ἀργυρᾶ** 'gold and silver cups', perhaps recalling those used in the libations of **32**.1. **ἐκ τῶν ἐγγὺς πόλεων:** but Egesta's only sizable neighbour is Selinus, which was not going to help. The story may have been elaborated by someone who recalled a story of Alcibiades borrowing Athenian state vessels at Olympia in 416 for his own entertaining and pretending that they were his own (Andoc. *Against Alcibiades* 29): Alcibiades is being played at his own game. **ἐσέφερον ἐς τὰς ἑστιάσεις ὡς οἰκεῖα ἕκαστοι** 'each carried them into (their own houses for) the banqueting (and passed them off) as their own'.

46.4 ἔκπληξιν: the key-word again, **33.**4 n, this time for a past 'shock' that is now causing the new shock of disappointment in the present.   **διεθρόησαν:** i.e. in general gossip, to be distinguished from the official report (**8.**3).

46.5 οἱ μέν: probably mainly the τριηρῖται, as the πρέσβεις are less likely to have returned on this campaign, senior men as they probably were.   **τὴν αἰτίαν ... ὑπὸ τῶν στρατιωτῶν:** cf. Plato, *Apol.* 38c, 'you will incur αἰτίαν ὑπὸ τῶν βουλομένων τὴν πόλιν λοιδορεῖν if you execute Socrates'.

47–50.1: THE DEBATE OF THE GENERALS

The generals had already had plenty of opportunity to discuss strategy. Some debate presumably did take place now because of the news from Rhegium and Egesta, though it is unlikely that this changed anyone's mind; it is still likely that Th. has brought together a series of discussions into one. Each general would now have had his say again, but the formal structure, with each speaking in turn and no further interchange, may also be Th.'s artificial reconstruction.

Scholarly debate has centred on which strategy was the wisest, or seemed so to Th.: cf. esp. Liebeschuetz 1968b: 292–7; Green 1970: 138–42; Laffi 1970: 292–7; Kagan 1981: 212–17; Cawkwell 1997: 17–18, 82–4; Lazenby 2004: 137–8. Readers are left to make up their own minds, though Th. may later indicate some approval for Lamachus' way of thinking (7.42.3, cf. **49** n.). The debate also illustrates further themes: the likelihood of disagreement within the split command, even though a single policy is agreed for now (**50.**1); the generals' contrasting temperaments and their different interpretations of their brief (**8.**2, **26.**1 nn., Mader 1993a); the importance of attracting allies, despite the disappointments of **44.**2–3, and the differing views on how to do it; the importance of prestige as well as military muscle; and, especially in Lamachus' speech (that is one reason why it is the longest), some insight into the strategic and tactical realities.

47 *The Speech of Nicias*

His emphasis echoes the brief at **8.**2, but (a) with Egesta, there is a sharpening from 'helping' the city (βοηθούς, **8.**2) to 'reconciling' it with Selinus; (b) with Leontini, his phrasing takes a pessimistic view of the likelihood of 'the course of the war leaving them any opportunity' (**8.**2) to do anything, and 'help' here (ὠφελῆσαι) is vaguer and weaker than ξυγκατοικίσαι, **8.**2; and (c) the city's injunction to 'act in the Athenians' best interests' is taken in a way that echoes Nicias' own limited reading of those interests. The effect is to omit the Syracusans completely, even though Nicias' own arguments at Athens had acknowledged that they were the real enemy and he will state this explicitly at 7.11.2 (see on ἐφ' ὅπερ below). Given that the scale of the expedition made this clear, it is not likely that the city's prestige would be enhanced by such a 'display of power' (ἐπιδείξαντας . . . τὴν δύναμιν) rather than humiliated by the climbdown; but Th. leaves readers to infer that for themselves, and some might have agreed with Nicias that this was now the least bad option. So Lazenby 2004: 137–8.   ἐφ' ὅπερ 'the purpose for which' (cf. 1.59.2), neuter rather than ἐφ' οὕσπερ, which would more unambiguously have suggested military action. He is less disingenuous at 7.11.2: 'the Syracusans, ἐφ' οὓς ἐπέμφθημεν'.   ἦν μὲν . . . τροφήν: this is clearly a response to the news of **46**, and that makes rhetorical sense: it prepares for his final emphasis on 'spending the city's own money', and allows the implication that the changed financial position justifies a limiting of Athens' ambitions to the minimum (Mader 1993a: 193–4). But one suspects that Nicias would have argued for the same strategy in any case.   ταῖς ἑξήκοντα ναυσίν, ὅσασπερ ἠιτήσαντο: 8.1.   καὶ οὕτω: i.e., after achieving that 'reconciliation'.   καὶ ἐπιδείξαντας μὲν τὴν δύναμιν . . . ἀποπλεῖν οἴκαδε: echoing **11**.4, though there it was his second-best option after not going at all.   τὴν ἐς τοὺς φίλους καὶ ξυμμάχους προθυμίαν: Nicias had not shown much enthusiasm for distant friends and allies at **10**.5 and **11**.7, but this is now the best way to make his case.   δι' ὀλίγου καὶ ἀπὸ τοῦ ἀδοκήτου 'for a short time and unexpectedly': δι' ὀλίγου again echoes **11**.4.   καὶ τῆι πόλει δαπανῶντας τὰ οἰκεῖα μὴ κινδυνεύειν: 'and not take risks with the city when spending its own resources'. The city itself had not been so reluctant to spend (**8** n.), but this is in character for Nicias: he had similarly concentrated on expense at **12**.1 and τῆι πόλει . . . κινδυνεύειν also echoes **10**.5.

48 *The Plan of Alcibiades*

As with Nicias, this too is in line with Alcibiades' earlier thinking, for at **17**.4–6 he had been optimistic about acquiring local allies and had stressed the 'barbarians', i.e. the Sicels. The confidence in the power of persuasion, especially his own, is also in character. The beginning is framed as a (good) response to Nicias; he is also more honest about the Syracusans as the main enemy, just as he was at **16–18**. He ignores the diplomatic failures in **44**, but those would hardly help his case. This was the plan that was eventually followed, and more states might have been won over had Alcibiades still been there to work his charm.   τὰς πόλεις: i.e. the Greek ones, as the τε ... καί construction with the Sicels shows: πόλις is felt as a Greek concept. He ignores the Phoenician settlements (2.6). **τοὺς μὲν ... τοὺς δέ:** the same distinction as at **34**.1 and **45** (nn.): the Syracusans' tribute-bearing subjects will be incited to revolt and their allies to switch sides. **πρῶτον** 'as a first step', as in πρῶτον ἤρξαντο πείθειν at **46**.2. **Μεσσηνίους:** **4**.6 n.; *IACP* 233–6. This prepares not just for **50**.1 but for **74**.1, where Alcibiades turns up at Messina to inflict damage rather than help. There was a good chance of winning the city over, as it was riven with *stasis* (5.5, **74**.1 n.). Understandably in view of its strategic importance, it had been the scene of fierce fighting in the 420s (4.24–5) after being taken first by Athens (3.90.3–4) and then by Syracuse (4.1). In the event it remained neutral in 415–413. **ἐν πόρωι ... Σικελίας** 'for they, more than anyone else, were positioned where one crosses to and approaches Sicily': see Maps 1 and 2. Cf. 7.4.7 (n.) and esp. 4.1.2 (425 BCE), the prospect that the Athenians might take as a base Messina, προσβολὴν ἔχον ... τῆς Σικελίας, and come at some point μείζονι παρασκευῆι: Intr., 21). **ἐφόρμησιν** 'base for attack': cf. **49**.4. **οὕτως ἤδη:** *then*, and not before, will be the time to attack. **οἱ μὲν ... οἱ δέ:** 'the latter ... the former ...', as often. Alcibiades punctiliously recites the diplomatic demands, but will have known that Syracuse at least was never likely to agree. If they had, his broader ambitions of **16–18** would have been frustrated. **κατοικίζειν** 'allow (us) to settle' the Leontinians. Cf. **50**.4.

49 *The Plan of Lamachus*

His beginning responds to Alcibiades' οὕτως ἤδη: no, better to strike immediately. Lamachus wastes no words on diplomatic niceties, but several of his emphases pick up narrative themes: the Syracusans as the enemy that mattered; the importance of psychology, especially the shock (ἔκπληξις, **49**.1 n.) of a sudden attack; the impact of sight (ὄψις x3; cf. esp. **30–32**.2 n.); the Syracusans' scepticism. He clearly has some knowledge about Syracuse just as Hermocrates has about Athens, though this particular intelligence is out of date (**49**.3 n.). Events will also support his view that military success will be necessary to gain those Sicilian allies (7.33.1 n.): οὕτως ἤδη (**49**.3) echoes Alcibiades' words as they reverse his sequence. The preference for Megara is a further response to Alcibiades and goes with the strategy: its closeness to Syracuse made it better for immediate action.

Lamachus' speech carries the authority of a military man, and it is often thought that Th. 'agreed' with him. This is inferred from **63**.2 (n.) and esp. 7.42.3, where Demosthenes avoids the errors of Nicias, who 'did not immediately attack Syracuse when he was an object of terror on his first arrival, but instead wintered in Catana . . .'. It certainly seems that Th. shared that criticism of Nicias, though it is unclear if 'immediately' there means exactly what Lamachus proposes here (see n. there). Still, both **63**.2 and 7.42.3 echo Lamachus' phrasing (nn.: cf. Hunter 1973: 97; Rood 1998: 169 n. 46), and it is reasonable to infer that Th. at least approved of his mindset – but he does not indicate that yet.   **ἄντικρυς:** with πλεῖν ἐπὶ Συρακούσας.   **τὴν μάχην:** 'the' battle here and at **49**.2, as Lamachus takes it for granted that there has to be one: it is a question only of where and when.   **ἐκπεπληγμένοι: 33**.4, **46**.4 nn.

49.2 τὸ γὰρ πρῶτον πᾶν στράτευμα δεινότατον εἶναι 'for, he said, every army is at its most frightening at the beginning': τὸ πρῶτον is adverbial. Echoed at 7.42.3 ἀφικόμενος γὰρ τὸ πρῶτον ὁ Νικίας φοβερός . . ., with Demosthenes' realisation that καί αὐτὸς ἐν τῶι παρόντι τῆι πρώτηι ἡμέραι δεινότατός ἐστι τοῖς ἐναντίοις; he consequently avoids a Nicias-like delay in order to shake (ἐκπλήξει) the enemy.   **ἀναθαρσοῦντας:** echoed at **63**.2.   **καὶ τῆι ὄψει καταφρονεῖν μᾶλλον** 'and are more contemptuous even (or 'also', καί) when they do catch sight'. Syracusan καταφρόνησις is another theme from earlier: it can be bad (**33**.3 n., **35**.1) or good (**34**.9 n.), but this would be the good sort – for Syracuse. Cf. again **63**.2 κατεφρόνησαν, and 7.42.3 ὑπερώφθη.   **μάλιστ' ἂν σφᾶς . . . μάχης:** σφᾶς = the Athenians (the nom. σφεῖς might be expected, but cf. **96**.1, 7.21.3), αὐτούς = the Syracusans; the infinitives correspond to optatives. For the repeated ἄν see **10**.4 n. κατὰ πάντα is then defined by the series of ways to instil such fear, 'sight', 'expectation', and 'danger'.   **τῶι αὐτίκα κινδύνωι τῆς μάχης:** for αὐτίκα qualifying a noun cf. **69**.3, **80**.5 (n.), 7.70.7, and for the word order see **33**.1 n.

49.3 ἐν τοῖς ἀγροῖς . . . ἥξειν: as 2.18.4 suggests that the Athenians might have been 'cut off from' the city in 431 if Archidamus had not delayed. This is the least convincing point, as by now the Syracusans were not so incredulous (**45**) and anyway it would take time to force a landing. But it was reasonable to think that many would seek refuge, and the possessions they left would be useful. For the apparently redundant μή after ἀπιστεῖν cf. e.g. 1.10.1, 2.101.1.   **ἐσκομιζομένων** 'as they made their way' (masc. gen. absolute), just as the Athenians ἐσεκομίζοντο at the beginning of the war, 2.18.4: see last n.   **χρημάτων:** especially money – there would be plunder from estate buildings, and captives to be sold as slaves as at **62**.3–4 – but also other stores: cf. **97**.5 n. and 7.25.1.   **κρατοῦσα:** i.e. after the expected battle (**49**.1 n.): the next step would be a siege.   **διαμελλήσειν περισκοποῦντας:** δια- and περι- both intensify, 'keep delaying while they looked around to see'.

49.4 ἐπαναχωρήσαντας: so the land attack would have been launched before they established their naval base. The ships would 'return' while most of the land force stayed to continue the siege. Lamachus glosses over the problems of disembarking that force in the first place, but these may not have been so difficult as modern readers might assume: cf. Kagan 1981: 216 n. 22; Lazenby 2004: 72, 138–9. **ἐφόρμησιν:** the best of the emendations. Lamachus may again be echoing Alcibiades' words (**48**): Messina might be good, but Megara was better. **τὰ Μέγαρα . . . ἃ ἦν ἐρῆμα:** 4.1–2 n., cf. **94**.1. In the event the Athenians made Catana their base, **51**.2–3, but that city could not yet be relied on, and deserted Megara would be easy to occupy. Its bay offered good anchorage; for differing views of its suitability in other respects see Green 1970: 141–2; Kagan 1981: 216. **ἀπέχοντα Συρακουσῶν οὔτε πλοῦν πολὺν οὔτε ὁδόν:** see Map 1. The distance is about 20 km.

50.1 *Decision*

Λάμαχος . . . ὅμως προσέθετο καὶ αὐτὸς τῆι Ἀλκιβιάδου γνώμηι: it is easy to see why Lamachus regarded Alcibiades' plan as less bad than Nicias', but Th. does not tell us why he gave up his own view. Plut. says of a later stage that Lamachus deferred, in that case to Nicias, because he was poorer and had less prestige (*Nic.* 15.2, cf. **62** n.): probably a guess, but a good one.

50.1–53: FIRST STEPS

Th. treats these opening moves briskly. There were opportunities for set-speeches, with Alcibiades urging locals to make an alliance rather as Brasidas had at Acanthus (4.85–7): instead the initiatives end abruptly, 'he sailed back to Rhegium' (**50**.1) and 'having failed, they sailed back to Catana' (**52**.2). Even the reception at Catana is achieved only once soldiers are in the city (**51**.1–2), and at Camarina it is not clear whether the Athenians put their case at all (**52**.1 n.). Th. will not have wished to anticipate material he was leaving for the Camarina debate of **75**.3–**88**.3, but the speed also indicates how swiftly Alcibiades' initiative falters. Still, there is no suggestion that the other plans would have been better: the grand sight of the fleet sailing around the E and S coasts (**52**.1) leads only to a quick return, with no hint of the impressed Sicilian reaction that Nicias expected (**47**); then the first fighting on land ends with Athenian plunderers cut off (**52**.2), not Syracusan farmers (**49**.3). The removal of Alcibiades himself (**53**) is likely to make things worse.

The briskness leads to some obscurity: no details of the topography are given (**50**.4–5 nn.), nor any explanation of the 'oaths' of **52**.1 (n.).

50.1 τῆι αὐτοῦ νηί 'in his own ship' (cf. **61**.6), following the pattern set by his great-grandfather Cleinias at Artemisium (Hdt. 8.17). The echo and the contrast may be sensed: Cleinias had there fought with distinction. **πόλει μὲν ἂν οὐ δέξασθαι, ἀγορὰν δ' ἔξω παρέξειν:** for ἄν + aor. inf. followed by fut. inf. cf. 1.127.2: it corresponds to 'we would not (opt.) . . . but we will (indic.)'. So Messina gives the same response as Rhegium, **44**.3.

50.2 ἑξήκοντα ναῦς: a regular size for a squadron of ships: cf. e.g. 1.112.3, 3.80.2, 3.91.1, 4.2.3, and **8**.1 n. **ἐκ πασῶν:** i.e. from all three detachments of **42**.1. These are no longer operating as separate bodies. **παρέπλεον** 'sailed along the shore'. **Νάξον: 3**.1 n. The city was a better bet than Messina, as even Nicias acknowledged (**20**.3), for it had suffered at the hands of Syracuse's allies in 425 (4.25.7–11). It duly offered a warmer welcome (**50**.3), then a winter base (**72**.1), and fought on Athens' side (**98**.1, 7.57.11). At some point it also contributed money (*IG* i³ 291a 1–2), but this may have been in 427–424 (**44**.2 n.). **ἕνα σφῶν αὐτῶν:** Lamachus or Nicias, as Alcibiades' rhetorical skills would be needed on the mission (**51**.1), but Th. does not say which. Perhaps he thought it did not matter, perhaps he did not know. Cf. **100**.1 n.

50.3 Κατάνην: 3.3 n.; Nicias counted it along with Naxos as a reliable ally, **20**.3 – a rare case where he was over-sanguine. Like Naxos, Catana made a substantial monetary contribution to Athens in, perhaps, 427–424: *IG* i³ 291 b col. 2.16–17. **ἐνῆσαν γὰρ αὐτόθι ἄνδρες τὰ Συρακοσίων βουλόμενοι:** cf. **51**.2, when they flee. The other evidence for *stasis* at Catana dates to the second quarter of the century (Berger 1992a: 18–19, *IACP* 206), but it is not surprising that trouble continued. **τὸν Τηρίαν ποταμόν:** the S. Leonardo river, some 18 km S of Catana and 35 km NNW of Syracuse: see Map 1. It is mentioned again at **94**.2. **ἐπὶ κέρως** 'in line'; cf. **32**.2. **τὰς ἄλλας ναῦς:** not 'other' than the 60 – the rest remained at Rhegium – but other than the ten that were sent ahead, **50**.4.

50.4 ἐς τὸν μέγαν λιμένα: see Map 4. This is its first mention, and Th. could have done more to explain the topography: cf. **99**.1 n. The Athenians apparently assumed that they would meet no resistance, for ten ships are not many: perhaps it could be taken for granted that they were coming to talk, as if under a flag of truce. **κατασκέψασθαι εἴ τι ναυτικόν ἐστι καθειλκυσμένον:** i.e. launched and afloat rather than hauled on to land (as Greek ships spent much of their time: Kopp 2016: 135). 'Manning' them would be a further phase (πληροῦσι . . . πληρούμενον, **52**.1). **ἀπὸ τῶν νεῶν:** with κηρῦξαι. Not many would hear, but word would soon get around of what had been said. **ὅτι Ἀθηναῖοι ἥκουσι . . . ἀπιέναι:** keeping the formal language of the proclamation, first in an indirect statement and then in indirect command. For the Ionian kinship cf. **6.**1 n.; for the alliance, **6.**2 n. and Intr., 30. The 'Leontinians in Syracuse' are those δυνατοί who had migrated to Syracuse in the late 420s and not subsequently left for Bricinnia (5.4.3–4). Nothing more is heard of them, and there could not have been many. This is gesture politics.

50.5 κατεσκέψαντο: echoing **50.**4, κατασκέψασθαι, and adding further elements to reconnoitre. 'The harbours' will include possibilities along the coast, including Trogilus, as well as the 'little harbour' (Map 4); the χώρα = the territory outside the city; 'from which they would have to base themselves in the fighting' acknowledges that they would need a base closer than Catana, and Catana itself could not yet be relied on. Plut. *Nic.* 14.5–7 tells of the capture of an enemy ship carrying a catalogue of Syracusan citizens, and the seers (μάντεις) worried that this might be the fulfilment of an oracle that 'the Athenians will take all the Syracusans'. Th. is usually silent about μάντεις (**69.**2, 7.50.4 nn.), but that story is anyway not in his manner.

51.1 καὶ ἐκκλησίας ... εἰπεῖν: the decision not to admit the army has already been taken (**50.**3), and so τὴν μὲν στρατιὰν οὐκ ἐδέχοντο is only the foil to the more important δέ clause, the invitation to the generals to speak. It is no surprise that, as at Messina, Alcibiades is the spokesman. **πυλίδα τινὰ ἐνῳκοδομημένην κακῶς** 'a postern-gate that had been badly walled up' or 'badly built into the wall'. **διελόντες** 'dismantle'. **ἐσελθόντες ἐς τὴν πόλιν ἠγόραζον** 'entered the city and went shopping', particularly for provisions. ἀγοράζω can just = 'spend time in the *agora*', but enough emphasis has fallen on 'granting an *agora*' (**44.**2–3, **50.**1) to make the meaning clear. ἐς τὴν πόλιν is to be taken with ἐσελθόντες (*pace* Chadwick 1996: 38, 'went shopping into the town', but ἀγοράζω as a verb of motion does not convince), and moved accordingly from its MS position. The behaviour is peaceable enough, though the intimidatory effect was not uncalculated.

51.2 οὐ πολλοί τινες: 1.1 n.

52.1 Καμαρίνης: the first mention in Bk. 6 of a city that will be important, but it is familiar from events in 427–424 as initially an ally of Leontini (3.86.2). The Athenians hastened there in 425 on hearing that it was being betrayed to Syracuse by a faction, but the outcome is unclear (4.25.7): in 424 the Camarinaeans gained Morgantine in return for a fixed payment to Syracuse (4.65.1). They responded favourably to the Athenian Phaeax in 422–1, 5.4.6. **ὡς, εἰ ἔλθοιεν, προσχωροῖεν ἄν:** the message proved over-optimistic. It probably came from just one faction: the divisiveness of 425 (last note) may well have continued.   πληροῦσι . . . πληρούμενον: 50.4 n.   ἁπάσηι οὖν τῆι στρατιᾶι: the fighting ships, at least; not much is heard of the transports once the military side is under way. The decision to send the full force is understandable for the Syracusan phase, as they might run into opposition. It is less clear why they all went on to Camarina, where diplomacy was the priority. If it was a show of strength it was heavy-handed, and did not work.   αὖθις 'in turn' (not 'again': they have not been to Camarina before).   ἐς τὸν αἰγιαλόν: rather than sailing straight into the harbour as at Syracuse (50.4). Camarina is, they hope, a friendly city, and needs to be asked first.   οἱ δ' οὐκ ἐδέχοντο: Th. passes very briefly over this: probably not just 'they did not receive the ships' but more broadly 'they did not admit the Athenians into the city', i.e. provide the sort of welcome that Naxos had given (50.3). The implication of their reply was 'we will admit that one ship and do no more'. On their later side-taking see 67.2, 88.1, 7.33.1, 7.58.1 with nn.   τὰ ὅρκια: Th. does not explain these 'oaths' further. It is normally taken as a term of 'the treaty from the time of Laches' of 75.3 (n.); so *HCT, CT*. Bauslaugh 1990: 158 prefers to assume a local compromise 'in which the opposing factions swore oaths to maintain neutrality, unless after proper deliberation the majority resolved to bring in one side or the other', but this seems less likely.   μιᾶι νηί . . . μεταπέμπωσιν: for similar stipulations cf 2.7.2, 3.71.1. Nothing precluded sending in an ambassador, presumably Alcibiades, on one ship to urge the Camarinaeans to come over. Perhaps they did, or perhaps the initial rebuff was so uncompromising that there was no point in asking. Whichever it was, Th. leaves it as ἄπρακτοι δὲ γενόμενοι.

52.2 ἁρπαγήν 'plunder'. The object will have been to sell the proceeds: cf. **49**.3 n.   τῶν Συρακοσίων ἱππέων . . . διαφθειράντων: the first blows of the campaign, and already an indicator of the Athenians' own cavalry problem: Intr., 6.

53.1 καταλαμβάνουσι: the historic present commands the reader/listener's attention for a pivotal moment.   τὴν Σαλαμινίαν ναῦν: the *Salaminia*, one of the two state triremes used for special missions. In 414 Aristophanes' Euelpides (**1**.2–5 n., **24**.3) is looking for somewhere to get away from it all: 'but nowhere beside the sea, where the *Salaminia* might pop up early one morning with a summonser' (κλητήρ, *Birds* 146–7).   ὡς κελεύσοντας: masc., i.e. the men in the *Salaminia*: cf. **44**.1 n.   ἐς ἀπολογίαν ὧν ἡ πόλις ἐνεκάλει: Th. picks up the story from **28–9**, but now these 'charges' are made by 'the city', not just individuals as at **28**.2. Alcibiades' enemies have evidently been active as they planned at **29**.3.   τῶν στρατιωτῶν . . . Ἑρμῶν: as at **27–29** Th. distinguishes the two outrages: some soldiers had been among those 'denounced with Alcibiades' for the Mysteries, and also some were denounced for the Herms. Strictly μετ' αὐτοῦ should refer only to the first group, for the testimonies against Alcibiades (μηνύματα) had concerned the Mysteries, **28**.1, **61**.1; it was only broader talk that implicated him with the Herms, **28**.2. Those now accused of the Herms mutilation (τῶν δέ) had presumably been denounced after their departure. On that sequence of denunciations cf. **27–29** n.

53.2 οὐ δοκιμάζοντες τοὺς μηνυτάς 'not subjecting the witnesses to proper scrutiny'. κατέδουν 'put in chains', from καταδέω, referring to suspects back in Athens: there had not yet been any chance to do the same to the accused here. χρησιμώτερον ... διαφυγεῖν 'regarding it as more helpful to investigate the matter rigorously and find out the truth than to allow, on the grounds of a denouncer's bad character, even an apparently good man to escape without examination once he had been accused'. τινά goes with χρηστόν, not πονηρίαν; the words pick up πονηρῶν and πάνυ χρηστούς. Th. now makes his indignation clear (cf. **27–29** n., **61**.2), and his language, esp. πονηρία, is similar to that used by Alcibiades himself at **89**.5, **92**.3 (nn.), and 8.47.2. Cf. Rawlings 1981: 113–15. βασανίσαι: generally 'investigate' (LSJ II.1), but with a hint of the 'torture' that might be involved (LSJ II.2). Yet what has led the Athenians astray is their believing so uncritically (ἀβασανίστως, 1.20.1) hearsay not only about the present – οὐ δοκιμάζοντες τοὺς μηνυτάς – but also about the past, **53**.3: cf. **54–59** n.

53.3 ἐπιστάμενος γὰρ ὁ δῆμος ἀκοῇ: ἐπίσταμαι does not always imply 'knowledge' rather than firm conviction (**37**.1 n.) and Th. is scathing about popular credulity when oral tradition is concerned (1.20.1, cf. **54**.1 and **54–59** n.), but thus far 'the people' were right: the end of the tyranny was harsh (**59**.2 n.) and the Spartans, not Harmodius and Aristogeiton, played a critical role in its overthrow (**59**.4 n). τὴν Πεισιστράτου καὶ τῶν παίδων τυραννίδα 'the tyranny of Peisistratus and his sons', taken as a single period: it is not implied that Peisistratus' individual reign also ended badly. For 'sons', including Hipparchus as well as Hippias, cf. **54**.5 n. οὐδ' ὑφ' ἑαυτῶν ... ἀλλ' ὑπὸ τῶν Λακεδαιμονίων: the excursus of **54–59** will go on to explain how, though **59**.4 will correct by adding 'and the Alcmaeonids' to 'the Spartans'. There is a double point. The Athenians had 'not even' (οὐδέ) overthrown the tyrants themselves; if they had, it would at least show that they had been able to cope. Still worse, their rescuers had been the Spartans; a new threat of tyranny now ran the risk of seeing the enemy within the city again. Sparta's role in ending the tyranny was seldom mentioned but seems to have been acknowledged

(Thomas 1989: 245–6), and is taken for granted at Ar. *Lys.* 1150–6 (411 BCE). ἐφοβεῖτο αἰεί: **59**.2 n.   πάντα ὑπόπτως ἐλάμβανεν: echoing **53**.2 to round off the paragraph, but πάντα there referred to the Herms and Mysteries scare; here it is even more wide-ranging.

54–59: THE END OF THE PEISISTRATIDS

At 1.20.1 Th. made his impatience clear: 'People pick up hearsay from one another about past events and accept without investigation (ἀβασανίστως) everything alike, even things that happened in their own country.' His prime example then (1.20.2) is exactly this one, the Athenians' mistaken views about the fall of the tyrants. That passage is echoed here, esp. at **54**.1: it is 'their own' tyrants here that the Athenians misremember (cf. 'in their own country' at 1.20.2), and they 'say nothing accurate' (cf. 'accept without investigation' there). In Bk. 1 ἀβασανίστως contrasts with his own rigorous cross-checking of everything that he has heard (1.22.1–3). It would be understandable if there was a similar concern here to parade his own investigative superiority (*HCT*), but in 415 such historical carelessness had effects in the here-and-now, and that is at least the surface justification for an expanded treatment. One paradox is that the Athenians were here carrying out a version of Th.'s own project, using past events to clarify similarities in the present (1.22.4). They were not even wrong about crucial facts, the harshness of Peisistratid rule at the end and the role of Sparta (**53**.3 n.). But there was more to it, and that was why they got things so wrong now: 'the surface analogy between the Peisistratid tyranny and Alcibiades' role is recognized as facile, misleading, and pernicious' (Connor 1984: 179).

Had the *dēmos* possessed greater insight, there were different parallels to find: that harshness was not explained by any intrinsic character of tyranny – the Peisistratids had hitherto been splendid – but by the suspicions unleashed by the *attack* on tyranny; personal passions can have big consequences; fearfulness, here that of Hippias, can precipitate the consequences most feared; the closer parallel to Hippias' final paranoia is found not in Alcibiades but in his enemies, πάντα ὑπόπτως ἀποδεχόμενοι (**53**.2, cf. **53**.3), and in the *dēmos*, χαλεπὸς . . . καὶ ὑπόπτης as it was (**53**.3, **60**.1, cf. **61**.1). That emphasis on the people's impetuosity is typical of Th.'s outlook (**63**.2 n., Intr., 6–7); in this respect the excursus carries thematic implications that extend beyond the Alcibiades affair, just as the digression on Pausanias and Themistocles illuminates Athenian and Spartan behaviour in ways relevant to more than its setting at 1.128–38.

The excursus expands 1.20.2, giving more detail of the killing itself (**57** nn.); 1.20 may well have been written in full knowledge of what he would write, perhaps had already written, here. One important new emphasis is the role of ἔρως (*CT*, Fornara 1968). That too could resonate with Alcibiades (Vickers 1995; Wohl 1999), notorious for his love life and sporting an image of Ἔρως on his shield (Plut. *Alc.* 16.2), though Th. himself has skirted around that theme with ἡ κατὰ τὸ σῶμα παρανομία (**15**.4 [n.]). The more destructive ἔρως in Th.'s account is that of the *dēmos* driving the Sicilian adventure (**24**.3 n.). Th. also adds to 1.20 the reasons for thinking Hippias the older son. He puts weight both on the inscriptional evidence (**54–5**) and on his own superior ἀκοή (**55**.1), and elaborately justifies his inferences. Fifth-century orators and sophists had developed a facility with arguments of εἰκός (**36**.3 n.), and that is on view here (εἰκός . . . οὐδὲ τοῦτο ἀπεοικότως . .'. οὐ μὴν οὐδ' ἂν κατασχεῖν δοκεῖ μοι, **55**.1–3).

An excursus often serves as a panel-divider, marking the end or beginning of a phase. Thus Hdt. places his excursus on the Alcmaeonids just after Marathon (6.121–4) and Th. his on Themistocles and Pausanias just before Pericles' decisive speech and the opening of the war (1.128–38): cf. also 7.57–8 n. Th. might have placed this excursus a little earlier, along with the description of the agitation at Athens, and attached it to the despatch rather than arrival of the *Salaminia*. That would have put it before the first fighting (**51–53**); placing it here intimates that Alcibiades' departure was an even more crucial turning-point (**61**.6).

Th. can be expected to be engaging with Hdt. 5.55–6 and 62–5 here, just as he seems to be in the further cases of historical carelessness at 1.20. He can certainly be seen as supplementing Hdt. by adding the erotic dimension. There are some Herodoteanisms of manner (nn.) too as he moves into Hdt.'s world, though fewer than in the excursus on Pausanias and Themistocles (Munson 2012: 250–6). These chapters also have the highest concentration of women in Th., another Herodotean characteristic, though they still remain marginal to the male manoeuvrings (Shannon-Henderson 2018: 94–5). Th. may be projecting his capacity to write Herodotean history but with a sharper critical edge: the lively narrative of **56–8** is unlike the austere manner of many of Th.'s excursuses (Schadewaldt 1929: 89–94), and bears comparison with Hdt. at his best. Still, Hdt. and Th. are at one on the important points that Hippias and not Hipparchus was tyrant (Hdt. 5.55.1), that the tyranny continued for four years after Hipparchus' death (Hdt. 5.55.1) in a harsher fashion than before (Hdt. 5.62.2, 6.123.2), and that the earlier phases of the tyranny were praiseworthy (Hdt. 1.59.6, cf. **54**.6 n.).

Hdt. is much fuller on the Spartan intervention (5.62–77, cf. **59**.4 n.). Th. might have made more of that, for it offered further parallels with the present: the danger of Spartan attack was soon to be in the air (**61**.2), and a new revolution would loom in 411 BCE after a similar four-year interval; the end of each story would be the departure of the targeted figure, there Hippias and now Alcibiades, into resentful partnership with Athens' most feared enemy. Like Athenagoras' reflections on democracy (**36–40** n.), the nervous atmosphere of 415 may give some long-distance preparation for that crisis of 411, but the narrative here dwells not on the successful overthrow of 511/10 but on the confusion and failure of four years earlier, and it is misdirected passion, not ideology, that Th. thinks most relevant. It is not clear that he is right about this. At several points his argument is weak (nn.), and the superiority of his own ἀκοή is simply asserted (**55**.1 n.); the only point on which he quotes independent evidence concerns the relative ages of the brothers. His own feelings about the *dēmos* may have clouded his judgement here.

It may be that there is also concealed polemic here against some other writer (Jacoby 1949: 158–65, *APF* 446, *HCT,* and others suggest Hellanicus), but the emphasis on the disastrous consequences of ἀκοή has most point if it is indeed oral tradition that is his primary target.

On the famous statues of Harmodius and Aristogeiton in the *agora* (Fig. 2, **54**.2 n.) see Azoulay 2017, who traces the shifting role they played in later ideological debates, and more briefly Vout 2018: 1–19. Azoulay argues (ch. 6) that the tyrannicides' memory received a new wave of veneration around the time that Th.'s history reached its final form, with Thrasybulus and the returning exiles of 404 seen as their spiritual descendants in liberating Athens. If so, Th.'s deflating treatment of the popular heroes would seem particularly pointed.

The bibliography on the excursus is extensive: see esp. Rawlings 1981: 101–17; Connor 1984: 176–80; Tsakmakis 1995: 176–225 and 1996; Rood 1998: 180–1; Ludwig 2002: 159–64; Stahl 2003: ch. 1; Meyer 2008; Pothou 2009: 144–51; Azoulay 2017; and *HCT* and *CT*.

54.1 Τὸ γὰρ Ἀριστογείτονος καὶ Ἁρμοδίου τόλμημα: in 514 BCE. As at 1.20.2, the names are taken as familiar. γάρ is surprising, as on the face of it **54**.1 contradicts rather than explains **53**.3 (next n.), but it introduces all **54–9** as filling out the bare mention of the liberation at **53**.3. For this use of γάρ to introduce embedded narrative see de Jong 1997. **ἀκριβὲς οὐδὲν λέγοντας:** yet at **53**.6 the Athenians are right about two important facts (n.). Still, (1) οὐδέν should not be taken literally, any more than crossly calling people 'totally ignorant' about something need imply that every proposition to which they would assent is false: cf. οὐδὲν ὑγιές,

2 Harmodius and Aristogeiton: Roman copies of lost bronze originals

'everything's a mess' (Ar. *Ach.* 955, *Eccl.* 325). (2) It is a familiar rhetorical device to begin a section with a striking but over-stated formulation that is then qualified: see Pelling 2019, index s.v. 'revision in stride'. (3) ἀκριβές also makes a difference, as one can know something vaguely without Th.'s own high standard of ἀκρίβεια (1.22.2, 5.26.5; cf. **55**.1). In particular, oral tradition will have made the tyrannicides' motives ideological rather than erotic (cf. intr. n. above), and is also unlikely to have matched Th.'s genealogical precision on Hippias' family (Kinzl 1973).   ξυντυχίαν 'incident'.   ἐγὼ ἐπὶ πλέον διηγησάμενος ἀποφανῶ: this is very Herodotean: with ἐπὶ πλέον cf. Hdt. 2.35.1 ἔρχομαι δὲ περὶ Αἰγύπτου μηκυνέων τὸν λόγον, and for ἀποφανῶ Hdt. 7.99.3 τὸ ἔθνος ἀποφαίνω πᾶν ἐὸν Δωρικόν . . .: cf. Thomas 2000: 227.

54.2 Πεισιστράτου γὰρ γηραιοῦ τελευτήσαντος: in spring 527. οὐχ Ἵππαρχος, ὥσπερ οἱ πολλοὶ οἴονται . . . ἔσχε τὴν ἀρχήν: the other version is found in [Plato], *Hipparchus* 228b–229d, where Socrates makes Hipparchus 'the eldest and wisest of Peisistratus' sons' and Hippias his successor after the assassination; the tone of that passage is hard to gauge, and various aspects seem tweaked to suit 'Socrates'' argument (Hirsch 1926). The killers were glorified as 'tyrannicides': every Athenian will have known the drinking-songs that celebrated the day when Harmodius and Aristogeiton 'killed the tyrant Hipparchus' or 'killed the tyrant and made Athens *isonomoi*' (*PMG* 893, 89, and 896). These would be in the minds of many when they viewed the famous bronze statues in the *agora* (Fig. 2, Azoulay 2017), replaced in 477/6 BCE after the originals were removed by Xerxes, and these could readily promote the assumption that Hipparchus was indeed tyrant: cf. **55**.4 n. Still, it is unclear how widespread that conception was. Hdt. refers casually to 'Hipparchus son of Peisistratus, the brother of Hippias the tyrant' (5.55.1); [Arist.] *Ath. pol.* 18.1 similarly makes Hippias succeed Peisistratus in the ἀρχή as the elder brother, though he also links Hippias and Hipparchus together as κύριοι τῶν πραγμάτων. Reference could also be made to 'the rule of the Peisistratids' or, as at **53**.6, 'of Peisistratus and his sons', and perhaps the family should be envisaged as ruling rather than any one son: so Lewis, *CAH* iv² 288 and Sancisi-Weerdenburg 2000: 13–15 ('a family business').

A better-informed debate can also be detected on who really deserved the credit for removing the tyrants, whether Harmodius and Aristogeiton, at least symbolically and perhaps by delayed effect (so e.g. Plato, *Symp.* 182c5–7 and Arist. *Rhet.* 2.1401b11–12), or Cleisthenes, the Alcmaeonids and, when mentioned at all, the Spartans. This played its part in the partisan exchanges that often surrounded the Alcmaeonids (cf. esp. Thomas 1989: ch. 5). Hdt. is here trenchant: 'thus the Alcmaeonids were the people who liberated Athens much more than Harmodius and Aristogeiton, so it seems to me' (6.123.2). Th. again agrees (**59**.4), though **53**.3 initially put more weight on the Spartans. ὧραι ἡλικίας λαμπροῦ 'renowned for his youthful beauty', lit. 'resplendent in the bloom of his youthfulness'. Athenians would already have an impression of that beauty from the *agora* statue. ἀνὴρ τῶν ἀστῶν, μέσος πολίτης 'a city-dweller, a citizen of middling status'. It would normally be hopeless for such a man to succeed as a rival to a tyrant's brother. εἶχεν αὐτόν 'was the lover in possession'. On the homosexual aspect, taken as read by Th. but ignored by Hdt., see *CT* 436–8.

54.3 πειραθείς: the active is standard for 'to make a pass at'. ὑπὸ Ἱππάρχου: [Arist.] *Ath. pol.* 18.1 says that the pass was made not by Hipparchus but by his younger brother Thessalus (**55**.1 n.), who was also the one responsible for humiliating Harmodius' sister (18.2); that passage stresses that Harmodius too was ἐρωτικός (18.1), probably signalling awareness of the usual account. That may be deliberately correcting Th. and may be right: multiple versions may have survived (Thomas 1989: esp. 261 and n. 68). If Th. knew that version one can see why he rejected it, as it was inconsistent with his reconstruction of the killers' motives at **57**.3. For a different view see *APF* 448–9 and Rhodes 1981: 227–8, 230. ἐρωτικῶς περιαλγήσας 'feeling a lover's anguish at this'. As at **54**.2 and **56**.2, Th. emphasises Aristogeiton (Tsakmakis 1995: 197), perhaps assuming that as the older man he would give the lead. This may be a minor further way in which he goes against the popular grain, for the drinking-song was often known as 'the Harmodius-song' (Azoulay 2017: 42, 72–3). μὴ βίαι προσαγάγηται αὐτόν: προσάγεσθαι, 'draw to oneself' or 'attract', puts it mildly. Getting sex by force (cf. βίαιον, **54**.4) was part of the tyrannical stereotype: Hdt. 3.80.5 has βιᾶται γυναῖκας, but boys might be victims too. Physical rape is not excluded, but the phrase includes using the power imbalance to leave the victim no real choice. ἐπιβουλεύει εὐθύς: Th. again puts more weight on Aristogeiton. ὡς ἀπὸ τῆς ὑπαρχούσης ἀξιώσεως 'in so far as he could, given his status'. A man of higher standing might do things differently, recruiting powerful collaborators and able to gain readier access to the tyrant's presence. κατάλυσιν τῆι τυραννίδι: such language is used by e.g. Arist. *Rhet.* 2.1401b11–12, and Plato, *Symp.* 182c57, but in terms of what Harmodius and Aristogeiton *achieved*. For Th. it is only an aspiration, one that existed even before the insult of **56**.1. Perhaps this suggests that ideology did play a part, but Th. may be presenting the aspiration as a *consequence* of the desire for revenge, repaying one hurt – at least the hurt anticipated, for the lovers could expect

Hipparchus to use force – with a very extreme one. There is also a matter of security, for if the tyrants remained in power any retaliation, or even Harmodius' refusal, would put the lovers in great danger. **56**.2–3 however does suggest more of a political dimension: see nn. there.

54.4 πειράσας: 54.3 n.   **βίαιον μὲν οὐδὲν ἐβούλετο δρᾶν:** thus far belying the stereotype, 54.3 n.   **ἐν τρόπωι ... προπηλακιῶν αὐτόν** 'made plans to humiliate him, but in a covert way so as to give the impression that it was not for this reason'. δή marks the disingenuousness: *GP* 231.

54.5 οὐδὲ ... ἐπαχθεῖς ἦσαν ... κατεστήσαντο: οὐδὲ γάρ marks this as both an explanation for Hipparchus' behaviour now and an additional comment on the reign: cf. Huitink–Rood on X. *Anab.* 3.4.36. The MSS have οὐδὲ ... ἐπαχθὴς ἦν ... κατεστήσατο, thus referring this only to Hipparchus. οὐδὲ ... ἐπαχθὴς ἦν might be possible, as a tradition survived of Hipparchus as the more agreeable brother ([Plato], *Hipparchus* 228b4–229a7, cf. [Arist.] *Ath. pol.* 18.1); but κατεστήσατο would only fit the version that Th. rejects, i.e. that Hipparchus was sole ruler. The move to plurals is easy, esp. in view of those that follow in ἐπετήδευσαν etc. Hipparchus can be regarded as participating in the 'family business' (**54**.2 n.) of ἀρχή, even if Hippias was 'the' tyrant: so also *Ath. pol.* 17.3 and 18.1, and that is assumed in 'the tyranny of Peisistratus and his *sons*' at **53**.6.   **ἀνεπιφθόνως:** whereas the stereotypical tyrant 'feels φθόνος against the ἄριστοι if they survive and live', Hdt. 3.80.4. Cf. **83**.2 n.   **ἐπὶ πλεῖστον δὴ τύραννοι οὗτοι:** that is, compared with other tyrants.   **ἀρετὴν καὶ ξύνεσιν:** high praise, for Th.: Theseus (2.15.2), Themistocles (1.138.3), Hermocrates (**72**.2), and the oligarchs of 411 (8.68.4) have ξύνεσις, Antiphon (8.68.1) and, strikingly, Nicias (7.86.5 [n.]), have ἀρετή, and Brasidas too has both (4.81.2). Hdt. praises Peisistratus himself in similar terms: 'then Peisistratus ruled the Athenians without disturbing the accustomed positions of honour (τιμαί) or changing the traditions (θέσμια), but administered the city on the basis of its existing traditions (ἐπί ... τοῖσι κατεστεῶσι), adorning it (κοσμέων) beautifully and well' (1.59.6). That is echoed here, esp. in καλῶς διεκόσμησαν and τοῖς πρὶν κειμένοις νόμοις, but Th. extends the praise to the sons, at least before 514.   **εἰκοστὴν μόνον πρασσόμενοι τῶν γιγνομένων** 'exacting only a 5 per cent tax on produce'. This goes causally with the main clause: this was enough to support the 'adornment', warfare, and sacrificing. [Arist.] *Ath. pol.* 16.4 says it was a δεκάτη, lit. 10 per cent. Perhaps one is wrong, perhaps it changed at some point, or perhaps δεκάτη is being used generically for a 'levy'.   **τήν τε πόλιν αὐτῶν καλῶς διεκόσμησαν:** on the tyrants' building cf. Andrewes, *CAH* iii². 3 410–15 and Lewis *CAH* iv² 294–7. Especially notable were temples to Athena and Olympian Zeus, but there were also, for instance, the altars of 54.6 and the Enneacrounos (2.15.5). καὶ τοὺς πολέμους διέφερον 'carried through their wars to a conclusion' (rather than cutting them short for lack of funds; cf. 1.11.2, 8.75.2): literally 'the' wars, as warfare was only to be expected in any extended period. One of these was to aid Plataea against Thebes in 519 (Hdt. 6.108), and there were interventions at Naxos (Hdt. 1.64.2) and Sigeum (Hdt. 5.94.1). Our information on that period is sketchy, and there were probably more. καὶ ἐς τὰ ἱερὰ ἔθυον: perhaps giving a more precise twist to Hdt.'s 'not changing the θέσμια' (1.59.6, quoted above).

54.6 αὐτὴ ἡ πόλις 'the city itself', without interference from the tyrant. τοῖς πρὶν κειμένοις νόμοις . . . ἐν ταῖς ἀρχαῖς εἶναι: again echoing Hdt. (see on ἀρετὴν καὶ ξύνεσιν above), but making it clear that Hdt.'s 'accustomed positions of honour' indeed remained but 'one of themselves' – perhaps family, perhaps including trusted followers – would occupy one of them. That clarification is necessary to explain the dedication of **54.7**. For the tyrants' management of the archonship see Lewis, *CAH* iv² 288–9. τὴν ἐνιαύσιον Ἀθηναίοις ἀρχήν: the annual eponymous archonship. τοῦ τυραννεύσαντος: here and at 55.1 (ἦρξεν) and 55.2 (τυραννεῦσαι) the force of the aor. is probably '*became* tyrant' (ingressive, *CGCG* 33.29), rather than indicating 'past only from the standpoint of writer and reader' (*HCT*). τῶν δώδεκα θεῶν βωμὸν τὸν ἐν τῆι ἀγορᾶι: in the NW corner of the *agora*. It was erected before 519, when the Plataeans became suppliants there (Hdt. 6.108.4). It was the centre-point from which distances were measured (Hdt. 2.7.1), and would be familiar even to many non-Athenians. ἄρχων 'as archon', probably in 522/1 BCE: ML 6 with comm. and Lewis, CAH iv² 289. Th. seems to imply that both altars were erected during the archonship, not just that in the *agora*, but does not quite say so. If he meant this, he may have been wrong about the second one (54.7 n.). ἐν Πυθίου: to be understood is e.g. τεμένει, as in the inscription. The precinct of Pythian Apollo in Athens was S of the Temple of Olympian Zeus on the right bank of the Ilissos.

54.7 προσοικοδομήσας . . . μεῖζον μῆκος τοῦ βωμοῦ 'enlarged the altar to a greater length', lit. 'built in addition a greater length of the altar'. As Th. does not quite bring out, the effacement may have been part of the purpose of the enlargement, not just an accidental by-product. τοῦ δ' ἐν Πυθίου . . . ἀμυδροῖς γράμμασι: the inscription survives (ML 11 = Fornara 37). Its letters are still clear, and so ἀμυδροῖς ('faint') probably refers to the wearing away of their red paint. The inscription is presumably quoted partly as a curiosity, partly to show that, at least on this occasion, 'one of themselves' was archon (54.6). It serves as a transition to the more adventurous epigraphic inferences of 55. μνῆμα τόδ'... τεμένει: the epigram is discussed by Page 1981: 240–1 and Petrovic 2007: 260–6. One might assume that the memorial was erected or inscribed before 511/10 and probably during the archonship itself of 522/1, but the lettering suggests a fifth-century dating. Arnush 1995 suggested that Peisistratus was allowed to return to Athens in the early 490s and commemorated his much earlier archonship; Viviers 1992: 86–9, 108–10 defended the 522 dating, and explained the letter-forms as the work of an Ionian mason or one under heavy Ionian influence.

55.1 "Ὅτι δὲ πρεσβύτατος ὢν Ἱππίας ἦρξεν: echoing 54.2 as Th. reverts to supporting that part of his claim. For the aor. see 54.6 n.   εἰδὼς μὲν καὶ ἀκοῆι ἀκριβέστερον ἄλλων ἰσχυρίζομαι: similarly echoing 54.1 ἀκριβὲς οὐδὲν λέγοντας, as Th. contrasts his own hearsay. His insistence strictly concerns only the brothers' relative age and status, but might also apply to his version of the 'erotic incident': he gives no other reason to accept it. He does not explain why he is so confident. It is not because there is evidential support concerning the relative ages, for that is added as a second point. Perhaps his audience is expected to remember the comparison of rival versions outlined at 1.22.2 [Intr., 2), but there he was concerned with eye-witnesses. Cf. Grethlein 2010: 218–20.   γνοίη δ' ἄν τις: such τις language is a predilection of Th. in such methodological passages: Rawlings 2010: 258–67. It is another Herodotean touch (Hdt. 1.134.1, 2.7.2).   τῶν γνησίων ἀδελφῶν: see on Θεσσαλοῦ... below.   ἡ στήλη ἡ περὶ τῆς τῶν τυράννων ἀδικίας: this *stēlē* has not survived. It was presumably erected after Hippias' expulsion in 511/10. If the *stēlē* recorded a formal prosecution or declaration of outlawry, the word ἀδικία may have figured in a preamble before listing precise charges; or the *stēlē* may have been a general celebration of the tyrants' departure; or the word may not have occurred at all, if Th. is paraphrasing before moving on to the list of names, the point that concerned him.   Θεσσαλοῦ μὲν οὐδ' Ἱππάρχου: for οὐδὲ... οὐδείς see LSJ οὐδέ A.II.2 and e.g. Hdt. 1.215.2 σιδήρωι δὲ οὐδ' ἀργύρωι χρέωνται οὐδέν. Thessalus (**54**.3 n.) is also mentioned at 1.20.2. Th. obviously takes these to be the two 'legitimate' (γνησίων) brothers. Two sons of Peisistratus by an Argive woman, Hegesistratus and Iophon, are mentioned by Hdt. 5.94.1 and [Arist.] *Ath. pol.* 17.4, which adds (not very plausibly) that Hegesistratus was another name for Thessalus. If by 'legitimate' Th. means 'sons of Peisistratus by his Athenian wife', that may be less a matter of retrojecting Pericles' citizenship law of 451 BCE, requiring citizen blood on both sides, than of assuming Peisistratus' relationship with the 'Argive γυνή' (Hdt. 5.94.1) to be extramarital. Hdt.'s description of Hegesistratus as a νόθος may make the same assumption (though cf. *APF* 445–6), but *Ath. pol.* 17.4 is explicit that they were married. So also Plut. *Cato mai.* 24.8, probably following *Ath. pol.* παῖδες . . . πρῶτον γῆμαι: yet Hdt. 5.65.1 spoke of the sons of 'the Peisistratids', plural.

Th.'s argument is not well expressed and would not have been strong even if it had been. The 'altar' shows only that Hippias had a son, not that his brothers did not, so all rests on the *stēlē*. The εἰκός argument (**54–59** n.) seems to assume that the *stēlē* was erected when Hippias already had five sons but his three younger brothers had not yet had time to marry: that is inherently implausible, especially as the *stēlē* could not have been put there till 511/10 when Hippias was already about 60 years old. Some argument along the lines that 'Hippias' sons were mentioned as being particularly important' as potential heirs would have been stronger. **Καλλίου τοῦ Ὑπεροχίδου:** the marriage would have been c. 550. This Callias (*APF* 450–2) was not necessarily related to the better-known fabulously rich family of the *genos* Kerykes (*APF* 254–70). Cleidemus, *FGrH* 323 F 15 made Hippias' wife the daughter of an ex-polemarch Charmus: that is not impossible if Hippias married twice.

55.2 τὸ πρεσβεύειν τε ἀπ' αὐτοῦ καὶ τυραννεῦσαι: closely connected ideas, so that one τό can go with both, 'being his eldest son and [therefore] becoming tyrant'. For the ingressive aor. see **54.6** n.

55.3 οὐ μὴν οὐδέ 'Nor, again . . .': *GP* 338–9. **ἂν κατασχεῖν** = ἂν κατέσχε in direct speech, an unreal condition in the past. **ποτέ:** without here a strong temporal sense, as with Engl. 'he would never have . . .'. **αὐτὸς δὲ αὐθημερὸν καθίστατο** 'and he would have been establishing himself [in power] on that very same day'. **ἀλλὰ . . . τῆι ἀρχῆι** 'but because the citizens had already become accustomed to fearfulness and the bodyguard to strict discipline, he was successful because he already had a good deal more than enough security [lit. 'a great surplus of security'], and he was not left at a loss as a younger brother in a position where he had not earlier been continuously familiar with power'. καὶ . . . καί co-ordinates the two clauses, the first explaining what was the case and the second what was not. The argument is open to the objection that it may have been a joint family rule (**54**.2 n.). **τοῖς μὲν πολίταις φοβερόν:** not altogether consistent with the insistence on the reign's earlier moderation (**54**.5–6), but one can be afraid even of a mild tyrant. **ἐς δὲ τοὺς ἐπικούρους ἀκριβές:** 'the', because it is taken for granted that a tyrant has bodyguards: cf. Hdt. 1.59.5, 98.2, Plato, *Rep.* 8.566b, 567d–e, and Pelling 2011: 429 on Plut. *Caes.* 57.7.

55.4 τοῦ πάθους τῆι δυστυχίαι . . . τὴν δόξαν τῆς τυραννίδος: the word-order emphasises τοῦ πάθους and τὴν δόξαν (**33**.1 n.). **ὀνομασθέντα**

'became famous'. Th. may be thinking particularly of the drinking-songs celebrating tyrannicide (54.2 n.), so that Hipparchus was assumed to be a tyrant as well (καί) as unfortunate victim.

56.1   δ' οὖν: resumptive, picking up the narrative from 54.3 and echoing its phrasing (πείρασιν/πειράσας,   προυπηλάκισεν/προπηλακιῶν). **ἀπαρνηθέντα:** despite its passive formation, this is the normal Attic aorist of the middle ἀπαρνέομαι, 'flatly reject'.   **ἐπαγγείλαντες . . . ἀπήλασαν:** plural after the singular προυπηλάκισεν: now Hippias as well as Hipparchus plays a part.   **κανοῦν οἴσουσαν:** to be a 'basket-carrier' was a considerable honour: 'during the reign of Erichthonius it was first established that maidens of respected standing (αἱ ἐν ἀξιώματι παρθένοι) should carry to the goddess the baskets containing the sacrifices, both in the Panathenaea and in the other processions' (Philochorus, *FGrH* 328 F 8). See Parker 2005: 223–6. Aristogeiton was of 'middling status' (54.2), but Th. has said nothing of Harmodius' family. Hdt. 5.57–61 argues that both were originally migrants from Eretria.   **ἐν πομπῆι τινι:** not the Panathenaea, as [Arist.] *Ath. pol.* 18.2 claims. That was still to come (56.2).   **διὰ τὸ μὴ ἀξίαν εἶναι:** perhaps a reference to her family (see above); perhaps an insinuation that she was not a virgin, an even worse insult.

56.2 μᾶλλον: perhaps 'more' than Harmodius himself, perhaps 'more' than he was enraged before (54.3).   **τὰ μὲν ἄλλα . . . ἐπέπρακτο:** the pluperfect momentarily stops the action: everything else had been set up, but they were waiting for the festival. Hdt. uses the same technique: cf. e.g. 6.24.2 with Hornblower–Pelling's n.   **τοὺς ξυνεπιθησομένους τῶι ἔργωι:** more than 54.3 (n.), this does suggest that there was more to it than a lovers' quarrel, and so does the expectation that others will join in impromptu, 56.3. Hippias himself already suspected plotting, 58.2.   **Παναθήναια τὰ μεγάλα:** Athens' greatest civic festival, celebrated in high summer: see Parker 2005: 253–69. The Panathenaea were celebrated every year, the Great Panathenaea one year in four. Its climax was this great procession, as later celebrated on the Parthenon frieze. Th. makes the choice of the festival a practical one, but if Hippias was so accessible (57.2) there would be alternative opportunities: there was emblematic significance too in choosing a festival so central to the city's sense of itself.   **τοὺς τὴν πομπὴν πέμψοντας** 'those who would take part in the procession'. For this hoplite contingent cf. Parker 2005: 260 and n. 27.   **ξυνεπαμύνειν δὲ εὐθὺς τὰ πρὸς τοὺς δορυφόρους ἐκείνους** 'and then they [οἱ ξυνεπιθησόμενοι] should immediately join in and defend them against the bodyguards', lit. 'in the matters with relation to the bodyguards': 'defend', because the expected picture is one of bodyguards rushing up immediately they see the attack.

56.3 ἀσφαλείας ἕνεκα: Hdt.'s Darius knew the danger of exposure once a plot was conceived, in that case against the usurper 'magus'. When it was suggested that more should be recruited, he retorts 'if you do that you will die miserably: someone will tell the magus for his own personal gain'. He also warns against delay: 'do it today, or I will tell the magus myself' (3.71.4–5). Now the delay till the Panathenaea itself magnified the risk.   **τοὺς μὴ προειδότας:** μή rather than οὐ because indefinite, 'people who would not have known beforehand'.   **καὶ ὁποσοιοῦν:** like καὶ ὁποσονοῦν at 4.37.1, in context this means 'however few'. The plotters are very confident.   **ἐκ τοῦ παραχρῆμα ἔχοντάς γε ὅπλα ἐθελήσειν σφᾶς αὐτοὺς ξυνελευθεροῦν** 'would be willing, given that they had weapons in their hands, to join in impromptu to set themselves free'. This, particularly the language of liberation, points to an ideological as well as a personal dimension, at least in the mentality expected in others: cf. **54**.3, **56**.2 nn.

57.1 καὶ ὡς ἐπῆλθεν ἡ ἑορτή: the festival lasted several days, but Th. focuses on the climactic procession.   **ἔξω:** the city wall (cf. ἔσω τῶν πυλῶν, **57**.3) ran through the Kerameikos. The procession started at the city's edge to allow a substantial distance so that many could watch (Parker 2005: 258). It would make its way to the acropolis and there present the goddess with her embroidered robe (*peplos*).   **διεκόσμει ... προῆισαν:** the two imperfects raise the suspense by dwelling on the last moments before the strike: Hippias was getting the different participants into order (officials, maidens, metics, hoplites, cavalry, sacrificial animals, etc.: Parker 2005: 259–61); meanwhile the assassins were stealthily moving to the front of the crowd, daggers at the ready. [Arist.] *Ath. pol.* 18.3 pictures it differently, with Hipparchus organising the procession and Hippias waiting on the acropolis. That may represent the author's own εἰκός inference on the most plausible way for the brothers to divide their roles (Fornara 1968: 407–9).

57.2 ὡς εἶδόν τινα τῶν ξυνωμοτῶν σφίσι διαλεγόμενον οἰκείως τῶι Ἱππίαι: σφίσι goes with ξυνωμοτῶν, τῶι Ἱππίαι with διαλεγόμενον. Such panicky confusion is a staple of assassination stories: on the Ides of March the plotters were similarly discountenanced by seeing one of their associates talking to Caesar, and then too the conversation was innocent (Plut. *Brut.* 16.2–3).   **εὐπρόσοδος:** a sign of a good ruler or commander (X. *Ages.* 9.2, *Anab.* 4.3.10, Plut. *Advice on public life* 823a), and one that could leave them vulnerable to attack (Dio 44.19.3, again of Caesar). Th. continues his stress on the Peisistratids' mildness before 514 BCE (**54**.5).   **μεμηνῦσθαι** 'that they had been denounced': the verb is used transitively as at 53.1.   ὅσον οὐκ ἤδη: a favourite idiom for such panicky expectation: cf. 8.96.3, Eur. *Hec.* 141, and X. *Hell.* 6.2.16 and 24.

57.3 προτιμωρήσασθαι: not quite in the oxymoronic sense of the rugby maxim 'get your retaliation in first': the τιμωρία is for the past insult, the προ- = before they are captured.   ὥσπερ εἶχον 'without more ado', lit. 'just as they were': another vivid touch. Cf. 8.41.3 and 42.1, and esp. Hdt. 2.121 δ.4, in the exciting story of Rhampsinitus.   ἔσω τῶν πυλῶν: 57.1 n.   παρὰ τὸ Λεωκόρειον καλούμενον 'next to the so-called Leokoreion'. Its location is uncertain: a site in the NW corner of the *agora* is possible. 1.20.2 and [Arist.] *Ath. pol.* 18.3 agree that this is where Hipparchus was killed as he was marshalling the procession. The brothers may each have been organising a different section, one outside and one inside the walls.   ὡς ἂν μάλιστα δι' ὀργῆς ὁ μὲν ἐρωτικῆς, ὁ δὲ ὑβρισμένος 'with all the anger one would expect, a lover's in the first case and driven by humiliation in the other'. The variation of construction with ὀργῆς is typically Thucydidean.   ἔτυπτον καὶ ἀποκτείνουσιν αὐτόν: the imperfect conveys the repeated strikes, another vivid touch; then for the critical act the historic present, the first since ἐπιβουλεύει (54.3) when it was all set in motion. The present tenses of διαφεύγει and ἀπόλλυται continue to immerse the reader in the action as it swiftly unfolds.

57.4 τοὺς δορυφόρους: their presence ('the' bodyguards) is again taken for granted, here with Hipparchus as at 55.3, 56.2, and 58.2 with Hippias.   ξυνδραμόντος τοῦ ὄχλου: perhaps to protect them as they anticipated at 56.2, perhaps just through excitement to see what had happened.   οὐ ῥαιδίως διετέθη 'was not gently dealt with': euphemistic for torture and then death. [Arist.] *Ath. pol.* 18.4–6 elaborates, with Aristogeiton naming many of Hippias' friends as accomplices, then intriguing Hippias by promising to expose many more: Aristogeiton mocked him for shaking the hand of his brother's killer on the deal, and Hippias stabbed him to death in fury – a 'melodramatic end' (Rhodes 1981: 233), and not at all in Th.'s manner even in so animated a narrative as this. Polyaenus 8.45 is more sensational still, with Aristogeiton's *hetaera* Leaena biting out her tongue under torture to stop herself revealing anything.

58.1 *Hippias' Response*

His calm effectiveness contrasts with the plotters' confused panic. [Arist.] *Ath. pol.* explicitly rejects this part of the story, presumably with Th. particularly in mind. For his reason see 58.2 n.   τοὺς πομπέας τοὺς ὁπλίτας 'the hoplites in the procession'.   ἀδήλως τῆι ὄψει πλασάμενος 'responding by arranging his features so as not to reveal anything', i.e. to avoid revealing (δηλοῦν) the truth; or perhaps 'inscrutably' (Spratt), not showing any emotion at all.   ἄνευ τῶν ὅπλων: an Attic *skyphos* of c. 460–450 depicts Harmodius and Hipparchus together with shields and helmets lying on the ground: Bicknell 1970, Azoulay 2017: 186. [Arist.] *Ath. pol.* 15.4, and Polyaenus 1.21.2 tell of a similar ploy of Peisistratus, with the *dēmos* at an armed display laying aside their weapons to hear him speak and then finding they had been disarmed. The story has probably migrated from one tyrant (it is uncertain which) to the other, but it is just possible that the same ploy worked twice, as it was regular practice to leave one's weapons to hear a speech: cf. 4.91. One should remember the practicalities. The clang of weaponry would make hearing difficult, crowding together with shields and spears would be awkward, and more could cram into a small space if they left the arms behind.

58.2 ἀνεχώρησαν: ἀν- economically paints a striking picture: Hippias will have gone up an incline to speak, the hoplites follow, and the bodyguards quietly remove the weapons behind and beneath them. Alberti prints ἀπεχώρησαν (H²: on that corrector see Intr., 36), but that has less appeal to the visual imagination.   **ὑπολαβεῖν** 'furtively remove'.   **εὐθὺς οὓς ἐπῃτιᾶτο:** so Hippias already had suspicions. Th. does not elaborate, perhaps taking for granted that tyrants generally had enemies to distrust. Again, this may suggest that ideology or general anti-tyrant feeling played a part in some minds.   **καὶ εἴ τις ηὑρέθη ἐγχειρίδιον ἔχων:** presumably under the armpit (Plato, *Gorg.* 469d, X. *Hell.* 2.3.23), perhaps in a sort of holster. The indic. suggests that some dagger-carriers were indeed discovered (cf. Wakker 1994: 276): so not just 'if anyone *might be* found', though H² (Intr., 36) emended to εὑρεθείη. These were presumably the ξυνεπιθησόμενοι τῶι ἔργωι of **56**.2.   **μετὰ γὰρ ἀσπίδος καὶ δόρατος εἰώθεσαν τὰς πομπὰς ποιεῖν:** [Arist.] *Ath. pol.* 18.4 rejects this part of the story 'for at that time they did not process in arms, but this was a later innovation by the *dēmos*'. In fact Th. seems right (Parker 2005: 260 n. 27).

59.1–2 Τοιούτωι μὲν ... ὑπάρχουσάν οἱ: Th. begins the rounding-off by echoing several phrases: with δι' ἐρωτικὴν λύπην cf. **54**.1 δι' ἐρωτικὴν ξυντυχίαν, **54**.3 ἐρωτικῶς περιαλγήσας, **57**.3 τὸν λυπήσαντα, and **57**.3 δι' ὀργῆς ὁ μὲν ἐρωτικῆς, ὁ δὲ ὑβρισμένος; with τῆς ἐπιβουλῆς cf. **54**.3; with ἡ ἀλόγιστος τόλμα cf. **54**.1, **56**.3, and **57**.3; with χαλεπωτέρα μετὰ τοῦτο ἡ τυραννίς cf. **53**.3. Some echoes also suggest reversals: ἐκ τοῦ παραχρῆμα περιδεοῦς echoes παραχρῆμα at **55**.3, **56**.3, and **57**.4, but the impromptu reactions have been different from those hoped for at **56**.3, with Hippias rather than onlookers seizing the moment; κατέστη echoes 54.5 κατεστήσαντο, first the tyranny established in mildness and then its turn to oppression. Harmodius took the insult χαλεπῶς (56.2), but it is the tyranny that now turns χαλεπωτέρα. See also 59.2 n. on φόβου and ἀσφάλειαν.   δι' ἐρωτικὴν λύπην . . . ἐγένετο: τε . . . καί link ἡ ἀρχὴ τῆς ἐπιβουλῆς and ἡ ἀλόγιστος τόλμα so closely that they can take the sing. verb ἐγένετο: cf. 7.44.1 n. δι' ἐρωτικὴν λύπην can go with both, as the love and the anguish were operative both at the beginning and at the strike: cf. 54.1 and 3 and esp. 57.3. C–S and others have taken ἐκ τοῦ παραχρῆμα περιδεοῦς just with ἡ ἀλόγιστος τόλμα, but it is better to take that too as qualifying both the ἀρχή and the τόλμα: fear at least played a part at the outset as well as at the strike, and it is not hard to imagine Aristogeiton's 'immediate' terror when he heard of his mighty rival.

59.2 τοῖς δ' Ἀθηναίοις: contrasting with Ἁρμοδίωι καὶ Ἀριστογείτονι: the lovers had their private vendetta, but the Athenians as a whole suffered for it.   χαλεπωτέρα . . . ἡ τυραννὶς κατέστη: so also Hdt. 5.55.1 and 62.2, [Arist.] *Ath. pol.* 19.1–2.   διὰ φόβου . . . ἀσφάλειάν τινα: for διὰ φόβου cf. 34.2 n. The fear (54.3, 59.1) and the concern for safety have now moved from tyrannicides to tyrant. In 415 such alarm transfers back to the *dēmos*, 53.3, along with the tyrant's χαλεπότης, 60.1 and 61.1.   τῶν τε πολιτῶν . . . καὶ πρὸς τὰ ἔξω: τε . . . καί ties the two points together to mark the paradox: killing one's fellow Athenians, looking abroad for safety.   ἔκτεινε καὶ . . . διεσκοπεῖτο: imperfects: he kept doing it. He exiled many too, [Arist.] *Ath. pol.* 19.1.   εἴ ποθεν . . . οἱ 'to see if he could identify some safe refuge that would be waiting for him if a revolution should come'. For ἀσφάλεια as 'source of safety' cf. 87.5.

59.3 γοῦν: the 'part proof' use (*GP* 441–3): the case of Lampsacus goes some way to demonstrating the generalisation that has preceded. Hippoclus took part in Darius' Scythian expedition at around this time (c. 513: Hdt. 4.138.1).   Ἀθηναῖος ὢν Λαμψακηνῶι: the word-order again (59.2 n.) emphasises the paradox – an Athenian joining with a Lampsacene! The cities had earlier been on bad terms (cf. Hdt. 6.37–8), but that brush had been with Miltiades as tyrant in the Chersonese, not with the Peisistratids. The point is more likely to be the surprising link with so minor a city.   αἰσθανόμενος . . . δύνασθαι: the choice of inf. rather than participle suggests 'believing that' rather than 'perceiving that': cf. 5.4.6, *CGCG* 52.24.   καὶ αὐτῆς σῆμα . . . ἔχον τόδε: by the time it was erected the sons were old enough to be 'tyrants' themselves, presumably succeeding their father either jointly or in succession. It looks therefore as if the tyranny continued after the Persian conquest of Lampsacus in 498 or 497 (Hdt. 5.117, *IACP* 987) – no surprise, if they could already be thought 'very influential with Darius'. **μέγα παρὰ βασιλεῖ Δαρείωι δύνασθαι:** a hint that Hippias is already thinking of his further move to the Persian court, **59**.4. **ἀνδρὸς ἀριστεύσαντος ... ἐς ἀτασθαλίην:** the third line is also quoted by Arist. *Rhet.* 1367b20–1 and attributed to Simonides, as such epigrams often were (inscribed epigrams did not state their composers): Lavelle 1986 and Petrovic 2007: 250–9 are inclined to accept Simonidean authorship, but Page 1981: 239–40 is unconvinced. It is uncertain when it was erected or by whom: perhaps Archedice's brothers, perhaps her sons. Th. does not imply that he has seen this inscription himself (ctr. **54**.7), but that does not mean that he did not. He might easily have travelled to Lampsacus during his Thracian exile. **πατρός τε καὶ ἀνδρὸς ἀδελφῶν τ' οὖσα τυράννων | παίδων τε:** the 'father' and 'husband' are clear, and for 'sons' see on καὶ αὐτῆς σῆμα above. The only 'brother' we know of was Peisistratus (**54**.6–7). Perhaps others were installed as tyrants in towns under Athens' control, as the elder Peisistratus imposed his son Hegesistratus at Sigeum (Hdt. 5.94.1); or perhaps the point is again that the tyranny was conceived as a 'family business' (**54**.2 n.), shared by all the sons (so Sancisi-Weerdenburg 2000: 14). **οὐκ ἤρθη νοῦν ἐς ἀτασθαλίην** 'was not carried away by this into thinking arrogantly': νοῦν is acc. of respect.

59.4 παυθεὶς ἐν τῶι τετάρτωι: 511/10 BCE. **ὑπὸ Λακεδαιμονίων καὶ Ἀλκμεωνιδῶν τῶν φευγόντων** 'by the Spartans and, among the exiles, the Alcmaeonids', echoing but also expanding **53**.3: this is the easiest way to unravel the genitive plurals. Th. does not need to go into detail, as the story is taken as familiar from Hdt. 5.62–5 and/or from oral tradition. **ἐχώρει ὑπόσπονδος ἔς τε Σίγειον καὶ παρ' Αἰαντίδην ἐς Λάμψακον:** generous treatment (cf. **54**.7 n.), as by then Athens controlled Sigeum (Hdt. 5.95.2) and might have excluded Hippias. 'Sigeum' would be known from Hdt. 5.65.3, 91.1, and 94.1, and Lampsacus could be inferred from the epigram: that does not prove that Hippias himself spent time there, but given the proximity to Sigeum and the presence of his daughter it was an easy guess. Doubtless there were oral traditions too. **ἐκεῖθεν δὲ ὡς βασιλέα Δαρεῖον:** he was still (or again) in Sigeum c. 504 (Hdt. 5.91.1, 94), and after that spent time with Artaphernes in Sardis (Hdt. 5.96). Th. clearly thinks that he also went to Darius himself and that he was at his court before leaving for the Marathon campaign. This may be right. **ἔτει εἰκοστῶι ... ἐστράτευσεν:** in 490 BCE, in fact the twenty-first year or (in archon years) the twenty-second, but Th. can be allowed to use a round number. Hippias' role at Marathon (Hdt. 6.102–20) is again taken as familiar.

60–61: ALCIBIADES RECALLED

The *Salaminia* arrived at **53**.1, and **53**.2–3 jumped back in time to describe the fearful atmosphere at Athens that had led to its despatch. The narrative now picks up the thread at Athens in that nervous phase, and so the events of **60**.1–**61**.5 took place earlier than the point that the Sicilian narrative had reached at **53**.1.

Various Peisistratid themes return here, though with shifts that emphasise that the *dēmos* is now directing events. Hippias had been fearful and suspicious (**59**.2); now it is the *dēmos* (**60**.1, **61**.1, cf. **53**.3), as ready to kill now (**60**.4–5) as Hippias was then. Anger drove the panicking Aristogeiton and Harmodius (**57**.4), and now drives the *dēmos* (**60**.2). Popular opinion was over-credulous about the tyrants (**54**.1, **60**.1); now the *dēmos* is again too quick to believe what it hears, thinking that τὸ σαφές has emerged (**60**.4, **61**.1), and Th. again knows better, for τὸ σαφές has never been known (**60**.2, cf. ἄδηλον, **60**.5). Once again a Spartan army is in the offing (**61**.2, cf. **53**.3, **59**.4); and again a precipitate action makes things worse. Cf. intr. n. to **54–59**.

Echoes may also be heard of the earlier passage on the Herms and Mysteries. Everything now seemed a matter of 'oligarchic and tyrannical conspiracy' (**60**.1 n.); at **27**.3 it had been 'revolutionary conspiracy and overthrow of the democracy' (cf. **28**.2), but 'tyrannical' now picks up the Peisistratid theme while also explaining the suspicions of, particularly, Alcibiades (cf. **15**.4).

60.1 μιμνησκόμενος ... χαλεπὸς ἦν τότε καὶ ὑπόπτης: this picks up the thread and echoes the language of **53**.3 ἐπιστάμενος γὰρ ὁ δῆμος ἀκοῆι ... χαλεπὴν (the word is used there of the tyranny, cf. **59**.2) ... πάντα ὑπόπτως ἐλάμβανεν. For ἐπίστασθαι cf. n. there: it is even more important here that it need not imply accurate 'knowledge'.   **τοὺς περὶ τῶν μυστικῶν τὴν αἰτίαν λαβόντας:** but it becomes clear that the hostility was against those charged concerning the Herms as much as the Mysteries, and that again, as at **27–9** (n.), the emphasis was first on the Herms and spread to the Mysteries. But this initial stress on the Mysteries prepares for the focus on Alcibiades, as the charge against him now centred on these (**61**.1).   **ἐπὶ ξυνωμοσίαι ὀλιγαρχικῆι καὶ τυραννικῆι:** for this train of thought and for ἐπί + dat. see **27**.3 n. This and 8.72.2 are the first occurrences of ὀλιγαρχικός in extant texts; here it may give some long-distance preparation for the revolutions of 411 (cf. **36–40, 54–60** nn.), while τυραννικῆι prepares for the more immediate focus on Alcibiades (**15**.4 n.). The combination 'oligarchic and (not 'or') tyrannical' may seem odd, but the *dēmos* may indeed have been fearful of both – or not have been clear what to fear.

The important aspect of both was that they were not democracy: cf. 3.62.3, a δυναστεία ὀλίγων ἀνδρῶν as 'neighbouring on tyranny'. The oligarchy of the 'Thirty Tyrants' in 404–403 (X. *Hell.* 2.4.1, etc.) would show how easily the terms could blur into one another.

60.2 πολλοί τε καὶ ἀξιόλογοι ἄνθρωποι: i.e. the πάνυ χρηστούς τῶν πολιτῶν of **53**.2. Th.'s indignation is clear. **ἐς τὸ ἀγριώτερόν τε καὶ πλείους ἔτι ξυλλαμβάνειν** 'to act with greater ferocity and make even more arrests'. Probably ἀγριώτερον is adverbial and to be taken with ξυλλαμβάνειν along with the direct obj. πλείους; but some may have heard τὸ ἀγριώτερον separately as an epithet-noun ('increased in ferocity') as in 8.24.4 ἐπεδίδου ... ἐπὶ τὸ μεῖζον, and understood a second ἐς τό before ξυλλαμβάνειν (so C–S and P–S). **ἀναπείθεται:** along with μηνύει at **60**.4, the historic presents point the two critical moments. Such moments often turn on persuasion, and hence πείθειν verbs attract a particularly large number of historic presents: cf. 7.39.2 and Jacquinod 2011. **εἷς τῶν δεδεμένων:** Andocides, as Th. surely knew: he had been imprisoned on the evidence of Diocleides (**27–29** n.; Andoc. *Myst.* 45). Why is he not named? Furley 1996: 52 suggests that Th. is protecting Andocides' reputation, but it is hard to detect such sympathy: he gives no hint of Andocides' own defence that the people he named were likely to be denounced anyway, and so he saved more lives than he was ready to sacrifice (*Myst.* 51–3). Perhaps it is rather a gesture of disapproval, denying him the respect, even the literary immortality, which naming him would give (Pelling 2000: 255–6 n. 4), but Th. elsewhere names people he would have thought πονηροί. Th.'s namings and non-namings are hard to reduce to any simple scheme: Hornblower *CT* ii: 135–7, Rood 2018: 153–6. **τῶν ξυνδεσμωτῶν τινος:** Th.'s account of this exchange in the prison is close to that of Andoc. *Myst.* 48–53, and if he wrote after 399 he may be drawing on that (Fornara 1980: 50–4). The fellow prisoner was his cousin Charmides according to Andoc. *Myst.* 48, a certain Timaeus according to Plut. *Alc.* 21.4–6. **εἴτε ἄρα καὶ τὰ ὄντα μηνῦσαι εἴτε καὶ οὔ:** καὶ ... καί emphasises that these are alternatives (*GP* 305), as at Plato, *Rep.* 5.471d, the case for having women on campaign εἴτε καί in the same ranks εἴτε καί in the rear. The focalisation here is uncertain: the fellow prisoner might himself have said 'whether true or not – that does not matter now', but this might equally be Th.'s comment. Andocides' own version was that he opposed the mutilation, but suffered an accident and was then falsely reported to his friends as planning to join in (*Myst.* 61–4): if that is right, he did not 'do it' (cf. δρασάντων τὸ ἔργον) but was certainly privy to the plan. It is a further question whether he knew if the men he denounced were guilty. Andoc. himself claims they were (*Myst.* 52–3, 55, 59: Pelling 2000: 33), but it was in his interest to say

COMMENTARY: 60.3–60.5

this. Plut. *Alc.* 21.5, 'it is better to make yourself safe by telling lies than to die in humiliation on the same charge', makes it clearer that, at least in Plut.'s view, he was lying. ἐπ' ἀμφότερα γὰρ εἰκάζεται 'conjectures are made in both directions'. εἰκάζεσθαι makes it clear that there is no decisive proof. περὶ τῶν δρασάντων τὸ ἔργον: 60.1 has left the impression that by τὸ ἔργον Th. means 'the Mysteries'; 60.4 will show that in fact Andocides' denunciation concerned the Herms, and *Myst.* 61–8 confirms this. The vagueness masks the jump from one to the other.

60.3 χρή, εἰ μὴ καὶ δέδρακεν, ... σῶσαι καὶ ... παῦσαι: καί may be emphatic, 'even if he did not actually do it', or may = 'even if he did not do it *as well*' (as confessing to it). χρή shows that it is an open question for the fellow prisoner whether Andocides 'did it'. Had it been an unreal condition ('even if you hadn't done it') the imperfect χρῆν would have been required: *CGCG* 34.17, *M&T* 415–16. ἄδειαν ποιησάμενον 'obtaining for himself immunity from prosecution'. καὶ τὴν πόλιν τῆς παρούσης ὑποψίας παῦσαι: Andoc. himself stresses this beneficial result of his actions (*Myst.* 50–1, 58–9, 61; *On his Return* 8). ἢ ἀρνηθέντι διὰ δίκης ἐλθεῖν 'than to deny it and come to court'. The structure of the sentence puts ἐλθεῖν into antithetical contrast with εἶναι, but in sense its contrast is with ὁμολογήσαντι μετ' ἀδείας. For διὰ δίκης ἐλθεῖν cf. Soph. *Ant.* 742.

60.4 κατ' ἄλλων: Andoc.'s own version was that only four of the men he named had not been denounced already (*Myst.* 52–3). He does not say how many other names he gave that had already figured on the other lists (**27–29** n.). μηνύει τὸ τῶν Ἑρμῶν: presumably to the ζητηταί (**27.2** n.), who would then have reported to the *dēmos* either directly or via the *boulē*. λαβών, ὡς ᾤετο, τὸ σαφές: but Th. has emphasised that matters were not really 'clear' at all (**60.2**). His scorn for popular credulity is as evident as in the Peisistratid excursus (**54–59** n.). καὶ δεινὸν ποιούμενοι: the phrase is a favourite of Hdt. (1.127.1, 7.163.1, 9.5.2, etc.), but cf. also Th. 1.102.4. The move from sing. to plural is easy: cf. 4.5 n. ὅσοι ξυνελήφθησαν 'as many as were captured'. These would largely be the men arrested earlier (**53.2, 60.2**). The others had presumably fled into exile. Still, Andocides' testimony probably led to further arrests, as **61.2** seems to imply (n.) and *Myst.* 52–3 may concede. ἐπανεῖπον ἀργύριον τῶι ἀποκτείναντι 'and in addition offered a sum of money to anyone who killed one of them'.

60.5 κἂν τούτωι ... περιφανῶς ὠφέλητο: the judgement may seem callous, and also surprising in view of Th.'s indignation at the treatment of respectable citizens (**27–29, 53.2, 60.2** nn.). But (1) the emphasis is partly on the ἄδηλον/περιφανῶς contrast: their guilt is unclear, but one thing that *is* clear is the benefit to the city . . . (2) . . . for the moment (ἐν τῶι παρόντι), Th. adds. The damage will come later, particularly because of the recall of Alcibiades, and the sentence prepares for the transition at **61**.1. (3) Forensic speeches, too, often stress the city's interests prominently: one strong reason for acquitting such a fine man or convicting such a scoundrel is that the city will benefit.   **ἄδηλον ἦν:** 'was' rather than 'is' (though it still 'is' unclear to Th. as well): as in ἐδόκει at **60**.1 and **60**.2, τότε at **60**.2, and ὡς ὤιετο at **60**.4, Th. keeps the focus on how things seemed at the time, and how little was certain.   **ἐτετιμώρηντο . . . ὠφέλητο:** the pluperfects round off this phase and reposition the narrative at the next stage, first at Athens (**61**.1–5) and then back in Sicily.   **ἡ . . . ἄλλη πόλις** 'the rest of the city'.

61.1 ἐναγόντων 'pressing the case': cf. **15**.2 n.   **τῶν ἐχθρῶν:** 8.65.2 describes the murder in 411 of the popular leader Androcles ὅσπερ καὶ τὸν Ἀλκιβιάδην οὐχ ἥκιστα ἐξήλασε; Plut. *Alc.* also names Androcles as Alcibiades' most vocal enemy before his departure, then Thessalus son of Cimon as mover of the eventual indictment (19.1–3 and 22.3, quoting the indictment verbatim).   **οἵπερ καὶ πρὶν ἐκπλεῖν αὐτὸν ἐπέθεντο: 28.2–29**.3. αὐτόν goes closely with ἐκπλεῖν (therefore not αὐτῶι), 'before he sailed'.   **χαλεπῶς οἱ Ἀθηναῖοι ἐλάμβανον:** again (**60**.1 n.) echoing **53**.3 and **59**.2 of the tyranny and **56**.2 of the tyrannicide.   **πολὺ δὴ μᾶλλον:** probably 'more than they had before' rather than 'more than with the Herms', but perhaps both.   **μετὰ τοῦ αὐτοῦ λόγου καὶ τῆς ξυνωμοσίας ἐπὶ τῶι δήμωι** 'with the same purpose and [i.e. 'namely', *GP* 291] the conspiracy against the people'. 'The' conspiracy, because this is focalised through the *dēmos*, and they now think of it as established fact.   **ἀπ' ἐκείνου:** to have originated 'from' him.

61.2 καὶ γάρ: 'introducing additional information (καί) which has explanatory force' (*CGCG* 59.66): cf. **103**.3.   **κατὰ τὸν καιρὸν τοῦτον ἐν ὧι περὶ ταῦτα ἐθορυβοῦντο:** this need not imply that it was after the events of **60**.2–4: see on πρὸς Βοιωτούς τι πράσσοντες below.   **μέχρι Ἰσθμοῦ παρελθοῦσα:** but not further. Presumably they heard that the Boeotian action, whatever it was (next n.), had fizzled out.   **πρὸς Βοιωτούς τι πράσσοντες** 'on some activity relating to the Boeotians': like Βοιωτῶν ἕνεκα, this may mean either planned co-operation or simply 'with an eye to'. Th. presents the expedition and its purpose as facts, whereas the notion that 'the city would have been betrayed' is only what 'was thought', ἐδόκει. Andoc. *Myst.* 45 also mentions this Boeotian development: the *boulē* imprisoned Andocides and the others, and on its advice the *stratēgoi* mobilised the Athenians in the city (see on κατέδαρθον ἐν Θησείωι below) at a time when 'the Boeotians had heard about these affairs and were on the frontier in arms'. That is, the Boeotians had already marched out when these actions were taken, and 'these affairs' will be the unrest and testimony that led to the arrests, not the arrests themselves. That is consistent with Th.'s chronology: the Athenians thought that the arrests *forestalled* the Boeotian initiative (καὶ εἰ μὴ ἔφθασαν . . .), and so it was already under way; then the pluperfect περιειστήκει at **61**.4 (n.) implies only that all this had contributed to the suspicions that then, some time after Andocides' denunciations, triggered the new move against Alcibiades. In that case the Boeotian and Spartan activity belongs shortly before **60**.2, i.e. before Andocides was arrested. Whatever the precise purpose of their initiative, the enemy probably hoped to exploit the crisis even if only to add to the unrest; the Athenians had good reason to be scared. By delaying mention of it to here Th. can emphasise the false rumour (Alcibiades was responsible) more than the sober truth, and again the *dēmos* emerges as unduly gullible. For speculation on what the Spartans were in fact up to see Pelling 2000: 24–5.   **πράσσοντες**: for the plural cf. **4**.5 n.   **εἰ μὴ ἔφθασαν δή**: δή adds an 'ironical tinge' (*GP* 229), 'implying, at most, that what follows is false; at least, that it not unquestionably true' (*GP* 233). One can almost hear the Athenians' mutual congratulations ('phew – we caught them in the nick of time') and sense Th.'s knowing scorn.   **κατὰ τὸ μήνυμα ξυλλαβόντες τοὺς ἄνδρας**: 'the' μήνυμα suggests the testimony given by Andocides himself, **60**.4, but it was Diocleides' earlier denunciations (**27–29** n.) that triggered most of the arrests: see on ὅσοι ξυνελήφθησαν, **60**.4. These are the thoughts of the *dēmos*, and they probably had both in mind.   **καί τινα μίαν νύκτα καὶ κατέδαρθον ἐν Θησείωι τῶι ἐν πόλει ἐν ὅπλοις**: Andoc. *Myst.* 45 gives more details: the *stratēgoi* instructed those in the city to come in arms to the *agora*, 'those within the long walls' (i.e. those living within the walls linking Athens and the Piraeus) to the Theseion, those in the Piraeus to the *agora* there, and the *hippeis* to the Anakeion; the *bouleutai* should sleep on the acropolis and the *prytaneis* in the *tholos* (i.e. their headquarters in the *agora*). That does not quite say that those living within the long walls should *sleep* in the Theseion, but is not inconsistent with that. The Theseion was probably N of the acropolis and SE of the *agora*; the Anakeion was nearby. See Travlos 1980: 577–8.

61.3 οἵ τε ξένοι τοῦ Ἀλκιβιάδου οἱ ἐν Ἄργει: for Alcibiades' Argive connections cf. **16**.6 and **29**.3 n.   **τοὺς ὁμήρους . . . κειμένους**: three hundred suspected of pro-Spartan sympathies who had been taken prisoner in 416 and placed in islands near the Attic coast (5.84.1).   **κειμένους**: here = the passive of τίθημι (**31**.1–2 n.); at 5.84.1 the verb is κατέθεντο.   **παρέδοσαν τῶι Ἀργείων δήμωι διὰ ταῦτα διαχρήσασθαι**: διὰ ταῦτα could give the reason for the handing over or for the execution or both. Alcibiades had been the one to round them up at 5.84.1; maybe he was now suspected of collusion with them, depositing them safely in preparation for a violent return, but if so Th. does not tell us.

61.4 περιειστήκει . . . ἐς τὸν Ἀλκιβιάδην 'had come round to settle on Alcibiades': for the pluperfect see **61.**2 n., and for περιίσταμαι ἐς cf. 7.18.3.   **ὥστε βουλόμενοι . . . ἐμεμήνυτο**: this brings the narrative almost back to the point of **53.**1, when the *Salaminia* arrived for Alcibiades and the others, but here the intention is more explicitly 'to bring him to trial and then kill him': a guilty verdict is taken as read. 'Him' rather than 'them': a similar fate might await the others, but there is not much interest in them (**61.**7 n.). For the present πέμπουσιν cf. **28.**1 n.   **ὧν πέρι ἄλλων ἐμεμήνυτο** = τοὺς ἄλλους περὶ ὧν ἐμεμήνυτο: cf. *GG* 1037 (for the omission of the article) and 1038.

61.5 θεραπεύοντες τό . . . μὴ θορυβεῖν 'taking care not to cause any disturbance with regard to the soldiers in Sicily, both their own and the enemy's': plural, as if εἰρήκεσαν rather than εἴρητο had preceded (cf. 2.53.4 with Rusten's n.). τό goes with θορυβεῖν ('hyperbaton', **11.**6 n.). The first τε might be expected to come immediately after θεραπεύοντες to co-ordinate with καὶ . . . βουλόμενοι, but the sentence is initially constructed as if θεραπεύοντες will introduce two parallel purposes; the second of these is then recast differently with 'the thought (or the construction) taking a different turn as it develops' (*GP* 519). θεραπεύω was also the verb used at **29.**3 of the *dēmos*' concern about the Argives and Mantineans. The blow to the Athenians' morale and the encouragement to the enemy would both be deleterious.   **τοὺς Μαντινέας καὶ Ἀργείους βουλόμενοι παραμεῖναι**: **29.**3 n.

61.6 τὴν ἑαυτοῦ ναῦν: 50.1 n.   **ἐν Θουρίοις**: where a Panhellenic colony had been founded in the 440s (*IACP* 304–7): see Map 2. The city's ethnic mix may have made it easier to slip away, for many there would have had little sympathy for Athens. Cf. **104.**2, 7.33.5 nn.   **ἐπὶ διαβολῆι**: picking up ξυνδιαβεβλημένοι. More than the formal denunciation is relevant: the general malicious talk made the result of the trial all too predictable.

61.7 ἤδη φυγὰς ὤν: ἤδη marks the crucial moment: this was the break from the city that would have such big consequences.   **ἐπὶ πλοίου** 'on a merchant ship': cf. **88.**9. We are not told what happened to 'his own ship': the Athenians probably appropriated it and sailed it back to Athens. It would be too conspicuous for Alcibiades to use.   **ἐς Πελοπόννησον**: first to Cyllene (**88.**9), and then he may well have gone to Argos (Plut. *Alc.* 23.1; Cawkwell 1997: 90) before Sparta. If so and if Th. knew it, he prefers to leave Alcibiades till he pops up in Sparta (**88.**9), as lost from the reader's view as he would have been from the Athenians'.   **ἐρήμηι**

δίκηι: the usual term for a trial *in absentia* (LSJ ἐρῆμος III). The defendant's case would then generally be lost by default: MacDowell 1978: 248–9. θάνατον κατέγνωσαν: it was also decreed that 'all priests and priestesses should formally curse' at least Alcibiades and perhaps the others. It was said that one priestess, Theano, refused (Plut. *Alc.* 22.5), but this may be a later fabrication (Sourvinou-Inwood 1988). καὶ τῶν μετ' ἐκείνου: at least some of these accompanied Alcibiades to Sparta (**88.**9), but they then fade out of the narrative.

62: END OF SUMMER 415

The first attempts to implement Alcibiades' diplomatic strategy of **48** had not gone well (**50–2**), though Catana had been seized (**51**). Plutarch is now scathing about these next operations: 'in the first place Nicias [whom Plut. assumes to be in control, **50.**1 n.] put distance between himself and the enemy when he went sailing around Sicily, and this boosted their morale; then he attacked Hybla, a tiny settlement, but left before capturing it; and finally he returned to Catana without achieving anything except the reduction of Hyccara, a barbarian place . . .' (*Nic.* 15.3–4). Plut. is here teasing out the implications he finds in Th.'s narrative; for the effect on Syracusan morale cf. **63.**2. The echoes of **47** (nn.) even suggest that Nicias is reverting to his more limited focus there on Egesta and Selinus. Still, diplomacy may not have been abandoned: presumably speeches were made at Himera (**62.**2), even if they were no more successful than those at Messina (**50.**1) and Camarina (**52**), and the approach to the Sicels (**62.**5) is a more peremptory equivalent of Alcibiades' plan to win them over (**48**). It was by now clear that the force would need to over-winter in Sicily, and the more allies and more resources the better.

CT associates with this expedition the fund-raising attested by *IG* i³ 291, but this is here taken as dating to 427–424: **44.**2 n.

62.1 οἱ λοιποὶ τῶν Ἀθηναίων στρατηγοὶ ἐν τῆι Σικελίαι: i.e. Nicias and Lamachus. Nicias is named soon enough (**62.**4), but Lamachus' name does not recur until **101.**6: cf. **62.**3 n. That silence may reflect his lack of influence (**50.**1 n.), though he will have had his say in decisions attributed to οἱ στρατηγοί (**64.**2). δύο μέρη ποιήσαντες τοῦ στρατεύματος καὶ λαχὼν ἑκάτερος: **42.**1 n. Alcibiades' departure necessitated some reorganisation, but ξύμπαντι immediately makes it clear that the two forces operated together. ἔπλεον ξύμπαντι ἐπὶ Σελινοῦντος καὶ Ἐγέστης: echoing Nicias' proposal to πλεῖν ἐπὶ Σελινοῦντα πάσηι τῆι στρατιᾶι, **47**: for ἐπί + gen. = 'in the direction of', **65.**1 n. This would be a surprisingly large fleet, but Nicias' concern had always been to make a display of force (**11.**4, **47**). The more distant Selinus is named first as the bigger town and as the stage expected to be the more important: Nicias knew what to expect from Egesta. In fact they did not reach Selinus at all. βουλόμενοι μὲν εἰδέναι τὰ χρήματα εἰ δώσουσιν οἱ Ἐγεσταῖοι: again picking up on the plan of **47**. μέν might be expected to follow εἰδέναι to co-ordinate with κατασκέψασθαι δέ, but such precise symmetry is often avoided: *GP* 371–3. 'The' money, taken as familiar, may refer just to the 30 talents of **46**.1, but given the other echoes it may be that Nicias' fallback request for τροφή for 60 ships (**47**) was reactivated. 30 talents was all that he got: **62**.4. κατασκέψασθαι . . . τὰ πρὸς Ἐγεσταίους: in **47** Nicias had talked of reconciling Selinus and Egesta ἢ βίαι ἢ ξυμβάσει. Plenty about these διάφορα had already been heard from the Egestaean ambassadors in Athens (**6**.1), but more could be learned on the spot, e.g. by inspecting the disputed territory, and putting it as 'their differences with the Egestaeans' suggests a readiness to ask the Selinuntines for their version.

62.2 παραπλέοντες δ' ἐν ἀριστερᾶι τὴν Σικελίαν: echoing παραπλεύσαντας at **47**. Sailing along the northern coast avoided duplicating the unsuccessful southern voyage at **50–1**. τὸ μέρος τὸ πρὸς τὸν Τυρσηνικὸν κόλπον 'the part facing the Tyrrhenian gulf', i.e. facing N: acc. in apposition with and more closely defining τὴν Σικελίαν. Ἱμέραν: see Map 1 and **5**.1 n. Himera was destroyed by the Carthaginians in 409 (*IACP* 199). The present tenses here and at 7.58.2 have been taken as an indication that this was written before that date, but that inference is uncertain: some settlement seems to have remained. Ἑλλάς: fem. adj. ὡς οὐκ ἐδέχοντο αὐτούς: Himera's population included many Dorians, even if the Chalcidians predominated (**5**.1 n., *IACP* 199). The city later openly supported Syracuse (7.1.3–5).

62.3 αἱροῦσιν: historic present for the expedition's most violent action. Ὕκκαρα: perhaps Monte d'Oro di Montelepre, perhaps Carini (cf. *CT* and *IACP* 177). Both towns are some 15 km W of Palermo (see Map 1), and near, though not actually on, the coast (cf. παραθαλασσίδιον). Σικανικὸν μέν, Ἐγεσταίοις δὲ πολέμιον: μέν . . . δέ notes the paradox: a Sican settlement might be expected to support Egesta (cf. **2**.3) against Greek Selinus (**4**.2). Timaeus, *FGrH* 566 F 23 and Diod. 13.6.1 say that Hyccara was Sicel rather than Sican and that view is preferred at *IACP* 177, but Th. is probably right. ἀνδραποδίσαντες τὴν πόλιν: a stark reminder of the realities of war. Other cities suffered similarly (Fragoulaki 2013: 323): this case was noteworthy because of the proceeds from the sale (**62**.4) and because some of the slaves end up as oarsmen in the Athenian fleet (7.13.2). παρέδοσαν Ἐγεσταίοις: a gesture in line with Alcibiades' policy of strengthening alliances (**48**), but practicalities also mattered: Athens could not afford to detach an occupying garrison, and could not expect to administer the town in the longer term. Cf. Euphemus' argument at **84** and **86**.3.   **πάλιν:** to be taken both with ἐχώρουν and περιέπλευσαν, as the position of μέν shows. The idea of going to Selinus was evidently abandoned.   **τῶι μὲν πεζῶι . . . ἐς Κατάνην:** they had to make room on the ships for the slaves, though some doubtless stayed on board as guards. The long march might not be easy. Did Lamachus lead it? One might assume so, but Th. does not tell us.

62.4 εὐθύς: probably retrospective: i.e. Nicias had moved on immediately from Hyccara leaving the main force to deal with its capture and enslavement. That explains the emphasis later in the sentence on his rejoining the στράτευμα.   **λαβὼν τάλαντα τριάκοντα: 46**.1, **62**.1 nn.   **ἀπέδοσαν** 'sold', though the middle is usual in that sense.   **ἐγένοντο:** on the plural with a neuter subj. see **13**.1 n.   **εἴκοσι καὶ ἑκατὸν τάλαντα:** if each was sold for 100 dr. that would mean 7,200 slaves, but the collection of material at *GSW* v. 242–3 suggests that 100 dr. would be towards the top end of usual prices, and probably the number was more like 10,000. Hyccara was evidently not a small place. The slaves recruited as oarsmen (7.13.2) were presumably sold to traders and then leased back as needed. The money mattered: by now the Athenians were short of cash (Kallet 2001: 104), especially if the contributions recorded at *IG* i³ 291 date to 427–424 rather than now (**44**.2 n.).

62.5 τοὺς τῶν Σικελῶν ξυμμάχους 'their allies among the Sicels'. **περιέπεμψαν:** the MSS have περιέπλευσαν, but the Sicels were inlanders. The intelligent corrector of H (**58**.2 n.) emended.   **κελεύοντες** 'urging' or 'telling them to' rather than 'ordering' (**13**.1 n.), but the Sicels might still have found this domineering. Still, some came (**65**.2).   **Ὕβλαν τὴν Γελεᾶτιν:** normally taken to be Paternò, some 18 km WNW of Catana. The name suggests a secondary foundation from (Greek) Gela, which would explain its enmity (cf. **67**.2), but Hybla was a Sicel town according to Diod. 11.88.6: cf. *IACP* 177 and Fragoulaki 2013: 294–5. Plut. *Nic.* 15.3 describes it as a πολίχνιον μικρόν, which is in line with Plut.'s dismissiveness (see intr. n. to **62**) but is probably right.   **καὶ οὐχ εἷλον:** the summer ends unimpressively.

63–71: EARLY WINTER 415–414: ATHENIAN SUCCESSES

The narrative takes on a new vigour: after the scrappy initiatives of the summer (**44–6, 50–2, 62**) the Athenians come up with a ruse that is wholly successful, followed by a battle where for the first time their initial hopes and confidence (**24**) appear justified. The energy contrasts too with the quiet noting of the summer's end at **62**.5; a slackening might then be expected, but for similar bursts of disconcerting autumn enterprise cf. 2.93, petering out at 2.94, and 8.2–3. The urgency fits the mindset of Lamachus (**49**), but Th. does not mention him (**62**.1 n.); οἱ στρατηγοί form the plan at **64**.1, and Nicias gives the speech at **68**. The sequence is bookended by the Syracusan cockiness of **63** and the increase in Athenian morale of **71**, and the interest in collective psychology is already clear (Intr. to Bk. 7, pp. 30–1). It was that cockiness that left the Syracusans vulnerable (**63, 65**.1), rather as Hermocrates warned (**33**.3).

63.1 τὴν ἔφοδον ... ὡς ἐπ' ἐκείνους ἰόντες: the variation of construction in parallel clauses is typical of Th.

63.2 τὸν πρῶτον φόβον καὶ τὴν προσδοκίαν: cf. **33**.5 n. on φόβος. This echoes Lamachus at **49**.2 τὸ γὰρ πρῶτον πᾶν στράτευμα δεινότατον εἶναι ... κατὰ πάντα ἂν αὐτοὺς ἐκφοβῆσαι ... τῆι προσδοκίαι ὧν πείσονται, and is itself picked up in Demosthenes' thinking at 7.42.3: see nn. on those passages.   **οὐκ εὐθὺς ἐπέκειντο:** this leaves it vague whether εὐθύς = 'immediately on arriving in Sicily', the context for Lamachus' advice at **49**, or 'immediately after occupying Catana': perhaps both, with the initial feeling of relief accentuated when the Athenians still failed to press the attack. 7.42.3 raises a similar issue: see n. there.   **κατά τε τὴν ἡμέραν ... ἔτι πλέον κατεφρόνησαν:** again echoing Lamachus at **49**.2 τῆι γνώμηι ἀναθαρσοῦντας ἀνθρώπους καὶ τῆι ὄψει καταφρονεῖν μᾶλλον and echoed at 7.42.3 ὅτι καὶ αὐτὸς ... τῆι πρώτηι ἡμέραι μάλιστα δεινότατός ἐστι τοῖς ἐναντίοις: cf. also Nicias at **23**.2.   **πλέοντες ... ἐφαίνοντο** 'they were evidently sailing ...', φαίνομαι + participle: **2**.2 n.   **τὰ ἐπ' ἐκεῖνα τῆς Σικελίας** '[the seas on] the far side of Sicily'.   **πειράσαντες** 'having made an attempt on' the city, active of πειράω, with e.g. τοῦ χωρίου understood.   **κατεφρόνησαν καὶ ἠξίουν:** the aor. κατεφρόνησαν is ingressive (**54**.6 n.); the imperfect ἠξίουν may also be 'began to', but more likely conveys sustained pressure.   **οἷον δὴ ὄχλος φιλεῖ θαρσήσας ποιεῖν** 'the sort of thing that a mob tends to do once it has become confident'. For the phrasing cf. 4.28.3 οἷον ὄχλος φιλεῖ ποιεῖν, there of the Athenians: the two *dēmoi* mirror each other. ὄχλος in a political context often conveys 'a tinge of contempt' (Dodds 1959: 204, cf. Hunter 1988–9; Saïd 2013: 203–4), and does so more regularly and strongly in Th. (cf. also **17**.2 and **89**.5 (nn.), 8.72.2, 8.86.5) and Plato (e.g. *Gorg.* 455a, *Rep.* 9.590b, *Euthyd.* 290a4) than in other authors; in a military context it is often pejorative in a different way, emphasising e.g. a lack of staying power (4.56.1, 4.126.6) or mere numbers that do not compensate for a lack of skill (2.88.2), but it can be more neutral as at **20**.4 and **64**.1.   **ἠξίουν τοὺς στρατηγοὺς ... ἄγειν** 'called on the generals to lead them'. It looks as if the decision remained one for the *stratēgoi*, but in a democracy such pressure might be hard to resist. ἐπειδή γε 'given that', explaining the Syracusans' thinking: *GP* 142, *CGCG* 48.4.

63.3 εἰ + indirect question: dependent on the verb of speaking implicit in ἐφύβριζον. **ξυνοικήσοντες... κατοικιοῦντες:** an elegantly and chiastically expressed gibe, with κατοικιοῦντες ('to settle others') contrasted with ξυνοικήσοντες ('to live there themselves with' – it is as if the Athenians are coming to be housemates or friendly neighbours); the οἰκ- of the verbs is also picked up in οἰκείαν, the Leontinians' 'own home'. Hermocrates will exploit a similar antithesis at **76.2**. Extra bite here comes from the earlier similarities to a colonising expedition: **1.2–5.3** and **23.2** nn., Intr., 1. Plut. may have read Th. too quickly or misremembered, for he has the weaker 'to live *with the Catanians* rather than to settle the Leontinians' (*Nic.* 16.1). **Λεοντίνους** 'Leontinians', the ethnic (**8.2** n.).

64.1 ἃ γιγνώσκοντες... μηχανῶνται: a monster sentence, with 104 words separating the subject (οἱ στρατηγοί) and the main verb (μηχανῶνται). Participial clauses summarise the generals' aims (βουλόμενοι) and their alertness to the difficulties (εἰδότες); a long parenthesis expands on the cavalry problem (τοὺς γὰρ... βλάπτειν ἂν μεγάλα), the hope that the plan would meet it (οὕτω δὲ... ἄξια λόγου), and the intelligence about a suitable base (ἐδίδασκον... ξυνείποντο); finally a repeated οἱ στρατηγοί is a reminder of the subject and πρὸς ἃ ἐβούλοντο of the clauses governed by βουλόμενοι. The structure mirrors the complex interplay of the factors and contrasts with the simpler sentences once events unfold, where verbal echoes will underline how everything goes according to plan (nn.), but this sentence is not generous to readers. Good oral delivery would make it easier for listeners. **πανδημεί:** a crucial element in the plan and in the ensuing reality: **64.3, 65.1, 67.2, 68.2**. **ἐν τοσούτωι** 'in the meantime', lit. 'in as much time (as this allowed)': cf. Ar. *Knights* 420. **ὑπὸ νύκτα: 7.2** n. **στρατόπεδον καταλαμβάνειν** 'to occupy [grounds for] a camp', as at **2.81.4**. **οὐκ ἂν ὁμοίως δυνηθέντες καὶ εἰ... ἐκβιβάζοιεν ἢ... γνωσθεῖεν** 'that their ability to do this would be different from (i.e. 'better than') what it would be if they were disembarking from ships against an enemy ready to receive them or were noticed making their way by land'. In direct speech they would say οὐκ ἂν ὁμοίως δυνηθεῖμεν. For this use of καί see **11.1** n. Many editors delete καί, which was possibly (not certainly) absent from the text used by the schol. and by Valla (Intr., 36): the translation would then be 'they would not be able to do this in the same way (i.e. 'so well') if they were disembarking...'. **τοὺς γὰρ ἂν ψιλοὺς... οἳ ξυνείποντο:** the indirect speech down to ἄξια λόγου conveys the generals' thinking, then the indicative ἐδίδασκον adds background in the narratorial voice.

Within the indirect speech βλάπτειν ἄν corresponds to an optative for the possibility they feared (in the direct-speech equivalent the subject would be οἱ ἱππεῖς, the object τοὺς ψιλοὺς καὶ τὸν ὄχλον), and the confident futures λήψεσθαι and βλάψονται convey what they now expected. For the repeated ἄν see **10**.4 n.; μεγάλα is internal acc. with βλάπτειν. **τὸν ὄχλον:** here neutral (**63**.2 n). **σφίσι δ' οὐ παρόντων ἱππέων:** the generals know their cavalry deficiency: Intr., 6. The Athenians presumably still had the 30 horsemen of **43** and those from Egesta (**62**.3), but Th. may ignore them here as so outnumbered as to be negligible; or perhaps they were away on herald duty (Bugh 1989: 48). **ὅθεν ... οὐ βλάψονται ἄξια λόγου** 'from which [they would operate and] not suffer serious harm' (internal acc.). The middle form of the future is used with a passive meaning also at 1.81.4. **ἐδίδασκον δέ:** δέ rather than γάρ, for receiving this information does not explain why Athenians wanted to occupy such a place; it is a helpful complement once the ambition is formed ('why, we know just the place . . .'). **τοῦ πρὸς τῶι Ὀλυμπιείωι χωρίου:** i.e. the land by (πρός + dat.) the temple of Olympian Zeus: this will play an important part in events, esp. at **70**, 7.4.6, and 7.37.2. The temple was at Le Colonne, W of the Great Harbour. There was a treasury in the temple (**70**.4), but that was not the reason for targeting the area here. **ὅπερ καὶ κατέλαβον:** a flash-forward – they *went on* actually to capture this area as well as (καί) just targeting it. The temple itself remained uncaptured (**71**.1). **Συρακοσίων φυγάδες:** this is the first we have heard of these, though their existence is no surprise given Syracuse's history of στάσις (**5**.1 n.). Th. characteristically delays their mention to the point when they become important: see Rood 1998 and Pelling 2000 and 2019, indexes s.v. 'delay, narrative'. **οὖν:** resumptive, after the long parenthesis: *GP* 428–9.

64.2 πέμπουσιν: historic present for the critical move. There is asyndeton (i.e. no connective particle), as τοιόνδε τι has already made the link. **τοῖς δὲ ... ἐπιτήδειον** 'but on just as good terms with the Syracusan generals, so they would think'. The ruse will be repaid in kind at 7.73.3, when some Syracusan horsemen pretend to be pro-Athenian and warn Nicias *not* to lead the army away at night. The model in historiography, and perhaps in real life, was Themistocles' two messages to Xerxes at Hdt. 8.75 and 110. **ἐν τῆι πόλει ἔτι ὑπολοίπους ὄντας τῶν σφίσιν εὔνων:** the Syracusan sympathisers in Catana were dominant at **50**.3, but **51**.2 had described their flight. Th. has characteristically delayed the important item that some remained. **ἔφη:** to the Syracusan generals (ἐκεῖνοι). He would of course have given the names. **ἠπίσταντο:** οὕς is understood from the preceding ὧν. ἐπίσταμαι need not mean firm 'knowledge'

(37.1 n.), but here it probably does: the people named would indeed be pro-Syracusan. What was false was the information.

64.3 αὐλίζεσθαι: presumably – so the informant implied – in a separate camp (*GSW* ii. 140), but perhaps billeted in private houses.   **ἀπὸ τῶν ὅπλων** 'away from their weapons', which – so it was implied – would be still in the camp.   **τὸ στράτευμα:** here and in the next line taken by most translators to be 'the camp', which according to the story would have been left with only a skeleton force; but that would require στρατόπεδον (which Herwerden conjectured), and στράτευμα should mean the fighting force itself as at **65.**2–3, **66.**1, and **67.**1. The Syracusans would indeed attack the camp, but they are encouraged to think that they would go on to defeat the whole army, presumably by moving on to round up those who, so they were told, would be trapped in the town.   **αὐτοί:** the Syracusan sympathisers: nom., because the informant claims to be one of them.   **ἠτοιμάσθαι:** this might be heard either as middle as at **17.**3 and **22**, 'and they had made preparations', or as passive as at 7.62.1, 'and preparations had been made'.

65.1 μετὰ τοῦ ... [παρεσκευάσθαι] ἐπὶ Κατάνην 'along with their general confidence also had thoughts of their own, even without this, of moving against Catana': an elaboration of the common idiom ἄλλοι τε καί, 'others and in particular'. παρεσκευάσθαι is a marginal gloss that has intruded into the text.   **τῶι ἀνθρώπωι** 'the fellow': the dismissive tone conveys that they should not have been taken in.   **ἀπερισκεπτότερον:** that is, they behave with less circumspection because they were already thinking on similar lines; there is also a hint of 'with less circumspection than they should have had'.   **ἤδη γὰρ ... παρῆσαν:** see **67.**2 n. for these reinforcements. γάρ explains why the Syracusans could go πανδημεί: these allies could be left to guard the city.   **πανδημεί:** echoing **64.**1, **64.**3: everything is going according to the Athenians' plan.   **αἱ ἡμέραι ἐν αἷς ξυνέθεντο ἥξειν:** 'day' rather than 'days' might be expected after ἡμέραν in the preceding sentence and ἡμέραι ῥητῆι (**64.**3), but this includes the march on the day before the attack.   **ἐπί** + gen., 'of motion *towards* or (in a military sense) *upon* a place', LSJ A.I.3.a. Contrast ἐπὶ Συρακούσας (acc.) at **65.**2, a more direct move 'to' and 'against'.   **τῶι Συμαίθωι ποταμῶι:** the Giarretta: see Map 1. They would then be some 50 km from Syracuse and 15 km from Catana. It was always optimistic to think that such a march could remain undetected by the Athenians.

65.2 ἠισθοντο αὐτοὺς προσιόντας: for the construction with acc. see **91.**6 n.   **ὅσοι ... προσεληλύθει:** including Sicels who had responded to the summons of **62.**5; the verb is singular because ἄλλος τις is the nearer subject. **τὰς ναῦς καὶ τὰ πλοῖα:** both fighting ships and transports. **ὑπὸ νύκτα:** 7.2 n. This again echoes 64.1. Evans 2016: 121 points out how unlikely it was that such a large fleet could stay unnoticed everywhere along the coast, even at night: still, even if it did not, news would not reach the Syracusan force until it was too late.

65.3 καὶ ... τε ... καί: capturing the simultaneous action in the two theatres. **ἐς τὸ κατὰ τὸ Ὀλυμπιεῖον** 'to the area close to [or 'opposite'] the Olympieion', but not including the Olympieion itself: 64.1 n. See Map 4. Alberti prints ἐς τὸν μέγαν λιμένα κατὰ τὸ Ὀλυμπιεῖον (H²), but the helpful addition is probably a conjecture of that enterprising scribe (58.2 n.). **τὸ στρατόπεδον καταληψόμενοι:** echoing 64.1, στρατόπεδον καταλαμβάνειν: hence 'the' camp, i.e. the one that they planned to establish. **ξύμπαντες ἤδη:** to be taken together, 'now reunited'.

66.1 αὐτοῖς: the Syracusans. **καθ᾽ ἡσυχίαν ... ἐπιτήδειον:** echoing ἐν ἐπιτηδείωι καθ᾽ ἡσυχίαν, 64.1. **χωρίον ἐπιτήδειον ... κρημνοί:** whether or not Th. had visited Syracuse himself (Intr., 3), only a small fraction of his audience would know the terrain, and his listeners and readers would not have the benefit of maps. The complexities of any landscape are hard to convey without such aids, and like other ancient writers (Pelling 1981, cf. Horsfall 1985) he provides a simplified model. He was not writing for scholars who would puzzle over the location of Dascon, or whether the landing was N or S of the river Anapus or both, or how the river could apparently play no part in the battle despite the destruction of the bridge (66.2). His points are the natural advantages of the site, the interval that the Athenians had secured to strengthen it still further, and the swift professionalism with which they set about it. One irony is that this well-appointed position will eventually contribute to the Athenian catastrophe when they are trapped there. Those who did not know would gather that the Anapus was an important river close by; specifying 'Dascon' is odder, as it looks like preparation for it to figure in the later narrative as with the Olympieion, but it does not. Perhaps it conveys Th.'s own mastery of the locale (Rawles 2015: 134), perhaps it creates the verisimilitude of circumstantial detail, or perhaps it is another case of his haphazard naming habits (**60.2 n.**).

The topography raises difficult questions that cannot be discussed here: cf. *HCT* 480–4; Green 1970: 157–60; Kagan 1981: 230–5; Lazenby 2004: 142–3. These concern both the landings (probably S of the river, at least in the main) and the battle (N of the river, Dover, Green, Kagan; S, Lazenby). Map 4 marks the battle as taking place to the north, but it is hard to be confident.

καὶ . . . τε . . . καὶ . . . καὶ . . . καί: the accumulated co-ordinates convey the site's multiple advantages, expanding ἐπιτήδειον without implying that the list is exhaustive ('a good site, and one in which . . .'). A decisive battle is to be expected (μάχης, ἐν τῶι ἔργωι) now that they are so close.   ἥκιστ' ἄν . . . λυπήσειν: ἄν + future inf. is rare in Attic Greek, but a high proportion of the cases are in Th. (M&T 208). The Athenians cannot expect to take on the enemy cavalry on even terms. The best they can aim for is to limit their effectiveness.   λίμνη: perhaps N of the river (Lazenby 2004: 143); or perhaps 'the large permanent pools of water . . . immediately behind the southern half of the shore' (HCT 479). The location of 'Lysimeleia' (7.53.2 and n.) is uncertain too, but may be the same.   παρὰ δὲ τό 'and in another direction'. The steepest cliffs are to the W and SW.

66.2 καὶ . . . καὶ . . . τε . . . καὶ . . . τε (if that is the right reading) . . . καὶ . . . καί: a second (cf. **66**.1 n.) conglomerate of co-ordinates collects the multiple activities of the Athenians. Sorting them out is not straightforward. (1) Perhaps καὶ ἐπὶ τῶι Δάσκωνι co-ordinates with παρά τε τὰς ναῦς, both go with σταύρωμα ἔπηξαν, and then ἔρυμά τε starts a separate point: they erected a stockade both to the ships and on Dascon, and also . . .: thus Dover, more explicitly at 1965: 74 than in HCT. In that case we might punctuate with a comma after Δάσκωνι. (2[a]) Or perhaps σταύρωμα ἔπηξαν governs παρά τε τὰς ναῦς only, and καὶ ἐπὶ τῶι Δάσκωνι looks forward, beginning a second clause that runs down to ἔλυσαν: they both (τε) built a stockade to the ships and (καί) on or to protect Dascon they (i) built τε a fort καί (ii) destroyed the Anapus bridge. If this is right, the bridge too would be in the area of Dascon, whether ἐπί + dat. here means 'to protect' (HCT 481) or, more likely, 'on' or 'at'. (2[b]) If however the less well attested ἔρυμά τι is read, the ἐπὶ τῶι Δάσκωνι clause runs only to ὤρθωσαν, and καὶ . . . ἔλυσαν is a third complete clause parallel to παρά τε τὰς ναῦς σταύρωμα ἔπηξαν and to ἐπὶ τῶι Δάσκωνι . . . ὤρθωσαν. In that case the bridge need not be close to Dascon. All of these are possible.   τῶι Δάσκωνι: of uncertain location: Diod. 13.13.3 suggests that it was also the name for a bay within the harbour. On one reading of the co-ordinate clauses (above), it should be near the bridge.   ἔρυμά τε: see above.   λογάδην: often used of 'picking out' stones for building. This would be the job of the λιθολόγοι, **44**.1 n.   τὴν τοῦ Ἀνάπου γέφυραν ἔλυσαν: presumably the bridge carrying the road to Helorus (**66**.3): it is not known where this crossed the river. Yet even after its destruction the river does not seem to have been a serious barrier in the manoeuvring and fighting that followed, and Green 1970 and HCT 483 both posit a second bridge, minor enough that the first could be described as 'the' bridge but substantial enough to allow easy transit. In a slightly later context Plut. *Nic.* 16.5 does mention 'bridges'.

66.3 παρασκευαζομένων: gen. absolute, setting the scene not just for ἐκώλυε but also for προσεβοήθησαν and ξυνελέγη. Th. could still have written παρασκευαζομένους as obj. of ἐκώλυε, but such needless genitive absolutes are particularly found when they come before the main clause: *CGCG* 52.32 n. 1. **ἐκ μὲν τῆς πόλεως οὐδεὶς ἐξιών:** these would be the 'Selinuntine and other allies' left to guard the city (**65**.1 n.). **προσεβοήθησαν:** aor. as they arrive, after the imperfect ἐβοήθουν as they were making their way (**65**.3). **τὸ πεζὸν ἅπαν ξυνελέγη:** it must by now have been close to the autumn sunset, given the early morning activity at Catana and then the long march back. **τὴν Ἑλωρίνην ὁδόν:** the road going S to Helorus. See Map 4.

67.1 τεταγμένον ἐπὶ ὀκτώ 'drawn up eight deep'. **ταῖς εὐναῖς:** i.e. where they had been sleeping (on the ground, *CHGRW* i. 162 [Krentz]). **ἐν πλαισίωι** 'in a square', the normal method when there were non-combatants (here τοὺς σκευοφόρους) to protect: cf. X. *Anab.* 3.2.36 and 3.4.19 with Huitink–Rood's nn. **ἐφορῶντας:** present tense: they should go there while keeping a close eye on developments. **τούτων τῶν ἐπιτάκτων** 'those in this additional formation'.

67.2 ὄντας πανδημεὶ Συρακοσίους καὶ ὅσοι ξύμμαχοι παρῆσαν: defining ὁπλίτας more closely, so ὄντας = 'consisting of . . .'. **ἐβοήθησαν:** aor. where Engl. would use a pluperfect (*CGCG* 33.40 n.1). The Selinuntine reinforcements were mentioned at **65**.1, but at that point the cavalry and archers would have been accompanying the fighting force going to Catana. **τὸ ξύμπαν ἐς διακοσίους** 'some two hundred in all', probably referring just to the Geloan cavalry rather than Selinuntines and Geloans together: cf. 7.33.1, where the Geloan cavalry still numbers 200 in 413. **καὶ Καμαριναίων ἱππῆς:** referred to again at **75**.3 and **88**.1. **ὅσον εἴκοσι . . . ὡς πεντήκοντα** 'about twenty' . . . 'around fifty', a characteristically Thucydidean variation. **ἔλασσον** rather than ἐλάσσονας: **1**.2 n. **καὶ τοὺς ἀκοντιστάς:** together presumably with the Camarinaean τοξόται mentioned in the parenthesis and the other 'stone-throwers, slingers, and archers' of **69**.2, ignored here as the least important.

67.3 προτέροις: i.e. they, not the Syracusans, would initiate the fighting. This is important at **69**.1. **κατά τε ἔθνη . . . παρεκελεύετο** 'gave encouragement along the following lines, addressed individually to each ethnic contingent as he went along the ranks and to the army as a whole'. Cf.

7.63–64.2, where in a similar pre-battle speech Nicias addresses separate points to allied sailors and to Athenians and ends καὶ ἐνθυμεῖσθε καθ᾽ ἑκάστους τε καὶ ξύμπαντες . . . He similarly moves along the ranks at 7.76 to give a final speech that partly echoes this one. At 4.94.2 Hippocrates too speaks ἐπιπαριὼν τὸ στρατόπεδον but only gets half way before the action starts: that makes it clearer that he repeated a similar speech to each contingent that he reached. That is probably also what is meant by κατά τε ἔθνη . . . ἕκαστα καὶ ξύμπασι here: the content was partly the same for everyone and partly adapted according to the men addressed, as Nicias varied his exhortations at 7.69.2, Agamemnon his at *Il.* 4.223–41, and the commanders theirs before Mantinea (5.69.1). Here at least Th.'s formulation does not raise the issue whether a single speech could have been audible to a large army (7.60.5 n.).

68 *Nicias Encourages the Troops*

With battle imminent his style is more forceful than in his earlier speeches, with few of the characteristics identified by Tompkins 1972 (**9–14** n.): the sentences are shorter, with fewer qualifying clauses, and he concentrates on realities rather than abstractions. The initial rhetorical questions immediately involve the audience, leading into 'we's that have something of the 'my fellow soldiers' style adopted by some later generals (Suet. *Diu. Iul.* 67.2: Dickey 2002: 288–90).

For such pre-battle exhortations cf. Cnemus and Brasidas (2.87) answered by Phormio (2.89); Demosthenes at 4.10; Pagondas (4.92) answered by Hippocrates (4.95); Brasidas at 4.126 and 5.9; the indirect speech summaries before Mantinea (5.69); and esp. Nicias himself (7.61–4) answered by 'Gylippus and the Syracusan generals' (7.66–7). Such speeches, often paired, became a traditional feature of later historiography (Lendon 2017b: 145–54), and mark the importance of the battle to come. Many of Nicias' points are conventional, though that does not imply that they were not made: he and Th. both knew that the same things often need to be said (7.69.2). For 'there is no need to say much' cf. 4.95.1, 5.9.1, 5.69.2; for the strength of the παρασκευή, 2.87.6; for the superiority of one's troops, e.g. 2.87.3–4, 4.95.3, 5.9.1, 7.63.4, 7.66.3–4; for the enemy's over-confidence, 2.89.1–3, 5.9.3–6; for ἐπιστήμη against τόλμα, 2.87.4, 2.89.2–5, 4.126.4; for the contrast of fighting at home and abroad, 4.92.1–6, 4.95.2, Hom. *Il.* 15.735–41; for the severe consequences of defeat, 4.92.4, 5.9.9, 7.61.1, 7.64.1, 7.68.2–3. The more striking features come in the second half, where the standard τόποι come in what the *enemy* generals would be saying: the Syracusans' advantage in being so close to friendly territory (2.87.6, 7.62.4); the risk to their country's survival (4.92.4, 7.61.1, 7.64.1, Hom. *Il.* 15.494–9, Aesch. *Pers.* 402–5); the prospect of a decisive victory (2.89.10, 4.95.2), here offered by their superior cavalry, **68.**3. The tone therefore becomes surprisingly downbeat, dwelling on the seriousness of the Athenian situation (ἀπορίαν) and the reasons for fear (φοβερωτέραν), **68.**4. Things were not that bad yet (nn.), but this fits the Nicias that the reader has come to know.

Unusually, there is no symmetrical speech on the Syracusan side. Th. would have found little that Nicias has left them to say, but anyway the Syracusan rush and confusion (**69.**1) will have left no time for speeches.

Such speeches often prefigure the future narrative, and here the anticipated events come in several waves. For the moment ἐπιστήμη will indeed outmatch τόλμα, just as in Phormio's battle in the Corinthian Gulf (2.90–2), but the Syracusans will be quick learners; the cavalry will soon become a critical advantage (**70.**3, 7.4.6, Intr., 6); the Athenians will eventually find it as hard to escape as Nicias foresees, with μὴ ῥαιδίως ἀποχωρεῖν by then carrying an even more terrifying significance (**68.**4 n.). Before the final battle Nicias' speech will echo this one (7.77), but then the Athenian πατρίς, not the Syracusan, will be at risk.

See also Luschnat 1942: 72–80; Leimbach 1985: 92–7; Iglesias Zoido 2007; Tsakmakis and Themistokleous 2013: 394–400.

68.1 μέν: answered by δέ at **68.**3, contrasting the reasons for confidence in the first half with those for fear in the second.   **ὦ ἄνδρες:** normally with an ethnic, e.g. ὦ ἄνδρες Ἀθηναῖοι (1.53.2) or Πελοποννήσιοι (1.53.4), or other qualifier (ὦ ἄνδρες ξύμμαχοι, 1.120.1, 5.9.9): here without, because Nicias is addressing both Athenians and allies as again at 7.63–4 (nn.). Cf. 7.77.7 n., beginning ὦ ἄνδρες στρατιῶται and again subdividing his audience.   **πάρεσμεν:** Nicias uses 'we' down to ἡμετέρας, **68.**3, then turns to 'you' at κτήσεσθε for the more homiletic second half: in the first half there is an affectation that no further advice is needed, as 'we' can all see our strength. For the first person πάρεσμεν after a vocative cf. 3.30.1. 'We are all in this together' is good bonding rhetoric here; it comes back pathetically in Nicias' final speech at 7.77.2, where suffering rather than confidence is shared.

68.2 ὅπου: as with Engl. 'where', 'the strict local sense occasionally passes into . . . a sense involving Time or Occasion', LSJ II.1.   **οἱ πρῶτοι:** the definite article is retained in the complement because it refers to the whole of a class (*CGCG* 28.6, 28.9).   **πάντα τινά** 'every individual', **31.**5 n.   **πανδημεί: 64.**1 n.   **ὥσπερ καὶ ἡμᾶς:** καί often reinforces ὥσπερ, as in e.g. 'just as our fathers did too', **18.**6: here and at 7.48.3 καί is retained even though the comparison is rejected.   **ὑπερφρονοῦσι**

μὲν ἡμᾶς: effective rhetorical use of the insults the troops had heard at 63.2–3.   ὑπομενοῦσι: future, as the accent shows.
68.3 τινι 'each' person (not 'someone'), as often in exhortations: **10**.5 n.   πολύ τε ἀπὸ τῆς ἡμετέρας αὐτῶν εἶναι: Nicias reverts to a point he made at Athens, **21**.2, **23**.2.   πρὸς γῆι οὐδεμιᾶι φιλίαι: Nicias exaggerates, for Naxos and Catana were not too far away; but getting there might not prove easy if the Syracusans won.   ἥντινα μὴ αὐτοὶ μαχόμενοι κτήσεσθε 'of any sort that you might win without fighting for it yourselves'.   εὖ οἶδ' ὅτι: parenthetical, **34**.7 n.   ὁ ἀγών: the ἀγών theme will become increasingly important: see Intr. to Bk. 7, p. 30.   ἐξ ἧς κρατεῖν δεῖ ἢ μὴ ῥαιδίως ἀποχωρεῖν: understood is 'not in our own country <but in a land>'. For the moment ἀποχωρεῖν can refer to withdrawal from the battlefield; the difficulty of 'going away' will become more severe and its significance broader at the end of Bk. 7.   οἱ γὰρ ἱππῆς πολλοὶ ἐπικείσονται: πολλοί is predicative, 'will attack in strength'.

68.4 τῆς τε οὖν ὑμετέρας αὐτῶν ἀξίας μνησθέντες: such exhortations often mention ancestors and civic pride. Nicias will do the same at 7.69.2, but for the moment he appeals rather to self-respect.   ἀπορίαν: again exaggerating. This prefigures the tone of his letter of 7.11–15, and that as well is too desperate too soon (nn.).

69–71 *The First Battle*

The description is unusually detailed, especially concerning the preliminaries (**69**) that Th. and other authors often pass over in silence. Thus this is the only pre-Hellenistic reference to the initial skirmishing of light troops (Wheeler 2007: 203–4) and Th.'s only reference to pre-battle sacrifice (Parker 2000: 304), though certainly the second and probably the first were regular. The detail can be seen as 'paradigmatic' (*CT*), illustrating other battles as well as this; but why here, when there have already been pitched battles in the earlier books? Perhaps because of the contrast with later battles in Bks. 6–7. This one fits that usual paradigm, and the more familiar the fighting the more Athenian experience tells; but later counterparts will be less regular, with the Syracusans the quicker to adapt (Intr., 33–4). The sharpest contrast is between the thunderstorm of **70**.1 and that of 7.79.3 (Paul 1987: 310–11). The Athenians handle the first with a calm rationality that the Syracusans lack, but they are so demoralised by the time of the second that it adds to their despair.

After Th. and partly drawing on him, battle narratives tended to become highly conventional, just as battles themselves often followed repetitive patterns: see esp. Lendon 2017a and 2017b, with extensive bibliography.

69.1 ἀπροσδόκητοι . . . ὡς ἤδη μαχούμενοι 'not expecting to fight straight away'. **οἱ δὲ καί:** i.e. those who had left for the city.   **ὡς δὲ ἕκαστός πηι τοῖς πλέοσι προσμείξειε καθίσταντο** 'took up their positions wherever each of them joined the throng'.   **προθυμίαι . . . τόλμηι . . . ἀνδρείαι . . . ἐπιστήμη:** picking up and expanding Nicias' ἐπιστήμη . . . τόλμα distinction of **68**.2, but giving the Syracusans due credit even in their defeat.   **τῶι δὲ ἐλλείποντι αὐτῆς καὶ τὴν βούλησιν ἄκοντες προυδίδοσαν** 'but because of their deficiencies in skill they involuntarily let down their good intentions too'.   **ἄν:** with ἐπελθεῖν, but attracted forward to second position in the clause (*CGCG* 60.7). The Syracusans' thinking was οὐκ ἂν ἐπέλθοιεν . . ., 'they [surely] wouldn't attack first': the boldness of the Athenian ploy had not yet shaken their mindset of **63**.

69.2 οἵ τε λιθοβόλοι καὶ σφενδονῆται καὶ τοξόται προυμάχοντο: it seems that these exchanges form a self-contained phase, and the sacrifices and trumpet-calls come after these, not before. It need not follow that the exchanges were simply 'formalistic, or ritualistic', expected to have little effect on the outcome (Pritchett *GSW* iv. 51–4, 5.62–3): at Sellasia in 222 BCE Cleomenes is disturbed when the skirmishing goes against him (Plb. 2.69.6), and defeated troops fleeing pell-mell might easily disrupt the hoplite line.   **λιθοβόλοι:** stone-*throwers* rather than slingers.   **τροπάς, οἵας εἰκὸς ψιλούς, ἀλλήλων ἐποίουν:** that is, in some areas one side inflicted a rout and in others the other, hence the plural τροπάς. οἵας εἰκός fits a paradigmatic presentation (**69–71** n.): this is what one would expect to happen.   **ἔπειτα δὲ μάντεις τε σφάγια προύφερον:** presumably after an earlier sacrifice in the camp to confirm the wisdom of fighting, though Th. (typically, **69–71** n.) does not mention it. For discussion whether these sacrifices too were 'divinatory', allowing the possibility of calling off the battle, see Pritchett, *GSW* i. 110, Jameson 1991: 203–4 and *CT*: probably they were, but the looked-for signs were 'simple and rarely known to fail' (Jameson 1991).   **σαλπικταί:** this is the Attic spelling (LSJ s.v. σαλπιγκτής, Threatte 1980–96 i: 574).

69.3 Συρακόσιοι . . . ὑπακούσονται: the Syracusans' thinking is closer than that of the Athenian side to Nicias' speech (περὶ πατρίδος, **68**.3); the Athenians strike notes that are both more positive (conquest) and more patriotic (cause the city no harm) than Nicias himself.   **μαχούμενοι:** the future tense ties this closely to the moment of closing, ἐχώρουν, effectively freezing the action before the first blow is struck.   **τὸ μὲν αὐτίκα . . . τὸ δὲ μέλλον . . .:** acc. of respect.   **τῶν δ' ἐναντίων . . . ἡσσώμενοι** 'and of those on the other side, the Athenians were fighting for alien land to make it their own, and to avoid harming their own land if they were defeated'. περί τε τῆς ἀλλοτρίας balances the Syracusans' περί τε πατρίδος, then for 'the

Argives and the independent among the allies' the construction shifts to infinitives of purpose (*M&T* 770), then shifts again with a new main verb for τό . . . ὑπήκοον.   τῶν ξυμμάχων οἱ αὐτόνομοι: including the Chians and Methymnaeans (**85**.2 [n.]): 7.57 draws more refined distinctions among the different sorts of ally.   τὴν ὑπάρχουσαν σφίσι πατρίδα 'the native land of their own', picking up the πατρίς theme but in a less patriotic vein. They just want to get home.   τὸ δ' ὑπήκοον τῶν ξυμμάχων: for the neut. collective cf. **35**.1 n. These seem the most susceptible to Nicias' emphasis on fear (**68**.3). There is nothing here of the shared pride in the empire that Nicias will appeal to at 7.64.3.   αὐτίκα: **49**.3 n.   εἶχον: for the plural cf. **4**.5 n.   ἔπειτα δὲ ἐν παρέργωι . . . ὑπακούσονται: a small example of Th.'s habit of ranking causes and motives as at 2.65.11 and 7.57.1: see Intr., 5.   εἴ τι ἄλλο . . . ὑπακούσονται 'in the hope that by helping in some other conquest they might make their own subjection (the Athenians) to them less harsh'.

70.1 ἐπὶ πολὺ ἀντεῖχον ἀλλήλοις: just as in Homer a period of equally poised battle can be broken by a sudden surge (*Il.* 12.415–71, 15.410–13 and 590–600; Latacz 1977: 187). But this is not just literary allusiveness: battles were like that.   τοῖς μὲν πρῶτον μαχομένοις . . . τοῖς δ' ἐμπειροτέροις: probably most commentators are right to take 'the more experienced' to be the Athenian side and 'those fighting for the first time' to be the Syracusan, at least in the sense that the 'more experienced' would be *predominantly* on the Athenian side. Emphasis has fallen on the Athenians' superior ἐπιστήμη (**68**.2, **69**.1), and Nicias stressed that they were ἀπόλεκτοι fighting a πανδημεί levy (**68**.2); cf. Hermocrates at **72**.3.   τὰ μὲν γιγνόμενα . . . τοὺς δὲ . . . παρέχειν: the weight falls on the δέ clause, and Th. does not imply that the Athenians were better meteorologists than the Syracusans. Their veterans were just more likely to say 'oh, it's just an autumn storm, and it's the enemy you need to be worried about'. See **69–70** n. for the Athenians' contrasting response to the thunderstorm of 7.79.3.   τοὺς δὲ ἀνθεστῶτας . . . παρέχειν 'and that they had a lot more to fear from the men facing them if those remained undefeated'. The participle with μή should be conditional (*CGCG* 52.40, *GG* 1611–12), and so the phrase does not quite convey 'alarm at the stubborn resistance of the enemy' (Spratt), though the Syracusans did indeed resist well for a time.

70.2 ὡσαμένων . . . κατέστη: so the Syracusan line crumpled from left to right, as the Athenians were in the centre (**67**.1). Th. as usual adopts what Lendon 2017a and 2017b calls a 'middle-hanging camera' approach, focusing on whole sections and not, Herodotus-like, zooming in on individual acts of valour.   παρερρήγνυτο: the παρ- is probably, as at 5.73.1, 'by the side' of the already defeated centre. It does not look as if the Athenian reserve was needed (**67**.1).

70.3 οἱ γὰρ ἱππῆς . . . εἶργον: as Nicias had foreseen, **68**.3. The Athenian archers and slingers were apparently less effective against cavalry than was expected (**43**). This is 'one of the decisive moments of the whole campaign' (*HCT*, cf. Kagan 1981: 236–42), as any follow-up could have led to a siege or possibly even a storming of the city. Polyaenus 1.39.2 has a story of the Athenians spreading caltrops (τρίβολοι, i.e. 'four-spiked implement[s] thrown on the ground to lame the enemy horses', LSJ) before the engagement: the horses either fled or were slaughtered by light-armed troops wearing special boots. If this refers to the same battle, it is hard to reconcile with Th.'s account (esp. ἀήσσητοι) even if it refers to an earlier stage, though it is possible that caltrops were spread along a corridor forward from the camp to protect the advance and any retreat. **εἴ τινας προδιώκοντας ἴδοιεν** 'whenever they saw anyone getting out ahead in the pursuit': for εἰ + opt. in a habitual condition in the past see *CGCG* 49.13, 15–16. **ἐπανεχώρουν . . . ἵστασαν:** imperfect: this is what they were doing while the Syracusans regathered and protected the Olympieion (**70**.4).

70.4 ἐς τὴν Ἑλωρίνην ὁδόν: see **66**.3 and Map 4. On most reconstructions the Syracusan lines would be N or NW of the Athenian, and they would therefore have fallen back to the N part of the road, near to the city. **ὡς ἐκ τῶν παρόντων ξυνταξάμενοι** 'forming up as best they could in the circumstances'. **ὅμως:** i.e. despite the obvious advantages of keeping the whole body together. On most reconstructions it would be no easy matter to get to the Olympieion, as the Athenian army lay between the Syracusans and the temple. The Syracusans had reason to fear for the treasure there.

71.1 πρὸς μὲν τὸ ἱερὸν οὐκ ἦλθον: Plut. *Nic.* 16.7 explains: 'the Athenians were eager to seize the nearby Olympieion, for there were many gold and silver dedications there, but Nicias deliberately delayed and allowed a Syracusan garrison to get there. His thinking was that, if the soldiers ransacked the treasure, the city would get no benefit from it while he would himself be held responsible for the impiety.' This is probably Plut.'s guesswork, building on his picture of Nicias as noted both for his piety and for his nervousness of the Athenian public, but he may well be right in pinpointing fear of sacrilege. Paus. 10.28.6 makes the same assumption, though he says that the Athenians did capture the temple but left its priest and the treasure unharmed. Diod. 13.6.4 similarly says that they had 'gained control of the Olympieion' the day before. If this version is early,

Th.'s insistence that they did not take it may be a tacit correction. ἐπὶ πυρὰν ἐπιθέντες: perhaps dividing the Athenians by tribes, so that the ashes from each tribe could be sent home separately (Arrington 2015: 34; Rubincam 2018: 99–100), but this is doubted by Rees 2018: 170: it would certainly be difficult to keep the remains separate as the pyre gradually collapsed. The Argives who died on the expedition were commemorated in their home town in a πολυάνδριον (Paus. 2.22.9), presumably either a 'communal burial-place' (LSJ) for the repatriated remains or a cenotaph (*GSW* iv. 152). A casualty list discovered in 1974 possibly commemorates these Argive dead (*SEG* 29.361, 33.293). περὶ ἑξήκοντα καὶ διακοσίους: Diod. 13.6.5 says 400. As with the Athenian casualties (ὡς πεντήκοντα) 'about' 260 might imply a rounding, but 260 is already less rounded than the multiples of 50 and 100 often found (Rubincam 1991) and it probably suggests instead some uncertainty as to the precise number. τὰ ὀστᾶ ξυνέλεξαν: the remains, probably bones more than ashes even after burning (Rees 2018). τὰ τῶν πολεμίων σκῦλα: clothes and especially weapons. Some would already have been used to make the τροπαῖον, **70**.3. ἀπέπλευσαν ἐς Κατάνην: Plut. was unimpressed: 'it was a famous victory, but Nicias did not exploit it at all . . .' (*Nic.* 16.8). Hermocrates exploits the same point at **79**.3.

71.2 αὐτόθεν: the word comes three times in the first half of the sentence, emphasising what was and what was not possible 'on the spot'. In the first case it = 'in the vicinity of the city', in the second and third 'in Sicily'. ἱπποκρατῶνται: a striking word, perhaps formed on the model of ναυκρατεῖν (**18**.5 n.) and here found for the first time in extant Greek. If Th. coined it, that reflects the importance of the idea in the campaign: Intr., 6. καὶ χρήματα δέ 'and money too'. καί co-ordinates with the preceding ἱππέας τε and the following τῶν τε πόλεων and τά τε ἄλλα; the addition of δέ is explained by Rijksbaron 1997b: 196–7 as 'setting off' the χρήματα from the previous item. The effect is to bind the cavalry and the money more closely together than the following items: these are the two requiring a combination of raising on the spot and fetching from home. Chiasmus – Athens, αὐτόθεν, αὐτόθεν, Athens – and balancing length of clauses reinforce the parallel. αὐτόθεν τε ξυλλέξωνται: it is possible that *IG* i³ 291 records the Sicilian contributions at this stage, but see **44**.2 n. μᾶλλον σφῶν ὑπακούσεσθαι 'would be more willing to do what the Athenians told them'. Such ὑπακούειν would be more voluntary than that imposed on the subject-allies (ὑπακούσονται, **69**.3), but could be a step in that direction: Euphemus will feel the need to reassure the Camarinaeans about this (**86**.3). ὅσων δέοι '[other things] in the quantities that would be needed'.

72–73: THE SYRACUSAN RESPONSE

Hermocrates responds decisively, and in a way that gives him considerably more power: one can increasingly understand why Athenagoras was suspicious (**38**.3, cf. **33–34** n., **36–40** n.). Equally striking is the shift of mood at Syracuse. The dismissiveness of **32**.3–**41**, esp. **35**, and the scorn of **63**.1 and **65**.1 (cf. **68**.2) have been dissipated by the reverse, and they 'vote everything that Hermocrates had told them to' (**73**.1).

Hermocrates finds the right things to say, and his claim that the defeat came from a lack of expertise rather than spirit echoes Th.'s own comment at **69**.1. ἀταξία (**72**.3) and ἀξύντακτος ἀναρχία (**72**.4 [n.]) are harsh, as the Syracusan line held for a long time and the cavalry did their job well, but may still be salutary in encouraging a disciplined training programme. His reassurance that this would make victory probable (κατὰ τὸ εἰκός) recalls the Corinthians' chirpy confidence of 1.121.4 that they can soon train themselves up to be the Athenians' naval equals (**72**.4 n.); but Hermocrates turns out to be right, at least eventually. For the similarities and contrasts in Gylippus' reassurance at 7.5.3–4 see n. there. Cf. Intr., 28–9.

On the style and structure of Hermocrates' remarks see Scardino 2012: 90–2. They might have been couched in direct speech, but Hermocrates is to be given a big speech soon enough (**76–80**).

72.1 ἀπέπλευσαν . . . διαχειμάσοντες: this foreshortens, for they initially sail only as far as Catana, though doubtless with the intention of moving on to Naxos. They eventually do so at **74**.2, then return to Catana before the end of winter at **88**.5.   **τοὺς σφετέρους αὐτῶν νεκρούς:** the emphasis may contrast these not just with those who died on the other side (**71**.1) but with those of their Sicilian allies.

72.2 Ἑρμοκράτης ὁ Ἕρμωνος . . . . ἐπιφανής: Hermocrates has been prominent in **32**.3–**40** and already in 4.58–65, but such thumbnail summaries need not imply that the characters are unfamiliar: they pick out the qualities relevant to what they are about to do or, especially, say (cf. Pericles, 1.139.4, and Alcibiades, **15** [n.]). Here Hermocrates' ξύνεσις will underpin his advice, while his experience and bravery make him an obvious choice if, as he recommends, στρατηγοὶ . . . ἔμπειροι are to be elected (**72**.4).   **ξύνεσιν: 54**.5 n.   **κατὰ τὸν πόλεμον:** either = 'in the war', i.e. 'this war' including the fighting of 427–424, or more generally 'in war' as at 2.100.2.   **ἐμπειρίαι τε ἱκανὸς γενόμενος καὶ ἀνδρείαι ἐπιφανής:** ἱκανός need not be lukewarm (**92**.5 n.), but in this case it may contrast with the stronger ἐπιφανής and pick up the contrast of **69**.1: the Syracusans lacked experience, but Hermocrates had sufficient; they were all brave, but Hermocrates especially so. οὐκ εἴα τῶι γεγενημένωι ἐνδιδόναι 'and told them not to give in to what had happened', i.e. not to be demoralised. Here as often (Intr., 28) Hermocrates recalls Pericles, so good at restoring confidence when the Athenians were unnecessarily fearful (2.65.9), as in his final speech when 'you were giving in to what had come your way' (ταῖς ξυμφοραῖς εἴκετε, 2.60.2).

72.3 γνώμην: here more 'spirit' or 'resolve', as with Gylippus at 7.5.4 and at e.g. 2.11.5 and 2.89.11, than 'judgement', as it was a clear mistake to have been duped into the march to Catana (**64–5**).   **ὅσον εἰκὸς εἶναι** 'as much as one might expect to be the case'.   **ἐμπειρίαι:** to be taken both with τοῖς πρώτοις τῶν Ἑλλήνων and with what follows: the Athenians were foremost in experience, and as far as experience was concerned it was laymen against experts. For figures involving τέχνη, a favourite of Plato, see Brock 2013a: 135 n. 93 and 148–52; they are less frequent in the fifth century than the fourth, and if Hermocrates really used the metaphor it would have been striking.

72.4 τὴν πολυαρχίαν: perhaps echoing Odysseus' οὐκ ἀγαθὸν πολυκοιρανίη (Hom. Il. 2.204), but Hermocrates does not continue, as Odysseus did, εἷς κοίρανος ἔστω: for the moment, a reduction to three is enough. Whether or not that allusion is sensed, any pre-existing suspicion that Hermocrates is building his path to tyranny (**33–4, 36–40** nn.) might well be strengthened.   **τῶν τε πολλῶν τὴν ἀξύντακτον ἀναρχίαν:** elaborating ἀταξίαν (**72**.4) and contrasting with πολυαρχίαν: too many commanders, too little obedience. The judgement is hard (intr. n. above), but it may include the slippings away to the comfy beds of home (**69**.1). It is hard to think that those were authorised.   **ἢν δὲ ὀλίγοι τε στρατηγοὶ γένωνται ἔμπειροι** 'if a few generals were appointed who were men of experience . . .'; not 'if a few generals became experienced', for experience does not come that easily, nor 'if generals were appointed that were few in number and men of experience', as that would require καί before ἔμπειροι.   **ὅπως ὡς πλεῖστοι ἔσονται:** developing the contrast of ἀναρχίαν ~ πολυαρχίαν: fewer leaders, more hoplites.   **προσαναγκάζοντες:** even here an authoritarian note might be heard: not a democratic 'we shall willingly train', but an expectation that the generals will use compulsion.   **ἐπιδώσειν γὰρ ἀμφότερα αὐτά:** the two qualities are both grammatically feminine but are picked up by the neuter: cf. **82**.4 and 3.97.3.   **τὴν μέν:** as usual of the nearer referent, i.e. their εὐταξίαν.   **μετὰ κινδύνων μελετωμένην:** just as the Athenians themselves, like the Spartans, ἐμπειρότεροι ἐγένοντο μετὰ κινδύνων τὰς μελέτας ποιούμενοι between the Persian and Peloponnesian Wars (1.18.3).   **τὴν δ' εὐψυχίαν . . . ἔσεσθαι** 'and their courage would grow even more confident when in combination with trust in their skill': cf. LSJ ἑαυτοῦ I for this comparative idiom for conveying progress or increase. The Corinthians at 1.121.4 were similarly blithe: 'once we have raised our ἐπιστήμη to the same level we will certainly win because of our εὐψυχία; . . . . their advantage in ἐπιστήμη is something we can match through μελέτη.' But the seamanship of Phormio would give the lie to that (2.83–90).

Here and at **75**.1 no mention is made of *maritime* training or of ship-building. Morakis 2015 infers that it was only the arrival of Gylippus and the Corinthian ships at 7.2 and 7.7.1 that redirected attention towards the sea.

72.5 τούς τε στρατηγοὺς καὶ ὀλίγους καὶ αὐτοκράτορας: τε is a sentence-connective (**18**.7 n.); καὶ . . . καί is then 'both . . . and'.   **ἦ μήν:** 'in oaths and pledges, usually in indirect speech' (*GP* 351).   **οὕτω γὰρ . . . παρασκευασθῆναι:** Xenophon's Ten Thousand came to think similarly: 'they thought that if they chose one leader, this would be better than πολυαρχία: this one man would be able to deploy the army by day or night, and if anything needed concealing it would be better concealed, and if swift action was needed there would be less danger of being too late; there would be no need for discussion, but whatever the one man decided would be implemented' (X. *Anab*. 6.1.18). X. may well have had this passage of Th. in mind (*CT*) and reconstructed the arguments that would be used.   **μᾶλλον ἂν στέγεσθαι . . . παρασκευασθῆναι:** corresponding to ἄν + optatives in direct speech.

73.1 Ἡρακλείδην τὸν Λυσιμάχου: not the same as the Heracleides of **103**.4.   **Σικανὸν τὸν Ἐξηκέστου:** he plays a role in Bk. 7 (46 and 50.1, a failed diplomatic mission; 70.1, commanding a wing in the naval battle).   **τούτους τρεῖς:** i.e. these three (and no more).

73.2 ἐς τὴν Κόρινθον καὶ ἐς τὴν Λακεδαίμονα πρέσβεις ἀπέστειλαν: as Hermocrates had recommended at **34**.3, there too with the request to send help quickly and to prosecute 'the war over there' more vigorously.   **ξυμμαχία** 'allied force': cf. X. *Hell*. 4.8.24, 'they sent a συμμαχία to Evagoras'.   **τὸν πρὸς Ἀθηναίους πόλεμον . . . τοὺς Λακεδαιμονίους:** as with Nicias at **10** and Hermocrates at **34**.3 (nn.) the assumption is that 'the' war is still continuing, even if covertly: cf. σαφέστερον, **88**.7. βεβαιότερον too revisits Nicias' preoccupations: now is the time for the Spartans to turn the unstable peace (**10**.2) into firm war. ἐκ τοῦ προφανοῦς and ὑπὲρ σφῶν link together, as part of the openness should be an explicitness that they are doing it for the Syracusans.   **ἀπαγάγωσιν:** readers and hearers might take the subject to be either 'the Spartans' (= 'force the removal of') or 'the Athenians' ('bring home').

74–75.2: PREPARATIONS FOR WINTER 415–414

74.1 εὐθύς: the new sense of urgency (**63–71** n.) continues. **ἐπὶ Μεσσήνην:** 48 n. The first diplomatic approach to Messina had been a disappointment (**50.**1), but their sympathisers' undercover activities had continued (ἃ μὲν ἐπράσσετο) and the success of **69–70** might well change a few minds. **ἃ μὲν ἐπράσσετο οὐκ ἐγένετο** 'their plotting did not come to anything', lit. 'what was being worked for [imperfect] did not happen [aor.]'. Alcibiades may have encouraged such plotting during his mission at **50.**1; if so, he will have known whom to denounce, but the pro-Syracusans probably had their suspicions already. **ὅτ' ἀπῄει ἐκ τῆς ἀρχῆς ἤδη μετάπεμπτος** 'when he was going away once recalled from his command'. The narrative flashes back to this treacherous behaviour some weeks earlier: it is mentioned now when it becomes relevant. Alcibiades disappeared in Thurii (**61.**6), some way N of Messina. Perhaps he doubled back, but more likely he found an opportunity to talk during his northward journey while still theoretically under guard: that is the impression left by Plut. *Alc.* 22.1, though this is probably Plut.'s own inference. Alcibiades was travelling in his own ship (**61.**6), and surveillance would be difficult. **ἐπιστάμενος ὅτι φεύξοιτο** 'knowing that he would be going into exile'. **μηνύει:** for the tense see **28.**1 n. **τοῖς τῶν Συρακοσίων φίλοις τοῖς ἐν τῆι Μεσσήνηι:** there had been earlier *stasis* in Messina in 424–422 (5.5.1), and there was more trouble in the 390s (Diod. 14.40, 88.5): *IACP* 234–5 and Berger 1992a: 54–6. **οἱ δέ:** i.e. 'the friends of the Syracusans', picked up and mildly redefined at the end of the sentence by οἱ ταῦτα βουλόμενοι once μὴ δέχεσθαι τοὺς Ἀθηναίους has clarified these 'wishes'. It is not one of Th.'s most elegant sentences, but this is better than taking οἱ δέ as the fiercer pro-Syracusans who did the killing (διέφθειραν) and οἱ ταῦτα βουλόμενοι as a larger body of people reluctant to side with Athens who then ἐπεκράτουν in the vote (*HCT*): the τε . . . καί connection suggests that the two verbs should have the same subject, and any στασιώτης committed enough to take up arms to exclude the Athenians would be strongly pro-Syracusan. **τούς τε ἄνδρας διέφθειραν πρότερον:** 'the' men killed are the pro-Athenian authors of the plotting (ἃ μὲν ἐπράσσετο). Engl. would use a pluperfect for διέφθειραν (*CGCG* 33.40 n.1): the killings had happened after Alcibiades' treachery but before the Athenian force arrived. τότε brings the narrative back to the present. **καί . . . καί:** the first καί coordinates ἐπεκράτουν with τούς τε ἄνδρας διέφθειραν, the second connects στασιάζοντες and ἐν ὅπλοις ὄντες. **ἐπεκράτουν μὴ δέχεσθαι** 'succeeded in winning a decision not to receive': cf. 5.46.4, ἐπικρατούντων . . . ταῦτα γίγνεσθαι. This was also the decision at **50.**1, but the Messinians at that point agreed to provide a market. This time it looks as if they rescinded that concession, for soon the Athenians τὰ ἐπιτήδεια οὐκ εἶχον, **74**.2.

74.2 περὶ τρεῖς καὶ δέκα: περί here qualifies a number that does not look like a rounding, and so it presumably points instead to Th.'s uncertainty: cf. **71**.1 n.   **ἐχειμάζοντο** 'were suffering because of the winter' or 'because of rough weather'.   **ὅρια** 'boundary posts'. The text is not certain, but ὅρια is noted as a variant in several MSS and seems to underlie the comments of the scholia. ὅριον is normally a 'boundary marker', but more than markers are needed around a camp: the context requires a barricade, presumably one distinct in type from σταυρώματα ('stockade'). The lexicographer Hesychius glosses the word as τείχισμα, φραγμόν ('fortification, paling'), ο 1220: that may be guesswork, but is likely to be right.   **διεχείμαζον** 'settled down and spent the winter', *CGCG* 33.52 n.1.   **ἐπί τε χρήματα καὶ ἱππέας:** as planned at **71**.2. Their thoughts, like the Syracusans' (**73**.2), end with a focus on reinforcements from Athens.

75.1 ἐτείχιζον δὲ καὶ οἱ Συρακόσιοι: thus begins the rival wall-building that will be so important. For the moment the Syracusans can do theirs unopposed, and have three projects (τε ... καὶ ... καί), the wall 'along the whole area facing Epipolae' and the two forts. Reconstructing the details on the ground is controversial, but here the view is accepted that this wall ran roughly N to S (Map 4): see esp. *HCT* 471–3 and Lazenby 2004: 144–5.   **τὸν Τεμενίτην ἐντὸς ποιησάμενοι** 'including Temenites within its perimeter'. The unfamiliar name is introduced without explanation, as with Dascon (**66**.1 n.), but this time 'Temenites' will play a role in future events: cf. **100**.2, 7.3.3. The name was due to the temple of Apollo Temenites, 'Apollo of the Precinct' (Cic. 2 *Verr.* 4.119), W of the city. That temple may now have been archaeologically identified: see *HCT* p. 472, *CT*, *IACP* 229.   **τὰς Ἐπιπολάς:** the plateau above the city, more fully described at **96**.2 when it begins to play a bigger part in the action.   **ὅπως μὴ δι' ἐλάσσονος εὐαποτείχιστοι ὦσιν** 'so that they might not be easy to enclose with a shorter wall', i.e. one cutting across from W to E: a N–S Syracusan wall would block off this possibility. See Map 4.   **ἢν ἄρα σφάλλωνται** 'if indeed they were to suffer a reverse'. Th. likes the combinations ἢν ἄρα or εἰ ... ἄρα (**24**.4, **33**.4, **41**.3, **78**.1): cf. *GP* 37–8, though Denniston's explanation, 'the hypothesis is one of which the possibility has only just been realized', is unsatisfactory. Here the Syracusans are by now very aware of the danger of a reverse. It rather signals that this is the less desired outcome, but one that needs to be taken into account: cf. Hdt. 8.109.5, Themistocles contriving his possible future at the Persian court ἢν ἄρα τί μιν καταλαμβάνῃ πρὸς Ἀθηναίων πάθος,

Wakker 1994: 346–7.   τὰ Μέγαρα φρούριον 'and Megara as a fort', i.e. Megara Hyblaea (**4**.1–2 n.). For the phrasing, stronger than 'a fort in Megara', cf. 2.32, ἐτειχίσθη δὲ καὶ Ἀταλάντη ὑπὸ Ἀθηναίων φρούριον. The site lay abandoned, and Lamachus had seen its strategic value (**49**.4).   ἐν τῶι Ὀλυμπιείωι: did the Syracusans leave the treasure there (**70**.4 n.), or did they move it to safety in the town? Th. perhaps did not know.   τὴν θάλασσαν προυσταύρωσαν ἧι ἀποβάσεις ἧσαν 'planted stakes along the edge of the sea where there were possible landing grounds'.

75.2 ἐστράτευσαν πανδημεὶ ἐπὶ τὴν Κατάνην: echoing the language of **64**.3 and **65**.1, but this time it is safe.   τῆς τε γῆς αὐτῶν: partitive gen., they ravaged 'part of their [the Catanaeans'] land'.   σκηνάς 'huts'.

75.3–88.2: THE CAMARINA DEBATE

Athenian envoys have spoken at other cities, especially Rhegium (**44**.3), Messina (**50**.1), Catana (**51**.1), and presumably Himera (**62** n.); there was also an earlier approach to Camarina (**52**.1 n.). Th. could have introduced a full-dress speech on one of those occasions, but prefers to delay one till here. This strengthens the panel-division given by winter 415–414, but there are further reasons. The Athenian speaker would generally have been Alcibiades, as explicitly at **51**.1. He will soon have a further speech (**89–92**), taking as ever a highly individualistic line; the less distinctive Euphemus is more suitable to convey how Athens as a whole was coming to view (or to say she viewed) her empire (**82–87** n.). Here, too, Hermocrates is present, affording a chance to see the arguments for both sides in a dilemma that would face several Sicilian cities, and so there is a 'paradigmatic' role as in the battle description of **69–71** (n.). That dilemma would shape differently as each side in turn seemed the more likely to win; there are hints of that too in the Camarinaean response (**88**.1 nn.).

Neither speaker says quite what might be expected from earlier speeches (nn.), and both put a strong emphasis on the realities of the present: that characterises both sides, but it illuminates the internal audience too, articulating the issues as they would present themselves to Camarinaean minds.

For Camarina cf. **52**.1 n.: in view of its shifting loyalties in the 420s it could easily be seen as a 'swing-city' that could go either way, and that too made it suitable as a paradigm for others. No doubt the factionalism of the 420s continued (4.25.7), but Th. does not muddy the waters by introducing local partisanship or speakers. One unusual feature is that Camarina had alliances not just with Athens (**75**.3 n.) but with Syracuse too (**80**.1 n.). The Camarinaeans cite that at the end to justify their neutrality (**88**.2), but it had not stopped them sending lukewarm support to the Syracusans already (**67**.2, **75**.3, **78**.4), and there are only casual mentions now of the alliances (**79**.1, **80**.1, **86**.2). **88**.2 therefore sounds more like an excuse than a real reason; self-interest, not moral or legal obligation, is what matters most.

On the debate see esp. de Romilly 2012: 110–15; Rawlings 1981: 117–22; Connor 1984: 180–4; Forde 1989: 61–5; Bauslaugh 1990: 156–60; Orwin 1994: 127–33; Price 2001: 146–7, 157–8, 165–9; Pelling 2012: 282–9 and 309–12; Tompkins 2015; and *HCT* and *CT*.

75.3 κατὰ τὴν ἐπὶ Λάχητος γενομένην ξυμμαχίαν: cf. **6**.2 n. Like 'the Leontini alliance in the time of Laches' mentioned there, this was contracted during 427–424 and not mentioned in Th.'s narrative of that campaign: Intr., 31. It may have involved the 'oaths' of **52**.1: see n. there. **εἴ πως** + opt. 'in the hope that': *CGCG* 49.25, **69**.3 n. **ὕποπτοι αὐτοῖς . . . μήτ' . . . πέμψαι . . . μὴ οὐκέτι βούλωνται . . . προσχωρῶσι δ'**: ὕποπτοι governs first μή + inf. (what they are suspected of having done), then two subjunctives, the first with μή (what it is feared they might do): the first construction is the equivalent of an indirect statement, the second of a fear clause (*CGCG* 43.1–3). The two are linked by μήτε . . . τε, with μὴ προθύμως brought forward for emphasis: that goes particularly with πέμψαι, but is relevant to the other clauses too – the Camarinaeans were suspiciously unkeen. **μήτ' ἐπὶ τὴν πρώτην μάχην πέμψαι ἃ ἔπεμψαν**: **67**.2. **ὁρῶντες τοὺς Ἀθηναίους ἐν τῆι μάχηι εὖ πράξαντας**: cf. the Athenians' hopes at **71**.2 and the Camarinaeans' own thinking now (**88**.2 n.). **φιλίαν**: as at **78**.1, not equivalent to ξυμμαχίαν though closely related to it (Price 2001: 139–40), and the two are often linked as at **34**.1 and **47**.1; φιλία may be assumed to underpin a ξυμμαχία, but one can have a friendship without an alliance (3.70.2, 5.94.1) and an alliance without friendship (3.12.1). Bauslaugh 1990: 56–64 and 158–9 n.35 argues that φιλία implies a promise of non-hostility but without the defined (if not always fulfilled) obligation to ξυμμαχεῖν if the other city were attacked: that may be too legally precise, but this may be what it often amounted to.

75.4 Εὐφήμου: this may well be the man who proposed a rider to the Egesta decree of (?) 418/7 (OR 166 = ML 37 = Fornara 81: **6** n.) concerning the treatment of future Egestaean envoys. If he took a particular interest in the area, he was a natural choice for a senior role in the expedition and now to act as a diplomat: he may well have had connections in Camarina too. But if so Th. does not say so. Cf. **81** n. **ξυλλόγου γενομένου τῶν Καμαριναίων**: not much is known of Camarina's constitution (*IACP* 204), but this assembly could make decisions (**88**.1–2).

76–80 *The Speech of Hermocrates*

The speech of the alliance-seekers might be expected to come first, as in the Corcyrean debate of 1.31–44, but Hermocrates seizes the initiative: he wants 'to get his denunciation in first' (**75.**4). That may just be because it happened that way in the real-life debate, but Hermocrates is thus characterised as hectoring, even bullying, whereas Euphemus is put on the defensive.

'Sicily for the Sicilians' was Hermocrates' rallying cry at Gela in 424 (4.59–64, cf. **33–4** n.): the islanders need to unite to fend off Athens. Much of the same comes here, with an additional layer of racial rhetoric: we Dorians should stick together (**79.**2, **80.**2–3) and show them what we are made of (**77.**1). That fits now as it did not in 424, as the Ionian cities are not now supporting Syracuse (**77.**1 n.): only the Dorians are left, though so far only Gela, Selinus, and in its lukewarm way Camarina have sent any help (**67.**2). There is accordingly a good deal of 'we' language. But the tone now is harder than at Gela, less inspirational and more recriminatory and, particularly at the end, threatening; κάλλιον (**80.**2) and μὴ αἰσχρῶς (**80.**5) may mark a move towards the more upbeat καλὸς ὁ ἀγών note (see Intr. to Bk. 7, p. 30), but for now the tone is intimidatory. Camarina had reason to fear Syracuse (**5.**3 n.), and Hermocrates exploits that nervousness rather than affecting any bland reassurance.

His style is punchy, as it was at **33–4**, and with some of the same mannerisms (nn.), including the sentences piling clause on clause as the arguments dovetail (**77.**1, **78.**1). There are differences too: he here favours crisp antitheses, sometimes with Gorgias-like wordplay (**76.**2 κατοικίσαι . . . ἐξοικίσαι; **76.**4 οὐκ ἀξυνατωτέρου, κακοξυνωτέρου δέ; **79.**2 ἀλόγως . . . εὐλόγωι; **79.**3 ξυστῶμεν . . . διαστῶμεν: cf. Gorg. *Helen* 5 ὑπ' ἔρωτός τε φιλονίκου φιλοτιμίας τε ἀνικήτου, or *Palamedes* 34 ταῦτα γὰρ προνοήσασι μὲν δυνατά, μετανοήσασι δὲ ἀνίατα; Tompkins 2015: 117–18). If γάρ was the keynote particle at **33–4** (n.), here the favoured constructions are μέν . . . δέ (17 x). and οὐκ . . . ἀλλά/δέ (17x). Dionysius of Halicarnassus found the antithetical wordplays 'frigid' (*Thuc.* 48), but they fit the argument's profusion of contrasts: the comparison of Athens' behaviour here and in the Aegean guides the choice between us and them (or 'me' and 'him', **78.**1 n.); the past gives the key to the future; words, especially any claim of justice (δικαίωμα, **79.**2, **80.**2), should not distract from deeds. Any obligations of alliance are given short shrift (**79.**1, **80.**1), and here the more recent past, the canny behaviour of Rhegium, provides the model (**79.**2). He assumes that the Athenians are hypocritical when they speak of such obligations (**76.**2, **77.**1) and that the Camarinaeans too will think in self-interested terms; he warns them not to try to be too clever (**78**.2). At **33-4** he played with alternative hypothetical futures, whereas here he looks to an alternative present: what would you have done if it had been you that Athens attacked (**78**.4)? His trenchant view of the Athenians' aims coincides with Th.'s own (**1**.1, **6**.1). At **80**.1 he intimates a claim to know more than he really can (n.), but even there he is proleptically right – a premature insight that turns out to be characteristic (Intr., 28–9).

76.1 καταπλαγῆτε: again the favourite Hermocrates word: **33**.4, **34**.4, **34**.6 with **36**.2 n. **δείσαντες**: with ἐπρεσβευσάμεθα, and governing τὴν παροῦσαν δύναμιν ... μὴ αὐτὴν καταπλαγῆτε and τοὺς ... λόγους ... μὴ ὑμᾶς πείσωσιν in variants of the 'I know thee who thou art' construction (**6**.3 n.), here with fear clauses rather than indirect questions. The opening brings in both the ἔργα/λόγοι contrast and the 'we' rhetoric: the Athenians are persuasive speakers, but you can already see, as we can, that their force is nothing to be afraid of.

76.2 προφάσει μὲν ἧι πυνθάνεσθε, διανοίαι δὲ ἣν πάντες ὑπονοοῦμεν: ἧι either by relative attraction for ἥν or ἥκειν is understood. This echoes Th.'s own view at **6**.1, but προφάσει has here and at **78**.1 resumed its connotation of 'explanation', 'pretext': see **6**.1 n. **κατοικίσαι ... ἐξοικίσαι** 'settle' ... 'displace', or more slickly in the internet age 'install' ... 'uninstall'. On the style see intr. n. above, and cf. the jeering ξυνοικήσοντες ... κατοικιοῦντες, **63**.3. **ἐκεῖ**: like ἐκεῖνα (**76**.3), used vaguely for 'over there' – Greece and the Aegean. **ἀναστάτους ποιεῖν**: as at Hestiaea in 446 (1.114.3) and more recently at Aegina (2.27.1), Potidaea (2.70.3), Scione (5.32.1), and Melos (5.116.4). Not that Syracuse's own record was spotless, as Hermocrates' hearers well knew: cf. **3**.3 n. (Naxos and Catana), **4**.2 (Megara), **6**.2 (Leontini), and above all **5**.3 (Camarina itself). **κατὰ τὸ ξυγγενές**: as fellow Ionians, **6**.1 n. **δουλωσαμένους ἔχειν** 'hold in a position of slavery', not quite equivalent to δουλώσασθαι but concentrating on the condition that results: *CGCG* 52.53. Stringent terms were imposed on Chalcis after the Euboean revolt in 446 (Plut. *Per.* 23.3–4, cf. Th. 1.114; ML 52 = Fornara 103 = OR 131). δουλωσαμένους puts it strongly, but this is not the time to mince words, and Hermocrates is also preparing for the stress on freedom at **76**.4 and **77**.1. **ὧν οἵδε ἄποικοί εἰσι: 3**.3 (n.).

76.3 τῆι δὲ αὐτῆι ἰδέαι: Engl. would say that their behaviour 'took the same shape'. Cf. 3.62.2, the claim that in not Medising the Plataeans were just siding with Athens, in a way that took the same ἰδέα as when they later 'Atticised' when Athens became the aggressor. **ἔσχον** 'came to have'. **πειρῶνται**: σχεῖν is understood. **ἡγεμόνες γὰρ γενόμενοι ἑκόντων τῶν τε Ἰώνων ... τιμωρίαι**: again (**76**.2 n.) similar to Th.'s own analysis, including the emphasis on 'Ionians' and on 'vengeance' (1.95.1, 96.1): for the 'willingness' cf. **82**.3 n. **καὶ ὅσοι ἀπὸ σφῶν ἦσαν** 'and of those coming from their own stock'. This may refer to Athens' grand claim to be the mother-city of all Ionians (7.57.4 with n.): the tautology with τῶν τε Ἰώνων would be rhetorically effective ('yes, Ionians, their own stock'). Alternatively it may identify Athens' colonies as a subgroup within the broader category that would include the mainland Ionians of Asia Minor; in that case καί = 'and more specifically' (LSJ s.v. A.I.2, *GP* 291). Hermocrates ignores e.g. Lesbos and Rhodes, members of the Delian League but neither Athenian colonies nor Ionian, but he is preparing to play the Dorian race card at **77**.1. Euphemus responds at **82**.3. **τοὺς μὲν ... ἐπενεγκόντες** 'charging some with desertion, some with attacking one another, and others with whatever plausible accusation they could use in each case'. The variation of construction is characteristic: the acc. λιποστρατίαν and the inf. στρατεύειν are both dependent on some verb such as αἰτιασάμενοι understood as the equivalent of αἰτίαν ... ἐπενεγκόντες. For Athenian chastisement for λιποστρατία cf. 1.99.1; the charge of 'fighting one another' refers especially to Samos and Miletus in 441/0 (1.115.2); εὐπρεπῆ may recall εὐπρεπῶς at **6**.1 (n.). These are stronger words than those in the authorial voice at 1.96–9 and than those of Hermocrates himself at 4.60–1. There may also be a faint echo of Hdt. 1.26.3, Croesus 'bringing different αἰτίαι against different people, bigger ones when he could find any but trivial in some cases': that would prepare for the clearer suggestion at **77**.1 that Athenians are the new equivalent of the Asiatic tyrant. **κατεστρέψαντο:** Hermocrates' keynote word for Athens' record and aspirations (**80**.4 n.), but Th. does not think it unfair (**1** n., **24**.3, 4.65.3), and Euphemus (**82**.3) and other Athenian speakers (1.75.4, 5.97) do not deny it.

76.4 καὶ οὐ περὶ τῆς ἐλευθερίας ... ἀντέστησαν: Hermocrates anticipates the 'we were worthy rulers because we were a beacon of freedom' argument often found in Athenian oratory (e.g. Lys. 2.47, Isoc. 4.98–9) and echoed at 1.75.1. Euphemus gives it an unexpected twist: **83**.1–2. **ἄρα:** marking 'the reality of a past event . . . as apprehended either during its occurrence: or at the moment of speaking or writing: or at some intermediate moment ("as it subsequently transpired")' (*GP* 36), here the last of these. **περὶ δὲ ... οὐκ ἀξυνετωτέρου, κακοξυνετωτέρου δέ** 'but the first were fighting to enslave people to themselves rather than to him [the Persian king], the second to change their master to one of equal intelligence but greater malevolence'. For the singsong wordplay see intr. n. to **76–80**. κακοξυνετωτέρου is likely to be a coinage of Th.: the word's only other extant occurrences are in passages quoting this one.

77.1–2 Ἀλλ' οὐ γὰρ δή ... ταύτηι μόνον ἁλωτοί ἐσμεν: despite his captiousness about the speech (76–80 n.), D. H. singles out this passage for praise: 'the language is clear and pure, it also has rapidity, beauty, intensity, grandeur, and incisiveness, and it is full of energetic emotion' (*Thuc.* 48). Ἀλλά ... γάρ 'marks the contrast between what is irrelevant or subsidiary and what is vital, primary, or decisive' (*GP* 101), esp. when 'breaking off' (*GP* 102): cf. e.g. Soph. *El.* 595 ἀλλ' οὐ γὰρ οὐδὲ νουθετεῖν ἔξεστί σε. This is the technique of παράλειψις, making a show of omitting an argument while ensuring that it is heard anyway (e.g. Dem. 18.100, 120, 138). In fact Hermocrates has already made the point. **τὴν ... πόλιν ... ἀποφανοῦντες ... ὅσα ἀδικεῖ:** again (76.1 n.) the 'I know thee who thou art' construction. **εὐκατηγόρητον** is a rare and striking word, also found in Antiphon fr. 51 'all of life is easy to blame'. It is probably a recent coinage of the rhetorical culture. **ἐν εἰδόσιν:** 'we'-rhetoric again (76.1 n.) – you Camarinaeans know that as well as we Syracusans. The phrasing may be a Hermocrates tic, as early in his Gela speech he asked τί ἄν τις ... ἐν εἰδόσι μακρηγοροίη; (4.59.2). Both passages may echo Pericles, reluctant to μακρηγορεῖν ἐν εἰδόσιν concerning the glorious deeds of their fathers' generation (2.36.4). The same deeds are in focus here, but seen from the victims' perspective. **πολὺ δὲ μᾶλλον ἡμᾶς αὐτοὺς αἰτιασόμενοι:** again as he had at Gela, 4.61.5–6. The 'we'-rhetoric continues but is wearing thin, as he is criticising not Syracuse but other Sicilians for not following Syracuse's example of resistance. **παραδείγματα:** again echoing Pericles' pride in the Athenians, παράδειγμα δὲ μᾶλλον αὐτοὶ ὄντες τισὶν ἢ μιμούμενοι ἑτέρους (2.37.1). Their imperialist way is now a παράδειγμα not to imitate, but of what to avoid. **τῶν τ' ἐκεῖ Ἑλλήνων ... ἐπικουρίας** then sets out what these παραδείγματα were, first (τε) the example given by 'the Greeks over there' further defined by ὡς ἐδουλώθησαν, then (καὶ) ταῦτα παρόντα σοφίσματα ... ἐπικουρίας in apposition to παραδείγματα. **ταῦτα ... ἐπικουρίας:** i.e. this is the form their σοφίσματα are taking here, with echoes of the ξυγγενῶν and ξυμμάχων language used in Greece in and after 480–479. Hermocrates was equally scathing about the 'alliance' excuse at 4.60.1. **οὐκ Ἴωνες τάδε εἰσίν:** cf. Stevens 1971 on Eur. *Andr.* 168 οὐ γὰρ ἔσθ' Ἕκτωρ τάδε, for this 'sarcastic or contemptuous' use of τάδε. At Gela Hermocrates had played down the Ionian–Dorian divide in the interest of his Pan-Sicilian theme (4.61.2, 64.3), but now the Ionian cities – Naxos, Messina, Catana, Leontini – are not supporting Syracuse, and Hermocrates can play the racial card (Price 2001: 156). See **76–80** n. **δεσπότην ... μεταβάλλοντες:** echoing ἐπὶ δεσπότου μεταβολῆι at **76**.4, but turning it to the subjects' discredit: they put up with it. **ἢ ἕνα γέ τινα** 'or someone or other', here dismissive: cf. Ar. fr. 506 K–A, 'the man has been wrecked by a book, or Prodicus, ἢ τῶν ἀδολεσχῶν εἷς γέ τις'. **Δωριῆς ἐλεύθεροι**

ἀπ' αὐτονόμου τῆς Πελοποννήσου τὴν Σικελίαν οἰκοῦντες: a fine climax, as each point adds extra precision: Dorians, free men, from the independent Peloponnese, with Sicily now as our home. αὐτόνομος and ἐλεύθερος are close but not identical in meaning, with αὐτόνομος giving the positive perspective of self-determination and ἐλεύθερος the absence of external domination: cf. Raaflaub 2004: 147–57. The linkage of the two is less clichéd here than it later became (e.g. Isoc. 4.117, Dem. 1.23, 18.305): we have imbibed our spirit from our origins in the Peloponnese, used to controlling its own destiny, and therefore will not put up with external bullying. At 5.9.1 and 7.5.4 Spartans show similar Dorian contempt for Ionians, and at 8.25 this leads Dorians into over-confidence and defeat (Alty 1982: 3–4).

77.2 ἕως ἂν ἕκαστοι κατὰ πόλεις ληφθῶμεν: Hermocrates had argued similarly at Gela: ξύμπαντες μὲν ἐπιβουλευόμεθα, κατὰ πόλεις δὲ διέσταμεν (4.61.2). ἐπὶ τοῦτο τὸ εἶδος τρεπομένους 'adopting this style', with a strong hint of shiftiness: cf. 8.56.2, of Alcibiades' manipulation of Tissaphernes. τοὺς μὲν . . . κακουργεῖν: Hermocrates affects to distinguish different Athenian tactics for different cities, but all three are things that he anticipates Euphemus will try here, causing a rift between Syracuse and Camarina, promising an alliance, and finding whatever honeyed arguments he can. διιστάναι: cf. **79**.3 and διέσταμεν at 4.61.2, quoted above: Tompkins 2015: 120. τοὺς δὲ . . . κακουργεῖν 'and harming others in whatever way they can by saying something alluring to each audience in turn'. καὶ οἰόμεθα . . . δυστυχεῖν; 'And do we think, as each distant neighbour is destroyed first, that the terror will not strike oneself too, and that the person who suffers before one suffers alone?' The singular is used as in τοῦ πέλας, **12**.1 n.

78.1 εἴ τωι ἄρα παρέστηκε 'if it has occurred to anyone . . .': so also Hermocrates at 4.61.2 παρεστάναι δὲ μηδενί ('let no-one think . . .'). ἄρα indicates a lively interest, and affects some surprise (cf. **75**.1 n.), that anyone should think that way. τὸν μὲν Συρακόσιον, ἑαυτὸν δ' οὐ . . . τῆς ἐμῆς . . . τῆς ἐμῆς . . . τῆς ἑαυτοῦ . . . τῆι ἐμῆι . . . ἐμοῦ . . . ἐμέ . . . τόν τε Ἀθηναῖον . . . τοῦ Συρακοσίου . . . τῆι δ' ἐμῆι . . . τὴν ἐκείνου: D. H. *Thuc.* 48 found the use of the singular 'wearisome' (κατακορές), but does not bring out that it is a mannerism of Hermocrates, parodied at **84**.3. The initial 'the Syracusan' could be seen as a continuation of the singular idiom of τοῦ ξυνοίκου (**77**.2 n.), and then 'my' and 'his' country follow easily: but ἐμοῦ, ἐμέ, and ἐμῆι are more in the style of his 4.64.1, 'I am providing a city that is the greatest . . . I am more likely to be attacking others than defending myself . . .'. Suspicions of his tyrannical manner (**33–4**, **36–40**, **38**.3 nn.) are not far away. ὑπέρ γε τῆς ἐμῆς targets anyone who accepts that the danger needs facing but does not want to do so *for Syracuse*: hence γε.   τοσούτωι δὲ καὶ ἀσφαλέστερον ὅσωι οὐ προδιεφθαρμένου ἐμοῦ 'and all the more safely for my not having been destroyed beforehand'.   τόν τε Ἀθηναῖον ... βούλεσθαι 'and the concern of the Athenian is not to exact punishment for the Syracusan's hatred but just as much to use me as a pretext for strengthening the other man's friendship', the 'other man' being the τις who may be thinking that way. D. H. found the whole sentence 'juvenile, overdone, and obscurer than what we call riddles' (*Thuc.* 48).

78.2   This sentence wins Dionysius' praise (*Thuc.* 48).   φθονεῖ: echoing Pericles on φθόνος as an inevitable concomitant of power (2.64.4–5). Alcibiades echoed that too, but to different effect: **16**.3 n.   σωφρονισθῶμεν 'be chastened', but retaining a sense of 'imparting σωφροσύνη': cf. 3.65.3, 8.1.3, and Euphemus' echoing σωφρονισταί, **87**.3. Engl. might put it as 'teach us a lesson'.   οὐκ ἀνθρωπίνης δυνάμεως βούλησιν ἐλπίζει 'he is indulging in wishful thinking that goes beyond human ability to fulfil', lit. 'he hopes a wish [internal acc.] that is not a property of human capacity'. Cf. 3.39.3 ἐλπίσαντες μακρότερα μὲν τῆς δυνάμεως, ἐλάσσω δὲ τῆς βουλήσεως.   οὐ γὰρ οἷόν τε ... ταμίαν γενέσθαι 'for it is not possible to dispense fortune in an exact match to desire', lit. 'for the same person simultaneously to dispense desire and fortune in the same way'. Hermocrates said something similar at 4.64.1, 'I am not so stupidly ambitious as to think that I am in command of τύχη in the same way that I can control my own thinking.' He again echoes Alcibiades, **18**.3 (ταμιεύεσθαι).

78.3   τοῖς αὑτοῦ ... φθονῆσαι 'perhaps one day he might lament his own evils and wish he could once again envy my good things'. ὀλοφυρθείς is probably middle in sense despite the passive formation. D. H. again thought this and the following sentence juvenile and overdone (*Thuc.* 48); Tompkins 2015: 121 defends.   ἀδύνατον ... προσλαβεῖν 'It is impossible for someone who has abandoned [me] and has not been willing to take on the extra dangers, ones concerning not words but deeds ...': λόγωι μὲν ... σωτηρίαν then explains the words/deeds contrast. 'It' remains unspecified: probably a vague 'to achieve what you would want' or 'to survive'. τοὺς κινδύνους προσλαμβάνειν may echo Hermocrates' programme in 424, but then (4.61.1) he was warning *against* 'taking on extra dangers' in language that echoed Pericles (1.144.1, 2.65.7: Intr., 28). By now, he argues, it is necessary to go the extra mile.   λόγωι ... σωτηρίαν: D. H. used this to round off his denunciation: 'an epigram inappropriate even for an adolescent.'

78.4 ὁμόρους ὄντας: Hermocrates stresses contiguity and danger rather than the relation of mother-city and colony: that is understandable, given that Syracuse had not treated her daughter well (5.3 n.). Euphemus will turn the 'neighbour'/'far away' theme differently, **82–87** n. In fact a mountain range separates the cities. **ἐκ τοῦ ὁμοίου** 'equally': see Rusten on 2.42.3 for Th.'s taste for this adverbial use of a preposition + neuter adj. **παρακελευομένους ὅπως μηδὲν ἐνδώσομεν φαίνεσθαι** 'to show yourselves encouraging us not to give in at all', φαίνεσθαι + participle (**2.2** n.). For ὅπως + fut. ind. after verbs of encouragement see *M&T* 355. **νῦν γέ πω:** taken closely together, 'at least up till now'.

79.1 τὸ δίκαιον πρός τε ἡμᾶς καὶ πρὸς τοὺς ἐπιόντας: τοὺς ἐπιόντας rather than 'the Athenians', for the importance will immediately be stressed of their being the attackers. Hermocrates was equally scathing about δίκαιον talk at 4.61.4. **ἤν** (i.e. ξυμμαχίαν) is followed by several constructions, first 'not in the case of friends', i.e. not when friends would be the shared enemy; then a conditional clause, '[in the case of enemies] if any of them were to . . .'; and finally an epexegetic inf. for what the alliance would commit them to doing. The variation is typical. The claim is that the ξυμμαχία amounts in technical terms to an ἐπιμαχία, a defensive alliance that applies only when one side is attacked, rather than a fuller commitment 'to have the same friends and enemies': the distinction is drawn at **1.44.1**, but is rarely explicit. An alliance could be interpreted in that way (cf. *CT* on 1.44.1), but the debate of **8–26** shows that the extent of any commitment could be anything but clear-cut. **ὅταν ὑπ' ἄλλων:** ἀδικῶνται is understood: 'under attack' is what is meant, but Hermocrates takes the chance to insinuate that this attack is unjust. **ἐπεὶ οὐδ' οἱ Ῥηγῖνοι . . . ξυγκατοικίζειν:** the next logical step is 'the Rhegians did not regard themselves as bound by their alliance [**44**.2 n.], so why should you?', but Hermocrates adds a second point to turn it into an *a fortiori* argument: if any city might be expected to act according to their alliance it would be Rhegium, as in that case it was reinforced by Chalcidian kinship (**4.6, 44.3** nn.).

79.2 ἐκεῖνοι: the Rhegians. **τὸ ἔργον τοῦ καλοῦ δικαιώματος ὑποπτεύοντες** 'suspecting the truth behind the fair-sounding justification'. **ἀλόγως σωφρονοῦσιν:** i.e. the Rhegians have no λόγοι to offer as justifications, but Hermocrates is being ironic: of course he thinks they have λόγος in the sense of 'reason'. For the oxymoron cf. Eur. *Bacch.* 940 παρὰ λόγον σώφρονας: there too the speaker Dionysus would say that the Bacchants have a deeper λόγος. **τοὺς μὲν φύσει πολεμίους . . . τοὺς δὲ ἔτι μᾶλλον φύσει ξυγγενεῖς:** again (**79.1** n.) there is some compression of argument, as the Syracusans are no 'closer' kin, either as Dorians or as Sicilians, than the Athenians are distant; but τοὺς μὲν φύσει πολεμίους compounds the idea of natural enemies because of (a) kinship and (b) hostile intent (cf. 4.60.1), and it is the second aspect that renders the Athenians ἔχθιστοι (cf. 7.68.2) and binds Camarina ἔτι μᾶλλον to Syracuse.

79.3 ἀλλ' οὐ δίκαιον, ἀμύνειν δὲ καὶ μὴ φοβεῖσθαι τὴν παρασκευὴν αὐτῶν: a further δίκαιον is understood with the infinitives. The sentence completes a ring with **79**.1, with what Hermocrates regards as a true δίκαιον trumping the false δίκαιον there and μὴ φοβεῖσθαι reversing δειλία; there is also a larger ring with **76**.1–2, with μὴ φοβεῖσθαι picking up μὴ αὐτὴν καταπλαγῆτε δείσαντες and δίκαιον reflecting the expected Athenian πρόφασις.   **οὐδὲ πρὸς ἡμᾶς ... διὰ τάχους:** cf. **71**.1 n.

80.1 ἀθρόους γε ὄντας 'provided we unite': Hermocrates had used the same language at 4.64.2, and Alcibiades will echo this passage at **91**.2.   **ἰέναι δὲ ἐς τὴν ξυμμαχίαν:** as at 5.30.5, a mix of the literal – marching troops – and the metaphorical: cf. 1.118.2 μὴ ταχεῖς ἰέναι ἐς τοὺς πολέμους, and 3.46.2 ἔλθοι ἂν ἐς ξύμβασιν.   **προθυμότερον: 6**.2 n.   **ἄλλως τε καὶ ἀπὸ Πελοποννήσου παρεσομένης ὠφελίας:** Hermocrates' careful words allow the meaning 'especially if', but many would take them as 'especially given that', conveying hard information that the Peloponnesians will send help. That will indeed happen (**93**.2), but Hermocrates does not know that yet, and this even goes beyond what Syracuse has asked for (**73**.2). Still, the phrase is dependent on εἰκός, what it is 'reasonable' to expect, and Hermocrates could have affected to be presenting only intelligent guesswork.   **οἳ τῶνδε κρείσσους εἰσί:** a sense-construction, with the plural picking up 'the Peloponnesians' implicit in ἀπὸ Πελοποννήσου.   **καὶ μὴ ... δοκεῖν:** still dependent on εἰκός, it is not reasonable for anyone (τωι = τινι) to think . . .   **τὸ ... βοηθεῖν:** in apposition to ἐκείνην τὴν προμηθίαν. For Syracuse's position as an ally of both sides see **75**.3–**88** n. and for the Athenian alliance **75**.3 n. It is not known when the Syracusan alliance was contracted: perhaps as early as their refounding in 461, **5**.3 n.

80.2 εἰ γὰρ ... σφαλήσεται ... περιέσται; for εἰ + fut. indic. see **6**.2 n.   **δι' ὑμᾶς μὴ ξυμμαχήσαντας:** close to the *ab urbe condita* construction (**3**.3 n.), but there is force in putting it so personally: the outcome will be because of *you*, and you will bear the consequences. Hermocrates' dismissal of neutrality as a compromise recalls the Athenians' at Melos (5.94–5), though their argument was different.   **τί ἄλλο ἤ** 'what was this other than ... ?'. A strong expostulation: cf. 3.58.5 and 5.98.1, where speakers are pleading for their lives.   **ἠμύνατε ... οὐκ ἐκωλύσατε:** aorist, as the sentence projects forward to the mindset of one looking back once

COMMENTARY: 80.3–80.5

the Syracusans have been defeated. σωθῆναι: inf. of what would have been the 'purpose or result' (it would be both) of their defending, had it happened: *CGCG* 51.16. κακοὺς γενέσθαι: 'be victorious' might be expected, but as with ἀδικῶσιν (**79**.1) Hermocrates adds the moral point. Euphemus echoes this at **86**.3. φίλους δὴ ὄντας: δή marks the Athenian disingenuousness (**54**.4 n.): 'friends', indeed . . . μὴ ἐᾶσαι ἁμαρτεῖν: more irony: be a true friend, and stop them 'going wrong'!

80.3 Ξυνελόντες . . . διαφυγεῖν: the summary is unusually full, adding extra perspectives (nn.) and putting some points more strongly (αἰεί, προδιδόμεθα, οὐκ ἄλλον τινὰ ἄθλον . . . λήψονται). For 'you already know this as well as we do' cf. **76**.2, **77**.1; for the Ionian/Dorian enmity, **77**.1; with Camarina's blameworthiness if Athens wins, **80**.2; with Camarina as the next victim, **77**.2, **78**; with the threat of slavery, **76**.2, **76**.4, **77**.1; and the summary ends, as the body of the speech did, with an appeal to honour (**80**.5 μὴ αἰσχρῶς, **80**.2 κάλλιον) conveyed with menace. D. H. singled out δεόμεθα . . . λήψονται as 'fine and worthy of imitation' (*Thuc.* 48). τε: connective τε (**18**.7 n.) is esp. frequent in summarising conclusions: Rusten 1989: 23. οὔτε τοὺς ἄλλους: a reminder that other Sicilian cities will face similar dilemmas: this is 'paradigmatic' (**75**.3–**88** n.). Those other cities may be included in those 'called to witness' the 'treachery', and that reinforces the threat of Dorian retribution. ἐπιβουλευόμεθα: a Hermocrates keynote (**33**.5, 4.60.1, 4.64.5, cf. **88**.7), and Alcibiades at least would not deny it (**18**.3). Euphemus throws it back at **86**.3. προδιδόμεθα: cf **34**.4 n. for this use of the present tense in lively predictions.

80.4 τῆς νίκης . . . λήψονται 'they will take as their prize of victory nobody other than the person who gave it to them'. ἆθλον is neuter, so τινά goes with οὐκ ἄλλον and ἆθλον is in apposition. The agonistic rhetoric so prominent in Bk. 7 (see Intr. to that book, 30) begins here as threat rather than inspiration.

80.5 ἤδη: emphatic: now is the time when you must choose. In fact the decision will effectively put it off: **88**.1 n. τὴν αὐτίκα ἀκινδύνως δουλείαν: for adverbs qualifying a noun see **49**.2 n. (again αὐτίκα), 8.64.5 τὴν ἀντικρὺς ἐλευθερίαν, and *CGCG* 26.18; but this is harsher as ἀκίνδυνον was an available alternative. Perhaps δουλείαν is here felt as close to an infinitive (so Dover 1965: 83), 'to play the slave'. ἢ κἂν περιγενόμενοι . . . διαφυγεῖν 'or, if you were to be victorious in our company, to avoid shamefully having these people as your masters and to escape hostile relations with us which would not be quick to end'. For ἢ καί introducing the second half of a disjunction see *GP* 306–7; Denniston's explanation is that 'ἤ separates two ideas objectively, in point of fact, while καί denotes that, subjectively, both must be kept before the mind', but it is simpler to see καί as emphasising that this 'too' is a possibility. ἂν περιγενόμενοι and μὴ ἂν βραχεῖαν γενομένην are the equivalent of potential optatives. **μὴ ἂν βραχεῖαν γενομένην:** a new point, delayed to give an even more clearly menacing end.

81 Τοιαῦτα... τοιάδε: τοιαῦτα as usual (**35**.1 n.) looking back, τοιάδε looking forwards (**8**.4, **15**.4, **19**.2, **32**.3, **35**.2, etc.). The transitional sentence is unusually terse, saying no more about Euphemus here than at **75**.4 (n.): contrast **15**, **36** and 3.41, Diodotus 'who in the first assembly too had been particularly vocal in opposing the execution of Mytileneans'. There may be advantage for Th. in his personal facelessness: **75**.3–**88**.2 n.

82–87 *The Speech of Euphemus*

Hermocrates' speech has indicated what pro-Athenian arguments were to be expected: a play for the high moral ground, stressing alliance obligations and denying any aspiration for a power-grab, combined with a rhetoric of 'liberation' from domineering Syracuse. The fourth-century *Rhetorica ad Alexandrum* also outlines the usual ways of arguing for an alliance (1424b27–1425a8): the potential allies are δίκαιοι, they have been helpful in the past, and are 'very powerful and a near neighbour'. Some speeches in Hdt. and Th. confirm these expectations. Hdt.'s Gelon points out the absence of any previous good turns when he rejects the Greek alliance (7.158.1–2); Th.'s Mytileneans counter the argument that Lesbos might seem 'far away' (3.13.5); his Corcyreans wish that they had been able to point to some past benefit that they have conferred (1.32.1) and claim that they have acted δικαίως (1.34.1).

Euphemus' argument is very different. Alliance obligations, including Camarina's own (**75**.3 n.), figure little, and τὸ δίκαιον figures only in passing (**82**.3–4, **86**.2). Instead he employs a rhetoric of frankness. He does not deny the Athenians' aspiration for as much power as possible, nor even that they have thoughts of 'staying' (**86**.3): that leaves it vague whether that implies only 'until our victory is complete' or a longer domination, though not 'enslavement' (**83**.4). His claim is that Athens' own interests require her to strengthen Camarina in order to keep Syracuse down, and so the implication is one of his city's relative weakness, not, as expected, of its strength. The 'near-at-hand' theme also takes a different turn, and it is *Syracuse*'s nearness that Euphemus emphasises (**84**.2, **86**.3); Athens is a distant power (**86**.3) and therefore needs Camarina as its local strong arm. That stress on distance also counters Hermocrates' scaremongering (there is nothing to fear from us . . .), while that on expediency meets his accusation of inconsistency: Ionian or Dorian, Athens has subdued those it needed to subdue and favoured those it needed to favour (**84**.2–**85**.2). λογ- words are recurrent (εὔλογον, **84**.2; ἀλόγως rebutted at **84**.3; οὐδὲν ἄλογον, **85**.1; λόγωι, **86**.2), countering Hermocrates' οὐ γὰρ δὴ εὔλογον of **76**.2: Athenian behaviour makes sense. How frank Euphemus is really being is a further question. Some of what he says is plausible (Brock 2013b: 54), but talk of 'liberation' (**87**.2) sits uneasily with Th.'s insistence that 'conquest' is in Athenian minds (καταστρέψεσθαι, **1**.1 n.), and many subject-states in the W had harder stories to tell about the Athenians' domination, however distant they might be. Cf. esp. Stahl 2011.

There are close verbal echoes of speeches at the beginning of the war (nn., cf. Rawlings 1981: 120–1), especially that of the Athenians at Sparta at 1.72–8: as in the Melian dialogue (5.85–113), Th. indicates the changing ways in which Athenians thought or at least talked about their ἀρχή. At Sparta there was more emphasis on τὸ δίκαιον; the shift can be seen either as an indication of moral decay or as a stripping away of hypocrisies (Pelling 2012: 306–12). In Bk. 1 the Athenians made much of their worthiness to rule (1.75), especially because of their leadership in the Persian Wars. Euphemus has some of this but is careful to limit the claims (**83**.1–2), with the same dismissiveness towards 'fancy words' as at Melos (οὐ καλλιεπούμεθα . . ., **83**.2, cf. 5.89.1). He emphasises instead that they were led, in the Persian Wars as now, by their own interest rather than by any liberating spirit: liberation is on offer to Camarina, or so he says (**87**.2–3), but only because that coincides with Athens' own security. The wishes of those subject allies, highlighted in Bk. 1, are here ignored (**82**.3 n.). Instead, as again at Melos, the emphasis is on the realities of power and the 'right' that this conveys (**82**.3, **85**.1, cf. 5.89, 105.2). Hermocrates himself would not have disagreed (4.61.5). There are continuities as well as contrasts with the past. The tyrant analogy has antecedents in Pericles and Cleon (**85**.1 n.); fear and security were already stressed in Bk. 1 (1.75.3–4); so was the insistence that the powerful will dominate (1.76.2). The talk has changed a little; the realities, less so.

The speech is skilfully planned (whether by Euphemus in reality or by Th. in reconstruction) as an answer to Hermocrates, whose argument and diction it echoes (nn.): cf. de Romilly 2012: 110–15. It begins by granting the eternal enmity of Ionians and Dorians, but using that to stress the need for Athens to defend itself against the Dorian Peloponnesians. This prompts the defence of the empire as 'reasonable' (εἰκότως, **82**.1 n.). The hard-headed ideology builds to a generality (**85**.1) which affords the transition to the second half, where Syracuse is seen as fitting the same pattern (**85**.3). The accusations mirror Hermocrates': now it is the

Syracusans that are using this as a mask for their own imperial ambitions; now it is their, not Athens', victim that Camarina is poised to become (86.3–5). Some of the same tropes are used too: you should be true to the arguments you would use yourselves (86.2, cf. 78.4); if you miss this opportunity, you will regret it (86.5, cf. 78.3). Euphemus cannot end with so naked a threat as Hermocrates did (80.5), as that would sit badly with his insistence that Athens cannot logistically remain. Still, his final stress on Athens' perpetual *potential* to intervene (87.4) may convey something of the same.

82.1 τῆς πρότερον οὔσης ξυμμαχίας: 75.3 n.   **τοῦ δὲ Συρακοσίου . . . ἔχομεν:** the beginning echoes not just that of the Athenians at Sparta (1.73.1: our embassy was not about this, but now we need to respond), but also that of Alcibiades at **16.1**. Alcibiades was justifying himself in words more appropriate to his city (**16–18** n.); here the civic context reasserts itself.   **ὡς εἰκότως ἔχομεν:** at Sparta the Athenians similarly set out to show ὡς οὔτε ἀπεικότως ἔχομεν ἃ κεκτήμεθα . . . (1.73.1), but the balance between different sorts of 'reasonableness' (εἰκός) has shifted. In Bk. 1 the emphasis was largely moral: we deserve it, especially because of the Persian Wars. Euphemus does not avoid moral justification completely (**82.3–83.1**), but his inflection of 'reasonableness' is more practical: given the predicament, our actions make sense. Cf. Pelling 2012: 307–9, and (with a rather different reading of the 1.73.1 passage) Stahl 2011: 35–6, 41–2.

82.2 τὸ μὲν οὖν μέγιστον μαρτύριον αὐτὸς εἶπεν: most explicitly at **80**.3, ἐπιβουλευόμεθα μὲν ὑπὸ Ἰώνων αἰεὶ πολεμίων. Cf. again the Athenians at Sparta, τεκμήριον δὲ μέγιστον αὐτὸς (Xerxes) ἐποίησεν (1.73.5).   **αἰεί ποτε πολέμιοι:** ποτε adds nothing in sense to αἰεί, but is used particularly when hostility (**89**.4, 2.102.2, 4.57.4, 8.85.3) or friendship (1.47.3, 3.95.1, 4.78.2) is in point.   **ἔχει δὲ καὶ οὕτως** 'and that is indeed how it is'.   **καὶ πλέοσιν οὖσι καὶ παροικοῦσιν:** just as the Syracusans are 'more numerous and neighbours' to the Camarinaeans: Euphemus insinuates that they too should consider how best to avoid subjection. ὑπακούω, fut. ὑπακούσομαι, more usually takes a gen. (hence the textual corruption, probably originating in a marginal gloss), but for the dat. cf. **69**.3, 2.61.1, 4.63.2.

82.3 μετὰ τὰ Μηδικά: Euphemus immediately shifts the emphasis from what would be most expected, τὰ Μηδικά themselves. The concentration on the later period keeps the focus on self-defence, first (μέν) against the Peloponnese, secondly (δέ) turning to the ἀρχή and explaining that that too had a defensive aspect; finally this straggling sentence turns to the moral dimension – the Ionians and islanders deserved it. **ναῦς κτησάμενοι** 'now that we had ships': their acquisition predated the Persian Wars (1.14.3, Hdt. 7.144), and so μετὰ τὰ Μηδικά governs only the 'freeing ourselves', not this participial clause. In 480–479 Athens accepted Spartan hegemony. **τῆς μὲν Λακεδαιμονίων ἀρχῆς καὶ ἡγεμονίας ἀπηλλάγημεν:** Hdt. 8.3.2 puts it in terms of the allies themselves removing the hegemony from Sparta and (implicitly) passing it on willingly to Athens. Th. has earlier made that allied willingness explicit, with the Spartans too voluntarily withdrawing (1.75.2, 1.95.7, 96.1); even Hermocrates granted that the Athenians' initial hegemony was willingly accepted (**76**.3). For Euphemus consent is irrelevant. **προσῆκον:** acc. absolute of an impersonal verb (*CGCG* 52.30), as at **84**.1. **ἢ καὶ ἡμᾶς:** καί as often in comparisons, **68**.2 n. **τῶν ὑπὸ βασιλεῖ πρότερον ὄντων:** skilfully turning Hermocrates' taunt of **77**.2 n.: yes, those allies were used to external rule, and so we did nothing out of the way. **καταστάντες οἰκοῦμεν:** Euphemus could simply have said κατέστημεν or καθέσταμεν, but οἰκοῦμεν directs attention back to the home front: we did what we did just to continue living our lives. Cf. **18**.7 and esp. **92**.5. **νομίσαντες ἥκιστ' ἂν ὑπὸ Πελοποννησίοις οὕτως εἶναι:** οὕτως initially looks back ('by becoming ἡγεμόνες . . .'), then δύναμιν ἔχοντες ἧι ἀμυνούμεθα explains further: for the fut. ind. see *CGCG* 50.24. Th.'s sketchy narrative in Bk. 1 did not emphasise self-defence against the Peloponnese, though 1.90–3 (the deception of Sparta needed while the Piraeus walls were being built) left no doubt that Spartan 'friendship' (1.92.1) in the early 470s coexisted with fear of what Athens might become (1.90.1). At Sparta in 432 the Athenians did mention fear of the Peloponnese, but as a reason for not *giving up* the empire (1.75.4), thus relating it to a later phase. **ἐς τὸ ἀκριβὲς εἰπεῖν** 'strictly speaking'. 7.49.3 and 1.138.3 (τὸ ξυμπᾶν εἰπεῖν) suggests that εἰπεῖν would be heard as absolute, 'so to speak', and ἐς τὸ ἀκριβές as = ἀκριβῶς as in ἐς τὸ φανερόν, 1.23.6, or ἐς τὸ πᾶν, Aesch. *Ag*. 682. **καταστρεψάμενοι:** as in his later ἀρχή language Euphemus gives up the blander phrasing of the earlier word ἡγεμόνες: cf. Wickersham 1994: 56–61. That fits this rhetoric of frankness, **82–87** n. **τούς τε Ἴωνας καὶ νησιώτας . . . δεδουλῶσθαι:** echoing Hermocrates, esp. **76**.2 κατὰ τὸ ξυγγενές . . . δουλωσαμένους (strictly only of Chalcis) and **77**.1 Ἴωνες . . . καὶ νησιῶται.

82.4 ἦλθον γὰρ ἐπὶ τὴν μητρόπολιν ἐφ' ἡμᾶς: many Ionians did participate in the campaigns of 490 and esp. 480–479, but they had little choice. Euphemus is treading on dangerous ground, as 'moving against their mother-city' is what he is now urging Camarina to do (**5**.3 n.). **ἀποστάντες:** both 'revolt' (LSJ ἀφίστημι B.2) and physically 'withdraw, leave' (LSJ B.1). Whole-scale western migration was sometimes aired then as an option (Hdt. 1.170.2), but was understandably not taken up. τὰ οἰκεῖα φθεῖραι: cf. 1.74.2 τὰ οἰκεῖα διαφθείραντες, of what the Athenians *did* do in 480. ὥσπερ ἡμεῖς ἐκλιπόντες τὴν πόλιν: the Athenian women and children moved to Troezen, Aegina, and Salamis during the invasion (Hdt. 8.41, etc.): cf. 1.18.2, 1.91.5. This became one of their proudest claims (Lys. 2.33–4, etc.), foregrounded by the Athenians at Sparta (1.73.4, 74.2–4); but that was very different from the permanent migrations that would have been necessary for Ionians. δουλείαν … τὸ αὐτὸ ἐπενεγκεῖν 'they wished for slavery themselves, and to impose the same thing on us'. For the neuter see **72**.4 n. Euphemus' dismissiveness is calculated to appeal to his Camarinaean audience, Dorians as they were (Price 2001: 102 n. 32).

83.1 ἄξιοί τε ὄντες ἅμα ἄρχομεν: Euphemus echoes 1.75.1 Ἆρ' ἄξιοί ἐσμεν, ὦ Λακεδαιμόνιοι …, but here 'worthiness' – their good deeds, the allies' bad – is only one of two reasons for the rule; the other (ἄξιοί τε is answered by ἅμα δέ, *GP* 513–14) reverts to self-protection. The effect is similar to rhetorical παράλειψις (**77**.1–2 n.). The glories of 480 will not be Euphemus' emphasis, but he gets them in anyway. ναυτικόν … ἐς τοὺς Ἕλληνας: ἀπροφάσιστον may pick up Hermocrates' contemptuous προφάσει, **76**.2: προφάσεις are not the Athenian way. 1.74.1 listed three contributions in 480, ἀριθμόν τε νεῶν πλεῖστον ('a little less than two thirds of the 400', it goes on; Hdt. 8.44 and 48 says 180 out of 378) καὶ ἄνδρα στρατηγὸν ξυνετώτατον (Themistocles) καὶ προθυμίαν ἀοκνοτάτην. Euphemus omits Themistocles; it would be unwise to awaken memories of Athens' wily trickster. τῶι Μήδωι ἑτοίμως τοῦτο δρῶντες 'doing this [i.e. provide ships and support] willingly for the Mede' rather than the Greeks. ἑτοίμως counters the obvious objection that they had no choice: perhaps not, but they did it 'readily'.

83.2 οὐ καλλιεπούμεθα ὡς … 'we do not use fancy words claiming that …'. Cf. 5.89.1, the Athenians at Melos: 'we do not come μετ' ὀνομάτων καλῶν, saying either that we rule δικαίως [cf. εἰκότως here] because of our defeat of the Mede or that we are now pursuing recompense for ἀδικία'. Those ambassadors excluded talk of justice more uncompromisingly; Euphemus has after all just made a strong claim that the subject-allies deserved their fate. καλλιεπέομαι is a rare word, not in itself pejorative (the servant at Ar. *Thesm.* 49 means it well when he describes Agathon as καλλιεπής, even if the word is thrown back at him mockingly, 60), but lending itself to a contrast with solid content: cf. the opening of Plato, *Apol.*, warning the jurors not to expect κεκαλλιεπημένους γε λόγους … ῥήμασί τε καὶ ὀνόμασιν of the sort Socrates' accusers have used (17b). ὡς ἢ τὸν βάρβαρον μόνοι καθελόντες … κινδυνεύσαντες: in fact

Euphemus *is* claiming that they rule εἰκότως (**82**.1 n.), so the weight falls on the participles: these are not his reasons for asserting it. Something like these claims would be known to Th.'s audience as staples of patriotic Athenian rhetoric: cf. esp. Lys. 2.20–47, beginning μόνοι γὰρ ὑπὲρ ἁπάσης τῆς Ἑλλάδος πρὸς πολλὰς μυριάδας τῶν βαρβάρων διεκινδύνευσαν (of Marathon, 20) and ending βέβαιον μὲν τὴν ἐλευθερίαν τῆι Εὐρώπηι κατηργάσαντο . . . ὑπὸ πάντων ἠξιώθησαν . . . ἡγεμόνες γενέσθαι τῆς Ἑλλάδος (of 480–479, 47). But Euphemus exaggerates each familiar claim even as he dismisses it, broadening the first and narrowing the second: see next two nn. **μόνοι καθελόντες:** echoing 1.73.4 φαμὲν γὰρ Μαραθῶνί τε μόνοι προκινδυνεῦσαι τῶι βαρβάρωι . . ., but there the claim was limited to Marathon. Euphemus' broadening to the whole Persian War makes it self-evidently false and goes with his dismissing it as immaterial; but the effect is to deflate, even parody, a cherished claim going back to Hdt. 9.27.5. Later authors however said similar things in earnest: Isoc. 16.27, Dem. 60.10; Thomas 1989: 223–4. But μόνοι was false even for Marathon: the Plataeans fought there too. Cf. Walters 1981. **ἐπ' ἐλευθερίαι τῆι τῶνδε . . . κινδυνεύσαντες:** for ἐπί + dat. see **27**.3 (n.). The familiar claim was that Athens led the way towards freedom for 'all Greece': see e.g. Lys. 2.20, quoted above, then 2.23, 25, 33, 34, 42; Isoc. 14.59; Plato, *Menex*. 239b, 241c. The claim Euphemus dismisses is narrower and was surely less often made, that they fought to liberate 'these people', i.e. the Ionians and islanders. It responds to **76**.4, but Hermocrates did not put it like this. **πᾶσι δὲ ἀνεπίφθονον τὴν προσήκουσαν σωτηρίαν ἐκπορίζεσθαι:** echoing 1.75.5 πᾶσι δὲ ἀνεπίφθονον τὰ ξυμφέροντα τῶν μεγίστων πέρι κινδύνων εὖ τίθεσθαι. The sense of φθόνος in ἀνεπίφθονον should not be lost: as at **54**.5 and 7.77.2–3, such power excites envy. Hdt. 7.139, acknowledging that his praise of Athens' contribution in 480–479 will be ἐπίφθονον . . . πρὸς τῶν πλεόνων ἀνθρώπων, may be in Th.'s or his audience's minds. As at **9**.1 (n.), προσήκουσαν combines 'our own' and 'befitting' for us to contrive.

83.3 ἀποφαίνομεν . . . τὰ ξυμφέροντα πράσσοντας 'we make this demonstration on the basis of the attacks that these people are launching against us and the suspicions, tending towards the more apprehensive, that you have yourselves: we know that those who are too fearfully suspicious get pleasure for the immediate future from hearing what appeals to them, but when it comes to action later they do what is in their interests'. ἀποφαίνομεν . . . εἰδότες perhaps echoes **77**.1 ἀποφανοῦντες ἐν εἰδόσιν, where Hermocrates makes these charges, and is also the counterpart of **76**.1, his fear that the opponents' words may be over-persuasive; it involves acknowledging that the Camarinaeans already suspect Athens' intentions, for that is why Hermocrates' argument carried some appeal. λόγου μὲν ἡδονῆι . . . τερπομένους also recalls Cleon's attack on slippery rhetoric at 3.38.5–7, with an audience delighted by its own cleverness; ἡδονὴ λόγων was then one of the obstacles to empire that Cleon categorised, 3.40.2. Here, though, instead of the expected 'but later regret it' (for which cf. **86**.5) the conclusion is that they will behave sensibly in the end, so they might as well decide to do so now.

83.4 γάρ: filling out ἀποφαίνομεν (*GP* 59, 'after an expression denoting the giving or receiving of information'), as at e.g. 2.48.3–49.1 οἷόν τε ἐγίγνετο λέξω . . . τὸ μὲν γὰρ ἔτος . . . It is better conveyed by a colon than by 'for'.   **οὐ δουλωσόμενοι . . . κωλύσοντες:** Euphemus leaves it tactfully (or tactically) unclear whether 'the Sicilians as a whole' (understood from τὰ ἐνθάδε) or 'our friends' (from μετὰ τῶν φίλων) are not to be enslaved but to be protected. Despite εἰρήκαμεν, Euphemus has not addressed this μετὰ τῶν φίλων aspect yet; it gives the transition to **84**.

84.1 προσῆκον . . . προσήκετε: picking up προσῆκον (**82**.3, also acc. absolute) and προσήκουσαν (**83**.2), with the same combination of 'fitting' and 'our own' as in the second passage (n.): our shared interest is already (ἤδη) enough to make you 'our own' people. That wordplay gives the transition to Euphemus' counter to the racial point, **84**.2, and is picked up by οἰκεῖον, **85**.1 n.   **κηδόμεθα:** echoing Hermocrates' κήδεσθαι, **76**.2.   **διὰ τὸ μὴ ἀσθενεῖς ὑμᾶς ὄντας ἀντέχειν Συρακοσίοις** 'and through your resisting the Syracusans, being strong enough to do so': μή with ἀσθενεῖς, not with ἀντέχειν.   **ἧσσον ἄν . . . βλαπτοίμεθα:** brachylogy for 'there is less chance that we would be harmed': not 'we would be less harmed', for it would prevent any harming at all. For this fear of Syracusan intervention cf. **6**.2, **10**.4 n.

84.2 εὔλογον κατοικίζειν: echoing and countering Hermocrates at **76**.2. For the λογ- language see **82–87** n.   **τοὺς ξυγγενεῖς αὐτῶν τοὺς ἐν Εὐβοίαι:** for the treatment of Chalcis see **76**.2 n., but ὑπηκόους is gentler than Hermocrates' δουλωσαμένους ἔχειν there.

84.3 τὰ μὲν γὰρ ἐκεῖ . . . τὰ δὲ ἐνθάδε 'for matters over there' and 'over here', accs. of respect.   **καὶ αὐτοί** 'even on our own'.   **ἀρκοῦμεν:** a play on ἀρκεῖν ~ ἀρχή may be felt: cf. X. *Cyr.* 5.5.16 ἀρξώμεθα δ', ἔφη, ἐκ τῆσδε τῆς ἀρχῆς, εἰ καὶ σοὶ ἀρκούντως δοκεῖ ἔχειν, and *Anab.* 2.6.20 ἀρκεῖν πρὸς τὸ ἀρχικόν.   **ὁ Χαλκιδεύς:** perhaps mocking Hermocrates' mannered use of the singular, **78**.1 n.   **δουλωσαμένους . . . ἐλευθεροῦν:** continuing (**84**.2 n.) the counter to Hermocrates' δουλωσαμένους ἔχειν (**76**.2), but Hermocrates did not talk of 'liberation': that is a subtle way of insinuating the idea as something that even an enemy concedes.

Euphemus then appropriates the claim at **87**.2. **ἀπαράσκευος ὢν καὶ χρήματα μόνον φέρων**: this puts it much more mildly than Hermocrates' 'enslavement'. For the distinction between ship-providing and tribute-paying allies cf. 1.99.3, where Th. forthrightly blames the allies themselves for choosing the second and consequently becoming ἀπαράσκευοι. As at **82**.3 (n.), Euphemus ignores any question of the allies' choice. **καὶ Λεοντῖνοι καὶ οἱ ἄλλοι φίλοι ὅτι μάλιστα αὐτονομούμενοι** 'both Leontinians and the other friends [are ξύμφοροι to us] by being as independent as possible'. Hermocrates' gibe had focused on the Leontinians; καὶ οἱ ἄλλοι φίλοι skilfully extends the counter to bring out the implications for Camarina too.

85.1 ἀνδρὶ δὲ τυράννωι ... ὅ τι μὴ πιστόν: Euphemus' tone is hardening: this is more sweeping than **83**.2, which was limited to necessary steps for security. He is not the first Athenian to draw the analogy with tyranny. Pericles had told the *dēmos* that its rule was like a tyranny (2.63.2), and Cleon had said that it *was* a tyranny (3.37.2). Such things were indeed said, and mocked: Ar. *Knights* 1111–14. Cf. Raaflaub 1979; Tuplin 1985; Pelling 2019: 86–7 and 144. **ἄλογον** is still countering the accusation of kinship inconsistency (**76**.2), and so is οἰκεῖον, building on the προσήκετε play at **84**.1: identity of interests is kinship enough.

85.2 καὶ γὰρ τοὺς ἐκεῖ ξυμμάχους ...: so Euphemus grants the legitimacy of drawing inferences from 'over there', but claims that Hermocrates has drawn the wrong conclusions. For ἐξηγεῖσθαι + acc. cf. 1.71.7. **ὡς ἕκαστοι χρήσιμοι** 'in whatever way each is useful'. **Χίους μὲν καὶ Μηθυμναίους ... περὶ τὴν Πελοπόννησον**: for these different types of allies see 1.99.2; 7.57 (nn.) mentions the Chians (§ 4) and Methymnaeans (§ 5) as ship-providing αὐτόνομοι (**77**.1 n.), and draws some further distinctions too. **χρημάτων βιαιότερον φορᾶι**: βιαιότερον is an adverb, χρημάτων φορᾶι defines how the manner is more forceful. 1.99 stressed that the rigour of the Athenians' exactions was unwelcome (ἀκριβῶς ἔπρασσον), but also presented the allies as free to choose which form of contribution they preferred: cf. **84**.3 n. Euphemus might however plausibly imply that the Chians and Methymnaeans would not have been allowed to continue in their chosen mode if it had not suited the Athenians too. **ἄλλους δὲ καὶ πάνυ ἐλευθέρως ξυμμαχοῦντας**: at 7.57.3 Th. similarly distinguishes between 'subjects' and 'independent allies', adding the further category (not relevant here) of mercenaries. **καίπερ νησιώτας ... περὶ τὴν Πελοπόννησον**: 7.57.7 includes Cephallenians and Zacynthians among the αὐτόνομοι, but adds that as islanders they had no choice but to support the masters of the sea. Euphemus' claim of generosity to εὔληπτοι islanders close to the Peloponnese also rings hollow after Melos, close to the Peloponnese (5.108) as it was.

85.3 ὥστε καὶ τἀνθάδε . . . καθίστασθαι 'So it makes sense for us to settle matters here too with an eye to our advantage and, as we say, to fear as far as the Syracusans are concerned.' εἰκός covers both what it makes practical sense for us to do and what it makes intellectual sense for Camarinaeans to believe that we are doing; 'fear ἐς Συρακοσίους' may embrace both our own fear of the Syracusans and, though he has not yet said this, the fear that we hope to inject into them. **ἀρχῆς . . . ὑμῶν** 'rule over you'. C–S, P–S, and *HCT* took 'you' here and in ξυστῆτε to include all other Sicilians, but it is important to keep the focus on the Camarinaeans, even if their compliance would pave the way to Sicilian domination (αὐτοὶ ἄρξαι τῆς Σικελίας): it is they who issued the invitation of **86.**1. Still, many of the same considerations applied to other cities too, and this suits the debate's 'paradigmatic' role (**75**.3–**88**.2 n.). **ἐπὶ τῶι ἡμετέρωι . . . ὑπόπτωι** 'through suspicions of us', with ἐπί + dat. as causal (LSJ B.III.1) and ἡμετέρωι the equivalent of an objective gen. ἡμῶν (*CGCG* 29.25). **βίαι ἢ καὶ κατ' ἐρημίαν . . . ἄρξαι τῆς Σικελίας** 'to rule Sicily themselves by force or even (καί) because there would be a vacuum if we were to leave without achieving our goals': in that case only minimal force might be necessary. Demosthenes similarly figures Philip as viewing greedily τὴν ἐρημίαν τῶν κωλυσόντων (*Phil.* 1.49). Hermocrates' bullying conclusion (**80**.5 n.) lent credence to this charge, and Camarinaeans anyway had first-hand experience of Syracusan aggression (**5**.3 n.). Euphemus might have reminded them of that, but perhaps he did not need to. **ἀνάγκη δέ** 'and that is what would have to happen'. **ἡμῖν:** with εὐμεταχείριστος. This would usually be a damaging admission, but it goes with the unusual strategy of stressing weakness rather than strength: **82–87** n. **οὔθ' οἶδ' ἀσθενεῖς ἂν ἡμῶν μὴ παρόντων πρὸς ὑμᾶς εἶεν:** balancing **84**.1, διὰ τὸ μὴ ἀσθενεῖς ὑμᾶς ὄντας ἀντέχειν Συρακοσίοις, to bookend this part of the argument.

86.1 ὅτωι . . . ἐλέγχει 'and anyone who disagrees is refuted by the facts themselves'. **τὸ γὰρ πρότερον ἡμᾶς ἐπηγάγεσθε:** the Camarinaeans were among those who asked Athens to intervene in 427 (3.86.2–3, **87**.2 n.). **προσείοντες** 'waving before us', like a threatening hand (Eur. *Her.* 1218). **εἰ περιοψόμεθα . . . κινδυνεύσομεν:** as the Egestaeans argued at **6**.2. Perhaps the envoys did indeed make the same argument in 427.

86.2 ἠξιοῦτε . . . πείθειν 'thought it right to persuade us' i.e. thought that we should find the argument persuasive: cf. **87**.1. **μείζονι πρὸς τὴν τῶνδε ἰσχύν:** ambiguous between 'bigger [than in 427–424] in response to these people's strength' and 'bigger than these people's strength requires'. The first suits the rhetorical strategy of maximising Syracuse's strength; the second points to the reason why, like e.g. the Rhegians (**44**.3), they might be 'suspicious'.   ὑποπτεύεσθαι: ἡμᾶς must be understood, with awkward changes of subject from the preceding ἀπιστεῖν and back to the second ἀπιστεῖν.

86.3 μέν γε: for this 'quasi-connective' use see *GP* 160: it introduces a reason, in this case for believing us rather than them (**86**.2), and γε emphasises the first limb of the μέν . . . δέ contrast.   ἐμμεῖναι 'to stay' – but till victory over Syracuse or still longer? Cf. **82–87** n.   μὴ μεθ' ὑμῶν = εἰ μὴ μεθ' ὑμῶν εἶμεν or ἐσόμεθα, hence μή rather than οὐ. 'You' is still primarily the Camarinaeans, with an element of flattery; but the extended relevance to the other Sicilian cities (**85**.3 n.) is increasingly felt.   γενόμενοι κακοί: mockingly echoing Hermocrates at **80**.2.   κατεργασαίμεθα 'were to reduce to subjection' the island, contrasting as at **11**.1 with κατασχεῖν (**9**.3 n.), 'to hold down'.   τῆι παρασκευῆι ἠπειρωτίδων: an aspect of the paradox of this island that is virtually a mainland (**1**.2 n.): they are equipped and trained for land-warfare, and hence not easy for a maritime power to control. Euphemus nods at another argument against drawing inferences from Athens' rule over the Aegean islands.   τῆς ἡμετέρας παρουσίας 'than our presence', i.e. than our force that is (temporarily) present.   ἐπιβουλεύουσι: echoing Hermocrates' keynote charge, **80**.3 n.   ἑκάστου   'for each undertaking'.   ἀνιᾶσιν: from ἀνίημι. Like ἐπιβουλεύουσι, this echoes what Alcibiades said of Athens itself, **18**.3 n.   καὶ ἄλλα ἤδη καὶ τὰ ἐς Λεοντίνους: accs. of respect. A fair point: the treatment of Leontini in 424–421 (**5**.4.2–4, **6**.2 n.) had been at odds with Hermocrates' conciliatory rhetoric at Gela in 424 (**4**.59–64, **76–80** n.).

86.4 ἀνέχοντας τὴν Σικελίαν μέχρι τοῦδε μὴ ὑπ' αὐτοὺς εἶναι 'acting as a check to prevent Sicily from falling under their sway until now': μή + inf. after a verb of preventing. Not 'being' under their sway, which would be αὐτοῖς.   ὡς ἀναισθήτους 'on the assumption that you do not realise what they are doing'.

86.5 ἀντιπαρακαλοῦμεν: a powerful word, not found in earlier extant literature: Plato uses it as Socrates summons Callicles towards a different life (*Gorg.* 526e).   τὴν ὑπάρχουσαν ἀπ' ἀλλήλων ἀμφοτέροις '[the safety] which each of us offers to the other'.   ἑτοίμην διὰ τὸ πλῆθος εἶναι ὁδόν: a mix of the metaphorical and the real, as the attacking Syracusans would literally make the journey but it is their numbers which mean that that 'path' is always open.   τῶι ὑπόπτωι: not quite 'the suspicion' but 'suspiciousness', the element of suspicion that is a recurrent feature of human psychology.   ὅτε οὐδὲν ἔτι περανεῖ παραγενόμενον ὑμῖν 'at a time when it will no longer achieve anything for you if it were to arrive'.

87.1 μήτε οἱ ἄλλοι: it is assumed that Syracuse will be repeating its calumnies elsewhere; that fits the debate's 'paradigmatic' quality (**75**.3–**88**.2 n.).   ἔτι ἐν κεφαλαίοις ὑπομνήσαντες: just as Hermocrates too ended with a round-up, **80**.3–5.   ἀξιώσομεν πείθειν: **86**.2 n.

87.2 φαμὲν γάρ . . . ἥκειν: Euphemus' slick antitheses begin in contrast (ἄρχειν μὲν . . . ἐλευθεροῦν δέ) but go on to underline consistency, both between 'here' and 'there' and between now and 427–424.   ἐλευθεροῦν: **84**.3 n.   ὑπ' αὐτῶν: Euphemus leaves 'them' unspecified: evidently 'the Syracusans', but the vagueness parallels ἄλλου and assimilates both to a single class of 'our enemies'.   πολλὰ δ' ἀναγκάζεσθαι πράσσειν, διότι καὶ πολλὰ φυλασσόμεθα: picked up by πολυπραγμοσύνη, **87**.3. This 'meddling hyperactivity' recalls the qualities characterised by the Corinthians at 1.70 – the restless vitality, the risk-taking, the irrepressibility – but this is the only time when Th. or his speakers use πολυπραγμοσύνη; they do talk of Athens as avoiding ἀπραγμοσύνη (Corinthians at 1.70.8, Pericles at 2.40.2, 2.63.2–3, and 2.64.4, cf. Alcibiades at **18**.6–7), but the positive antonym is e.g. δραστήριος (2.63.3, cited at **18**.6 n.), 'active' rather than 'hyperactive'. Euphemus is ironically appropriating a word that is generally pejorative (Allison 1979): why, this terrible hyperactivity of ours might actually be quite useful to you . . . For a similar turning of the hostile gibe cf. Eur. *Supp.* 577–8, with wordplay along the same lines:

> *Herald:* πράσσειν σὺ πόλλ' εἴωθας ἥ τε σὴ πόλις.
> *Theseus:* τοιγὰρ πονοῦσα πολλὰ πόλλ' εὐδαιμονεῖ.

καὶ νῦν καὶ πρότερον . . . οὐκ ἄκλητοι, παρακληθέντες δὲ ἥκειν: in 427 they were invited by 'the allies of the Leontinians', i.e. 'the Chalcidian cities and Camarina' (3.86.2–3); now it had been Egesta and the Leontinian exiles. Despite Euphemus' claim to be summarising, he has mentioned this invitation only at **86**.1–2, and it was not to justify their presence but to remind the Camarinaeans of the argument they had then used.

87.3 μήθ' ὡς δικασταί . . . μήθ' ὡς σωφρονισταί 'neither as judges nor as chasteners'. The first recalls the Athenians at Sparta, 'we do not take you to be δικασταί either of us or of the Corinthians', 1.73.1; the second echoes Hermocrates' warning not to try to teach the Syracusans a lesson (σωφρονισθῶμεν), **78**.2.   ὃ χαλεπὸν ἤδη: possibly with ἀποτρέπειν (ἡμᾶς) πειρᾶσθε – we are already too far committed to be deterred – but possibly with ὡς σωφρονισταί: we do not take kindly to hearing moral sermons.   καθ' ὅσον δέ τι . . . χρήσασθε 'to whatever extent a portion of our hyperactivity and character leads to your sharing the same interests as us, take that portion and exploit it'. τι probably goes with καθ' ὅσον, adding a softening tone (cf. Hornblower–Pelling on Hdt. 6.52.6): there is again (87.2 n.) some irony, and a suggestion that that 'extent', and any concomitant apprehension, should not be very great given the immense range of Athenian πολυπραγμοσύνη. πολὺ δὲ πλείους τῶν Ἑλλήνων καὶ ὠφελεῖν: a stronger claim even than Pericles' 'none of our subjects doubts that they have worthy masters' (2.41.3): it is rare for Athens' empire to be justified in terms of the benefits to the ruled, though Lys. 2.56–7 and Isoc. 4.101–9 have a try. But here the argument is carefully phrased: see next n.

87.4 ἐν παντὶ γὰρ πᾶς χωρίωι . . . σώιζεσθαι: the claim is not that Athenian intervention is always to the allied state's good; it is rather that the *threat* of such intervention is a check against the worst abuses. Underlying it is the likelihood that Athens might support the democratic side in *stasis* (cf. 3.82.1), and so those deterred from plotting or injustice would typically be real or aspiring oligarchs. For ἐν παντὶ γὰρ πᾶς cf. 7.87.6 n.   **καὶ ὧι μὴ ὑπάρχομεν** 'even in a place where we have no presence already'.   **ἀδικήσεσθαι:** this middle form of the fut. inf. is used with passive sense: cf. 5.56.2.   **διὰ τὸ ἑτοίμην . . . κινδυνεύειν** 'because the expectation is always at hand for the one [the potential victim] that he may in some way get help from us and for the other [the oppressor] that, if we come, he cannot avoid fear of being in danger'. In the first case ἐλπίς is as much 'hope' as 'expectation'.   **ὁ μὲν ἄκων σωφρονεῖν, ὁ δ' ἀπραγμόνως σώιζεσθαι:** the μέν and δέ have swapped sides, as here ὁ μέν is the oppressor and ὁ δέ the victim. The qualities have swapped around too: now Athens is a sort of σωφρονιστής after all (87.3), and its πολυπραγμοσύνη generates a welcome ἀπραγμοσύνη for the vulnerable people left in peace. ἄκων σωφρονεῖν also echoes and rivals Hermocrates' oxymoronic ἀλόγως σωφρονεῖν, **79**.2.

87.5 τὴν κοινὴν . . . ἀσφάλειαν 'this shared safety that is now at hand both for the requester (= me/the Athenians) and for you'.   **ἐξισώσαντες τοῖς ἄλλοις μεθ' ἡμῶν τοὺς Συρακοσίους** 'after joining with us in reducing the Syracusans to the same level as the others' i.e. the other Sicilian cities as in μήτε οἱ ἄλλοι in **87**.1. The MSS reading τοῖς Συρακοσίοις would have to go with ἀντεπιβουλεῦσαι and leave ἐξισώσαντες as intransitive, 'making yourself equal to the other states' (cf. 5.71.2); but it is being able to match Syracuse rather than the other cities that should be the climax of the argument. Camps' 1955 emendation suits the rhetoric well, as Syracuse will survive but with its wings clipped, and that is why Camarina will be needed as a counterweight that can 'plot against' the city on even terms. This also conveys a final reassurance that Athenian aims in Sicily are limited, not aimed at annihilating their great rival but just at re-establishing a balance of power. καὶ ἀντεπιβουλεῦσαί ποτε ἐκ τοῦ ὁμοίου μεταλάβετε 'take in turn the opportunity even to plot against them one day on even terms'. Euphemus again (86.3 n.) takes up Hermocrates' ἐπιβουλεύειν refrain: such plotting may be the stuff of inter-*polis* relations (18.3 n.), and why should not Camarina have her turn?

88.1–2 *Camarina's response*

88.1 ἐπεπόνθεσαν 'had experienced', pluperfect: this may include 'while listening to the speeches', but the tenses of the rest refer also to their previous decisions (aor. ἔπεμψαν) and to their pre-existing and surviving attitudes (imperfect ἦσαν, ὤιοντο, ἐδόκει). The speeches have not changed these, except in forcing them to formulate their position more explicitly (88.2). κατὰ τὸ ὅμορον ... ἐγγὺς ὄντας: confirming the importance of the 'near-at-hand' motif that Hermocrates exploited (78.4) and to which Euphemus gave an unexpected twist (82–87 n.). τοὺς ὀλίγους ἱππέας: 'the' few horsemen, because taken as familiar from 67.2, giving their number as 20. The 50 archers mentioned there are ignored here. τὸ λοιπὸν ἐδόκει αὐτοῖς ὑπουργεῖν μὲν τοῖς Συρακοσίοις μᾶλλον ἔργωι: ἐδόκει rather than ἔδοξεν, referring to their settled intention before and during the debate. τὸ λοιπόν contrasts with ἐν τῶι παρόντι, μᾶλλον with ἔλασσον and ἔργωι with λόγωι: in fact and in future they will do more (though as little as possible) for the Syracusans, but in word and now they will convey even-handedness. ἐν δὲ τῶι παρόντι: this conveys some provisionality: they will wait upon events, and their stance may change. They will in fact step up their assistance to Syracuse as the tide turns (7.33.1; cf. 58.1), responding to success then just as they have now (ἐπειδὴ ... ἐγένοντο). τῆι μάχηι: **67–70**.

88.2 ἀμφοτέροις οὖσι ξυμμάχοις σφῶν ... εὔορκον δοκεῖν εἶναι: 75.3–88.2 n. ἐν τῶι παρόντι: echoing ἐν δὲ τῶι παρόντι, 88.1, but now this is part of their message, not just their thinking. If so, they may have intended this to offer some hope to both sides.

88.3–93: DIPLOMACY, WINTER 415–414

88.3–6 rounds up various decisions and initiatives taken in Sicily. Apart from noting the move to Catana after early activity in Naxos, there is no implication that they are listed in chronological order, which Th. may not have known.

88.3 ἐν τῆι Νάξωι ἐστρατοπεδευμένοι: 74.2.   **τὰ πρὸς τοὺς Σικελοὺς ἔπρασσον**: continuing the initiatives of **48** and **62**.5.   **ὅπως** + fut. indicative: **11**.7 n.

88.4 οἱ μὲν πρὸς τὰ πεδία ... τῶν δὲ τὴν μεσόγειαν ἐχόντων: Th. distinguished earlier between subject and independent Sicels (**34**.1 and **45**, cf. **48**, 3.103.1), but has delayed their geographical locations till now, when they are about to become important: **94**.3, **103**.2, 7.1.4–2.4, 7.32. He makes it clear that there are exceptions to his generalisations: μᾶλλον, οὐ πολλοί (but some), πλὴν ὀλίγοι. On the Sicels and their sympathies see Fragoulaki 2013: 292–8; Pope 2017.   **οὐ πολλοὶ ἀφειστήκεσαν**: pluperf., so these 'breakings away' were not the result of these approaches. It cannot have been easy: Hermocrates had been concerned to 'firm up' these allies (**34**.1) and the Syracusans had sent 'guards' (**45**). Carlà 2014 suggests that these οὐ πολλοί are the same as the '300' slaves that Polyaenus 1.43.1 records as defecting to Athens after an unsuccessful revolt (cf. 7.48.2 n.); but Th.'s rebels sound like free, though not wholly autonomous, 'subjects' rather than slaves or even serfs.   **αἱ οἰκήσεις εὐθὺς πλὴν ὀλίγοι μετὰ τῶν Ἀθηναίων ἦσαν**: rather awkwardly, the fem. οἰκήσεις is picked up by masc. ὀλίγοι in a 'sense-construction' and then serves duty for their inhabitants as subject of κατεκόμιζον. The formulation brings out that these were scattered 'settlements' rather than the coastal πόλεις, and had therefore been more difficult and less important for Syracuse to control.   **καὶ πρότερον αἰεί**: i.e. they were not just independent now, they had also (καί) always been so.   **πλήν**: here conjunction rather than preposition, so ὀλίγοι rather than ὀλίγων: cf. 2.21.2 and e.g. Soph. *Ajax* 1238 οὐκ ἄρ' Ἀχαιοῖς ἄνδρες εἰσὶ πλὴν ὅδε;   **κατεκόμιζον** 'brought down' to Naxos on the coast.   **εἰσὶν οἵ**: idiomatic for 'some', therefore the present tense. The plural verb tends to be preferred for the nom. (cf. 7.44.8), the singular ἔστιν οὕς/ὧν/οἷς (**88**.6, cf. 1.6.5, 3.92.5, 5.72.4, 7.11.2) for the oblique cases.   **χρήματα**: Sicel monetary contributions to the Athenians are attested in *IG* i³ 291, dated by *HCT* and *CT* to 415–413 BCE; if the 427–424 dating preferred here (**44**.2 n.) is right, those mentioned here will represent further requests and payments.

88.5 τοὺς δέ: a further προσαναγκάζειν is understood, 'they were prevented from forcing others': cf. **102**.2, 7.56.2.   **φρουρούς τ' ἐσπεμπόντων**: present tense, so these were further garrisons to complement the 'guards' sent at **45**.   **τόν τε χειμῶνα ... διεχείμαζον**: the imperfect is both inceptive and durative: some weeks or months of winter had already passed (**63**.1), but they now settled down to and then continued their over-wintering. τὸν χειμῶνα can be taken as either internal acc. or acc. of duration of time.   **κατεκαύθη ὑπὸ τῶν Συρακοσίων**: **75**.2.

88.6 ἐς Καρχηδόνα: 15.2 n. Relations between Carthage and Syracuse were not good, and within a few years they will be at war: see Intr. to Bk. 7, p. 35). Alcibiades will shortly talk of Carthage too, but as a potential Athenian target (**90**.2): the current feelers may have been as much to reassure as in the hope of help (ὠφελεῖσθαι). **περὶ φιλίας: 75**.3 n. **εἰ δύναιντό τι ὠφελεῖσθαι** 'in the hope of getting some help', εἰ + opt. (*CGCG* 49.25). **Τυρσηνίαν:** three penteconters arrived in the spring, **103**.2, and Etruscan land forces play a part at 7.53.2–54: cf. 7.57.11. On Athenian–Etruscan relations see Fragoulaki 2013: 283–7, arguing that a sense of ancestral kinship (4.109.4) played a part. For the possibility that some cavalry also came from Campania see **98**.1 n. **ἔστιν ὦν: 88**.4 n. **καὶ αὐτῶν** 'even of their own accord', without waiting to be asked: they were already 'at odds with the Syracusans' (7.57.11). **περιήγγελλον ... ὡς ἅμα τῶι ἦρι ἑξόμενοι τοῦ πολέμου:** thus putting into action the plan they formulated at **71**.2. On περιήγγελλον see also 7.18.4 n. The Sicels duly 'provided many allies' in the following spring, **103**.2. **ἵππους σφίσιν ὡς πλείστους πέμπειν:** cf. Intr., 6. They probably asked for horsemen as well, and that is what they get at **98**.1 (n.). **τὸν περιτειχισμόν** 'the circumvallation': 'the', because a siege is now taken to be inevitable. This had been foreseen from the outset, and the 'stone-gatherers and 'carpenters' (**44**.1 n.) were already there. What they needed was the materials. **πλινθεῖα** 'brick-making moulds'. **σίδηρον:** perhaps for tools – 'stone-working σιδήρια' are mentioned at 4.4.2 – as well as for clamps and dowels.

88.7 Οἱ ... ἀποσταλέντες πρέσβεις: 73.2. This was not necessarily later than the actions listed in **88**.3–6: after that round-up, the narrative now reverts to Greece, first Sparta and then (**93**.4) Athens. **τούς τε Ἰταλιώτας ἅμα παραπλέοντες:** at least Rhegium, Epizephyrian Locri, and Croton lay on the route, and probably Thurii and Taras too. Locri and Taras were already anti-Athenian (**44**.2 n.), but had not, it seems, sent help and are not listed as active Syracusan allies at 7.58; Thurii was broadly pro-Athenian (7.35.1), but not ferociously so (**104**.2, 7.33.6 nn.); Rhegium was biding its time; and 7.35.1 suggests that Croton was trying to stay out of it. **ὡς καὶ ἐκείνοις ὁμοίως ἐπιβουλευόμενα** 'as aimed against them as well'. **κατὰ τὸ ξυγγενές:** as mother-city, **3**.2.

88.8 πάσηι προθυμίαι: 6.2 n. Something might be made of the alliteration of ψ–φ–π–π–π in oral delivery. **τόν τε αὐτοῦ πόλεμον** 'the war there'. 'The', as it is taken as continuing, in line with the views of Nicias, Hermocrates, and Th. himself (**10**.2, **34**.3, 5.26.2). But Th. has not recorded any hostilities in that theatre since the small-scale fighting of **7**. **σαφέστερον:** cf. ἐκ τοῦ προφανοῦς, **73**.2.

88.9 Ἀλκιβιάδης: last heard of at **61.**7 (n.), and τότε refers back to then. The detail of his journey is delayed till here, together with his nervousness about the reaction he will get at Sparta: that nervousness is important background for his speech.   **τῶν ξυμφυγάδων:** **61**.7 n.   **Κυλλήνην:** in the NW corner of the Peloponnese. He may have gone on to Argos (**61.**7 n.), but Th. passes quickly to the encounter that will matter.   **ὑπόσπονδος:** i.e. with a promise of safe conduct.   **διὰ τὴν περὶ τῶν Μαντινικῶν πρᾶξιν:** not just the battle of 418, but Alcibiades' whole construction of the anti-Spartan alliance, going back to his deception of the Spartan envoys in 420 (5.43–6, **15** n.): cf. **89.**2–3. This was a matter of pride for him in Athens (**16.**6), of embarrassment now.

88.10 καὶ ξυνέβη ἐν τῆι ἐκκλησίαι … τοὺς Λακεδαιμονίους: after Euphemus' many echoes of the speeches of 432 (**82–87** n.), there is now an echo of their occasion: then too the Corinthians and other allies came to Sparta, denounced the Athenians in the assembly (ξύλλογος, 1.67.3), and tried to spur the Spartans into action (παροξῦναι, 1.67.5, cf. παρώξυνε here).   **τὰ αὐτὰ καὶ τὸν Ἀλκιβιάδην** 'the same things as Alcibiades': καί as in ὁμοίωι καί, **11.**1 n. τὰ αὐτά is internal acc. with both δεομένους and πείθειν. The reader already knows that the Corinthians and Syracusans will be taking a common line (ξυναναπείθοιεν, **88.**7); what now 'came about' was that they were urging the same as Alcibiades.   **πείθειν** 'urge' or 'try to persuade'; 'successfully persuade' would require the aor. πεῖσαι.   **τῶν τε ἐφόρων καὶ τῶν ἐν τέλει ὄντων**   'the ephors and the (other) authorities', cf. τῶι δὲ Πάχητι καὶ τοῖς Ἀθηναίοις, 3.33.2. The five ephors exercised great power – a change in ephors brings a change of policy at 5.36 – but others had authority too, notably the two kings and the council of elders: see *OCD*[4] on 'ephors' and '*gerousia*'.   **κωλύοντας** 'telling them not to' (cf. **62.**5 n. on κελεύοντες) rather than 'preventing' – they could not 'prevent' it without being present in force – but still hardly necessary: the Syracusans had no intention of making terms if they could avoid it.

89–92 *The Speech of Alcibiades*

Many of Th.'s speeches and debates reinforce a pre-existing mindset: Athens was already bent on going to Sicily (**8–26**), Syracuse was not ready to be fully persuaded (**32.**3**–41**), Camarina continued to prevaricate (**75.**3–**88.**2), Athens was already repenting over Mytilene (3.36–49), Melos was always going to fight on (5.89–113). Alcibiades' speech here is one that makes a difference. The Spartan decision at **93.**1–2 is not the one they were minded to take before (**88.**10), and all Th.'s emphasis falls on the impact of that speech, with the Syracusan and Corinthian pleas lost from view. This is despite the comparatively small proportion given to practical advice (**91**.4–**92**.1), backed up by his version, not necessarily wholly accurate, of Athens' aims (**90–91**.1) and of the danger to the Peloponnese if Syracuse falls (**91**.2–3). The beginning and end, almost half the speech, is about Alcibiades himself, with two separate λύσεις διαβολῆς (**16**.1 n.), first countering the hostility he expects because of his past behaviour vis-à-vis Sparta (**89**), then defending his conduct towards Athens (**92**.2–5), before an upbeat appeal in the last half-sentence to Spartan ambition and pride.

At **16–18** (n.) Alcibiades was already speaking of himself in terms more fitting to a city, and here too he treats himself and the cities as equivalent entities: there is even some magnificence in such shameless egotism. If Sparta (**89**.2) or Athens (**92**.3–4) has treated him poorly, he has behaved 'justly' (**89**.3 δικαίως) in retaliating; he has regarded his political line as 'just' (**89**.6 δικαιοῦντες), and he also 'thinks it right' (**92**.2 and 5, ἀξιῶ) that nobody should think the worse of him; any indignation was 'unreasonable' (**89**.3, οὐκ εἰκότως). This involves a bold redefinition of patriotism (**92**.3–4): a πατρίς that does not give him his due deserves nothing, does not even deserve the name. He does not appeal to honour or obligation or Dorian unity: such arguments would not sit easily on the lips of a renegade. Instead he appeals, as nakedly as Euphemus at Camarina, to his audience's own interests. He should be believed, so he claims, because he is an Athenian insider and he knows (**90**.1 εἴ τι πλέον οἶδα, **91**.1 τὰ ἀκριβέστατα εἰδότος, **92**.5 τὰ μὲν Ἀθηναίων οἶδα): listen, and learn (**90**.1, **91**.1 μάθετε). This is a 'rhetoric of authority' (Chlup 2006); the tone is didactic. But is he speaking the truth? The Spartans had experienced his duplicity before (5.43–6), and had every reason to be suspicious now. As it happens, he is talking straight when he identifies areas of Athenian weakness and the right courses for Sparta (**91**.4–**92**.1), and the Spartans do learn from his 'teaching' and accept his superior knowledge (**93**.1 διδάξαντος . . . νομίσαντες παρὰ τοῦ σαφέστατα εἰδότος ἀκηκοέναι). It is less clear that they believed his claims about Athens' intentions, or that they would have been right to do so.

He begins with a series of short, firm sentences, several linked as at **17**.1–2 by καὶ . . . καὶ . . . καί (Tompkins 1972: 212–13, **16–18** n.), others linked with staccato connections (**89**.4 and **89**.6 nn.): every point in his favour is so simple, it might seem (**89**), and even his own political career is couched in conservative terms likely to appeal to Spartan tastes (**89**.6 n.). A more complex sentence weaves together the threatening multiplicity of Athenian aspirations (**90**.3): this leads on to a catalogue of the dangers for Sparta unless it acts, with menacing (**6**.2 n.) uses of εἰ and εἰ μή with future indicatives (**91**.1, 3, 4). Comparatively little is said about the situation in Sicily (**91**.2), but it is delivered with the same dogmatic

confidence as his generalisations in Athens (**17**.2–5): they underpin the
particular advice he gives, with further sentence complexity to convey the
medley of necessary measures (**91**.4) and of advantages to be got from
occupying Decelea (**91**.7). The language finally turns in a more sophistic
and abstract direction as the flurry of words defends this innovative view
of patriotism (**92**.4). He does well to delay this to the end: such egoistic
over-cleverness was not likely to appeal to Spartans, but by then he has
persuaded them of the practical advantages.

   On the speech see esp. Cawkwell 1997: 89–90; Forde 1989: 96–115;
Debnar 2001: 203–17; Price 2001: 258–62; Mack 2015: 144–6, and *HCT*
and *CT*. Allison 2006 gives a vigorous defence of Alcibiades: 'Th. delivers
a message to [the Athenians] about the man they destroyed' (164).

89.1 τῆς ἐμῆς διαβολῆς . . . τῶι ὑπόπτωι μου 'about the personal attacks
on me . . . because of the suspicions of me': the beginning is as self-centred as ever (Gribble 1999: 210–11). At **16**.1 too he began with the need
to defend himself.   τὰ κοινά 'the matters of common interest'.

89.2 τῶν δ' ἐμῶν προγόνων . . . τὴν ἐκ Πύλου ξυμφοράν: Alcibiades
begins, as he did at **16**.1, with a mention of his ancestors, but here too
(cf. n. there) there is a twist: he claims to have tried to outdo them in
pro-Spartanism and repair the damage they had done to the relationship. At 5.43.2 Alcibiades was indignant that in making the peace of
421 the Spartans 'had ignored him because of his youth and paid him
no respect on the grounds of the proxeny of old: his grandfather had
renounced this, but Alcibiades thought in terms of renewing it by taking
care [θεραπεύων] of the prisoners from the island' (i.e. Sphacteria: **10**.2
n.). The Spartans then had preferred the help of Nicias and Laches, and
in 420 Alcibiades had retaliated with the trick of 5.44.3–46. The consequence was the souring of Athens–Sparta relations and Athens' alliance
with Argos, Mantinea, and Elis (5.47).   τὴν προξενίαν ὑμῶν κατά τι
ἔγκλημα ἀπειπόντων: Alcibiades leaves this 'complaint' tactfully vague.
The renouncer was Alcibiades' grandfather, also called Alcibiades, and its
occasion was probably the Athens–Sparta split of 462 (1.102). The proxeny – a commitment of a citizen of city A to promote within that city the
interests of city B – went back at least to the mid sixth century: cf. *HCT*
and *CT* on 5.43.2.   πάλιν ἀναλαμβάνων: this is again vague, and need
not imply any official recognition on Sparta's part (though Plut. *Alc.* 14.1
calls Alcibiades '*proxenos* of the Spartans'): cf. 'thought in terms of renewing it' at 5.43.2, quoted above.   τὴν ἐκ Πύλου ξυμφοράν: ξυμφορά is
the favoured word for that Spartan disaster, **10**.2 n. ἐκ + gen. suggests '*as
a result* of Pylos', not so much the capitulation there as the humiliation
that followed for Sparta (4.40) and the city's continual requests to get the

prisoners back (4.41.3-4). It is not known whether Alcibiades supported those requests; his 'care' (ἐθεράπευον, cf. 5.43.2, quoted above, and Plut. *Alc.* 12.1) is more likely to have consisted in trying to make their custody more (but still not very, for they were kept in chains, 4.41.1) comfortable. ὑμεῖς πρὸς Ἀθηναίους καταλλασσόμενοι: in the negotiations of 421 that culminated in the 'Peace of Nicias' (**9–14** n.). τοῖς μὲν ἐμοῖς ἐχθροῖς: presumably Nicias in particular, though 5.43.2 specifies Laches as well, the proposer of a year-long truce in 423 (4.118.11). ἀτιμίαν: strong language (Dover 1974: 236–42), which would be justified only if in 421 other Athenians had shared Alcibiades' own expectations of the role he might play. This is not quite as confrontational as the 'you Spartans are yourselves to blame' of the Corinthians (1.69.1) and the Plataeans (3.55.1), but still implies that his listeners are part of the explanation for the state of affairs that they do not like.

89.3 πρός τε τὰ Μαντινέων καὶ Ἀργείων 'to the cause of' [or 'the business concerning'] 'the Mantineans and Argives': not just to the Mantineans and Argives themselves, but to his agitation that led to the treaty of 420 (5.47) and indirectly to the battle of Mantinea in 418: **16**.6 n. ὅσα ἄλλα ἠναντιούμην ὑμῖν 'and to however many other matters there were in which I opposed you': ὅσα after πρός, then internal acc. with ἠναντιούμην. Alcibiades is again vague, but he persuaded Patrae to strengthen its fortifications (5.52.2), invaded Epidaurus (5.53), worked in Argos to strengthen their Athenian alliance (Plut. *Alc.* 15.4–5), and supported the reduction of Melos ([Andoc.] 4.22–3). ἀναπειθέσθω: here 'persuaded *back*', made to change his views (so the schol.): cf. 5.80.2, 8.52, Hdt. 6.23.2, 8.143.1. διότι καὶ τῶι δήμωι προσεκείμην μᾶλλον 'because in addition [to opposing you] I leant more towards the people . . .' ἐνόμιζε . . . ἡγήσηται: the tenses are important: even if people thought that way in the past, let them realise that it would be wrong to be angry on those grounds (οὕτως) now.

89.4 τοῖς γὰρ τυράννοις αἰεί ποτε διάφοροί ἐσμεν: for αἰεί ποτε cf. **82**.2 n. This is an oddly oblique way to begin his answer to the 'democratic' charge, but Alcibiades is also implicitly warding off suspicions of his own tyrannical inclinations, **15**.4, as well as appealing to Spartan pride in their traditional opposition to tyrants (1.18.1). His ancestors are treated more positively here than at **89**.2; Th.'s audience might recall the defence of the Alcmaeonids as μισοτύραννοι at Hdt. 6.121–4, though Hdt. there glosses over some awkward counter-examples (see Hornblower–Pelling's n.). πᾶν δὲ τὸ ἐναντιούμενον τῶι δυναστεύοντι δῆμος ὠνόμασται: some may have heard τῶι δυναστεύοντι as neuter, some as masculine. As stated, the claim comes close to being simply false, though it builds on the positions of 'tyranny' and 'democracy' at opposite extremes of the political spectrum. Δῆμος and 'democracy' can be theorised as embracing all citizens, not just the lower classes (2.37.1, cf. Arist. *Pol.* 1291b30–40, Forde 1989: 100–1), but still many of the cities opposing Xerxes were not democracies and within a state ὁ δυναστεύων often had to fear an elite: that is the point of Thrasybulus' advice to his fellow tyrant Periander at Hdt. 5.92ζ. τὰ πολλά 'in most respects' (not 'many', which would not have the definite article), internal acc. with ἕπεσθαι: this prepares for the following claim to have been more moderate than the norm, and so is best punctuated with a colon after ἕπεσθαι.

89.5 τῆς ... ὑπαρχούσης ἀκολασίας 'than the prevailing indiscipline'.   τὸν ὄχλον: as he moves from his family to those deplorable 'others' he adopts the pejorative word for the *dēmos* that they egged on: **63**.2 n.

89.6 ἡμεῖς δὲ τοῦ ξύμπαντος προέστημεν: picking up ἡ προστασία of **89**.4: 'we' are still his family. τοῦ ξύμπαντος contrasts with ὄχλος, conveying that his family presided (itself a big claim) over everyone, not just the mob. For the concept of προστασία τοῦ δήμου, cf. **35**.2 and esp. [Arist.] *Ath. pol.* 28, simplifying Athens' political history into a sequence of προστάται.   ἐν ὧι σχήματι ... ξυνδιασώιζειν: Alcibiades is playing to his audience at Sparta, proud of its long-standing constitution (1.18.1) and apprehensive of over-clever innovation (Archidamus at 1.84.3). As for Alcibiades himself, Th. explicitly endorses Phrynichus' view that he 'was no more wedded to oligarchy than democracy' (8.48.4).   καὶ ὅπερ ἐδέξατό τις 'and [the constitutional form, σχῆμα] that had been handed down to one', lit. 'that one had received': 'one' rather than 'we/us', because it is couched as a general maxim.   ξυνδιασώιζειν: ξυν- conveys that this was going along with the consensus.   δημοκρατίαν γε: γε directs attention to the word and concept 'democracy', almost 'democracy in itself'.   καὶ ἐγιγνώσκομεν 'we also [as well as inheriting it] recognised it for what it was'.   καὶ αὐτὸς οὐδενὸς ἂν χεῖρον, ὅσωι καὶ λοιδορήσαιμι 'and I would be second to none in recognising what democracy was, [outstripping others] to the same degree as I might also do in the abuse I could pour on it': Alcibiades likes potential optatives (**16–18** n.). The thought is compressed and the passage is usually but unnecessarily emended. Again a colon or a dash is better than a full stop before ἀλλά ... λέγοιτο: 'I could say a lot, but there is no need'.   ὁμολογουμένης ἀνοίας: 'folly' may reflect the particular charge that a *dēmos* was too uneducated to make intelligent decisions: Athenagoras defended democracy against the charge at **39**.1. Alcibiades may have shared the contempt he affects – cf. **17**.4 n. for a possible foretaste – but he may just have been telling the Spartans what they would like to hear; cf. the cynicism about his constitutional principles at 8.48.4, quoted on ἐν ὧι σχήματι . . . above.   αὐτήν: some hearers might have taken δημοκρατίαν to be the 'it', some πόλιν.   ἡμῖν: the reference of 'we' has probably shifted from 'my family' (**89**.4 n.) to οἱ φρονοῦντές τι, with the implication that those with any sense would of course have welcomed revolution had it been safe to do so.

90.2 ἐπλεύσαμεν: no connective particle is needed as μάθετε ἤδη has already given the link: **64**.2 n.   **πρῶτον μέν, εἰ δυναίμεθα, Σικελιώτας καταστρεψόμενοι:** thus far this chimes with Th.'s own analysis and phrasing at **1**.1.   **μετὰ δ' ἐκείνους αὖθις καὶ Ἰταλιώτας:** the Syracusans tried to persuade the Italians of this, **88**.7, but Th. has said nothing in the authorial voice to support it.   **καὶ τῆς Καρχηδονίων ἀρχῆς καὶ αὐτῶν ἀποπειράσοντες** 'and to make an attempt on Carthage's empire and the Carthaginians themselves' i.e. not just to detach subject-states (especially Corsica and Sardinia) from Carthage but also to add Carthage itself to their empire. Th. gives this as Alcibiades' own dream, **15**.2, and according to Hermocrates Carthage's fear, **34**.2, but again there has been no authorial indication that this ambition was broadly shared: cf. **15**.2 n. Neither Italy nor Carthage figures in Alcibiades' picture of Athens' prospects, however rosily painted, at **16–18**. The last mention of Carthage was as a potential Athenian ally rather than victim, **88**.6 n.

90.3 ἤδη τῆι Πελοποννήσωι ἐμέλλομεν ἐπιχειρήσειν: there has so far been talk of a possible Sicilian/Peloponnesian attack on Athens (**6**.2, **11**.3, **36**.4, cf. **86**.1), but none of a combined Athenian/Sicilian move against the Peloponnese; still, some such attack would be a natural corollary of a greatly expanded Athenian empire in the W.   **πολλοὺς δὲ βαρβάρους μισθωσάμενοι:** despite the mention of Carthage and the current importance of Athens' non-Greek allies (**88**.4, **88**.6 nn.), Alcibiades passes over the possibility of Athens acquiring non-Greek subjects: barbarians would have to be hired. His focus is firmly on the threat that Athens might rule the *Greek* world (τοῦ ξύμπαντος Ἑλληνικοῦ ἄρξειν).   **Ἴβηρας:** the geographical range of Alcibiades' scaremongering becomes even wider. He may be thinking of Carthaginian dependencies in Spain.   **ἄλλους τῶν ἐκεῖ ὁμολογουμένως νῦν βαρβάρων μαχιμωτάτους** 'and others acknowledged to be currently the most effective fighters of the barbarians over there': left menacingly vague.   **ἐχούσης τῆς Ἰταλίας ξύλα ἄφθονα:** this at least is not exaggeration: Meiggs 1982: 462–6.   **αἷς τὴν Πελοπόννησον**

πέριξ πολιορκοῦντες ... καταπολεμήσειν: echoing the Athenian strategy in 431, when they had sought alliances with Corcyra, Cephallenia, Acarnania, and Zacynthus as a way of 'defeating the Peloponnese by surrounding her' (πέριξ τὴν Πελοπόννησον καταπολεμήσοντες, 2.7.3). The echo brings out how much has changed, at least in Alcibiades' presentation: now the talk is of subjection, not of alliances; and the Periclean strategy of coastal raids (2.23.2–3, 25, 30, etc.) has changed to a more permanent blockade.   ἐντειχισάμενοι 'walling in' i.e. besieging: to be distinguished from ἐπιτείχισις, 'fortifying' a city that one has already occupied 'against' the enemy, 91.6 and 93.2.   καὶ τοῦ ξύμπαντος Ἑλληνικοῦ ἄρξειν 'rule over the whole Greek world as well': Alcibiades had dangled that prospect at 18.4, but even he had immediately drawn back to 'or at least we will damage the Syracusans'.

90.4 τι αὐτῶν 'any one of those plans': cf. **92**.1 (n.) and 5.26.5 for τις as 'many a one' (LSJ II.1).

91.1 ὅσοι ὑπόλοιποι στρατηγοί 'as many generals as are left...'. Th. could have said 'two' and named them; the tone is not necessarily dismissive, for this is not the time to downplay the danger; more likely he is indicating that even if one general falls out there will be a stream of replacements. It is also probable that Nicias' lukewarmness was known at Sparta just as at Syracuse (**34**.6), and this may be a warning not to entertain false hopes that Athens might draw back.   εἰ + fut. indic.: again at **91**.3 and 4, and cf. **6**.2 n.   τἀκεῖ: vague neuter pl. encompassing both 'your interests there' and 'your allies there'.   μάθετε ἤδη: repeated from **90**.1 as the didactic tone continues.

91.2 Σικελιῶται ... περιγένοιντο: laying the foundation for his advice: the Sicilians are ἀπειρότεροι (and so need an experienced general to guide them); but they might even now (καὶ νῦν ἔτι) survive if they can unite (and are more likely to do so if they see signs of energy from Sparta).   ξυστραφέντες ἁθρόοι: Hermocrates' refrain. Cf. esp. **80**.2.   μάχηι τε ἤδη πανδημεὶ ἡσσημένοι: **67–70**, with πανδημεί echoing a recurrent word there (**64**.1 n.).   καὶ ναυσὶν ἅμα κατειργόμενοι: this was not yet true and is strictly part of Alcibiades' prediction (ἔσονται), but it might easily be heard as conveying what was already the case.   ἀντίσχειν: this is best accented thus (present infinitive of ἀντίσχω) here and at 1.117.3, but as ἀντισχεῖν (aor. inf. of ἀντέχω) at 1.141.6 where a single battle is in point.

91.3 ἔχεται: present tense of a lively and confident prediction: **34**.4 n. ἐπιπέσοι: Alcibiades speaks of this danger in terms appropriate to the attacking forces themselves (7.29.3 and 5).

91.4 τις: μῆτις might be expected, intensifying the preceding μή (*CGCG* 56.4), but cf. **10.5, 68.**3 nn. for this exhortative use of τις.   **στρατιάν τε ἐπὶ νεῶν πέμψετε:** this is not taken up by the Spartans to any extent (**93.**2 n.), but Alcibiades' speedy move on to his 'still more useful . . .' suggestion may hint that he did not expect it to be: it is more a further way of underlining the urgency.   **οἵτινες:** sense construction with στρατιάν.   **αὐτερέται . . . ὁπλιτεύσουσιν:** as the Athenians sent to Mytilene, 3.18.4.   **ἄνδρα Σπαρτιάτην ἄρχοντα** 'a Spartiate man to command'. The successes of Brasidas in N Greece (423–421 BCE) lent plausibility to the idea that a strong and gifted commander could make all the difference: Debnar 2001: 210.   **προσαναγκάσηι:** προσ- may convey 'force them *to*' do so, as at **72.**4 and **88.**5, or 'force these *in addition*' to those willingly accepting this, or both: there is similar ambiguity at 7.18.4, 4.87.2, 5.42.2, and 8.76.6.

91.5 φανερώτερον: cf. **73.**2 (n.), **88.**8.   **ἐκπολεμεῖν** might be heard as either transitive, 'stir up matters here to war' (cf. X. *Hell.* 5.4.20), or intransitive with τὰ ἐνθάδε as internal acc., 'fight the war here'.

91.6 τειχίζειν τε χρὴ Δεκέλειαν: the idea of ἐπιτείχισις/ἐπιτειχισμός – a hostile fortification in Attic territory – was not in itself new: both the Corinthians and Pericles had envisaged the possibility at the war's outset (1.122.1, 142.4), and it had been aired again in 422/1 (5.17.2). But this is the first mention of Decelea, so important later: further details of the place are left to 7.19.2 and 7.27–8 (n.). It lay on the slopes of M. Parnes, about 18 km N of Athens. Hdt. 9.73.2 says that the Spartans deliberately spared Decelea when ravaging Attica during 'the war that happened much later [than 479] between Athens and Sparta', presumably the Archidamian War: so grateful were they for the help legendarily given them by the Deceleans when Theseus had abducted Helen and they were searching for her. If Hdt. is right, this indicates (a) Sparta's readiness to move now to a harder and more pragmatic line, and (b) Th.'s downplaying of such religious and mythical motivations.   **καὶ μόνου αὐτοῦ νομίζουσι . . . οὐ διαπεπειρᾶσθαι** 'and think that this is the only thing among those [to be expected] in the war that they have not experienced'. Alcibiades is flattering his audience, indicating that this is the only opportunity they have missed. He may be over-generous: they had ravaged Attica extensively in the yearly invasions up to 424 (cf. esp. 3.26.3), but *Hell. Oxy.* 12.5 says that the country suffered relatively little then in comparison with the invasions after 413.   **αἰσθάνοιτο . . . πυνθανόμενος:** if there is a distinction between αἰσθάνοιτο and πυνθανόμενος, it may be between initial uninformed opinion and its later confirmation, but perhaps Alcibiades is just waxing pompously redundant. αἰσθάνομαι + acc. (rather than gen.) + participle is favoured for intellectual and visual rather than auditory perception (*CGCG* 52.20): cf. 65.2, 7.2.2, 7.81.1.   ἐπιφέροι 'bring to bear on them', a slightly grandiose-sounding extension of such uses as ὅπλα (7.18.2) or πόλεμον (7.56.2) ἐπιφέρειν.   δεινά 'things to fear', their weak spots.

91.7 ἃ δέ: internal acc. with both ὠφελούμενοι and κωλύσετε.   κατεσκεύασται 'fitted out': not just the homesteads around the countryside but the farm equipment, the stored and harvested produce, and – particularly – the slaves.   αὐτόματα 'spontaneously', without needing any action on your part: again, runaway slaves are particularly in point, especially from the important silver mines at Laureion. This proved realistic: 7.27.5 says that more than 20,000 deserted.   καὶ τὰς... ἀποστερήσονται: ἀποστερεῖν can take a double acc. of the thing taken and the person it is taken from, and in the passive the person then becomes the subject and the acc. is retained for the thing (*CGCG* 35.15); here that is combined with the alternative construction of ἀποστερεῖν with gen. (τῆς... προσόδου ἧσσον διαφορουμένης), or this may be heard as gen. absolute. The realism of Alcibiades' prophecies is mixed; 7.27 sets out what actually happened. Crops were indeed extensively damaged and food transport into the city was impeded (7.27.5). Decelea in N Attica was a poor base to interfere with Laureion in the S, but slaves from the mines did desert in numbers (see above). Income 'from the courts' plays on the stereotype of Athens as litigation-crazy (Ar. *Clouds* 208, *Birds* 41, *Peace* 505, and esp. *Wasps*), doubtless a prejudice that Spartans relished, and perhaps Alcibiades is unrealistically envisaging a court standstill (so schol.) and therefore no private income from jury-pay; or maybe the δίκαι ἀπὸ συμβόλων are meant (1.77.1, ps.-Xen. *Ath. Pol.* 1.16), suits heard at Athens between Athenians and individuals from the subject-states. The implication would be that they are rigged in Athens' favour, but with allied defections such hearings would cease.   μάλιστα δὲ... ὀλιγωρήσουσιν: predicated on the assumption that a burst of Spartan energy will generate allied rebellion. Alcibiades gives no reason for thinking this will happen now when it had not happened extensively during the Archidamian War.   διαφορουμένης 'being transported', carried across the sea to Athens as φόρος, 'tribute'.   τὰ παρ' ὑμῶν.. . πολεμεῖσθαι 'that you were now waging full-scale war', lit. 'that what is coming from you is warfare now waged in a full-scale way'. Cf. 4.23.2 τὰ περὶ Πύλον ὑπ' ἀμφοτέρων κατὰ κράτος ἐπολεμεῖτο.

92.1 τι αὐτῶν 'any one of those things'.   προθυμότερον: 6.2 n.   ἐν ὑμῖν 'depends on you', it is a choice for you to make. Stirring language: cf. e.g. Hdt. 3.85.2, 6.109.3, Soph. *OT* 314, Eur. *Alc.* 278.

92.2 χείρων οὐδενὶ... δοκεῖν... οὐδὲ ὑποπτεύεσθαι: this wards off two different negative assessments, (1) being rated lower morally for lack of patriotism and (2) being suspected of insincerity or recklessness.   **φιλόπολις:** a rare word, used three times in this ch. and elsewhere in Th. only at 2.60.5, Pericles' proud claim for himself: the contrast between the two 'patriotisms' is felt (Bassi 2007: 197–203). The word can be used of friendly gods (Aesch. *Sept.* 176, Ar. *Wealth* 720, cf. Pi. *O.* 4.18) as well as of humans who show their loyalty (Ar. *Lys.* 546, Plato, *Rep.* 5.470d, 6.503e and, with irony, *Apol.* 24b).   **οὐδὲ ὑποπτεύεσθαί μου ἐς τὴν φυγαδικὴν προθυμίαν τὸν λόγον** 'nor should what I say arouse suspicion on grounds of showing an exile's enthusiasm', a phrase that shows linguistic virtuosity as well as rhetorical slipperiness: it is the first appearance of φυγαδικός in extant texts. The obvious point is 'the reckless zeal *of a refugee*' (LSJ), carried away by animosity into giving over-aggressive advice: he counters that he has every reason to wish to damage his native city. A sceptical Spartan might react by thinking that the stronger the animosity, the more likely it would be to warp the man's judgement.

92.3 φυγάς τε γὰρ... ὠφελίας 'I am in flight from the iniquity of those who drove me out, not from helping you, if you will do what I say': a forced antithesis as Alcibiades navigates this tricky ground. πονηρ- words come easily to his lips when he talks about his enemies: cf. **89**.5 and, echoing this passage, 8.47.2.   **καὶ πολεμιώτεροι... γενέσθαι** 'and no worse enemies are you who somewhere caused harm to your own enemies than those who forced their own friends to become enemies': Alcibiades leaves it unclear whether he means 'enemies' to their own state, Athens, thus justifying his actions as patriotic after all, or just to himself. He veers between claiming to state a general truth (οἱ... οἱ...) and tying it down to the specific case (ὑμεῖς). The jingling wordplay is clever rather than convincing.

92.4 τό τε φιλόπολι... ἐπολιτεύθην 'I apply my patriotism not in [the world of] the injustice I am now suffering, but [in the world] where I played a politician's role in safety'. Despite its passive form, ἐπολιτεύθην can serve as the aor. of middle πολιτεύομαι.   **ἐπὶ πατρίδα οὖσαν ἔτι** 'against a native land that still exists': this leaves it unclear whether Athens is no longer a native land just for him or for anyone, having lost all moral claim to such a title.   **ἀνακτᾶσθαι:** this moves more clearly to 'recover *for myself*', and recalls language used of exiled pretender-rulers 'getting back their ἀρχή': cf. Hdt. 1.61.3, 6.83.1, Aesch. *Cho.* 237. The word can later mean 'reinstate' more generally (cf. LSJ and e.g. Cassius Dio 53.2.4, of 'restoring temples'), but it is unclear that Alcibiades' or Th.'s audience would here feel any ambiguity.   καὶ φιλόπολις οὗτος ὀρθῶς ...: a breathtaking claim, for Alcibiades is saying not simply that other loyalties (to family, to tribe, to gods, to faction) may on occasion outweigh τὸ φιλόπολι (Pusey 1940), nor even that his exile transforms the moral calculus by weakening any demands of loyalty (Gribble 1999: 127–8): he claims that τὸ φιλόπολι can *consist in* trying to recover one's country, whatever that may require. It is an extreme example of the distortion of language identified at 3.82.4 as a feature of *stasis* (Thompson 2013), and a Spartan audience, ideologically respectful of civic authority, was particularly unlikely to be impressed: Forde 1989: 107–8 n. 27; Debnar 2001: 210–11 n. 28.   οὐχ ὃς ἂν ... μὴ ἐπίηι, ἀλλ' ὃς ἂν ... πειραθῆι: ἂν + subj. because generalising, 'the sort of person who ...'.   ἀναλαβεῖν 'get back', 'regain' (LSJ ἀναλαμβάνω II.1): like ἀνακτᾶσθαι (above), this suggests 'for myself', not just 'restore'.

92.5 ἀξιῶ τε: echoing ἀξιῶ at **92**.1, first what the Spartans should not do and now what they should.   καὶ ἐς κίνδυνον καὶ ἐς ταλαιπωρίαν πᾶσαν: 'every' is attracted into the gender of the nearer noun: cf. **97**.1 οὔτε πλοῦν οὔτε ὁδὸν πολλήν.   τὸν ὑφ' ἁπάντων προβαλλόμενον λόγον 'what everyone says ...', and Alcibiades goes on as if he is quoting a proverb. If so, the proverbial version would presumably be 'if someone can hurt you a lot, they can also benefit you a lot': again (**92**.3 n.) Alcibiades mixes the generalised and the specific, tying this maxim down to the particular case ('if *I* hurt *you*' ...). What seems to have been more proverbial is 'make friends knowing they can become enemies and enemies knowing they can become friends': cf. Soph. *Ajax* 678–82, perhaps adapting a saying of Bias of Priene, with Finglass 2011 ad loc.   ἱκανῶς 'quite enough', as often suggesting more than just 'sufficiently': cf. e.g. Hdt. 3.4.1 καὶ γνώμην ἱκανὸς καὶ τὰ πολέμια ἄλκιμος; Antiphon *Tetr.* 1.β.2 ἱκαναὶ λῦπαι.   ὅσωι 'according to the degree that ...', here without an explicit comparative or superlative, but there is a comparison implied: he has superior knowledge of Athens – superior to that of others, superior also to his intelligent guesswork about secretive (5.68.2) Sparta.   καὶ αὐτοὺς ... βουλεύεσθαι: still dependent on ἀξιῶ.   περὶ μεγίστων δὴ τῶν διαφερόντων 'the things that matter most', lit. 'the biggest things that make a difference'. The tone grows more grandiloquent as the peroration builds.   τά τε ἐκεῖ βραχεῖ μορίωι ξυμπαραγενόμενοι μεγάλα σώσητε: τά τε ἐκεῖ ... μεγάλα are to be taken together despite the lengthy jump between them ('hyperbaton'): this is again a sign of the language's elevation, contrasting the 'small' proportion of Sparta's resources committed and the 'great things' – not just cities but interests and prospects – that would be protected.   τὴν τε οὖσαν καὶ τὴν μέλλουσαν δύναμιν: i.e. not just the power that exists but the greater version to be feared if the war goes Athens' way, **90**.3–4. **καὶ τῆς ἁπάσης Ἑλλάδος ἑκούσης καὶ οὐ βίαι, κατ' εὔνοιαν δὲ ἡγῆσθε:** a resonant conclusion, with an implied comparison with the 'rule of Greece' (ἄρξειν, in contrast to ἡγῆσθε here) by force that Athens was envisaging, **90**.3. There is a recollection too of the beginning of the war when 'general goodwill tended very much towards the Spartans, most particularly because they proclaimed they were liberating Greece' (2.8.4). Th.'s audience after 404 might well reflect that, once Sparta had won, their rule was very different, and did little to earn goodwill.

93 Decisions

93.1 διανοούμενοι μὲν καὶ αὐτοὶ πρότερον 'who already had thoughts of their own of . . .': not mentioned at **88**.10, but the focus then was on their lukewarm intentions concerning Sicily.   **μέλλοντες δ' ἔτι καὶ περιορώμενοι:** typical Spartan behaviour according to the Corinthians in 432 (μελληταί, 1.70.3). Sparta had certainly been strangely inactive in summer 415, at least in Th.'s record. For περιορᾶσθαι, 'circumspection', cf. **103**.2 and 7.33.2, in both cases of Sicilian cities biding their time before choosing a side.   **ἐπερρώσθησαν:** ῥώμη, especially in its psychological aspects (**31**.1 n.), will soon become an even more important theme: see 7.7.4 n. and intr. to Bk. 7, p. 30. Th. continues to emphasise Alcibiades alone. The Syracusan and Corinthian pleas may have carried more weight than Th. implies (Brunt 1952: 71–2 = 1993: 26–7; Kagan 1981: 257; Salmon 1984: 332), but Sparta had often resisted Corinthian pressure before and one should not underrate the energising effect of charismatic rhetoric.   **διδάξαντος:** cf. **89–92** n. for Alcibiades' didactic tone.   **παρὰ τοῦ σαφέστατα εἰδότος:** echoing τὰ ἀκριβέστατα εἰδότος, **91**.1.

93.2 ὥστε τῆι ἐπιτειχίσει τῆς Δεκελείας προσεῖχον ἤδη τὸν νοῦν: they may have 'applied their mind' to fortifying Decelea, but for the moment that is all they did: Alcibiades had to 'teach' them again a year later (7.18.2 ἐδίδασκε τὴν Δεκέλειαν τειχίζειν) and tell them to get on with it. τὸ παραυτίκα therefore as often (**83**.3, 1.127.1, 1.134.2, 3.56.7, 5.65.6) marks a contrast with something else that is delayed: this, unlike Decelea, is to be done immediately.   **πέμπειν:** after προσεῖχον τὸν νοῦν, as = διενοοῦντο.   **τιμωρίαν** 'help' (LSJ II): this is the change from the thinking of **88**.10. The Spartans do not in fact send *much* help (Green 1970: 171–2; Kagan 1981: 257–9), but if Th. is right about the discretion granted Gylippus this may be as much his choice as theirs.   **Γύλιππον τὸν Κλεανδρίδου:** the first introduction of this major figure. For his father

Cleandridas, disgraced in 446 BCE, see **104.**2 n.: Gylippus was possibly an adopted son, if Ael. *VH* 12.43 is right in calling him a μόθαξ and if that means one of lesser birth adopted as a 'foster-brother' by a young Spartiate. Clearly, neither that status nor his father's scandal had prevented his rise to a position of trust. His father's connection with Thurii (**104.**2 n.) may have played a part in his selection for this mission. His own career too would end in disgrace and exile, accused of embezzlement when serving with Lysander (Plut. *Lys.* 16, *Nic.* 28.4, Diod. 13.106.8–9). **προστάξαντες ἄρχοντα τοῖς Συρακοσίοις** 'assigning as a commander to the Syracusans', i.e. the Syracusans as a whole: μετ' ἐκείνων then narrows to their ambassadors present in Sparta. The language is rather peremptory, given that the Syracusans had not requested a commander, **88.**7–8: that was Alcibiades' idea. There seems to have been no thought of sending Alcibiades himself (Green 1970: 168). There were limits to Sparta's trust in him.   **ποιεῖν ὅπηι . . . τοῖς ἐκεῖ:** the broad discretion allowed Gylippus resembles that given the Athenian generals, **26.**3.

93.3 τοὺς Κορινθίους: i.e. the Corinthian ambassadors, **88.**8: they will take these instructions home and pass them on to the authorities.   **οἱ** 'to him', dative of the reflexive pronoun.   **ἐς Ἀσίνην:** near the SE tip of Messenia.   **παρασκευάζεσθαι . . . ἑτοίμας εἶναι πλεῖν:** the jump from 'they [the Corinthians] should prepare' to 'they [the ships] should be ready' is harsh.   **ἀνεχώρουν:** i.e. the Syracusan and Corinthian ambassadors.

93.4 ἡ ἐκ τῆς Σικελίας τριήρης . . . ἐπί τε χρήματα καὶ ἱππέας: 74.2. Much narrative space has intervened since, but this need not correspond to a great time-lag: cf. **88.**3–6, **88.**7 nn.   **τήν τε τροφὴν καὶ τοὺς ἱππέας:** but Th. does not say how much or how many, leaving that to their arrival, **94.**4. The τροφή is probably equivalent to the χρήματα, i.e. the funds that could be used to support the troops.   **καὶ ὁ χειμὼν . . . ὃν Θουκυδίδης ξυνέγραψεν: 7.**4 n.

94–95: SPRING 414

An attack ἅμα τῶι ἦρι is planned and expected (**71.**2, **74.**2, **88.**6); now it comes, with εὐθὺς ἀρχομένωι (**94.**1) underlining the urgency, but not much is achieved, and the Athenians are soon back in Catana, **94.**3, **94.**4. They can do little until their reinforcements arrive (**94.**4), already marked at **71.**2 and **74.**2 as of critical importance. Little happens in Greece either (**95**), and the usual scuffles go on without, as yet, much of an eye on Sicily: after Sparta's positive response at **93.**1–2, more might be expected than their passive role at 95.1. The war resumes in earnest in the summer, with the near-synchronism of the two sides' moves on Epipolae (97.1–2).

94.1 οἱ ἐν τῆι Σικελίαι Ἀθηναῖοι: in contrast with those at home (93.4). 'Sicilian Megara' also underlines that the narrative has moved back to the W.   Μεγάρων τῶν ἐν τῆι Σικελίαι: Megara Hyblaea (4.1 n.). Lamachus had seen the advantages of the site (49.4 n.); the Syracusans had fortified it at 75.1.   οὕς: i.e. 'the Megarians', sense-construction after 'Megara'.   ὥσπερ καὶ πρότερόν μοι εἴρηται: 4.2 n. Such uses of 'I' to refer to himself as narrator are rare in Th. (only here and 5.1.1), though frequent in Hdt.: Gribble 1998: 44, 64; Brock 2003: 8–9. Possibly, then, a long-distance recollection of the Herodotean manner of **1.2–5.3** (n.)?

94.2–3 ἀποβάντες...ἐμπιμπράντες: an extraordinary accumulation of participles and verbs enumerating all the actions in sequence.   ἐδῄωσαν τοὺς ἀγρούς: as was often done early in the season, though more often in early summer (2.47.2) than at the beginning of spring: corn cannot be burnt while still green, and the best time for crop-burning is mid May to mid June (Hanson 1998: 50–1, 219–20). Perhaps on this occasion it was a matter of burning stored grain (Hanson), but given Th.'s phrasing it is more likely that it was destroyed by trampling. For the aor. ἐδῄωσαν see on ἐδῄουν below.   ἔρυμά τι τῶν Συρακοσίων: the Syracusans had 'made Megara a φρούριον' at **75**.1, but ἔρυμά τι sounds less impressive ('either an improvised breastwork or a stronghold similarly constructed', Watson-Williams 1962: 103), possibly part of the more elaborate fortification.   αὖθις καὶ πεζῆι καὶ ναυσὶ παρακομισθέντες: καὶ πεζῆι seems illogical after 'again', as there was no mention at **94.1** of a synchronised land movement to Megara; still, there may have been one, with παρέπλευσαν there focusing on the more important aspect and καὶ πεζῆι now mattering more as the Syracusan land forces will have been alerted. Maybe, though, the audience simply takes the illogicality in its stride.   ἐπὶ τὸν Τηρίαν ποταμόν: **50**.2 n. The Athenians are pulling back to the N.   ἀναβάντες 'moving inland' from the shore.   ἐδῄουν ... ἐνεπίμπρασαν: imperfects for actions still in process when they encounter the Syracusans, whereas the earlier ἐδῄωσαν referred to a completed action. The σῖτος may have been stored grain.   τισὶν οὐ πολλοῖς: **1**.1 n. (on οὐ πολλῶι τινι ὑποδεέστερον).

94.3 Κεντόριπα, Σικελικὸν πόλισμα: Centoripa/Centorbi, some 35 km inland and WNW of Catana: see *IACP* 207–8 and Fragoulaki 2013: 297–8. It was 'a Sikel community under strong Hellenic influences' (Fragoulaki 2013); the local ruler was probably the Demon who was *proxenos* of the Athenians along with his brother Archonides (7.1.4 n., Pope 2017: 412). During the winter most inland Sicels had already come over to the Athenians (**88.4–5**). The need for this ὁμολογία may suggest that the process was not yet complete, or that this pre-existing goodwill now led to a more formal agreement. The Centoripans give valuable aid at 7.32.   τῶν τε Ἰνησσαίων καὶ τῶν Ὑβλαίων: Hybla (**62**.5 n.) was midway betwen Centoripa and Catana; Inessa (*IACP* 177 and 185) was presumably nearby. 3.103.2 describes it as a Σικελικὸν πόλισμα and notes that the Syracusans controlled its acropolis in winter 426–425.

94.4 τούς τε ἱππέας ... καὶ τάλαντα ἀργυρίου τριακόσια: as anticipated at **71**.2 and requested at **74**.2 and **93**.4 (nn.), hence 'the' horsemen, taken as familiar, without 'the' horses to go with them. Th. has not so far said how much had been requested, and gives numbers only here. Kallet 2001: 109 infers that 'the response . . . was less than requested'; or this may be the usual narrative delay (**64**.1, **74**.1 nn.) until the numbers are about to be relevant.   ἄνευ τῶν ἵππων ... ὡς αὐτόθεν ἵππων πορισθησομένων: as the Athenians in Sicily had apparently anticipated, for they had asked for horses locally at 88.6 (n.); they arrive at **98**.1. Cf. **37**.1 n. The phrasing of **71**.2 (n.) already implied an element of local gathering, and **74**.2 and **93**.4 specified only 'horsemen'.   μετὰ σκευῆς: cavalrymen would provide their own saddles, bridles, etc.   καὶ τάλαντα ἀργυρίου τριακόσια: the payment is recorded in the Athenian accounts (OR 170 = ML 77 = Fornara 144, lines 73–7). It was probably authorised in March, with a further small allocation 17 days later.

95.1 ἐπ' Ἄργος στρατεύσαντες Λακεδαιμόνιοι: cf. **7**.1–2 (n.).   Κλεωνῶν: on the road between Corinth and Argos, 120 stades (Strabo 8.6.19 i.e. about 25 km) N of Argos. The Spartans were taking a long detour to the N. Cleonae had fought on the Argive side at Mantinea (5.67.2).   σεισμοῦ δὲ γενομένου ἀπεχώρησαν: the earthquake would be taken as a bad omen. They invaded again later in the summer (**105**.1).   τὴν Θυρεᾶτιν: long disputed border territory, a plain about 20 km long on the E coast. Hdt. 1.82 recounts a battle of 300 champions from each city to decide ownership c. 546 BCE.   λείαν: probably mainly livestock, though perhaps including some slaves.   ἣ ἐπράθη ταλάντων οὐκ ἔλασσον πέντε καὶ εἴκοσι: for neuter/adverbial οὐκ ἔλασσον see **1**.2 n.; for the omission of ἣ cf. 4.44.6. As οὐκ ἔλασσον suggests, this was an unusually large sum, and this is probably why it is mentioned; but it pales in comparison with the 120 talents realised from Hyccara (**62**.3–4).

95.2 Θεσπιῶν: for Thespiae *IACP* 457–8. Its constitution was an oligarchy based on a property qualification. Relations with neighbouring Thebes were often strained, and in 423 the Thebans had destroyed the Thespians' walls 'charging them with pro-Athenian sympathies

(4.133.1). The flight of survivors now 'to Athens' confirms that those charges were not without foundation. οὐ κατέσχεν 'did not succeed', intransitive. ξυνελήφθησαν: and were doubtless killed.

96–103: SUMMER 414: THE BATTLE OF THE WALLS BEGINS

The narrative is dense, the manoeuvres and constructions complex, and the modern student finds it difficult to follow them even with the aid of a map (here Map 4). Th.'s ancient audience had no such visual aid, and listeners would find it even harder than readers who could check back through the book-roll for any detail they had missed. Th. assumes an audience that already knows something of what will follow (**99**.4 n.), and he introduces without further explanation several places or features he has not mentioned before, e.g. 'the meadow' at **96**.3, 'Euryelus' at **97**.2, 'Syce' and 'the circle' at **98**.2, 'the precinct' at **99**.3, and 'the little gate' at **100**.1, though the context normally conveys to the audience what is important. In some other cases Th. does provide locations, distances, and orientations, but still even an audience with total concentration would tend to accumulate these as disparate facts, not combine them into a coherent bird's-eye view of the whole topography. Modern critics find this dismaying (e.g. 'the description of the topography is too rudimentary to evoke an image of the battleground or to enable us to properly understand the military tactics', Funke and Haake 2006: 381), but they may find it more confusing than his ancient listeners and readers would do. They would be used to geography presented more 'hodologically' i.e. as a description of the gradually mounting experience as a traveller goes, and less as a bird's-eye view: see e.g. Purves 2010, and for Hdt. Barker, Bouzarovski, Pelling, and Isaksen 2016. They would expect their view to be built up piecemeal, and pick up whatever detail they needed to know for each manoeuvre as it came. Given the difficulty of conveying the complexity of real terrain, they might also accept and even welcome a simplified model (**66**.1 n.).

It matters more that they grasp the critical importance of these siegeworks and countermeasures, and note the rhythm of Athenian victories and Syracusan reverses. The recurrent τροπαῖον στήσαντες/ἔστησαν (**97**.5, **98**.4, **100**.3, **103**.1) sounds a refrain; so do the Syracusan 'retreats into', or 'towards', 'the city' (**97**.4, **98**.3, **100**.1, **101**.4, **102**.3–4). All builds to the theme of Syracusan depression of **102**.4 and **103**.3–4 (Rood 1998a: 171–2), and ensures that Gylippus arrives when the dangers are at their most intense. That narrative pattern is as old as the *Odyssey*, and often recurs (Pelling 1988: 237–8 on Plut. *Ant.* 48). Syracusan disorganisation, slackness, and low confidence (**98**.3, **99**.2, **100**.1, **101**.3) also prepare for the difference a Spartan general can make. But Lamachus' death (**101**.6) and Nicias' illness (**102**.2) and misreading of the danger (**104**.3) presage the turning of the tide.

96.1 ὡς ἐπύθοντο . . . ἰέναι: 'the Athenians (as a whole)' is understood with μέλλοντας, as it is not just the horsemen who will attack. The Syracusans (**37**.1) are as aware as the Athenians (**21**.1, **71**.2, **74**.2, **88**.6) of the importance of the cavalry: Intr., 6.   τῶν Ἐπιπολῶν: first mentioned at **75**.1, but the fuller description comes here. See Map 4.   σφᾶς . . . ἀποτειχισθῆναι: rather than the expected σφεῖς: **49**.2 n.   τὰς προσβάσεις 'the approaches', esp. those out of sight of the city. Th. does not say where: presumably Euryelus in particular (**97**.2 n.), but there are also some possible pathways to the N (Drögemüller 1969: 76–7, 115; Green 1970: 183).

96.2 οὐ γὰρ ἂν ἄλληι 'by any other way', in Engl. as in Greek combining 'by any other method' (than by stealing in unnoticed) and 'by any other route'.   δυνηθῆναι: standing for an optative in direct discourse.   ἐξήρτηται 'lies hanging from', but it is not clear what this means: later authors who imitate the phrase (Strabo 7.1.3, Plut. *Ant.* 46.4) may not have understood it correctly. *HCT* may be right in taking it as 'the rest [i.e. except 'the approaches'] of the tract [of Epipolae itself] has steep edges', but it may also mean that the rest of the terrain [except Epipolae] all forms part of the elevation culminating in Epipolae itself. In that case the point is that, given that the city side is visible, the approaches that needed guarding were in the other directions.   ἐπιφανὲς πᾶν ἔσω 'all visible from inside (the city)'. Th. may here simplify, as Epipolae itself only becomes visible from the slightly elevated ground a little to the N of the city (*HCT* p. 473); perhaps, then, ἔσω extends to that ground, which was now on the city side of the wall of **75**.1. Still, πᾶν may refer not to the plateau of Epipolae but to the part of 'the rest of the terrain' (see last note) that slopes down 'as far as the city'. If there is some simplification it does not affect Th.'s point: the Athenians could hardly stay unnoticed if they approached Epipolae from the city side.

96.3 ἐς τὸν λειμῶνα παρὰ τὸν Ἄναπον ποταμόν: N of the river: see Map 4. The audience will know from **66**.2 that the Anapus was an important river, but no more. Despite 'the' meadow, this was not mentioned at **66**, though it is no surprise near a λίμνη (**66**.1).   οἱ περὶ τὸν Ἑρμοκράτη στρατηγοί: 'the' generals, the ones elected at **73**.1; they presumably entered office only now. Th. implies that this was why the muster happened now, and it was a coincidence that the Athenians were on the move (**97**.1). Th.

is explicit there that this movement was undetected (ἔλαθον), but intelligence may have been received by one side or the other (or both: Green 1970: 187–8) that something could be expected soon.   ἑξακοσίους λογάδας: who will have a role to play at 7.43.4.   ἐξέκριναν πρότερον: Engl. would translate with a pluperfect: cf. *CGCG* 33.40.   Ἄνδρου: part of the Athenian empire, and Diomilus may have been exiled as one of an anti-Athenian faction.   ὅπως . . . εἶεν . . . παραγίγνωνται: cf. 7.17.4 for a similar combination of the alternative opt. and subj. constructions in purpose clauses. Cf. *CGCG* 45.3, though neither of these instances suits the observation there that in such cases 'the subjunctive tends to highlight the purpose more immediately relevant for the subject of the verb'.

97.1 ταύτης τῆς νυκτός, <ἧι> τῆι ἐπιγιγνομένηι ἡμέραι ἐξητάζοντο ἐκεῖνοι: so the Athenian movement came before that of **96**, and the rather awkward expression is necessary to make that clear: deletion of <ἧι> . . . ἐκεῖνοι (as preferred by *HCT*) would leave ταύτης τῆς νυκτός ambiguous between the night before and the night after. The switch from temporal sequence means that only in retrospect does the reader realise that the Syracusan foresight and discipline of **96** were already too late: cf. ἤδη here. Verbal echoes (ἔλαθον, **97**.1 ~ **96**.1; παραγενέσθαι, **97**.2 ~ **96**.3) emphasise how, from the Syracusan perspective, it has all gone wrong.   **Λέοντα:** see Map 4, though its precise location on the northern edge is uncertain. Th. does not mention it again.   **ἓξ ἢ ἑπτὰ σταδίους:** about 1–1.25 km: cf. **97**.3 n. **Θάψον:** briefly mentioned at **4**.1. See map 2.   **οὔτε πλοῦν οὔτε ὁδὸν πολλὴν ἀπέχει:** but Th. does not give distances (about 10 km as the crow flies, but rather more by either land or sea) as with Leon. On the gender of πολλήν see **92**.5 n.

97.2 διασταυρωσάμενος: i.e. erected a barricade of stakes across the neck of the isthmus. This could be done relatively quickly.   **φθάνει:** historic present for the climactic moment, as with ἀποθνήισκει at the culmination of the fighting (**97**.4).   **τὸν Εὐρύηλον:** not previously mentioned; it becomes important again as the most convenient ascent at 7.2.3 and 7.43.2. This is at the extreme W angle of Epipolae (see Map 4), but Th. does not tell his audience that; what matters is that it is out of Syracusan sight and closer to the Athenian force than to the Syracusans.

97.3 ὡς ἕκαστος τάχους εἶχε: as in ἀτακτότερον, **97**.4, the difference from the orderly parade of **96** is marked.   **οἱ περὶ τὸν Διόμιλον ἑξακόσιοι:** **96**.3.   **στάδιοι . . . οὐκ ἔλασσον ἢ πέντε καὶ εἴκοσι:** about 4 km, with the last part uphill: no wonder they were out of formation, and doubtless out of breath. As with Leon (**97**.1 n.) Th. gives the distance, and the audience can contrast the two (though the distance at **97**.1 is from Leon to the nearest point of Epipolae, not Euryelus itself: *HCT* 468). For neuter/ adverbial οὐκ ἔλασσον see **1**.2 n.; for the length of Th.'s 'stade', **1**.2 n. and 7.19.2 n.   ἀποθνήισκει: **97**.2 n.

97.5 στήσαντες ... ἀποδόντες ... ἐπικαταβάντες ... ἐπαναχωρήσαντες: as at **94**.2–3 (n.) the stacking of participles conveys a rapid sequence in strict order, as the burst of Athenian energy continues.   **ἐπὶ τῶι Λαβδάλωι ... ὁρῶν πρὸς τὰ Μέγαρα:** see Map 4. Th. does here give a more precise position and orientation, indicating that the Athenians were most concerned with the N approaches.   **τοῖς χρήμασιν:** especially money, needed to buy supplies, but also more generally 'possessions': cf. **49**.3 n.

98.1 ἦλθον ἔκ τε Ἐγέστης ἱππῆς τριακόσιοι ... ὡς ἑκατόν: at **88**.6 the Athenians had requested 'horses' from the Sicels and Egesta, and probably asked for horsemen too, as envisaged at **71**.2. In any case, that is what they now get. Diod. 13.44.1–2 reports that at some point 800 cavalry from Campania were hired to help Athens: the item and the figure are accepted, perhaps too readily, by Frederiksen 1968: 12–14. If they ever arrived and if Th. knew about them it is strange that he does not mention them: that number would have made a big difference. Cf. 7.57.11 n.   **καὶ Ἀθηναίων ὑπῆρχον πεντήκοντα καὶ διακόσιοι: 94**.4.   **πεντήκοντα καὶ ἑξακόσιοι ἱππῆς:** they are still outnumbered: the Syracusans were able to field at least 1,200 at **67**.2. But they are now able to compete, and are immediately successful (**98**.4).

98.2 τὴν Συκῆν ... τὸν κύκλον: despite the 'the's, neither has been mentioned, and all the audience can infer is that these are on Epipolae. 'The circle' swiftly becomes important, esp. at **102**, and Th. may have chosen to leave more detail until then, but 'the fig-tree' is not mentioned again and it is hard to see that the audience needs to know about it. Perhaps Th. carelessly assumes the audience know more than they have been told, or perhaps he is writing for readers who might visit and do their own reconstruction, as so many have tried to do since: 'the fig-tree' would be a useful pointer as long as it survived. For the location see *HCT* 473–4 and Green 1970: 192, followed here in Map 4.   **καθεζόμενοι** 'taking their position' (not at all 'sitting down', given the frantic activity): cf. e.g. 2.18.1, 2.19.1.   **ἐτείχισαν:** aor. rather than imperfect for the completed construction: ctr. ἐτείχιζον, **99**.1 (n.).   **ἔκπληξιν:** this language of sudden shock played a part in the Syracusan rhetoric the year before (**36**.2, **76**.1 nn.); it now transfers to the realities of war, where it will be important in tracking morale. In two separate arcs Syracuse will first suffer and finally inflict progressively more severe ἔκπληξις/κατάπληξις: Athenians are hit by it at 7.21.4 and 24.3, then Syracusans at 7.42.2–3 and

43.6, and this is in turn reversed decisively at 7.69.3, 70.6, 71.7, 72.4 and 8.1.2. ἐπεξελθόντες: echoing οὐκ ἐπεξῆισαν at 97.5, as the Syracusans think of doing now what they did not do then. καὶ μὴ περιορᾶν 'and not look on and let them'.

98.3 διεσπασμένον τε καὶ οὐ ῥαιδίως ξυντασσόμενον: the winter training programme (**72**.4) had not been as effective as Hermocrates had there hoped. The disorder repeats itself at 7.3.3. ἐκώλυον: conative imperfect. λιθοφορεῖν: **44**.1 n.

98.4 φυλὴ μία τῶν ὁπλιτῶν: the army was organised on the basis of the Cleisthenic tribes, so this would be a tenth of the hoplite strength of the Athenians themselves, therefore about 150 men (cf. **43**). Most of the allies were deployed in separate units (**67**.1), though those from Athenian cleruchies retained their tribal identities and presumably stood with their fellow tribesmen.

99.1 ἐτείχιζον . . . παρέβαλλον: inceptive imperfects, but also conveying that the action continued for some time (*CGCG* 33.52 n.1). τὸ πρὸς βορέαν τοῦ κύκλου τεῖχος: possibly just 'a wall to the north of the circle', with τὸ πρὸς βορέαν as a separate adverbial phrase, but more likely '*the* wall to the north of . . .', taking τό with τεῖχος: 'the', because a series of walls could be presumed to be the next step. παρέβαλλον 'deposited alongside' the line of the wall. ἐπὶ τὸν Τρωγίλον καλούμενον αἰεί 'continuously all the way to the place called Trogilus': see Map 4 and *HCT* 474–5, to be preferred to Drögemüller 1969: 84–90 and Green 1970: 194–6. Trogilus is mentioned again at 7.2.4. ἧπερ βραχύτατον . . . τὸ ἀποτείχισμα 'the place affording them the shortest distance for the fortification from the Great Harbour to the sea on the other bank': see Map 4. The distance from the circle to Trogilus is about 3 km; for the stretch from the circle to the harbour, 1.5–2 km, see **103**.1 n. The audience are assumed as at **50**.4 to know that there was a 'Great Harbour', and can infer that as harbours are in inlets they will be bordered by at least one neck of land: that makes 'the sea on the other bank' understandable. The stretch to Trogilus would be the N section of this 'walling off' (ἀποτείχισμα) of the city; the S will be started at **101**.1.

99.2 οὐχ ἥκιστα . . . τῶν στρατηγῶν: to be taken together, 'not least among the generals'. μάχαις . . . τρέπεσθαι: the accumulation of co-ordinates and the confusion of different 'they's create a straggly sentence, and one can almost hear the hasty and improvised rethinking: better to build a lower wall – that will block them off – but what if they come to stop us? Send just a part of our forces, and plant stakes – that will in any case distract them from their own building. The repeated φθάσειαν . . . φθάνειν introduces the important preoccupation. **πανδημεί:** a keyword of the previous summer's tactics, 64.1 n. Alcibiades' prediction of 91.2 might seem to be coming true. **ὑποτειχίζειν . . . γίγνεσθαι:** the word ὑποτειχίζειν is not found again until Appian and Cassius Dio, and the noun-forms ὑποτείχισμα (**100.1**) and ὑποτείχισις (**100.3**) nowhere else at all. It should mean either 'build a lower wall' (C–S: cf. κάτωθεν τοῦ κύκλου, **99.3**) or 'build a wall up to meet . . .', i.e. to 'intercept' (P–S, Marchant): in most places it would be both, as the Athenians controlled the higher ground, and interception was the aim. The words down to γίγνεσθαι are then best taken as (a) 'it seemed better to build a (lower/ intercepting) wall where they (the Athenians) were going to build their wall, and, if they [the Syracusans] succeeded in getting their wall built first, for there to be barriers cutting off the Athenians (from completing the fortification)'. With the scholiast, this takes ἀποκλήσεις γίγνεσθαι along with ὑποτειχίζειν as dependent on ἄμεινον ἐδόκει εἶναι. Alternatively (b), the implied subject of φθάσειαν might be 'the Athenians' and καὶ . . . ἀποκλήσεις γίγνεσθαι taken with ἔμελλον. The translation will then be '. . . where they (the Athenians) were going to build their wall and, if they succeeded in doing so first, there would be barriers cutting off the city'. In that case, though, the switch of subject is harsh when e.g. ἀποκλήσειν τὴν πόλιν would have sufficed, and the purpose of the Athenian fortification is anyway already clear. The plural ἀποκλήσεις also favours (a): the Syracusans' plan to cut off the fortifications to both S and N. A comma after τὸ τεῖχος is here added to Alberti's text to clarify the meaning along these lines. **εἰ ἐπιβοηθοῖεν:** i.e. 'the Athenians'. **μέρος . . . τὰς ἐφόδους:** i.e. they would not allow themselves to be drawn into a full-scale battle, but just send a detachment to occupy 'the approaches' and erect and defend a stockade to protect the construction force. These will be the 'approaches' to the (usually lower) ground where the Syracusans would be working on the fortification; 'the' stakes probably = 'the ones you would expect' for such a defence. The combination of φθάνειν and προκαταλαμβάνοντες is not quite pleonastic (C–S, P–S, Spratt), for each side seeks to pre-empt the other and the Syracusans hope to get their pre-emption in first. **ἐκείνους . . . τρέπεσθαι:** corresponding to an opt. in direct speech. For the reduplicated ἄν (though the text is uncertain) see **10.4** n.: it puts extra weight on πάντας – they would have to stop building and fight us, all of them.

99.3 ἀπὸ τῆς σφετέρας πόλεως: with ἀρξάμενοι: their construction started from the walls of their city. **κάτωθεν τοῦ κύκλου τῶν Ἀθηναίων ἐγκάρσιον τεῖχος ἄγοντες:** see Map 4 for this 'cross-wall', 'below' the circle on (probably) the sloping ground between the plateau and the marsh; but the uninformed listener or reader would assume that this would aim to cut across the wall just mentioned N of the circle. In fact this cross-wall would initially be directed more to the S, close to the grove. τάς τε ἐλάας ἐκκόπτοντες τοῦ τεμένους: not a thing to do lightly: such behaviour had caused religious outrage at Corcyra in 427 BCE (3.70.4). But times were desperate, and the Syracusans could claim to be *defending* Apollo Temenites, for this is presumably the 'precinct' of the temple that gave its name to the 'Temenites' of 75.1 (n.) and 100.2. Th. again writes as if the audience knows more of the topography than he has said (98.2, 99.1 nn.).

99.4 αἱ δὲ νῆες τῶν Ἀθηναίων οὔπω ... ἐς τὸν μέγαν λιμένα: this explains why the Syracusans did not need to concern themselves with defence on the Harbour side. Th.'s wording implies an audience that knows that the ships did later sail into the Great Harbour (102.3), but many more would know that the expedition featured a great sea-battle in the Harbour than would be familiar with e.g. 'the circle' or 'the fig-tree'. ἐκράτουν τῶν περὶ τὴν θάλασσαν 'had maritime supremacy', controlling any potential activity connected with the sea. Th. does not explain why the Athenians, so proud of their maritime skill, did not challenge that domination. Green 1970: 191–3 criticises the Athenian generals sharply for their failure to do more to implement a naval blockade.

100 The chapter is carefully constructed (Yaginuma 1990): first a massive sentence (100.1), where the subordinate clauses set out first the thinking on both sides and then their simultaneous actions (Syracusan separation of forces, Athenian destruction of the water supply), then continuing more elaborately to the Athenian perception of Syracusan slackness and, in the long-delayed main clause, their attack. The action that follows is narrated in short, snappy sentences and clauses, with a historic present for the decisive moment, αἱροῦσι τὸ σταύρωμα (100.2), and then co-ordinated aorists for the swift sequence of events, κατέφυγον ... ξυνεσέπεσον ... ἐξεκρούσθησαν ... διεφθάρησαν. δίχα γιγνομένοις: that is, with some of them working on their own wall and others attacking the Syracusans. φυλὴν μίαν καταλιπόντες: the audience can assume or infer that the Syracusans, like the Athenians (98.4 n.), brigaded their troops on a tribal model. If, as seems likely, the Syracusans had three tribes, those left on guard would still be quite numerous. ποτοῦ ὕδατος 'of drinking water', with οἱ ὀχετοί but transposed into the relative clause, as in 2.45.1 παισὶ δ' ὅσοι τῶνδε πάρεστε. διέφθειραν: perhaps just by hacking through them, but poisoning cannot be excluded: the Athenians (wrongly) thought the Spartans might have poisoned their wells at the beginning of the war

(2.48.2). **τηρήσαντες** 'having watched out for' this opportunity: cf.
2.4. **προύταξαν:** προ- implies that others were to follow: cf. **100.**2 n.
on οἱ διώκοντες. **τῶν ψιλῶν τινὰς ἐκλεκτοὺς ὡπλισμένους:** rather than
regular hoplites because these were likely to be faster runners. **μετὰ
τοῦ ἑτέρου στρατηγοῦ . . . μετὰ τοῦ ἑτέρου:** Th. does not say which general
did which; perhaps he did not know, perhaps it did not matter (cf. **50.**2
n.). It allows him to continue his non-naming of Lamachus (**62** n.) until
his death (**101.**6). **εἰ ἐπιβοηθοῖεν** 'in case they (the Syracusans) should
send help'. At **99.**2 the Syracusans had planned to send just 'a part of
their army' if the Athenians were to attack *their* construction parties. The
tables have been turned. **τὸ σταύρωμα τὸ παρὰ τὴν πυλίδα** 'the palisade by the little gate', presumably part of the larger stockade. Th. has not
mentioned this 'little gate' before, and the audience would be bemused:
possibly a postern through the city wall close to where the new cross-wall
abutted, but more likely in the Temenites προτείχισμα that he goes on to
mention. This second interpretation adds more to the narrative, as this
will then be the gate through which both sides burst (**100.**3); but it is an
extreme example of the way that topographical information is fed to the
audience only piecemeal (**96–103** n.).

100.2 τὸ προτείχισμα τὸ περὶ τὸν Τεμενίτην: presumably part of the winter wall enclosing Temenites of **75.**1: see Map 4. Readers and hearers
are expected to have good memories. **οἱ διώκοντες:** maybe just the
advance force of 300, but some of those attacking τὸ σταύρωμα τὸ παρὰ
τὴν πυλίδα may have been able to join in. **τινές . . . οὐ πολλοί: 1.**1 n.

100.3 διεφόρησαν τοὺς σταυροὺς παρ' ἑαυτούς: for use in their own
fortification.

101–2 Another (cf. **100** n.) carefully constructed sequence, this time setting the scene with two measured sentences on first the Athenian and then
the Syracusan fortification moves and countermoves. Imperfect tenses
describe what they were about (ἐτείχιζον . . . ἀπεσταυροῦν . . . παρώρυσσον);
action comes in **101.**3, but with the focus still firmly on the same theatre:
the fleet move, so important in itself, is given in only a subordinate clause.
As at **100.**2, historic presents describe the climactic activity (ἐπιχειροῦσιν . . .
αἱροῦσιν, **101.**3). The main fighting itself is dismissed perfunctorily (καὶ
μάχη ἐγένετο, καὶ ἐν αὐτῆι ἐνίκων οἱ Ἀθηναῖοι); the greater significance will
come in what looks initially like a mere mopping-up but instead produces
further critical moments and further historic presents, first in quick succession χωροῦσι . . . τρέπουσι . . . ἐσβάλλουσιν (**101.**5), then for the most
important point of all ἀποθνήισκει, then φθάνουσιν (**101.**6) and, for the
dangerous follow-up attack on the circle, πέμπουσιν and αἱροῦσι (**102.**1–2).

So Lamachus finally re-enters the narrative for the first time since **50.**1, but only to die (**101.**6): cf. **66.**2 n. That leaves only Nicias of the three generals, and another critical element, his illness, is also here introduced, for the moment a stroke of luck (**102.**2), for the future a calamity.   τοῦ κύκλου: **99.**1 n.   ἀπὸ τοῦ κύκλου . . . τοῦ ἕλους: the imperfect ἐτείχιζον is inceptive, 'from the circle they began to fortify the cliff . . . with a wall', though it also conveys that this took some time. The wording initially suggests that the circle bordered the cliff, and starting from it they could fortify the cliff-edge as the first stretch of the the περιτείχισμα; but τὸ πρὸς τὸν κρημνόν (**101.**3) indicates that there was first a distance, perhaps very short, from circle to cliff. Thus begins the fortification on the S side of 'the circle': see Map 4. 'The marsh' is Lysimeleia (7.53.2 n.). Readers/ listeners with a good memory (cf. **100.**2 n.) may remember from the battle of the Anapus that the plain included a lake (though not there a 'marsh') and was bordered by cliffs (**66.**1), which they would now gather were the cliffs of Epipolae. Even if they did not, Th. now goes on to convey the topography that needs to be known.   ἥπερ αὐτοῖς βραχύτατον ἐγίγνετο ἐς τὸν λιμένα τὸ περιτείχισμα: this economically clarifies the relation of this wall to the N one (**99.**1): that wall was to cover the shortest distance 'from the great harbour to the other sea', this one the equivalent 'to the harbour', so descending in the opposite direction. The echo of **99.**1 (ἥπερ βραχύτατον ἐγίγνετο . . . τὸ ἀποτείχισμα) brings out the symmetry. ἀποτείχισμα is used there because on its own the northern wall would just 'wall off' one approach, περιτείχισμα here because the southern one would complete the circumvallation, even though in itself it constituted a further 'walling off' (**101.**2).

101.2   καὶ αὐτοί: with both ἐξελθόντες and ἀπεσταύρουν: while the Athenians were fortifying, the Syracusans too went out and set about their defences.   ἀπεσταύρουν . . . παρώρυσσον: see Map 4. Digging a trench through a marsh would be barely possible and certainly unpleasant, but the Syracusans would concentrate on the firmer areas; the Athenians would have trouble anyway riding or fighting through the flooded parts. But they find a way: **101.**3.

101.3   τὸ πρὸς τὸν κρημνόν: 101.1 n.   ἐπιχειροῦσιν αὖθις τῶι τῶν Συρακοσίων σταυρώματι καὶ τάφρωι:** thus resuming (αὖθις) the attack of **100.**1–2, but extending it to the new S stockade as well, as 'the trench' and 'the marsh' make clear.   τὰς μὲν ναῦς . . . ἐς τὸν μέγαν λιμένα τὸν τῶν Συρακοσίων: they arrive at **102.**3. Thus, in a subordinate clause, an order is reported that was to prove momentous. For now it sounds like, and at **102.**3 it acts as, a diversionary operation (μέν) for the primary concern (δέ), the fighting over the fortifications.   καταβάντες ἀπὸ τῶν

Ἐπιπολῶν ἐς τὸ ὁμαλόν καὶ διὰ τοῦ ἕλους: so following the path of the projected S wall, as the echo of **101.1** makes clear.   θύρας: not 'doors' – not many would be to hand – but any flat panel: LSJ I.8. The Syracusan guards must have been slack if they did not notice such activity in this dawn half-light (ὄρθρον).

101.4 μάχη ἐγένετο: presumably in the plain (τὸ ὁμαλόν, **101.1** and 3). See Map 4. Particularly alert readers and listeners may realise that we are in the vicinity of the battle of the Anapus, **67–71**. This is then confirmed, and built on, by mentions of 'the river' (i.e. the Anapus) and 'the bridge' (cf. **66**.2), and those with less complete memories will gather from those what they need to know.   ἐνίκων 'were victorious', imperfect, as often with νικάω when it is the result rather than the moment of victory that matters: *CGCG* 33.18, Huitink–Rood on Xen. *Anab.* 3.2.13.   τὸ δεξιὸν κέρας . . . ἐπὶ τῶι εὐωνύμωι: the Syracusans would be attacking from E to W or from SE to NW somewhere N of the Anapus, with the left wing closer to the river: see Map 4.   παρὰ τὸν ποταμόν 'along the river' – or so any reader or listener would take it unless puzzled by trying to match it to the terrain. The river is the Anapus, and the men were making for the bridge (wherever that was: **66**.2 n.) in order to cross to the S: whether that meant a flight W or E depends on the location of battle and bridge. They would not be safe even across the bridge, despite τὸ ἀσφαλές at **101.6**, as the Athenians could cross too. But the Syracusans would have a better chance of making it to the fortified Olympieion (**64**.1 n).   οἱ τῶν Ἀθηναίων τριακόσιοι λογάδες: **100**.1 n. Again their speediness is needed here.   τὴν γέφυραν: presumably the bridge of **66**.2, rebuilt over the winter.

101.5 προσπεσόντων αὐτῶν: 'they' might include both the Athenian λογάδες, 'falling into' the hoplites in their flight (LSJ προσπίπτω I.1), and the Syracusan pursuers, 'falling upon' them in attack (LSJ I.2).   ἡ πρώτη φυλὴ τοῦ κέρως: i.e. 'the first' they came to, the φυλή closest to the river. For the tribal organisation see **98**.4 n.

101.6 ὁ Λάμαχος . . . ἀποθνήισκει: so at last he is mentioned again (**66**.2 n.), for the first time since **50**.1. The focus zooms in to narrate this crucial scuffle, but it is not in Th.'s manner to give colour or detail. By contrast Plut. *Nic.* 18.3 describes a single combat of Lamachus against Callicrates, 'a spirited fighter', which left both men dead. That may go back to an early source, perhaps Philistus.   ἐπιδιαβάς: probably 'crossing over against' the Syracusans, rather than (LSJ) 'crossing over in addition to' the troops that had already crossed.   τάφρον τινά: presumably not the Syracusans' trench of **101**.2–3, at least as far as Th. knew, as he would have said τὸν τάφρον; more likely an irrigation trench connected with the marsh. This helps to explain why Lamachus became 'isolated': it was difficult for troops to leap across in numbers.   ἐς τὸ ἀσφαλές: 101.4 n.

102.1 οἱ πρὸς τὴν πόλιν αὐτῶν . . . καταφυγόντες: 101.4. αὐτῶν is taken with οἱ . . . καταφυγόντες, not with πόλιν: 'those of them . . .' i.e. the Syracusans.   τοὺς κατὰ σφᾶς Ἀθηναίους: the Athenian left wing, now lacking its general Lamachus. It is unclear whether this squaring-up led to any fighting, as Th. immediately switches his focus to the more dramatic development.

102.2 τὸ μὲν δεκάπλεθρον προτείχισμα: again the definite article does not indicate anything already mentioned, nor could a 'ten-*plethron* wall' be a regularly expected feature: the size of any 'advance wall' would depend on the individual case. 'Ten *plethra*' (approximately 300 m) is doubtless a rough estimate. It may not have covered the full circumference if the surrounding terrain in places offered sufficient protection.   διεκώλυσεν: αἱρεῖν and διαπορθεῖν are understood.   ἔτυχε γὰρ ἐν αὐτῶι δι' ἀσθένειαν ὑπολελειμμένος: the first we have heard of any illness, possibly but not certainly the kidney-disease that will become so important (7.15.1 [n.], 77.2); but for the moment it is lucky that he was there. He had been well enough to lead half of the force at **100.1**.   τὰς γὰρ μηχανάς: ladders, scaffolding, etc.   ξύλα: perhaps including some of the wood collected at **99.1** and the captured σταῦροι of **100.3**, lying in the space between the προτείχισμα and the τεῖχος.

102.3 τῶν Ἀθηναίων ἀποδιωξάντων τοὺς ἐκεῖ: presumably these were from the Athenian right wing who had finished their pursuit at **101**.6; the left wing were still engaged (**102.1**). Sight-lines are here important. Flames from the circle, close to the cliff-edge, were visible from below, and the ships sailing into the harbour could be seen by the Syracusan attackers.   βοήθεια 'a relieving force'.   καὶ αἱ νῆες . . . κατέπλεον ἐς τὸν μέγαν λιμένα: yet at **99**.4 the Syracusans were in control of the sea. If there was any fighting, Th. does not tell us; but perhaps the Syracusan focus, not just Th.'s own, was on the land.   ὥσπερ εἴρητο: 101.3.

102.4 οἱ ἄνωθεν: perhaps simply = οἱ ἄνω (Spratt: cf. 3.68.3, 7.63.2), but -θεν may also be influenced both by ὁρῶντες and by ἀπῆισαν: they both 'see' and will 'go away' *from* above. Cf. 7.79.2 n.   μὴ ἂν . . . ἱκανοὶ γενέσθαι: the inf. is the equivalent of a potential opt., with μή rather than οὐ after νομίσαντες (*M&T* 685).

103.1 ἀπὸ τῶν Ἐπιπολῶν . . . τείχει διπλῶι: see Map 4. ἀπετείχιζον is inceptive imperfect as at **101**.1. Th. characteristically delays further detail until this wall becomes relevant at 7.2.4: it becomes clear that its length would be a little more than 7 or 8 stades i.e. less than 2 km, so rather shorter than the N wall of **99**.1. The reader/listener will understand, as the Syracusans did at **102**.4, that now the ships had arrived the Athenians would focus on this S wall to the harbour. This 'double wall' would offer protection as stores were transported from the ships: the two walls probably splayed out in a V to cover all the ships anchored close to shore in the harbour. The walls would also block the natural route from the city into the hinterland (Drögemüller 1969: 92–3).

103.2 τὰ δ' ἐπιτήδεια . . . ἦλθον δὲ καὶ . . . καὶ ἐκ τῆς Τυρσηνίας . . . καὶ τἆλλα: the co-ordinated string catalogues all the things that are going well, followed by a shift of focus (**103**.3) to the mirroring despondency on the other side.   ἐσήγετο ἐκ τῆς Ἰταλίας: perhaps by boat to Naxos or Catana and then by land, or perhaps directly into the harbour if the Syracusan maritime domination of **99**.4 was felt to be ended: cf. **102**.3 n.   πανταχόθεν: strongly put (e.g. Taras would still be hostile), accentuating how well things were going with waverers picking what looked like the winner.   ἦλθον . . . πολλοὶ ξύμμαχοι 'many came as allies . . .', beyond those whose support was already clear at **65**.2, **88**.3–6, **94**.3 and **98**.1. Cf. **88**.4 n.   περιεωρῶντο 'were being circumspect', middle: **93**.1 n.   ἐκ τῆς Τυρσηνίας: **88**.6 n. Their troops will be important at 7.53–4.   προυχώρει αὐτοῖς ἐς ἐλπίδας 'were progressing so as to encourage their hopes' (not quite 'were going as they hoped').

103.3 καὶ γάρ: 'introducing additional information (καί) which has explanatory force' (*CGCG* 59.66): cf. **61**.2. It may give an extra reason either for Athens' reading of events ('the Syracusans too' thought the Athenians were going to win) or for their buoyancy (the peace-feelers from the demoralised enemy). Th. may here overstate Syracusan despondency, and after the war survivors may have exaggerated for effect; but we cannot be sure. For the interest in morale see Intr. to Bk. 7, pp. 30–1.   πολέμωι μὲν . . . τοὺς δὲ λόγους: the force of the μὲν . . . δέ is 'their thinking was . . ., and their talk was of making terms'.   οὐδὲ ἀπὸ τῆς Πελοποννήσου 'not even from the Peloponnese', despite the assurances their ambassadors had heard at Sparta, **93**.2.   ἦκε: as the present ἥκω is perfect in meaning ('I have come'), this imperfect = a pluperfect.   καὶ πρὸς τὸν Νικίαν: there is no reason to think that these approaches were made secretly, though Nicias did have his covert sources (7.48.2 n.): οὗτος γάρ . . . implies that, had Lamachus still been alive, he would have been approached too.

103.4 οἷα δὲ εἰκός . . . 'as one would expect with people who . . .'.   πολλὰ ἐλέγετο πρός τε ἐκεῖνον καὶ πλείω ἔτι κατὰ τὴν πόλιν: chiastically reversing the order of τοὺς δὲ λόγους ἔν τε σφίσιν αὐτοῖς . . . καὶ πρὸς τὸν Νικίαν. This order then gives the transition into the result of that internal talking. **καὶ γάρ τινα καὶ ὑποψίαν:** for καὶ γάρ see **103.**3 n. The second καί goes with ὑποψίαν: they 'even' went so far as to start suspecting one another. **τοὺς στρατηγούς τε ἐφ' ὧν αὐτοῖς ταῦτα ξυνέβη:** those, including Hermocrates, who were elected at **73.**1 but had only recently assumed office (**96.**3 n.). **ἔπαυσαν, ὡς ἢ δυστυχίαι ἢ προδοσίαι τῆι ἐκείνων βλαπτόμενοι:** this vindictiveness and suspicion of unsuccessful generals is reminiscent of Athens (cf. Intr., 7–8, 33), but Syracuse is content just to terminate their office rather than fine, exile, or execute: it might after all just be bad luck, δυστυχία. That may itself indicate the hostility of the gods and therefore be a reason to drop a general; Nicias' good luck was correspondingly a reason for wanting him to serve (**17.**1 [n.]). **Ἡρακλείδην καὶ Εὐκλέα καὶ Τελλίαν:** not the Heracleides son of Lysimachus of **73.**1, as he was one of those now ejected. None of these three is mentioned again by Th., but Heracleides and Euclees are probably the same as the generals at Ephesus in 409 (Xen. *Hell.* 1.2.8): that Heracleides is 'son of Aristogenes'.

104: GYLIPPUS

Thus, at the nadir of Syracusan fortunes (**96–103** n.), enters the man who will make the big difference. He shares the despondency himself, especially as the news he hears is even worse than the reality (ἐψευσμέναι, **104.**1). His journey is described slowly, at a time when every day counts (Rengakos 2006: 294); then his arrival in the W is anything but impressive, and his hopes of a town where he expected to find a welcome (**104.**2) turn out to be as unfounded as the Athenian expectations the previous year (**44.**2–3). A storm at sea then ensures a ragged arrival at the city where he does find succour, Taras, not quite as alone and exhausted as Odysseus at Scherie but still in something of that vein. Nicias understandably finds nothing to worry him in the news, **104.**3. But anyone used to narrative rhythm will sense from the phrasing there that this will change; the little word πω confirms it. Many readers and listeners would already know enough to be aware how dramatic that change will be.

104.1 Γύλιππος . . . νῆες: 93.2–3. **ἐφοίτων** 'kept coming': the word conveys regular and repeated movement. **πᾶσαι ἐπὶ τὸ αὐτὸ ἐψευσμέναι** 'all giving false information to the same effect'. This need not imply any deliberate intent to deflect or even to deceive Gylippus, just a tendency towards exaggeration in a crisis. **οὐκέτι . . . οὐδεμίαν:** the two negatives

intensify one another rather than cancelling each other out: *CGCG* 56.3–
4.   **Πυθὴν ὁ Κορίνθιος:** first mentioned here: cf. 7.1.1, 70.1.   **δυοῖν
δὲ Κορινθίαιν:** at **93**.3 Gylippus had told the Corinthians to send two ships
immediately to Asine and prepare 'as many ships as they had in mind' to sail
when required. These are presumably those two advance ships.   **πρὸς
ταῖς σφετέραις δέκα:** the 'ten' include the advance two: 7.7.1 n. Only here
and indirectly does Th. indicate how many ships the Corinthians had
decided to send in response to Gylippus' instructions (last n.). This would
have required deliberation during the winter, but Th. did not interrupt his
narrative to mention that.   **δέκα Λευκαδίας δύο καὶ Ἀμπρακιώτιδας τρεῖς:**
both Leucas and Ambracia were Corinthian colonies (*IACP* 355, 365).
These ships would have been picked up at Leucas; the crews presumably
travelled there with the rest of the Corinthian ships.

104.2   πρεσβευσάμενος κατὰ τὴν τοῦ πατρός ποτε πολιτείαν, 'sent ambassadors to make overtures in line with the citizenship his father had once
possessed'. Gylippus' father Cleandridas had been embroiled in the scandal of 446 when King Pleistoanax had been accused of accepting a bribe
from Pericles to abandon a campaign (2.21.1, Plut. *Per.* 22.3); Cleandridas
fled into exile, was condemned to death *in absentia*, but became a citizen
of Thurii, probably when the city was founded in 444–443, and commanded armies there (Polyaenus 2.10, Strabo 6.1.14). For the possibility,
no more, that Cleandridas was regarded as one of the city's *oikistai* see
CT; if so and if Th. knew it he does not say so, preferring to leave the
approach low-key. – The text is uncertain: OCT and *CT* prefer the less
well attested καὶ τὴν τοῦ πατρὸς ἀνανεωσάμενος πολιτείαν , 'and renewed the
citizenship of his father'. In that case Gylippus would be resuscitating a
past connection rather as Alcibiades tried to 'revive' his family's Spartan
proxeny (5.43.2, cf. **89**.2 n.) and the Thurians would be making a conciliatory gesture even as they rebut his request for support. But it is hard
to go against the weight of the MSS, and ἀνανεωσάμενος may reflect an
explanatory guess that has worked its way into the text.   **οὐ δυνάμενος
αὐτοὺς προσαγαγέσθαι:** Thurii continued to support Athens, though less
enthusiastically than Athens wished (7.33.6 n., 35.1, 7.57.11): cf. **88**.7
n.   **τὸν Τεριναῖον κόλπον:** the geography is bewildering, as Terina
is on the wrong side (the W) of S. Italy: see Map 2. Most likely Th. is
thinking of the waters SW of Point Iapygia (**30**.1 n.), and got the name
wrong.   **πάλιν:** more likely to be heard with χειμασθείς, 'storm-tossed
again', than with προσμίσγει. The bedraggled Trojan refugees started the
book similarly, **2**.3: cf. Intr., 14.

104.3   ὑπερεῖδε 'viewed with contempt', LSJ ὑπεροράω II.2. At **33**.3
Hermocrates had urged the Syracusans not to καταφρονεῖν their enemy;

Nicias now makes the mistake. ληιστικώτερον . . . παρεσκευασμένους 'prepared in a more pirate-like way'. At 1.10.4 Th. pictures the Greek ships in the Trojan War as 'not being covered over but ληιστικώτερον παρεσκευασμένα in the old-fashioned way' i.e. without protection overhead or leather screens on the sides (*CT* ad loc.). Such a fitting-out was suited to picking off individual ships or coastal raiding rather than to a full naval battle, and Nicias will have assumed from the small number that this was the plan.

105: GREECE SUMMER 414

The break between, in the traditional division, Bks. 6 and 7 is a light one, but it is not baseless (Intr., 14). The arrival of Gylippus is one turning-point; these open hostilities between Athens and Sparta mark another milestone, as Th. explains. That gives these scuffles a different feel from those of **7** (n.), for this is not quite business as usual. Th. does not speculate on why the Athenians chose to escalate: Sparta had not yet occupied Decelea (**93**.2 n., 7.19.1). But they will have heard of the Spartan deliberations of **88**.7–**93**, and known that Gylippus was on his way.

105.1 καὶ Λακεδαιμόνιοι ἐς τὸ Ἄργος ἐσέβαλον: resuming the abandoned operation of **95**.1 (n.). This καί is the first of a 'both . . . and . . .' with καὶ Ἀθηναῖοι . . .; αὐτοί τε καὶ οἱ ξύμμαχοι mildly redefines Λακεδαιμόνιοι.   τῆς γῆς τὴν πολλήν 'the greater part of the land' as at 2.56.4, not just 'much of the land' which would be τῆς γῆς πολλήν (Diod. 16.25.2, etc.): cf. **7**.1, τῆς τε γῆς οὐ πολλήν.   αἵπερ: i.e. 'the ships', a remarkable ascription of agency that recalls Hdt. 5.97.3, the Athenian ships that were the ἀρχὴ κακῶν . . . Ἕλλησί τε καὶ βαρβάροισι, and through the 'window' of that passage *Il.* 5.63, the ships of Paris that became ἀρχέκακοι for all the Trojans (πᾶσι Τρώεσσι): cf. Dillery 2018: 211, suggesting that the memory of the Herodotus passage recalls the herald Melesippus' gloomy prediction in 431 that this day μεγάλων κακῶν ἄρξει for the Greeks (2.12.3). It was all beginning again for the Athenians at the beginning of the Bk. (**6**.1 n.); now it is the same for both sides.   αὐτοῖς: 'for them', as in the datives in the Hdt. and *Il.* passages quoted above.

105.2 ληιστείαις ἐκ Πύλου: after the Athenian refusal to withdraw their garrison from Pylos in 421 (5.35.7–8), largely conducted by refugee helots (4.41.2, 5.56.3), and extracting 'much booty' (5.115.2).   καὶ περὶ τὴν ἄλλην Πελοπόννησον: not mentioned earlier. They may have taken place during the operations in the Argolid, 5.53–6; but small-scale raiding, more or less approved by the city, may have happened at any time without making it into Th.'s narrative. **μᾶλλον ἤ . . . μετά τε Ἀργείων καὶ Μαντινέων ξυνεπολέμουν:** not implying that the Argives and Mantineans were mounting such joint missions but without Athens, only that such a united operation of all three might have been possible. In fact Argos had contented itself with raiding Phlius: **105**.3 n. **κελευόντων . . . ἀπελθεῖν** 'urging them to do no more than put to shore with arms in Laconia, join them in ravaging a very small part of it, and then go home'. **Πυθοδώρου καὶ Λαισποδίου καὶ Δημαράτου:** Pythodorus is unlikely to be the general exiled in 424 for his perceived failure in Sicily (4.65.3, Intr., 31), but may well be the signatory to the peace and alliance of 421 (5.19.2, 24.1). Laispodias crops up again as an ambassador to Sparta from the oligarchic rulers in 411 (8.86.9), and is probably the man ridiculed by Aristophanes (*Birds* 1567–9) for the way he wore his cloak and by Eupolis (*Demes* fr. 107 K–A) for something concerning his calves: see Dunbar 1995: 716–17. Demaratus is not mentioned elsewhere. **ἀρχόντων:** Th. leaves their precise status vague (generals or navarchs?). **Ἐπίδαυρον τὴν Λιμηράν:** in SE Laconia (*IACP* 580): see Map 3a. **Πρασιάς:** in E Laconia, 50 km N of Epidaurus Limera (*IACP* 586): see Map 3a. **ὅσα ἄλλα** 'a certain number of others', LSJ ὅσος III.2. **τοῖς Λακεδαιμονίοις . . . ἐποίησαν** 'and afforded the Spartans a reason for self-defence against the Athenians that was now easier to argue'. The Sicilian narrative began with an interest in Athenian προφάσεις (**6**.1 [n.]), and the focus now switches to the other side. The point is picked up at 7.18.2–3 (n.), which makes it clear that this is not merely a matter of pretexts. The Spartans really thought that this time they had right on their side. τοῦ ἀμύνεσθαι is itself part of the Spartan case: they are only defending themselves.

105.3 **οἱ Ἀργεῖοι ἐσβαλόντες ἐς τὴν Φλειασίαν:** just as they had in winter 417–416 and again in 416 (5.83.3, 115.1): cf. **7**.1 n. **τῆς τε γῆς** 'part of their land': **75**.1 n.

WORKS CITED

Alberti, J. B. 1972–2000: *Thucydidis historiae* i–iii. Rome.
Allen, P. 2018: *The political class: why it matters who our politicians are.* Oxford.
Allison, J. W. 1979: 'Thucydides and πολυπραγμοσύνη', *AJAH* 4: 10–22.
 1989: *Power and preparedness in Thucydides.* Baltimore and London.
 1997: *Word and concept in Thucydides.* Atlanta.
 2006: 'A citizen's defense: Alcibiades speaks', in M Skortsis (ed.), *III international symposium on Thucydides: the speeches*: 156–75. Athens.
Alty, J. 1982: 'Dorians and Ionians', *JHS* 102: 1–14.
Ampolo, C. 1987: 'I contributi alla prima spedizione Ateniese in Sicilia (427–424 A.C.)', *PdP* 42: 5–11.
Andrews, J. A. 2009: 'Athenagoras, *stasis*, and factional rhetoric (Thucydides 6.36–40)', *CPh* 104: 1–12.
Antonelli, L. 1996: 'La falce di Crono: considerazioni sulla prima fondazione di Zancle', *Κώκαλος* 42: 315–25.
Arafat, K. 2013: 'Marathon in art', in C. Carey and M. Edwards (eds.), *Marathon – 2,500 years (BICS* Supp. 124): 79–89.
Arnush, M. 1995: 'The career of Peisistratos son of Hippias', *Hesperia* 64: 135–62.
Arrington, N. T. 2015: *Ashes, images, and memories: the presence of the war dead in fifth-century Athens.* Oxford.
Asheri, D. 1992: 'Sicily, 478–31 BC', in D. M. Lewis, J. Boardman, J. K. Davies, and M. Ostwald (eds.), *The Cambridge Ancient History* v (2nd ed., Cambridge): 147–70.
Avery, H. C. 1973: 'Themes in Thucydides' account of the Sicilian expedition', *Hermes* 101: 1–13.
Azoulay, V. 2017. *The tyrant-slayers of ancient Athens: a tale of two statues* (tr. J. Lloyd: French original 2014). Oxford.
Badian, E. 1992: 'Thucydides on rendering speeches', *Athen.* 80: 187–90.
Bakker, E. J. 1997: 'Verbal aspect and mimetic description in Thucydides', in Bakker (ed.), *Grammar as interpretation: Greek literature in its linguistic contexts* (*Mnem.* Supp. 171, Leiden): 7–54.
 2006: 'Contract and design: Thucydides' writing', in Rengakos and Tsakmakis 2006: 109–29.
Balot, R., S. Forsdyke, and E. Foster (eds.) (2017): *The Oxford handbook to Thucydides.* Oxford.
Baragwanath, E. and E. Foster (eds.) 2017a: *Clio and Thalia: Attic comedy and historiography* (*Histos* Supp. 6: https://research.ncl.ac.uk/histos/SV6ClioandThalia.html).

2017b: 'Introduction', in Baragwanath and Foster 2017a: 1–24.
Barker, E., S. Bouzarovski, C. Pelling, and L. Isaksen (eds.) 2016: *New worlds from old texts: revisiting ancient space and place*. Oxford.
Bassi, K. 2007: 'Spatial contingencies in Thucydides' *History*', *ClassAnt* 26: 171–218.
Bauslaugh, R. A. 1990: *The concept of neutrality in classical Greece*. Berkeley and Oxford.
Berger, S. 1992a: *Revolution and society in Greek Sicily and Southern Italy* (*Historia* Einzelschr. 71). Stuttgart.
1992b: 'Seven cities in Sicily', *Hermes* 120: 421–4.
Bicknell, P. J. 1970: 'The Harmodios skyphos in the Villa Giulia', *AC* 39: 159–60.
Bloedow, E. F. 1993: 'Hermocrates' strategy against the Athenians in 415 B.C.', *AHB* 7: 115–24.
1996: 'The speeches of Hermocrates and Athenagoras at Syracuse in 415 B.C.: difficulties in Syracuse and in Thucydides', *Historia* 45: 141–58.
Boedeker, D. 2001: 'Heroic historiography: Simonides and Herodotus on Plataea', in D. Boedeker and D. Sider (eds.), *The new Simonides* (Oxford), 120–34.
Bolmarcich, S. 2014: 'Beyond the three-barred sigma: IG i³ 11', in J. Bodel and N. Dimitrova (eds.), *Ancient documents and their contexts: first North American congress of Greek and Latin epigraphy (2011)* (Leiden and Boston): 54–66.
Bonner, R. J. 1920: 'The book divisions of Thucydides', *CPh* 15: 73–82.
Bosworth, A. B. 1992: 'Athens' first intervention in Sicily: Thucydides and the Sicilian tradition', *CQ* 42: 46–55.
Bowie, A. M. 2007: *Herodotus: Histories book VIII*. Cambridge.
Bowra, C. M. 1960: 'Euripides' epinician for Alcibiades', *Historia* 9: 69–79, repr. in *On Greek Margins* (Oxford, 1970): 34–48.
Braccesi, L. and G. Millino 2000: *La Sicilia greca*. Roma.
Bremmer, J. 1995: 'Religious secrets and secrecy in classical Greece', in H. G. Kippenberg and G. G. Stroumsa (eds.), *Studies in the history of Mediterranean and Near Eastern religions* (Leiden, New York, and Cologne), 61–78.
Brock, R. 2003: 'Authorial voice and narrative management in Herodotus', in Derow–Parker 2003: 3–16.
2013a: *Greek political imagery from Homer to Aristotle*. London, New Delhi, New York, and Sydney.
2013b: 'Athens' Sicilian expedition: contemporary scenarios of its outcome', in Powell 2013: 49–70.

2013c: 'Cleon's colourful language', in U. Bultrighini and E. Dimauro (eds.), Ὅμηρον ἐξ Ὁμήρου σαφηνίζειν: *omaggio a Domenico Musti: atti del convegno internazionale, Chieti 13-14 dicembre 2011* (Lanciano): 137–46.
Brunt, P. A. 1952: 'Thucydides and Alcibiades', *REG* 65: 59–96, repr. in his *Studies in Greek history and thought* (Oxford, 1993): 17–46.
Bugh, G. R. 1989: 'Thucydides 6.43 and 6.64.1: the case of the thirty missing Athenian horsemen', in R. I. Curtis (ed.), *Studia Pompeiana et Classica in honour of Wilhelmina F. Jashemski* ii (New Rochelle, NY): 25–31.
Camp, J. McK. 2015: 'Excavations in the Athenian agora 2008–2012', *Hesp.* 84: 467–513.
Camps, W. A. 1955: 'Thucydides vi. 87, 5', *CR* 5: 17.
Canevaro, M. 2019: 'La délibération démocratique à l' assemblée athénienne: procédures et stratégies de légitimation', *Annales HSS* 74: 339–81.
Carlà, F. 2014: 'Ein Sklavenaufstand in Syrakus (414 v. Chr.)', *Incidenza dell'Antico* 12: 61–89.
Casali, S. 2010: 'The development of the Aeneas legend', in J. Farrell and M. C. J. Putnam (eds.), *A Companion to Vergil's Aeneid and its transmission* (Chichester and Malden, MA): 37–51.
Cawkwell, G. L. 1997: *Thucydides and the Peloponnesian War.* London and New York.
2005: *The Greek wars: the failure of Persia.* Oxford.
Ceccarelli, P. 2019: 'Nomi propri e tradizioni storiche nel racconto erodoteo sulle Termopili', in M. B. Savo (ed.), *Specola historicorum. Tradizione e trasmissione dei testi storiografici nel mondo greco* (Tivoli): 35–73.
Chadwick, J. 1996: *Lexicographica graeca: contributions to the lexicography of ancient Greek.* Oxford.
Chambers, M. H., R. Gallucci, and P. Spanos 1990: 'Athens' alliance with Egesta in the year of Antiphon', *ZPE* 83: 38–63.
Chaniotis, A. 2009: 'Travelling memories in the Hellenistic world', in R. Hunter and I. Rutherford (eds.), *Wandering poets in ancient Greek culture: travel, locality and pan-Hellenism* (Cambridge): 249–69.
Chlup, J. T. 2006: 'The rhetoric of authority: Alcibiades' speech to the Spartans in Thucydides', *Cahiers d'Études Anciennes* 42: 299–325.
Christ, M. T. 2001: 'Conscription of hoplites in classical Athens', *CQ* 51: 398–422.
Clarke, K. 2008: *Making time for the past: local history and the polis.* Oxford.
Congiu, M., C. Miccichè, and S. Modeo (eds.) 2012: *Dal mito alla storia. La Sicilia nell'Archaiologia di Tucidide* (*Atti del VIII Convegno di studi, Caltanisetta, 21-22 Maggio 2011*). Caltanisetta and Rome.

Connor, W. R. 1984: *Thucydides*. Princeton.
1985: 'The razing of the house', *TAPA* 115: 79–102.
Cordano, F. 1987: 'Contributo onomastico alla storia di Camarina arcaica', Κώκαλος 33: 121–7.
Cornford, F. M. 1907: *Thucydides mythistoricus*. London.
Crane, G. 1996: *The blinded eye: Thucydides and the new written word*. Lanham, MD and London.
Cusumano, N. 2011: '"Ἔκπληξις e κατάπληξις: shock e resilienza in Tucidide', Ὅρμος: *Ricerche di Storia Antica* 3: 36–54.
Davies, J. K. 1971: *Athenian propertied families*. Oxford.
2007: 'The Phokian Hierosylia at Delphi: quantities and consequences', in N. Sekunda (ed.), *Corolla Cosmo Rodewald* (Gdansk), 75–96.
De Angelis, F. 2016: *Archaic and classical Greek Sicily: a social and economic history*. Oxford.
De Jong, I. J. F. 1987: *Narrators and focalizers: the presentation of the story in the Iliad*. Amsterdam.
1997: 'γάρ introducing embedded narratives', in Rijksbaron 1997a: 175–85.
De Romilly, J. 1956: 'La crainte dans l'oeuvre de Thucydide', *C&M* 17: 119–27.
1976: 'Alcibiade et le mélange entre jeunes et vieux: politique et médecine', *WS* 10: 93–105.
2012: *The mind of Thucydides* (tr. E. T. Rawlings, Cornell): originally *Histoire et raison chez Thucydide* (Paris, 1956, 2nd ed. 1967).
Debnar, P. 2001: *Speaking the same language: speech and audience in Thucydides' Spartan debates*. Ann Arbor.
Delebecque, E. 1965: *Thucydide et Alcibiade*. Aix-en-Provence.
Derow, P. and R. Parker (eds.) 2003: *Herodotus and his world*. Oxford.
Desmond, W. 2006: 'Lessons of fear: a reading of Thucydides', *CPh* 101: 359–79.
Dickey, E. 2002: *Latin forms of address: from Plautus to Apuleius*. Oxford.
Dillery, J. 2018: 'The past in the present and the limits of history: two Greek cases', in R. Rollinger (ed.), *Conceptualizing past, present and future: proceedings of the ninth symposium of the Melammu project held in Helsinki/Tartu May 18–24, 2015* (Münster): 207–28.
Dillon, M. P. J. 2003: '"Woe for Adonis": but in spring not summer', *Hermes* 131: 1–16.
Dodds, E. R. 1959: *Plato: Gorgias*. Oxford.
Dougherty, C. 1993: 'It's murder to found a colony', in C. Dougherty and L. Kurke (eds.), *Cultural poetics in ancient Greece: cult, performance, poetics* (Cambridge): 178–98.

2014: 'Ships, walls, men: classical Athens and the poetics of infrastructure', in K. Gilhuly and N. Worman (eds.), *Space, place, and landscape in ancient Greek literature and culture* (Cambridge): 130–70.
Dover, K. J. 1953: 'La colonizzazione della Sicilia in Tucidide', *Maia* 6: 1–20; German translation in Herter 1968: 344–68.
　1955: 'Anapsephisis in fifth-century Athens', *JHS* 75: 17–20, repr. in *The Greeks and their legacy* (Oxford, 1988): 188–93.
　1965: *Thucydides: Book VI* (school edition). Oxford.
　1974: *Greek popular morality in the time of Plato and Aristotle*. Oxford.
Drögemüller, H.-P. 1969: *Syrakus: zur Topographie und Geschichte einer griechischen Stadt* (Gymn. Beiheft 6). Heidelberg.
Dunbar, N. V. 1995: *Aristophanes: Birds*. Oxford.
Edmunds, L. 1975: *Chance and intelligence in Thucydides*. Cambridge, MA.
Evans, R. 2016: *Ancient Syracuse: from foundation to fourth century collapse*. London and New York.
Fantasia, U. 2012: 'Quanto è "grande" la Sicilia? L'*archaiologia* siciliana (Th. 6, 2–5) nel suo contesto', in Congiu, Micciché, and Modeo 2012: 13–29.
Fauber, G. M. 2001: 'Hermocrates and Thucydides: rhetoric, policy, and the speeches in Thucydides' *History*', *ICS* 26: 37–51.
Feddern, S. 2016: 'Thucydides' *Methodenkapitel* in the light of the ancient evidence', in V. Liotsakis and S. Farrington (eds.), *The art of history: literary perspectives on Greek and Roman historiography* (*Trends in Classics* supp. vol. 41, Berlin and Boston): 119–44.
Figueira, T. J. 2015: 'Modes of colonisation and elite integration in "archaic Greece"', in N. R. E. Fisher and H. van Wees (eds.), *'Aristocracy' in antiquity: redefining Greek and Roman elites* (Swansea): 313–47.
Finglass, P. 2011: *Sophocles: Ajax*. Cambridge.
　2018: *Sophocles: Oedipus the King*. Cambridge.
Flower, M. A. 2009: 'Athenian religion and the Peloponnesian War', in O. Palagia (ed.), *Art in Athens during the Peloponnesian War* (Cambridge): 1–23.
Forde, S. 1989: *The ambition to rule: Alcibiades and the politics of imperialism in Thucydides*. Ithaca and London.
　2012: 'Thucydides and "realism" among the classics of international relations', in Harloe and Morley 2012: 178–96.
Fornara, C. W. 1968: 'The "tradition" about the murder of Hipparchus', *Historia* 17: 400–24.
　1980: 'Andocides and Thucydides', in S. M. Burstein and L. A. Okin, *Panhellenica: essays in ancient history and historiography in honor of Truesdell S. Brown* (Lawrence, KA): 43–55.

Forrest, W. G. 1975: 'An Athenian generation gap', *YCS* 24: 37–52.
Forsdyke, S. 2001: 'Athenian democratic ideology and Herodotus' *Histories*', *AJPh* 122: 329–58.
Foster, E. 2017: 'Aristophanes' Cleon and post-Peloponnesian war Athenians: denunciation in Thucydides', in Baragwanath and Foster 2017a: 129–52.
Foster, E. and D. Lateiner (eds.) 2012: *Thucydides and Herodotus*. Oxford.
Fowler, D. 2000: *Roman constructions: readings in postmodern Latin*. Oxford.
Fowler, R. L. 1996: 'Herodotus and his contemporaries', *JHS* 116: 62–87, repr. in R.V. Munson (ed.), *Oxford readings in classical studies: Herodotus* i. Oxford 2013: 46–83.
Fraenkel, E. 1950: *Aeschylus: Agamemnon*. Oxford.
Fragoulaki, M. 2013: *Kinship in Thucydides: intercommunal ties and historical narrative*. Oxford.
Frangoulidis, S. A. 1993: 'A pattern from Homer's *Odyssey* in the Sicilian narrative of Thucydides', *QUCC* 44: 95–102.
Frederiksen, M. W. 1968: 'Campanian cavalry: a question of origins', *Dialoghi di Archeologia* 2: 3–31.
Freeman, E. A. 1891–4: *A history of Sicily from the earliest times*. Oxford.
Fulkerson, L. 2012: 'Alcibiades πολύτροπος: Socratic philosopher and tragic hero?', *Histos* 7: 269–98.
Funke, P. and M. Haake 2006: 'Theaters of war: Thucydidean topography', in Rengakos and Tsakmakis 2006: 369–84.
Furley, W. D. 1996: *Andokides and the Herms: a crisis in fifth-century Athenian religion* (*BICS* Supp. 65). London.
Galinsky, C. 1969: *Aeneas, Sicily, and Rome*. Princeton.
Garvie, A. F. 2009: *Aeschylus: Persae*. Oxford.
George, C. H. 2014: *Expressions of time in ancient Greek*. Cambridge.
Golden, M. 2015: 'The geography of Thucydides', in L. L. Brice and D. Slootjes (eds.), *Aspects of ancient institutions and geography: studies in honor of Richard J. A. Talbert* (Leiden and Boston): 199–216.
Gomme, A. W. 1920: 'Notes on Thucydides Book VI', *CR* 34: 81–5.
1951: 'Four passages in Thucydides', *JHS* 71: 70–80.
Gomme, A. W., A. Andrewes, and K. J. Dover 1945–1981: see Abbreviations, *HCT*.
Graf, F. 2000: 'Der Mysterienprozeß', in L. Burckhardt and J. von Ungern-Sternberg (eds.), *Große Prozesse im antiken Athen* (Munich): 114–27.
Graham, A. J. 1964: *Colony and mother city in classical Greece*. Manchester.
2001: *Collected papers on Greek colonization*. Leiden.
Gray, V. J. 2017: 'Thucydides and his continuators', in Balot, Forsdyke, and Foster 2017: 621–39.

Green, P. 1970: *Armada from Athens*. London, Sydney, Auckland, and Toronto.

Greenwood, E. 2017: 'Thucydides on the Sicilian expedition', in Balot, Forsdyke, and Foster 2017: 161–77.

Grethlein, J. 2010: *The Greeks and their past: poetry, oratory, and history in the fifth century BCE*. Cambridge.

2013: *Experience and teleology in ancient historiography: 'futures past' from Herodotus to Augustine*. Cambridge.

Gribble, D. 1998: 'Narrator interventions in Thucydides', *JHS* 118: 41–67.

1999: *Alcibiades and Athens: a study in literary presentation*. Oxford.

2006: 'Individuals in Thucydides', in Rengakos and Tsakmakis 2006: 438–68.

2012: 'Alcibiades at the Olympics: performance, politics, and civic ideology, *CQ* 62: 45–71.

forthcoming: 'Power and pararitual: Alcibiades and the mysteries', in T. Duff (ed.), *Alcibiades: his ancient reception* (Swansea).

Griffiths, G. T. 1961: 'Some habits of Thucydides when introducing persons', *PCPhS* 7: 21–33.

Hammond, N. G. L. 1973: 'The particular and the universal in the speeches in Thucydides' *History*', in Stadter 1973: 49–77.

Handley, E. W. 1953: '-sis nouns in Aristophanes', *Eranos* 51: 129–42.

Hansen, M. H. 1980: 'Perquisites for magistrates in fourth-century Athens', *C&M* 32: 105–25.

1987: *The Athenian assembly in the age of Demosthenes*. Oxford.

1991: *The Athenian democracy in the age of Demosthenes: structure, principles and ideology* (tr. J. A. Crook). Oxford.

Hanson, V. D. 1998: *Warfare and agriculture in classical Greece*. Berkeley.

Harloe, K. and N. Morley (eds.) 2012: *Thucydides and the modern world: reception, reinterpretation and influence from the Renaissance to the present*. Cambridge.

Harman, R. S. 2018: 'Metahistory and the visual in Herodotus and Thucydides', in A. Kampakoglou and A. Novokhatko (eds.), *Gaze, vision and visuality in ancient Greek literature* (Berlin): 271–88.

Harris, E. M. 2014: 'Nicias' illegal proposal in the debate about the Sicilian expedition' (Thuc. 6.14)', *CPh* 109: 66–72.

2016: 'Alcibiades, the ancestors, liturgies, and the etiquette of addressing the Athenian assembly', in V. Liotsakis and S. Farrington (eds.), *The art of history: literary perspectives on Greek and Roman historiography* (*Trends in Classics* supp. vol. 41, Berlin and Boston): 145–56.

Hawthorn, G. 2012: 'Receiving Thucydides politically', in Harloe and Morley 2012: 212–28.

Hemmerdinger, B. 1948: 'La division en libres de l'oeuvre de Thucydide', *REG* 61: 104–17.
Henry, A. 1992: 'Through a laser beam darkly: space-age technology and the Egesta decree (I.G. i³ 11)', *ZPE* 91: 137–46.
  1995: 'Pour encourager les autres: Athens and Egesta encore', *CQ* 45: 237–40.
Herter, H. 1954: 'Pylos und Melos: ein Beitrag zur Thukydides-Interpretation', *RhM* 97: 316–43, repr. in Herter 1968: 369–99.
  (ed.) 1968: *Thukydides (Wege der Forschung* 98). Darmstadt.
Hesk, J. 2015: 'Thucydides in the twentieth and twenty-first centuries', in Lee and Morley 2015: 218–37.
Heubeck, A. 1980: 'Πρόφασις und kein Ende (zu Thuk 1.23)', *Glotta* 58: 228–36.
Hinrichs, F. T. 1981: 'Hermokrates bei Thukydides', *Hermes* 109: 46–59.
Hirsch, M. 1926: 'Die athenischen Tyrannenmörder in Geschichtsschreibung und Volkslegende', *Klio* 20: 129–67.
Hong, L. and S. E. Page 2004: 'Groups of diverse problem-solvers can outperform groups of high-ability problem solvers', *Proceedings of the National Academy of Sciences* 101.46: 16385–9.
Hornblower, S. 1994a: 'Introduction', in S. Hornblower (ed.), *Greek historiography* (Oxford): 1–72.
  1994b: 'Narratology and narrative techniques in Thucydides', in S. Hornblower (ed.), *Greek historiography* (Oxford), 131–66, repr. in his *Thucydidean themes* (Oxford 2011): 59–99.
  2004: *Thucydides and Pindar: historical narrative and the world of epinikian poetry*. Oxford.
Hornblower, S. and C. Pelling 2017: *Herodotus: Histories book VI*. Cambridge.
Horsfall, N. 1985: 'Illusion and reality in Latin topographical writing', *G&R* 31: 197–208.
Hunt, P. 2006: 'Warfare', in Rengakos and Tsakmakis 2006: 384–413.
Hunter, V. J. 1973: *Thucydides: the artful reporter*. Toronto.
  1988–9: 'Thucydides and the psychology of the crowd', *CJ* 84: 17–30.
Iglesias Zoido, J. C. 2007: 'The battle exhortation in ancient rhetoric', *Rhetorica* 25: 141–58.
Jacoby, F. 1949: *Atthis: the local chronicles of ancient Athens*. Oxford.
Jacquinod, B. 2011: 'πείθω et le présent historique chez Thucydide', in Lallot, Rijksbaron, Jacquinod, and Buijs 2011: 89–113.
Jameson, M. H. 1991: 'Sacrifice before battle', in V. D Hanson (ed.), *Hoplites: the classical Greek battle experience* (London): 197–227.
Janko, R. 1997: 'The physicist as hierophant: Aristophanes, Socrates and the authorship of the Derveni papyrus', *ZPE* 118: 61–94.

Jebb, R. 1880: 'The speeches in Thucydides', in E. Abbott, *Hellenica: a collection of essays on Greek poetry, philosophy, history and religion* (Oxford and Cambridge): 266–323.

Johnson, L. M. 2015: 'Thucydides the realist?', in Lee and Morley 2015: 391–405.

Joho, T. 2020: 'Alcibiadean mysteries and longing for "absent" and "invisible things" in Thucydides' account of the Sicilian expedition', *HSCPh* 113: 115–58.

  forthcoming: *Language and necessity in Thucydides' history*. Oxford.

Jordan, B. 1975: *The Athenian navy in the classical period: a study of Athenian naval administration and military organization in the fifth and fourth centuries BC*. Berkeley.

  2000a: 'The Sicilian expedition was a Potemkin fleet', *CQ* 50: 63–79.

  2000b: 'The crews of Athenian triremes', *AC* 69: 81–101.

Jost, K. 1935: *Das Beispiel und Vorbild der Vorfahren bei den attischen Rednern und Geschichtsschreibern bis Demosthenes*. Diss. Basel.

Jouanna, J. 1980: 'Politique et médecine. La problématique du changement dans le *Régime des maladies aiguës* et chez Thucydide (livre VI)', in M. Grmek and F. Robert (eds.), *Hippocratica – Actes du Colloque hippocratique de Paris, 4–9 Septembre* 1978 (Paris), 299–319, tr. as 'Politics and medicine: the problem of change in *Regimen in Acute Diseases* and Thucydides (Book 6)', in *Greek medicine from Hippocrates to Galen: Selected Papers* (ed. P. van der Eijk, tr. N. Allies: Leiden and Boston, 2012): 21–38.

Kagan, D. 1981: *The Peace of Nicias and the Sicilian expedition*. Ithaca.

Kallet, L. 2001: *Money and the corrosion of power in Thucydides: the Sicilian expedition and its aftermath*. Berkeley, Los Angeles, and London.

  2013: 'Thucydides, Apollo, the plague and the war', *AJPh* 134: 355–82.

Keene, E. 2015: 'The reception of Thucydides in the history of International Relations', in Lee and Morley 2015: 355–72.

Kelly, A. 2015: 'Stesichorus' Homer', in P. J. Finglass and A. Kelly (eds.), *Stesichorus in context* (Cambridge): 21–44.

  forthcoming: 'Homer and Hipponax', in V. Cazzato and E. Prodi (eds.), *The limping muse: Hipponax the poet* (Cambridge).

Kelly, D. 1996: 'Oral Xenophon', in I. Worthington (ed.), *Voice into text: orality and literacy in ancient Greece* (Leiden): 149–63.

Kinzl, K. H. 1973: 'Zu Thukydides über die Peisistratidai', *Historia* 22: 504–7.

Kitto, H. D. F. 1966: *Poiesis: structure and thought*. Berkeley.

Knox, B. M. W. 1968: 'Silent reading in antiquity', *GRBS* 9: 421–35.

Kohl, W. 1977: *Die Redetrias vor der sizilischen Expedition (Thukydides 6,9–23)*. Meisenheim am Glan.
Konstan, D. 1987: 'Persians, Greeks and empire', *Arethusa* 20: 59–73.
Kopp, H. 2016: *Das Meer als Versprechen: Bedeutung und Funktion von Seeherrschaft bei Thukydides*. Göttingen.
Kremmydas, C. 2017: '*Ēthos* and logical argumentation in Thucydides' assembly debates', in S. Papaioannou, A. Serafim, and B. da Vela (eds.), *The theatre of justice: aspects of performance in Greco-Roman oratory and rhetoric* (Leiden and Boston): 93–113.
Kurke, L. 1991: *The traffic in praise: Pindar and the poetics of social economy*. Ithaca.
La Torre, G. F. 2012: 'L'*archaiologhia* tucididea e la cronologia delle più antiche colonie greche di Sicilia', in Congiu, Micciché, and Modeo 2012: 31–44.
Laffi, U. 1970: 'La spedizione ateniese in Sicilia del 415 a.C.', *RSI* 82: 277–307.
Lallot, J, A. Rijksbaron, B. Jacquinod, and M. Buijs (eds.) 2011: *The historical present in Thucydides: semantic and narrative function = Le présent historique chez Thucydide: sémantique et fonction narrative*. Leiden.
Landemore, H. 2013: *Democratic reason*. Princeton.
Latacz, J. 1977: *Kampfparänese, Kampfdarstellung und Kampfwirklichkeit in der Ilias, bei Kallinos und Tyrtaios*. Munich.
Lateiner, D. 1977: 'No laughing matter: a literary tactic in Herodotus', *TAPA* 107: 173–82.
  2012: 'Oaths: theory and practice in the *Histories* of Herodotus and Thucydides', in Foster–Lateiner 2012: 154–84.
  2018: '*Elpis* as emotion and reason: hope and expectation in the Greek historians', in G. Kazantzidis and D. Spatharas (eds.), *Hope in ancient literature, history, and art (Trends in Classics* supp. vol. 63): 133–51.
Lavelle, B. M. 1986: 'The dating and patronage of the Archedike-epigram', *Hermes* 114: 240–4.
Lazenby, J. F. 2004: *The Peloponnesian war: a military study*. London and New York.
Lebow, R. N. 2012: 'International relations and Thucydides', in Harloe and Morley 2012: 197–211.
Lee, C. and N. Morley (eds.) 2015: *A handbook to the reception of Thucydides*. Chichester.
Leighton, R. 1999: *Sicily before history: an archaeological survey from the Palaeolithic to the Iron Age*. London.
Leimbach, R. 1985: *Militärische Musterrhetorik: eine Untersuchung zu den Feldherrnreden des Thukydides*. Stuttgart.

Lendon, J. E. 2017a: 'Battle description in the ancient historians, part I: speeches, results, and sea-battles', *G&R* 64: 39–64.
— 2017b: 'Battle description in the ancient historians, part II: structure, array, and fighting', *G&R* 64: 145–67.
Liebeschuetz, W. 1968a: 'The structure and function of the Melian dialogue', *JHS* 88: 73–7.
— 1968b: 'Thucydides and the Sicilian expedition', *Historia* 17: 289–306.
Liotsakis, V. 2015: 'Texts of religious content in Thucydides and the implied ancient reader', *RFIC* 143: 278–317.
Loomis, W. T. 1998: *Wages, welfare costs and inflation in classical Athens*. Ann Arbor.
Loraux, N. 1986: *The invention of Athens: the funeral oration in the classical city* (tr. A. Sheridan; French original 1981). Cambridge, MA.
Low, P. 2007: *Interstate relations in classical Greece: morality and power*. Cambridge.
— 2020: 'Remembering, forgetting, and rewriting the past: Athenian inscriptions and collective memory', in C. Constantakopoulou and M. Fragoulaki (eds.), *Shaping memory in ancient Greece: poetry, historiography, and epigraphy* (*Histos* Supp. 11): 235–68: https://research.ncl.ac.uk/histos/SV11ShapingMemoryinAncientGreece.html.
Ludwig, P. W. 2002: *Eros and polis: desire and community in Greek political theory*. Cambridge.
Luginbill, R. 1999: *Thucydides on war and national character*. Boulder, CO.
Luraghi, N. 1991: 'Ricerche sull'*archeologìa italica* di Antiocho di Siracusa', in L. Bracchesi (ed.), *Hesperìa 1: Studi sulla Grecità di Occidente* (Roma): 61–88.
— 1992: 'Fonti e tradizioni nell'*archaiologìa siciliana* (per una rilettura di Thuc. 6, 2–5', in L. Braccesi (ed.), *Hesperìa 2: Studi sulla Grecità di Occidente* (Roma): 41–62.
— 2002: 'Antioco di Siracusa', in R. Vattuone (ed.), *Storici greci d'Occidente* (Bologna): 55–89.
Luschnat, O. 1942: *Die Feldherrnreden im Geschichtswerk des Thukydides*. Leipzig.
Ma, J., N. Papazarkadas, and R. Parker (eds.) 2009: *Interpreting the Athenian empire*. London.
MacDowell, D. M. 1962: *Andokides: On the Mysteries*. Oxford.
Mack, W. J. G. B. 2015: *Proxeny and polis: institutional networks in the ancient Greek world*. Oxford.
Mackie, C. J. 1996: 'Homer and Thucydides: Corcyra and Sicily', *CQ* 46: 103–13.
Macleod, C. 1974: 'Form and meaning in the Melian dialogue', *Hist.* 23: 385–400, repr. in Macleod 1983: 52–67.

Macleod, C. 1978: 'Reason and necessity: Thucydides 3.9–14, 37–48', *JHS* 98; 64–78, repr. in Macleod 1983: 88–102.
— 1979: 'Thucydides on faction (3.82–3)', *PCPS* 205: 52–68, repr. in Macleod 1983: 123–39.
— 1983: *Collected essays*. Oxford.
Maddoli, G. 2010: 'La παλαιά ξυμμαχία fra Atene e Leontini nel quadro della politica occidentale ateniese', *Klio* 92: 34–41.
Mader, G. 1993a: 'Rogues' comedy at Segesta: Alcibiades exposed?', *Hermes* 121: 181–95.
— 1993b: 'Strong points, weak argument: Athenagoras on the Sicilian expedition (Thucydides 6.36–38)', *Hermes* 121: 433–40.
— 2013: 'Fear, faction, fractious rhetoric: audience and argument in Thucydides' Syracusan antilogy (Thucydides 6.33–40)', *Phoenix* 67: 237–62.
Malkin, I. 1987: *Religion and colonization in ancient Greece*. Leiden.
— 2002: 'Exploring the validity of the concept of "foundation": a visit to Megara Hyblaia', in V. Gorman and E. Robinson (eds.), *Oikistes: studies in constitutions, colonies, and military power in the ancient world, offered in honor of A. J. Graham* (Leiden): 195–225.
— 2003: '"Tradition" in Herodotus: the foundation of Cyrene', in Derow and Parker 2003: 153–70.
— 2005: 'Herakles and Melqart: Greeks and Phoenicians in the middle ground', in E. S. Gruen (ed.), *Cultural borrowings and ethnic appropriations in antiquity* (Oriens et Occidens 8, Stuttgart): 238–57; rev. version in Malkin 2011: 119–41.
— 2011: *A small Greek world: networks in the ancient Mediterranean*. Oxford.
Maltagliati, G. 2020: 'Persuasion through proximity (and distance) in the Attic orators' historical examples', *GRBS* 60: 68–97.
Marinatos, N. 1980: 'Nicias as a wise advisor and tragic warner in Thucydides', *Phil.* 124: 305–10.
— 1981: *Thucydides and religion* (Beiträge zur klass. Phil. 129). Königstein.
Marincola, J. 1997: *Authority and tradition in ancient historiography*. Cambridge.
— 2001: *Greek historiography* (*Greece & Rome new surveys in the Classics* 31). Oxford.
— (ed.) 2007a: *A companion to Greek and Roman historiography*. Malden, MA.
— 2007b: 'Speeches in classical historiography', in Marincola 2007a: 118–32.
Matthaiou, A. P. 2004: 'περὶ τῆς IG i³ 11', in A. P. Matthaiou and G. E. Malouchou (eds.), Ἀττικαὶ Ἐπιγραφαί: Πρακτικὰ Συμποσίου εἰς μνήμην *Adolf Wilhelm (1864–1950)* (Athens): 99–122.

Matthaiou, A. P. 2011: τὰ ἐν τῆι στήληι γεγραμμένα: six Greek historical inscriptions of the fifth century B.C. Athens.
Mattingly, H. B. 1963: 'The growth of the Athenian empire', *Hist.* 12: 257–73.
McCutcheon, R. W. 2015: 'Silent reading in antiquity and the future history of the book', *Book History* 18: 1–32.
Meiggs, R. 1982: *Trees and timber in the ancient Mediterranean world*. Oxford.
Meritt, B. D. 1957: 'Greek inscriptions', *Hesp.* 26: 198–221.
Meyer, E. 2008: 'Thucydides on Harmodius and Aristogeiton, tyranny, and history', *CQ* 58: 13–34.
Mitchel, F. 1964: 'The Athenian plague: new evidence inviting medical comment', *GRBS* 1964: 101–12.
Moggi, M. 2005: 'Demos in Erodoto e Tucidide', in G. Urso (ed.), *Popolo e potere nel mondo antico* (Pisa): 11–24.
Moles, J. L. 1993: 'Truth and untruth in Herodotus and Thucydides', in C. Gill and T. P. Wiseman (eds.), *Lies and fiction in the ancient world* (Exeter): 88–121.
Morakis, A. 2011: 'Thucydides and the character of Greek colonisation in Sicily', *CQ* 61: 460–92.
2015: 'The fleet of Syracuse (480–413 B.C.E.), *Historika* 5: 263–76.
Moreno, A. 2007: *Feeding the democracy: the Athenian grain supply in the fifth and fourth centuries BC*. Oxford.
Morrison, J. S. 1984: '*Hyperesia* in naval contexts in the fifth and fourth centuries BC', *JHS* 104: 48–59.
Morrison, J. S. and R. T. Williams 1968: *Greek oared ships, 900–322 B.C.* Cambridge.
Morrison, J. V. 2004: 'Memory, time, and writing: oral and literary aspects of Thucydides' *History*', in C. J. Mackie (ed.), *Oral performance and its context* (*Mnem.* Supp. 248, Leiden and Boston): 95–116.
2006: *Reading Thucydides*. Columbus, OH.
2007: 'Thucydides' *History* live: reception and politics', in C. Cooper (ed.), *Politics and orality: orality and literacy in ancient Greece* (Leiden and Boston): 217–33.
Moscati, S. 1985: 'Tucidide e i Fenici', *RIFC* 113: 129–33.
Munson, R. V. 2012: 'Persians in Thucydides', in Foster and Lateiner 2012: 241–77.
Murray, H. A. 1961: 'Two notes on the evaluation of Nicias in Thucydides', *BICS* 8: 33–46.
Murray, O. 1990: 'The affair of the mysteries: democracy and the drinking group', in O. Murray (ed.), *Sympotika: a symposium on the symposion* (Oxford): 148–61.
2014: 'Thucydides and Apollo Archegetes', *ASNSP* 6: 447–73.

Naiden, F. S. 2006: *Ancient supplication.* New York.
Nývlt, P. 2014: 'Was Alcibiades an informant of Thucydides?', *Act. Ant. Hung.* 54: 381–91.
Ober, J. and T. Perry 2014: 'Thucydides as a prospect theorist', *Polis* 31: 206–32.
O'Connor, J. S. 2011: *Armies, navies, and economies in the Greek world in the fifth and fourth centuries BCE.* Diss. Columbia.
O'Connor, S. 2016: *Some observations on pay for Athenian military forces at Potidaea (432–430/29 B.C.) and in Sicily (415–413 B.C.)*, Arctos 50: 107–24.
Orwin, C. 1994: *The humanity of Thucydides.* Princeton.
Osborne, R. 1985: 'The erection and mutilation of the Hermai', *PCPS* 211: 47–73.
  1998: 'Early Greek colonization: the nature of Greek settlement in the West', in N. Fisher and H. van Wees (eds.), *Archaic Greece: new approaches and new evidence* (London): 251–69.
Osborne, R. and S. Hornblower (eds.) 1994: *Ritual finance politics: Athenian democratic accounts presented to David Lewis.* Oxford.
Ostwald, M. 1986: *From popular sovereignty to the sovereignty of law: law, society, and politics in fifth-century Athens.* Berkeley, Los Angeles, and London.
Page, D. L. 1959: *History and the Homeric Iliad.* Berkeley, Los Angeles, and Cambridge.
  1981: *Further Greek epigrams: epigrams before 50 A.D from the Greek anthology and other sources not included in 'Hellenistic epigrams' or 'The garland of Philip'.* Cambridge.
Papazarkadas, N. 2009: 'Epigraphy and the Athenian empire: re-shuffling the chronological cards', in Ma, Papazarkadas, and Parker 2009: 67–88.
Parker, R. 1996: *Athenian religion: a history.* Oxford.
  2000: 'Sacrifice and battle', in van Wees 2000: 299–314.
  2005: *Polytheism and society at Athens.* Oxford.
Paul, G. M 1987: 'Two Battles in Thucydides', *EMC/CV* 31: 307–12.
Pelling, C. 1981: 'Caesar's battle-descriptions and the defeat of Ariovistus', *Latomus* 40: 741–66.
  1988: *Plutarch: Life of Antony.* Cambridge.
  1991: 'Thucydides' Archidamus and Herodotus' Artabanus', in M. A. Flower and M. Toher (eds.), *Georgica: Greek studies in honour of George Cawkwell* (*BICS* Supp. 58) : 120–42.
  1992 : 'Plutarch and Thucydides', in P. A. Stadter (ed.), *Plutarch and the historical tradition* (London): 10–40, repr. in Pelling 2002: 117–41.

2000: *Literary texts and the Greek historian*. London. Most of ch. 6 ('Thucydides' speeches', pp. 112–22) is reprinted in Rusten 2009: 176–87.
2002: *Plutarch and history: eighteen studies*. London.
2007: 'Aristagoras', in E. Irwin and E. Greenwood (eds.), *Reading Herodotus* (Cambridge): 179–201.
2009: 'Bringing autochthony up to date: Herodotus and Thucydides', *CW* 102: 471–83.
2011: *Plutarch: Life of Caesar*. Oxford.
2012: 'Aristotle's Rhetoric, the *Rhetorica ad Alexandrum*, and the speeches in Herodotus and Thucydides', in Foster and Lateiner 2012: 281–315.
2013: 'Xenophon's and Caesar's third-person narratives – or are they?', in A. Marmodoro and J. Hill (eds.), *The author's voice in classical and late antiquity* (Oxford): 29–73.
2014: 'Thucydides', in C. Pelling and M. Wyke, *Twelve voices from Greece and Rome: ancient ideas for modern times* (Oxford): 65–82.
2019: *Herodotus and the Question Why*. Austin.
2021: 'Gomme's Thucydides and the idea of the historical commentary', in S. Harrison and C. Pelling (eds.), *Classical scholarship and its history: essays in honour of Christopher Stray* (Stuttgart and Berlin): 219–47.
Petrovic, A. 2007: *Kommentar zu den simoneidischen Versinschriften*. Leiden and Boston.
Piccirilli, L. 2000: 'La tradizione extratucididea relativa alla spedizione ateniese in Sicilia del 415–413', in *Terze giornate internazionali di studi sull'area Elima* (Pisa): 823–48.
Pinney, T. 1974–81: *The letters of Thomas Babington Macaulay*. Cambridge.
Pope, S. 2017: 'The Athenians and the Sikels in the late fifth century B.C.', in D. W. Rupp and J. E. Tomlinson (eds.), *From maple to olive: proceedings of a colloquium to celebrate the 40th anniversary of the Canadian Institute in Greece* (Athens): 401–19.
Porciani, L. 2007: 'The enigma of discourse: a view of Thucydides', in Marincola 2007a: 328–35.
Poschenrieder, T. 2011: 'Material constraints in Thucydides' representation of history', in Rechenauer and Pothou 2011: 145–57.
Pothou, V. 2009: *La place et le rôle de la digression dans l'œuvre de Thucydide* (*Hist*. Einzelschr. 203). Stuttgart.
Powell, A. 1979: 'Religion and the Sicilian expedition', *Historia* 28: 15–31.
(ed.) 2013: *Hindsight in Greek and Roman history*. Swansea.
Price, J. J. 2001: *Thucydides and internal war*. Cambridge.

2013: 'Difficult statements in Thucydides', in Tsakmakis and Tamiolaki 2013: 435–46.
Pulleyn, S. 1997: *Prayer in Greek religion*. Oxford.
Purves, A. C. 2010: *Space and time in ancient Greek narrative*. Cambridge.
Pusey, N. M. 1940: 'Alcibiades and τὸ φιλόπολι', *HSCPh* 51: 215–31.
Quinn, J. C. 2018: *In search of the Phoenicians*. Princeton.
Raaflaub, K. 1979: '"Polis tyrannos": Zur Entstehung einer politischen Metapher', in G. W. Bowersock, W. Burkert, and M. C. J. Putnam (eds.), *Arktouros: Hellenic studies presented to B. M. W. Knox on the occasion of his 65th birthday* (Berlin and New York): 237–52.
   1989: 'Perceptions of democracy in fifth-century Athens', *Cl&Med* 40: 32–70.
   2002: 'Herodot und Thukydides. Persischer Imperialismus im Lichte der athenischen Sizilienpolitik', in L. M. Günther and N. Ehrhardt (eds.), *Widerstand, Anpassung, Integration. Festschrift für Jürgen Deininger zum 65. Geburtstag* (Stuttgart): 11–40.
   2016: 'Die große Herausforderung: Herodot, Thukydides und die Erfindung einer neuen Form von Geschichtsschreibung', *HZ* 302: 593–622.
Rawles, R. 2015: 'Lysimeleia (Thucydides 7.53, Theocritus 16.84): what Thucydides does not tell us about the Sicilian expedition', *JHS* 135: 132–46.
Rawlings, H. R. 1975: *A semantic study of PROPHASIS to 400 BC* (*Hermes* Einzelschr. 33). Wiesbaden.
   1981: *The structure of Thucydides' history*. Princeton.
   2010: 'Thucydidean epistemology: between philosophy and history', *RhM* 153: 247–90.
   2016: κτῆμά τε ἐς αἰεί . . . ἀκούειν, *CPh* 111: 107–16.
   2017: 'Writing history implicitly through refined structuring', in Balot, Forsdyke, and Foster 2017: 195–209.
Rechenauer, G. and V. Pothou (eds.) 2011: *Thucydides – a violent teacher? History and its representations*. Göttingen.
Rees, O. 2018: 'Picking over the bones: the practicalities of processing the Athenian war dead', *Journal of Ancient History* 6: 167–84.
Rengakos, A. 2006: 'Thucydides' narrative: the epic and Herodotean heritage', in Rengakos and Tsakmakis 2006: 279–300.
Rengakos, A. and A. Tsakmakis 2006: *Brill's companion to Thucydides*. Leiden and Boston.
Rhodes, P.J. 1972: *The Athenian Boule*. Oxford.
   1981: *A commentary on the Aristotelian Athenaion Politeia*. Oxford.
   1994: 'The ostracism of Hyperbolus', in Osborne and Hornblower 1994: 85–98.

Ridgeway, W. 1888: 'Thucydides VI. 2', *CR* 2: 180.
Rigsby, K. J. 1987: 'Phocians in Sicily: Thucydides 6.2', *CQ* 37: 332–5.
Rijksbaron, A. (ed.) 1997a: *New approaches to Greek particles: proceedings of the colloquium held in Amsterdam, January 4–6, 1996, to honour C. J. Ruijgh on the occasion of his retirement.* Amsterdam.
  1997b: 'Adverb or connector? The case of καὶ . . . δέ', in Rijksbaron 1997a: 187–208.
  2011: 'The profanation of the Mysteries and the mutilation of the Hermae: two variations on two themes', in Lallot, Rijksbaron, Jacquinod, and Buijs 2011: 177–94.
Robinson, E. W. 2000: 'Democracy in Syracuse, 466–412 B.C.', *HSCPh* 100: 189–205.
Robinson, E. W. 2011: *Democracy beyond Athens: popular government in the Greek classical age.* Cambridge.
Rogkotis, Z. 2006: 'Thucydides and Herodotus: aspects of their intertextual relationship', in Rengakos and Tsakmakis 2006: 57–86.
Rood, T. 1998: *Thucydides: narrative and interpretation.* Oxford.
  1999: 'Thucydides' Persian Wars', in C. S. Kraus (ed.), *The limits of historiography: genre and narrative in ancient historical texts* (Leiden, Boston, and Cologne): 141–68, repr. in Rusten 2009: 158–75.
  2006: 'Objectivity and authority: Thucydides' historical method', in Rengakos and Tsakmakis 2006: 225–49.
  2012: 'Thucydides', in I. de Jong (ed.), *Space in ancient Greek literature: studies in ancient Greek narrative* 3 (Leiden and Boston): 141–59.
  2017: 'Thucydides, Sicily, and the defeat of Athens', *Ktèma* 42: 19–39.
  2018: 'Thucydides' in K. de Temmerman and E. van Emde Boas (eds.), *Characterization in ancient Greek literature: studies in ancient Greek narrative* 4 (Leiden and Boston): 153–71.
Roos, E. 1962: 'Athens Vertragsverhältnis zu Egesta im 5 Jahrh. v. Chr.', *Op. Ath.* 4: 9–29.
Rosivach, V. J. 1987: 'Autochthony and the Athenians', *CQ* 37: 294–306.
  2012: 'The *thētes* in Thucydides 6.43.1', *Hermes* 140: 131–9.
Rubel, A. 2013: *Fear and loathing in ancient Athens: religion and politics during the Peloponnesian war* (tr. M. Vickers and A. Piftor; German original 2000). Durham.
Rubincam, C. 1991: 'Casualty figures in the battle descriptions of Thucydides', *TAPA* 121: 181–98.
  2018: 'How were battlefield dead counted in Greek warfare?', *AHB* 32: 95–105.
Rusten, J. S. 1989: *Thucydides: the Peloponnesian war book 2.* Cambridge.
  (ed.) 2009: *Oxford readings in Thucydides.* Oxford.

Rutter, N. K. 2000: 'Syracusan democracy: "most like the Athenian"?', in R. Brock and S. Hodkinson (eds.), *Alternatives to Athens: varieties of political organization and community in ancient Greece* (Oxford): 137–51.
Saïd, S. 2013: 'Thucydides and the Masses', in Tsakmakis and Tamiolaki 2013: 199–224.
Salmon, J. B. 1984: *Wealthy Corinth: a history of the city to 338 BC*. Oxford.
Sammartano, R. 2012: 'Tucidide e gli Elimi: quali barbari?', in Congiu, Micciché, and Modeo 2012: 159–80.
— 2018: 'L'Apollo *Archegetes* di Naxos e l'identità dei Sicelioti', *Historika* 8: 69–89.
Sancisi-Weerdenburg, H. 2000: 'The tyranny of Peisistratos', in Sancisi-Weerdenburg (ed.), *Peisistratos and the tyranny: a reappraisal of the evidence'* (Amsterdam): 1–15.
Sawyer, E. 2015: 'Thucydides in modern political rhetoric', in Lee and Morley 2015: 529–47.
Scardino, C. 2012: 'Indirect discourse in Herodotus and Thucydides', in Foster and Lateiner 2012: 67–96.
Schadewaldt, W. 1929: *Die Geschichtsschreibung des Thukydides*. Berlin.
Schein, S. L. 2013: *Sophocles: Philoctetes*. Cambridge.
Schütrumpf, E. 2011: '"As I thought that the speakers most likely might have spoken . . .". Thucydides *Hist.* 1.22.1 on composing speeches', *Phil.* 155: 229–56.
Seaford, R. 2000: 'The social function of Attic tragedy: a response to Jasper Griffin', *CQ* 50: 30–44.
Seager, R. 1967: 'Alcibiades and the charge of aiming at tyranny', *Historia* 16: 6–18.
Shannon-Henderson K. 2018: 'Women in Thucydides: absence and inferiority', in A. Tsakiropoulou-Summers and K. Kitsi-Mytakou (eds.), *Women and the ideology of political exclusion: from antiquity to the modern era* (London): 89–103.
Shanske, D. 2007: *Thucydides and the philosophical origins of history*. Cambridge.
Shipley, G. 2011: *Pseudo-Skylax's Periplous: the circumnavigation of the inhabited world*. Bristol.
Smart, J. D. 1972: 'Athens and Egesta', *JHS* 92: 128–46.
Smith, D. G. 2004: 'Thucydides' ignorant Athenians and the drama of the Sicilian expedition', *Syllecta Classica* 15: 33–70.
— 2009: 'Alcibiades, Athens, and the tyranny of Sicily', *GRBS* 49: 363–89.
Sommerstein, A. H. 1990: *Aristophanes: Lysistrata*. Warminster.
— 2013: *Menander: Samia*. Cambridge.

Sourvinou-Inwood, C. 1988: 'Priestess in the text: *Theano Menonos Agrylethen*', *G&R* 35: 29–39.
Stadter, P. A. 1973 (ed.): *The speeches in Thucydides*. Chapel Hill.
  1989: *A commentary on Plutarch's Pericles*. Chapel Hill.
  2017: 'Characterization of individuals in the history', in Balot, Forsdyke, and Foster 2017: 283–99.
Stahl, H.-P. 1973: 'Speeches and course of events in books six and seven of Thucydides', in Stadter 1973: 60–77; rev. version in Stahl 2003: 173–88.
  2003: *Thucydides: man's place in history* (German original 1966). Swansea.
  2011: 'War in Thucydides: veneer remover – veneer fabricator', in Rechenauer and Pothou 2011: 29–48.
Steiner, D. 2005: 'For want of a horse: Thucydides 6.30–2 and reversals in the Athenian civic ideal', *CQ* 55: 407–22.
Stevens, P. T. 1971: *Euripides: Andromache*. Oxford.
Stradis, A. 2015: 'Thucydides in the staff college', in Lee and Morley 2015: 425–45.
Taplin, O. 1993: *Comic angels and other approaches to Greek drama through vase-painting*. Oxford.
Thomas, R. 1989: *Oral tradition and written record in classical Athens*. Cambridge.
  1992: *Literacy and orality in ancient Greece*. Cambridge.
  2000: *Herodotus in context*. Cambridge.
Thompson, C. 2013: 'Thucydides, Corcyra, and the meaning of words', *Anc. Phil.* 33: 273–89.
Threatte, L. 1980–96: *The grammar of Attic inscriptions* i–ii, Berlin and New York.
Tompkins, D. P. 1972: 'Stylistic characterization in Thucydides: Nicias and Alcibiades', *YCS* 22: 181–214.
  1993: 'Archidamus and the question of characterization in Thucydides', in R. M. Rosen and J. Farrell (eds.), *Nomodeiktes: Greek studies in honor of Martin Ostwald* (Ann Arbor): 99–111.
  2013: 'The language of Pericles', in Tsakmakis and Tamiolaki 2013: 447–64.
  2015: 'Gorgias in the real world: Hermocrates on interstate *stasis* and the defense of Sicily', in C. A. Clark, E. Foster, and J. P. Hallett (eds.), *Kinesis: the ancient depiction of gesture, motion, and emotion* (Ann Arbor): 116–27.
  2017: 'The death of Nicias: no laughing matter', in Baragwanath and Foster 2017a: 99–128.
Tosi, R. 2018: 'Per una rilettura di Thuc. I 22, 1', *Eikasmos* 29: 165–82.

Travlos, J. 1980: *Pictorial dictionary of ancient Athens* (2nd ed.; 1st ed. 1971). London.
Trevett, J. 1992: *Apollodoros the son of Pasion*. Oxford.
  1995: 'Nikias and Syracuse', *ZPE* 106: 246–8.
Tsakmakis, A. 1995: *Thukydides über die Vergangenheit*. Tübingen.
  1996: 'Thukydides VI.54.1 und Herodot', *Phil.* 140: 201–13.
  2017: 'The speeches', in Balot, Forsdyke, and Foster 2017: 267–81.
Tsakmakis, A. and M. Tamiolaki (eds.) 2013: *Thucydides between history and literature (Trends in Classics* supp. vol. 17). Berlin and Boston.
Tsakmakis, A. and C. Themistokleous 2013: 'Textual structure and modality in Thucydides' military exhortations', in Tsakmakis and Tamiolaki 2013: 391–408.
Tuplin, C. J. 1985: 'Imperial tyranny: some reflections on a classical Greek political metaphor', in P. Cartledge and D. Harvey, *CRUX: Essays in Greek history presented to G. E. M. de Ste Croix* (London): 348–75.
Van Emde Boas, E. 2017: 'Analyzing Agamemnon: conversation analysis and particles in Greek tragic dialogue', *CPh* 112: 411–34.
Van Wees, H. (ed.) 2000: *War and violence in ancient Greece*. London.
  2004: *Greek warfare: myths and realities*. London.
  2006: 'Mass and elite in Solon's Athens: the property classes revisited', in J. Blok and A. Lardinois (eds.), *Solon of Athens: new historical and philological approaches* (Leiden): 351–89.
Vatri, A. 2017: *Orality and performance in classical Attic prose*. Oxford.
Verdenius, W. J. 1954: 'καί, "and generally"', *Mnem.* n.s. 7: 38.
Vickers, M. 1995: 'Thucydides 6.53.3–59: not a "digression"', *DHA* 21: 193–200.
Viviers, D. 1992: *Recherches sur les ateliers de sculpteurs et la cité d'Athènes à l'époque archaïque: Endoios, Philergos, Aristoklès*. Gembloux.
Vössing, K. 2005: 'Objektivität oder Subjektivität, Sinn oder Überlegung? Zu Thukydides' γνώμη im "Methodenkapitel" (1,22,1)', *Hist.* 54: 210–15.
Vout, C. 2018: *Classical art: a life history from antiquity to the present*. Princeton.
Wakker, G. C. 1994: *Conditions and conditionals: an investigation of ancient Greek*. Amsterdam.
  1997: 'Emphasis and affirmation: some aspects of μήν in tragedy', in A. Rijksbaron (ed.), *New approaches to Greek particles* (Amsterdam): 209–32.
Wallace, R. W. 1992: 'Charmides, Agariste and Damon: Andokides 1.16', *CQ* 42: 328–35.
Wallinga, H. T. 1993: *Ships and sea-power before the great Persian War: the ancestry of the trireme*. Leiden.

Walters, K. R. 1981: '"We fought alone at Marathon": historical falsification in the Attic funeral oration', *RhM* 124: 206–11.
Wassermann, F. M. 1947: 'The Melian dialogue', *TAPA* 78: 18–36.
Watson-Williams, E. 1962: 'ἔρυμα: Thuc. I. 11', *Eranos* 62: 101–4.
Weidgen, J. 1927: 'Zum Thukydidestext II', *RhM* 76: 307–36.
Welch, D. A. 2003: 'Why international relations theorists should stop reading Thucydides', *Review of International Studies* 29.3: 301–19.
Westlake, H. D. 1958a: 'Thucydides II, 65, 11', *CQ* 52: 102–10, repr. in Westlake 1969: 161–73.
  1958b: 'Hermocrates the Syracusan', *Bulletin of the John Rylands Library* 41: 239–68, repr. in Westlake 1969: 174–202.
  1960: 'Athenian aims in Sicily, 427–414 B.C.: a study in Thucydidean motivation', *Hist.* 9: 385–402, repr. in Westlake 1969: 101–22.
  1969: *Essays on the Greek historians and Greek history*. Manchester.
Wheeler, E. L. 2007: 'Land battles', in *CHGRW* 1: 186–224.
Whitmarsh, T. 2016: *Battling the gods: atheism in the ancient world*. London.
Wickersham, J. 1994: *Hegemony and Greek historians*. Lanham, MD.
Wilamowitz-Moellendorff, T. von 1917: *Die dramatische Technik des Sophokles*. Berlin.
Willi, A. 2008: *Sikelismos: Sprache, Literatur und Gesellschaft im griechischen Sizilien (8.–5. Jh. V. Chr.)*. Basel.
Winkler, J. 1990: *The constraints of desire*. New York and London.
Wiseman, T. P. 2018: review of K. Sandberg and C. Smith (eds.), *Omnium Annalium Monumenta: Historical Writing and Historical Evidence in Republican Rome* ii (2018), *Histos* 12: I–XXIII.
Wohl, V. 1999: 'The Eros of Alcibiades', *ClassAnt* 18: 349–85.
Yaginuma, S. 1990: 'Thucydides 6.100', in E. Craik (ed.), *'Owls to Athens': essays on classical subjects for Sir Kenneth Dover* (Oxford): 281–5.
Yunis, H. 1991: 'How do the people decide? Thucydides on Periclean rhetoric and civic instruction', *AJPh* 112: 179–200.
  2001: *Demosthenes: On the crown*. Cambridge.
Zaccarini, M. 2018: 'What's love got to do with it? *Eros*, democracy, and Pericles' rhetoric', *GRBS* 58: 473–89.
Zahrnt, M. 2006: 'Sicily and Southern Italy in Thucydides', in Rengakos and Tsakmakis 2006: 629–55.
Zuchtriegel, G. 2018: *Colonization and subalternity in classical Greece: experience of the nonelite population*. Cambridge and New York.

INDEX

1 GENERAL

Aborigines: 102
Abydus: 144, 184
Acanthus: 214
Acarnania: 295
'Acesta': 100
Achradina: 106
Acrae: 111
Acragas: 29, 32, 34, 35, 107, 109, 112, 115, 161
Acron: 35
Actaeon: 106
Adonia: 16, 169, 170
Aegean Sea: 178, 186, 207, 265, 266, 283
Aegina: 34, 177, 266, 278
Aeneas: 100-1, 209
Aeschylus: 35
Agamemnon: 5, 251
Aglaophon: 148
Alcibiades: 2-7, 9, 11, 19-22, 24-8, 32, *et passim*, esp. 122-76, 211-12, 235-41, 289-301; style of speaking, 146, 290-1, 293, 298; wealth, 143
Alcmaeonids: 218, 220, 223-4, 234, 292
Alexander of Macedon: 147
Alliances: 32, 112, 146, 271, 274; see also under individual cities and states
Ambracia: 317
Amphipolis: 1, 131
Anakeion: 239
Anapus river: 248, 249, 305, 312-13
Anaxilas of Rhegium: 110
Andocides: 171-2, 236-9
Androcles: 175, 238
Andromachus: 171, 172
Andros: 306
Antimnestus: 110
Antiochus, Syracusan historian: 31, 35, 96-7, 100-2, 105, 110
Antion: 100
Antiphemus of Rhodes: 109
Antiphon, Athenian archon in 418/7 BCE: 113
Antiphon, executed in 411 BCE: 225
Aphrodite: 209

Apollo Archegetes: 105
Apollo Temenites: 310
Arcadia: 150, 163
Archedice: 233-4
Archers: 123, 124, 163, 168-9, 206, 250, 256, 286
Archias: 106
Archidamus, king of Sparta: 127, 154, 162, 186, 190, 193, 213, 293
Archonides: 30, 302
Argos: 119-20, 143, 150, 155, 163, 176, 178, 206, 227, 239, 240, 225-7, 254-5, 289, 291-2, 303, 319
Aristogeiton: 218, 221-35
Aristophanes: 33, 116, 120, 132, 144, 167, 185, 217, 319
Aristophon: 148
Aristotle: 11, 19, 34, 149
Artabanus: 122, 160
Artaphernes: 234
Artas: 30
Artemis: 207
Artemisium: 215
Asclepiades (?): 14 n. 45
Asine: 301, 317
Assyria: 133
Athena: 225
Athenagoras: 6, 24, 25, 27, 33, 95, 111, 158, 162, 179, 184-204, 221, 258, 294
Athens: Sicilian alliances, 30-2, 112-14, 116-18, 132, 140, 155, 159, 162, 263-4, 271; as 'tyrant city', 13, 28, 129, 156, 275, 281; decision to go to Sicily, 415 BCE, 123-4; earlier dealings with Syracuse, 29-35; expedition of 427-424 BCE, 2, 21, 30-2, 94; handling of its great men, 28-9; leadership, 5-7, 28, 142, 175; plague, 135-6, 169-70; pressure from Egesta, 112-19; resilience after 413 BCE, 4; similarities with Syracuse, see Syracuse; views of empire, 27-8, 155-6, 274-86; war aims, 31, 93, 114-16, 123, 125, 139, 161, 162, 167, 210-11, 267, 275, 294

342

Atossa: 23
Audience(s): 8–14, 19, 23, 24
Aulis: 181
Ausoni: 100–1
Autochthony: 99–100, 152

Bacchylides: 35
Bias (Herodotean sage): 122
Black Sea: 9, 183
Boeotia: 121, 131, 238–9
boulē: 140, 169, 172, 237–9
Brasidas, Spartan general: 214, 225, 251, 296
Bricinnia: 216
Byzantium: 144

Cadmus of Zancle: 110
Caecilius Metellus, L.: 102
Caesar, C. Iulius, dictator: 139, 183, 230
Calabria: 102
Call-ups: 169, 181
Callias, Hippias' father-in-law: 228
Callicrates of Syracuse: 313
Callisthenes, historian: 126
Camarina: 9, 21, 26, 27, 29–32, 34, 111–12, 115, 118, 156, 161, 214, 216–17, 241, 250, 257, 263–90; alliance with Athens, 30–1, 117, 263–4, 274; alliance with Syracuse, 263–4; *stasis* at, 216–17
Campania: 101, 288, 307
Carthage: 22, 26, 35, 103, 143, 188, 189, 191, 203, 288, 294
Casmenae: 111
Catana: 30, 34, 107, 115, 161, 213–6, 241, 243, 246–7, 250, 253, 258–9, 263, 266, 268, 286, 301, 315
Catherine the Great: 177
Cavalry: 6, 121, 161–3, 180, 197, 217, 245–6, 249–50, 252, 256–8, 288, 303, 305, 307
Centoripa: 302–3
Cephallenia: 205, 281, 295
Chalcedon: 144
Chalcidice: 121, 131, 132
Chalcis: 104, 107–12, 115, 161, 207, 242, 266, 271, 277, 280, 284
Charicles: 173–4
Charmides, Athenian prisoner: 236
Charmus, Hippias' father-in-law: 228
Charybdis: 97
Chios: 132, 205, 255, 281

chorēgia: 148
Cicero: 8 n. 26
Cimmerians: 133
Cimon: 175, 238
'Circle': 304, 307–14
Civil strife: *see* stasis
Claudius, emperor: 26
Cleandridas, father of Gylippus: 300–1, 317
Cleidemus, historian: 228
Cleinas, father of Alcibiades: 141, 215
Cleisthenes of Athens: 156, 223
Cleobulus, Spartan ephor: 130
Cleomenes III of Sparta: 254
Cleon: 13, 27, 33, 35, 126, 128, 153, 156, 159, 166, 185, 194–5, 198–9, 201, 275, 280, 281
Cleonae: 303
Cnemus: 251
Colonisation: 1, 93, 95–111, 165, 245
Corax: 35, 152, 296
Corcyra: 11 n. 38, 29–30, 115, 139, 154, 178, 185, 192, 205, 295, 310; Corcyrean debate (1.31–44), 20, 24, 118, 123, 265, 274
Corinth: 13, 26, 27, 106, 111, 118, 120, 121, 123, 131, 161, 171, 189–91, 203, 258, 260, 284, 289, 296, 300, 301, 303, 317; Corinthians' characterisation of Athens and Sparta at 1.69–71, 22, 28, 129, 132, 135, 158, 167, 189, 193, 284, 292, 300
Corinthian Gulf: 139, 252
Corn: 31, 94, 120, 161, 302; *see also* grain
Cornford, Francis: 18
Crataimenes: 109–10
Craterus: 169
Cratippus: 4
Crete: 109, 169, 206
Croesus: 23, 156, 267
Croton: 207, 288
Cyclopes: 99
Cyllene: 240, 289
Cylon of Athens: 144
Cyme: 109
Cyrene: 105
Cyzicus: 144

Darius I of Persia: 23, 230, 234
Dascon, founder of Camarina: 111

INDEX

Dascon, locality in Syracuse: 111, 248, 249, 262
de Jong, Irene: 17
Decelea: 291, 296–7, 300, 318
Deinomenids at Syracuse: 29, 198
Delphi: 35, 105, 106, 109–10, 119, 127, 161
Demaratus, Athenian general: 319
Demeter: 170
Democracy: 6–7, 122–3, 153, 195, 200–2, 292–4
Demon of Centoripa: 302
Demosthenes, Athenian general: 25, 28, 165, 212–13, 244, 251
Demosthenes, fourth-century politician and orator: 25, 140, 195, 282
Demostratus: 124, 168, 169
Diagoras of Melos: 170
Diocleides: 171, 172, 236, 239
Diodotus: 19, 129, 195, 202, 274
Diomilus, exiled from Andros: 306
Dion: 121
Dionysius I of Syracuse: 34, 186, 195, 198
Dionysius of Halicarnassus: 11, 14 n. 45, 36–7, 97, 265, 269–70, 273
Dodona: 119
Dorians: 30, 34, 35, 104, 107, 109, 118, 205, 242, 265–9, 272–3, 275, 278, 290
Ducetius: 29, 35
Duris of Samos: 150

Egesta: 34–5, 100–2, 115, 209–10; alliance with Athens, 32, 113–14, 116–17, 132, 140, 155, 159, 242–3, 264; and Athenian war-aims, 125, 139, 210, 241–2; and Selinus, 1, 32, 34, 112, 140, 209, 241–2; pressure on Athens to intervene, 1, 32, 112–19, 122, 124, 154, 159, 242, 284; support in fighting, 162, 197, 208, 242, 246, 307; wealth, 124, 161, 208–9, 241–2
Egypt: 155, 183
Elea: 35
Eleusinian Mysteries: 167, 170–1, 174, 218–19, 235, 237
Elis: 131, 150, 291
Elymi: 35, 100, 102
Empedocles: 35
Emporion: 100
Enneacrounos: 226

Entimus, Cretan: 109
Ephorus: 98, 103, 104, 107
Epicharmus: 35
Epidamnus: 106
Epidaurus Limera: 319
Epidaurus: 180, 292
Epipolae: 9, 262, 302, 305–7, 312
epiteichismos: 296, 300
Eretria: 109, 229
Erichthonius: 229
Eryx: 100, 102, 124, 209
Etna: 101, 107
Etruscans: 35, 288; *see also* Tyrrhenians
Euarchos: 107
Euboea: 16–17, 104, 106, 109, 112, 178, 266
Euclees, Syracusan general: 316
Euphemus: 13, 25, 27–8, 115, 133, 146, 147, 155, 243, 257, 263–86, 289, 290
Eupolis: 319
Euripides: 9, 35, 148, 152, 284
Euryelus: 304–7
Eurymedon, Athenian general: 31, 94

Fear: 19–20, 21–22, 151, 179, 188, 193, 219, 233, 235–6, 277, 282

Gela: 35, 105, 107–12, 161, 206, 243, 250, 265; conference of Gela, 424 BCE, 31, 186–9, 191, 199, 265, 268–9, 283
Gelon: 29, 35, 108, 111, 198, 274
Gomme, A. W.: 4–5, 12
Gorgias: 35, 152, 265
Grain: 16, 30, 120, 163–4, 170, 302; *see also* corn
Great Harbour: 9, 12, 15, 177, 184, 215, 246, 308, 310, 312
Gylippus: 2, 14, 30, 101, 251, 258, 259, 260, 300–1, 304, 316–18

Habron, Athenian archon in 458/7 BCE: 113
Hagnon, Athenian general: 180
Harmodius: 218, 221–35
Hecataeus: 157
Hegesistratus: 227–8
Hell-Fire Club: 171
Hellanicus: 100–2, 221
Hellenica Oxyrhynchia: 4
Helorus: 249, 250
Heracleides son of Aristogenes: 316

Heracleides son of Lysimachus: 260, 316
Heracles: 106, 158
Hermes and Herms: 170–3, 217–18, 235, 237–8
Hermocrates: 3, 7, 21, 24, 25, 27–9, 31, 33, *et passim*, esp. 183–204, 257–88; style of speaking, 186, 191, 193, 258, 265–6, 269, 270; suspicions of tyrannical ambition, 34, 186–7, 195, 198, 202–3, 258–9, 269
Herodotus: 5, 10, 12–14, 16, 18, 23, 24 n. 59, 31 n. 75, 32–3, 95–106, 122, 126, 133, 177, 184, 195, 208, 209, 220, 223, 227, 237, 255, 267, 274, 277, 279, 302, 304, 318
Hesiod: 99, 182
Hestiaea: 266
Hieron of Syracuse: 35, 105, 107, 198
Himera: 35, 97, 110, 111, 115, 161, 241, 242, 263
Himeras river: 29
Hipparchus, son of Peisistratus: 218–35
Hippias, Athenian tyrant: 218–35
Hippoclus: 233
Hippocrates of Gela: 105, 110, 111
Hippocrates, Athenian general: 154, 251
Hippocratic corpus: 5
Homer: 10, 12–13, 15, 18, 23, 97, 99, 126, 184, 255, 259, 304, 326
Hope: 19–20, 32, 139, 147, 167, 285
Horse-breeding and equestrian competition: 137, 147–8
Hybla: 241, 243, 303
Hyblon: 107–8
Hyccara: 241–3, 303
Hyperbolus, Athenian politician: 122, 142, 143, 183

Iapyges: 101–2, 154
Iberians: 100, 294
Ilissos: 226
Inessa: 303
Ionian Sea: 139, 191
Ionians: 34–5, 104, 115, 125, 157, 216, 265–9, 273, 275, 277–9
Iophon: 227
Italus: 102
Italy: 9, 29–30, 32, 35, 100–3, 110, 154, 178, 207, 294

Kale Akte: 29
Kerameikos: 230

Labdalon: 307
Laches, Athenian general: 94, 116–17, 217, 264, 291–2
Lade, battle of (494 BCE): 110
Laestrygonians: 99
Laispodias, Athenian general: 319
Lamachus: 25, 27, 28, 123, 125, 163, 190, 210–14, 215, 241, 243, 244, 263, 302, 305, 311–15
Lamis: 107
Lampsacus: 233–4
Laughter: 194
Laureion: 297
Leaena: 231
Leokoreion: 231
Leon: 306–7
Leontini: 30, 32, 34, 35, 97, 99, 104, 105, 107, 112, 115–18, 122, 125, 127, 136, 139, 140, 152, 159, 207, 210, 212, 216, 245, 266, 268, 281, 283, 284; alliance with Athens, 30 and n. 71, 112–14, 117–18, 155, 209, 264
Lesbos: 205, 267, 274
Leucas: 317
Ligyes/Ligurians: 100
Lindos: 109
Little Harbour: 216
Livy: 195
Locri, Epizephyrian 30, 207, 288
Lydia: 133
Lysander: 177, 301
Lysimeleia: 249, 312

Macedonia: 121, 147
Mantinea: 150, 163, 176, 178, 206, 240, 291–2, 319; battle and campaign of (418 BCE), 1, 17, 27, 120–1, 146–7, 150, 251, 292, 303, 319
Marathon, battle of (490 BCE): 13, 31 n. 75, 220, 234, 279
Mardonius: 160, 167
Medes: 110, 133, 154, 278
Megabyxus: 200
Megara (in Greece): 106, 107, 131, 206
Megara Hyblaea: 96–7, 104, 107–8, 110, 112, 118, 212, 214, 263, 266, 302, 307
Melesippus, Spartan herald: 318

INDEX

Melos and Melian dialogue: 9, 17–20, 28, 93, 98, 115, 117, 129, 130, 132, 139, 157, 170, 190, 266, 272, 275, 278, 282, 289, 292
Menecolus, founder of Camarina: 111
Mercenaries: 154, 163, 168, 176, 206, 281
Messenia: 110
Messina: 21, 26, 27, 29, 31, 34, 115, 161, 212, 214, 215, 216, 241, 261, 263, 268; *stasis* at, 261; Straits of, 98, 103
Metapontum: 31, 34, 207
Methone: 121
Methymna: 205, 255, 281
Meton: 16
Miletus: 9, 208, 267
Miltiades, Athenian statesman and tyrant in Chersonese: 233
Morale: 116, 131, 155, 179, 181, 240, 241, 244, 300, 307, 315
Morgantine: 216
Motye: 103–4
Mylae: 111
Myletidae: 111
Mytilene: 132, 140, 274, 296; Mytilenean debate (3.36–50), 25, 35, 122, 123, 140, 198, 289

Naxos: 30, 104, 107, 115, 161, 215, 217, 226, 253, 258, 266, 268, 286, 287, 315
Nemea: 148
Nicias: 1, 5–8, 15, 18–30, *et passim*, esp. 122–76, 210–11, 251–3; his illness, 128, 166, 305, 312, 314; Peace of Nicias, 126, 130, 147; sounding Spartan, 127, 129, 130, 132; style of speaking, 126–9, 136, 141, 164–5, 251
Notium: 145

Oaths: 113, 120, 122, 214, 217, 264
Oenotrians: 101–2
Oligarchs and oligarchy: 10, 34, 120, 135, 160, 198–9, 200–2, 235–6, 285, 293, 303
Olympia: 35, 161, 209
Olympic games: 146–8
Olympieion: 246, 248, 256–7, 263, 313
Opici: 101–2, 109
Oral tradition: 218, 221, 223, 234

Orneae: 120–1
Oroetes: 208
Ortygia: 106
Ostracism: 34, 122, 142
Otanes: 200

Pagondas: 154, 251
Palice: 35
Pammilus: 108
Panathenaea: 229–30
Panormus: 104
Pantacyas river: 107
Parmenides: 35
Parnes: 296
Paros: 200
Patrae: 292
Pausanias, Spartan regent: 97, 143, 144, 219–20
Pay rates: 124, 180
Peisander: 173–4
Peisistratus and Peisistratids: 9, 218–35, 237
Pelasgians: 102
Perdiccas: 121
Periander: 293
Pericles: 1, 4, 6–8, 13–14, 21–2, 27–8, 33, 35, 119, 122–9, 132, 134, 137, 139, 141–59, 175, 180–7, 190, 193, 195–7, 201, 203, 220, 227, 258–9, 268, 270, 275, 281, 284–5, 295–6, 298, 317
Perieres: 109–10
Persephone: 170
Persia: 28, 95, 116, 133, 154, 179, 233–4, 262, 267; Persian Wars, 29, 188–9, 275
Phaeax, Athenian politician: 32, 207, 216
Philistus, Syracusan historian: 31, 100, 101, 111, 313
Phlius: 120, 319
Phocis: 101, 102, 104
Phoenicians: 34, 103–4, 212
Phormio: 151, 184, 251–2, 260
Phrynichus, Athenian politician: 293
Phrynichus, comic poet: 172
Phrynichus, tragic poet: 9
Pindar: 35, 146, 149
Piraeus: 177, 239, 277
Pittacus: 122
Plataea: 97, 226, 279; battle of (479 BCE) 13, 31 n. 75; Plataean debate (3.52–68), 24, 97, 176, 266, 291

Plato: 141, 200, 259
Pleistoanax, Spartan king: 317
Plutarch: ix, 15, 32-3, 35, 94, 125, 169, 241, 245, 256
Point Iapygia: 178, 183, 191, 192, 206, 317
Polyaenus: 209, 231, 232, 256, 287, 317
Polycrates of Samos: 208, 209
Polyzelos: 35
Potidaea: 115, 266
Prasiae: 319
proxenoi: 30, 125, 291, 302, 317
prytanis: 140-1, 239
Pylos: 130, 131, 291, 318
Pyromachus: 148
Pythen, Corinthian general: 317
Pythian Games: 148
Pythodorus, Athenian general exiled in 424 BCE: 31, 319
Pythodorus, signatory to Peace of Nicias: 319
Pythonicus: 171

Rhegium: 26, 30-1, 34, 110, 160, 207, 210, 214, 215, 263, 265, 271, 288; alliance with Athens, 30, 162, 207, 271
Rhodes: 94, 109, 169, 205-6, 267

Salaminia: 217, 235, 240
Salamis, battle of (480 BCE): 12, 31 n. 75, 278
Samos: 110, 267
Sandanis: 122
Sardinia: 294
Sardis: 234
Scione: 17, 266
Scythes: 110
Seers: 16, 93, 216, 254
Selinus: 1, 35, 97, 108, 161, 186, 209; and Egesta, 1, 32, 34, 112-13, 116, 140, 241-2; role in fighting, 243, 250, 265; wealth, 161
Sellasia, battle of (222 BCE): 254
Selymbria: 144
Sicania: 101
Sicans: 99, 100, 102, 242
Sicanus river: 100
Sicanus, Syracusan general: 260
Sicels: 29, 34, 35, 100, 102, 103, 111, 154, 161, 211-12, 241, 242, 243, 247, 287-8, 303, 307
Sicelus: 101

Sigeum: 226, 234
Simonides: 13, 234
Siwah: 119
Slingers: 163, 169, 205, 206, 250, 254, 256
Socrates: 15-16, 223, 278
Soloeis: 104
Solon: 23, 205
Sophocles, Athenian general: 31
Sophocles, tragic poet: 12, 17, 144, 299
Spain: 294
Sparta: active on Attic border in 415 BCE, 235, 239-41; and Argos, 120; and Boeotia, 238-9; and religion, 18; and Sicily, 30; discussions in autumn 415 BCE, 289-301; ephors, 130, 289; role in expelling the Peisistratids, 218-9, 221, 223-4, 234-5; winter 415-14 BCE, 301-4, 318-19
Sphacteria: 206, 291
Stade: 98
stasis: 10, 29, 32, 34, 112, 120, 152-3, 166, 199, 206, 212, 215, 261, 285, 299
Stoa Poikile: 13
Syagrus: 195
Syce: 304, 307
Symaethus river: 247
Syracuse: and Egesta, 1; and Leontini, 117-18; and Selinus, 116; constitution, 34, 184; earlier dealings with Athens, 29-35; foundation, 96-7, 106; growth of power within Sicily, 29-30, 106-11; politics at, 184-5, 195; similarities with Athens, 6, 28-9, 33-4, 161, 186, 189, 316; *stasis*, 34, 111, 112, 153, 246

Tacitus: ix, 26, 195
Taras: 35, 191-2, 207, 288, 315, 316
Tegea: 150
Teisias: 35, 152, 296
Tellias, Syracusan general: 316
Temenites: 262, 310-11
Terias river: 215, 302
Terina: 317
Teucer: 171, 172, 174
Thapsus: 107, 306
Theano: 241
Thebes: 226, 303-4
Themistocles: 97, 150, 176, 219-20, 225, 246, 262, 278
Theocles or Thoucles: 104, 107
Theopompus: 4

Thermopylae, battle of (480 BCE): 31 n. 75
Theseion: 239
Theseus: 225, 284, 296
Thespiae: 303
Thessalus, denouncer in 415 BCE: 174, 175
Thessalus, son of Peisistratus: 224, 227, 238
thētes: 200, 205
Thrace: 1–3, 114, 131, 132, 234
Thrasybulus of Athens: 221
Thrasybulus of Miletus: 208, 293
Thrasybulus of Syracuse: 198
Thucydides: and democracy, 6–7; and religion, 18, 119, 296; book-divisions, 14–15, 318; composition of history, 1–3; concern with future audience, 10–11; gathering information, 1–3, 227; judgement of Sicilian expedition, 4–8; publication or circulation of History, 3, 8, 31 n. 75; ranking of explanations, 5, 10, 114, 182, 255; sources, 96; speeches, 22–9 *and see Index 2*, 'speeches'; travels, 3, 234, 248
Thurii: 30, 34, 207, 240, 261, 288, 301, 317
Thyreatis: 303
Timaeus of Tauromenium, historian: 99, 100, 111, 242
Timaeus, Athenian prisoner: 236
Torone: 17
Trierarchy: 124, 180–2

Trinacria: 100, 110
Troezen: 278
Trogilus: 216, 308
Trotilus: 107
Troy and Trojan War: 5, 12, 13, 14, 18, 20, 96, 100–4, 106, 166, 317, 318; *see also* Homer
Tyndarides of Syracuse: 198
Tyranny: as Athenian preoccupation, 144, 235–6; associations with Olympic success, 149; bodyguards, 228–9, 231; Peisistratids, 219–35; tyrannicides celebrated, 221–4; tyrant city: *see* Athens
Tyrrhenian Gulf: 242
Tyrrhenians: 154, 288, 315; *see also* Etruscans
Tzetes, Ioannes: 37

Valla, Lorenzo: 36, 196, 245
Virgil: 100, 101, 184

Warner figures: 122
Wilamowitz-Moellendorff, Tycho von: 17

Xenares, Spartan ephor: 130
Xenophon: 3, 8–9, 18, 260
Xerxes: 13, 16, 23, 122, 157, 177, 179, 182–4, 188–90, 194, 223, 246, 276, 293

Zacynthus: 124, 169, 281, 295
Zancle: 100, 109–11, 115

2 LANGUAGE, STYLE, AND NARRATIVE TECHNIQUE

Adverb qualifying noun: 213, 273
Alliteration: 127, 133, 191, 288
Assonance: 127
Asyndeton: 246, 294
Audience address: 251, 252
Auditory effects: 177, 184

Catalogues: 205
Chiastic arrangement: 99, 114, 134, 202, 245, 257, 315–16
Closure: 14, 15, 177
Co-ordinate clauses accumulated: 249, 257, 308, 310, 315
Conditional clauses: 117, 131, 156, 182, 228, 232, 237, 255, 256, 262–3, 271

Delay, narrative: 93, 124, 239, 246, 261, 287, 289, 301, 303, 315

Eikos reasoning: 196, 197, 220, 228, 230, 272, 276, 278–9, 282
Ethnographic style: 32, 97, 99, 102, 105
Expressions of time: 105–6

First-person statements: 99, 302
Focalisation: 17, 179, 236, 238
Free indirect discourse: 17

Hearing syntax in different ways: ix, 98, 99, 110, 131, 139, 157, 168, 187, 292–3, 294

Hexameter rhythm: 195
Hypallage: 150
Hyperbaton: 134–5, 136, 240, 299
Hypophora: 199
'I know thee who thou art' construction: 119, 150, 266, 268
Imagery: athletic, 150, 158, 176, 253, 273; blending and mixing, 151–2, 157–8, 201; canine, 199; craft, 259; erotic, 1, 166–7; medical, 141, 158–9; stewardship, 156, 270
Intertextuality: 12–14, 16
'Introduction' of characters: 125, 141, 145, 194, 258, 300

Linguistic difficulty: 11, 36–7
Litotes: 139

Metaphor: 131–2, 139, 146, 150, 156, 157, 163, 166, 179, 208–9, 259, 272, 283

Naming and non-naming: 136, 168, 192, 203, 236, 248, 311; *see also* 'speaking names'
Narrator interventions: 99

Opening: 15, 93, 129, 195, 266
Optative constructions favoured: 129, 131, 133, 146, 293
Oracular tone: 118, 127
Oral performance: ix, 8–11, 245, 288

Panel-dividers: 95, 220, 263
Paradigmatic descriptions: 26, 253, 254, 263, 273, 282, 284
Paraleipsis: 268, 278
Parataxis: 146
Participle: conditional, with μή, 255; dominant (*ab urbe condita*), 106, 272; impersonal, 165, 277; stacked, 302, 207
Personification: 204, 318
Plural verb with neuter plural subject: 138–9, 243
Polyptoton: 118, 133
Preposition + neuter adjective: 271
Progressive correction: 17, 223
Prolepsis: 95, 110, 143
Proverbs: 134, 139, 149, 154, 156, 299

Psychological interest: 190, 212, 244, 283–4, 300; *see also Index 1*, morale
Relative clauses loosely attached: 141, 149
Revision in stride: *see* progressive correction
Rhetorical tropes and clichés: 'as I persuade myself', 187; autonomy and freedom, 269; beacon of freedom, 267, 278–9; closeness to friendly territory, 251–2; consistency, 128; consequences of defeat, 251–2; denigration of opponents' motives, 195; enemy over-confidence, 251; home and abroad, 251; 'I have often said before', 198; 'if you miss this chance you will regret it', 276; initial overstatement, 223; λύσις διαβολῆς, 146, 290; 'my own view', 129; 'near at hand', 271, 274–6, 286; pity as Athenian virtue, 117; playing with derogatory alternatives, 202; prospect of victory, 251; race, 94–5, 265, 266–9, 271–2, 280; rhetoric of authority, 290; rhetoric of frankness, 274–5, 277; rhetoric of liberation, 274–5; skill against daring, 251; 'someone will say', 199–200; superiority of our troops, 251; 'there is no need to say much', 251; 'truth universally acknowledged', 134; unpopular truths, 128–9; we are all in this together, 252; we are the patriots, 140; we are well prepared, 251; we deserved our empire, 278–9; we fought alone at Marathon, 279; we gave up our homes, 278; 'we' rhetoric, 130, 131, 187, 251, 252, 265–6, 268.
Ring composition: 150, 183, 272

Sense-construction: 206, 272, 287, 296, 302
'Speaking names': 27, 194
Speeches: 22–9, *then esp.* 122–3, 126, 145–6, 160, 184–5, 186–7, 190, 194–5, 203, 250–2, 263–4, 265–6, 274–6, 289–91
Summers and winters, arrangement by: 93, 303

INDEX

Tense:
  Aorists: 113, 166, 229, 272-3, 310;
    focalising through narratorial
    viewpoint, 179; ingressive, 226,
    228, 244
  Imperfects, conative, 193, 308;
    durative, 94, 244, 286, 287;
    favouring internal points of view,
    179; in unreal conditions, 237;
    inceptive, 93, 103-4, 178, 205,
    244, 287, 308, 312, 314; 'of
    intention', 95; preliminary to
    main action, 205; repetitive, 231,
    233; scene-setting 116, 230, 250,
    256, 302, 311
  Perfect: conveying continuing result
    of past action, 129, 151; perfect
    subjunctive, 151; perfect with
    present sense, 315
  Pluperfect: 113-4, 116, 129,
    144, 159, 239, 240, 286, 287,
    315; as action-freezing, 229; as
    repositioning the narrative, 238;
    other tenses used when Engl. would
    use pluperfect, 250, 261, 306
  Present: 136, 174; historic, 174,
    217, 231, 236, 240, 242, 246,
    306, 310, 311; in lively predic-
    tions of the future, 191, 273, 295
Topographical description: x, 3, 9-10,
    94, 214-15, 248, 304, 307, 310,
    311, 312

Variation of construction: 125, 143, 162,
    167, 204, 231, 244, 250, 267, 271
Verbs of hindrance or prevention: 98,
    175, 283
Verbs of hoping or expecting: 166
Visuality: 13, 15, 167, 177-9, 182-4,
    232

Year-endings: 121, 301

3 GREEK

ἀγάλλω: 204
ἀγοράζω: 216
αἰεί: 155-6, 292
αἰσθάνομαι: 233, 247, 296-7
αἰτία: 114-15
ἀκριβής: 158
ἀλλά . . . γάρ: 268
ἄλλοι τε καί: 124, 247
ἀμιλλάομαι: 181
ἄν + future infinitive: 249
ἄν + subjunctive: 299
ἄν repeated: 131, 156, 192, 213, 246,
    309
ἀνακτάομαι: 298
ἀναλαμβάνω: 299
ἀναμιμνήισκω: 117
ἀναπείθω: 292
ἀναψηφίζω: 140
ἄνοια: 149, 293-4
ἀντικρούω: 208-9
ἀντιπαρακαλέω: 283
ἀντιτίθημι: 155
ἀπαρνέομαι: 229
ἀπαρτάω: 163
ἄπειρος: 32, 94-5
ἀπιστέω: 213
ἀποδίδωμι: 243
ἄρα: 168, 262-3, 267, 269

ἀρετή: 225
ἀρκέω: 280
ἄρχω: 147
ἀσφάλεια: 20, 166, 233, 285
αὐτίκα qualifying noun: 213, 273
αὐτόθεν: 162, 163, 168, 257, 303
αὐτόνομος: 269
ἀφαιρέομαι: 203
ἀφίστημι: 277
ἄχθος: 145

βασανίζω: 218
βοάω: 175

γάρ introducing embedded narrative:
    221
γιγνώσκω: 159
γνώμη: 23 n. 58, 259; παρὰ γνώμην, 193
γοῦν: 233
δ' οὖν: 145, 229
δεινός: 179
δέος: 188; see also Index 1, 'fear'
δή: 132, 166, 239, 273
διά + genitive: 135
διαβολή: 143, 176, 240; see also λύσις
    διαβολῆς
διαγιγνώσκω: 176
διαπολεμέω: 196-7

INDEX

διδάσκω: 129, 300
δυναστεία: 198
δυσέρως: 138

ἑαυτοῦ + comparative: 260
ἐγγύς/ἐγγύτατα: 102
εἰ ... ἄρα: 168, 262–3
εἰ + future indicative: 117, 272, 290, 295
εἰ + optative: 256, 264, 288
εἰ + subjunctive: 162
εἰ not suggesting doubt: 178, 184
εἰ δὲ μή: 191
εἰκάζω: 182
εἰσὶν οἵ: 287
ἐκπλήσσω, ἔκπληξις: 133–4, 186, 196, 210, 307–8
ἑκὼν εἶναι: 141
ἔλασσον: 98, 168, 250, 307
ἐλεύθερος: 129, 267, 269, 279, 280
ἐλπίς: 147, 155, 167, 270, 285, 315; see also Index 1, 'hope'
ἐμπίπτω: 166
ἐξαιρέω: 166
ἐξαρτάω: 305
ἐπάγομαι: 115, 130
ἐπειδή γε: 245
ἐπηλυγάζω: 196
ἐπί + accusative: 185
ἐπί + dative: 173, 180, 235, 249, 279, 282
ἐπί + genitive: 241, 247
ἐπιβοάω: 147
ἐπιβουλεύω: 273, 283, 286
ἐπικαλέομαι: 116
ἐπίσταμαι: 197, 218, 235, 246–7
ἐπιτυγχάνω: 199
ἐρήμη δίκη: 240–1
ἔρις: 182, 194
ἔρως: 166–7, 177, 220, 224, 233
ἔστιν οὕς: 287
ἔτι καὶ νῦν: 100
ἔτι: 118
εὔελπις: 167
εὐκατηγόρητος: 268
εὐπρεπῶς: 114–5
ἐχόμενος: 105

ἢ καί: 273–4
ἢ μήν: 260
ἢ που γε δή: 197
ἤδη: 178, 184, 204, 205, 208, 212, 240, 248, 273, 280, 306

ἤν ... ἄρα: 262–3
ἡσυχία: 21–2, 129, 132, 156, 168, 191, 198, 248
ἤτοι ... ἤ: 198

θάμβος: 183
θεραπεύω: 176, 240, 291–2
θεωρία: 105, 147
θύρα: 303

ἰδέα: 266
ἴδιος: 137, 139, 142–5, 147–8
ἱκανός: 258–9, 299
ἱπποκρατέω: 257
ἰσο- compounds: 149, 200
ἰσομοιρέω: 201–2
ἰσονομία: 200

καί expressing comparison: 133, 162, 245, 281, 289
καὶ γάρ: 238, 315, 316
καὶ μήν: 153
κακόξενος: 267
καλλιεπέομαι: 278
καταπλήσσω, κατάπληξις: 134, 188, 196, 198, 203, 266, 307
καταστρέφω: 94, 267, 277, 294
καταφρονέω: 134, 187, 193, 194, 213, 244, 317–18
κατέχω: 129, 132–3, 202
κεῖμαι: 184, 239
κελεύω: 137–8, 243, 289, 319
κενός: 180–1
κληρόω: 204
κωλύω: 289

λαμβάνω: 17
λιθοβόλος: 254
λιθολόγος: 206
λογοποιέω: 198
λωφάω: 135–6

μαλακός: 138, 176
μελετάω: 135
μέλλω: 132, 162, 300
μέν ... γε: 283
μέν ... δέ ... δ' αὖ: 199
μετέωρος: 131–2
μή or οὐ: 155, 159, 230, 255, 283, 314

ναυτικόν: 30
νικάω: 303
νόμος: 148

ξύγκειμαι: 196
ξυμφορά: 130–1, 291
ξύνεσις: 196, 201, 202, 225, 258

οἰκίζω: 99, 104, 107–8
οἰωνός: 172–3
ὁμιλέω: 151
ὅμιλος: 153
ὁμοιοτρόπως: 161
ὄνομα: 189
ὀξύς: 135
ὅπου: 252
ὅπως + future indicative: 135, 138, 271, 287
ὀργή: 151
ὅριον: 262
ὁρμάομαι: 113–14, 129, 159
ὅς/ὅστις: 105
ὅσον οὐκ ἤδη: 231
οὔ or μή: *see* μή
οὐδὲ γάρ: 225
ὄχλος: 152–3, 161, 179, 244, 246, 293

πανδημεί: 245, 247, 250, 252, 263, 195, 309
πάντως: 160
παρανομία: 144, 175
παρασκευή: 94, 95, 118, 159, 179, 205, 283
πείθω: 289
πειράω: 224, 244
περιοράομαι: 198–9, 300, 315
περίπλους: 97–8
πλέθρον: 314
πλήν as conjunction: 287
πόθος: 167
ποιέω: 174
πολιτεύομαι: 298
πολυπραγμοσύνη: 284–5
πορθμός: 102
ποτε: 228, 276, 292
πρίν + subjunctive: 132, 176
πρίν in superlative phrases: 139, 179
πρόθυμος: 115
προσ- and προ- prefixes: 115

προσάγομαι: 224
προσαναγκάζω: 296
προσήκω: 127, 146, 279, 280, 281
προτιμωρέομαι: 231
πρόφασις: 114–15, 126, 266, 278

σαλπικτής: 254
-σις compounds: 170
σπένδομαι: 120
στόρνυμι: 157
στράτευμα: 247
σφάλλω: 133, 145, 167
σωφρονίζω: 270, 284

τάδε: 268
ταμιεύομαι: 156
τε as connective: 136, 159, 260, 273
τε, positioning: 140, 142, 240
τέκτων: 206
τηρέω: 102, 311
τις: 95, 187, 253, 268–9, 296
τό + infinitive: 136, 155, 166
τό μή + infinitive: 98
τρίβολος: 256
τρίβω: 158

ὑπακούω: 257, 276
ὑπηρεσία: 181
ὑπὸ νύκτα: 120–1, 245, 248
ὑποτειχίζω, ὑποτείχισμα, ὑποτείχισις: 309

φαίνομαι + infinitive or participle: 99, 208, 244, 271
φαῦλος: 158, 161–2
φθόνος: 149, 225, 270, 279
φιλόπολις: 298–9
φόβος: 188; *see also Index 1*, 'fear'
φοιτάω: 316
φυγαδικός: 298
φυλοκρινέω: 156

χρή or χρῆν: 237

ὥστε + optative: 189
ὥστε introducing sentence: 155